JERUSALEM, ALEXANDRIA, ROME

SUPPLEMENTS

TO THE

JOURNAL FOR THE STUDY OF JUDAISM

Editor

JOHN J. COLLINS

The Divinity School, Yale University

Associate Editor

FLORENTINO GARCÍA MARTÍNEZ

Qumran Institute, University of Groningen

Advisory Board

J. DUHAIME – A. HILHORST– P.W. VAN DER HORST
A. KLOSTERGAARD PETERSEN – M.A. KNIBB – J.T.A.G.M. VAN RUITEN
J. SIEVERS – G. STEMBERGER – E.J.C. TIGCHELAAR – J. TROMP

VOLUME 82

JERUSALEM, ALEXANDRIA, ROME

*Studies in Ancient Cultural Interaction
in Honour of A. Hilhorst*

EDITED BY

FLORENTINO GARCÍA MARTÍNEZ

AND

GERARD P. LUTTIKHUIZEN

BRILL
LEIDEN · BOSTON
2003

This book is printed on acid-free paper.

Library of Congress Cataloging-in Publication data

Jerusalem, Alexandria, Rome : studies in ancient cultural interaction in honour of A.
  Hilhorst / edited by Florentino García Martínez and Gerard P. Luttikhuizen.
    p. cm. — (Supplements to the Journal for the Study of Judaism, ISSN 1384-2161 ; v. 82)
    Includes bibliographical references and indexes.
    ISBN 90-04-13584-7 (alk. paper)
      1. Christian literature, Early—History and criticism. 2. Literature, Ancient—History and
  criticism. I. Hillhorst, A. II. García Martínez, Florentino. III. Luttikhuizen, Gerard P. IV.
  Series.

BR67.J47 2003
270.1—dc22
                                                                    2003057886

BR
67
.J47
2003

ISSN 1384-2161
ISBN 90 04 135847

PRINTED IN THE NETHERLANDS

CONTENTS

PREFACE

The present volume has been compiled by colleagues and friends as a respectful tribute to Dr. Antonius Hilhorst (Ton to his friends). It will be presented to him on the occasion of his 65th birthday, which coincides with his retirement as Associate Professor of New Testament Studies and Early Christian Literature at the Faculty of Theology and Religious Studies of the University of Groningen.

Although he has worked at a Department of Biblical Studies for most of his academic career, Ton has always remained a classical scholar. Trained in classical philology at the Catholic University of Nijmegen under the supervision of Professor Christine Mohrmann, he is equally at home in the Greek and Latin literatures, in the New Testament, Hellenistic Judaism, the Church Fathers and the Latin literature of the Middle Ages and the Renaissance. His profound familiarity with all these languages and literatures allows him to see them as part of a continuum, mutually interacting over a long period of time.

Ton's scholarly bibliography is collected at the end of this volume and ranges from his dissertation, *Sémitismes et latinismes dans le Pasteur d'Hermas*, and his monumental edition of the *Visio Pauli*, to one of his latest published articles "Poésie hébraïque et métrique grecque. Les témoignages des Anciens, de Philon d'Alexandrie à Boniface de Mayence." It clearly reveals three constants running through all his published work (in French, English, German, Spanish and Dutch), not only when dealing with New Testament Apocrypha and other early Christian texts, the topics deareast to his heart, but also when studying Greek and Latin classic authors or the Church Fathers, or when working with the Hebrew and the Greek Old Testament, the New Testament, Philo, Josephus or other Hellenistic Jewish authors.

The first of these constants is the prominence of *philology*, which constitutes the fundament of all his published research, text editions and interpretations alike. But Ton, although a notorious lover of Dictionaries and Grammars, never stops at philology. Taking it as his starting point, Ton has further explored the continuum of literatures in order to unveil the fecundating process of transmission, assimilation and reaction among the texts, which we call *interaction*. This is

the second constant in his work. Ton has pursued this interaction
of texts of different origins and various periods, studying it not only
at the level of the languages (primarily Greek, Latin, and Hebrew/
Aramaic), but also at the level of cultures and religions. A third constant in Ton's research is that his interest in the interaction of languages and cultures of the past is not merely antiquarian, but is
aimed at *keeping this cultural heritage alive* and making it more accessi-
ble. This interest is evident from his numerous translations of lesser
known early Christian texts, and particularly from the tremendous
effort invested, together with his wife Carolien Hilhorst-Böink, in the
annotated Dutch translation of the *Legenda Aurea*, which will soon be
published.

The title of the present volume, *Jerusalem, Alexandria, Rome: Studies
in Ancient Cultural Interaction*, tries to reflect the various interests of the
dedicatee, his approach to languages and literatures as forming part
of a continuum, and his attention to the interactions between the
different literary corpora at the levels of language and culture. The
23 contributions deal with different literary compositions from various cultural areas and different times, but all of them represent the
constants appearing in Ton's scholarly work.

Five of these contributions deal specifically with the interaction of
the Old Testament with later Jewish or Christian writings: Michael
Knibb, "The Use of Scripture in *1 Enoch* 17–19," Gerard Luttikhuizen,
"The Critical Rewriting of Genesis in the Gnostic *Apocryphon of John*,"
János Bolyki, "'Never Repay Evil with Evil.' Ethical Interaction
between the Joseph Story, the Novel *Joseph and Aseneth*, the New
Testament and the Apocryphal Acts," Jacques van Ruiten, "The
Four Rivers of Eden in the *Apocalypse of Paul* (*Visio Pauli*). The
Intertextual Relationship of Genesis 2:10–14 and the *Apocalypse of
Paul* 23:45," and Arie van der Kooij, "The Interpretation of Meta-
phorical Language: A Characteristic of LXX-Isaiah."

Two contributions are devoted to the interaction of Greek motives
in Jewish and Christian literature: Anders Klostergaard Petersen,
"Between Old and New—The Problem of Acculturation Illustrated
by the Early Christian Usage of the Phoenix Motif," and István
Czachez, "The Eagle and the Tree: A Homeric Motif in Jewish and
Christian Literature."

The *Martyrium* literature, perhaps Ton's dearest field of study, has
certainly not been forgotten. Jan Bremmer, "The Vision of Saturus
in the *Passio Perpetuae*," and Boudewijn Dehandschutter, "The Text

of the Martyrdom of Polycarp Again. (With a Note on the Greek
Text of Polycarp, *ad Phil.*),'' bear witness to Ton's long involvement
with this literature during the many years of preparation of a text-
critical edition of the *Martyrium Pionii* in all the languages in which
it has been preserved as well as a voluminous commentary, a work
he will now have the leisure to bring to completion.

Other contributors explore the influences of Greek writings within
a Jewish context at the level of philology, like Natalio Fernández
Marcos, "Theodoret's Philological Remarks on the Language of the
Septuagint," and Florentino García Martínez, "Greek Loanwords on
the Copper Scroll," at the level of theological ideas in a Greek composition, like John Collins, "Life and Death in Pseudo Phocylides," or in
a Hebrew one, like Günter Stemberger, "'Moses Received Torah . . .'—
Rabbinic Conceptions of Revelation," at the level of the influence
of literary compositions, like Monika Pesthy, "The Three Nets of
Belial from Qumran to the *Opus Imperfectum in Matthaeum*," and
Johannes Tromp, "Origen on the *Assumption of Moses*," or at the level
of *realia*, like Eibert Tigchelaar, "The White Dress of the Essenes
and the Pythagoreans," and Ed Noort, "Βεθαβαρα τὸ τοῦ ἁγίου Ἰωάννου
τοῦ Βαπτίσματος. Remarks about Storied Places at the Jordan, John
the Baptist and the Madaba Mosaic Map."

Six contributions move beyond the chronological frame of the
Supplements to the Journal for the Study of Judaism, but all of them faith-
fully represent the same principles of interaction in the continuum
of literary texts that characterise Ton's research. Jan den Boeft, *Aeterne
rerum conditor.* Ambrose's Poem about 'Time,'" and Antoon Bastiaensen,
"Augustine of Hippo Preaching on John the Baptist," explore the
interaction of the Biblical text in Latin dress in poetic or homiletic
texts of Latin Church Fathers; Marc Van Uytfanghe, "La saveur
biblique du latin mérovingien: l'exemple de la *Vie de Sainte Rusticule*,
Abbesse à Arles (VIIᵉ siècle)," unveils the influence of the Biblical
on Merovingian Latin; Gerard Bartelink, "*Illitteratus* in Early Christian
and Medieval Texts. Church and Illiteracy," pursues the influence
of the only mention of illiteracy in the New Testament in later
Christian texts, and Martin McNamara, "The Irish Legend of the
Antichrist," offers a complete dossier of the Antichrist topic in Ireland.
Finally, Miekske van Poll-van de Lisdonk, examines "Erasmus' Note
on Gal 4:25. The Connection between Mount Sinai and Jerusalem,"
one example of the philological work of Erasmus on the Greek text
which lies at the basis of his Latin translation.

Since each contribution can be read on its own, we have decided
to present them arranged in the alphabetical order of the names of
the authors.

A domain where all Ton's scholarly qualities have come to the
fore is in his work as a reviewer—there are more than a hundred
reviews in his bibliography—and as Book Review Editor of the *Journal
for the Study of Judaism*. His erudition, the breadth of his knowledge,
his precision, his attention to detail, his gentleness and his uncom-
promising *acribia*, make each one of these reviews a model of the
genre. These same qualities have made Ton an esteemed member
of the Board of the *Journal for the Study of Judaism* since 1981, and
of the Board of the *Supplements to the Journal for the Study of Judaism*
since its inception in 1996. Since 1998 he has been the Editorial
Secretary and Books-Review Editor of the *JSJ* and, happily for all
of us, Ton has agreed to continue for a while in these functions,
providing the same unfailing service to the scholarly community.

The editors and all the contributors to this volume feel that this
publication is merely a token of gratitude, their own and that of the
academic community throughout the world, to the dedicatee for a
life-long dedication to scholarship. We thank Annemieke ter Brugge,
who prepared the index of references to ancient texts and the list
of abbreviations, and Eva Hilhorst for the photograph of her father.
Ad multos annos, Ton!

Florentino García Martínez and Gerard P. Luttikhuizen

ABBREVIATIONS

ADAJ	*Annual of the Department of Antiquities of Jordan*
ANRW	*Aufstieg und Niedergang der römischen Welt*
ARN	Avot de Rabbi Nathan
ASTI	*Annual of the Swedish Theological Institute*
ATD	Das Alte Testament Deutsch
BAR	*Biblical Archaeology Review*
BBB	Bonner biblische Beiträge
BETL	Bibliotheca Ephemeridum Theologicarum Lovaniensium
BG	Berlin Codex
BKAT	Biblischer Kommentar, Altes Testament
BZAW	Beihefte zur Zeitschrift für die neutestamentliche Wissenschaft
CAD	*The Assyrian Dictionary of the Oriental Institute of the University of Chicago*
CC(S)L	Corpus Christianorum: Series latina
CIJ	*Corpus inscriptionum judaicarum*
CIL	*Corpus inscriptionum latinarum*
CPG	*Clavis patrum graecorum*
CSEL	Corpus scriptorum ecclesiasticorum latinorum
DJD	Discoveries in the Judaean Desert
DTT	*Dansk teologisk tidsskrift*
EPRO	Études préliminaires aux religions orientales dans l'empire romain
ETL	Ephemerides Theologicae Lovanienses
GCS	Die griechischen christlichen Schriftsteller der ersten [drei] Jahrhunderte
GRBS	*Greek, Roman, and Byzantine Studies*
HUCA	*Hebrew Union College Annual*
HTKAT	Herders theologischer Kommentar zum Alten Testament
HTR	*Harvard Theological Review*
JAOS	*Journal of the American Oriental Society*
JbAC	*Jahrbuch für Antike und Christentum*
JEH	*Journal of Ecclesiastical History*
JJS	*Journal of Jewish Studies*
JNES	*Journal of Near Eastern Studies*
JNSL	*Journal of Northwest Semitic Languages*
JQR	*Jewish Quarterly Review*
JSHRZ	Jüdische Schriften aus hellenistisch-römischer Zeit
JSJ	*Journal for the Study of Judaism in the Persian, Hellenistic, and Roman Periods*
JSJS	Supplements to *JSJ*
JSNT	*Journal for the Study of the New Testament*
JSP	*Journal for the Study of Pseudepigrapha*
JTS	Journal of Theological Studies
KAT	Kommentar zum Alten Testament
KAV	Kommentar zu den apostolischen Vätern
LCL	Loeb Classical Library
NedTT	*Nederlands theologisch tijdschrift*
NovT	*Novum Testamentum*
NTOA	Novum Testamentum et Orbis Antiquus
OBO	Orbis Biblicus et Orientalis
OLD	Old Latin Dictionary

PG	Patrologia graeca
PGL	*Patristic Greek Lexicon*
PL	Patrologia latina
PTS	Patristische Texte und Studien
RAC	*Reallexikon für Antike und Christentum*
RB	*Revue biblique*
RE	*Realencyklopädie für protestantische Theologie und Kirche*
REAug	*Revue des études augustiniennes*
RevBén	*Revue bénédictine*
RevQ	*Revue de Qumran*
RGG	*Religion in Geschichte und Gegenwart*
RTL	*Revue théologique de Louvain*
SBLEJL	Society of Biblical Literature Early Judaism and its Literature
SBLSCS	Society of Biblical Literature Septuagint and Cognate Studies
SBLTT	Society of Biblical Literature Texts and Translations
SC	Sources Chrétiennes
SHANE	Studies in the History of the Ancient Near East
SNTSMS	Society for New Testament Studies Monograph Series
ST	*Studia theologica*
STDJ	Studies on the Texts of the Desert of Judah
SVTP	Studia in Veteris Testamenti pseudepigrapha
TBN	Themes in Biblical Narrative
TDNT	*Theological Dictionary of the New Testament*
TDOT	*Theological Dictionary of the Old Testament*
ThWAT	*Theologisches Wörterbuch zum Alten Testament*
ThLL	Thesaurus linguae latinae
ThZ	*Theologische Zeitschrift* (Basel)
TSAJ	Texte und Studien zum antiken Judentum
TWNT	*Theologische Wörterbuch zum Neuen Testament*
VC	*Vigiliae christianae*
VCSup	Vigiliae christianae Supplements
VT	*Vetus Testamentum*
WBC	Word Biblical Commentary
WUNT	Wissenschaftliche Untersuchungen zum Alten und Neuen Testament
ZDPV	*Zeitschrift des deutschen Palästina-Vereins*
ZPE	*Zeitschrift für Papyrologie und Epigraphik*

ILLITTERATUS IN EARLY CHRISTIAN AND MEDIEVAL TEXTS: CHURCH AND ILLITERACY

Gerard J.M. Bartelink*

The Latin term *illitteratus* (*inlitteratus, illitteratus*), translation of the Greek *agrammatos*, refers like its antecedent to different levels of education. In texts of the classical period it especially denotes a person who was not literarily or scientifically cultivated. Seneca formulated it as follows: "Thus we call illiterate a person who is not completely uncultivated but who did not receive a higher education."[1] Also in medieval texts this meaning—beside that of "one who cannot read and/or write"—remained current. When John of Salisbury stressed the desirability that a monarch should be a man of letters, he quoted a sentence ascribed to the Roman king Konrad III: "For an illiterate king is like a crowned ass."[2]

In late Latin texts, however, *illitteratus* is also often used to denote the lowest level of education: a person who, not having received school-teaching at all, cannot read and write. An interesting example from non-Christian texts is to be found in Columella, who remarked that such a completely illiterate person yet may be able to administer an estate in a reasonable way.[3] King Theodoric (around 525) is called *illitteratus*, because, during the ten years of his reign, he did not succeed in writing the four letters with which he had to sign his official decrees.[4]

In this article, written on the occasion of the retirement of Ton Hilhorst—who once, some fifty years ago, was my student in classical

---

* Nijmegen.

[1] Seneca, *De beneficiis* 5,13,3: *sic illitteratum dicimus non ex toto rudem, sed ad altiores litteras non perductum*; cf. H.-I. Marrou, *Saint Augustin et la fin de la culture antique* (Paris, 1938), 559: *"(Litterae) . . . ne désigne pas nécessairement les connaissances élémentaires qu'enseigne le litterator, l'instituteur."*

[2] John of Salisbury, *Polycraticus* 524D: *quia rex illitteratus est quasi asinus coronatus.* Cf. E.R. Curtius, *Europäische Literatur und Lateinisches Mittelalter* (Bern-München, 1961³), 185.

[3] Columella, *De re rustica* 1,8,4: *potest etiam illitteratus (sc. vilicus) . . . rem satis commode administrare.*

[4] *Anonymus Valesianus* 14,79: *rex Theodoricus illitteratus erat et sic obrutu sensu, ut in decem annos regni sui quattuor litteras subscriptionis edicti sui discere nullatenus potuisset.*

Greek at the Carmellyceum in Oldenzaal—, texts from early Christian and medieval sources have been collected. They concern chiefly the second category of *illitterati*, those who cannot read and/or write (synonyms: *sine litteris, litteras nescientes* or *ignorantes, litteris ineruditi*) and are divided into three groups (clergy, monks, laymen).

Those who cannot read or write stay in the twilight of history. Because of the scanty information about them it is practically impossible to indicate the percentage of *illitterati* in Antiquity or in the early Middle Ages. At any case, there must have been clear differences between town and country, between the numerous provinces of the vast Roman Empire and between the various periods.[5]

It is generally known that statistic analysis of Egyptian papyrus texts—the most extensive material we possess—did not yield much concrete results, the material being too limited for such an analysis of the degree of illiteracy.[6] More fruitful was the method of H.C. Youtie, who tried to study the social significance of the established cases of illiteracy: from which environment did these persons originate, which career did they make? It appeared that the social strata were not homogeneous as to the knowledge of reading and writing and that *agrammatos* could also denote a person who did not know Greek, but was able to read Demotic or Coptic texts.[7] Making use of the hagiographic material, Eva Wipzycka rightly noticed that the role of the Church in the process of alphabetisation in Egypt should not be neglected; it stimulated the reading of the Bible and of popular pious texts.[8]

In *Act. Ap.* 4:13,[9] the only biblical text where *illitteratus* (*sine litteris*) figures, the apostles Peter and John are called illiterate (Greek: *agram-*

---

[5] See, for instance, Ewa Wipzycka, "Le degré d'alphabétisation en Égypte byzantine," *Revue Aug.* 30 (1984) 279–296.

[6] Cf. E. Majer-Leonhard, *Agrammatoi* (Diss. Frankfort, 1913); R. Calderini, "Gli agrammatoi nell' Egitto greco-romano," *Aegyptus* 30 (1950) 14–41.

[7] H.C. Youtie, "Agrammatos: An Aspect of Greek Society in Egypt," *Harvard Studies in Classical Philology* 75 (1971) 161–176; *Id.*, "Hypographeus: the social Impact of Illiteracy in Graeco-Roman Egypt," *Zeitschrift für Papyrologie und Epigraphik* 17 (1973) 201–221; *Id.*, "Because they do not know Letters," *Zeitschrift für Papyrologie und Epigraphik* 19 (1975) 101–108.

[8] See E. Wipzycka, "Le degré d'alphabétisation," 285: "D'ailleurs, le rôle stimulant de l'évangélisation n'était pas restreint à la mise en place d'un vaste appareil ecclésiastique, mais s'étendait à la propagation de la lecture de l'Écriture et des textes de dévotion, dont la connaissance était inséparable de la foi."

[9] Vulgata: *Videntes autem Petri constantiam et Ioannis, comperto quod homines essent sine litteris* (Vet. Lat. h: *illitterati*) *et idiotae, admirabantur.*

matos). Here we find a paradoxical opposition: though being illiterate, they speak clearly and with wisdom about divine things so as to stagger the members of the Jewish sanhedrin. It is a text which had many echoes in early Christian writings.[10]

A similar contrast between illiteracy and inspired wisdom *in religiosis* can be found also in *Adversus haereses* of Irenaeus of Lyons: Barbarian people accepting the Christian faith and bearing in their heart the salvation that was written by the Spirit without paper and ink, believed although they were illiterate, but in their faith they possessed great wisdom.[11]

And four centuries later, Gregory the Great, on account of the prosperous progress of the conversion of the Angli, alluded also to *Act. Ap.* 4:13. In a letter to Augustine, the first bishop of the Angli (601), he compared the first mission in the history of the Church with the missionary activities of his own time. Just as God chose illiterate persons as His apostles to show that conversion was not a matter of human wisdom, He also worked great things among the Angli through feeble men.[12]

In the *Tractatus* of Chromatius of Aquilea we find the opinion that the expansion of Christianity seemed the more stupendous, because that it was preached in the beginning by very simple men: "Thus (Christ) did not chose noble and rich men of this world (this could make the preaching suspect) nor the wise men of this world (then one could think that they had convinced humanity by secular wisdom), but He elected fishermen, illiterate en uneducated people, ignorant of profane erudition. Thus the grace of the Redeemer would be obvious."[13]

---

[10] See, for instance, Minucius Felix, *Octavius* 16,5: *inlitteratos, pauperes, imperitos de rebus caelestibus disputare.*

[11] Irenaeus, *Adv. haer.* 3,4,1: *sine charta et atramento scriptam habentes per Spiritum in cordibus salutem . . .; qui sine litteris . . . crediderunt; . . . propter fidem perquam sapientissimi sunt.*

[12] Greg. Magn., *Registrum* XI, 36: *Qui ut mundum ostenderet non sapientia hominum sed sua se virtute convertere, praedicatores suos, quos in mundum misit, sine litteris elegit, haec etiam modo faciens, quia in Anglorum gentem fortia dignatus est per infirmos operari.* Cf. Jerome, *In Matthaeum* 1,4,19 (CCSL, 77, 23): *piscatores et inliterati mittuntur ad praedicandum ne fides credentium non virtute Dei sed eloquentia et doctrina fieri putaretur* (almost literally borrowed by Beda, *In Marcum* 1,358–361 (CCSL, 120, 446). The combination *homines illitteratos et piscatores* also in Jerome, *In Sophoniam* 3:10–13 (CCSL, 76A, 703: opposed to the literate scribes and Jewish priests).

[13] Chromatius of Aquilea, *Tractatus* 16, *In Matth.* 4:18–25, CCSL, 9A, 263: *Non ergo nobiles mundi aut divites elegit, ne suspecta fieret praedicatio, non sapientes saeculi, ut per sapientiam saeculi persuasisse humano generi crederentur, sed elegit piscatores, illitteratos, imperitos, indoctos, ut aperta esset gratia Salvatoris.*

In the series of commentators of *Act. Ap.* 4:13, Beda, already on the border of the Middle Ages, explained *sine litteris* by a reference to the Greek text. From *agrammatos* he deduced that the author did not mean that the apostles could not read or write, but that another level is meant here: They did not command the *ars grammatica*, they had no literary knowledge.[14]

THE CLERGY

When in the second century the organisation of leadership in the Christian communities had assumed its definite shape, this implied that a certain education of the clergy was required. A priest should at least be able to read, for it was an important part of his task to read the Bible and the liturgical texts. Though there was no special training of the clergy, as a rule, some scientific training was considered indispensable and was often clearly appreciated. Sometimes a candidate did not fulfil the minimum requirements. Toward the end of the third century circumstances could even lead to the ordination of a completely illiterate bishop,[15] though this will have been an exceptional case. Our sources mention especially problematic situations. Gregory of Nyssa wrote an interesting letter about the requirements a candidate had to meet.[16]

In the fifth and sixth century, in the West it was often difficult to find able candidates for the priestly office. No doubt, it was more difficult in the country than in the towns. It was for this reason that the council of Vaison (A.D. 529) decreed that the parish-priests in the villages were obliged to educate young *lectores* who might be able to edify the rural Christian communities.[17]

---

[14] Beda, *Liber retractationis in Actus Apostolorum* (PL, 92, 1008): *"Sine litteris" dicit non quod litteras nescirent sed quod grammaticae artis peritiam non haberent; namque in Graeco apertius pro hoc verbo agrammati, hoc est inlitterati habetur.* Beda alludes also to *Act. Ap.* 4:13 in his *In Cantica Canticorum libri VI* (PL, 91, 1067): *oblitus gratiae Dei quae etiam inlitteratis et idiotis scripturarum archana revelavit.* Cf. Origenes, *Contra Celsum* 8,47; 6,2 (the apostles were too uneducated to have preached successfully by human means alone).

[15] Cf. *Didascaliae apostolorum* 3,1–18 (ed. Erik Tidner, Berlin, 1963, 5); *Constitutiones apostolorum* 2,1–2 (being unlearned does not necessarily disqualify for bishop's office).

[16] Cf. Gregory of Nyssa, *Ep. 17* (ed. G. Pasquali, *Gregorii Nysseni Epistulae, Editio altera*, Leyden, 1959, 51–58).

[17] *Iuniores lectores* (cf. can. 1 et alibi). See K.J. v. Hefele – H. Leclercq, *Histoire des Conciles II* (Paris, 1909ff.), 1110–1115.

Since the Merovingian period (after 500) the Church started to set up here and there its own schools with the main purpose to assure a summary education of the clergy. The situation was so deplorable that some priests, though being able to read, possessed only little knowledge of liturgical Latin texts. Gregory of Tours describes the hilarity caused by a priest who made a hash of Latin words.[18] According to Caesarius of Arles many people among his audience—"and perhaps some priests also"—liked to have valuable beautifully bound books, but kept them hidden in the bookcases. They did not read them themselves nor presented them to others to read. They were not aware that it was of no use to possess books without reading them.[19]

Speaking about the holy priest Sanctulus, Gregory the Great remarks that sanctity of life can compensate lack of education:[20] "We know that the venerable Sanctulus hardly possessed any knowledge of the rudiments of reading and writing. But as love is the fulfilment of the Law, he observed the whole Law in his love of God and his neighbour. What he did not know externally, lived in him internally in his love . . . Let us compare his learned ignorance with our ignorant science."

Canons of some local synods prescribe explicitly that a deacon or a priest must at least be able to read and write. Particularly in Merovingian Gaul, which suffered under a sharp cultural decline, the Church tried to counter the decline with such prescriptions. An illiterate (*sine litteris*) should not be ordained priest or deacon (council of Orleans, A.D. 533).[21] A good fifty years later (A.D. 589) the council of Narbonne (can. 11) similarly prohibited the bishop from

---

[18] Cf. Gregory of Tours, *Virtutes Martini* II,1 (Scriptores rer. Merov. I,2, 609): *Sed cum presbyter ille nescio quae rustice festiva verba depromeret, multi eum de nostris irridere coeperunt.*

[19] Caesarius of Arles, *Sermo* 1,20 (Morin I, 18): *multi sunt, et forte aliqui religiosi qui plures libros et satis nitidos et pulchre ligatos habere volunt, et ea ita armariis clausa tenent, ut illos nec ipsi legant, nec aliis ad legendum tribuant: ignorantes quod nihil prodest libros habere, et eos propter mundi impedimenta non legere.*

[20] Gregory the Great, *Dialogi* 3,37,19–20: *Scimus certe quia isdem venerabilis vir Sanctulus ipsa quoque elementa litterarum bene non noverat, sed quia plenitudo legis est caritas (Rom. 13:10), legem totam in Dei ac proximi amore servavit, et quod foras in cognitione non noverat, ei intus vivebat in amore . . . Comparemus, si placet, cum hac nostra indocta scientia illius doctam ignorantiam.*

[21] *Concilia Galliae A. 511–A. 695*, cura et studio Caroli de Clercq (CCSL, 148A; Turnholti, 1973), 101: *Presbyter vel diaconus sine literis vel si baptizandi ordinem nesciret nullatenus ordinetur.*

ordaining a candidate who could not read (*litteras ignorantem*).[22] Moreover, it was prescribed that an illiterate (*litteris inheruditus*), being ordained before and not functioning well, should lose his stipend, when, owing to his indolence, he did not correct his deficiency. And if he did not mend his ways, he should be sent to a monastery.

Around 400 the lack of priests was a real problem in the Church of North-Africa. In some parishes there was no deacon, not even an illiterate one. Bishop Aurelius of Carthage, as appears from the Acts of the council of Carthage (A.D. 401),[23] proposed to send one of the bishops to Italy to submit the problems to the bishops of Rome and Milan.

For the situation in South-Italy around 600 a letter of Gregory the Great to bishop John of Squillacium is illuminating. Gregory remarked among other things that an illiterate ought not to be ordained priest.[24] In the Middle Ages there were sometimes similar problems. Illiteracy could be a reason to discharge a priest from his office. In his *Dialogus miraculorum* (ca. 1220), Caesarius of Heisterbach presents the example of a priest (*sacerdos idiota*) who pleads his cause with pope Innocentius, a *vir litteratissimus*. Touched by his simple words, the pope agrees that he may retain his parish, *quam propter illitteraturam perdere merito debuerat.*[25]

THE MONKS

Among the monks in the deserts of Egypt and Syria there were many illiterates. In monastic writings the illiterate monk, who, confronted with learned and literate heathens, nevertheless appears to be wiser than his visitors, is a stereotypical figure. Such an episode

---

[22] *Ibid.*, 256: *Amodo nulli liceat episcoporum ordinare diaconum aut presbiterum literas ignorantem; set si qui ordinati fuerint, cogantur discere. Qui vero diaconus aut presbyter fuerit literis inheruditus et desidiose legere vel implere officium distulerit et in ecclesia paratus ad omnia non fuerit, ab stipendio reiciendum . . . Aut quid erit in ecclesia Dei, si non fuerit ad legendum exercitatus? Et si perseveraverit desidiose, et non vult proficere, mittatur in monasterio, quia non potest nisi legendo edificare populum.*

[23] *Concilia Africae A. 345–A. 525*, cura et studio C. Munier (CCSL, 149; Turnholti, 1974), 194: *tanta indigentia clericorum est, multaeque ecclesiae ita desertae sunt, ut ne unum quidem diaconum vel inliteratum, habere reperiantur.*

[24] *Registrum* II 37: *Praecipimus autem, ne umquam illicitas ordinationes facias . . . aut ignorantem litteras.*

[25] Caesarius of Heisterbach, *Dialogus miraculorum* 6,29 (ed. J. Strange, Cologne-Bonn-Brussels, 1841; anast. reprint Ridgewood, 1966, 381).

is to be found for the first time in the *Vita Antonii* of Athanasius, the prototype of Christian biography. The pagan philosophers, trying to test the wisdom of Anthony, were impressed by his intelligent answers.[26] Anthony did not receive a profane education ("*grammata* cannot in the *Vita* refer to elementary education in how to read and write,")[27] but this was compensated by his spiritual wisdom.[28]

This contrast between learned men and the illiterate monk recalls *Act. Ap.* 4:13. In this connection, a passage in Cassian asks for our attention, where the true spiritual wisdom of a saint is opposed to secular erudition. The latter, according to Cassian, can be compared with a tree that only has useless leaves, whereas the first is like a tree loaded with fruits.[29] It is this situation that has been characterised by the oxymoron *docta ignorantia*.[30]

The monk-bishop Martin of Tours fits also in this category: Sulpicius Severus characterized him as an illiterate who had the gift of wisdom and was able to explain the Scripture.[31]

The Rule of Pachomius prescribed that everyone who wanted to become a monk but was unable to read, should be obliged to learn it. Every day, at the first, third and sixth hour, he should apply before his teacher in the monastery. He had to learn the letters, then the syllables and the words. When someone was but little motivated, supervision should be exercised so that he should not neglect to practise reading.[32] All the monks should be able to read the Bible.

---

[26] *Vita Antonii* 73,1 (old Latin translation): *qui litteras nesciebat*; 73,3 *quia videbant tantum intellectum in homine inlitterato quem dicunt idiotam*. Like here, in *Vita Antonii* 85,5 the Greek *idiotès* has been rendered with two words in the old Latin translation: *Unde enim homini inlitterato et idiotae tantam et talem mentem, nisi quia diligitur a Deo?*

[27] See S. Robinson, *The Letters of St. Anthony*. Origenist Theology, Monastic Tradition and the Making of a Saint (Bibliotheca Historico-Ecclesiastica Lundensis 24; Lund, 1990), 141; cf. also G. Garitte, "A propos des lettres de S. Antoine l'ermite," *Le Muséon* 52 (1939) 13–39.

[28] Cf. *Vita Antonii* 66,2.

[29] Cassianus, *Conlationes* 14,16,6–7.

[30] Cf. Gregory the Great, *Dial.* 3,37,20 (the *docta ignorantia* of the priest Sanctulus); id., *Dial.* 2, Prol. (the well-known characterizing of Benedict: *scienter nescius et sapienter indoctus*); id., *Hom. in ev.* 35,8 (Stephanus of Rieti: *lingua rustica—docta vita*).

[31] J. Fontaine, *Vie de S. Martin* (Sources Chrétiennes 133–135; Paris, 1967), 1075: "La même contradiction paradoxale entre l'inculture et la facilité à parler avec profondeur et clarté des choses de Dieu, est ici constatée en la personne de Martin. Le thème est parallèle à celui de l'opposition entre oratores et piscatores." See also: M. Hirschberg, *Studien zur Geschichte der 'simplices' in der alten Kirche* (Berlin, 1944); M. Bambeck, "Fischer und Bauer gegen Philosophen: ein christlicher Topos in Antike und Mittelalter," in: *Mittellateinisches Jahrbuch* 18 (1983) 29–50.

[32] *Praecepta* 139 (A. Boon, *Pachomiana Latina* [Louvain, 1932], 50): *Et si litteras*

Essentially there should be in the Pachomian monasteries nobody who could not read. This is the more remarkable as in the country of Upper-Egypt, where most of the monasteries were built, illiteracy was widespread.

In the first monastic Rules of the Occident we also find the prescription that all the monks in a monastery should learn to read. Thus in the Rule of Caesarius of Arles it says that: "they must learn the letters" (*litteras discant*). The same prescription was inserted in the Rules of Aurelianus, successor of Caesarius as bishop of Arles, and of Ferreolus, bishop of Uzès.[33] Only after mastering that facility, could the monks consecrate themselves to the reading of the Bible (*lectioni vacare*), for which activity a part of the order of the day had been reserved. It is noteworthy that *lectio* in these Rules was limited to the reading of the Holy Scripture and that profane authors remained beyond the horizon of the monks.

Laymen

Whereas the profane school of Antiquity survived in the Greek East,[34] in great parts of the Occident it fell into decay after the German invasions. In Gaul the former school disappeared nearly completely around 500, but in Italy it held its own longer. The Church tried to remedy this deficiency by founding monastery schools and later on Episcopal and cathedral schools. Although they were principally intended to educate the future clergy and the monks, the lack of secular schools caused children of well-to-do parents who did not enter into holy orders, to be sent to these schools as well.[35]

---

ignorabit, hora prima et tertia et sexta vadet ad eum qui docere potest et qui ei fuerit delegatus, et stabit ante illum, et discet studiosissime cum omni gratiarum actione. Postea vero scribentur ei elementa, syllabae, verba ac nomina, et etiam nolens legere compelletur. Et omnino, nullus erit in monasterio qui non discat litteras.

[33] Cf. Caesarius, *Regula ad monachos* 14 (PL, 67, 1100); *id.*, *Regula ad virgines* 17 (PL, 67, 1109) *Omnes litteras discant*; Aurelianus, *Regula ad monachos* 32 (PL, 67, 391) and *Regula ad virgines* 26 (PL, 68, 402) *Litteras omnes discant*; Ferreolus, *Regula ad monachos* 11 (PL, 66, 963) *Omnis qui nomen vult monachi vindicare, litteras ei ignorare non liceat.*

[34] See Marguerite Harl, "Église et enseignement dans l'Orient grec au cours des premiers siècles," in: *Église et Enseignement*. Actes du Colloque du Xe anniversaire de l'Institut d'Histoire du Christianisme de l'Université Libre de Bruxelles, Édités par Jean Préaux (Brussels, 1977), 17–31.

[35] See Blumenkamp, art. *Erziehung* (*RAC* 6,537ff.); H.-I. Marrou, *L'histoire de l'éducation dans l'Antiquité classique* (Paris, 1965^6); P. Riché, *Éducation et Culture dans l'Occident barbare, VIe–VIIe siècles* (Paris, 1973^3).

A new type of school was developed, providing for other wants. Classical Latin learnt by the study of the traditional school authors was no longer needed and was replaced by biblical Latin. Texts about *illitterati* in the sixth and seventh century are scanty. It should, for instance, be noticed that they scarcely figure in Merovingian hagiography. Nearly all these saints are described as children of *nobiles* or even *nobilissimi parentes*, receiving an education in the *studia liberalia*. They should be exemplary in all respects and of these qualities a noble origin was also a part. In the Merovingian period only the elite went to school and the great mass was illiterate.[36]

But the sources mention also some exceptions. So Walaricus, abbot of Leuconay, looking after his sheep as a boy, wanted to learn the alphabet like the boys of noble origin.[37] Pirenne argued that at that time there must have been in Gaul some lay schools where boys were prepared for the official service and where also talented children of simple freeborn men were admitted. So we read in Gregory of Tours that Leobardus was sent to school at the usual age. Not yet knowing that he later would choose the religious life, he was prepared for the official service.[38] Even in the primitive situation of the Merovingian period, there was need of some *notarii* for the land registry, tributes, jurisdiction and commerce. A homily of Caesarius of Arles informs us that merchants who were not able to write, engaged book-keepers (*mercenarii litterati*), who conducted their correspondence and posted up the books.[39]

As in Italy under the Ostrogoths, in Spain under the Visigoths and in North-Africa under the Vandals, there were some remnants of the profane school in an adapted form in Gaul south of the Loire in the sixth century.

---

[36] See F. Graus, *Volk, Herrscher und Heiliger im Reich der Merowinger. Studien zur Hagiographie der Merowingerzeit* (Praha, 1965), 362–363; H. Pirenne, "De l'état de l'instruction des laïques à l'époque mérovingienne," *Rev. Bén.* 46 (1934) 164–177.

[37] *Vita Walarici* 1 (ed. B. Krusch, *Script. rer. Merov.* IV, 161): ʿ*Puerulus . . . oviculas patris sui ibidem per pascua laeta circumagens, . . . audivit in locis vicinorum propinquis qualiter nobilium parvulorum mos est doctoribus instruere scolas. Exin tali desiderio provocatus, tabellam sibi faciens, cum summa veneratione humilique prece a praeceptore infantium depoposcit ut sibi alfabetum scriberet et notitiam litterarum insinuaret* (the value of this source is however questionable, since this *Vita* is dating only from the eleventh century).

[38] Gregory of Tours, *Vitae patrum* 20 (ed. B. Krusch, *Mon. Germ. Hist., Script. rer. Merov.* III, 741): *qui tempore debito cum reliquis pueris ad scolam missus . . . nesciens se clericum esse futurum, iam ad dominicum parabatur . . . ministerium.*

[39] Caesarius of Arles, *Sermones* (PL, 39, 2325).

Only a few illiterates are expressly mentioned. One of them is Servulus, a paralytic at Rome (around 600), who had his regular place in the portico of San Clemente. In a homily, Gregory the Great speaks with appreciation of his interest in the Scripture, which however he cannot read. From the alms he received he bought codices of the Bible, which he made others read to him. Thus he became familiar with the biblical texts.[40]

Biblical stories, painted on the church walls or in mosaic, had a decorative function but were also intended to be a support for the illiterate. A well known text from the beginning of that tradition in the Occident (around 400) is to be found in the poems of Paulinus of Nola, who remarks that the biblical scenes decorating the *basilica nova* of Saint Felix can tell those who cannot read—and most of the visitors of that church were, as Paulinus says, peasant people—what others can read in the biblical texts.[41]

In the Greek Church similar ideas had been developed. Thus Nilus of Ancyra (first half of the fifth century) declares that Old and New Testament stories on church walls are meant for "the illiterate who were unable to read the Holy Scripture."[42]

Theodoret of Cyrus presents a pagan antipode. There are pagans, he says, who are unable to read and for whom in any case the works of the Greek poets and philosophers about the mythological stories are beyond their horizon. To deceive also these simple people, the devil taught painters and sculptors to make pictures and statues of the gods and to represent mythological scenes, that are to be seen everywhere, not only in the pagan temples but also in the squares and streets of the towns.[43]

---

[40] Gregory the Great, *Hom.* 15,5 (PG, 76, 1133D–1134A): *Nequaquam litteras noverat, sed Scripturae Sacrae sibimet codices emerat, ut religiosos quosque in hospitalitate suscipiens, hos coram se legere sine intermissione faciebat; . . . ut iuxta modum suum plene sacram Scripturam disceret, cum, sicut dixi, litteras funditus ignoraret.* The same story in *Dial.* 4,15,3.

[41] See Paulinus of Nola, *Carmen* 27, 511–516 and 542–555: *Sancti Pontii Meropii Paulini Nolensis Carmina* (CSEL, 30) edidit Guilelmus de Hartel. Editio altera supplementis aucta curante Margit Kamptner, Vindobonae 1999, 285–286: *picturas fucatis agmine longo/porticibus* (510–511)—*turba frequentior hic est/ rusticitas non cassa fide neque docta legendi* (547–548)—*cernite quam multi coeunt ex omnibus agris* (552)—*longinquas liquere domos* (554).

[42] Nilus of Ancyra, *Letter to the Prefect Olympiodorus, Epistularum Liber* IV 61 (PG, 79, 577D).

[43] Theodoret of Cyrus, *Curatio affectionum Graecarum* 7,6 (Sources Chrétiennes, 57; ed. P. Canivet, Paris, 1958), 296.

Besides images on the walls of the churches, an exemplary manner of life can also support the words of the preacher for those who
do not know the letters of the alphabet, as Gregory the Great remarks
in a letter. In this way these people can learn the intentions of the
Bible.[44] And in another passage he says that the illiterate come into
contact with the Scripture when they see how it is put into practice
by those who live according to the words of the Scripture.[45]

Well known are other passages where Gregory gives his opinion
about the role of images in the churches:[46] "Pictures are used in
churches so that those who are ignorant of letters may at least read
by seeing on the walls what they cannot read in books (*codicibus*)."[47]
And: "What writing (*scriptura*) does for the literate, a picture does for
the illiterate looking at it, because the ignorant see in it what they
ought to do; those who do not know letters read in it. Thus especially for the nations (*gentibus*), a picture takes the place of reading . . . Therefore you ought not to have broken that what was placed
in the church in order not to be adored but solely to instruct the
minds of the ignorant" (transl. L. Duggan).[48]

---

[44] Gregory the Great, *Registrum* III, 13 (to Agnellus of Fundi): *Tua praedicatione qui
litteras nesciunt, quid divinitus praecipiatur, agnoscant . . . Sicque te in cunctis operibus exhibere
festina, ut scripturam constrictionemque* (= *scripturam constrictam*: a summary of the Scripture)
te habeant, quicumque aut neglegit aut non potest lectione formari.

[45] Cf. Gregory the Great, *In Ezech. II, Hom. 10,18* (CCSL, 142, 394): *Qui (sc.
adhuc carnaliter vivunt) et si fortasse litteras ignorant et praecepta Dei legere non valent, certe in
multorum fidelium conversatione bona quae imitentur vident. Ecce in Ecclesia voces sancti Evangelii
atque apostolorum sonant, ecce exempla bene viventium cotidie hominum oculis opponuntur*; Caesarius
of Arles, *Sermo* 75,3: *et lectionem divinam aut ipsi frequentius relegamus, aut si nos ipsi legere non possumus, illos qui legunt . . .*

[46] See the texts in *S. Gregorii Magni Registrum Epistularum libri* VIII–XIV, ed.
D. Norberg (CCSL, 140A; Turnholti, 1982): IX 209 (768); XI 10 (873–876); cf.
also L.G. Duggan, "Was Art really the 'Book of the illiterate'?," *Word and Image* 5
(1989) 227–251.

[47] *Reg.* IX 209 (First Letter to Serenus): *Idcirco enim pictura in ecclesiis adhibetur, ut
hi qui litteras nesciunt saltem in parietibus videndo legant, quae legere in codicibus non valent.*

[48] *Reg.* XI 10 (Second Letter to Serenus): *Nam quod legentibus scriptura, hoc idiotis
praestat pictura cernentibus, quia in ipsa ignorantes vident quod sequi debeant, in ipsa legunt qui
litteras nesciunt; unde praecipue gentibus pro lectione pictura est* (cf. 875: *Ut nescientes litteras
ipsam historiam intendentes, quid dictum sit discerent*). Cf. H.L. Kessler, "Pictorial Narrative
and Church Mission in Sixth-Century Gaul," in: *Studies in the History of Art* 16 (1985)
76; P. van Dael, "Biblical Cycles on Church Walls: pro lectione pictura," in: J. den
Boeft – M. van Poll-van den Lisdonk (eds), *The Impact of Scripture in Early Christianity*
(Supplements to *VC* 44; Leiden, 1999), 122–133.—In medieval acts, charters and
other documents it is noticed sometimes that witnesses are unable to write their
name; for instance in a Yugoslav charter from 1383: 'The above-mentioned witnesses from the town Durazzo, those who are able to write as well as those who

To summarise: Though *illitteratus* figures only once in the Bible (*Act. Ap.* 4:13), this passage is significant. The apostles Peter and John, though being illiterate, speak with wisdom about divine things. As to the clergy, though a special education did not exist, there were minimum requirements a candidate had to fulfil. Even in the times of the wandering of the nations and in the Merovingian period canons of local synods prescribed that a deacon or a priest must at least be able to read and to write. As to the monks, the Rule of Pachome prescribed that everyone who wanted to become monk and was unable to read, should be obliged to learn it. The same prescription is to be found in the first monastic Rules of the Occident. When monastery schools were founded, by lack of secular schools also children of well-to-do parents were sent there.

are not' (*Lexicon Latinitatis Medii Aevi Iugoslaviae*, Zagreb 1969, 554: *subscripti testes, licterati* (= *litterati*) *et Illicterati, de eadem civitate Duracii*). Who was unable to write, marked a sign with his own hand. See also Niermeyer, 971, s.v. *signum* (hand mark) *Quia litteras ignoro, . . . manu mea signum feci* (*Formula Visigothorum* nr. 7, 578).

"HE MUST GROW, I MUST DIMINISH" (JOHN 3:30): AUGUSTINE OF HIPPO PREACHING ON JOHN THE BAPTIST

ANTOON A.R. BASTIAENSEN*

The *corpus* of augustinian *sermones* includes at least eighteen sermons on John the Baptist. As to the contents of these sermons, there is a sharp distinction between those preached on 24 June, celebrated as John's birthday, and those preached on 28 August (or 27 December), celebrated as the day of his martyrdom on King Herod's orders. Not only is there a great difference in number: three on John's passion as against fifteen on his nativity, but the contents are very different as well. The sermons on his martyrdom are moralizations. Commenting on Herod's oath, which, contrary to his own desire, caused the death of the martyr, they warn against the dangers of swearing. The sermons on John's birth (one of these, *sermo* 293A,[1] has much gained in length by Dolbeau's discoveries)[2] are of an explicitly dogmatic character: their point is the difference between John and Christ in the historical process of incarnation and redemption. We start with Augustine's preaching on John's passion.

THE SERMONS ON THE PASSION

Of these sermons only three survive, 307, 308 and 94A. *Sermo* 307 begins with a subject that recurs in almost all the sermons, including those on the birth, viz. the interpretation of John's words (John

---

* Nijmegen.

[1] The sermons are numbered according to P.P. Verbraken, *Études critiques sur les sermons authentiques de saint Augustin* (Instrumenta Patristica 12; Steenbrugis-Hagae Comitis, 1976) and *Id.*, "Mise à jour du Fichier signalétique des sermons de saint Augustin," in *Aevum inter utrumque. Mélanges offerts à G. Sanders* (Instrumenta Patristica 23; Steenbrugis-The Hague, 1991), 481–490), where also for each sermon—except for those discovered lately by F. Dolbeau, *Augustin d'Hippone. Vingt-six sermons au peuple d'Afrique* (Collection des Études Augustiniennes. Série Antiquité 147; Paris, 1996)— the edition to be consulted (PL, PLSuppl, CCL and G. Morin, *Augustini Sermones post Maurinos* (Miscellanea Agostiniana 1; Roma, 1930) is indicated.

[2] Dolbeau, *Augustin d'Hippone*, 484–495

3:30): "He (Christ) must grow, I must diminish," which Augustine
takes to be borne out by Christ, who grew by being raised up on
the cross, and John, who diminished by having his head cut off.
Then the opposition is pointed out between the malignity of the two
women, Herodias and her daughter, and Herod's respect for John,
a respect that is, however, overridden by the sense of obligation
induced by the oath, which results in the death of John. It is a dangerous thing, therefore, to confirm a statement or promise by oath,
for you don't know whether you can keep to your word or not. So,
Christ tells us not to swear. That God Himself confirms by oath (cf.
Ps 109[110]:4: "The Lord has sworn, and he will not repent of it")
is not surprising, for God cannot lie. And Augustine concludes by
mentioning—a favourite topic of his—that, as a youth, he himself
used to swear, but that he had succeeded in ridding himself of this
evil. In *Sermo* 308 the dilemma is pictured of Herod, caught between
sinning by not keeping his oath and sinning by killing John. The
Bible knows of other similar situations. David had sworn to kill
Nabal, but at Abigail's request he did not keep his oath (1 Sam
25:22–33). He chose the less of two evils, but he had much better
not sworn at all. In view of man's possibility of hiding his thoughts
a declaration or promise on oath proves wrong. If someone on whom
we are dependent forces us to do something bad and makes us swear
to it, we are both guilty, but his guilt is worse: he commits a double murder, on his own soul and on ours. *Sermo* 94A centres on the
love of truth. John had told Herod the truth on his adulterous marriage with Herodias: his witnessing to this truth brought about his
death. Every Christian must bear witness to the truth, take sides
with Jesus Christ against the devil. It was against the devil that the
martyrs had to fight, but every Christian must always take up arms
against him. Illustrative is a habit of speaking of the monks. In
Numidia, to the west, Augustine says, the *servi Dei*, i.e. the monks,
in mutual asseverations use the formula *si vincas*: "as sure as I wish
you to be victorious"; in Augustine's own region and in the regions
more to the east the monks' formula is *per coronam tuam* "by your
crown." Both expressions indicate that the religious profession was
seen as martyrdom, i.e. a life-and-death struggle against the devil.
And Augustine addresses his listeners in the same way: "I adjure
you *per coronam vestram* always to fight against the devil." A similar
asseveration appears in a sermon for Christmas, *Sermo* 196,4,4: "I
adjure you by him who was born today." There is no denying a

certain inconsistency in Augustine's attitude, for in his other declarations all formulas of swearing are dismissed. But expressions in
connection with spiritual well-being, apparently, were considered
innocent, in opposition, for example, to the formulas condemned in
Sermo 180,6,6: *per deum* "by God" and *testis est deus* "God is my witness," because they often misuse the name of God to confirm lies
and other false declarations.

The Sermons on the Birth

1. Sermo *287*

The sermons for John's birthday are of a quite different nature.
Their contents can be summarised in the words: John the Forerunner's
and Christ the Lord's place in the history of salvation. Though varied and at times gripping, the preaching always elaborates on this
one theme. The same biblical scenes are evoked, the same words
from the Bible quoted and explained in the same way, the same
side-reflections made, the same formulas used. Exemplary is *Sermo*
287, a sermon from the last years of Augustine's life, abruptly ended
because of the heat (and perhaps of the preacher's tiredness): although
cut short the sermon presents practically the whole range of Augustine's
usual statements on the subject. It runs as follows. The celebration
of John's birthday is a very special event. The birthdays of Christ
and of John are the only birthdays the Church celebrates, proof of
the exceptional greatness of this man, called also by Christ the greatest of those born of women (Matt 11:11). But John declares that he
who comes after him, i.e. Jesus Christ, ranks before him (John 1:15).
If John is the greatest of men, Christ must be more than man. He
is God, the Word that was in the beginning, that was with God and
was God (John 1:1). But Christ has a birthday too, for the Word
has become flesh (John 1:14). As the Word of the Father he was
not born, but by his birth in the flesh he became a human being,
so that we celebrate his birthday. Of both John and Christ the birth
was miraculous, announced by an angel: one, the servant and forerunner, was born of a barren woman and a man advanced in years;
the other, the Lord and possessor, was born of a virgin without a
man. John, who wished to be inferior to his Lord, said: "I am not
worthy to untie the thong of his sandal" (John 1:27); even had he
been worthy, the kneeling and bending down would already have

been a humiliation; but he made himself as small as possible and crept under the rock, for he was a lamp, and feared to be extinguished by a gust of pride. John wanted himself to diminish and Christ to grow (John 3:30): therefore the light of day after John's birthday on 24 June diminishes, and after Christ's birthday on 25 December increases; and for the same reason John died shortened by being beheaded and Christ died lengthened by being raised on the cross. Mary, on hearing that she would conceive in her womb, asked the angel how this could be, since she had no husband; and the angel answered that she would conceive by the overshadowing of the power of the Most High (Luke 1:34–35). No lust would be involved, no passion, no heat, no *aestus*. Then, interrupting himself, the bishop says: "But we ourselves suffer now from heat, *aestus*: let us stop."

2. *The other sermons*

It is an untimely conclusion, but most of what in Augustine's eyes the subject required had been said, as a global comparison with the other birthday-sermons makes clear. In these sermons, however, some supplements and particulars occur that ask for our attention. They are of a twofold nature: some expand on themes that belong to the main subject, others discuss attendant points, mainly in connection with the never ending fight against unorthodox doctrine and practice.

DISCUSSION OF THE ESSENTIAL THEMES

I am going to discuss here four themes which Augustine considers essential: 1) the theme of *verbum*, "word," against *vox*, "voice"; 2) the theme of *lucerna*, "lamplight," against *lumen, lux, sol*, "daylight," "sunlight"; 3) the aspect of the different circumstances of the two births, in particular the different reactions of Zechariah and Mary; 4) the aspect of the different season and the different passion. It is always a word of the Bible that marks the start of Augustine's explanations.

As to the first theme, "word" against "voice," there is a complication in that this theme fascinated Augustine not only as a pastor but also as an anthropologically interested critical philosopher, who asks questions like "what is language?," "how do I grasp what you say?," "how does a thought in my mind come to live in your mind too?." Although aware that his audience did not always keep up

with the flight of his ideas—and apologising for it—, he never tired
of talking to his flock about the wonderful process of "word" and
"voice" in human relationship (*Sermo* 288,3–4; 289,3; 293A,5–11;
293B,2). But in the end he always turned to the word of the Bible,
drawing from it a double spiritual sense. On the one hand, interpreting the text on the *vox clamantis in deserto*, the "voice crying in
the wilderness" (Matt 3:3), he emphasizes that John is the voice
heralding the coming of the pre-existent eternal Word (*Sermo* 288,2;
289,3; 290,4,4; 292,4,4; 293,2–3; 308A,2; 293A,5; 293B,2; 293C,1;
293D,2); on the other hand, interpreting the text on the *vox sponsi*,
the "voice of the bridegroom" (John 3:29), he states that the Word
incarnate is voice itself, the voice of the Father, heard first of all by
John, who, as a friend, hears the voice of the bridegroom, Christ
(*Sermo* 293D,3). In the whole of the birthday-sermons the mystery of
the Word and its attendant voice is the most discussed subject.

But the opposition "lamplight"—"daylight," "sunlight" also found
much favour with the bishop, commenting on Christ's word about
John: *ille erat lucerna ardens et lucens*, "he was a burning and shining
lamp" (John 5:35). John was a lamp, that is to say: he spread not
his own, but a borrowed light, borrowed from the self-existent, all-
enlightening light, Christ, the Word of God. That light cannot be
extinguished, in contrast to a lamp, the light of which is always acci-
dental and in danger of being blown out by a gust of wind. Augustine
in this context always refers to the *ventus superbiae*, the "squall of
pride," from which John, humiliating himself before Christ, is shielded
(*Sermo* 66,1; 289,4; 290,1,1; 293,3; 293D,1). Elsewhere it is noted
that the *lucerna*, the lamplight, bears witness to the *dies*, the daylight,
for Christ is called *dies*: the lamplight, John, was needed, because
the daylight was hidden and only by remaining hidden could follow
its path to Calvary (*Sermo* 293D,2; cfr. 1 Cor 2:8: "if the rulers of
this age had understood the wisdom of God, they would not have
crucified the Lord of glory"). Another reason why the lamplight was
needed was that sick eyes cannot stand the daylight (*Sermo* 128,1,1;
293,4). But John wasn't the only one to shed light. The apostles too
were luminous, for Chist called them *lux mundi*, the "light of the
world," adding that a *lucerna*, a lamp, is not put under a bushel, but
on a stand to give light to all in the house (Matt 5:14–16). That
stand, according to Augustine, was the cross of Christ, in which Paul
as a *lucerna* gloried (Gal 6:14): we too may glory in that cross, provided we realise that we are *lucernae* and, by practising humility, avoid

being blown out. The sermon ends with a corker: "in the end we
are all equal: just look into the graves."

The word *lucerna* struck another responsive chord with Augustine
in that it reminded him of the verses 17 and 18 of Psalm 131 in
the Latin version he was acquainted with: *Paravi lucernam Christo meo;
inimicos eius induam confusionem; super ipsum autem florebit sanctificatio mea,*
"I have prepared a lamp for my anointed; his enemies I will clothe
with shame, but upon himself my sanctification will flower." In the
first words *paravi lucernam Christo meo* Augustine perceived a clear mention of the two: John, the lamp, announcing Christ who was to
come. The question, then, follows: who are the enemies that will be
clothed with shame? The tekst of *Sermo* 308A,6 put it quite plainly:
inimici Christi aperti, qui, nisi Iudaei?, "who else but the Jews are Christ's
open enemies?" There are hidden enemies too, all those who lead
evil and impious lives, *inique et impie viventes.* But the enemies who
put up an open fight against Him during his life were the Jews, the
Scribes and Pharisees: they argued and quarrelled with him and he
refuted them and put them to shame (cf. Matt 21:27); in their thirst
for revenge they tortured and killed him, for they are the tenants
who put the son of the owner of the vineyard to death (Luke 20:15).
Augustine accepts the charge against the Jews, insinuated somehow
by the text of the Gospel, that they were the murderers of the
Messiah, the Son of God (*Sermo* 128,1,2; 293,4; 293D,3–4; 308A,1;
cf. *Enarr. in ps.* 131, 27 and *Tract. in Ioh.* 2,9). In connection with
this charge we find only once or twice a reference to contemporary
Jews (*Sermo* 293D,4: "day by day the Jews are confounded, but they
don't convert themselves," *cotidie confunduntur [Iudaei] et non convertun-
tur*). Because statements about John and Jesus always touch upon the
transition from the Old to the New Testament, Augustine focuses
on the Jews of that period, looked upon as Christ's adversaries. From
his point of view a condemnation is understandable, but we cannot
but deplore his position.

Augustine was also fascinated by the different circumstances of
John's birth and the birth of Christ. In nearly all the sermons the
different situation is emphasised. John was born of an old, hitherto
childless, couple, Jesus of a young woman, who preserving her vir-
ginity, *integritas,* and not knowing the passion of lust, *aestus libidinis,*
was overshadowed by the Holy Spirit (*Sermo* 289,1; 290,1,1. 4,4;
291,5; 293,1; 293A,2; 293B,3; 293C,1). Augustine speaks with respect
and tenderness of Mary, the young virgin, a woman in her prime,

in the springtime of life, *virgo primaeva, iuvencula crescens, iuvencula florens*. Most charming is the conclusion of *Sermo* 291, picturing a conversation between the preacher, Mary and the angel of the Annunciation on the topic of the grace bestowed on Mary. The preacher addresses Mary: you were virgin when you conceived him, you remained virgin when you gave birth to Him: "where did you get this privilege?," *unde tibi hoc*? Mary answers: I shy away (*verecundor*) from telling you about my bliss myself; listen to the salutation of the angel and acknowledge your salvation; believe him as I did, and let the angel tell you where I got this privilege, *unde mihi hoc*. The preacher asks the angel: where did Mary get this privilege?, *unde Mariae hoc*? And the angel: I said this, as I greeted her: *ave, gratia plena*. Mary, here, is not a Greek *Theotokos*, but a Latin *Madonna*.

Mary is not only graced by her corporal *integritas*. Hers was also a spiritual *integritas*, a purity of faith, an innocent way of life. The comparison with Zechariah, Augustine remarks, is revealing. It is a nearly identical miraculous message they both receive, but "equal voice, unequal heart," *similis vox, dissimile cor* (*Sermo* 291,5): doubt prevails in Zechariah's heart, not in Mary's (cf. Luke 1:11–22. 29–38). She believes without hesitation, only asks how this is to come about, since she has no husband. Zechariah is told that he loses his speech for the time being, Mary that she is blessed among women, that Gods power will overshadow her and that she will be mother of the Son of God (*Sermo* 290,4,4; 291,5; 293B,4; 293C,1).

In yet another way Augustine underscores the difference between the birth of John and that of Jesus. In many sermons (*Sermo* 287,3,4; 288,5; 289,5; 293A,6; 293B,3; 293E,2 en 293D,5), there appears, sooner or later, sometimes most unexpectedly, a reflection on the birthdays of the two and on the character of their martyrdom. It is a curious thing that the two subjects go together, except in *Sermo* 293,1, where mention is made of the birthdays only. Augustine's explanation, based on John's words: "He must grow, I must diminish," *Illum oportet crescere, me autem minui* (John 3:30), as we have seen above, runs as follows. Christ is superior, John inferior: look at the data of their births: at the day of Christ's birth, 25 December, the days begin to increase, at that of John, 24 June, to diminish; look also at their passion: Christ's death was an increase, an elevation—he was raised on the cross—, John's death was a decrease, a diminution— he was beheaded—. It looks as if the two topics and their combination was a more or less obligatory part of Augustine's preaching, expected and appreciated also by the audience. It has to do with the popular character of the sermons, but both the frequency and the combination attract our attention. The question whether this was a traditional or a special arrangement will be treated further on.

DISCUSSION OF INCIDENTAL THEMES

With the themes hitherto discussed Augustine's starting point is always the word of the Bible on the personality and the mission of John and Jesus. It is, in other words, the subject treated, the birth of John, that guides Augustine's thought. The situation alters when questions of faith and morality present themselves. Augustine's lasting concern for the purity of doctrine and the correctness of behaviour of his flock sometimes leads him to discuss questions that have no direct relationship with the subject, John the Baptist. Indirectly, this subject was likely to lead to confrontations with Donatists and Pelagians about the hotly debated questions of doctrine and practice regarding the sacrament of baptism. But other points of doctrine or conduct too could turn up in the course of a sermon. There was a variety of religions in North Africa: how do they appear in Augustine's preaching on John the Baptist?

1. The old pagan religion

In the course of the fourth century catholic orthodoxy had gained much ground in North Africa, but even in the first decades of the fifth century its dominance was far from being undisputed. There was the *vetus superstitio*, the old pagan religion, that still had to be reckoned with. In *Sermo* 279 of the year 401—not related to John's birthday—the conversion is related of a pagan called Faustinus: the sermon concludes with the remark: the pagans get old, they decrease in number; they will finish either by conversion or by extinction, *veterescunt, minuuntur: finientur aut credendo aut moriendo*. In a sermon on John's birthday in the same year (*Sermo* 293B) the preacher condemns the relics of polytheism, the still popular rites and festivities of the past. The conclusion of the sermon is revealing. A worried pastor admonishes his flock. We must not dishonour John's birth—John's birthday coincided with a traditional midsummer festival—with the "relics of sacrilegious worship, those foolish and ludicrous celebrations," *reliquiae sacrilegiorum, . . . studia atque ioca vanitatum*—: yes-

terday, with children kindling fires, smoke and stench were all over
our town: why doesn't the older generation stop these youngsters? I
must complain about that; and this complaining won't end until the
old pagan religion has wholly disappeared, *consummetur*, and the new
religion has definitely established itself, *perficiatur*.

2. *The Jews*

In Augustine's days the Jews were numerous in North Africa. But
the condemnation of the Jews, mentioned above, is an ideological
one, directed first of all at the Jewish contemporaries of Christ. As
for Augustine's Jewish contemporaries, in his sermons on John the
Baptist he censures them only in passing.

3. *The Manichees*

Among Augustine's earliest adversaries the Manichees, his old co-
religionists, were prominent. But if I am not mistaken, clear references to their doctrine or practice are lacking in the sermons on
John. There could be a connection with the rapid disappearance of
the Manichaean menace, noted by Lancel (386–388).

4. *The Donatists*

Very sharp is the discussion with the Donatists and the refutation
of their opinion that baptism administered by a sinner or heretic is
invalid and rebaptism required. The subject-matter of the preaching
being John the Baptist and his activity at the river Jordan, it was
inevitable that questions would arise concerning the Donatist baptismal practice. In two sermons, both dating from the year 400
approximately, at the height of the controversy, the conflict erupts.
In *Sermo* 292,2,2; 4,5–8, Augustine, in a pointed argumentation (in
the second person singular), takes the Donatists to task for their practising and justifying rebaptism. The formula *ego baptizo*, "I baptise,"
he says, doesn't imply that the minister is owner of the baptismal
grace; nor does the allegory of the good tree bearing good fruit and
the bad tree bearing bad fruit (Matt 7:17–18; Luke 6:43) mean that
the fruit of baptism is not wholly the work of Christ, but depends
also on the moral quality of the minister. For that matter, John baptised Christ, and who dares to say that he is the tree and Christ the
fruit? In the other sermon—the passage in question has become

available thanks to Dolbeau's discoveries (*Sermo Dolbeau* 10, 13–16)—
Augustine refutes the argument of the Donatists that, if Paul ordered
the rebaptism of those who had been baptised by John (Acts 19:1–7),
they too had the right and the obligation of rebaptising those who
had been baptised by an unworthy minister. Augustine replies: the
baptism Paul declared insufficient was John's, not Christ's. Christ's
baptism is valid, independently of the minister's merits.

5. *The Arians*

In spite of their condemnation at the Council of Nicea in 325 the
Arians, and their allies, the Eunomians, built up a strong position
in the course of the fourth century. In Augustine's eyes both were
dangerous heretic sects, because their doctrine was detrimental to
the divine nature and the personality of the Son, Gods consubstan-
tial Word. At first, they did not have large numbers of adherents in
North Africa, but political and other developments had caused a
regular stream of immigrants, many Arians among them, to come
to North Africa and mix up with the local population. Not only in
Carthage, but in Hippo too Arians had made their appearance,[3] and
more than once Augustine entered into a discussion with them. At
the end of *Sermo* 229O, preached during Easter-week about the year
420, he mentions with great joy that an Arian debater, who with
three colleagues had challenged him, at the end of the dispute had
abjured Arius and had become a catholic. Some years before, in a
sermon on the birth of John, he had emphasised, appealing to the
catholicity of the audience (*utique catholici auditis*), that the Son is not
an inferior God; the one God is Father, Son and Holy Spirit; only
because of his divine nature the Son could be the Mediator between
God and man (*Sermo* 293,7). Without doubt Augustine warned here
his flock against the faulty Arian conception of God. In a much earlier sermon, preached before 400, Augustine, commenting on the
scene of Jesus' baptism, when the Holy Spirit descended and the
voice was heard of the Father (Matth 3:16–17 and parallel places),
likewise had defended the equality of the three Divine Persons (*Sermo*

---

[3] In *Sermo* 46,8,18 Augustine says: *eunomiani non sunt in Africa*. But in the course
of the years a growing number of Arians had come to Hippo: see A.-M. La
Bonnardière, *Recherches de chronologie augustinienne* (Paris, 1965), 92–101, and S. Lancel,
Saint Augustin (Paris, 1999).

308A,4–5): the anti-Arian tenor stands out. And possibly the same holds good for an undated and in bad form transmitted sermon, in which, with a reference to Paul's Epistle to the Philippians (Phil 2:6), Augustine maintains the equality of the Son with respect to the Father (*Sermo* 293E,2).

6. *The Pelagians*

Of the discussions with the Pelagians we perceive echoes in at least one, and perhaps two sermons, both dating probably from the first phase of the conflict, in the years 412–416. In the first one (*Sermo* 290,6,7) the preacher, expanding on a comparison between Zechariah and Mary, quotes the verse of Mary's *Magnificat: Esurientes implevit bonis et divites dimisit inanes* (Luke 1:53). Prototypes of the *divites* to be sent empty away and of the *esurientes* to be filled with good things are the Pharisee and the tax collector (Luke 18:10–14), the Pharisee priding himself on his righteousness, the tax collector humbly asking for pardon. To them and to all those who are like them the word of the Gospel applies: "everyone who exalts himself will be humbled, and he who humbles himself will be exalted" (Luke 14:11). And because all good gifts come from God, man must not arrogantly attribute justice to himself. Because of the emphatic character of the orator's statements the Maurist editors think that he attacks the Pelagian view of man's self-reliance in matters of salvation. But this could be doubted, because the line of thought is augustinian in itself, irrespective of an anti-Pelagian context. The evidence is much greater in the other sermon (*Sermo* 293,8–11), where, in a comparison of John and Christ, it is forcefully stated that Christ, as the only Mediator between God and man, is the Saviour of all human beings, newborn babies included: *per unum salvamur, maiores, minores, senes, iuvenes, parvuli, infantes* (*Sermo* 293,8). There is only one door, and babies, just as grown-ups, have to pass through it. That is why a mother, prompted by her faith, runs with her baby to the church to have it baptised, *testis est mater fideliter currens cum parvulo baptizando ad ecclesiam* (*Sermo* 293,10). That running to the church appears whenever Augustine defends infant baptism against the Pelagians: *Sermo* 174,7,8; 176,2,2 (the babies cannot run on their own, but because they want to be baptised, they run on other people's legs, *alienis pedibus currunt*); *De peccatorum meritis et remissione et de baptismo parvulorum* 1,18,23 (they are brought to the church by the pious fear of their

running relatives, *suorum currentium pio timore portantur*); *Contra Iulianum*
1,7,31 (throughout the world mothers run daily with their children
to Jesus Christ, *matres quotidie toto orbe terrarum . . . ad Christum Iesum . . . cum
parvulis currunt*); further *De nuptiis et concupiscentia* 2,2,4; *De natura et origine animae* 2,9,13; 3,10,14; *De civitate dei* 13,4 (to run to Christ's grace,
ad Christi gratiam currere), *Epist.* 131,7,21; 8,23.24.

TYPICALLY AUGUSTINE

Our last discussion concerns the question: what is typical of Augustine
in all this? I think that two points in this respect deserve our attention, one regarding the arrangement of the subject-matter in the sermons, the other regarding a detail of stylistic character. As for the
first point, in the foregoing we have seen that Augustine, in his
preaching on John, usually develops the same ideas. It can hardly
be doubted that this constant recurring of the same pattern is a particular of Augustine. A case in point, in my view, is the remarkable
explanation of the scriptural text *Illum oportet crescere, me autem minui*
(John 3:30). As we have seen, Augustine proposes a double analogy. That Christ is the superior, John the inferior is reflected on
one hand by the birthdays of the two, the birthday of Christ marking the increase, that of John the decrease of the daylight, on the
other hand by the fact that Christ was elevated by the crucifixion,
John diminished by the decapitation. Is this speculation Augustine's
own invention or an inheritance of the past? We must of course take
into account the Latin idiom. The opposition *crescere—minuere/minui*
was used for the indication of the increase and decrease of the shape
of the celestial bodies. In Plinius Maior we read in 2,95: *sidera . . . cresce-
rent minuerenturque*; in 37,181: *crescentis minuentisque sideris speciem*; the
same combination applies to the moon in 2,58, as in Vegetius, *De
re militari* 3,42: *diverso lunae crescentis minuentisque statu*. It is therefore
understandable that John's *Illum oportet crescere, me autem minui* was
seen in connection with he increase and decrease of the light of day.
That this text could also be seen with relation to the different martyrdom of the two results from the existence of the expressions: *capite
(de)minuere, capitis (de)minutio*, indications for an administrative declaration of death, a deprivation of civil rights. The term *caput* in its
original sense, in combination with *(de)minuere*, suggested the idea of
decapitation, and *crescere*, correspondingly, of elevation on the cross.

Was Augustine the first to propose the double analogy? A consultation of the *Biblia Patristica* for the text of John 3,30 (including the quotations of the original Greek: ἐκεῖνον δεῖ αὐξάνειν, ἐμὲ δὲ ἐλαττοῦσθαι) tells us that writers of the first four centuries didn't present this explanation: in the relevant passages in their works the double analogy is not found.[4] A pseudo-ambrosian sermon, hesitantly attributed to the Maximus of Turin who is considered by some scholars as a contemporary of Augustine, has the theme of the increase and decrease of the daylight, not that of the two forms of martyrdom. There is, however, so much uncertainty as to the identity and the period of life of this Maximus that a dependence on him on the part of Augustine cannot be seriously contemplated—should there be a relationship, it would probably be the other way round.[5] It cannot be doubted, I think, that Augustine's handling of the biblical word is of his own invention, an adaptation to the taste of his audience. We know that after his ordination to the priesthood he took to a careful study of Holy Scripture. Is this explanation of the passage of the Gospel (John 3:30) and many another exegetical peculiarity in the preaching on John the Baptist perhaps the fruit of the exegetical study of the rhetor Augustine, preparing for his functioning as minister of the Word?

Remarkable in a more stylistic respect is, in my view, the regular use, in the discussion with the Pelagians, of the verb *currere* in passages that picture mothers and other members of the family "running" with the new-born babies to the church in order to have them baptised by the priest. This expressive *currere*, indicating haste resulting from decidedness, equally bears Augustine's stamp. We don't find it in Cyprian's *Epistula* 160, a text, repeatedly quoted by Augustine, in which infant baptism is defended. Ambrose, in *De Abraham*

---

[4] Tertullian, *De oratione* 1,3; Clement of Alexandria, *Stromata* 6,94,6; Origen, *Catenae in Iohannem* 520,12; 521,1; *Commentarius in epist. ad Romanos* 178,1 (see the study of J.T. Lienhard, "Origen and Augustine: Preaching on John the Baptist," *Augustinian Studies* 26 (1995) 37–46, for the difference between Origen's view of John and the much more christological interpretation of Augustine); Basil of Caesarea, *De baptismo* 1,2,4; Ambrose, *De patriarchis* 11,47; *Expositio evang. secundum Lucam* 2,81; 7,12. *Biblia Patristica. Index des citations et allusions bibliques dans la littérature patristique 1–6* (Paris, 1975–1995).
[5] Maximus of Turin, *serm.* 99 *extr., de natale domini salvatoris*, 1 (A. Mutzenberger [CCL, 23; Turnholti, 1962], 394): *in nativitate Christi dies crescit, et in Iohannis nativitate decrescit*; on Maximus as possible contemporary of Augustine, see Mutzenbecher, XXXV.

2,11,80–81, also defends infant baptism, but in a much more theoretical way: there is no question of "running to the church to the
baptismal font." In *De Noe et arca* 19,70 it is said of Jews, convert-
ing to the Christian faith, that they "run to the font and ask for
instruction in the faith," *currunt ad fontem, doctrinam expetunt*: the font,
here, is not the baptismal font, but the fountain of Christian doctrine. In *Expositio evang. sec. Lucam* 7,29 and 6,35 a repentant sinner
is said to run to the church, *currere ad ecclesiam*, and to run to do
penance, *currere ad paenitentiam*. But the image of mothers hastening
with their babies to the font is not evoked. Nor does Jerome employ
currere in that context:[6] translating Origen (*Hom. Origenis in Lucam* 14)
he formulates in a neutral way; "children are baptised for the for-
giveness of sins," *parvuli baptizantur in remissionem peccatorum*. It is the
strongly felt need to express himself as forcefully as possible in this
important matter that led Augustine to this drastic and provocative
turn of phrase. It is no literary oratory, but an elementary kind of
eloquentia, characteristic of the preacher Augustine. And Caesarius of
Arles, in this point too, plagiarises Augustine, as he writes (*Sententia
de gratia* 101):[7] "while the parents run with their children to the baptismal font," *dum cum ipsis parvulis currunt parentes ad baptismum*.

---

[6] I checked all Ambrose's and Jerome's *currere*-passages with the help of Chadwick-
Healy's computerized PL-edition.
[7] PLSuppl., 4,531.

AETERNE RERUM CONDITOR:
AMBROSE'S POEM ABOUT "TIME"

JAN DEN BOEFT*

Quid est ergo tempus? Si nemo ex me quaerat, scio; si quaerenti explicare uelim, nescio. In this characteristic manner Augustine words an experience which had earlier been described by Plotinus concerning time and eternity: ἐναργές τι παρ᾽ αὐτοῖς περὶ αὐτῶν ἐν ταῖς ψυχαῖς ἔχειν πάθος νομίζομεν, "we think that we have a clear and distinct experience of them in our own souls" (tr. A.H. Armstrong), but as soon as we try to examine both notions more closely, we are baffled: ταῖς γνώμαις ἀποροῦντες.[1] Augustine goes on to note that the past does no longer exist, the future does not exist yet and the present cannot be present forever. Does time really exist? One seems compelled to conclude: *tendit non esse*, "time tends to pass into nothingness." In any case, time differs radically from eternity. God is eternal, man lives in time: *domine, pater meus aeternus es; at ego in tempora dissilui, quorum ordinem nescio, et tumultuosis uarietatibus dilaniantur cogitationes meae.*[2] Being "temporal" can be a painful experience: one feels (Augustine is, of course, far more personal: *I* feel) quite distressed.

The eleventh book of the *Confessiones* is fascinating in that it makes so clearly manifest that philosophical analysis is not necessarily a merely abstract exercise, but can lead to shattering discoveries which involve one's entire person. Nevertheless, it is primarily a philosophical way to deal with time. There are other ways in which time can be experienced. For this we may turn to Augustine's teacher in Milan, bishop Ambrose.[3] In his explanation of *in principio fecit deus caelum et terram* (Gen 1:1) he introduces Exod 12:2 *mensis hic initium mensuum erit uobis.* This concerns the feast of Passover, *quod ueris initio celebratur*, a very apt time for the creation: *inde mundi capi oportebat exordium, ubi erat oportuna omnibus uerna temperies. Unde et annus mundi*

---

* Utrecht.
[1] August., *Conf.* 11.17, Plotinus, *Enn.* 3.7.1. See E.P. Meijering, *Augustin über Schöpfung, Ewigkeit und Zeit. Das elfte Buch der Bekenntnisse* (Leiden, 1979), 57ff.
[2] August. *Conf.* 11.39.
[3] See for a survey of the relations between Augustine and Ambrose E. Dassmann in *Augustinus-Lexikon*, vol. I, 270–285.

*imaginem nascentis expressit, ut post hibernas glacies atque hiemales caligines
serenior solito uerni temporis splendor eluceat.* This set the tone for the
future; the chronological sequence of time brings with it that each
year the earth produces new seeds and buds, and thus repeats what
God had said in Gen 1:11: *germinet terra herbam faeni seminans semen
secundum genus et secundum similitudinem et lignum fructiferum faciens fructum.*
Regeneration mirrors generation and therefore the Israelites left Egypt
in spring and Easter is celebrated in spring.[4]

This is an entirely different view of time, and also one which lends
itself to be operationalized in poetical form. The penetrating analyses of book 11 of the *Confessiones* might perhaps also be turned into
poetry, for instance in the shape of philosophical hymns, but, if so,
these would primarily appeal to the intellect, less to the senses. But
there is more. Ambrose's handling of time in his discussion of the
crucial subject of creation forms a perfect match with the early Christian tradition, in which time was arranged in the yearly recurring
feasts and each day in a number of specific moments. These moments
had been indicated explicitly or implicitly by God himself. During
the first three Christian centuries various daily horaria of prayer were
developed. According to Robert Taft it is impossible to harmonize
the evidence, which cannot be fitted "into one system or horarium
without doing violence to the facts."[5] One of the most interesting
schedules is the one described in Hippolytus' *Apostolic Tradition*, ch.
41. The status and indeed the text of this work pose many problems, but the essential content of the chapter in question is not disputed. Some, not all, of the times which are commended for prayer
are directly based on Scripture, e.g. the third hour: *in hac enim hora
uisus est Christus cum fixus est in ligno,*[6] the ninth: *illa uero hora in latere
Christus punctus aquam et sanguem fudit,* midnight, because then the entire
creation rests for a moment to praise the Lord, at the cock's crow:
illa enim hora gallo cantante fili Israhel Christum negauerunt.[7]

Among the Ambrosian hymns the authenticity of which is certain
or highly probable there are four pertaining to a specific time of the

---

[4] Ambr., *Hex.* 1.13–14.

[5] Robert Taft, S.J., *The Liturgy of the Hours in East and West* (Collegeville, 1986), 27.

[6] The precise time is only mentioned in Mark 15:25: ἦν δὲ ὥρα τρίτη καὶ
ἐσταύρωσαν αὐτόν. Cf. the first verses of Ambrose's relevant hymn: *Iam surgit hora
tertia/qua Christus ascendit crucem.*

[7] Cf. Ambr. *in Luc.* 10:75: *Ubi tamen negat Petrus? Non in monte, non in templo, non in
sua domo, sed in praetorio Iudaeorum, in domo principis sacerdotum. Ibi negat, ubi ueritas non est.*

day. These can be regarded as precursors of Prudentius' *Cathemerinon*, but with a vital difference: Ambrose's hymns had a liturgical function. The first verses of the four hymns are in chronological order of the time of day: *Aeterne rerum conditor* (cock's crow), *Splendor paternae gloriae* (morning), *Iam surgit hora tertia*, *Deus creator omnium* (evening). In all four the time of day is clearly indicated: *praeco diei iam sonat* (1.5), *uerusque sol inlabere* (2.5), *grates peracto iam die/et noctis exortu preces* (4.9–10). The idea that the various times of the day have a specific function and meaning and thus testify to a deliberate order, is also indicated, though usually indirectly, with one telling exception. The first stanza of *Aeterne rerum conditor* consists of a succinct poetic statement about God's arrangement of time(s). One is justified to regard this stanza as "programmatic" for daily round hymns in general. The text runs as follows:

> Aeterne rerum conditor,
> noctem diemque qui regis,
> qui temporum das tempora,
> ut alleues fastidium.

The prominent place of *aeterne* and the remarkable phrase in vs. 3 emphasize the same contrast as was felt by Augustine in the passage quoted above from *Conf.* 11.39. In itself the first verse might be regarded as the equivalent of the first verse of the evening song: *Deus creator omnium*, but changing places would be unthinkable. In the present hymn God's eternity is focussed and contrasted with the temporality of his creation. As to the third verse, in their articles and comments scholars try to come to terms with the precise syntactical structure and the meaning of *temporum . . . tempora*. No doubt this refers to God's arrangement of the subdivisions of time (hours, months, seasons etc.). Judging from Prudentius, *Cathemerinon* 5.2 *qui certis uicibus tempora diuidis*, Prudentius understood it in this way.[8] Remarkably, however, if not downright amazingly, Ambrose's masterly use of polyptoton seems wasted on the learned readers. I am unable to think of a better way to express time's plurality over against eternity's singularity. One comes across other fine and functional specimens of polyptoton in ancient poetry and rhetoric, but here the iconic handling of this figure of speech by Ambrose is truly outstanding.

---

[8] Cf. also August. *civ.* 22.24.5: *Quam grata uicissitudo diei alternantis et noctis!*

The so-called *gallicinium*-hymn has been often studied and commented upon. If we restrict ourselves to the past two decades, three
important papers can be mentioned and two commentaries, one of
"usual" proportions by J. Fontaine and another by A. Franz with a
tremendous size.[9] Judging by the various interpretations, Ambrose's
poem contains a very intricate pattern of meanings of an allegorical
nature. Fontaine often detects "un double sens," e.g. the cock's crow
has functions which are "à la fois pratiques et symboliques." Earlier,
Charlet had argued that the words of the hymn "suggèrent au
chanteur une triple interprétation, une compréhension à trois niveaux."
Franz goes one better with four "mögliche Verständnisweisen." In
the detailed interpretation one comes across many remarkable statements. According to Fauth the first stanza implies "eine personale
Überblendung von Deus Pater und Dei Filius," which is linked with
Ambrose's "bekanntermassen besonders betonten trinitarischen Disposition"; in *segregans* (vs 8) Fontaine detects this connotation: "une sorte
de préfiguration du Jugement de Dieu"; before this verse, *uiantibus*
(vs 7) in the view of Franz can refer to "die Pilgerschaft der Gläubigen
durch die Nacht dieses Erdenlebens." Now there is no reason to
belittle the vast learning of the named scholars and I for one gladly
acknowledge to have learned much from their exercises, which can
indeed be helpful to understand the hymn. Yet there is something
unsatisfactory or, to put it more bluntly, simply wrong with their
approach. The fundamental flaw is that the character of *Aeterne rerum
conditor* disappears from sight. It is not a theological essay disguised
by its metrical form, but first and foremost, or rather: exclusively, a
lyrical poem. In this respect it is fairly ominous that none of the
scholars referred to seems to have sensed the poetical value of the

---

[9] W. Fauth, "Der Morgenhymnus Aeterne rerum Conditor des Ambrosius und
Prudentius Cath. 1 (ad galli cantum)," *JbAC* 27/28 (1984/5) 97–115; J.-L. Charlet,
"Richesse spirituelle d'une hymne d'Ambroise: *aeterne rerum conditor*," *La Maison-Dieu*
173 (1988) 61–69; P. Siniscalco, "Linguaggio della poesia e linguaggio della prosa:
un esempio fortunato in Ambrogio di Milano (*Aeterne rerum conditor*—hex. 5,24, 88s.),"
*Polyanthema (Studi di letteratura cristiana antica offerti a Salvatore Costanza = Studi Tardoantichi
VII [1989]) 151–165; Ambroise de Milan, *Hymnes*. Texte établi, traduit et annoté
sous la direction de Jacques Fontaine (Paris, 1992), 143–175; Ansgar Franz, *Tageslauf
und Heilsgeschichte. Untersuchungen zum literarischen Text und liturgischen Kontext der Tagzeithymnen
des Ambrosius von Mailand* (St. Ottilien, 1994), 147–276. The last-named author very
often refers to Joh. Kayser, *Beiträge zur Geschichte und Erklärung der Kirchenhymnen*
(Paderborn, 1886), 81–103, reprinted with a few minor alterations in *Id.*, *Beiträge
zur Geschichte und Erklärung der ältesten Kirchenhymnen* (Paderborn, 1881), 149–169.
Inexplicably, Franz continually spells the author's name as "Kaiser".

polyptoton *temporum . . . tempora*. As was argued above, this expresses how time is experienced, not analysed or discussed.

It would be pedantic to present a complete "alternative" commentary here. Instead I shall only try to explain my own approach, which entails that here and there a specific verse will be singled out. First, however, the attention should be drawn to two remarkable facts; a) the poem contains very few qualifying adjectives: *aeterne* (1), *profundae* (6),[10] and *nocturna* (7), a scarcity which in lyrical poetry is quite surprising; b) the large amount of finite verbal forms, half of which in the third person singular. All verbs denote an action, not a situation. Taken together, these linguistic facts express that something is happening all the time. Time moves on. After the first stanza, in which the basic principles were stated, the second stanza opens the description of the gradual development of one particular division of time. *Praeco diei iam sonat* (vs 5) deserves careful attention. Franz dilates exuberantly on the two nouns, but he is not interested in the verb, which Fontaine regards as a "métonymie pour le mot propre *canit*." This is also a sign of a another curious fact, viz. that, whereas the poet only introduces the word *gallus* in vs 18 (!), both commentators straightaway substitute *praeco diei* by "coq" and "Hahn."[11] Most amazing, however, especially in view of the lavish attention paid to *praeco* and *sonat*, is the absence of any note on *iam*, as if this is a mere stopgap. In fact, it is a precious colouring of the statement. In their analysis of the discourse functions of *iam* Kroon and Risselada i.a. found that *iam* can focus on the "the element . . . which runs counter to a particular . . . expectation."[12] With the simplest of devices the poet achieves much: we immediately know that a) the scene is set in the night, and b) contrary to what may have been expected, the night suddenly draws near its end: *iam* provides precisely the tinge of urgency which is needed here. The first aspect is dwelt upon in vss 6–8, which imply that the sound which in vs 5

---

[10] Fontaine aptly refers to *noctemque profundam* (Verg. *Aen.* 4.26 and 6.462).

[11] Note that the cock in Ambr. *Hex.* 5.88 is only the last of the *nocturnae aues*, the persuasive description of which begins in 5.84. See e.g. 5.85 *habet etiam nox carmina sua, quibus uigilias hominum mulcere consueuit, habet et noctua suos cantus; quid enim de luscinia dicam, quae peruigil custos, cum oua quodam sinu corporis et gremio fouet, insomnem longae noctis laborem cantilenae suauitate solatur.* The last part has been inspired by *interea longum cantu solata laborem* (Virgil, *Georgica* 1.293).

[12] C. Kroon and R. Risselada, "The Discourse Functions of *iam*," in: B. García-Hernández, *Estudios de Lingüística Latina* (Madrid, 1998), 429–445.

was recognized as the announcement of daybreak had been heard
earlier, though with a different function: in vs 7 it takes over the
function of light in the deep darkness of the night, whereas the polyptoton in vs 8 seems to hint at the various parts of the night: the
sound makes a division between them. The ancients' division of the
night is complicated by the scarcity of clear evidence. See Appendix 3 for a brief survey.

The text of the hymn is paralleled by a passage in *Hexameron*
5.88,[13] which can be found in Appendix 2. As can be seen, this parallel becomes quite clear in the third stanza. Its first two verses are
the counterpart of *hoc ipse lucifer excitatus oritur caelumque inluminat*. Note
that the sound awakens the morning star, the one who "brings light,"
and secondly, how the poetic version differs from the prosaic one,
not merely by deviant wording, but above all by the entirely different
perception of the poet: what he sees, is not the arrival in the sky of
light, but the sky's liberation from darkness. The poet perceives the
processes of nature differently. When one reads on, it becomes clear
that vss 9–10 contain only the first vignette of a series, which is held
together by the anaphoric use of *hoc*. All four are expressed with an
equally masterful economy of words. After the sky the earth and the
sea are represented by a well chosen individual scene, in which "liberation" is the indirectly hinted at common element, and the quartet
culminates in the crucial moment of Peter's repentance at daybreak.
As could be expected, instead of enjoying the poetic visualisation,
commentators prefer to detect all allegorical meanings and conno-
tations one could possibly think of. This entails some remarkable
consequences. In vs 11 the majority of scholars, gathered in a very
handy list by Franz,[14] want to emend mss *errorum* into *erronum*. Fontaine
curiously regards the mss reading as the "lectio difficilior." It seems
far more likely that the rare word *erro* was unknown to a copier at
a vital stage of the tradition. Moreover, those who refer to *Hex.* 5.88
latro suas relinquit insidias are on firm ground. Even in case one sur-
mises that Ambrose first of all meant the demons, *erro*, "vagabond,"
is quite apt. Precisely in this small philological problem the commentators' basic assumption is decisive. Franz dislikes the interpretation
"die im Dunkel der Nacht schleichende Missetäter," because "gerade

---

[13] See for a sober and careful comparison the paper of Siniscalco mentioned in
note 9.
[14] Franz, *Tageslauf*, 214–5.

durch diese Version die mehrdimensionale Sinnstruktur des Liedes zerstört wird." Theological exegesis shall prevail! Precisely for this reason it is surprising that he has failed to exploit the hidden etymology of "night" in vs 12: *quod nocet, nox* (Varro, *De lingua latina* 6.6).

Vs 16 deserves close attention for two reasons. In the first place *canente*, which in retrospect brings a change in the syntactical construction of anaphorically placed *hoc*: it now becomes clear that *hoc* is not a simple abl. causae, but the Head of an ablative absolute. Its late appearance is functional: only now the sound is identified as the crowing of a cock. Secondly, what is the tense of *diluit*? Franz provides some helpful references to other passages in Ambrose in which this verb is used in a comparable context, and then revels in its range of meanings: "in einem reizvollen Spannungsfeld zwischen metaphorischem und halbmetaphorisch-konkretem Sinn." However, he pays no attention to the fact that *diluit* can be both present and perfect tense. Of course, the incident in the courtyard of the high priest's house took place some 350 years before, and the perfect tense is apt to refer to it (cf. Fontaine's "a lavé"), but within the series *soluit* (10), *deserit* (12), *colligit* (13) it can also be present tense. In the actual liturgical performance Peter's repentance is revived, just as in the hymn *Iam surgit hora tertia* the verb in the second verse *qua Christus ascendit crucem* refers to a past act, but which the singers experience at that precise moment of their singing. More important, however, is the firm embedding of the scene of Peter's repentance in the arrangement of time. Important as it is for all Christian believers—after all it concerns the rock of the Church—, in itself it is only one of the scenes picturing daybreak. To put it into other words: it is not Peter washing away his guilt which prompts reflections on the symbolism of daybreak, but the other way round: the scene of repentance appears in its natural place in time, in accordance with the chronological order which God wanted. Peter's reaction is indeed "timely." It also marks the transition to the consequences which daybreak entails: we must all act in accordance.

Therefore, the second half of the hymn begins with a convincing exhortation: *surgamus*, "let us rise." Elsewhere I have argued that the structure of the last four stanzas is also determined by Eph 5:14 *surge qui dormis et exsurge a mortuis, et illuminabit tibi Christus.*[15] Ad vs 32

---

[15] J. den Boeft, "Three Ambrosiana," in: *L'esegesi dei padri latini delle origini a Gregorio Magno* (Studia Ephemeridis Augustinianum, 68; Rome, 2000), 540–1.

soluamus Franz rightly notes that this subjunctive at the end parallels *surgamus* halfway. What happens in between? In the fifth stanza
those who are still lying in bed are activated by the cock. For Franz
"entspannen die Verse ein dichtes Bedeutungsgeflecht" and Fontaine,
who in general is more reserved, also notes all sorts of symbolic con-
notations. In my view, however, these verses have been satisfactorily, indeed excellently, explained by Kayser: "Trefflich ist die
Steigerung, welche in den drei letzten Versen der aufmerksamen
Beobachtung entgegentritt. Iacentes, die noch ruhig im Schlafe daliegen
weckt er auf; die zwar aufgewacht, aber noch schlaftrunken und
schlafsüchtig (somnolentos) auf dem Lager sich hin und her wälzen,
increpat, schilt er; die, obwohl ganz erwacht, sich mit klarem
Bewußtsein aufzustehen weigern (negantes), klagt er ihrer Trägheit
wegen an, arguit."[16] I only add that the deviation from the parallelism of vss 18–20 is also due to the fact that *dormientes*, which has
the same metrical pattern as *somnolentos*, could not be used, because
it would merely repeat *iacentes*. Fontaine draws attention to "les asso-
nances finales néanmoins assemblées en séries de deux (-at, -it, -itur)."

One can take a further step and say that here the poet makes
full use of the unclassical stylistic device of rhyming in order to
emphasize the intrinsic connection between the actions: rhyme has
an iconic function here. The seven brief statements are asyndetically
placed, but made visible as the mutually connected elements of a
series by rhyme. The various things which happen at the cock's crow
belong together. Some readers may be ready to grant that Kayser's
view of the fifth stanza is convincing, but add that the sixth stanza
surely can only be understood as testifying to a typically Christian
spirituality: *spes, salus, fides*, and perhaps above all *lapsis*. Yet, the three
nouns have an age-old pedigree as important values of Roman culture and society, and as to *lapsis*, the exclusively Christian meaning
is not immediately necessary. The verb *labi* can be used about people who have come to grief: *multos, fortunae iniuria lapsos, sustentat atque
erigit* (Quintil. *Decl.* 260, p. 63, l. 24), or have sunk to an inferior
state: *regia (crede mihi) res est succurrere lapsis* (Ov. *Pont.* 2.9.11), or who
have made a mistake: *orabant puniret noxios, ignosceret lapsis* (Tac. *Ann.*
1.44.1), *aut vos, qui sero lapsum revocatis, amici* (Prop. 1.1.25).

---

[16] Kayser, *Beiträge*, 89–90, bzw. 157. The author rejects the idea that *negantes* indicates the "Verleugner": "dadurch würde ja mit einem Male ein ganz fremdes
Moment herangezogen" (o.c. 90, bzw. 157).

The common element in the four verses of the sixth stanza is daybreak brightening the outlook of those who are in some sort of dis-
tress. In view of what follows in the seventh stanza (*labentes, lapsus*)
the typically Christian sense of *lapsus*, "guilty of apostasis," cannot
be ruled out, but its presence is more subtle: what the poet is con-
triving in the fifth and sixth stanzas, is a gradual development of
the "physical" aspects to a point where it glides into the "spiritual"
experiences which are intrinsically linked to early morning. In both
stanzas this time of day is explicitly expressed and *gallo canente* is now
continued with *Iesu . . . respice*, as in the biblical text: *Et continuo adhuc
illo loquente cantauit gallus. Et conuersus Dominus respexit Petrum* (Luke
22:60–61).

Three things are worthy of notice here: 1) Jesus' looking at Petrus
occurs only in the version of Luke. 2) Whereas ἐνέβλεψεν in the original text only has a literal meaning: Jesus looked at Peter, the Latin
verb *respicere*, apart from "to look back at" (OLD s.v. 2b), can mean
"to show concern for" (OLD s.v. 8a and b): *Libertas, quae sera tamen
respexit inertem* (Verg. *Buc.* 1.27). This ambiguity is made good use of
in vs 25:3) Precisely this element of Luke's version is used only at
this point of the hymn, not in vss 15 and 16, where the scene of
Peter's repentance was the fourth of a series in which liberation was
the binding factor. In the seventh stanza, however, an entirely different
viewpoint is in place: Jesus' support of failing human beings.[17] In
the final stanza the morning light appears. Kayser's paraphrase of
its contents is again economic and clear: "Indess ist es heller geworden; das aufdämmernde Licht der Morgenröthe erinnert den Dichter
an das ewige Licht, welches Christus ist. Waren die Anfangsworte
an den Schöpfer gerichtet, die Schlussworte wenden sich an den
Erlöser, daß er sein himmlisches Gnadenlicht auch dem Geiste aufge-
hen lassen wolle."[18] Only at this point the spiritual aspect is explicitly mentioned: *sensibus, mentis*. At daybreak Jesus is prayed to shine
in the hearts of men and to dispel their sleep. He will, of course,
fulfil these vows and so the singers' immediate reaction should be

---

[17] Remarkably, *et conuersus Dominus respexit ad Petrum* is not commented on by
Ambrose in his *in Luc.*, but in *in psalm.* 45.15. Having quoted Ps 39:2 *expectatus expec-
taui dominum, et respexit me*, he then continues with: *quem dominus respexit saluat. Denique
in domini passione cum titubaret Petrus sermone, non mente—licet ipse Petri sermo titubantis
fidelior sit quam doctrina multorum—, respexit eum Christus et Petrus fleuit, quo proprium lauit
errorem. Ita quem uoce uisus est denegare, lacrimis fatebatur.*
[18] Kayser, *Beiträge*, 97, bzw. 164.

their due sound. The sequence at daybreak is therefore: sound awakens light, sound and light awaken man, man responds by sound.

In conclusion I can be brief. Scholars tend to interpret Ambrose's hymns in the same way as learned early Christian exegetes interpreted Scripture. In Franz this tendency has found its apex. However, such an interpretation was only feasible in the case of the Bible, in which every single sentence, even every single word was filled with all sorts of allegorical and spiritual meanings. But, as Augustine emphasized, the authors of Scripture should not be imitated: *Non ergo expositores eorum ita loqui debent, tamquam se ipsi exponendos simili auctoritate proponant, sed in omnibus sermonibus suis primitus ac maxime ut intellegantur elaborent.*[19]

"Taking pains to make oneself understood" is precisely what the lyrical poet Ambrose did in his hymns, above all in *Aeterne rerum conditor*. He did not endeavour to put theological doctrines into correct metrical form or to achieve imitations of biblical texts with various levels of meaning. His contribution was an entirely different one, viz. to word his poetical perception of time, in this case the earliest phase of daybreak. The first stanza of his poem expresses the creator's arrangement of time, for man's sake (*ut alleues fastidium*). After this introduction the text of the poem follows what is happening both in nature and in man, when daybreak is in progress. From beginning to end lyrical perception, which deviates from down-to-earth factuality, is given a voice, in subtle forms, as the polyptoton *temporum . . . tempora*, the selection of short vignettes representing sky, earth and sea (vss 9–14), the functional use of rhyme in vss 18–24, the timely use of *iam* in vs 5 etc. This typically lyrical way of looking at reality is in Ambrose's case inspired by an early Christian conviction about creation, in which physical and spiritual aspects are integrated. Peter's repentance (vss 15–16) is on the same level as the sailor's regaining of strength (vss 13–14). The return of hope, well-being and confidence in vss 21–24 does not occasion some sort of symbolic comparison with daybreak. If anything, it is the other way round: this is the time God has determined for such experiences. Such a view of time is not at all surprising. Even the most important facts in the history of salvation also took place at their proper time: *Uespere passus est Christus . . . Mane resurrexit* (Ambr. *in Ps.* 45:14).

---

[19] August. *doctr. chr.* 4.8.22.

Time plagues the brain of philosophers, and not merely as a problem for the intellect, appealing to their resources of disciplined thinking, but even, as Augustine's analysis in book 11 of the *Confessiones* shows, as an "existential" question. In the vita activa, however, time can be primarily perceived as a salutary arrangement, in which God's purpose becomes visible. Such a perception lends itself to be poetically expressed. Both ways of coming to terms with time can yield impressive results, as is shown by Augustine and Plotinus on the one hand, and by Ambrose in a great hymn, which deserves to be liberated from all superfluous exegetical overweight and to be enjoyed on its own terms, as lyrical poetry.[20] Such an interpretation is by no means revolutionary or iconoclastic. It is in fact supported by R. Herzog in his seminal study of Prudentius' poetry, which indeed deserves to be treated "allegorically." Comparing *Aeterne rerum conditor* with *Cathemerinon* 1, he notes: "Der wichtigste Unterschied ist, daß das vorstehende Lied des Ambrosius die Schwelle zur Allegorie noch nicht überschreitet."[21]

APPENDIX 1

Aeterne rerum conditor,
noctem diemque qui regis,
et temporum das tempora,
ut alleues fastidium.

Praeco diei iam sonat,
noctis profundae peruigil,
nocturna lux uiantibus,
a nocte noctem segregans.

Hoc excitatus Lucifer
soluit polum caligine,
hoc omnis erronum chorus
uias nocendi deserit.

Hoc nauta uires colligit
pontique mitescunt freta;
hoc ipse petra ecclesiae
canente culpam diluit.

---

[20] This is, of course, something entirely different from the level of the *sensus literalis* in Franz's four stages model.

[21] Reinhart Herzog, *Die allegorische Dichtkunst des Prudentius* (Zetemata, Heft 42; Munich, 1966), 67.

Surgamus ergo strenue;
gallus iacentes excitat
et somnolentos increpat;
gallus negantes arguit.

Gallo canente spes redit,
aegris salus refunditur,
mucro latronis conditur,
lapsis fides reuertitur.

Iesu, labentes respice
et nos uidendo corrige;
si respicis, lapsus cadunt
fletuque culpa soluitur.

Tu lux refulge sensibus
mentisque somnum discute,
te nostra uox primum sonet
et uota soluimus tibi.

APPENDIX 2

Ambrosius, *Hexameron* 5.88–89 after the text of Schenkl's edition:

Est enim galli cantus suauis in noctibus—non solum suauis, sed etiam
utilis, qui quasi bonus cohabitator et dormitantem excitat et sollicitum
admonet et uiantem solatur processum noctis canora significatione
protestans. hoc canente latro suas relinquit insidias, hoc ipse lucifer
excitatus oritur caelumque inluminat, hoc canente maestitiam trepidus
nauta deponit omnisque crebro uespertinis flatibus excitata tempestas
et procella mitescit, hoc <canente> deuotus adfectus exsilit ad pre-
candum, legendi quoque munus instaurat, hoc postremo canente ipsa
ecclesiae petra culpam suam diluit, quam priusquam gallus cantaret
negando contraxerat, istius cantu spes omnibus redit, aegri releuatur
incommodum, minuitur dolor uulnerum, febrium flagrantia mitigatur,
reuertitur fides lapsis, Iesus titubantes respicit, errantes corrigit, denique
respexit Petrum, et statim error abscessit, pulsa est negatio, secuta con-
fessio. quod non fortuito accidisse, sed ex sententia domini lectio docet.
sic enim scriptum est, quia dixit Iesus ad Simonem: *non cantabit gallus,*
priusquam me ter neges. bene fortis in die Petrus, nocte turbatur et ante
galli cantum labitur et labitur tertio, ut scias non inconsulta effusione
sermonis esse prolapsum, sed mentis quoque nutatione turbatum. idem
tamen post galli cantum fit fortior et iam dignus quem Christus aspi-
ciat; *oculi* enim *domini super iustos.* Agnouit uenisse remedium, post quod
iam errare non posset, et in uirtutem ab errore mutatus amarissime
fleuit, ut lacrimis suis lauaret errorem. (89) respice nos quoque, domine
Iesu, ut et nos propria recognoscamus errata, soluamus piis fletibus
culpam, mereamur indulgentiam peccatorum.

APPENDIX 3

The ancients divided the night in several parts. In the Roman army's encampments the four "watches" were in Ambrose's time measured with the "water-clock": *in quattuor partes ad clepsydram sunt diuisae uigiliae, ut non amplius quam tribus horis nocturnis necesse sit uigilare* (Vegetius, *Epitome rei militaris* 3.8.17). There are, however, also indications that Greeks and Romans in some way measured the time of night with the crowing of the cock at certain moments. In Aristophanes' *Ecclesiazusae* the women have organized a meeting of the *ecclesia* before dawn. Consequently, the men arrive too late for their attendance fee. "You have no chance," Blepyros says to Chremes, οὐδ' εἰ μὰ Δία τότ' ἦλθες, ὅτε τὸ δεύτερον/ἀλεκτρυὼν ἐφθέγγετο (390–391). A scholion ad loc. notes ὁ γὰρ ἀλεκτρυὼν τρίτον κοκκύζει. At the end of a wedding-song of Theocritus the singers announce their return very early in the morning, when πρᾶτος ἀοιδός will let himself be heard. Juvenal 9.107 mentions a moment *ad cantum . . . galli secundi*. The Romans had various non-military divisions of the night, e.g. *uespera, conticinium, intempesta nox, gallicinium, lucifer* (Varro apud Servius ad *Aen.* 2.268). This seems to come near Ambrose's text. However, Censorinus, *De die natali* 24.1–3, and Macrobius, *Saturnalia* 3.1.12 differ considerably from Varro

Remarkably, there seems to be no really satisfactory survey of this matter. The most helpful contributions I could find are Ludolph Dissen, "De partibus noctis et diei ex divisione veterum," in *Id.*, *Kleine lateinische und deutsche Schriften* (Göttingen, 1839) 130–150, and David Brady, "Alarm to Peter in Mark," *JSNT* 4 (1979) 42–57. The latter's point of departure is the fact that, in contrast to the parallel reports in Matthew, Luke and John, the Gospel of Mark (or rather a large number of manuscripts of this Gospel) in ch. 14 mentions that the cock crew ἐκ δευτέρου (vs 72) at Peter's third denial, in accordance with Jesus' prediction that he would deny him three times before the cock had crown δίς (vss 30 and 72). The editors of the standard edition are not certain about the text, as can be seen in the apparatus criticus and as is explained by B.M. Metzger in his *Textual Commentary on the Greek New Testament* ad loc. Assuming the correctness of "twice," Hans Kosmala devoted two interesting short studies to "The Time of the Cock-crow," which can be found in vol. II of his *Studies, Essays and Reviews* (Leiden, 1978), 76–81. Kosmala marshals evidence from the Middle East and from classical literature, but in this respect Brady has somewhat more to offer, i.a. a few remarkable passages from travellers' reports on the crowing of cocks as a method of measuring time in the nineteenth and twentieth centuries. He finally concludes that Mark's "twice" probably does not refer to specific periods of the night.

It may have become clear that uncertainty reigns, and it should also be added that Ambrose's enigmatic *a nocte noctem segregans* does not necessarily refer to the same division of the night as could be hinted at in Mark 14:30 and 72.

"NEVER REPAY EVIL WITH EVIL":
ETHICAL INTERACTION BETWEEN THE JOSEPH STORY, THE NOVEL *JOSEPH AND ASENETH*, THE NEW TESTAMENT AND THE APOCRYPHAL ACTS

JÁNOS BOLYKI*

Believers of both Judaism and Christianity must face the question raised by A. Hilhorst: "Christianity may have proclaimed a message of peace, but it met with violence from the beginning."[1] Can a god-fearer react with peacefulness and good deeds to hostility? Both religions give positive answers to this question. Now, within the frames of Biblical tradition we want to deal with a writing, the origin of which is still debated. It is not sure whether it belongs to the Jewish, the Christian or both traditions. This is a Hellenistic novel called *Joseph and Aseneth* (= *Jos. Asen.*). A famous scholar of Hellenistic religious novels, Tibor Szepessy thinks that *Jos. Asen.* is a Christian novel.[2] An important evidence to this is the ethical admonition of *Jos. Asen.*: "a pious man never repays evil with evil" (28:5 and repeated elsewhere). This admonition is not without example in the NT, either. The writer of a recent English language book also shares Szepessy's opinion.[3] The majority of scholars, however, regards *Jos. Asen.* as a Jewish novel[4] or as a story composed by a god-fearer.[5] It

---

* Budapest.
[1] A. Hilhorst, "The Apocryphal Acts as Martyrdom Texts: The Case of the Acts of Andrew," in J. Bremmer (ed.), *The Apocryphal Acts of John* (Kampen, 1995), 1. In this footnote, let me express my gratitude and honor to Mr. Hilhorst, in the name of myself and the Theological Faculty of the Károli Gáspár Reformed University at Budapest.
[2] T. Szepessy, *Az apokrif apostolakták és az antik regény (Apocryphal Acts of the Apostles and the Antique Novel)*. Antik Tanulmányok (AntTan) XXXVIII (1994) 127, note 56.
[3] R.S. Kraemer, *When Aseneth Met Joseph. A Late Antique Tale of the Biblical Patriarch and His Egyptian Wife, Reconsidered* (New York, 1998), 245.
[4] V. Aptowitzer, *Asenath, the Wife of Joseph. A Haggadic Literary-Historical Study* (HUCA, 1; New York, 1924), 286; Chr. Burchard, *Untersuchungen zu Joseph und Aseneth* (WUNT, 8; Tübingen, 1961), 99; D. Sänger, "Bekehrung und Exodus. Zum jüdischen Traditionshintergrund von 'Joseph und Aseneth,'" *JSJ* 10 (1979) 11; *Id.*, "Jüdisch-hellenistische Missionsliteratur und die Weisheit," *Kairos* (1981/4) 231; G.W.E. Nickelsburg, "Joseph and Aseneth," in *Jewish Literature Between the Bible and Mishnah* (London, 1981), 258; G. Bohak, *Joseph and Aseneth and the Jewish Temple in Heliopolis* (Atlanta, 1996), XIII.
[5] Kraemer only mentions and does not share this view, *op. cit.* 272–273.

is obvious that neither the author nor the date[6] can be discovered
for sure. In the absence of all these data let us concentrate on the
origin and usage of the norm "never repay evil with evil" by studying the interaction of Jewish and Christian ethical texts.

I

We find incredibly parallel lines in *Jos. Asen.* and the Apostolic parenesis. According to the former, Levi, Joseph's wise and prophetic
brother calms Simeon in his murderous anger (he wanted to kill the
Pharaoh's son) with the following words: ἡμεῖς ἀνδρὸς θεοσεβοῦς
παῖδές ἐσμεν καὶ οὐ προσήκει ἀνδρὶ θεοσεβεῖ ἀποδοῦναι κακὸν ἀντὶ
κακοῦ (*Jos. Asen.* 23:9), that is: "We are men who worship God, and
it does not befit us to repay evil with evil." On the other hand,
Aseneth, the heroine thus cheers up her defeated brothers-in-law
(Joseph's sons born from his female slaves), who earlier had risen
up against her but now fear the vengeance of their victorious brothers: οἱ ἀδελφοὶ ὑμῶν εἰσιν ἄνδρες θεοσεβεῖς καὶ μὴ ἀποδιδόντες κακὸν
ἀντὶ κακοῦ τινι ἀνθρώπῳ (*Jos. Asen.* 28:4), that is: "our brothers are
men who worship God and do not repay anyone evil for evil." She
also comforts her ardent brother-in-law: μηδαμῶς, ἀδελφέ, ἀποδώσεις
κακὸν ἀντὶ κακοῦ τῷ πλησίῳ σου (28:14), which means: "By no
means, brother, will you do evil for evil to your neighbor." And
finally we might quote Levi's words, who prevents his youngest
brother Benjamin from killing his defeated and wounded enemy: οὐ
προσήκει ἀνδρὶ θεοσεβεῖ ἀποδοῦναι κακὸν ἀντὶ κακοῦ οὐδὲ πεπτωκότα
καταπατῆσαι, οὐδὲ ἐκθλῖψαι τὸν ἐχθρὸν ἕως θανάτου (29:3), that is:
"it does not benefit a man who worships God to repay evil for evil
nor to trample underfoot a fallen man nor to oppress his enemy till
death."

These very words can be found in the texts of the Apostolic letters (Rom 12:17; 1 Thess 5:15; 1 Pet 3:9). In Rom 12:17 we read:
"never pay back evil for evil (μηδενὶ κακὸν ἀντὶ κακοῦ ἀποδιδόντες),
let your aims be such as all men count honorable" (NEB). In 1
Thess 5:15 the Apostle says: "See to it that no one pays back wrong
for wrong, but always aim at doing the best you can for each other

---

[6] The date of the novel is placed somewhere between 150 B.C.E. and the 4th
century C.E. Cf. Kraemer, *op. cit.* 237–239.

and for all men." At last, 1 Pet 3:9 reads: "Do not repay wrong with wrong, or abuse with abuse; on the contrary, retaliate with blessing."

How can these parallelisms be explained? The question leads us to the problem of *ethical interaction*. Is there a way from the Christian writings and the oral tradition to *Jos. Asen.* and back, especially concerning the norm of "a man who worships God never repays evil with evil"? First we consider this question on the basis of tradition- and redaction criticism and second, from a community point of view that lies behind these works (conflicts of the community, *Sitz im Leben*).

II

Since the novel's date of writing is uncertain, *Jos. Asen.* and the New Testament ethical parenesis (theoretically at least) can relate to each other in four different ways.

1. *Jos. Asen. is the earlier one.* Then—in part—it could have influenced Christian parenesis. To what extent could *Jos. Asen.* be a source of Christian parenesis? It certainly could. We must know two things about this. The first is that Christian parenesis did absorb certain Jewish Hellenistic thoughts.[7] Such was R. Meir's (*ca.* 150 B.C.E.) saying about repaying evil with good.[8] They never absorbed anything without distinction, though! Christian parenesis did not accept, for example a very special ethical feature of *Jos. Asen.*: the form "it does not befit a man who worships God" (οὐ προσήκει ἀνδρὶ θεοσεβεῖ). The word προσήκει is not found in NT. In the acceptance of Hellenistic pagan and Jewish ethical teaching the main criterion was that the accepted material should have corresponded to the original teaching of Jesus, in our case about loving our enemies (Matt 5:38–48; Luke 6:27–36). The Christian parenesis accepted Jesus' words only by shaping them according to its need and actual situation. J. Piper raises two interesting questions about the similarities and dissimilarities

---

[7] About the sources of Christian parenesis in general: P. Vielhauer, *Geschichte der urchristlichen Literatur* (New York-Berlin, 1975), 53. Regarding 1 Pet 3:9, cfr. P.J. Achtemeier, *1 Peter. A Commentary on First Peter* (Minneapolis, 1996), 223.

[8] "God said to Moses: Imitate me: since I repay evil with good, you should also pay back good for evil."

of Jesus' words with the Christian parenesis.[9] If both the love command in Matthew and Luke and the love parenesis of the Apostolic
letters can be traced back to Jesus, why are they so apparently
different? If the *vox Jesu* was indeed the common source, how can
we find the continuity (the path of tradition) between Jesus' word
and the ethical-parenetic forms?[10] He shows that the oral parenetic
tradition can be discovered as early as in the first Christian Church
and Jesus' command on loving our enemies was very much a part
of it. He even dares to say that if we are able to get to know anything about this oral tradition, it is that the "do not repay evil with
evil" formula is always followed by a positive command, like in Rom
12:17: "let your aims be such as all men count honorable." In 1
Thess 5:15: "always aim at doing the best you can for each other
and for all men." And finally in 1 Pet 3:9: "retaliate with blessing."
These clauses necessarily follow the negative formula: "never repay
evil with evil." Nevertheless, behind the formula "repay evil with
blessing" it is not difficult to recognize the antithesis of the Sermon
on the Mount, as it reflects Jesus' words: "pray for your persecu-
tors" (Matt 5:44). Similarly, the already quoted Rom 12:17 is also
followed by a positive formula in verse 18: "live at peace with all
men." This also leads us to the Sermon on the Mount: "make your
peace with your brother" (Matt 5:24). Thus, in the Christian parenesis we find Jesus' original command in the second part of the
"negative formula—positive formula" sequence. The negative formula itself (never repay evil with evil) goes back to the Hellenistic-
Jewish ethics. According to Piper, the Christian church interpreted,
paraphrased and applied Jesus' command to love our enemies, especially in the catechetical teaching. Various examples show us how
the same thought gained new and new emphasis in the course of
its development. This is how Hellenistic-Jewish and Christian ideas
(rooted in Jesus' teaching) also merged into Christian parenesis, in
a way that the latter was the criterion of acceptance for the former.
So, it might be possible that *Jos. Asen.* influenced NT parenesis.

2. *The oral tradition of the NT is earlier than the Joseph novel.* In this case
we count with Christian influence in the ethical world of *Jos. Asen.*

---

[9] J. Piper, *"Love your enemies." Jesus' Love Command in the Synoptic Gospels and in the
Early Christian Paraenesis* (Cambridge, 1979).
[10] *Ibid.*, 171.

What is more, *Jos. Asen.* must be a novel of Christian background, then. Had the book not a Christian origin, it would not have incorporated Christian elements but it would have rather refused them. Then, is *Jos. Asen.* a Christian book?

Arguments that support this option are: *Jos. Asen.* has parallels with Christian parenesis not only in the "never repay evil with evil" formula, but in many other rules concerning the behavior of "a man who worships God": an ἀνήρ θεοσεβής does not kiss a non-believing woman, because her lips are defiled by the food offered to idols; such man does not have premarital sexual relationships (*Jos. Asen.* 8:5–7), he does not hit anyone who is unable to defend him/herself; although he is ready to protect himself from the enemy, he does not kill (*Jos. Asen.* 29:3). These are not the only arguments for a Christian origin. The scene of washing the feet also recalls a NT motif (John 13:1–20; *Jos. Asen.* 20:1–5), similarly the sacramental nature of the divine comb, the sign of the cross pressed in the comb and the blood coming out of it (cf. 1 Cor 11:23–26; *Jos. Asen.* 16:17) and other motives.

Arguments against the Christian origin of *Jos. Asen.* are: Christians never used the term θεοσεβής as their self-designation, mainly it was used by the Jewish diaspora community for themselves or for pagans who were attracted to them (Acts 2:5; 10:2). Another argument is of ethical nature: if *Jos. Asen.* was a Christian writing, its repeated ethical admonition (never repay evil with evil) would be only a mutilated version of the original Christian standard (negative formula + positive formula) and of Jesus' love command. This is not too plausible. We are left with one more argument (supporting the Christian origin of *Jos. Asen.*), which can count for the lack of any positive formula (like "retaliate with blessing" or "aim at doing the best you can") found in early Christianity. If we accept Kraemer's hypothesis[11] about the initial writing of the document in the 3rd century and a redaction of it in the 6th, there must have been a later Christian author or redactor who kept only the negative formula (never repay evil with evil) purposefully without any positive clause (e.g. "aim at doing the best you can") in order to create a more authentic *oeuvre*, that is the age of the Patriarchs, when such positive clause simply did not exist.

---

[11] *Ibid.*, 296 (cf. note 3).

3. *A third option is "simultaneity."* Of course, not that of exact dates
(we saw that it is impossible for the moment). Here "simultaneity"
means one age, one sociological-cultural environment and mutual
interactions, in the same way as the *Testament of the Twelve Patriarchs*[12]
is simultaneous with *Jos. Asen.* and the NT. In this writing the original Qumran background was shaped by a Hellenistic-Jewish layer
and by a later Christian interpolation. It demands benevolence only
towards compatriots or fellow members of the same religious community. There are a few interesting exceptions, though. According
to *T. Benj* 4:21 "The good man hath not a dark eye; for he showeth
mercy to all men, even though they be sinners, even though they
devise evil concerning him. So he that doeth good, overcometh the
evil, being shielded by Him that is good." *T. Jos* 18:2 claims even
more: "if any one seeketh to do evil unto you, do ye by well-doing
pray for him, and ye shall be redeemed of the Lord from all evil."
In *T. Gad* 6:7 we read: "if he (your enemy) be shameless, and abideth
in his wrongdoing, even then forgive him from the heart, and give
the vengeance to God." These texts are ethically compatible with
the "never repay evil with evil" maxim. Unfortunately, scholars differ
in identifying the date and the layer responsible for these views
(Qumran-influenced, Hellenistic-Jewish or Christian). That is why we
call these writings ethically "contemporary" or "simultaneous" with
both *Jos. Asen.* and the NT parenesis—avoiding the question of exact
sources and dating. This very "simultaneity" can also apply to the
relationship of *Jos. Asen.* and the parenetic writings of the NT. A
special case of non-chronological "simultaneity" would exist here, if
we regarded the admonition "never repay evil with evil" a Hellenistic-
Stoic proverb or saying, which was well-known in the contemporary
Mediterranean world. If it was so, it might have penetrated both
the novel *Jos. Asen.* and the ethics of NT epistles. According to Piper
the so-called Middle-Stoa was the most widespread ethical teaching
in the Eastern coast of the Mediterranean Sea just before Jesus was
born and the soil the Church sprang from was undoubtedly imbued
with Stoic philosophy.[13] For example, Seneca, the representative of
contemporary Stoicism, was very much interested in the rightful
behavior of the wise man towards his enemies: "We shall never

---

[12] Its date is still debated among scholars, i.e. between 100 B.C.E. and 200 C.E.,
cf. Piper, 43.
[13] Piper, 26.

cease ... to give aid even to our enemies" (*De Otio* 1,4). "And so let your thoughts follow this trend: 'He has not repaid me with gratitude: what shall I do?' Do as the gods, those glorious authors of all things, do, they begin to give benefits to him who knows them not, and persist in giving them to those who are ungrateful ... Let us imitate them: let us give even if many of our gifts have been given in vain" (*De Beneficiis* VII.30.2. and 5). "If you are imitating the gods, you say, 'then bestow benefits also upon the ungrateful'; for the sun rises also upon the wicked, and the sea lies open to pirates" (*De Beneficiis* IV.26). It is worth to mention another thinker of the age, Epictetus, who has one idea common with the First Letter of Peter. "If therefore you start from this point of view you will be gentle with the man who reviles you" (*Enchiridion* 42).[14] It is interesting that the Greek original of the verb "revile" is in the same context in 1 Pet 3:9 "Do nor repay wrong with wrong, or abuse with abuse." It seems to be natural that such a popular ethical concept could have easily ended up in aphorisms and maxims that later influenced the authors of both *Jos. Asen.* and the NT ethical teachings. For the application of aphorisms—although in a different context—a good example is one from the *Bacchae* of Euripides (794k) "It is hard for you to kick against the goad," later used by Luke in Acts 26:14, there said by Jesus to the protesting Paul, before his conversion in Damascus.[15] We find very instructive parallels for the interconnectedness of different cultures and for a common heritage of aphorisms and sayings in the genre of anonymous "gnomologia" prepared by Jewish authors in order to prove that the monotheistic-ethical heritage of Moses and the Hellenistic Greek philosophers are not too far from each other.[16]

4. *The fourth option.* There is still a *fourth option*, in many respects a most plausible one: *Jos. Asen.* and the NT epistles had the same ethical-parenetic sources. This is by no means impossible, since the whole OT and its ethical material was a common heritage for them. We can reckon with two such OT sources: the wisdom-literature and the Joseph stories (Gen 37:39–50).

---

[14] Quotations of Seneca and Epictetus are taken from Piper, *op. cit.*, 21 and 25.
[15] A. Vögeli, "Lukas und Euripides," *ThZ* 9 (1953) 415–438.
[16] N. Walter, "Pseudepigraphische jüdisch-hellenistische Dichtung: gefälschte Verse auf Namen griechischer Dichter," in *JSHRZ*, Bd. IV., Lieferung 3 (Gütersloh, 1983), 175–181, 244–254.

As to the *wisdom-literature*, first we mention Prov 17:13: "If a man repays evil for good, evil will never quit his house." Ethics do not begin with repaying evil with good. That is the highest achievement of it. The minimum is not to repay good with evil. This "minimum-ethics" could be developed independently in both Jewish and Christian parenesis until the "never repay evil with evil" formula was born. The MT text of Prov 20:22 also applies here: "Do not say: I repay evil with evil!" This is very close to the "never repay evil with evil" norm of the ethics of *Jos. Asen.* and the NT epistles. NT parenesis not only accepted and further developed the norms of wisdom-literature about forgiving evil and repaying it with good, but also quoted them. Ps 34:12–16 (about self-temperance and peacefulness) echoes in 1 Pet 3:9–12: "blessing is the inheritance to which you yourselves have been called." At the same time, this is a dogmatic argument for the norm "never repay evil with evil"! In the other above quoted parenesis locus from Rom 12:17 and its context we see other quotations from the OT wisdom-literature. In 12:16b from Prov 3:7: admonition to humbleness. In Rom 12:17a from Prov 17:13: we should not repay good with evil; and in 12:17b from the LXX version of Prov 3:4. Verse 20 reminds us of Prov 25:21f.: "if your enemy is hungry, give him bread to eat; if he is thirsty, give him water to drink." What else is this, if not a positive-practical application of the "never repay evil with evil" formula?

Those who seek OT influence in the "never repay evil with evil" formula of NT parenesis often refer to the wisdom-literature. We think that it is also worthwhile to examine the Joseph story of Genesis, especially chapter 50.

III

When we look at the Joseph story of Genesis as a possible background for the NT parenesis and the ethics of *Jos. Asen.*, we step on a new path, not only in view of the examined material but of the method as well. It is not about pure textual criticism in the sense of tradition- and redaction criticism. It is about the *Sitz im Leben*[17] and the ethical conflicts[18] of tradition-making communities. The

---

[17] Piper, 26.
[18] Ritoók Zs. – Sarkady J. – Szilágyi J., *A görög kultúra aranykora* [The Golden Age of the Greek Culture] (Budapest, 1984), 284–286.

conflicts in literature (e.g. in the Greek tragedies) always picture the collision of opposing ethical convictions, either they are rooted in the different social development of different cultures or in the tension of paradigm-shifts caused by an inner development of a certain society.[19] This is similar in the Joseph stories of Genesis. We think that besides the wisdom-literature, these stories could also influence the parenesis of the novel *Jos. Asen.* and the Apostolic epistles.

In the Joseph stories (Gen 37:39–50) we find all the three sources of Genesis (Jahwist, Elohist and the Priestly Writing), but in the text (Gen 50:20) and its context (Gen 50:15–17:19–20)[20] we are most interested in the work of the Elohist. The Elohist lived after the broke up of Judah and Israel (ca. 930 B.C.E.), but well before the exile of the 6th century. Perhaps he experienced the Assyrian devastation of Israel (722 B.C.E.), but we cannot be sure about that. Both his view of history, reflected in the Joseph story, and his theological-ethics show the influence of his own situation. Just as the country was torn apart after 930, the larger family of Jacob was also broken up into the smaller families of Joseph and his brothers. As Jacob was unable to keep his family together, in the case of a country it was also impossible to go on living in tribal structures at the time of the Elohist. As Joseph managed to become a high rank officer of the Pharaoh and to rescue his needy and homeless family, the Elohist also felt that it was necessary to find a way of surviving among the great political powers of his age. Joseph is the early image of Moses: as Moses rescued his people from Egypt, Joseph also rescued his family by settling them down in Egypt.[21] As Moses stood up against the Pharaoh for the sake of his people, Joseph also stood up together with the Pharaoh for the sake of his family (people). As Joseph's life was jeopardized by his brothers, the survival of Israel and Judah was also jeopardized by different interest groups, who despised the covenant made between God and the elected people.

Joseph's story was written not only for the purposes of historical analogies and lessons. There are also theological and ethical lessons

---

[19] *Ibid.*, 442.

[20] To the exegesis, origin and theology of the story see: G. von Rad, *Das erste Buch Mose* (ATD; Berlin, 1956), 374–379; K. Westermann, *Genesis* (Neukirchen, 1982), 230–233. 298k.; L. Ruppert, *Die Josephserzählung der Genesis* (München, 1965), 195–199. 219. 226. 228–231, etc.; H. Seebass, *Geschichtliche Zeit und theonome Tradition in der Joseph-Erzählung* (Gütersloh, 1978), 83–124.

[21] Ruppert, *op. cit.*, 226–57.

in the story, powerfully reflecting to history. Who governs history? What are the reasons for the sufferings (Joseph sold by his brothers, the country divided, the people goes into exile) experienced through the history? How should a victorious one behave towards his defeated enemies or rebellious brothers? Gen 50:20 answers these questions: "You meant to do me harm; but God meant to bring good out of it by preserving the lives of many people, as we see today." In Hebrew the two predicates of the main clause are expressed by the same verb (*chasab*). It shows that God is the Lord of the events and history, no one can resist his plans, for God uses even the resistance to fulfill his eternal plans. Although Joseph was sold as slave by his brothers, this very crime opened a way before him to Egypt, where he would be able to save them during the famine. It is clear why Joseph, understanding the divine providence, does not intend to take revenge on his brothers. He does not want to be a judge over them ("Am I in the place of God?"), to repay evil with evil. Many scholars notice that this behavior was a theological-ethical source from the wisdom-literature variants to the theme: "A man's heart may be full of schemes, but the Lord's purpose will prevail" (e.g. from Prov 16:1.9.33; 19:21; 20:24; 21:1.31). This is true for Gen 50:20, for Joseph recognized (and wanted to make his brothers recognize) that God's guidance was above their lives. Still, the main sapiential example is in Prov 20:22: "Do not think to repay evil for evil, wait for the Lord to deliver you." We think that this is the common source of the novel *Jos. Asen.* and the NT parenesis in the light of both the lexical content and the situation.

In Gen 50:20 Joseph refrains from revenge, because (1) he had realized that the evil committed against him has been changed for good and useful by God. (2) For this reason it is not his responsibility to punish the evil deeds: God is the one who makes judgment. (3) What is more, he realized that this was not only his story: the purpose of what happened was "preserving the lives of many people" (during the famine).

All what has been said so far is also true for the novel *Jos. Asen.*, independently of a date B.C.E. or C.E., and independently of the novel being a Jewish or a Christian work. The novel and especially its second part (chs. 22–29) enlarges the story of Genesis in a Haggadic way: after the death of their father, the brothers born of slave women rebel against Joseph and Aseneth. Together with the evil son of the

Pharaoh they decide to kill Joseph. In the battle following, Aseneth, Joseph and his blood brothers prevail and have mercy on the defeated half-brothers, Aseneth's brothers-in-law. It is natural that a theory was formed to explain this scenario by saying that this is all about (a) the inner conflict of the first century large Jewish diaspora in Alexandria, and (b) the external conflict between the diaspora and the non-Jewish citizens of the city. The author wants to encourage his contemporaries by retelling and updating these 1300-year-old stories. As far as the inner conflict is concerned the half-brothers serving the Pharaoh's son symbolize the compromising Jews in the diaspora against the faithful ones. The evil Pharaoh who succeeds the former good Pharaoh symbolizes the shift in the earlier and peaceful life of the diaspora into a more endangered one. *Jos. Asen.* 28:4 (and its repetitions) say that "a pious man never repays evil with evil" inviting the diaspora into a peaceful and harmonic inner life, on the basis of OT reminiscences, especially of Gen 50:20. It is not sure if this peacefulness also applies to the Egyptians, because in the story of *Jos. Asen.* we read about the exterminating of a great number of Egyptian soldiers (*Jos. Asen.* 27:5–6).

The Apostolic epistles must have applied to themselves the warnings of Prov 20:22 and Gen 50:20 (never repay evil with evil), for both in the Christian church and out of it they have been faced with the relevance of the question "What shall we do to those who have wronged us?" (cf. Matt 6:12b). On the one hand they had to cope with the inner social and cultural tensions of every young religious community, and on the other hand they had to form a new and efficient behavior against the external threats of the authorities and other social groups. Nevertheless, in the parenesis of the Apostolic epistles we do not find exclusively negative admonitions, but also a great deal of positive formulations, like in Rom 12:17 "let your aims be such as all men count honorable," in 1 Thess 5:15 "always aim at doing the best you can" and 1 Pet 3:9 "on the contrary, retaliate with blessing." We saw that these admonitions go back to Jesus' teaching about loving our enemies (Matt 5:38–48; Luke 6:27–36). Piper mentions four motivations that lead from Jesus' command to the parenesis. The first was the experience of God's all surpassing grace in Jesus, the second was the expectation of the final eschatological blessing in the obedience to the command about loving our enemies, the third was the new birth after baptism and experiencing the eschatological feeling of being a part of God's people and the fourth was the realization of the necessity of a completely renewed mind. Of course we do not find such motivations in *Jos. Asen.*

It is not easy to decide when the admonition "never pay back evil for evil. Let your aims be such as all men count honourable" applies to inner conflicts of the congregation and when it applies to external conflicts. Rom 12:17 most probably referred to the behavior towards those outside, for it exhorts to "all men count honourable." 1 Thess 5:15 clearly indicates that "doing the best we can" is necessary not only within the congregation but also outside of it. 1 Pet 3:9 is very specific in that it pleas for only those who did wrong to the congregation.

It seems that although the OT roots in the novel *Jos. Asen.* and the NT parenesis are the same, the latter supplements them with a positive admonition, which is an application of Jesus' general love command to the Christians' situation. Thus, the novel *Jos. Asen.* is either earlier than the NT epistles (NT epistles show Jesus' influence while *Jos. Asen.* does not), or we have an novel author of enormous "empathy" and talent, who refrained from showing more than OT ideas in order to create a more authentic scenario and timing (the age of Joseph patriarch).

IV

Let me say a few words on the aftermath of the formula "never repay evil with evil" in the apocryphal acts written in the late 2nd and 3rd centuries. The *Acts of John* 81 mentions that John thus rebukes someone, who regards a criminal unworthy of the resurrection: "We have not learned, my child, to render evil for evil" (Οὐκ ἐμάθομεν, τέκνον, κακὸν ἀντὶ κακοῦ ἀποδοῦναι). The term "learned" most probably refers to the parenetic admonitions received in the catechetical teaching of the church. The theological–ethical explanation of this admonition is beautiful, it is worth to quote at least a part of it: "for God, though we have done much ill and no good toward him, hath not given retribution unto us, but repentance." It proves that the admonition was part of the catechetical teaching, the personal *pastoratio* and the genre of Christian novel as well. We may add the genre of the Christian sermon: in the *Acts of Thomas* 58 (Thomas' sermon to all people, not only to the Christian ones) we find the formula without further explanation. Although the negative formula is almost identical in the apocryphal document and in *Jos. Asen.* 23:9; 28:5.10.14 and 29:3, we can be very sure that it was not borrowed from the novel but from the apostolic admonitions.[22]

---

[22] J. Bolyki, "Miracle Stories in the Acts of John," in J. Bremmer (ed.), *The Apocryphal Acts of John* (Kampen, 1995), 30. A different opinion from mine: P.J. Lallemann, *The Acts of John* (Leuven, 1998), 146.

THE VISION OF SATURUS IN THE
PASSIO PERPETUAE

Jan N. Bremmer*

One of Ton Hilhorst's main interests has always been the genre of the *Acta Martyrum*. In fact, it was probably the work that I did with Jan den Boeft on these *Acta* in the early 1980s that first brought us into contact. He may therefore be interested in some observations on a *Passio* that has long intrigued both of us, the *Passio Perpetuae et Felicitatis* (henceforth: *Perpetua*).[1] Whereas most scholars have concentrated on Perpetua and her visions, the vision of Saturus, her spiritual guide, has been somewhat neglected by modern critics.[2] That is why we venture to offer our erudite colleague the following contribution, in which we will look first at Saturus himself and the text of his vision (§ 1), then examine his welcome in heaven (§ 2) and conversation with clergy on earth (§ 3), and conclude with a few observations on the vision as a whole.[3]

1. SATURUS AND (THE TEXT OF) HIS VISION

Saturus first makes his entry onto the martyrological scene in a vision of Perpetua, where she sees him preceding her to heaven and remarks:

---

* Groningen.

[1] I quote the *Passio Perpetuae* from J. Amat, *Passion de Perpétue et de Félicité suivi des Actes* (Paris, 1996); the other *Acta martyrum*, where possible, from A.A.R. Bastiaensen et al., *Atti e passioni dei martiri* (Milan, 1987), and the *Passio Montani et Lucii* (henceforth: *Montanus*) from the new edition by F. Dolbeau, "La Passion des saints Lucius et Montanus," *REAug* 29 (1983) 39–82. For the translations I have gratefully adapted those of H. Musurillo, *The Acts of the Christian Martyrs* (Oxford, 1972).

[2] Cf. E. Corsini, "Proposte per una lettura della 'Passio Perpetuae'," in *Forma futuri. Studi in onore del Cardinale Michele Pellegrino* (Turin, 1975), 481–541 at 509 note 64: "Ignorata o quasi dalle testimonianze antiche relative alla *Passio*, la visione di Saturo non ha avuto fortuna neanche presso la critica 'storica'"; but see J. Amat, *Songes et visions. L'au-delà dans la littérature tardive* (Paris, 1985), 122–28; P. Habermehl, *Perpetua und der Ägypter* (Berlin, 1992), 171–77.

[3] I freely use and update some of the results of J. den Boeft and J. Bremmer, "Notiunculae martyrologicae II," *VC* 36 (1982) 383–402, and of my studies *The Rise and Fall of the Afterlife* (London and New York, 2002), 57–64; "Perpetua and Her Diary: authenticity, family and visions," in W. Ameling (ed.), *Märtyrer und Märtyrerakten*

"he who later had given himself up spontaneously on account of us
(because he had instructed us): he had not been present when we
were arrested" (4.5).[4] Evidently, he was the catechist of Perpetua and
her group. However, he does not seem to have been a cleric, since
he is nowhere given a clerical rank and clearly rates himself lower
than a bishop or a presbyter (14.3: § 3). And indeed, in the time of
Tertullian a catechist could be a layman.[5] Saturus is a typical slave
name,[6] which suggests that he was a freedman, just like some of the
others named in his vision (§ 3). It must have been pure chance that
he was not arrested together with his pupils, since the little that we
know about the persecutions under Septimius Severus indicates that
they targeted catechumens and their instructors.[7]

After having reported the four visions of Perpetua, the editor of
Perpetua continues with the observation: "But the blessed Saturus has
also issued into circulation (*edidit*) his own vision, which he wrote
with his own hand" (11.1). Bastiaensen (*ad loc.*) interprets *edidit* as
narravit and Amat translates "fait connaître," but there seems to be
no reason why we should not take *edidit* in its technical sense as giving a manuscript to a friend on the understanding that he would
make further copies and initiate circulation.[8] The more so, since it
is explicitly stated that he wrote down the vision *ipse*,[9] perhaps even as
part of a larger report. It was not unusual among the early Christians
to write in prison—witness Paul, Ignatius, Perpetua and the first part
of *Montanus*, which was written *de carcere* (12.1)—and these letters and
reports must have served to encourage the fellow faithful.[10]

(Stuttgart, 2002), 77–120, and "Contextualizing Heaven in Third-Century North
Africa," in R.S. Abusch and A.Y. Reed (eds.), *In Heaven as it is on Earth: Imagined
Realms and Earthly Realities in Late Antique Religions* (Cambridge, 2003).

[4] It was considered a special honour to lead the way to martyrdom, cf. Cyprian,
Ep. 6.4, 28.1.1–2, 39.2.1, 60.1.2.

[5] Hippolytus, *Apost. Trad.* 19: *sive clericus est qui dat (doctrinam) sive laicus*; Tertullian,
De praes. haeret. 3.5; Cyprian, *Ep.* 29.1.2, 73.3.2.

[6] M. Lamberz, *Die griechischen Sklavennamen* (Vienna, 1907), 29–30; H. Solin, *Beiträge
zur Kenntnis der griechischen Personennamen in Rom* I (Helsinki, 1971), 68–70.

[7] P. Keresztes, "The Emperor Septimius Severus: a precursor of Decius," *Historia*
19 (1970) 564–78 at 570; A. Alcock, "Persecution under Septimius Severus," *Enchoria*
11 (1982) 1–5, a papyrus re-edited by H.-M. Schenke, *Enchoria* 18 (1991) 86–88;
A. Daguet-Gagey, "Septime Sévère, un empereur persécuteur des chrétiens?," *REAug*
47 (2001) 3–32.

[8] For this sense of *edere* see most recently T. Dorandi, *Le style et la tablette* (Paris,
2000), 103–28; R. Nauta, *Poetry for Patrons* (Leiden, 2002), 121–4.

[9] This is also stressed in 14.1.

[10] For more examples see P. Franchi de' Cavalieri, *Scritti agiografici*, 2 vols (Rome,

It is not fully clear in which language Saturus had left behind this description. Fridh has demonstrated that both the Latin and the Greek version of Saturus' vision have a prose rhythm different from the parts of *Perpetua* by Perpetua and the editor. This points to an originally independent "edition" of Saturus' vision, although we do not know in what form. Fridh favours a Greek original,[11] but his discussion seems to show rather that in some passages the Greek version went back to a better Latin version than has eventually come down to us, just as the Greek version of Perpetua's visions sometimes displays knowledge of a better Latin *Vorlage* than our present text. As he himself notes, the words *"et coepit Perpetua graece cum illis loqui"* (13.4) also occur in the Greek version, where they look rather strange. Fridh tries to solve the problem by stating that Saturus tells his vision in a manner "très simple et naïve," but the far from *naïve* manner in which the internal problems of the Carthaginian church are treated in his vision (13), the mention of Perpetua's Greek, and his many conversations in Latin (4.6, 17.1–2, 18.7, 21.1 and 4) all make it highly unlikely that Saturus originally wrote in Greek.[12]

Whereas Van Beek and Amat do not rate the Greek version very highly in their constitution of the text, it has recently been persuasively argued that in some passages this version offers better readings than our most important manuscript, A.[13] In particular, it has preserved the name of Perpetua's home town Thuburbo Minus (2.1), which is not found in the Latin version, and the name of the predecessor of Hilarianus, Minicius Opimianus (6.3), if in a somewhat garbled form.[14] Moreover, in Saturus' vision Amat accepts the Latin Iocundum (11.8), but the Greek version's Ἰουκοῦνδον clearly points to the correct Iucundus. The spelling Iocundus is not attested in Latin literature or inscriptions until Late Antiquity (*ThLL s.v.*) and probably is a secondary corruption. Similarly, Amat accepts "Saturninus" in A as the name of Iucundus' fellow martyr, but both the

---

1962), I.213–14; R. Lane Fox, *Pagans and Christians* (Harmondsworth, 1986), 471; add Cyprian, *Ep.* 22.2.1.

[11] Å. Fridh, *Le problème de la Passion des Saintes Perpétue et Félicité* (Gothenburg, 1968), 12–45 (prose rhythm), 46–83 (priority of Greek version).

[12] Fridh is clearly biased towards the priority of the Greek version, as is shown by his unpersuasive discussions of 11.8 (67–8), 11.9 (68–71), 12.1 (71–2) and 12.5 (74–5).

[13] See the important review of Amat's edition by C. Mazzucho, *Rivista di Storia e Litteratura Religiosa* 36 (2000) 157–67.

[14] See Bremmer, "Perpetua and Her Diary," 82, 91–2 (also on the spelling Minicius).

Greek version and three of the Latin manuscripts (B, D, E²) have
"Saturus." As this was a common name, there seems to be no reason not to accept it into the text: the name Saturninus may well
have been introduced in an attempt to avoid confusion.

So what did Saturus see in his vision?

> [11] We had undergone martyrdom, he said, and parted from the
> flesh, and were carried towards the east by four angels who did not
> touch us with their hands. But we moved along not on our backs fac-
> ing upwards, but as though we were climbing up a gentle hill. And
> after having passed the first world, we saw an intense light, and I said
> to Perpetua (for she was at my side): "This is what the Lord promised
> us. We have received his promise."
>
> And while we were being carried by those four angels, a great space
> appeared which was just like a park, with rose bushes and all kinds
> of flowers. The trees were as tall as cypresses, and their petals were
> constantly falling. There, in the park, there were four other angels
> more splendid than the others. When they saw us, they paid us homage
> and said to the other angels in admiration: "Look, they are here! Look,
> they are here!"
>
> And those four angels who were carrying us were impressed and
> set us down. And on our own feet we went through the park along
> a broad road. There we met Iucundus, Saturus, and Artaxius, who
> had been burned alive in the same persecution, as well as Quintus,
> who had died as a martyr in prison. And we asked them where the
> others were.[15] The angels said to us: "First come and enter and greet
> the Lord."
>
> [12] And we came to a place whose walls seemed to be constructed
> of light. And four angels stood before the gate of that place, who
> dressed us with white robes as we went in. And we entered and heard
> the sound of voices in unison chanting endlessly: "Holy, holy, holy."
> And we saw someone sitting in the same place who looked like an
> old man, with white hair but a youthful face, whose feet we did not
> see. And on his right and left were four elders, and behind them there
> stood several other elders. And entering with admiration we stood
> before the throne, and four angels lifted us up and we kissed him, and
> he touched our faces with his hand. And the other elders said to us:
> "Let us rise." And we rose and gave the kiss of peace. And the elders
> said to us: "Go and play." And I said to Perpetua: "You have what
> you want." And she said to me: "Thanks be to God that I am hap-
> pier here now, although I was happy in the flesh."

---

[15] I follow Bastiaensen in reading: *Et quaerebamus de illis ubi essent ceteri*, whereas
Musurillo puts a full stop after *essent*.

[13] And we went out, and before the gate we saw Bishop Optatus on the right and Aspasius the presbyter teacher on the left, apart from one another and looking sad. And they threw themselves at our feet and said: "Make peace between us, because you have departed and left us behind like this." And we said to them: "Are you not our bishop and you the presbyter? How can you fall at our feet?" And we were moved and embraced them. And Perpetua started to talk to them in Greek, and we drew them apart into the park under a rose arbour. And while we were talking to them, angels said to them: "Let them enjoy themselves. And if you have any quarrels, forgive one another." And they made them confused and they said to Optatus: "Scold your flock, because they assemble before you as if they had returned from the circus and were discussing the different teams." And it thus seemed that they wanted to close the gates. And we recognised there many brethren, and also martyrs. All of us were fed by an indescribable smell that satisfied us. Then I woke up full of joy.

2. SATURUS' WELCOME IN HEAVEN

Saturus starts by observing that they had died and were carried by four angels towards the east. The passage is a clear example of the widespread belief among the early Christians that martyrs would not have to wait, but could immediately ascend to heaven.[16] This is also confirmed by Saturus' eastwards destination (*in orientem*), since the early Christians believed that Paradise was situated in the east, a normal location already in intertestamentary literature.[17] However, Saturus did not go unaccompanied. The presence of Perpetua at his side is a nice confirmation of the close association between teacher and pupil that we can also notice in Perpetua's first vision (4.6).[18] Moreover, they were accompanied by a group of four angels, a specific number that is already attested in Jewish tradition:[19] Saturus clearly was not without a certain feeling of importance.

---

[16] For many examples see Bremmer, *Rise and Fall*, 58; add Cyprian, *Ep.* 31.3, 55.20.3, 58.3.1 and *Ad Fort. praef.* 4, 13.

[17] *Gen* 2.8; *T. Job* 52.10; *1 Enoch* 32.2; *2 Enoch* 31.1, 42.3; *4 Ezra* 5.21, cf. F. Dölger, *Sol salutis* (Münster, 1925²), 173–81; S. de Blaauw, *Met het oog op het licht. Een vergeten principe in de oriëntatie van het vroegchristelijk kerkgebouw* (Nijmegen, 2000).

[18] C. Osiek, "Perpetua's Husband," *J. Early Christ. Stud.* 10 (2002) 287–90 unpersuasively suggests that Saturus might have been Perpetua's husband. The text does not provide any indication for such a relationship.

[19] J. Michl, "Engel II," *RAC* 5 (1962) 60–97 at 89–90 (four angels around God's throne), and "Engel IV," *ibidem*, 109–200 at 183–4 (other groups of four angels).

Rather intriguingly, Saturus relates that they went "as if climbing a gentle hill." Apparently, heaven was somewhere above them. Similarly, Perpetua had to climb a high ladder (4.3), and in the *Passio Mariani* (6.9–10) Marian had to ascend a high tribunal.[20] Moreover, heaven is situated beyond "the first world," just as Paradise lies *extra mundum* in *Montanus* (7.5). No further details are provided regarding its geography, except that they already saw *lucem immensam* before their actual arrival in heaven. Light was perhaps the most striking feature of the Christian paradise,[21] and in this way its brightness is particularly stressed.

On arrival, just like Perpetua in her first vision (4.8), they saw a great open space which looked like a *viridiarium*, "park." The term is also used by Cicero (*Att.* 2.3.2) in the context of the *Cyropaedia*, but here probably refers to the wonderful parks of the Roman grandees in North Africa, which we can still admire on the mosaics and which ultimately derived from the Persian *paradeisoi*.[22] Such a representation of heaven as a kind of "paradise" was not abnormal in intertestamentary literature.[23] In this case the park was full of flowers, with very tall roses in particular.[24] Amat connects the rose with funerary customs,[25] but such a meaning seems to be out of place here. Roses were the spring flowers *par excellence*, and their mention suggests a mild climate in heaven:[26] spring also became *de rigueur* in Roman descriptions of the Golden Age and the *locus amoenus*.[27]

---

[20] See also L. Beirnaert, "Le symbolisme ascensionnel dans la liturgie et la mystique chrétiennes," *Eranos Jahrb.* 19 (1950) 41–63; F. Graf, "The Bridge and the Ladder: Narrow Passages in Late Antique Visions," in Abusch and Reed, *In Heaven as it is on Earth* (note 4).

[21] Bremmer, *Rise and Fall*, 60, 124, 126.

[22] For these Roman wild parks see F. Olck, "Gartenbau," *RE* 7 (Stuttgart, 1912), 768–841 at 838; M. Blanchard-Lemée *et al.*, *Mosaics of Roman Africa*, tr. K.D. Whitehead (London, 1996), 167–77; M. Guggisberg, "Vom Paradeisos zum 'Paradies'. Jagdmosaiken und Gartenperistyle in der römischen Herrschaftsarchitektur Nordafrikas und Siziliens," *Hefte Arch. Sem. Univ. Berns* 17 (2000) 21–39. Persian *paradeisoi*: Bremmer, *Rise and Fall*, 109–19.

[23] For various examples see A. Hilhorst, "A Visit to Paradise: Apocalypse of Paul 45 and Its Background," in G.P. Luttikhuizen (ed.), *Paradise Interpreted* (Leiden, 1999), 128–39 at 136f.

[24] The picture of roses as tall as trees is very rare, but note Hesychius ρ 394: ῥοδῆ: αὐτὸ τὸ δένδρον.

[25] Amat, *Songes et visions*, 125.

[26] Note also the moderate climate in the picture of the underworld in [Plato], *Axiochos* 371D.

[27] Spring flowers: Nisbet and Hubbard on Horace, *C.* 1.38.4. Golden Age: Verg.

This does not exclude the possibility that the roses also carry a different meaning, as we will soon see.

A mild climate in heaven is also mentioned in a sermon, formerly believed to have been by Cyprian, which probably dates to the first years of the 250s and may well have originated in Carthage itself. After a graphic picture of the torments that awaited the unrighteous, the author continues with the pleasures of paradise:

> where in the verdant fields the luxuriant earth clothes itself with tender grass, and is pastured with the scent of flowers; where the groves are carried up to the lofty hill-top, and where the tree clothes with a thicker foliage whatever spot the canopy, expanded by its curving branches, may have shaded. There is no excess of cold or of heat, nor is it necessary that in autumn the fields should rest, or, again in the young spring, that the fruitful earth should bring forth her bounty. All things are of one season: fruits are borne of a continued summer, since there neither does the moon serve the purpose of her months, nor does the sun run his course along the moments of the hours, nor does the banishment of the light make way for night. A joyous repose possesses the people, a calm home shelters them, where a gushing fountain in the midst issues from the bosom of a broken hollow, and flows in sinuous mazes by a course deep sounding, at intervals to be divided among the sources of rivers springing from it.[28]

In this sermon that had to intimidate and stimulate the imagination of the faithful, torments and pleasures are of course much more elaborated than in Saturus' vision, but the idea of a pleasant climate with eternal light, *lux perpetua*, is crystal clear.

The rose trees Saturus saw were as tall as cypresses.[29] Tall trees were desirable for their shade and therefore also occur in other pictures of wonderful gardens, such as in that of Alcinoos in the *Odyssey* (7.114), in that encountered by Socrates and Phaedrus in Plato's *Phaedrus* (230B) and, still, in a garden in the late fourth-century *Visio Pauli* (24), where Paul sees *arbores magnas et altas valde* before entering Paradise. But what do the petals of the rose trees do? The Latin

---

G. 2.149–50; Ovid, *Met.* 1.107 with F. Bömer *ad loc.*, *F.* 5.207–8; Lucian, *VH* 2.12; Claud. *Epithal.* 55.

[28] Pseudo-Cyprian, *De laude martyrii* 21, translation adapted from R.E. Wallis, *The Writings of Cyprian* II = *Ante-Nicene Christian Library*, vol. 13 (Edinburgh, 1894), 245–6, cf. Amat, *Songes et visions*, 155–6. For date and place see the concise discussion by J. Doignon in R. Herzog and P.L. Schmidt (eds.), *Handbuch der lateinischen Literatur der Antike IV* (Munich, 1997), 578.

[29] Servius on Vergil, *Ecl* 1.25: *cupressus vero arbor est maxima*.

manuscripts unanimously state that they *cadebant sine cessatione*, and the Greek version confirms the antiquity of this text. Yet falling petals are somewhat surprising, since Cyprian (*Carm.* 6.227) writes about Paradise: *nulla cadunt folia*. That is why Amat's edition of *Perpetua* has followed Robinson's emendation *canebant*, as some descriptions of the *locus amoenus* stress the melodious sound of leaves.[30] Yet these interpretations clearly fit the leaves of trees, whereas our passage concerns petals of roses. Such a continuing rain of rose petals must have created a pleasant, fragrant (below) atmosphere in which to converse, and to lie on roses was considered the height of hedonism;[31] in fact, roses already occur in Orphic(-like) descriptions of the underworld.[32] Even so, there is something idiosyncratic about the detail.

Saturus, Perpetua and their angels now met another group of four angels, who were clearly higher in rank, as they guided them to the place where God was sitting on his throne. With them they walked on a broad road that apparently crossed the park (*stadium*). Such roads cannot have been unusual, as it is repeatedly mentioned regarding *paradeisoi* that they provided possibilities for walking.[33] Here they met three martyrs, Iucundus, Saturus and Artaxius, who had been burned to death in the same persecution. The names are illustrative of the "multicultural" nature of the Roman empire, but also strongly suggest that they were freedmen. Iucundus is an impeccably Latin name; Saturus is a Greek name, and Artaxius was probably a native Armenian, since several Armenian kings of that name are known.[34] The probability that they were freedmen would fit the nature of their execution—the *vivicomburium* was a not uncommon penalty for the lower classes, but also for Christian martyrs;[35] the names and the penalty thus also tell us something about the social level from which the Carthaginian Christians were recruited. The fourth mar-

---

[30] See the discussions by A. Dieterich, *Nekuia* (Leipzig, 1913²), 34; Fridh, *Le problème*, 59–61 and V. Saxer, *Bible et hagiographie* (Berne, 1986), 92–4. F. Dolbeau, *REAug* 37 (1987) 315 proposes *candebant*, but this is less convincing, as *sine cessatione* presupposes an action and roses hardly *candent*.

[31] Nisbet and Hubbard on Horace, *C.* 1.5.1.

[32] Pindar, fr. 129.3 Maehler; Aristophanes, *Frogs* 448.

[33] Bremmer, *Rise and Fall*, 116.

[34] R. Schmitt, "Artaxerxes, Ardašir und Verwandte," *Incontri Linguistici* 5 (1979) 61–72.

[35] Cf. *Mart. Polycarpi* 12–6; *Mart. Carpi, Papyli et Agathonicae* (Greek) 37–44; *Mart. Pionii* 20–1; *Passio Philippi* 11–13; Eus. *MPal. passim*; F.J. Dölger, *Antike und Christentum* 1 (Münster, 1929), 243–57; J.-P. Callu, "Le jardin des supplices au Bas-Empire," in *Du châtiment dans la cité* (Rome, 1984), 313–59.

tyr was a certain Quintus, who had already died in prison. Such a fate was also not uncommon. Cyprian (*Ep.* 22.2) provides a list of a whole group of Christians who had died in prison from bad conditions; in fact, even one of Saturus' group, Secundulus, had died before he could be executed for his faith (14). As both our passage and that of Cyprian demonstrate, such a, so to speak, premature death did not deprive Christians from the coveted title of *martyr*.[36]

From the park the martyrs arrived at God's palace. Fridh compares the distinction between Paradise and palace in *2 Enoch* (8 and 20), where the former is situated in the third heaven and the latter in the seventh, but in the African imagination the two are clearly in the same space; similarly, Marian heads for the *praetorium* of the heavenly judge through a wonderful landscape (*Passio Mariani* 6.11–12). Amat (*ad loc.*) compares the palace of Cupid in Apuleius' *Metamorphoses* (5.1) but, in contrast to the elaborate description of that building,[37] Saturus is very reticent. He only mentions that its walls were built of light, another example of the prominence of light that we have already encountered.

At the entrance, the martyrs had to put on new, white clothes; this is already the colour typical of the saints in heaven in *Revelation* (6:11, 7:9,13,14).[38] Such a change of clothes is also attested in *2 Enoch* (22:8–10) and the *Ascensio Isaiah* (9:2), and was probably a standard motif in early Apocalypses. On entering, they heard people singing in unison "Holy, holy, holy."[39] The words are a straight quotation

---

[36] Note also *Montanus* 2; Eus. *HE*. 5.2.3.

[37] See. S. Brodersen, "Cupid's Palace—A Roman Villa (Apul. *Met.* 5, 1)," in M. Zimmerman *et al.* (eds.), *Aspects of Apuleius' Golden Ass II* (Groningen, 1998), 113–25; G. Brugnoli, "Il palazzo di Amore nella Favola di Amore e Psiche di Apuleio e nell' Asino di Machiavelli," *Fontes* 3, 5–6 (2000) 83–98.

[38] For many more examples see U. Körtner and M. Leutzsch, *Papiasfragmente. Hirt des Hermas* (Darmstadt, 1998), 386 note 71 and 480 note 202; see also the contribution by Eibert Tigchelaar in this volume. For the heavy dependence of *Perpetua* on *Revelation* in its description of the afterlife see R. Petraglio, "Des influences de l'*Apocalypse* dans la *Passio Perpetuae* 11–13," in R. Petraglio *et al.* (eds.), *L'Apocalypse de Jean. Traditions exégétiques et iconographiques. III*[e]*–XIII*[e] *siècles* (Genève, 1979), 15–29; A.P. Orbán, "The Afterlife in the Visions of the Passio SS. Perpetuae et Felicitatis," in A.A.R. Bastiaensen *et al.* (eds.), *Fructus Centesimus. Mélanges offerts à G.J.M. Bartelink* (Steenbrugge and Dordrecht, 1989) 269–77; Th. Heffernan, "History becomes Heilsgeschichte: the Principle of the Paradigm in the Early Christian *Passio Sanctarum Perpetuae et Felicitatis*," in U. Goebel and D. Lee (eds.), *Interpreting Texts from the Middle Ages* (Lewiston, 1994), 119–38.

[39] For the chant see L. Koenen, *ZPE* 31 (1978) 71–6; add *I. Alexandreia* 187; C. Böttrich, "Das 'Sanctus' in der Liturgie der hellenistischen Synagoge," *Jahrb.*

from one of the visions of Revelation (4:8), where the beasts round
the throne of God "rest not day and night, saying, Holy, holy, holy.
Lord God Almighty, which was, and is, and is to come"; the Greek
form of the words may well point to its use in contemporary liturgy.[40]
The object of their praise is God himself, represented as a man with
grey hair and a youthful face. As has often been seen, the background to this picture is Revelation 1:14, where it is said of God
that "his head and his hairs were white like wool, as white as snow."
Yet, at the same time, his youthful face refers to Christ: the same
fusion between God and Christ that we can see in the visions of
Perpetua, where it is often difficult to establish whether she sees God
or Christ.[41] Why are God's feet invisible? Amat (*ad loc.*) thinks that
this expresses Gods "caractère surhumain," whereas Bastiaensen (*ad
loc.*) suggests that it indicates "il mistero che circonda la figura di
Dio." Neither of these explanations is really persuasive, and we may
wonder whether the detail is not the reflection of the same picture
in Revelation, where it is said that God was "clothed with a garment down to the foot" (1:13), even though a bit later his feet are
said to be "like unto fine brass" (1:15).

On either side of God there were four elders, and elders also
stood behind him. Amat and Bastiaensen (*ad loc.*) understandably
compare the elders of Revelation (4:10), who worship God, but in
our passage they play a role in the reception and are able to give
various indications as how to behave *coram Deo*. That is why it is
attractive to follow Brent Shaw's suggestion that these *seniores* also
reflect a lesser known African clerical order. Shaw notes the occurrence of these church authorities in Tertullian (*Apol.* 39.4–5) and
here in *Perpetua*, but observes that there is a "considerable gap in
the literary evidence during the entire mid-century before elders are
mentioned again in an African context."[42] However, we can point
to a passage that possibly closes the mid-century gap. According to
the *Passio sancti Felicis episcopi* (1), in A.D. 303 the Roman *curator rei
publicae* Magnilianus ordered the *seniores plebis* of a village not far from

f. Liturgik u. Hymnologie 35 (1994–95) 10–36; D.G. Martínez, *Baptized for our sakes: a
leather trisagion from Egypt (P. Mich. 799)* (Stuttgart and Leipzig, 1999); A. di Bitonto
Kasser, "Due nove testi cristiani," *Aegyptus* 79 (1999) 93–106.
 [40] L. Duchesne, *Origines du culte chrétien* (Paris, 1925), 182.
 [41] See Bremmer, "Perpetua and Her Diary," 103, 118.
 [42] B. Shaw, *Rulers, Nomads, and Christians in Roman North Africa* (Aldershot, 1995),
Ch. X ("The Elders of Christian Africa"), 210.

THE VISION OF SATURUS

Carthage to be brought to him, since bishop Felix had gone to Carthage. Shaw well observes that in the text the *seniores* are the highest church authority after the bishop, that is before the priest and the readers. Now in a letter by Firmilian to Cyprian (*Ep.* 75.4.3), originally written in Greek in the autumn of 256 but translated into Latin in Cyprian's secretariat, Firmilian states that "we find it needful that each year *seniores et praepositi* should come together." Given the prominence of the *seniores* after the bishop in the *Passio Felicis* and the familiarity of the term *presbyteri* in Africa, the occurrence of *seniores* in our text may well be another testimony to the prominence of this somewhat obscure group in the African church.

Once again a group of four angels is present to lift up Saturus and Perpetua in order to give God a kiss. The kiss looks like a greeting kiss,[43] but God's response hardly signifies the washing away of the tears as Amat and Bastiaensen (*ad loc.*) suggest—in any case, neither the Latin nor the Greek easily provides that meaning.[44] The touching of their faces suggests intimacy, but the absence of reciprocity in kissing also indicates a certain distance between God and the martyrs. The Latin then rather abruptly proceeds with "Let us stand," whereas the Greek has: "Let us stand and pray." One cannot escape the idea that at this point in the Latin text something has gone wrong, since just before it was said that the martyrs were standing before God's throne (12.5). Can it be that they had first fallen flat on their face in front of God in order to do him obeisance, just like Enoch (*2 Enoch* 4)? In any case, the custom to end a prayer with a "kiss of peace" (*osculum pacis* or *pax*) is well attested in Carthage from Tertullian onwards.[45]

The *seniores* dismissed Saturus and Perpetua with the words *Ite et ludite*. The phrase is not that easy to understand. Bastiaensen (*ad loc.*) probably rightly observes that it denotes "felicità escatologica," even though he provides no clear parallels, but his comparison with Dinocrates' play is hardly persuasive, since the little boy plays *more infantium* (8.4), which cannot be expected of Saturus and Perpetua.

---

[43] For such a kiss see K. Thraede, "Friedenskuss," in *RAC* 8 (1972) 505–19 at 507–11.

[44] *Contra* Amat, *Songes et visions*, 126 note 126; Bastiaensen *ad loc*. Both the Latin *de manu sua traiecit nobis in faciem* and the Greek περιέλαβεν τὰς ὄψεις are unique.

[45] K. Thraede, "Ursprünge und Formen des 'Heiligen Kusses' im frühen Christentum," *JbAC* 11–12 (1968–69) 124–80 at 150–3, who does not mention our passage.

We might perhaps think of contemporary pagan funerary iconography on the sarcophagi, which displays a clear dominance of a "freudig-
festliche Thematik" with its many Dionysiac scenes.[46] Can it be that
we see here its Christian counterpart?

This part of the vision is concluded by a brief dialogue between
Saturus and Perpetua. The latter introduces her concluding sentence
with *Deo gratias*, an expression which already occurs in Tertullian's
De patientia, 14.4, as Bastiaensen and Amat (*ad loc.*) observe, but, more
importantly, also concludes the end of Marian's vision (*Passio Mariani*
6.15). It fits the intense expectation of the life everlasting displayed
by Perpetua's own vision that Saturus here lets her comment that
she is now even more *hilaris* in heaven than on earth.[47]

3. Conversation with the Clergy on Earth

After their meeting with God, Saturus and Perpetua leave His palace,
and it is striking that the stress on play and *hilaritas* is rather abruptly
succeeded by sadness and discontent: one cannot fail to note an art-
ful disposition in this part of the vision, which clearly aims at con-
trasting the elevated position of the martyrs in heaven with the
troublesome situation of the clergy on earth. Before the gate, they
saw their bishop and one of his presbyters, a *presbyter doctor*, far away
from one another. They are not said to be martyrs, and the sequel
shows that they are in fact still alive. Amat (*ad loc.*) states without
argument that Optatus was bishop of Carthage. Although this is not
supported by the text, his conversation in Greek (below) and the reference to the circus factions seem indeed to fit better a bishop of
Carthage than that of Saturus' small town of Thuburbo Minus.
Optatus is one of the very few African bishops known by name from
the period before Cyprian.[48] This relative absence of early bishops
in our tradition may well be an indication of their modest position
before Cyprian greatly increased the importance of the function.
Names taken from participles ending in *-atus* were preponderant in

---

[46] See the stimulating observations of P. Zanker, *Die mythologischen Sarkophagreliefs
und ihre Betrachter* (Munich, 2000), 10f.

[47] For the spiritual connotation of *hilaris* see Amat *ad loc.*

[48] See the list in G.W. Clarke, *The Letters of St. Cyprian of Carthage I* (New York
and Ramsey, 1984), 158.

Africa and typical for slaves, freedmen and soldiers.[49] Aspasius' Greek name also points to an origin as a freedman.[50] His function, *presbyter doctor*, which is attested only in Africa, must have been that of a specialised class of presbyters, viz. those who had to teach the catechumens or potential clerics.[51] Optatus' and Aspasius' names, then, add to the indication of a strong presence of freedmen among Africa's first Christians, as already suggested by the names of Iucundus, Saturus and Artaxius (§ 2).[52]

The standing apart of both clerics is evidently symbolic of the dissensions within their congregation, and it is remarkable that they prostrate themselves before the lay persons Saturus and Perpetua. Their humiliation is so striking that the text calls attention to it by letting Saturus and Perpetua exclaim: "Are you not our bishop (*papa*) and you presbyter?" Although *papas* was not unknown in Latin and probably introduced by the Greek speaking *paedagogi*,[53] *papa* seems to have been re-introduced into Christian usage via the Greek speaking community that formed the basis of the African Christian congregation.[54] Whereas originally a form of address attested first in Tertullian (*Pud.* 13.7), we can note here its development towards a title for a bishop, which is already complete by the time of Cyprian (*Ep.* 23, 30–1, 36).[55] After this exclamation, Saturus and Perpetua embrace the dissenting couple, another sign of the martyrs' superiority—although perhaps not without a slight hint of condescension on the part of Saturus.

The context does not elucidate why Perpetua now starts to speak with them in Greek. Tertullian's use of Latin in the majority of his

---

[49] R. Syme, "'Donatus' and the Like," *Historia* 28 (1978) 588–603 = Syme, *Roman Papers III*, ed. A.R. Birley (Oxford, 1984), 1105–19.

[50] In the West, the name is less rare than that of Artaxius, see *CIL* 5.1099, 13.11207 and 11441.

[51] For this rarely mentioned function see H. Janssen, *Kultur und Sprache* (Diss. Nimwegen, 1938), 39–43; add Cyprian, *Ep.* 29.1.2 and *Acta Saturnini, Dativi et sociorum* 10; for the value of the latter *Acta* see A.R. Birley, "A Persecuting Praeses of Numidia under Valerian," *JTS* 42 (1991) 598–610.

[52] Add these examples to G. Schöllgen, *Ecclesia sordida?* (Münster, 1985), 249.

[53] See E. Courtney on Juv. 6.633.

[54] For Greek examples see Dionysius Alex. *apud* Eus. *HE.* 7.7.4; Origen, *Dialogus cum Heraclide* 1.20, *Hom. 1 in Samuel, Epistula ad Africanum* 11.85.49; Gregory Thaumaturgos, *Epist. Can.*, can. 1. *Papa* was very popular as a name in Asia Minor, cf. C. Brixhe and M. Özsait, *Kadmos* 40 (2001) 163.

[55] For the title see most recently C. Pietri, *Roma christiana*, 2 vols (Rome, 1976), II.1609–12.

treatises seems to indicate that this was the language of the majority of his audience, but the higher, educated strata of the Carthaginian
population, including the Christian community, evidently spoke or
understood Greek.[56] Can it be that Perpetua wanted to speak to
Optatus and Aspasius without being understood by other people, as
they took the clergy aside under a rose arbour? However this may
be, the mention of the rose arbour is probably not without significance
and one more indication of the importance of Saturus and Perpetua
in comparison with the quarreling clergy. In early Christianity, red
roses were symbolic of the blood of the martyrs, just as their thorns
could symbolise the martyrs' torture. This symbolism already occurs
in Cyprian, and would stay alive until the fifth century.[57] By asso-
ciating themselves with the rose, then, Saturus and Perpetua stressed
their pre-eminent position.

It was apparently not enough that the martyrs addressed the clergy;
the angels also had to contribute to putting them into their rightful
place. They sternly address the clergy, and mention of the martyrs'
refrigerium once again presents the reader with the difference between
the eschatological joy of the martyrs and the all too earthly difficulties
of the clergy.[58] Moreover, in addition to these none too angelic exhortations, Optatus is reprimanded because he apparently keeps his flock
insufficiently disciplined. The angels compare the behaviour of his
parishioners with those of the supporters of the horse racing teams
of the circus (*de factionibus*).[59] We do indeed have interesting evidence
that these chariot races roused the passions of the Carthaginians,
since in Carthage several curses have been found against the char-
ioteers or their horses, which start to appear from the second century A.D. onwards.[60] Apparently, ancient supporters did not behave

---

[56] G. Schöllgen, "Der Adressatenkreis der griechischen Schauspielschrift Tertullians,"
JbAC 25 (1982) 22–7; T. Barnes, *Tertullian* (Oxford, 1985²), 67–9.

[57] See the passages offered by J. den Boeft and J. Bremmer, "Notiunculae
Martyrologicae," *VC* 35 (1981) 43–56 at 53 and "Notiunculae Martyrologicae II,"
397–9; add Cyprian, *De op. et eleemos.* 26; Hier. *Ep.* 54.14; Paulinus of Nola, *Carm.*
18.146ff.

[58] For the eschatological connotation of *refrigerium* see Bastiaensen on *Perpetua* 3.4.

[59] Bastiaensen (*ad loc.*) comments: "I fedeli, divisi in fazioni come nei giochi del
circo, si gettano contro il loro vescovo," but *factiones* are the teams, not the supporters, cf. A. Cameron, *Circus Factions* (Oxford, 1976), 14.

[60] A. Audollent, *Defixionum Tabellae* (Paris, 1904), 234–44; D.R. Jordan, "A Survey
of Greek Defixiones Not Included in the Special Corpora," *GRBS* 26 (1985) 151–97,
no's 138–41 and Jordan, "New defixiones from Carthage," in J.H. Humphrey (ed.),
The Circus and a Byzantine Cemetery at Carthage I (Ann Arbor, 1988), 117–34.

that differently from modern football hooligans.[61] The angels compound their reprimands by pretending to close the gates. Which gates? The text is curiously vague at this point, but they can hardly be other than the gates of Paradise. The Old Testament does not provide any explicit information about such gates, but the mention in *Genesis* (3.23) of cherubs guarding the entrance to Paradise provided the stimulus for later generations to introduce walls.[62] And, clearly, no walls without gates.

In addition to the garden-like appearance of heaven, we are struck by the stress on the presence of many others there: Perpetua sees "many thousands of people" and Saturus "many of our brethren." This multitude of people fits the description of heaven as a large place. The idea frequently recurs in early Christian epitaphs, where the dead are said to have joined the *beati, iusti, electi* and *sancti,* whereas the pagan deceased of the period wander by themselves in the Elysian Fields.[63] But who were these heavenly people? Saturus notes: *Et coepimus illic multos fratres cognoscere, sed et martyras.* In earlier discussions of some elements of Saturus' vision, I followed Musurillo's translation of the last three words ("martyrs among them") and argued that Tertullian's reproduction of this passage, "on the day of her passion the most heroic martyr Perpetua saw in the revelation of Paradise only martyrs there,"[64] deviously canvasses his own exclusivist views about admission into heaven, since *Perpetua* does not contain such a passage and the vision of Saturus explicitly contradicts his words.[65] This interpretation has recently been disputed by Dolbeau, who states that the "opposition" between *Perpetua* and Tertullian "est indiscutable, mais seulement en anglais, car le texte latin de *PPerp* présente une certaine ambiguité."[66] Dolbeau probably means that

---

[61] For the riotous behaviour of these supporters, which became even worse over time, see Cameron, *Circus Factions,* 271–96; M. Matter, "Factions et spectacles de l'hippodrome dans les papyrus grecs à Hermoupolis de Thebaide. Etude preliminaire," *Ktema* 21 (1996) 151–56; M. Whitby, "The violence of the circus factions," in K. Hopwood (ed.), *Organised Crime in Antiquity* (London, 1998), 229–54.

[62] See the *Apocalypse of Moses* 17:1; *bKetubbot* 77b; *bShabbath* 119b; *Vita Adam* 31:2, 40:2.

[63] G. Sanders, *Licht en duisternis in de Christelijke grafschriften,* 2 vols (Brussels, 1965), II.661–8 (Christians), 691–2 (pagans).

[64] Tert. *An.* 55.4: *Quomodo Perpetua, fortissima martyr, sub die passionis in revelatione paradisi solos illic martyras vidit,* etc.

[65] Thus Bremmer, "The Passion of Perpetua and the Development of Early Christian Afterlife," *NedTT* 54 (2000) 97–111 at 101 and *Rise and Fall,* 59.

[66] F. Dolbeau, *REAug* 47 (2001) 382.

the Latin can equally mean "brethren who were also martyrs," but is he right?

Let us look again at the passage. G. Chiarini (*apud* Bastiaensen, *Atti*, 135) follows Musurillo ("martyrs among them") by translating *sed et martyras* with "e tra essi anche dei martiri"; Bastiaensen suggests "those of the brothers who were martyrs" or "the brothers who were also martyrs"; Amat translates with "tous des martyrs" in her edition, and Charles Hill with "many brethren, and moreover martyrs."[67] These translations demonstrate that the meaning of *sed et* is not immediately transparent, although these words are crucial to a proper understanding of the sentence. So what do they mean? The combination *sed et* also occurs elsewhere in *Perpetua*. After the visions of Perpetua, the editor continues with mentioning that Saturus also (*sed et Saturus*) put his vision into circulation (11.1). And Felicitas *in magno erat luctu* (15.2) because she was prevented from martyrdom by her pregnancy. *Sed et conmartyres graviter contristabantur* that they would leave her behind (15.3). In these cases the combination *sed et* clearly mentions two different categories (Perpetua and Saturus; Felicitas and her fellow martyrs), of which the contrast is not particularly marked. This is indeed a development in post-classical Latin, which can also be noticed in Tertullian and Apuleius, where the combination *sed et* is regularly "mehr weiterführend als adversativ," but always seems to mention two (or more) different categories.[68] Although in post-classical Latin *sed et*, in the meaning of *sed etiam*, can also appear without a preceding *non modum* (*LHSz* II.518–9), the translation "and also martyrs" is probably more attractive than the equally possible "but also martyrs," since the categories of brethren and martyrs are not necessarily exclusive. I would therefore conclude that Saturus saw "many brethren, and also martyrs" in heaven.

Tertullian's interpretation strongly suggests that he wanted to limit entry into heaven to martyrs only, and he was not unique in this respect. In our tradition, the words *sed et* are attested only in the two best manuscripts, Amat's A (Van Beek's 1) and D (Van Beek's 2),

---

[67] A.A.R. Bastiaensen, "Tertullian's reference to the *Passio Perpetuae* in *De Anima* 55.4," *Studia patristica* 12.2 (Berlin, 1982), 790–95; Ch. Hill, *Regnum Caelorum. Patterns of millennial thought in Early Christianity* (Grand Rapids and Cambridge, 2001²), 154.

[68] E. Löfstedt, *Zur Sprache Tertullians* (Lund and Leipzig, 1920), 62, who compares Tertullian, *De idololatria* 10: *quaerendum autem est etiam de ludimagistris, sed et ceteris professoribus litterarum*; Apuleius, *Met.* 7.7, 8.16, 10.6, etc.

whereas they are omitted in the other testimonies. This omission
suggests that, like Tertullian, their scribes preferred a heaven with
only martyrs. Such a preference may have been an uneasy com-
promise between the competing early Christian views of an immediate entry into heaven of all saints or the Irenean notion of a waiting
in Hades for the resurrection.[69]

It is somewhat surprising that Saturus only now notes the wonderful smell in heaven. Can this have been influenced by Perpetua's
first vision, in which she wakes up with a wonderful taste in her
mouth? Bastiaensen and Amat (*ad loc.*) suppose that the motif derives
straight from the New Testament (2 Cor 2:14–5 and Eph 5:2).[70] Yet
the idea of supernatural fragrance already occurs in the *Homeric Hymn
to Demeter*, and probably is an inheritance from pagan tradition,[71]
even if Christians had already appropriated the motif before Saturus.[72]
Influence from Perpetua's vision at this point is indeed not impossible, since Saturus' phrasing of his waking up, *expertus sum*, is identical to Perpetua's *experta sum* at the end of her first vision (4.29),
whereas this form of the participle does not occur elsewhere before
the fourth century.[73] Saturus' joy (*gaudens*) reflects the joy of the
Christians in their suffering, which is often attested and also occurs
elsewhere in *Perpetua*.[74] Perpetua tells us that of all her kin her father
would be the only one who would not derive joy from her suffering
(5.6), and when the crowd demanded that Perpetua and her fellow
martyrs should be scourged by the group of *venatores*, they "rejoiced
at this that they had obtained a share in the Lord's sufferings" (18.9).
On this "happy note," then, Saturus' vision concludes.

Conclusion

When we now look back at the vision, we can see that it consists
of two parts, which demonstrate the esteem and importance of Saturus

---

[69] Hill, *Caelum regnorum*, 155.

[70] Amat, *Songes et visions*, 127 still saw here a direct reference to "la croyance
archaïque" that souls and demons fed themselves with perfumes.

[71] W. Déonna, *Euôdia. Croyances antiques et modernes* (Genève, 1939), 163–267; N.J.
Richardson, *The Homeric Hymn to Demeter* (Oxford, 1974), 252–3.

[72] B. Kötting, *Ecclesia peregrinans*, 2 vols (Münster, 1988), II.23–33 ("Wohlgeruch
der Heiligkeit"); G. Buschmann, *Das Martyrium des Polykarp* (Göttingen, 1998), 301–9.

[73] Bastiaensen *ad loc.* who refers to *ThLL s.v.*

[74] See Bremmer, "Perpetua and Her Diary," 94f.

both in heaven and on earth. In the first half (11–12), Saturus elaborately describes his entry and reception in heaven. This part shows the esteem he enjoys from God and the heavenly host of angels and *seniores*. The reader is left in no doubt that we have to do here with somebody who is held in high regard by the heavenly hierarchy. At the same time, the vision must also have confirmed and strengthened (if that was necessary) his role as the spiritual guide of Perpetua and his other fellow martyrs.

The second part of the vision (13) demonstrates the importance of the martyr on earth, even if via a heavenly meeting. The clergy pays its respect to the martyrs, and the martyrs are free to reproach the clergy, assisted in this respect by angels. We have no information about the immediate context of the quarrels alluded to in the vision, but given the pre-eminence of martyrs and *confessores* in the early Church it is easy to imagine tensions between them and the slowly developing hierarchy, such as becomes all too visible in the letters of Cyprian.[75]

Finally, the terrible events in New York in September 2001 and the continuing stream of Palestinian suicides in Israel raise the harrowing question as to the nature and identity of the people who "happily" die for a cause they espouse, as well as the conditions that facilitate the voluntary giving up of everything for what many may consider a mistaken ideal. Such an investigation would of course go beyond the limits of this contribution.[76] Yet both Perpetua's and Saturus' visions clearly demonstrate that the strong belief in a welcoming hereafter can be a powerful stimulus in bearing torture and execution.[77] Similarly, the highjackers of the WTC-planes carried a description of the Islamic Paradise with them,[78] and Paradise also

---

[75] A. Brent, "Cyprian's Reconstruction of the Martyr Tradition," *JEH* 53 (2002) 241–68.

[76] Such an investigation is only gradually becoming possible. See especially C. Reuter, *Mein Leben ist eine Waffe. Selbstmordattentäter—Psychogramm eines Phänomens* (Munich, 2002); note also some of the websites discussed by J.W. van Henten, "Internet Martyrs and Violence: Victims and/or Perpetrators," in J. Bekkenkamp and Y. Sherwood (eds.), *Vocabularies of Violence, The Bible in the Twenty-first Century* 3 (Sheffield, 2003).

[77] For belief in immortality as an important Christian "compensator" see the interesting reflections of R. Stark, *The Rise of Christianity* (Princeton, 1996), 163–89.

[78] This is clear from the widely reported finding of an Arabic manuscript in the suitcase of Mohammed Atta, which was strangely left behind when he flew the first plane into the WTC tower; a fragment of the same manuscript was found in the wreckage of the plane that crashed in Pennsylvania. For a discussion and English

seems to have played a role in the motivation of the Chechens who occupied a Moscow theatre in October 2002 with fatal consequences for themselves and many of the theatre-goers.[79] Heaven still exerts a powerful influence on earthly imaginations, however difficult this is for us secularised Westerners to accept.[80]

translation see D. Cook, "Suicide Attacks or 'Martyrdom Operations' in Contemporary Jihad Literature," *Nova Religio* 6 (2002) 7–44.

[79] I conclude this from the fact that a female "kamikaze" wrote down a prayer for a Russian, who had shown interest in her, and told him: "If you recite this very often, you will join us in Paradise," cf. C. van Zwol, "De gijzeling in Moskou van uur tot uur," *NRC Handelsblad*, Zaterdags Bijvoegsel 2/3–11–2002.

[80] For information and comments I am most grateful to Jan den Boeft, Ruurd Nauta and Stelios Panagiotakis. Kathleen Coleman kindly and carefully corrected my English.

LIFE AFTER DEATH IN PSEUDO-PHOCYLIDES

John J. Collins*

The subject of life after death is introduced parenthetically in the Sayings of Pseudo-Phocylides (97–115), in the context of an exhortation on moderation and equanimity. As is typical of aphoristic collections, sayings are juxtaposed because of thematic association rather than strict consequential logic. Advice on moderation in grief is followed by admonitions against disturbing graves or dissolving the human frame.[1] This, in turn, leads to the reflections of life after death. The passage, beginning at vs. 103, reads as follows:

> καὶ τάχα δ' ἐκ γαίης ἐλπίζομεν ἐς φάος ἐλθεῖν
> λείψαν' ἀποιχόμενων. Ὀπίσω δὲ θεοὶ τελέθονται
> ψυχαὶ γὰρ μίμνουσιν ἀκήριοι ἐν φθιμένοισιν
> πνεῦμα γὰρ ἐστι θεοῦ χρῆσις θνητοῖσι καὶ εἰκών
> σῶμα γὰρ ἐκ γαίης ἔχομεν κἄπειτα πρὸς αὐγὴν
> λυόμενοι κόνις ἐσμέν. ἀὴρ δ' ἀνὰ πνεῦμα δέδεκται . . .
> πάντες ἴσον νέκυες, ψυχῶν δὲ θεὸς βασιλεύει
> κοινὰ μέλαθρα δόμων αἰώνια καὶ πατρὶς ᾍδης
> ξυνὸς χῶρος ἅπασι πένησί τε καὶ βασιλεῦσιν
> οὐ πολὺν ἄνθρωποι ζῶμεν χρόνον ἀλλ' ἐπίκαιρον
> ψυχὴ δ' ἀθάνατος καὶ ἀγήρῳ ζῇ διὰ παντός

The passage is translated as follows by van der Horst (with my own variations in parentheses):

> For (and) in fact[2] we hope that the remains of the departed will soon (perhaps) come to the light again out of the earth. And afterwards they become gods.
> For the souls remain unharmed in the deceased (among the dead).
> For the spirit is a loan from God to mortals, and his image.

---

* Yale.

[1] W.T. Wilson, *The Mysteries of Righteousness. The Literary Composition and Genre of the Sentences of Pseudo-Phocylides* (TSAJ, 40; Tübingen, 1994) claims that vss. 9–131 are structured according to the four cardinal virtues, and relates vss. 55–96 to moderation, but 97–121 to courage. Vss. 97–98, however, are clearly concerned with moderation.

[2] There is no Greek counterpart for "in fact."

For we have a body out of earth, and when afterwards we are resolved
again into earth we are but dust; but the air has received our spirit. . . .
All alike are corpses, but God rules over the souls
Hades is our common eternal home and fatherland,
a common place for all, poor and kings.
We humans live not a long time but for a season.
But our soul is immortal and lives ageless forever.[3]

This short passage appears to contain a bewildering range of different
ideas about the afterlife. The hope that the remains will come to
light out of the earth follows on an admonition against dissolving
the human frame, and so would seem to imply a physical resurrection. In contrast, several statements affirm the immortality of the
soul. But here again there is a complication. According to vs. 105,
"souls remain unharmed among the dead," but the air (ἀήρ) receives
the spirit (πνεῦμα). Most scholars assume that the soul and the spirit
are one and the same, but some have argued that they should be
distinguished. Finally, the statement that Hades is our common eternal home echoes an older eschatology, whereby the shade descends
to Hades and there is neither physical resurrection nor ascent of the
spirit to the heavens.

Scholarly assessments of this confusing passage are of two kinds.
On the one hand, H.C. Cavallin refers to "the unharmonized juxtaposition of contradictory ideas about afterlife."[4] Van der Horst cites
with approval a dictum of Arthur Darby Nock about "the widespread tendency of language about the afterlife to admit inconsis-
tencies."[5] Johannes Thomas suggests that the author is stringing
together whatever ideas are brought to mind by the theme of death.[6]
Pascale Derron claims that Pseudo-Phocylides assembles ideas of
afterlife that were current in his time, and declines to make a synthesis.[7] Such eclectic juxtaposition of ideas is typical of aphoristic
wisdom, and Pseudo-Phocylides was no philosopher. On the other
hand, Felix Christ and Ulrich Fischer have tried to find a coherent

---

[3] Trans. P.W. van der Horst, *The Sentences of Pseudo-Phocylides* (SVTP, 4; Leiden,
1978), 95.
[4] H.C. Cavallin, *Life After Death. Paul's Argument for the Resurrection of the Dead in I
Cor 15. Part I. An Enquiry into the Jewish Background* (Lund, 1974), 153.
[5] A.D. Nock, *Essays on Religion and the Ancient World* (Oxford, 1972) I. 507, n. 19.
Cf. Van der Horst, *The Sentences*, 188–9.
[6] J. Thomas, *Der jüdische Phokylides* (NTOA, 23; Fribourg-Göttingen, 1992), 206.
[7] P. Derron, *Pseudo-Phocylide. Sentences* (Paris, 1986), 25.

doctrine of life after death in Pseudo Phocylides.[8] Christ, who refers to the passage as "ein typisch synkretistisches Amalgam,"[9] argues for a tripartite anthropology, involving body, soul (ψυχή) and πνεῦμα, each of which is assigned a different place after death, until they are brought together in the resurrection. Fischer also affirms a tripartite anthropology, but he denies that Pseudo Phocylides envisions resurrection of the body. Consequently, he denies that all three elements are combined again at the resurrection.[10]

The disagreements between these scholars involve two main issues. First, does Ps. Phocylides envision physical resurrection? And if so, how is this idea related to the belief in immortality of the soul? Second, does Pseudo-Phocylides assume a bi-partite (body-soul) or a tri-partite (body-soul-spirit) anthropology? A third question is raised indirectly: how does Pseudo-Phocylides relate to the spectrum of Jewish ideas about the afterlife in the centuries around the turn of the era?

Physical Resurrection?

An apparent belief in physical resurrection is expressed in verses 103–104: "we hope that the remains of the departed will perhaps come to the light again out of the earth." This is characterized by van der Horst as "a very literalistic doctrine of the resurrection," which was "typically Jewish and very un-Greek."[11] There were in fact many stories in the Greek world of individuals who had returned from the dead, but most educated Greeks would have found the resurrection of the physical body incomprehensible or ridiculous.[12] It is not quite accurate, however, to say that such an idea was typically Jewish.[13] Jewish texts from the second century B.C.E. to first

---

[8] F. Christ, "Das Leben nach dem Tode bei Pseudo-Phokylides," *Theologische Zeitschrift* 31 (1975) 140–7; U. Fischer, *Eschatologie und Jenseitserwartung im Hellenistischen Diasporajudentum* (BZNW, 44; Berlin, 1978), 125–43.
[9] Christ, "Das Leben nach dem Tode," 147.
[10] Fischer, *Eschatologie*, 140.
[11] Van der Horst, *The Sentences*, 185.
[12] D.B. Martin, *The Corinthian Body* (New Haven, 1995), 114. Martin insists, correctly, that the usual contrast between Jewish and Greek views on this subject is oversimplified and ultimately misleading (p. 110).
[13] The classic contrast of Jewish and Greek eschatology is that of O. Cullmann, "Immortality of the Soul or Resurrection of the Dead," in K. Stendahl, ed., *Immortality and Resurrection* (New York, 1965), 9–35.

century C.E. exhibit a wide range of conceptions of life after death, and only rarely affirm resurrection of the physical body.[14] Interestingly enough, some of the earliest texts that emphasize the physical character of the resurrection, such as 2 Maccabees 7 and *Sib Or* 4:181–2, were written in Greek, by authors who came from the Diaspora.[15] Nonetheless, belief in physical resurrection was atypical of Diaspora Judaism, and it is quite alien to the philosophically sophisticated works of Philo or the *Wisdom of Solomon*. 4 Maccabees, which deals with the same story of martyrdom as 2 Maccabees 7, eliminates the references to physical resurrection. Jewish epitaphs from the Greek-speaking Diaspora down to the end of the first century only rarely express any hope for an afterlife, and then speak of the flight of the soul to the holy ones[16] or of astral immortality.[17] Since the *Sentences* are steeped in Greek moral philosophy, it is rather surprising to encounter a literalistic belief in physical resurrection here.

The reference to "the remains of the departed," in vss. 103–4, follows an admonition against dissolving the human frame (ἁρμονίην ἀναλυέμεν).[18] Fischer points out that these verses (102 and 103) are linked only by καὶ, not by any words indicating a causal connection (such as γάρ). Instead, vss. 103–4 are linked to vs. 105 ("For the souls remain unharmed among the dead"). Fischer infers that the souls are the "remains," and so that Pseudo-Phocylides does not affirm bodily resurrection, but only immortality of the soul. But, as van der

---

[14] This is recognized by van der Horst, *The Sentences*, 185. On the range of Jewish conceptions see G.W.E. Nickelsburg, *Resurrection, Immortality and Eternal Life in Intertestamental Judaism* (Harvard Theological Studies, 26; Cambridge, MA, 1972); Cavallin, *Life After Death*; J.J. Collins, "The Afterlife in Apocalyptic Literature," in A.J. Avery-Peck and J. Neusner, ed., *Judaism in Late Antiquity. Part 4. Death, Life-After-Death, Resurrection and The World-to-Come in the Judaisms of Antiquity* (Leiden, 2000), 119–39.

[15] 2 Maccabees describes events in Jerusalem, but it is an abridgement of the work of one Jason of Cyrene, and the Greek style betrays a better Hellenistic education than is likely to have been available in Jerusalem. *Sib Or* 4 is usually thought to have been composed in Syria or Asia Minor.

[16] W. Horbury and D. Noy, *Jewish Inscriptions of Graeco-Roman Egypt* (Cambridge, 1992), 69 (inscription no. 33 = CIJ 1510).

[17] CIJ 788. P.W. van der Horst, *Ancient Jewish Epitaphs* (Kampen, 1991), 123–3.

[18] Christ, "Das Leben nach dem Tode," 141, suggests that this is a polemical reference to the practice of gathering bones into ossuaries for secondary burial. Van der Horst, *The Sentences*, 184, insists that "there is not the slightest hint of the use of ossilegia in this text," and supports the view that it refers to the dissection of cadavers, which was practiced in Alexandria. It is difficult to see, however, how the admonition would not apply to the practice of secondary burial, which most certainly involved the dissolution of the human frame.

Horst has pointed out, "there are no parallels for λείψαν᾽ ἀποιχομένων in the sense of souls, whereas its use for the bodily remains of the dead is common."[19] Λειψάνα can be used for remains other than physical; for example, the remains of good people are their deeds.[20] But Fischer's solution would require that the word be used here in a way that is without parallel. The reference to physical resurrection cannot be denied.

But Pseudo-Phocylides is not necessarily so committed to belief in physical resurrection as the usual translations would suggest. The Greek reads:

καὶ τάχα δ᾽ ἐκ γαίης ἐλπίζομεν ἐς φάος ἐλθεῖν
λείψαν᾽ ἀποιχόμενων. Ὀπίσω δὲ θεοὶ τελέθονται

Van der Horst notes that τάχα can mean either "soon" or "perhaps, probably," and declares that "in view of vs. 104b the first meaning is here the most feasible."[21] He translates "soon," and in this he is in agreement with all recent commentators. But Pseudo-Phocylides was no apocalyptic visionary, and there is no other hint in the poem of imminent eschatology. I would suggest that "perhaps" is the more appropriate translation here.[22] This is the only time in this passage where he speaks of hope.[23] In contrast, he categorically affirms the immortality of the soul twice (105, 115). Of that he has no doubt. The resurrection of the physical body is acknowledged as a possibility to be hoped for. Presumably, the author was aware that some Jews held this belief, and he affirms it tentatively. The subject is raised here by the admonition against "dissolving the human frame" but the admonition is not made contingent on the belief. Rather, the hope of resurrection is introduced as a supplementary supporting consideration. The tone is speculative rather than certain.

Vs. 104b, "and afterwards they become gods" does not in any way require that the resurrection take place soon. While earlier scholars found this statement shocking in a Jewish text, it is now widely

---

[19] Van der Horst, *Essays on the Jewish World of Early Christianity* (NTOA, 14; Fribourg-Göttingen, 1990), 36.

[20] H.G. Liddell and R. Scott, *A Greek-English Lexicon*, revised and augmented by H.S. Jones with the assistance of R. McKenzie (Oxford: Clarendon, 1940), 1037.

[21] Van der Horst, *The Sentences*, 185.

[22] This was already suggested by L. Schmidt, in a review of J. Bernays, *Ueber das phokylideische Gedicht*, in *Jahrbücher für classische Philologie* 3 (1857) 510–19.

[23] Van der Horst adds "in fact" without any basis in the Greek.

recognized that it is simply a variant of a common Jewish belief, that the righteous are elevated to heaven after death to shine like stars or become companions of the angels (who are often called אלהים, gods, in contemporary Hebrew texts, such as the Dead Sea Scrolls).[24] The point at issue here is how this belief can accommodate a hope for physical resurrection. Normally, the soul or spirit was thought to ascend to heaven, and while this might still have bodily form, it was what St. Paul would call a "spiritual body" (σῶμα πνευματικόν). In the words of Plutarch, "we must not violate nature by sending the bodies of good men with their souls to heaven."[25] Even St. Paul was emphatic that "flesh and blood cannot inherit the kingdom of God" (1 Cor 15:50). It must first be transformed into a different kind of body. Pseudo-Phocylides does not discuss the transformation, but he allows space for it by claiming that physical resurrection and apotheosis are sequential stages in the afterlife. This attempt to accommodate different eschatological conceptions as stages in a process is typical of the apocalyptic literature of the late first century C.E. So, for example, *4 Ezra* affirms both a messianic reign on earth and a new creation, by having the messiah reign for 400 years and then die, to make way for a return to primeval silence and a new creation (*4 Ezra* 7:28–31). In the New Testament, Revelation similarly provides for a reign on earth for 1,000 years, followed by a new heaven and a new earth. The account of the resurrection in *2 Baruch* is especially relevant to Pseudo-Phocylides:

> For the earth will certainly then restore the dead it now receives so as to preserve them: it will make no change in their form, but as it has received them, so it will restore them, and as I delivered them to it, so also will it raise them. For those who are then alive must be shown that the dead have come to life again, and that those who had departed have returned. And when they have recognized those they know now, then the judgement will begin . . . (*2 Bar* 50:2–4).[26]

Then, after the judgement, the appearance of both righteous and wicked will change: the righteous "will be transformed so that they

---

[24] J.J. Collins, "Powers in Heaven. God, Gods and Angels in the Dead Sea Scrolls," in J.J. Collins and R.A. Kugler, *Religion in the Dead Sea Scrolls* (Grand Rapids, 2000), 1–28. For the belief that the righteous would be raised up to heaven after death see Dan 12:2; *1 Enoch* 104:2–6.

[25] Plutarch, *Romulus*, 28.8. See Martin, *The Corinthian Body*, 113.

[26] Trans. R.H. Charles, revised by L.H. Brockington, in H.F.D. Sparks, *The Apocryphal Old Testament* (Oxford, 1984), 869.

look like angels" (51:5), while the wicked become decaying shadows of their former selves. *2 Baruch*, then, provides both for physical resurrection and for transformation to an angelic state. These were originally two quite distinct conceptions of the afterlife, but in the later apocalypses different traditions are combined. Pseudo-Phocylides is engaging in a similar synthesis of distinct traditions.

SOUL AND SPIRIT

The form of afterlife that is most emphatically affirmed by Pseudo-Phocylides is the immortality of the soul, which is asserted in vss. 105 and 115. The first of these statements is somewhat puzzling: ψυχαὶ γὰρ μίμνουσιν ἀκήριοι ἐν φθιμένοισιν. Van der Horst translates: "for the souls remain unharmed in the deceased." The initial impression here is that the soul remains alive in the dead body. But then in vs. 108 we are told that the air receives the spirit. Vss. 111–113 suggest that the soul lives on in Hades. In light of the latter point, the phrase ἐν φθιμένοισιν in vs. 105 is better translated as "among the dead" (i.e. in Hades). Most commentators assume that the soul (ψυχή) and the spirit (πνεῦμα) are one and the same, and consequently find a contradiction between vss. 105 and 108.[27] Christ and Fischer, however, argue that Pseudo-Phocylides is making a threefold distinction between body, soul and spirit.[28] So vs. 105 begins ψυχαὶ γὰρ, vs. 106 πνεῦμα γάρ, and vs. 108 σῶμα γάρ. In this reading, each element goes to a different place at death: the body returns to dust, the soul goes to Hades, and the spirit goes up to the air.

Pseudo-Phocylides' understanding of the make-up of the human being draws on the opening chapters of Genesis. The statement that the body is from earth and returns to dust (vss. 107–8) echoes Gen 3:19. The reference to the image of God in vs. 106 alludes to Gen 1:27. The mention of the spirit, πνεῦμα, derives from Gen 2:7b, which reads in the LXX:

Ἐνεφύσησεν εἰς τὸ πρόσωπον αὐτου πνοὴν ζωῆς, καὶ ἐγένετο ὁ ἄνθρωπος εἰς ψυχὴν ζῶσαν.

---

[27] E.g. van der Horst, *The Sentences*, 189.
[28] Christ, *Das Leben nach dem Tode*, 144; Fischer, *Eschatologie*, 140.

As Philo explains: that which he breathed in was nothing else than divine spirit (οὐδὲν ἦν ἕτερον ἤ πνεῦμα θεῖον).²⁹ Philo also links the in-breathing of the spirit to the imprint of the image of God: "Moses likened the fashion of the reasonable soul to no created thing, but averred it to be a genuine coinage of that dread Spirit, the Divine and Invisible One, signed and impressed by the seal of God, the stamp of which is the Eternal Word. His words are 'God in-breathed into his face a breath of Life;' so that it cannot but be that he that receives is made in the likeness of Him Who sends forth the breath. Accordingly we also read that man has been made after the image of God."³⁰ More precisely, Philo held that the human being "was made a likeness and imitation of the Logos when the divine breath was breathed into his face."³¹ He is very specific that "it is in respect of the Mind, the sovereign element of the soul, that the word 'image' is used."³² The image then is not the human being as a whole, but is imprinted on the mind by the divine spirit.

Both the formulation of Gen 2:7b and the various statements of Philo on the image of God invite a distinction between ψυχή and πνεῦμα. This distinction has been discussed extensively in the context of 1 Corinthians 15, where St. Paul draws a contrast between the σῶμα ψυχικόν that is buried and the σῶμα πνευματικόν that is raised. In his Harvard dissertation, Birger Pearson argued that the distinction was derived from Hellenistic-Jewish exegesis of Genesis.

At least some Hellenistic philosophers distinguished between the soul and the mind (νοῦς), with the latter being the higher element. So, for example, Plutarch wrote that "every soul partakes of mind; none is completely irrational or deprived of mind,"³³ but souls are also mixed to varying degrees with the flesh and passions. Pearson contends that the Hellenistic Jewish authors substituted πνεῦμα for νοῦς as the divine element (or alternated between the two terms and related this to Gen 1:27, where humanity is created in the image of

---

²⁹ *De Opif.* 135.
³⁰ *Plant* 18–19.
³¹ *De Opif.* 139. Compare also *Det* 83. See G. Sterling, "Wisdom among the Perfect: Creation Traditions in Alexandrian Judaism and Corinthian Christianity," *NovT* 37 (1995) 355–84 (especially 357–67) and, in general, J. Jervell, *Imago Dei. Gen. I 26f. im Spätjudentum, in der Gnosis und in den paulinischen Briefen* (Göttingen, 1960).
³² *De Opif.* 69; Cf. *Spec. Leg.* I 81 and many other passages.
³³ Plutarch, *de genio Socratis*, 591 D–F.

God).[34] Philo does not in fact draw a clear distinction between ψυχή and πνεῦμα, and sometimes uses them interchangeably.[35] He distinguishes between the mind, as the dominant part of the soul, and the soul as a whole,[36] but can also refer to the soul as a divine fragment from the upper air (ἡ δὲ ψυχὴ αἰθέρος ἐστίν, ἀπόσπασμα θεῖον).[37] It does not appear that a distinction between soul and spirit was a standard part of Hellenistic Jewish exegetical tradition.[38] Nonetheless, the occasional distinction between ψυχή and πνεῦμα in the exegesis of Genesis is illuminating for the case of Pseudo-Phocylides.[39] If ψυχή and πνεῦμα are one and the same, then vs. 108 is contradictory to the statements about the souls in vss. 105 and 111. While it is possible that Pseudo-Phocylides is merely stringing together traditional sentiments, without regard for consistency, an interpretation that does not posit incoherence must be preferred.

If ψυχή and πνεῦμα are distinguished here, the implication is that the element by which human beings share in the image of God is withdrawn at death. According to vss. 107–108, the body becomes dust and the air receives the spirit. Thus far Pseudo-Phocylides reflects a quite traditional anthropology. We may compare the account of death in Qoheleth: "the dust returns to the earth as it was, and the spirit returns to God who gave it" (Qoh 12:7).

But what then of the soul? Two things are said about it. First, it "is immortal and lives ageless forever" (115). Second, the place where it lives on is the Netherworld, or Hades. According to vs. 108 it remains "unharmed among the dead" (ἐν φθιμένοισιν). The statement that "God rules over the souls" (111) conjures up a picture of a god of the Netherworld, such as Pluto or Osiris, except that for

---

[34] Pearson, *The Pneumatikos-Psychikos Terminology*, 11–12. It should be noted that non-Jewish authors could also refer to the higher part of the self as πνεῦμα. See Martin, *The Corinthian Body*, 275, n. 64.

[35] R.A. Horsley, "Pneumatikos vs. Psychikos: distinctions of Spiritual Status among the Corinthians," *HTR* 69 (1976) 271–2. See also D. Winston, *Logos and Mystical Philosophy in Philo of Alexandria* (Cincinnati, 1985), 27–42 on Philo's concept of the ψυχή.

[36] *Her.* 55: "We use 'soul' in two senses, both for the whole soul and also for its dominant part, which properly speaking is the soul's soul."

[37] *Leg. All.* 3.161.

[38] Josephus, in his paraphrase of Gen 2:7 says that God injected a spirit into Adam, and a soul (*Ant* 1.34), but even here it is possible that he is using a hendiadys, and that the two are regarded as the same.

[39] Pseudo-Phocylides has not been part of the discussion of the *psychikos-pneumatikos* distinction.

the Jewish author this God is also the God of the living. Vs. 112 continues: "Hades is our common home." The idea that the soul lives on in Hades is found already in Homer. In the words of Albrecht Dihle: "The soul goes to the underworld and may sometimes show itself to a living person in a dream prior to burial of the corpse, taking on the appearance of the living man for this purpose. In the underworld it leads a shadowy existence which has little to do with the self of man . . . Nothing is expected of the shadowy existence of the ψυχή in the underworld."[40] This concept was essentially similar to the Hebrew נפש which also lived on in Sheol as a shade. The Platonic idea of the immortal soul was quite different from this, and implied a much fuller life after death, since the soul was now the seat of the personality. While the older ideas of the afterlife were repudiated by philosophers, they lived on in popular religion into the Hellenistic age.[41] Consider, for example, an epitaph from the "land of Onias" at Leontopolis: "'How old were you when you slipped down into the shadowy region of Lethe?' At twenty years old I went to the mournful place of the dead . . . 'Childless I went to the house of Hades.' May the earth, the guardian of the dead, be light upon you."[42]

Precisely how Pseudo-Phocylides understood the immortal soul is unclear. It seems to be immortal by its nature: immortality is not a reward for righteousness.[43] Nothing is said of a judgement after death; the reference to Hades as "our common home" suggests that there is no separation of righteous and wicked, at least initially. If the spirit is withdrawn, the life of the soul must be diminished, but Pseudo-Phocylides appears to view it positively. The fact that the soul remains unharmed means that it is available for resurrection. Again, we are given no indication as to whether everyone is to be raised.[44] We should hardly expect that everyone would "become

---

[40] A. Dihle, "ψυχή in the Greek World," *TDNT* 9 (1974) 609.

[41] See the classic study of E. Rohde, *Psyche. The Cult of Souls and Belief in Immortality among the Greeks* (New York, 1925), 524–7.

[42] W. Horbury and D. Noy, *Jewish Inscriptions of Graeco-Roman Egypt* (Cambridge, 1992), 90 (no. 38 = *CIJ* no. 1530).

[43] Pearson, *The Pneumatikos-Psychikos Terminology*, 21, asserts that "no Jew, not even Philo, could go so far as to assert with Plato that the soul was immortal by its very nature and therefore incapable of mortality." This does not hold true for Pseudo-Phocylides.

[44] Note that Dan 12:2, the classic biblical attestation of resurrection, does not

gods." If the resurrection is selective, this might explain the rather tentative formulation of Pseudo-Phocylides: "we hope that the remains of the departed will perhaps come to the light again." The resurrection would presumably require that the spirit be again united with the soul and the bodily remains.[45]

CONCLUSION

Pseudo-Phocylides was not a philosopher, but a purveyor of conventional ideas. There is no doubt that he relied on traditional formulations, and these stand in some tension with each other. Much remains unclear in his exposition of the afterlife. Nonetheless, the judgement that the passage consists of "the unharmonized juxtaposition of contradictory ideas" is hardly justified. If the reading proposed here is correct, Pseudo-Phocylides combined different ideas of the afterlife, but strung them together in a way that achieved a measure of coherence. After death, the physical body returns to the earth, the soul goes to Hades, and the spirit returns to the air, to God. The immediate expectation after death, then, conforms to the popular conception of Hades, which is copiously attested in epitaphs, Gentile and Jewish, throughout the Hellenistic period. Since the soul remains unharmed, however, Pseudo-Phocylides can affirm the widespread belief in the immortality of the soul, even though that belief, in its philosophical formulations, envisioned something rather different from a shadowy afterlife in Hades. Hades, however, was not the end. Pseudo-Phocylides affirmed the hope that bodily remains would again come to light out of the earth. This hope was grounded in Jewish rather than Greek traditions, but was by no means commonplace in Judaism. It is expressed tentatively here, as a hope rather than as a firm belief. Unlike the immortality of the soul, it was not guaranteed for everyone. The ultimate hope was to "become gods," by exaltation to the heavens or the stars, as envisioned in Jewish apocalypses from early second century B.C.E. on.

These ideas about the afterlife seem to be cobbled together from popular beliefs and traditions. Pseudo-Phocylides lacks the philosophical sophistication of Philo, or even of the *Wisdom of Solomon*,

---

imply that everyone will be raised. See J.J. Collins, *Daniel* (Hermeneia; Minneapolis, 1993), 392.

[45] Contra Fischer, *Eschatologie*, 140.

and the visionary certainty of the apocalypses. The poem has usually been assumed to have been composed in Alexandria, but the
evidence of this assumption is very slight. Vs. 39: "strangers should
be held in equal honor with citizens" certainly has resonance in an
Alexandrian context in the first century c.e.[46] The other main argument for Alexandrian provenance, the supposed reference to the dissection of corpses in vs. 102, must be considered doubtful, as the
reference may be to the Jewish practice of secondary burial. There
is nothing at all to tie Pseudo-Phocylides to any specific location outside of Egypt.[47] The closest parallel to his view of the afterlife is perhaps the passage cited above from *2 Baruch*, but Pseudo-Phocylides
adds to this a Hellenistic veneer, by speaking of Hades and of the
immortality of the soul. The *Sentences* certainly come from a Greek-
speaking environment. Egypt remains the most likely candidate. But
at least on the matter of the afterlife, it attests to a form of Jewish
belief that is rather different from that of Philo or the *Wisdom of
Solomon*, and may be more reflective of popular ideas about death
and the hereafter. Whatever its provenance, this poem is an intrigu-
ing witness to the variety of Judaism in the Hellenistic period.

---

[46] Compare Philo, *De Vita Mosis* 1.35 argues that strangers should be regarded
as settlers and friends, who are near to being citizens. *Wis* 19:13–16 complains that
the Egyptians practiced the most bitter hatred of strangers.
[47] *Pace* J. Barclay, *Jews in the Mediterranean Diaspora* (Edinburgh, 1996), 336.

THE EAGLE ON THE TREE:
A HOMERIC MOTIF IN JEWISH AND
CHRISTIAN LITERATURE

István Czachesz*

This study examines the peculiar occurrences of the eagle in the *Paraleipomena Jeremiou* (= *Par. Jer.*) and the *Acts of Philip* (= *Acts Phil.*) The parallels between those two episodes have been first noticed by F. Amsler.[1] Elsewhere I compared the two texts with each other as well as Jewish and Christian parallels.[2] The *Apocryphon of John* (= *Ap. John*) has not yet been examined in this context.[3]

I

The *Par. Jer.* is an originally Jewish writing with a Christian ending and perhaps with Christian interpolations.[4] According to this book, the prophet Jeremiah accompanied the people of Jerusalem to the Babylonian exile, whereas his disciples Baruch and Abimelech stayed in Jerusalem. Later on (6.15–7.12), an angel dictates a letter to Baruch, and God sends an eagle (*aetos*) to deliver the letter to Jeremiah. Baruch calls the eagle "chosen (*eklektos*) from among all birds of heaven" and "king of the birds." Finally he instructs it to fly "straight as a speeding arrow" in the power of God. The eagle flies to Babylon,

---

* Groningen.

[1] F. Amsler, *Acta Philippi*, vol. 2: *Commentarius* (Turnhout, 1999), 172.

[2] I. Czachesz, *Apostolic Commission Narratives in the Canonical and Apocryphal Acts of the Apostles* (Diss. Groningen, 2002), 149–154.

[3] Professor Florentino García Martínez has called my attention to this parallel. Professor Jan N. Bremmer kindly read the manuscript and made useful suggestions about the Greco-Roman material.

[4] The book is also known as *2 Baruch, 3 Baruch, 4 Baruch,* "The rest of the words of Baruch," or "The rest of the words of Jeremiah." Cf. Herzer, *Paralipomena Jeremiae* (Tübingen, 1994), 1. I quote the text after Kraft and Purintun, *Paraleipomena Jeremiou* (Missoula, Mont., 1972). Herzer, *op. cit.*, 177–192, dates the Jewish text between 125 and 132, the Christian ending (9.10–32) a little after 136. He rejects the idea of other Christian interpolations in the text. Recently Schaller, *Paralipomena Jeremiou*, 678–681, suggested A.D. 118–132 as the date of the Jewish writing, but left open the question of the date of the Christian redaction.

and sits on a post or tree (*xylon*) outside the city. Then (7.13–23)
Jeremiah comes along with a funeral procession. The eagle greets
Jeremiah, and tells him it brought a letter from Baruch and Abimelech.
The prophet praises God and calls the people together. When the
people arrive, the eagle comes down on the corpse and revives it.
The people are astounded and cry out, "This is the God who
appeared to our fathers in the wilderness through Moses, and now
he has appeared to us through this eagle."

   The *Ap. John* is a Gnostic Christian writing. Its shorter version
was written in Greek in the late second or early third century A.D.;
later in the third century, it underwent a major redaction, which
resulted in the longer version. Both versions were translated into
Coptic in the fourth century.[5] The *Ap. John* is a Gnostic paraphrase
of the story of creation, a subject that is reflected in a number of
Nag Hammadi texts.[6] After the rulers and authorities create Adam,
the Father gives him Reflection (*epinoia*) as a helper. The Chief Ruler,
Yaldabaoth, desires Reflection, but he cannot reach her, as she is
hidden in Adam. He therefore creates the woman, whom Adam
recognises as his "fellow-essence." In the short version, Reflection
teaches them: "From the tree, in the form of an eagle, she taught
them to eat of knowledge, so that they might remember their perfection, for both had undergone the fall in ignorance" (*NHC* III.30.17–21).[7]
In the long version, it is the Saviour who teaches the couple: "I
appeared in the form of an eagle on the tree of knowledge, which
is the Reflection from the Providence of pure light, that I might
teach them and awaken them out of the depth of sleep. For they
were born in a fallen state and they recognised their nakedness"
(*NHC* II.23.26–33).[8]

   A Christian writing from late antiquity, the *Acts Phil.* (second half
of the fourth century), reports a similar epiphany of Jesus (3.5–9).[9]

---

   [5] The *Apocryphon of John* has survived in four Coptic manuscripts: *Nag Hammadi
Codices* II, III, IV, and *Codex Papyrus Beroliensis* 8502. For a synopsis and translation
of the texts, see M. Waldstein and F. Wisse, *The Apocryphon of John. Synopsis of Nag
Hammadi Codices II,1; III,1; and IV,1 with BG 8502,2* (Leiden, 1995). Waldstein and
Wisse, *ibid.*, 1, date the short version to the early third century. If Irenaeus knew
the text, it dates to the second century; cf. G. Luttikhuizen, "A Gnostic Reading
of the Acts of John," in J.N. Bremmer (ed.), *The Apocryphal Acts of John* (Kampen,
1995), 119–152 at 124–125.
   [6] Cf. Luttikhuizen, "Gnostic Reading," 125.
   [7] In *BG* 60.19–61.7 Reflection teaches "him" (Adam).
   [8] *NHC* IV,1 does not contain this passage.
   [9] Text in F. Bovon *et al.*, *Acta Philippi*, vol. 1: *Textus* (Turnhout, 1999), 89–95.

When the apostle Philip prays and beseeches the Lord Jesus to reveal himself, suddenly a huge tree appears in the desert. Philip sits down under the tree and begins to eat. When he looks upwards, he catches glimpse of the "image of a huge eagle," the wings of which are "spread out in the form (*typos*) of the true cross." Philip addresses the "magnificent eagle," and asks it to take his prayers to the Savior. He calls it "chosen (*eklektos*) bird," the beauty of which is "not of this place." Suddenly he realizes that it is the Lord Jesus Christ "who revealed himself in this form (*typos*)." The apostle praises the Lord, and Jesus (still in the form of an eagle) exhorts the apostle.

A further text to be mentioned is *2 Baruch* (*Syrian Apocalypse of Baruch*). In *2 Baruch* 77 an eagle (*nešraaʾ*) delivers the letter of Baruch. The Most High, Baruch claims, created the eagle so that it may be elevated (*mʾalay*) above all flying creatures. Baruch also instructs the bird not to rest anywhere until it arrives at the people beyond the Euphrates.

Given the evident parallels between the three texts, can we establish a literary dependence between them? In his commentary on the *Acts Phil.*, Amsler (see note 1 above) suggests the *Par. Jer.* as a possible source of the eagle epiphany. *2 Baruch*, in turn, has been suggested as a source of the *Par. Jer.*[10]

The relation of the texts has to be re-examined for different reasons. First, the *Ap. John* has not yet been examined in this context. Second, the identification of *2 Baruch* as the source of the eagle motif leaves unexplained a highly interesting feature of the *Par. Jer.*, the *Ap. John*, and the *Acts Phil.*, namely, the theriomorphic epiphanies. Whereas the eagle appears as a positive symbol in both religions,[11] the epiphany of God or Jesus in the form of an eagle is unusual. The eagles in the *Acts Phil.* and the *Par. Jer.* do not appear in dreams or visions. The heroes encounter them on the road at daytime, and identify them as appearances of the deity. There is, however, no trace of regarding the animal as an epiphany in *2 Baruch*. Provided that the writer of the *Par. Jer.* took the motif from the *2 Baruch*, there must have existed a different source that inspired the theriomorphic representation of God. Third, the *Par. Jer.*, the *Ap. John*,

---

The Greek *Acts of Philip* contains fifteen "acts" plus the martyrdom text. For the dating of the text cf. Czachesz, *op. cit.*, 136, note 1.

[10] Herzer, *op. cit.*, 72–77; Schaller, *op. cit.*, 670–673.

[11] Cf. Czachesz, *op. cit.*, 151–153; add E.R. Goodenough, *Jewish Symbols in the Greco-Roman Period*, vol. 8 (New York, 1958), 121–145.

and the *Acts Phil.* represent the deity not simply as an eagle, but rather as an eagle on a tree.

In this study, I will argue that Homer was the main source of the motif of the "eagle on the tree" for Jewish and Christian literature. I will examine how the *Par. Jer.*, the *Ap. John*, and the *Acts Phil.* used the Homeric motif and how the three writings relied on each other.

II

The eagle was an important symbol in both Greek and Christian religions, and to a lesser degree, it played a positive role also in Judaism. The mutual associations between the eagle, the king, and the supreme god were so widespread in ancient cultures that it should be little surprising when Jewish and Christian texts call the eagle the king of birds and associate it with God or Jesus.[12] Instead of proceeding from a general comparison of the role of the eagle in those literary and religious traditions, I depart from the specific feature that the eagle passages in the *Par. Jer.*, the *Ap. John*, and the *Acts Phil.* have in common. The deity appears in the form of an eagle that sits on a pole or tree in our texts. There are parallels to this particular motif in Homer.

Gods appear in the form of birds or are compared to birds in a number of Homeric passages.[13] In two cases, gods sit on a tree in the form of birds: *Iliad* VII.58–61 and XIV.286–291.

In Book VII of the *Iliad*, Apollo convinces Pallas Athena to stop the fight and let the war be decided in a battle of two. Apollo inspires Hector to suspend the battle, and Agamemnon stops the Achaeans. Then "Athena and Apollo of the silver bow in the likeness of (*eoikôs*) vultures sat on the lofty oak of father Zeus who bears the aegis, rejoicing in the warriors."[14] After casting lots, Aias goes forth to fight with Hector. Their combat, however, remains unfinished when evening

---

[12] D'Arcy Wentworth Thompson, *A Glossary of Greek Birds* (Oxford, 1936), 2–16; Th. Schneider and E. Stemplinger, "Adler," in Th. Klauser (ed.), *RAC*, vol. 1 (Stuttgart, 1950), 87–93; C. Hünemörder, "Adler," in H. Cancik and H. Schneider (eds.), *Der neue Pauly*, vol. 1 (Stuttgart-Weimar, 1996), 115–116.

[13] Cf. J. Pollard, *Birds in Greek Life and Mythology* (London, 1977), 155–161. G.G. Kirk, *The Iliad: A Commentary*, vol. 2 (Cambridge, 1990), 239–240; P. Friedrich, "An Avian and Aphrodisian Reading of Homer's *Odyssey*," *American Anthropologist* 99 (1997) 306–320, Appendix.

[14] *Iliad* VII.58–61, trans. W.F. Wyatt in LCL.

falls. The parties agree to hold armistice and bury the dead. The second, perhaps less interesting text is *Iliad* XIV.286–291. At this place we read that Hypnos climbed the highest tree on Ida to observe Zeus without beings seen by him. Hypnos sits there like (*enalinkios*) a bird that has a clear sound and is called either *chalkis* or *kymindis*.[15]

The question whether these texts and many other Homeric passages about birds are metamorphoses or similes has generated endless scholarly debates for centuries. Did the gods put on the form of birds, did they become birds for a time, or were they only similar to birds in some respect? The problem becomes especially interesting if we relate it to the *Par. Jer.* and the *Acts Phil.* Whereas the rest of early Christian and Jewish literature uses the image of the eagle as a simile or metaphor, these two writings seem to surpass that level and describe theriomorphic epiphanies. Could they rely on Homer in doing so?

Authors made up various lists of Homeric passages that are likely candidates for being metamorphoses, and *Iliad* VII is one of the key texts. In fact, most authors have taken this locus as a case of metamorphosis. It is impossible to summarize the whole research at this place, yet it is worth mentioning four characteristic opinions in order to gain a general overview of the discussion. Nilsson marshals evidence from Mycaenean archeology to prove that birds were not only attributes of gods, but also their actual forms of appearance.[16] He reads Homer against that archeological background, and concludes that in a number of passages (also in *Iliad* VII.49) gods appear in the form of birds.[17]

In a well-argued study, F. Dirlmeier[18] attempted to dissolve the "phantom" of bird-gods. He examined the issue in general, and six passages in particular that had been widely quoted as metamorphoses. The first and the second items on Dirlmeier's list are our two examples from the *Iliad*. He concluded that all of his texts could be understood as finding similes referring to the motion of the birds.[19]

---

[15] The meanings of neither *chalkis* nor *kymindis* are known. For different ancient and modern explanations, see Pollard, *op. cit.*, 158–159. More recently see J.N. Bremmer, *Greek Religion* (Oxford, ²1999), 7.

[16] M.P. Nilsson, *Geschichte der griechischen Religion*, vol. 1 (Munich, ³1967), 290–292.

[17] Nilsson, *op. cit.*, 349 (note 4).

[18] F. Dirlmeier, *Die Vogelgestalt Homerischer Götter* (Heidelberg, 1967).

[19] Dirlmeier, *op. cit.*, 35.

J. Pollard[20] describes several Homeric passages as "transformations" of the gods into bird form, including *Iliad* VII.61. He also
writes about "half complete" transformations (e.g., *Odyssey* 5.337) and
"mere similes" (e.g., *Iliad* XIII.62f.). Pollard remarks that the Homeric
gods rarely appear in their own shape, except when consorting with
one another. He notices that the presence of a god could be inferred
from some internal crisis often coincident with the sudden appearance of a bird, and suggests that the importance given to "bird transformations" in such cases may well derive from the Bronze Age view
that a god's presence was indicated by the presence of a bird.[21]

A. Schnapp-Gourbeillon lists three passages that she takes for metamorphoses, two of which are our examples.[22] She bases her argument on the whole context of Homer. When the gods appear as
humans, sometimes the metamorphosis is so perfect, that the heroes
do not recognize them.[23] This metamorphosis is often expressed by
the same word (*eoikôs*)[24] that we find in *Iliad* VII.59.[25] Whereas the
appearance of the gods as humans hides them, their subsequent
metamorphosis into a bird sometimes reveals their identity. In Book
1 of the *Odyssey*, for example, Athene appears in a human form to
Ulysses' son Telemachos, who recognizes her only when she flies
away like a bird.[26]

Finally, Walter Burkert warns against attributing theriomorphic
beliefs to the Greeks. In the Minoan-Mycenaean religion, birds could
be understood as epiphanies of gods, but "the owl of Athena, the
eagle of Zeus, and the peacock of Hera-Juno are little more than
heraldic animals for the Greeks."[27] "Myth, of course," Burkert remarks,
"toys with animal metamorphoses."[28]

[20] Pollard, *op. cit.*, 154–161.
[21] Pollard, *op. cit.*, 159.
[22] A. Schnapp-Gourbeillon, *Lions, héros, masques. Les interpretations de l'animal chez Homère* (Paris, 1981), 185–190.
[23] Dirlmeier, *op. cit.*, 16, reminds us to the elementary fact that Homeric gods have human forms also on the Olympus. One may answer, however, that they still need metamorphosis to assume the form of a particular human person.
[24] *Iliad* XXIV.347; *Odyssey* 13.222.
[25] Schnapp-Gourbeillon, *op. cit.*, 189, finds that the comparison of humans to animals follows a similar logic as the metamorphosis of the gods. The hero *is* a lion for a short moment.
[26] *Odyssey* 1.320. This is probably the passage that Schnapp-Gourbeillon, *op. cit.*, 188, has in mind. The word *anopaia* is much debated, but it does not influence the meaning of the sentence.
[27] W. Burkert, *Greek Religion* (trans. J. Raffan; Cambridge, Mass., 1985), 65.
[28] Burkert, *op. cit.*, 64.

It seems almost impossible to judge what the Greeks actually meant by the animal metamorphoses in the Homeric texts, and how they understood those passages from the classical period onward. There might have been great differences in the reading of such passages across time and space. In the second century A.D., Tatian ridicules the metamorphoses of the Greek gods into various animals.[29] Although he does not mention Homeric texts in particular, it is likely that Christians of the same mind as Tatian were inclined to see (ridiculous) metamorphoses also in Homer. Animal metamorphoses were acceptable "toys" in Greek literature. They were, in contrast, highly unacceptable for most Jewish and Christian authors.[30]

III

The motif of the eagle on the tree also played an important role in Greek art. Although we cannot fully exhaust that topic at this place, it will be useful to mention some examples. Birds sitting on posts or idols are widespread on Minoan representations: "Birds are seen to perch on the double axes at sacrifice in the Ayia Triada sarcophagus, on the columns from the Shrine of Dove Goddess, and on the heads of the idols form the Late Minoan period."[31]

A series of Cretan coins from Gortyn shows Europa as a young woman on a tree, with an eagle appearing on many of the coins.[32] Cook reads the series as a cartoon depicting the union of Europa with Zeus in the form of an eagle.[33] The scene, of course, also reminds one of the myth of Zeus and Leda. On one of the coins, Europa holds a scepter with a bird.[34] Another coin from Asia Minor shows Artemis Eleuthera on a tree.[35]

Pausanias describes the eagle on a pillar or scepter several times. He reports that before the altar of Zeus *Lykaios* there are two pillars

---

[29] Tatian, *Address to the Greeks* 10; cf. Tertuallian, *Ad nationes* 2.13.

[30] For *Revelation* 5–7 see below. In the *Acts of John*, Jesus changes his appearance several times, but never appears as an animal; cf. H. García , "La polymorphie du Christ. Remarques sur quelques définitions et sur de multiples enjeux," *Apocrypha* 10 (1999) 16–55.

[31] Burkert, *op. cit.*, 40–41.

[32] A.B. Cook, *Zeus*, vol. 1 (Cambridge, 1914), 528–529.

[33] Cook, *op. cit.*, 532–533.

[34] Cook, *op. cit.*, 529, fig. 399; cf. p. 532.

[35] Burkert, *op. cit.*, 86.

on the east, "on which there were of old gilded eagles."[36] A scepter
with an eagle sitting on it is held by the Zeus statues at Olympia[37]
and Megalopolis.[38] Pindar, Sophocles, and perhaps also Aristophanes,
refer to similar scepters.[39]

In the Roman world, the eagle was the most important military
symbol.[40] During his second consulship (104 B.C.), Marius established
it as the supreme standard of the legions.[41] The eagle standard (*aquila*)
consisted of an eagle with stretched wings and a thunderbolt in its
claws, sitting on a post with handles. The *aquilae* enjoyed religious
veneration.[42] The same symbol could also signify the honour of single persons. The triumphant warlord carried an ivory scepter (*scipio
eburneus*) with an eagle.[43] In the imperial period, the consuls and the
emperors wore this decoration. When Juvenal (born in A.D. 67)
ridicules the exhibitionism of the praetors, he mentions "the bird
that stands on the ivory scepter."[44]

IV

Which of the above-mentioned occurrences of the "eagle on the
tree" motif influenced the writers of the *Par. Jer.*, the *Ap. John*, and
the *Acts Phil.*? Did they use the image of the Roman military stan-
dards? If the second Jewish war was the *Sitz im Leben* of the *Par.
Jer.*, the author(s) had an immediate and long-lasting impression of
the *aquilae*. They could easily decipher the symbolism of the eagle

---

[36] Pausanias 8.38.7. Trans. W.H.S. Jones in LCL; cf. Nilsson, *op. cit.*, 398.
[37] Pausanias 5.11.1.
[38] Pausanias, *Description of Greece* 8.31.4.
[39] Pindar, *Pythian Odes* 1.6; Sophocles, fragm. 884 (Radt). For Aristophanes, see
Pollard, *op. cit.*, 143.
[40] J. Yates, "Signa militaria" in W. Smith, ed, *A Dictionary of Greek and Roman
Antiquities* (London, 1875), 1044–1046; A.R. Neumann, "Aquila," in K. Ziegler
et al. (eds.), *Der kleine Pauly*, vol. 1 (München, 1979), 478; Y. Lafond, "Feldzeichen,"
in H. Cancik and H. Schneider (eds.), *Der neue Pauly*, vol. 4 (Stuttgart-Weimar,
1996), 458–462.
[41] Pliny the Elder, *Natural History* 10.16.
[42] Valerius Maximus, *Memorable Words and Deeds* 6.1.11 writes about *sacratae aquilae*.
Cf. Neumann, *op. cit.*
[43] Dionysius of Halicarnassus, *Roman Antiquities* 3.61; Valerius Maximus, *Memorable
Words and Deeds* 4.4.5. Cf. W.H. Gross, "Skeptron," in *Der kleine Pauly*, vol. 5 (Munich,
1979), 327; R. Hurschmann, "Stab, Stock, Knüppel," in H. Cancik and H. Schneider
(eds.), *Der neue Pauly*, vol. 11 (Stuttgart-Weimar, 2001), 884–885. In the latter example, there is a *scipio eburneus* but no explicit mention of the eagle.
[44] Juvenal, *Satires* 10.43, *da nunc et volucrem sceptro quae surgit eburno*.

with the thunderbolt, interpreting the figure as a storm-god.[45] However, it is difficult to believe that they were so much grasped by the image that they used it to represent their own deity in a religious legend. The *Par. Jer.* (similarly to the books of *Esdra* and *Nehemia*) condemns the mingling of Jews with foreigners and reports that Jeremiah was grieved when his afflicted compatriots prayed to a foreign god for deliverance (6.16–17; 7.30). Further, the eagle of the *Par. Jer.* is a symbol of life rather than war. It is never associated with war against Israel's enemies, but it resuscitates a corpse (7.19). Apart from the formal coincidence, it is difficult to find arguments for identifying it with the image of the Roman military standard *aquila*.

For similar reasons, it is unlikely that this motif was inspired by any of the Greco-Roman eagle images representing Zeus or Juppiter. To the reality of the second Jewish war, we have to add two historical records of instances when the image of an eagle scandalized the Jews. The first instance is the "desolating sacrilege," the altar that Antiochus Epiphanes set up in the temple, which most probably contained the winged image(s) of Zeus Olympius or Baal Shamem.[46] That the remembrance of this event was living is shown by the references of the New Testament.[47] The second case occurred under Herod the Great, who placed the image of an eagle above the temple gate, but had to remove it because of the general uproar.[48]

The influence of Greco-Roman tradition on the *Par. Jer.* was more subtle. The pagan idols of the day must have been overtly offensive for a Jew who wrote that his people must separate themselves from the foreigners and their gods. Yet, the same Jewish person had some Greek education, and therefore knew Homer. He was, in part, favorably disposed toward the image of the eagle, to which the Jewish Scriptures often compare God, God's court, or the faithful.[49] He probably relied on *2 Baruch* (in some form) when he had the eagle deliver the letter of Baurch to the Diaspora. In someone who was

[45] For a comparison of Zeus and Near Eastern storm-gods, see M.L. West, *The East Face of Helicon* (Oxford, 1997), 115–116, 580–581.

[46] *Daniel* 9:27; *2 Maccabees* 6:2. Cf. S. Schroer, *In Israel gab es Bilder* (Freiburg, 1987), 352–53; K. Koch, *Daniel* (Neukirchen-Vluyn, 1986), 136–140; D. Wenham, "Abomination of Desolation," in D.N. Freedman (ed.), *The Anchor Bible Dictionary*, vol. 1 (New York, 1992), 28–31.

[47] Matthew 24:15.

[48] Josephus, *Jewish Antiquities* 17.146–163; *Jewish War* 1.650–653.

[49] Exod 19:4; Ps 103:5; Isa 40:31; Ezek 1:10.

familiar with Homer, this motif evoked the role of the eagle as Zeus' messenger in Homer.[50]

Why did the author think of *Iliad* VII in particular? One may immediately object that the Homeric text mentions "vultures" (*aigypioi*), whereas the bird in the *Par. Jer.* is an "eagle" (*aetos*). This problem can be solved if one considers that the two species were often confused in antiquity and the usage of the two names varied.[51] The same ambiguity characterizes the Hebrew *nešer*, and probably the Syriac *nešraa'* used in *2 Baruch*.[52] The difference between the Homeric *fēgos* (oak) and the *xylon* in the other text is also not decisive, because the latter had a wide range of meanings, including pole, cut wood, and living tree.[53]

In order to understand why *Iliad* VII is a likely source for the *Par. Jer.*, we have to examine the broader context of the episode in both writings. The *Par. Jer.* reports that Jeremiah asked a place from the king to bury the dead of his people. When the eagle arrives, the people are busy carrying a corpse to bury it outside the city. This motif has its own significance in the narrative. Burying the dead was a pious act, of which the famous example was Tobit.[54] Living in the Assyrian diaspora, Tobit "performed many acts of charity to his kindred." He buried the corpses that he found outside the city, and went into much trouble doing this. The author of the *Par. Jer.* could have borrowed from the popular story of Tobit.[55] In the *Iliad*, the burying of the dead is discussed in detail after the metamorphosis of the two deities. The battlefield is already filled with corpses (VII.327–335) and the cease-fire gives an opportunity to collect them.

---

[50] E.g., *Iliad* XXIV.290–321 etc. Cf. A.B. Cook, *Zeus*, vol. 2/2 (Cambridge, 1925), 1360–1361.

[51] D'Arcy Wentworth Thompson, *A Glossary of Greek Birds*, 5–6, 25–26; Pollard, *op. cit.*, 76, quoting W.R. Halliday.

[52] L. Koehler and W. Baumgartner, *The Hebrew and Aramaic Lexicon of the Old Testament*, vol. 2 (Leiden, 1995), 731. R. Payne Smith (ed.), *Thesaurus Syriacus*, vol. 2 (Oxford, 1901), 2479, s.v. *nešraa'*, does not indicate the polysemy.

[53] H.G. Liddel *et al.* (eds.), *A Greek-English Lexicon With a Revised Supplement* (Oxford, 1996), s.v.

[54] Tobit 1:17–2:8; cf. Sirah 7:33; 38:16. See especially *4 Ezra* 2:23: "When you find any who are dead, commit them to the grave and mark it, and I will give you the first place in my resurrection."

[55] Note that the delivery of Baruch's letter by the eagle is another motif that was originally related to the Assyrian diaspora. According to *2 Baruch* 77:19–25, the eagle took the letter to the "nine and a half tribes," whereas the letter to Babylonia was entrusted to three men.

Vultures are likely to appear under such circumstances, which probably explains why the two deities choose this particular form. If the author of the *Par. Jer.* already had in mind the motif of the eagle (probably from *2 Baruch*) and the burying of the dead (probably from *Tobit*) and also knew Homer, it is not any more surprising that he came upon *Iliad* VII.58–61.

May this sound speculative, one should keep in mind that the epiphany of God as an eagle on a tree is quite strange in the context of Jewish literature. Consequently, it is difficult to give it a self-evident explanation to it. I hope to have shown that *Iliad* VII.58–61 is at least a very likely source for that motif. Of course, that parallel does not explain every detail of the episode. Whereas sudden recognition has its parallels in Homer (see, for example, *Odyssey* 1.320 above), the resuscitation of the corpse by an eagle is unique to the *Par. Jer.* This feature is not Homeric, and must be read against the background of Hellenistic, Jewish, and Christian miracle stories.[56]

In the short version of the *Ap. John*, Reflection (*epinoia*) sits on a tree "in the form of an eagle" (*nthe nouaetos* or *mpesmot nouaetos*). The relevant Homeric passages use similar expressions (*eoikôs* or *enalinkios*, see above). A similar phrase, in contrast, does not occur in either *2 Baruch* or the *Par. Jer.* Further, in the *Ap. John*, Reflection teaches Adam (and his wife), but does not do anything that resembles those two texts. It can be concluded that the short text of the *Ap. John* relied on the classical imagery of the eagle on the tree, possibly on Homer. Although it is later than *2 Baruch* and the *Par. Jer.*, it was probably not influenced by them. The longer text of the *Ap. John* dates to the middle or end of the third century. In this version, the eagle is not any more identified as Reflection, but rather as the Saviour. When the long version of the *Ap. John* was made, the eagle was already known as a symbol of Christ.[57] In the early third century, Hippolytus of Rome commented on *Revelation* 12.14:[58] "[The text is about] the two wings of the great eagle, that is to say, the faith of

---

[56] Luke 7:11–15; Philostratus, *The Life of Apollonius of Tyana* 4.45; *Mekhilta Beshallah* 1 (referring to 2 Kings 4:32–36). Cf. W. Cotter, *Miracles in Greco-Roman Antiquity. A Sourcebook* (London, 1999), 45–46 and *passim*; J. Blenkinsopp, "Miracles: Elisha and Hanina ben Dosa," in J.C. Cavadini (ed.), *Miracles in Jewish and Christian Antiquity* (Notre Dame, 1999), 57–81.

[57] Cf. Amsler, *op. cit.*, 172–173; Czachesz, *op. cit.*, 153.

[58] "The woman was given the two wings of the great eagle, so that she could fly from the serpent into the wilderness." (*New Revised Standard Version*).

Jesus Christ, who, in stretching forth His holy hands on the holy
tree, unfolded two wings, the right and the left, and called to Him
all who believed upon Him, and covered them as a hen her chick-
ens." The reviser of the *Ap. John* evidently felt that the eagle on the
tree must symbolise the Saviour rather than Reflection.

The *Acts Phil.* was not composed in its present form before the
end of the fourth century. From this time there is archaeological evidence of the eagle symbolising Christ on the cross. An eagle on a
cross is depicted on a sarcophagus and an eagle with a cross on its
chest decorates a capital of a fourth century cathedral.[59] Likewise,
the *Acts Phil.* reports that the "wings of the eagle were spread out
in the form of the cross." The text is not unique in fourth-century
Christianity in employing an eagle on a tree to *symbolise* Christ on
the cross. It remains unique, however, as far as the eagle in the narrative *is* Christ who acts and speaks.

The closest parallel to the scene is found in the long version of
the *Ap. John*, where the Saviour teaches Adam and his wife in the
form of an eagle sitting on a tree: "I appeared in the form of an
eagle on the tree of knowledge, which is the Reflection from the
Providence of pure light, that I might teach them and awaken them
out of the depth of sleep. For they were both in a fallen state and
they recognised their nakedness. Reflection appeared to them as a
light and she awakened their thinking" (*NHC* II.23.26–35). We can
compare this passage with *Acts Phil.* 3.8 (A): "Speaking from the
mouth of the eagle, as it were, Jesus said to Philip, 'Behold I bless
you on account of your prayer, and humiliate myself to you in my
glory. I will strengthen you with my light before the ones who are
ignorant of me'." The concept of "light" and "ignorance" are common
to the two passages, which increases the possibility of literary dependence. The *Acts Phil.* also seems to have been acquainted with other
writings known to us from the Nag Hammadi Codices: *Letter of Peter
to Philip, Gospel of Philip, Gospel of Mary*.[60] In the fourth century, the
widely accepted symbolism of Christ as an eagle made it unprob-
lematic for the *Acts Phil.* to borrow the motif from the *Ap. John*.

The borders between comparison, symbolism, and metamorphosis were fluid in Homer as well as in early Christian literature.

[59] Schneider and Stemplinger, "Adler," 92; A. Negev, "Elusa," in D.N. Freedman,
ed, *Anchor Bible Dictionary*, vol. 2 (New York, 1992), 484–487 at 486.
[60] Cf. Czachesz, *op. cit.*, 136–148.

Schnapp-Gourbeillon argues that in Homer "the hero who is compared to a lion *is* the lion."[61] In the well-know passage of Revelation 5–6, the Lamb in the heavenly court *is* Christ. However, Revelation situates the whole account in the heavenly court, clearly separating it from (while emphasising its importance for) the events on earth. The *Ap. John*, where the Saviour appears in the form of eagle, clearly belongs to the same genre of revelation (*BG* 20.19–22.16). The *Acts Phil.*, in contrast, stresses the aspect of metamorphosis in a way unique among early Christian writings. Philip says, "How did you, who are mighty, appear on the top of this tree?" In the subsequent sentences, there is a gradual transition to the subject of Christ's incarnation. This association also supports the interpretation that the author viewed the eagle episode as a metamorphosis. Homeric gods show considerably more inclination to appear in the form of (or change into) animals in a story than God or Christ in Jewish and early Christian literature. It is remarkable that Philip asks the eagle to carry his prayers to God. Although the eagle carries letters in *2 Baruch* and the *Par. Jer.*, the motif could have been taken directly from Homer and Greek mythology, where the eagle is featured as Zeus' messenger.[62] The parallels with *2 Baruch* and the *Par. Jer.* cannot be neglected; however, their role as sources of the eagle episode in the *Acts Phil.* seems less important than it has been suggested.

---

[61] Schnapp-Gourbeillon, *op. cit.*, 189.
[62] Cf. note 50 above.

THE TEXT OF THE *MARTYRDOM OF POLYCARP* AGAIN (WITH A NOTE ON THE GREEK TEXT OF POLYCARP, *AD PHIL.*)

Boudewijn Dehandschutter*

The study of the *Martyrdom of Polycarp* (= *Mart. Pol.*) has led us on several occasions to make considerations on the textual transmission of this precious document.[1] A number of years ago, we were able to publish the readings of the codex Atheniensis, a "new" manuscript belonging to the hagiographical transmission of the menologies.[2] At that time, a colleague of ours, none other than A. Hilhorst who is honoured by this "Festschrift," made us aware of the reference to a text of *Mart. Pol.* in a catalogue on "neglected" manuscripts in the Bibliotheca Vallicelliana at Rome, published by S. Lucà.[3] We hope that the present contribution may serve as a (late) compensation for the kind information given to us so many years ago.

Our curiosity about the Vallicellian codex arose even more when it became clear that in the manuscript the text of *Mart. Pol.* was preceded by Polycarp's *Letter to the Philippians* (= *Pol. Phil*). But we are afraid we must disappoint the reader already: the Vallicellianus does not contain a full Greek text of *Pol. Phil.*! However, some more information about the Vallicellian manuscript SI 20 must be given first.

The codex is rather voluminous, containing 138 folios, according to Lucà's catalogue to be dated 1700–1702.[4] Above the section starting with the text of *Pol. Phil.* figures the year 1701. It might be added immediately that, only speaking about *Mart. Pol.*, such a recent

---

* Leuven.

[1] See B. Dehandschutter, *Martyrium Polycarpi. Een literair-kritische Studie* (BETL, 52; Leuven, 1979), 27–129; also *Id.*, "The Martyrium Polycarpi: A Century of Research," in *ANRW* II, Religion Band 27,1 (Berlin, 1993), 485–522. On the Coptic story about Polycarp known as the "Harris" fragments, see F.W. Weidmann, *Polycarp & John. The Harris Fragments and their Challenge to the Literary Tradition* (Notre Dame, 1999), and our response in *VC* 55 (2001) 104–107.

[2] B. Dehandschutter, "A 'New' Text of the Martyrdom of Polycarp," *ETL* 66 (1990) 391–394.

[3] S. Lucà, "Manoscritti greci dimenticati della biblioteca Vallicelliana," *Aug* 28 (1988) 661–702, cf. 677.

[4] Cf. S. Lucà, *art. cit.*, 677.

date is not exceptional. The fragmentary Jerusalem codex (BHG 1560c) dates from the seventeenth century, and the Ottobonianus 92 (BHG 1560a), actually a copy from the Vindobonensis, dates from the sixteenth century.[5]

More remarkable is the context in which the writings that concern us are transmitted. *Pol. Phil.* and *Mart. Pol.* (resp. ff. 20–23 and 23–29v) are preceded by some (pseudo-)Athanasian *spuria*.[6] After *Mart. Pol.* follows the curious *Letter of Maria Cassobolita to Ignatius*[7] and a text of the *Martyrdom of Ignatius* (ff. 31v–35).[8] Then a large number of (pseudo-) Chrysostomian writings are copied, interrupted by some other, as a rule short materials (pseudo-Justin, Marcus Eremita, Maximus Confessor).[9] The codex finds its conclusion with fragments of Ignatian Letters, the last one being the beginning of Ignatius, *ad Romanos* (ff. 136v–137).

The Text of *Mart. Pol.* in the Codex Vallicellianus

A first confrontation with the text leads to the following observations:

(1) The codex gives the text of *Mart. Pol.* according to the division in 22 chapters as is usual from the first printed editions on.
(2) In the margin some alternative readings are offered.[10]
(3) The scribe has used the margin also to indicate some biblical references.[11]
(4) The scribe knows the text of *Mart. Pol.* with the additional chapters 21 and 22 as available in codd. BPH and A, remaining on the whole congruent only with B. It is this observation we want

---

[5] See on this our *Martyrium Polycarpi* (1979), 33–34.
[6] Cf. CPG 2261 and CPG 2240.
[7] The Greek text of this Letter was first published by I. Vossius, see F.X. Funk, *Patres apostolici*, vol. I (Tübingen, 1901), LXV.
[8] About this text cf. CPG 1036; also B. Dehandschutter, "Ignatiusbriefe," in RGG IV (2001) 34–36.
[9] Cf. S. Lucà, *art. cit.*, pp. 677–678.
[10] They are 2,1   χρή pro δεῖ;
            ἀνατιθέναι vel ἀναθεῖναι pro ἀναρεθῆναι;
      8,1   συμβεβληκότων pro συμβεβηκότων;
      12,2 Ἀσίας pro ἀσεβεῖας;
      12,3 ζῶντα ante τὸν πολύκαρπον.
[11] They are 2,3 – 1 Cor 2:9;
      7,1 – Matt 26:55;
      9,1 – Deut 31:23;
      10,2 – Rom 13:1/Tit 3:1.

to substantiate with some comments on the text of the *Mart. Pol.* in the Vallicellianus.

From the very beginning the text *of the inscriptio* poits to an acquaintance with B in the reading Φιλαδελφίᾳ (loco Φιλομηλίῳ). This reading is not completely exclusive, as codex P offers the same "mistake."[12] In many other cases where our codex is corresponding with B, it is again at instances that B is joined by other witnesses, such as the well-known cases of ὁ τύραννος in 2,4, or ἀσεβείας in 12,2.[13] But as a matter of fact one can conclude that the B-text appears more exclusive: our manuscript offers readings peculiar to B in 6,2 with the remarkable κληρονόμος (loco κεκληρωμένος). In 7,2 the scribe follows the exclusive reading τινες ἔλεγον εἰ (loco καὶ εἰ) singular to B. In 17,2 our codex adds ταφῇ after σῶμα, again = B; the same happens *ibid.* with αὐτόν omitted before πυρός. In 19,2 the Vallicellianus shares with B the omission of Ἰησοῦν Χριστὸν τὸν σωτηρα τῶν ψυχῶν ἡμῶν, but then our scribe restores the text deliberately as καὶ κυβερνήτην τῶν ψυχῶν καὶ σωμάτων: "the Lord is the governor of our souls and bodies."[14]

Faced with this situation the pressing question is obviously: can the text of the Vallicellianus be taken as an independent witness to B? In our opinion some doubts are justified. One must envisage the possibility that the text of our codex has derived from one of the first printed editions of *Mart. Pol.* This possibility is all the more the case as the early editions rely almost exclusively on B. This codex was the basis for the first printed text of *Mart. Pol.* by James Ussher in 1647,[15] and Ussher's text was used by Cotelier for his famous edition of the "Apostolic Fathers" in 1672. As the scribe of the Vallicellianus entitles his text of *Mart. Pol.* with exactly the same words as Cotelier: Τῆς Σμυρναίων Ἐκκλησίας περὶ μαρτυρίου τοῦ ἁγίου Πολυκάρπου Ἐπιστολὴ ἐγκύκλιος (which is not Ussher's), we are

---

[12] See on this our *Martyrium Polycarpi* (1979), 52, n. 107; 175, n. 443.

[13] *Martyrium Polycarpi* (1979), 76–77; 91–92. Or see again the striking Μαίων and στρατιου in ch. 21, readings shared by B and P.

[14] There is not much need to call attention to blunders such as 14,2 ἡμετέρας instead of ἡμερας!

[15] Comp. J.A. Fischer, "Die ältesten Ausgaben der Patres Apostolici. Ein Beitrag zu Begriff und Begrenzung der Apostolischen Väter," in *Historisches Jahrbuch* 94 (1074) 157–190; 95 (1975) 88–119.

inclined to see in Cotelier's text the source of *Mart. Pol.* as it appears in the Vallicellianus!

Apart from the title, there are other indications. The division of the text into twenty-two chapters, unknown in the manuscripts, and even not used by Ussher, appears in Cotelier's edition. The marginal biblical references correspond again with Cotelier, and the same is true of the marginal readings. The only difference is that the scribe of the Vallicellianus did not take notice of some variants chosen from the Eusebiustext, as Cotelier did. But the comparison with Eusebius became something important in the later editions, from the time of the re-edition of Cotelier by Clericus (Clericus is the one to provide the reader with something like a critical apparatus).

There is one more reason to think of Cotelier: in his edition the texts of *Pol. Phil.* and *Mart. Pol.* are printed subsequently (this is not the case in Ussher's work, the Letter and the Martyrdom being separated over two volumes).[16] In the light of the evidence as we have it now, we cannot but conclude that the text of *Mart. Pol.* in the Vallicellianus has no independent value as a witness to the text, and can only serve to demonstrate how early Cotelier's textedition became influential.[17]

THE TEXT OF *POL. PHIL.* IN THE CODEX VALLICELLIANUS

The preceding conclusion doesn't seem very encouraging with regard to a brief consideration of the text of *Pol. Phil.*, though our first excitement about the presence of a text of *Pol. Phil.* in the Vallicellianus might be forgivable. It is sufficiently well known that the Greek text of *Pol. Phil.* is deficient: all available manuscripts show a contamination of *Pol. Phil.* and the *Epistle of Barnabas* in as much as *Pol. Phil.* § 9 ἀποθανόντα καὶ δι' ἡμᾶς runs into *Barnabas* § 5 ὑπὸ τὸν λαόν etc.[18] It means that *Pol. Phil.* is known further by the Latin translation,[19]

---

[16] The edition of the Ignatian and Polycarpian Letters being from 1644, that of the Martyrdom from 1647.

[17] See *Martyrium Polycarpi* (1979) 57–58; the text of Cotelier remained *the* text of *Mart. Pol.*; only with Jacobson (1838) a full collation of all known manuscripts is at the basis of the text edition.

[18] See the description of the matter regarding the *Letter of Barnabas*: F.R. Prostmeier, *Der Barnabasbrief* (KAV, 8; Göttingen, 1999).

[19] It is not for nothing that a recent commentator such as J.B. Bauer has given

except for a quotation in Eusebius *H.E.* III,36 from *Pol. Phil.* 9 and 13. The scribe of the Vallicellianus is fully aware of the gap: following the textual divisions into chapters, he notes after § 9 λειπει concluding his presentation of the text with the Greek from Eusebius for § 13 which is indicated as ιγ. This text ends abruptly with ἡμῶν ἀνηκούσαν as the quotation of Eusebius does. It is almost obvious that the Cotelier edition put the text at the scribe's disposal: the latter followed his model until the interruption after § 9, and could borrow the Greek text of § 13 from its insertion in the Latin translation which follows in Cotelier.

In this situation surprises are not to be expected in the Greek text, but it will be permitted to point out one detail which also offers some curiosity with regard to the early editions of *Pol. Phil.* If our scribe had had only one manuscript of the Polycarpian letter before him, he would certainly have been aware of the fact that the Greek text of *Pol. Phil.* 4,3 reads not ἡμῶν σκοπεῖται but μωμοσκοπεῖται. There is no manuscript to sustain the former reading; remarkably enough it has been introduced in the text instead of the latter by the early editors, Ussher, Cotelier, Clericus. The last one however adds in a note: "*In exemplari* μωμοσκοπεῖται *scriptum est: quam vocem qui non intellexerunt* ἡμῶν σκοπεῖται *legendum esse existimaverunt . . .*".[20] It is indeed quite possible that early editors were unfamiliar with this *terminus technicus* from the Jewish-hellenistic sacrificial language.[21] In each case our scribe has not had any afterthought, simply following Cotlier's ἡμῶν σκοπεῖται, in spite the latter's marginal note (which refers to the manuscript reading).

The conclusion to be drawn from these short observations on the text of *Pol. Phil.* in the Vallicellianus cannot differ much from what has been said about *Mart. Pol.* There is no independent witness, the text offers all evidence of straight dependence from Cotelier's edition.

It remains difficult to explain why some one has collected and written down so different writings in one and the same codex, except that it could have served as a kind of writing exercise.[22] However,

---

full weight to the Latin translation, cf. *Die Polykarpbriefe* (KAV,5; Göttingen, 1995), 15–18, 87–93.

[20] Cf. J.B. Cotelier, *Sanctorum Patrum qui temporibus apostolicis floruerunt opera . . .*; we have used the re-edition by Clericus of 1724, cf. p. 185.

[21] However the verb μωμοσκοπεῖν can be read also in *1 Clement* 41,2.

[22] The suggestion is made by S. Lucà for some manuscripts described by him, but not for SI 20, cf. *art. cit.*

we can end this contribution on a positive note: the text of *Pol. Phil.* and *Mart. Pol.* attracted someone so much that he has copied these precious *Polycarpiana* as complete as possible, instead of limiting himself to some extracts or fragments.

THEODORET'S PHILOLOGICAL REMARKS
ON THE LANGUAGE OF THE SEPTUAGINT

Natalio Fernández Marcos*

In the Preface to the Questions of Kings, dedicated to Hypathios, Theodoret comments on the reason for the obscurity of the Scripture. In his opinion it is due to the fact that the Greek translators intended to do a literal translation. He goes on to assert that this ἀσάφεια affects the translations from Latin into Greek in the same way; these translations are also full of obscurity.[1]

The issue of the obscurity of the Scripture was commonplace in Theodoret's time. Moreover, since Origen, almost everything has been said on the secret meaning of the prophecies, the Old Testament as a parable of Jesus, and the true meaning of the texts concealed in the obscure forms of the discourse.[2] As a matter of fact, Theodoret shares these traditional arguments concerning the prophetic texts; these speak in an enigmatic way (προφητικῶς καὶ αἰνιγματωδῶς) because they conceal a secret meaning.[3] But for the historical books he attributes the obscurity of the text to the literal character of the translation adducing, as an example, contemporary Greek texts translated from the Latin. In other words, in the historical books, Theodoret does not link obscurity and mystery but simply remind us of the philological devices that can hinder the true understanding of texts. Theodoret, as other Antiochene authors, was aware of a wide tradition of *Scholia* devoted to the elucidation of Homer and other classical authors. Many of their linguistic observations are made following

---

* Madrid.

[1] Αἴτιον δὲ γε τῆς ἀσαφείας, καὶ τὸ σπουδάσαι τοὺς ἑρμηνεύσαντας περὶ πόδα τὴν ἑρμηνείαν ποιήσασθαι· ταὐτὸ δὲ τοῦτο πάσχουσι καὶ οἱ τὴν Ἰταλῶν φωνὴν εἰς τὴν Ἑλλάδα μεταφέροντες χλῶτταν· Πολλῆς γὰρ ἀσαφείας κἀκεῖνα μεστά, cf. N. Fernández Marcos – J.R. Busto Saiz, *Theodoreti Cyrensis Quaestiones in Reges et Paralipomena. Editio Critica* (TECC, 32; Macrid, 1984), 3 (= QRP).

[2] M. Harl, "Origène et les interprétations patristiques grecques de l'"obscurité" biblique," *VC* 36 (1982) 334–371; D. Barthélemy, "Eusèbe, la Septante et 'les autres,'" in *La Bible et les Pères, Colloque de Strasbourg (1–3 Octobre 1969)* (Paris), 51–65 (Reprint in D. Barthélemy, *Études d' histoire du texte de l'Ancien Testament* [OBO, 21; Fribourg-Göttingen, 1978], 179–194).

[3] J.-N. Guinot, *L'exégèse de Théodoret de Cyr* (TH, 100; Paris, 1995), 151–165.

the steps of this tradition. Moreover the technical terms employed belong to the practice of the *Scholia* literature.[4]

As I have pointed out elsewhere, Theodoret ignores the Hebrew but he invests much effort in explaining the Greek transliteration of Hebrew words with recourse to the ancient collections of the *Onomastica Sacra*, the material of the "three younger translators," Josephus and other Hebrew traditions.[5] Theodoret presents a wide set of comments on the Hebraisms (ἰδιώματα) of the Septuagint; they are scattered throughout his questions and commentaries.[6] These Hebrew idioms were extensively treated by other members of the Antiochene school, such as Diodor of Tarsus, Theodor of Mopsuestia and particularly Hadrian.[7] I wish to concentrate on some lexical terms of the Septuagint that, according to Theodoret, needed to be explained for his contemporary readers. They point to the fact that the sacred language of the translation was no longer fully understood in 5th century Antioch. These examples reflect a concrete stage of the reception of the Septuagint and are a witness of the evolution and renovation of the Greek language.[8]

In Theodoret's *Questions to the Octateuch* and in his *Questions to the Kings and Chronicles*, a number of questions arise which are specifically concerned with lexicographical problems that I consider to be worthy of comment.

Εἴδωλον/ὁμοίωμα: In the question 38 to Exodus corresponding to the text of Ex 20:4 "You shall not make for yourself an idol," Theodoret explains the distinction between both terms with the following words: "The idol has no substance; the image, however, is a form and representation of something. Since the Greeks fashion the forms that do not exist, Sphinxes, Tritons and Centaurs, and the

---

[4] A. Leonas, "Patristic Evidence of Difficulties in Understanding the LXX: Hadrian's Philological Remarks in *Isagoge*," in B.A. Taylor (ed.), *X Congress of the International Organization for Septuagint and Cognate Studies, Oslo, 1998* (SBLSCS, 51; Atlanta, 2001), 393–414.

[5] N. Fernández Marcos, "Teodoreto de Ciro y la lengua hebrea," *Henoch* 9 (1987) 39–54.

[6] J.-N. Guinot, *L'exégèse*, 346–350.

[7] Cf. F. Goessling, *Adrians Eisagoge eis tas theias graphas* (Berlin, 1887) and C. Schäublin, *Untersuchungen zu Methode und Herkunft der antiochenischen Exegese* (Köln-Bonn, 1974), 123–139.

[8] M. Harl, "Le renouvellement du lexique des Septante d'après le témoignage des recensions, révisions et commentaires grecs anciens," in *Id., La langue de Japhet. Quinze études sur la Septante et le grec des Chrétiens* (Paris, 1992), 145–165.

Egyptians (fashion) forms dog-faced and bull-headed, the author calls idols the copies of things not having existence; but (he calls) images the representations of existing things like sun and moon, stars, men, beasts, reptiles and beings such as those."[9]

Εἴδωλον is one of the various translations of the Septuagint for the Hebrew *pesel*, idol or image of a god, cut from stone, shaped from clay, carved from wood or cast from metal.[10] The rest of the interpreters translate this passage by γλυπτός, sculpture. Ὁμοίωμα is used for the Hebrew *těmūnāh*, a copy or representation.

Nevertheless Theodoret reads the text within the Greek system of references without connection to the Hebrew *Vorlage*. In Greek the word εἴδωλον is coloured by the Homeric and classical meaning of phantom, ghost, unsubstantial form. The Hesychian Lexicon according to the Homeric and classical tradition records as synonym the word σκιά.[11] Theodoret's comments are worked in the frame of this tradition; as a result, he confirms a semantic shift far removed from the original meaning of *pesel*. The Septuagint translation by εἴδωλον was the starting point of a new meaning developed by Theodoret with concepts drawn from Greek and Egyptian mythology.

τελεσφόρος/τελισκόμενος: They are *hapax legomena* in the Septuagint to Deuteronomy 23:17(18). They reproduce a double translation of πόρνη and πορνεύων in the same verse for the Hebrew *qĕdešah* (female prostitute) and *qādēš* (male prostitute).[12] Theodoret's explanation points to the pagan mysteries religions: the first would mean the person who introduces or acts as a guide to the mysteries; the second, the person introduced or initiated into the mysteries.[13] Again a double translation in the Septuagint plus the cultural context of the Greek

---

[9] Τὸ εἴδωλον οὐδεμίαν ὑπόστασιν ἔχει· τὸ δὲ ὁμοίωμα, τινός ἐστιν ἴνδαλμα καὶ ἀπείκασμα, ἐπειδὴ τοίνυν ἕλληνες ἀναπλάττουσι τὰς οὐχ ὑφεστώσας μορφάς, σφίγγας καὶ τρίτωνας καὶ κενταύρους· καὶ αἰγύπτιοι κυνοπροσώπους καὶ βουκεφάλους, εἴδωλα καλεῖ τὰ τῶν οὐχ ὑφεστώτων μιμήματα· ὁμοιώματα δὲ τὰ τῶν ὑφεστώτων εἰκάσματα, οἷον ἡλίου καὶ σελήνες, ἀστέρων, ἀνθρώπων, θηρίων, ἑρπετῶν, καὶ τῶν τούτοις παραπλεσίων, N. Fernández Marcos – A. Sáenz-Badillos, *Theodoreti Cyrensis Quaestiones in Octateuchum. Editio Critica* (TECC, 17; Madrid, 1979), 127,7–13 (= QO).
[10] T. Muraoka, *Hebrew/Aramaic Index to the Septuagint, Keyed to the Hatch-Redpath Concordance* (Grand Rapids, MI, 1998).
[11] K. Latte, *Hesychii Alexandrini Lexicon* II (Hauniae, 1966), 25.
[12] J.W. Wevers, *Notes on the Greek Text of Deuteronomy* (SBLSCS 39; Atlanta, 1995), 372.
[13] Τελεσφόρον καλεῖ δὲ τὸν μυσταγογοῦντα, τελισκόμενον δὲ τὸν μυσταγογούμενον, QO, 248, 19–20.

religion produces a new meaning and a new reading confirmed by
Theodoret's commentary which is different from that of the original.

μανδύας/ἀρκαδίκιν/μαντίον: When Jonathan made a covenant with
David he stripped himself of the robe (ἐπενδύτην), and gave it to
David, as well as the garment (μανδύαν), as a sign of their friendship (1 Kings 18:4).[14] Probably the word μανδύας was no longer
understood among Theodoret's readership and he judges it necessary to explain it with a list of synonyms which were more common in the 5th century A.D.: "it is a kind of upper garment. I think
it is either a kind of garment or what most people call a mantle."[15]
It is worth noticing Theodoret's method to elucidate the meaning
of the word in question. He recurs to the context and the substitution of words that have been employed by the other translators. He
realises that in 1 Kings 4:12 when a man of Benjamin running from
the battle line came with his clothes torn, the Septuagint read διερ-
ρηγμένα τὰ ἱμάτια, while Aquila translated μανδύαν διερρηγμένον.
Likewise he observes that in 2 Kings 10:4 the King of the Ammonites
seized David's envoys, shaved off half the beard of each, cut off their
garments (μανδύας) . . . and sent them away. Aquila used this time
χιτών. These words are well represented in Lampe's Lexicon of
Patristic Greek, and μανδύας found a place even in the Lexicon of
Hesych, probably via Theodoret.[16]

χλίδων/βραχιάριον: When an Amalekite informs David of Saul's
death he adds: "I took the diadem on his head and the bracelet
(χλίδωνα) on his arm" (Hebrew 'es 'adah, 2 Kings 1:10). Theodoret
dedicates a question to elucidate the meaning of this word: "a golden
ornament that is put around the arms or the wrists of the hands";
he adds that Aquila calls it βραχιάριον.[17] However, when he comments
2 Kings 8:7 on the gold shields (Hebrew šelet, "small circular shield")
that were carried by the servants of Hadadezer, translated in the

[14] For the books of Kings, I quote according to the Septuagint, that is 1–4 Kings,
corresponding to 1–2 Samuel and 1–2 Kings of the Hebrew.
[15] Τί ἐστι μανδύας; Εἶδος ἐστιν ἐφεστρίδος. Οἶμαι δὲ ἢ ἀρκαδίκιν εἶναι, ἢ τὸ
παρὰ τῶν πολλῶν μαντίον ὀνομαζόμενον, QRP, 39,5–7.
[16] G.W.H. Lampe, A Patristic Greek Lexicon (Oxford, 1968) and K. Latte, Hesychii
Lexicon II, 627.
[17] Κόσμος ἐστὶ χρυσοῦς, ἢ τοῖς βραχίοσι περιτιθέμενος, ἢ τοῖς καρποῖς τῶν χειρῶν,
QRP, 64,5–6.

Septuagint by χλίδωνας τοὺς χρυσούς, Theodoret registers a different interpretation of Aquila, τοὺς χρυσοὺς κλοιούς ("gold collars").[18] In this case the context did not serve to clarify the meaning, since he overlooks Symmachus's interpretation φαρέτρας τὰς χρυσᾶς ("gold quivers for the arrows"). The semantic field may extend from an ornament to a kind of defensive weapon. But the source of this semantic shift lies in the Septuagint translation that uses the same Greek words for two different Hebrew terms, a phenomenon well attested in translation Greek and the source of manifold confusion.

πλινθίον/πλαίσιον: The word πλινθίον appears exclusively in the Antiochene text since the majority text of the Septuagint transliterates, according to the Hebrew, the patronymics or names of peoples: "Banaiah son of Jehoiada was in command of the Cherethites and the Pelethites" (2 Kings 20:23). However Antiochene translates those names καὶ Βαναίας υἱὸς Ἰοαδδαὶ ἐπὶ τοῦ πλινθίου καὶ ἐπὶ τους δυνάστας.[19] Theodoret explains the word without reference to the Hebrew or to the transliteration of other manuscripts: "I think that πλινθίον is called what is named πλαίσιον by the external writers. And this is a kind of line of battle of the army in the form of a square."[20] Theodoret goes so far as to imagine Baneas in command of a kind of a royal "guard de corps" and compare him with the *magister* of the Romans who was entrusted with the command of the royal infantry, shield-bearers and spear-bearers. One can no longer speak of a semantic shift but of a new meaning created by the Antiochene interpretation, far removed from that of the original. This interpretation has also been the object of Theodoret's comments. It is a witness of the richness and novelty of the Septuagint read and understood as a literary piece on its own.

In a few cases Theodoret specifically records the distinction between the biblical use and the term current in the common language of

---

[18] QRP, 83,7–8.
[19] N. Fernández Marcos – J.R. Busto Saiz, *El texto antioqueno*, I, 153. The Antiochene is followed by the Old Latin. Since it is only attested in the Antiochene text, this meaning is lacking in the general lexica and the lexica of the Septuagint; however it is registered in E.A. Sphocles, *A Greek Lexicon of the Roman and Byzantine Periods*, Leipzig 1914 (Reprint: Hildesheim-New York, 1975).
[20] Πλινθίον οἶμαι καλεῖσθαι, ὃ παρὰ τοῖς ἔξω συγγραφεῦσι πλαίσιον ὀνομάζεται. Εἶδος δὲ τοῦτο στρατιωτικῆς παρατάξεως τετράγωνον ἐχούσης τὸ σχῆμα, QRP, 108, 9–11.

his time. These observations open a window on the history of the Greek language and constitute a contribution to Greek lexicography.

χιτὼν ἀστραγαλωτός: It is the long robe with sleeves worn by Tamar when she was raped by her brother Amnon (2 Kings 13:18–19). The meaning of the Hebrew word *pas* is not clear, perhaps "tunic composed of variegated pieces": that is how it has been translated by the Septuagint in Gen 37:23.32 (Joseph's tunic), χιτὼν ποίκιλος; or "tunic reaching to the ankles," as was understood by Josephus.[21] This term is peculiar to the Antiochene text and, consequently, ignored until now by the lexica of the Septuagint. Aquila and the rest of the Septuagint translate it by καρπωτός,[22] "reaching to the ankle or wrist," while Symmachus prefers χειριδωτός, "sleeved." Theodoret mentions Josephus's interpretation and that of Aquila, "a tunic embroidered with anklebones," but, what is more important, records the current name given by his contemporaries (οἱ νῦν δέ), that is, πλουμαρικός.[23]

νωτοφόρος/ὠμοφόρος: Theodoret alludes to one of the officers of Solomon, Ahikam, who is in command of the burden-bearers (3 Kings 2:34). This section is lacking in the Hebrew but he recurs to the parallel passages of Chronicles (2 Chr 2:1[2].17[18]; 34:13) where the Hebrew word *sabal* is translated by νωτοφόρος, and he continues ὠμοφόρους δὲ οἱ νῦν ὀνομάζουσιν.[24]

ἐπωμίς/ἀκαδίκιν: From the extension of the first and unique question to 1 Chronicles one can deduce the problem represented by David dancing before the ark. Moreover, in 1 Chr 15:17 it is said that "David wore a linen ephod" only. In addition to this behaviour that provoked Michal's despise (2 Kings 6:14–16), David was not a priest and was dressed with a priestly robe. Theodoret points out that he has explained the meaning of the ephod several times,

---

[21] τὸν μέχρις ἀστραγάλων διήκοντα, Josephus, *Ant* 3.158.

[22] It is worth emphasizing that this passage belongs to the καίγε-section of Kings. This fact may explain the agreement between the majority text of the Septuagint and Aquila.

[23] Τὸν δὲ χιτῶνα τὸν ἀστραγαλωτὸν, ὁ μὲν Ἀκύλας καρπωτὸν ὠνόμασεν, ἀντὶ τοῦ καρποὺς ἐνυγασμέννους ἔχοντα· οἱ νῦν δὲ αὐτὸν καλοῦσι πλουμαρικόν, QRP, 92,15–93,1.

[24] QRP, 130,1–3.

in the 60th question to Exodus (QO 143,10–27), in the 17th question to Judges (QO 301, 18–25), and in the 5th question to 1 Kings (QRP 8,5–9). He has provided different synonyms such as ἐφεστρίς, the translation of Symmachus, ἐπωμίς, and that of Aquila, ἐπένδυμα. But now, in defence of David, he makes a distinction between sacred vests and profane robes. Consequently it is clear that David, being a pious man, a friend of God did not dare to dress a sacred vest. The text says only that when he was dancing before the ark he did not wear the royal dress but only a shoulder's tunic that now is called ἀρκαδίκιν.[25]

In other cases Theodoret, in the way of the ancient scholiasts of Homer and other classical authors, elucidates a less common word with a short explanation as in 1 Kings 20:19.20. Jonathan informs David of his strategy. On the third day he shall go a long way down . . . Jonathan will shoot three arrows to the side of it. The Septuagint uses in both cases the verb τρισσεύω, "to do a thing thrice or for the third time." Theodoret comments on the first occurrence: Τὸ δὲ τρισσεύσεις ἀντὶ τοῦ τρεῖς ἡμέρας ἀναμενεῖω, and concerning the second, Τὸ δὲ τρισσεύσω ἀτὶ τοῦ τρεῖς ἀφήσω στχίζας, that is I will shoot three arrows.[26] The whole question is full of philological remarks. The Hebrew transliteration ἀματτάρα (maṭṭarah), "target" according to the book of interpretation of Hebrew names[27] is translated by "trench" (τάφρος) by the Greeks, φοσσάτον by the Romans and σκοπός, "target," by the Syrians. Interestingly enough, David shall remain beside the stone there (1 Kings 20:19) and the Antiochene text translates correctly παρὰ τω λιθω ἐκείνῳ, but the rest of the Septuagint transliterates τὸ ἐργάβ, interpreted or guessed by Theodoret as "cave or hollow place" from the context of 20:41 where David rises from the ἀργόβ. Theodoret's interpretation is taken almost with the same words from Diodor.[28]

Likewise, it is not clear what kind of apostasy is alluded to at 3 Kings 14: 37–38 (= 14:23–24 in Hebrew), probably there were male temple prostitutes (qādeš) in the land. In any case the Septuagint translates this Hebrew term by σύνδεσμος (reading probably qešer),

---

[25] Ἀλλὰ διδάσκει ὁ λόγος ὡς ἡγούμενος τῆς κιβωτοῦ καὶ χωρεύων, οὐ τὸ βασιλικὸν περιεβέβλητο σχῆμα, ἀλλ᾽ ἐπωμίδα μόνην, ἥν νῦν καλοῦσιν Ἀρκαδίκιν, QRP, 252,17–18.

[26] QRP, 44,9–10 and 16–24.

[27] On this book cf. QRP, LXI, note 3.

[28] Cf. N. Fernández Marcos – J.R. Busto Saiz, *El texto antioqueno*, I, 63.

"revolt?" instead of *qādeš*. Theodoret explains in the manner of the scholiasts, Τὸ δὲ σύνδεσμος ἀντὶ τῆς ἀποστάσεως τέθεικε.[29]

φοιβάω: In Deut 14:1 the Hebrew text says: "You must not lacerate yourselves or shave your forelocks for the dead." The Septuagint translates: οὐ φοιβήσετε, οὐκ ἐπιθήσετε φαλάκρωμα ἀνὰ μέσον τῶν ὀφθαλμῶν ὑμῶν ἐπὶ νεκρῷ. The verb φοιβάω is a *hapax legomenon* in the Septuagint. The difficult comprehension of this verb can be deduced from the correction of most of the manuscript tradition towards a form of φοβέω/-οῦμαι.[30] Aquila translates it by the verb κατατέμνειν, the same verb used by the Septuagint for the hitpoel of *gadad* when the priests of Baal (1 Kings 18:28) cut themselves with swords. The Complutensian Polyglot adheres to the meaning of the Hebrew word and uses the verb κόπτειν. The Septuagint clearly tries to reinterpret the prohibition within a new framework. The meaning of φοιβάω is "to cleanse, to purify" from a root originally signifying "to be bright, radiant." This is how it has been interpreted by Dogniez[31] and Wevers.[32] Moreover, Wevers tries to see a semantic shift in this translation that betrays the Alexandrian origin of the translation, since the rites of purification played an important role in the Egyptian religion. However, Lust prefers the mantic interpretation and interprets the Greek word as "to seek oracular ecstasy."[33]

Be that as it may, Theodoret's explanation for his readers of the 5th century confirms the mantic interpretation, within the new context of the Greek religion: καὶ διὰ μὲν τοῦ οὐ φοιβήσετε, τὰς μαντείας ἐξέβαλε. φοῖβον γὰρ τὸν ψευδόμαντιν ἐκάλουν τὸν Πύθιον.[34] Theodoret connects the verb with Apollo's epithet. Unfortunately this connection does not solve the problem of the meaning since the sense remains unexplained.[35] But Theodoret is aware of the multiple forms

[29] QRP, 165,12–13.
[30] Cf. J.W. Wevers, *Septuaginta. III, 2 Deuteronomium* (Göttingen, 1977), 192.
[31] C. Dogniez, *La Bible d' Alexandrie. 5 Le Deutéronome* (Paris, 1992), 203: "vous ne ferez pas de purification."
[32] J.W. Wevers, *Notes on the Greek Text of Deuteronomy*, 240: "I would translate: You must not engage in purificatory rites." The translator avoided the notion of gashing oneself in favor of the notion of purification. Possibly the substitution was an oblique reference to Egyptian funerary customs in which the corpse was cleansed with various spices."
[33] J. Lust, E. Eynikel, K. Hauspie, *A Greek-English Lexicon of the Septuagint, II*, (Stuttgart, 1996).
[34] QO, 241,24–242,2.
[35] "Das wort φοῖβος, das dem Namen des Apollon vorangestellt wird, ist noch

of divination in the Greek tradition. Interestingly enough, he does not comment Deuteronomy 18:10–14 where the Septuagint records no less than eight kinds of magic and divination forbidden to the Hebrews. However, question 29 to Leviticus[36] is entirely devoted to the ventriloquists (ἐγγαστρίμυθος),[37] called by the Greeks ἐντερομάν-τεις, in the idea that the demons speak from the belly. Moreover, questions 72, 73 and 74 to 1 Kings are given over to the female ἐγγαστρίμυθον of Endor (1 Kings 28), especially question 73. Question 52 to 4 Kings explains a new kind of diviners, the γνῶσται, that, in his opinion, are the diviners by means of the liver, different from the diviners by means of the flight of the birds (οἰωνισμός) and from the divination through words.[38] And when he comments 2 Chronicles 35: 19a according to the Septuagint, a verse missing in Hebrew, he links the κερεσείμ to the list of diviners.[39] Josiah set the Temple in order with his reform burning all kinds of ventriloquists, diviners by the words, *terafim* and *kereseim* in the land of Judah and in Jerusalem. This word in the Septuagint probably resulted from a mistaken transliteration of *qedesim* the male Temple prostitutes mentioned in 4 Kings 23:7, through a confusion in Hebrew of the similar consonants *daleth/res*. Theodoret is aware of the multiform kind of divination among the Greeks and includes them in the ranks of the diviners. No matter that in QRP 239,2 he interprets the Καδησίμ mentioned in 4 Kings 23:7 simply as δαίμονες.

δυσεντερία/ἕδρα/φαγέδαινα: When the Philistines captured the ark of God they were stricken with tumours (1 Sam 5:6.9.12). The Hebrew word ʿ*epholim* (ketiv)/*tehorim* (qere) points to a kind of disease, generally translated by tumours or hemorrhoids.[40] The Septuagint

---

völlig unerklärt," cf. M.P. Nilsson, *Geschichte der griechischen Religion* I (München, 1967³), 559.

[36] QO, 181,11–14.

[37] For the semantic shift of this word in Late Antiquity from a seer-diviner by means of his belly-voice to a conjurer of the dead or necromancer, due to the translation of the Septuagint see S. Torallas Tovar – A. Maravela-Solbakk, "Between Necromancers and Ventriloquists: The ἐγγαστρίμυθοι in the Septuagint," *Sefarad* 61 (2001) 419–437.

[38] QRP, 217,1–5 and 236,8–10: Κλήδων δέ ἐστιν ἡ διὰ λόγων παρατήρησις· οἰωνισμὸς δὲ ἡ διὰ πτηνῶν. Γνώστας δὲ οἶμαι τοὺς δι᾽ ἥπατος μαντευομένους κληθῆναι.

[39] QRP, 299,1–2: Τὸ δὲ Κερεσεὶμ εἶδος εἶναι μαντείας ὑπολαμβάνω.

[40] P. Kyle McCarter, *I Samuel* (AB 8; New York, 1984⁴), 117–124. The correction of the scribes means that the written text, probably alluding to hemorrhoids, was considered improper for public reading.

translates regularly this term by the plural of ἕδρα: εἰς τὰς ἕδρας or ἐν ταῖς ἕδραις, "in the seats, on the buttocks," without mentioning specifically the kind of disease. Theodoret remarks that the Philistines were not willing to recognise the difference between his god Dagon and the God of Israel and therefore they succumbed to various diseases (ποικίλοις παθήμασι). Subsequently he mentions the name of the disease in the Septuagint, ἕδρα, followed by the name given by Aquila, φαγέδαινα,[41] and the name given by Josephus, δυσεντερία.[42] Theodoret is concerned with the harmony of the Scripture, τῆς θείας γραφῆς συμφωνία.[43] At first sight the different names of the disease, this apparent διαφωνία, seem to contradict the due harmony of the Scripture. Then he provides a description of the different phases of the disease to solve the problem as if it were a medical diagnosis. Theodoret explains that the disease begins with the ἕδρα, it becomes a dysentery, and finally ends with a cancerous sore.[44] It is not the only case where Theodoret manifests his medical knowledge. When he comments on Solomon's wisdom (3 Kings 4:29–33), following a tradition already present in Hellenistic Jewish writers, he states that the authors of medical works draw many of their remedies from Solomon, such as which part of the animals is appropriate for each disease (ἀλεξιφάρμακον) like the bile of the hyena, the fat of the lion, the blood of the bull or the meat of the vipers.[45]

CONCLUSION

These brief notes confirm Theodoret's philological approach to the Scripture in the line of other Antiochene authors. In the explanation of the word he follows the principles of the ancient interpreters of Homer, especially Aristophanes of Byzantium and Aristarchus, in the Hellenistic Alexandria. He learnt, like the other Antiochenes, to elucidate the Scripture from the Scripture with the recourse to par-

---

[41] In fact, in 1 Sam 5:6 Aquila uses the verb φαγεδαινίζω.
[42] Josephus, *Ant* 6,3.
[43] Cf. the Preface to the QO, 3,18–19.
[44] QRP, 14,11–14: Ἀλλὰ μηδεὶς διαφωνίαν νομιζέτω τὰς διαφόρους ἐκδόσεις. Τὴν γὰρ δυσεντερίαν τὸ τῆς ἕδρας διεδέξατο πάθος· τὸ γὰρ συχνὸν τῆς ἐκκρίσεως τὸ τῆς ἐκκρίσεως κατέκαυσε μόριον, εἰς φαγέδαιναν δὲ τῷ χρόνῳ τὸ ἕλκος μετέπεσε.
[45] QRP, 135,10–14. Other testimonies of Theodoret's knowledge of the medical terms in J.-N. Guinot, *L'exégèse de Théodoret*, 435–438 and Ch. Schäublin, *Untersuchungen*, 151.

allel passages and other linguistic devices in the same way that Homer could only be clarified from Homer.[46] The Antiochenes in their aim to elucidate the literal meaning of the Scripture had recourse, not only to the Christian *Onomastica Sacra* and biblical glossaries, but also to pagan lexica and diverse florilegia.[47] The lexical component of Theodoret's exegesis is more developed than that of Origen.[48] To clarify the obscure passages of the biblical text, Theodoret uses the same method of the pagan *Scholia* for the less common words of the classical authors that need to be translated to the vocabulary of the current language. In Theodoret the lexical comments prevail over the syntactical or stylistic observations concerning the biblical Greek. To clarify the obscure words he does not look to the Hebrew but to contemporary Greek hermeneutics. His questions to the Octateuch and to the historical books, with the constant recourse to the *realia* and the linguistic illustration transmit an scholarly atmosphere concerned with the hermeneutics of Scripture at the most factual level. Hadrian's *Eisagoge* focuses on the figures of speech and figures of language. It can be considered to be the first treatise on biblical semantics. There can be no exegetical practice without first caring for the literal and factual understanding of the text. Theodoret concentrates on the lexical remarks. But both share the same aim, to help the students and readers in the correct interpretation of the Scriptures. At the end of the *Eisagoge*, Hadrian compares the reader who wants to approach the Scripture to a traveller through an unknown land. He is obliged to know the main directions so as not to go astray. In a similar way, pupils who want to learn the Bible have first to know the content or target, then the proprieties of the Scripture, its figures and *tropoi*, but to no lesser extent, the clear translation of the words as a kind of sign which will guide them safely towards their goal.[49]

---

[46] Cf. B. Neuschäfer, *Origenes als Philologe* I and II (Basel, 1987), I, 276–285: Ὅμηρον ἐξ Ὁμήρου σαφηνίζειν. A principle associated with Aristarchus but not attested before Porphyry. The same method was used for showing the consonance (συμφωνία) of the Scripture, in particular between the Old and New Testament.

[47] Ch. Schäublin, *Untersuchungen*, 95–108.

[48] In spite of the new insights on Origen as philologist emphasized by B. Neuschäfer, *Origenes*, 140–155.

[49] οὐχ ἥκιστα δὲ τὴν τῆς κατὰ τὴν λέξιν ἑρμενείας σαφήνειαν, οἷα δή τινα σημεῖα τῆς ὁδοιπορίας προσυποδεικνύναι, δι' ὧν τότε ἀσφαλὲς καὶ βέβαιον αὐτοῖς ὑπάρχοι πρὸς τὸ προκείμενον, Gössling, *Hadrian's Eisagoge*, 132.

May these pages serve as a tribute to Ton, who, since the beginning of his brilliant academic career, has contributed in a singular manner, to clarify the influence of foreign languages like Hebrew and Latin on the evolution and renovation of postclassical Greek.

GREEK LOANWORDS IN THE *COPPER SCROLL*

Florentino García Martínez*

The *Copper Scroll* (3Q15) is certainly the most remarkable manuscript of the whole collection known to us under the name "Dead Sea Scrolls."[1] Its unique support (two thin plates of almost pure copper), its contents (a dry list of hiding places of treasures) and its language (a Hebrew rather different from the other manuscripts), place it in a unique position among the collection of manuscripts from the Dead Sea. It is little wonder that the number of studies dedicated to unravelling its "mystery" could by now fill a well stocked library.[2]

---

* Leuven-Groningen.

[1] The first complete edition (with transcription of the Hebrew text, drawings of the Scroll and English translation) was the much disputed book by J.M. Allegro, *The Treasure of the Copper Scroll* (London, 1960). It was preceded by the publication of a French and of an English translation by J.T. Milik in "Le rouleau de cuivre de Qumran (3Q15). Traduction et commentaire topographique," *RB* 66 (1959) 321–357, and "The Copper Document from Cave III of Qumran. Translation and Commentary," *ADAJ* 4–5 (1960) 137–155. The official edition was prepared by J.T. Milik, "Le rouleau du cuivre provennant de la grotte 3 (3Q15)," in M. Baillet, J.T. Milik et R. de Vaux (eds.), *Les 'Petites grottes' de Qumrân* (DJD, 3; Oxford, 1962), 198–302 (= DJD, 3) A new edition by E. Puech, prepared on the occasion of the restoration of the Scroll by the laboratories of the EDF—Valectra on 1994–1996, is soon to appear in the Series STDJ.

[2] P. Muchowski, "Bibliography of the Copper Scroll (3Q15)," *Folia Orientalia* 26 (1989) 65–70 lists the most important publications up to the 1980's. The following titles complete this bibliography up to 2002.

M. Bar-Ilan, "The Process of Writing the Copper Scroll," in *Copper Scroll Studies*, 198–209. K. Beyer, *Die aramäischen Texte vom Toten Meer. Ergänzungsbad* (Göttingen, 1994) (3Q15: *Die Kupferrolle*, 224–233). G.J. Brooke and P.R. Davies (eds.), *Copper Scroll Studies* (JSPSup, 40; Sheffield, 2002). R. Bertholon, N. Lacoudre, J. Vasquez, "The Conservation and Restoration of the Copper Scroll from Qumran," in *Copper Scroll Studies*, 12–24. P.R. Davies, "John Allegro and the Copper Scroll," in *Copper Scroll Studies*, 25–36. H. Eshel, "Aqueducts in the Copper Scroll," in *Copper Scroll Studies*, 92–107. J.E. Elwolde, "3Q15: Its Linguistic Affiliation, with Lexicographical Comments," in *Copper Scroll Studies*, 108–121. R. Fidler, "*Inclusio* and Symbolic Geography in the Copper Scroll," in *Copper Scroll Studies*, 210–225. F. García Martínez – E.J.C. Tigchelaar, *The Dead Sea Scrolls. Study Edition* (Leiden-Grand Rapids, 2000) (3Q15, Vol. I, 232–239). S. Goranson, "Sectarianism, Geography, and the Copper Scroll," *JJS* 43 (1992) 282–287; *Id.*, "Further Reflections on the Copper Scroll," in *Copper Scroll Studies*, 226–231. J.E. Harper, "26 Tons of Gold and 65 Tons of Silver," *BAR* 19 (1993) 44–45. F. Jiménez Bedman, "Los términos (סום y סמה) en el *Rollo de Cobre* (3Q15)," *Miscelánea de Estudios Arabes y Hebreos* 45 (1996) 27–35; *Id.*, "Lexical Analysis of the Copper Scroll from the Perspective of Mishnaic

One of the characteristic of the scholarly work of Ton Hilhorst, since his seminal *Semitismes et Latinismes in the Pastor of Hermas*,[3] has been the search for cross-fertilisation among the Classical and Semitic cultures. It seems fitting, therefore, to honour his 65th birthday by looking once again at another unique feature of this composition:

Hebrew," in J. Targarona and A. Sáenz Badillos (eds.), *Jewish Studies at the Turn of the 20th Century. Volume I* (Leiden, 1998), 27–35; *Id.*, "El misterio del Rollo de Cobre (3Q15)," en J. Trebolle Barrera (ed.), *Paganos, Judíos y Cristianos en los Textos de Qumrán* (Trotta: Madrid, 1999), 229–241; *Id.*, *El misterio del Rollo de Cobre de Qumrán. Análisis lingüístico* (Biblioteca Midrásica, 25; Estella, 2002). W. Johnson, "Professor Henry Wright Baker: The Copper Scroll and his Career," in *Copper Scroll Studies*, 37–44. I. Knohl, "New Light on the Copper Scroll and 4QMMT," in *Copper Scroll Studies*, 233–256. A. Lange, "The Meaning of *Demaᶜ* in the Copper Scroll and Ancient Jewish Literature," in *Copper Scroll Studies*, 122–138. J.M. Laperrousaz, "Méthodologie et datation des mansucrits de la mer Morte: le *Rouleau de cuivre* 3Q15," in G. Brooke and F. García Martínez (eds.), *New Qumran Texts and Studies* (STDJ, 15; Leiden, 1994), 233–241. J.K. Lefkovits, *The Copper Scroll (3Q15): A Reevaluation, A New Reading, Translation, and Commentary* (STDJ, 25; Leiden, 1999); *Id.*, "The Copper Scroll Treasure: Fact or Fiction? The Abbreviation ככ versus ככרין," in *Copper Scroll Studies*, 139–154. B. Lesley Segal, "The Copper Scroll: Novel Approaches," in *Copper Scroll Studies*, 271–275. J. Lübbe, "The Copper Scroll and Language Issues," in *Copper Scroll Studies*, 155–162. M. Lunderberg and B. Zuckerman, "When Images Meet: The Potential of Photographic and Computer Imaging Technology for the Study of the Copper Scroll," in *Copper Scroll Studies*, 45–57. P. Mandel, "On the Duplicate Copy of the Copper Scroll (3Q15)," *RevQ* 16 (1993), 74. P.K. McCarter, "The Mysterious Copper Scroll. Clues to Hidden Temple Treasure," *Bible Review* 8/4 (1992), 34–41; *Id.*, "The Copper Scroll Treasure as an Accumulation of Religious Offerings," in M.O. Wise et al. (eds), *Methods of Investigation of the Dead Sea Scrolls and the Khirbet Qumran Site. Present Realities and Future Prospects* (Annals of the New York Academy of Sciences, 722; New York, 1994), 461–463. L. Morawiecki, "The Copper Scroll Treasure: a Fantasy or Stock Inventory? *Qumran chronicle* 4 (1994) 169–74. P. Muchowski, *Zwój miedziany (3Q15). Implikacje spornych kwestii lingwistycznych* (International institute of Ethnolinguistic and Oriental Studies, Monograph Series, 4; Postnan, 1993); *Id.*, "Dysorthographic Forms *hapôn* and *ᶜakôn* on 3Q15," in Z. Kapera (ed.), *Intertestamental Essays in Honour of Józef Tadeusz Milik* (Qumranica Moglianensia, 6; Krakow, 1992), 131–133; *Id.*, "Language of the Copper Scroll in the Light of Phrases Denoting the Directions of the World," in *Methods of Investigation of the Dead Sea Scrolls and the Khirbet Qumran Site*, 319–327; *Id.*, "Two Proposals of Reading in the Eight Column of 3Q15," *The Qumran Chronicle* 4 (1994) 183–185; *Id.*, "The Origin of 3Q15: Forty Years of Discussion," in *Copper Scroll Studies*, 257–270. S.J. Pfann, "*Kelei Demaᶜ*: Tithe Jars, Scroll Jars and Cookie Jars," in *Copper Scroll Studies*, 163–179. E. Puech, "Quelques résultats d'un nouvel examen du Rouleau de Cuivre (3Q15)," *RevQ* 18 (1997) 163–190; *Id.*, "Some Results of the Restoration of the Copper Scroll by EDF Mécénat," in L. Schiffman et al. (eds.), *The Dead Sea Scrolls Fifty years After Their Discovery* (Jerusalem, 2000), 884–894; *Id.*, "Some Results of a New Examination of the Copper Scroll (3Q15), in *Copper Scroll Studies*, 58–89. L.H. Schiffman, "The Architectural Vocabulary of the Copper Scroll and the Temple Scroll," in *Copper Scroll Studies*, 180–195. H. Stegemann, *Die Essener, Qumran, Johannes der Täufer und Jesus. Ein Sachbuch.* (Freiburg, 1993), 104–108. B. Thiering, "The Copper Scroll: King's Herod Bank Account?," in *Copper Scroll Studies*, 276–287. L. Tov, "Some

the presence of Greek words in Hebrew clothing. Greek loanwords are nothing unusual in the Hebrew and Aramaic literature of the time,[4] and they represent a constant feature in later Rabbinic literature.[5] In the Qumran collection of manuscripts, however, the *Copper Scroll* is the only place in which they appear. The assertion of E. Qimron: "There are no Greek and Latin loans, though some scholars consider such words as מגדל 'tower' as denoting a military structure to be Greek or Latin loan translations,"[6] remains true even today, after the publication of the totality of the manuscripts. As a token of friendship to Ton, I would like to bring together the elements of this unique feature of the *Copper Scroll* and to offer some reflections thereupon.

Palaeographical Observations Regarding the Cover Art," in *Copper Scroll Studies*, 288–290. M.O. Wise, "David J. Wilmot and the Copper Scroll," in *Copper Scroll Studies*, 291–310. A. Wolters, "The Copper Scroll and the Vocabulary of Mishnaic Hebrew," *RevQ* 14 (1990) 483–495; *Id.*, "Apocalyptic and the Copper Scroll," *JNES* 49 (1990) 145–154; *Id.*, "Literary Analysis and the Copper Scroll," in Z. Kapera (ed.), *Intertestamental Essays in Honour of Józef Tadeusz Milik*, 339–352; *Id.*, "History and the Copper Scroll," in *Methods of Investigation of the Dead Sea Scrolls and the Khirbet Qumran Site*, 285–298; *Id.*, *The Copper Scroll: Overview, Text and Translation* (Sheffield, 1996); *Id.*, "The Shekinah in the Copper Scroll: A New Reading of 3Q15 12.10," in S. Porter and C.A. Evans (eds.), *The Scrolls and the Scriptures: Qumran Fifty Years After* (JSPSup, 26; Sheffield, 1997), 282–291; *Id.*, "*The Copper Scroll*," in P. Flint and J. VanderKam (eds.), *The Dead Sea Scrolls after Fifty Years: A Comprehensive Assessment*. Vol. I (Leiden, 1998), 302–323; *Id.*, "Copper Scroll," in L.H. Schiffman and J.C. VanderKam (eds.), *Encyclopedia of the Dead Sea Scrolls*. Vol. I (New York, 2000), 144–148; *Id.*, "Palaeography and Literary Structure as Guides to Reading the Copper Scroll," in *Copper Scroll Studies*, 311–333.

[3] A. Hilhorst, *Sémitismes et latinismes dans le Pasteur d'Hermas* (Græcitas Christianorum Primæva 5; Nijmegen, 1976).

[4] In the list of musical instruments which appears in Daniel 3:5.7.10 and 15, some of the musical instruments carry Greek nouns. It includes three stringed instruments with Aramaic names taken from Greek: קיתרוס (according to the *Ketib*, the *Qere* reads קתרוס) which is obviously the zither, from κιθάρις or κιθάρα; סבכא, from σαμβύκη, a small triangular harp, the Latin *sambuca*; פסנתרין, from ψαλτήριον, the psaltery, a stringed instrument with a *testudo* or sounding board above the strings, the Latin *psalterium*. We also find the סומפניה, from Greek συμφωνία, the double flute or bagpipe. See P. Grelot, "L'orchestre de Daniel III, 5,7,10,15," *VT* 29 (1979) 23–38. For a very convenient comparison of the names given in the different witness, see K. Koch and M. Rösel, *Polyglottensynopse zum Buch Daniel* (Neukirchen-Vluyn, 2000), 60–69.

[5] S. Krauss, *Griechische und Lateinische Lehnwörter im Talmud, Midrasch und Targum*, I–II (Berlin, 1898–1899) (reprint Olms, Hildesheim, 1964). Even if one accepts the meaning of Immanuel Löw, who revised the work and prepared the Register, and who reduces the quantity of loanwords (vol. II, p. 622), there remain more than enough to prove my point.

[6] E. Qimron, *The Hebrew of the Dead Sea Scrolls* (Harvard Semitic studies, 29; Atlanta, GA. 1986), 117.

There can be no doubt that both the author and the engraver of the *Copper Scroll* were somehow familiar with the Greek language, a fact made evident by the presence of groups of Greek letters at the end of certain entries in the first columns of the Scroll. These letters (always in groups of two or three) are placed at the end of the line[7] and, with one exception,[8] are clearly separated from the Hebrew text by a longer or shorter empty space. On all but one occasion[9] these letters follow the expression of a quantity, be it in numerical symbols (on three occasions)[10] or in numbers (on three other occasions).[11] For this reason, Ullendorf suggested we read these letters as expressions of numerical value.[12] While it is true that Greek letters were used (like Roman or Hebrew letters) to express numerical values,[13] the values of the Greek letters used in the *Copper Scroll* do not correspond to the values expressed in the document in Hebrew.[14] In addition, it is completely unclear why, after having clearly expressed the value of the hidden treasures in Hebrew, the author would again repeat the same value cryptically in Greek. B. Thiering[15] suggests a variant of this interpretation which gives numerical value to the Greek letters but this is even less plausible. According to her they are intended to refer to separate deposits of Greek coins, the quantity of which being indicated by the central letter (gold), by the right letter (silver) and the left letter (copper) respectively. But this system is not attested elsewhere and the relationship to the precious metals seems completely arbitrary. Most scholars consider the letters to be abbreviations of Greek names. This interpretation was first proposed

---

[7] Col. 1:4 : KEN; col. 1:12: ΧΑΓ; col 2:2: HN; col. 2:4 ΘE; col. 2:9: ΔI; col.3:7: TP; col. 4:2: ΣK (Milik, DJD 3, 288, considers the first letter uncertain: "La première lettre grecque est un σ, χ, ξ en surcharge sur une autre lettre?" DJD, 3, 288. ΣK is read by Allegro, *The Treasure*, 39, and by all other editions.

[8] In 2:4, where ΘE is written directly after the number sixty five, וחמש ששין, because the Hebrew text extends practically to the end of the line. E. Ullendorf, "The Greek Letters of the Copper Scroll," *VT* 11 (1961) 227–228, reads the letters as ΞE in order to obtain the value sixty-five in Greek, but, although badly written, the reading of Θ can be considered palaeographycally assured.

[9] In 1:12 where it follow the description of the place, "the cave of the ablutions."

[10] In 2:2 (42 ככרין), 3:7 (40 ככ), and 4:2 (14[. . .] ככ)

[11] In 1:4: (seventeen ככרין), 2:2 (sixty-five עשתות זהב), 2:9 (ten ככרין),

[12] Ullendorf, "The Greek Letters," 227: "Connection between the numerical values of these letters and their context is too striking to invoke mere coincidence."

[13] Their use is well attested even on Jewish coins.

[14] See Lefkovits, *The Copper Scroll*, 499 and 502 for a comparison of the values given by Ullendorf and the current values of the preserved letters.

[15] Thiering, "The Copper Scroll: King's Herod Bank Account?," 287.

by B. Pixner[16] who understood them as the names of the people responsible for the treasures in the Jerusalem area and identified them with people mentioned in the writings of Josephus. Pixner's hypothesis has been adopted or adapted by many other scholars.[17]

Although for the present author, as for other scholars like Milik[18] or Lefkovits,[19] the precise meaning of these letters cannot be ascertained, their presence on the scroll provides a solid proof that both the author and the engraver of the *Copper Scroll* were somehow familiar with the Greek language. This is thus sufficient to seriously consider the possible presence of Greek loanwords in the *Copper Scroll*.[20]

1. DELIMITATION OF THE GREEK LOANWORDS

Although the majority of scholars agree that the *Copper Scroll* does indeed contain a number of Greek loanwords, the precise number is difficult to ascertain. There is as yet no consensus on the number of Greek loanwords in the manuscript or on the identity of the words that should be considered as such. The reason for this uncertainty is related to some of the problems posed by the manuscript itself.

The first problem is caused by the peculiar writing of the manuscript and by its support. Cross has classified this script among the

---

[16] B. Pixner, "Unravelling the Copper Scroll Code. A Study on the Topography of 3Q15," *RevQ* 11/43 (1983) 323–361, p. 335

[17] For example, Beyer, *Ergänzungsband*, 225–227, who keeps three of the names proposed by Pixner and changes the four others; H. Stegemann, *Die Essener*, 107–108, who understands the names as corresponding to the owners of the deposits kept in the Temple treasury and described in the *Copper Scroll* (for items 1 and 4 members of the House of Abbiadene, mentioned by Josephus); for L. Tov, "Palaeographical Observations" 289–290, who assumes no less than 25 different scribes at work on the *Copper Scroll*, the Greek letters would be the signatures of the experts who filled the value of the hidden treasure inscribed by the scribes who have written the place only known to them where the treasures were buried.

[18] DJD, 3, 221: "Je n'ai trouvé aucune explication plausible pour la présence et la signification de ces syllabes grecques dispersées dans un document hébreu."

[19] Lefkovits, *The Copper Scroll*, 504: "Thus, the significance and mystery of the Greek letters in the Scroll may remain unsolved."

[20] Since the origin of the *Copper Scroll* and its relationship to the other documents found at Qumran is still a much disputed matter, recourse to the presence of Greek manuscripts in caves 4 and 7 of Qumran and in other finds of the Desert of Judah (for a complete list of those Greek documents cf. DJD, 39, 215–220), or the use of some Greek letters in the cryptic alphabet used in 4Q186 would not suffice to prove the case.

"Vulgar semiformal" Herodian hands, with a mix of formal and cursive forms." While he notes that this script is well adapted to be inscribed on hard surfaces, he also recognises that "the script of the Copper Document exhibits an excessively wide variety of letter forms."[21] This variety of forms (which has lead Lefkovits to postulate "several scribes"[22] and L. Tov to suggest no less than 25 different hands at work in its 12 columns),[23] together with the practically identical form of several letters, such as *b/k, d/r, h/ḥ, w/y/z*, etc. has resulted in a wild variety of readings of many words. The additional fact that the scribe does not always separate words (more often than not, in fact, he employs a sort of *scriptio continua*), frequently uses medial forms of several letters in final position (always in the case of *mem*) and often uses final forms in medial position, has simply encouraged the multiplicity of readings. Finally, some of the phonetic characteristics apparent in the document, such as the obvious weakening of the gutturals *'/h* and *'/ḥ* (which has also affected the *r*), the neutralisation of the *r/n*, the confusion of the sibilants *s/š*, or the substitution of the sonorous *g/k*, have lead the copyist to confound several letters. This element, together with the real (or assumed) errors introduced during the process of copying the document, has led to an even greater multiplication of readings proposed by the scholars.[24]

As a result of these factors, the document has been transcribed in a variety of often widely differing ways. This has led in turn to several different proposals suggesting loanwords for words in the text that would appear to be foreign to the Hebrew language. What follows is a list of the Greek and Latin loanwords that have been identified so far, in the chronological order of the publications in which the identifications appeared, starting with the book of John Allegro.

---

[21] F.M. Cross on DJD, 3, 217.

[22] J. Lefkovits *The Copper Scroll*, 454: "Several scribes were involved in engraving the Copper Scroll, a fact reflected in the script."

[23] L. Tov, "Palaeographical Observations," 288: "I suggest that the scroll was not written by one scribe, as is generally assumed by scholars, but by 25 different ones."

[24] For examples of these phonetic changes in the *Copper Scroll* see F. Jiménez Bedman, *El misterio del Rollo de Cobre*, 154–162.

1.1 *Allegro 1960*

Although Allegro's interest was centred on the topographical identification of the locations mentioned in the *Copper Scroll* and the potential discovery of the treasures to which it refers, his notes to the
translation of the published transcription recognise the following words
as loanwords:

פרסטלון περίστυλον. Allegro reads in 1:6–7: "šbḥṣr hyrsṭlwn" and
translates "which is in the Court of the Peristyle."[25] His note to the
passage leaves no doubt about the identification of פרסטלון as a
Greek loanword from περίστυλον: "= *peristulon* 'a colonnade round
a temple or the court of a house,' and thus here the Outer Court,
or Court of the Gentiles, surrounded by porticoes."[26]

איסתרין στατήρ. Allegro reads in 9:3: "'ystryn 'rbʿ" and translates
"four staters"[27] from the Greek στατήρ, as his note makes explicit:
"'(y)styr = Gk *stater* = the old shekel = the common (provincial *selaʿ*
or *tetradrachma*.")[28]

אסטאנ στοά. The final nun is clearly written in the medial form.[29]
Allegro reads in 11:2: "h'sṭ'n" which he translates as "Portico" and
again his note to the word makes clear he has identified it as the
Greek loanword στοά: "Red. *sṭ'n* for *'ysṭb', y'sṭww'* (Jastr. *Dict.* 54ᵃ);
Syr *'esṭʿwa'* = Gk *stoa* 'porch, portico.'"[30]

אכסדרנ ἐξέδρα. Also here the final nun is clearly written in the
medial form. Allegro has recognised this loanword in 11:3 and 11:5,
reading respectively "h'ksdrn" and "b'ksdr'".[31] The notes on both
these words are very instructive. With respect to 11:2 he writes:
"Rdg. *'ksdrn* for *'ksdr'* (cf. n. 263), GK *exedra*; as the vestibule of a
tomb chamber" while in the second: "Rgd. *b'ksdr'* for text's *bhkshr'*
(the *r* has been inserted above and between de *h* and the *'aleph*; for
the confusion of *ḥ* [sic] and *d*, cf. n. 84)."[32] This means in practice

---

[25] Allegro, *The Treasure*, 33. The omission of the *p* on his transcription (*hyrsṭlwn*)
is certainly a printing error.

[26] *Ibid.*, 136.

[27] *Ibid.*, 49.

[28] *Ibid.*, 157.

[29] *Ibid.*, 53. The final *nun* is clearly written as medial, a phenomenon which happens often in this scroll: באמצענ 4:7; שבעינ 4:12; ככרינ 7:16; מנ 9:10; האכסדרנ 11:3,
with no apparent reason, since on many other occasions the final form is employed.

[30] *Ibid.*, 164.

[31] *Ibid.*, 53.

[32] *Ibid.*, 164.

that he has adapted the clear reading of the manuscript in line 5
to his reading of the word in line 3.

In addition to these four Greek loanwords, Allegro also suggested
a couple of loanwords from Latin. In 1:9 he reads "w'pwryn" and
notes: "'*apwryn* for '*ampôrîn* = *amphora*" "two handled vase, pitcher,
used for oil, wine, honey, etc."[33] The word is indeed known as a
Latin loanword in Rabbinic literature, although the *nun* is not elided:
אנפורין may be a variant plural form (the attested form is feminine
אנפוראות). Also with *nun* אנפוריא or אנפורין is also attested as a Greek
loanword from ἐμπορία.[34] The reading of *-yn*, however, seems palaeo-
gaphically very difficult. Beyer, who also recognises the word as a
Latin loanword, prefers the more plausible reading ואמפורת with a *-t*
in place of the *-yn*, and translates "(25 Liter-)Amphoren."[35] Milik
reads ואמפורד, which seems palaeographically equally possible since it
is difficult to distinguish *d* and *r*.[36]

The other Latin loanword identified by Allegro (ביא *via*) does not
seem necessary, since the Hebrew word (which should be read either
בבואה or בביאה, in both cases from the verb בוא, "when coming,"
or "at the entrance") makes sense on its own. In 5:13 Allegro reads:
"bby' hmzrḥy" which he translates: "in the eastern road."[37] The corresponding note explains the reason: "Rdg. *biyyā'* (= latin *via*) "road,
highway" here appar. masc., rather than *bî'ah* 'entrance,' in which
case the defining *mzrḥy* would lack both art. and fem. termination."[38]
The separation between the *he*, which in this instance is attached to
the preceding *aleph* but clearly separated from the following *mem*, has
no basis in the manuscript, not even according to Allegro's drawing, and the grammatical problem which forces him to make the
separation is non-existent; it is due to his reading of *zayin* instead of
yod in the following word. If this word is read (with Milik and the
majority of other scholars) as מירחו "from Jericho," there is no reason to introduce *via* into the text.

Allegro thus clearly recognised four Greek loanwords in the *Copper
Scroll*: περίστυλον, στατήρ, στοά, and ἐξέδρα. He was very close to

---

[33] *Ibid.*, 137.
[34] Krauss, *Griechische und Lateinische Lehnwörter*, II, 61; M. Jastrow, *A Dictionary of the Targumim, the Talmud Babli and Yerushalmi, and the Midrashic Literature*, I, 87.
[35] Beyer, *Ergänzungsband*, 225–226,
[36] DJD, 3, 284
[37] Allegro, *The Treasure*, 41.
[38] *Ibid.*, 140.

identifying a fifth: λάγηνος or λάγυνος. In 1:9 he reads: "blgyn" and translates "of *lôg* vessels."[39] In his note to the passage, Allegro suggests we read בלגין as a plural or plural form of the Biblical *lôg*, a liquid measure used in the Temple, the contents of which would amount to about one pint. The same note also suggests, however, the alternative reading of the word as the singular, *lagîn*: "or rd. sing. *lagîn* 'flagon,' [smaller than a *kad* 'jug, pitcher' (cf. VII 16) and larger than a *kôs* 'cup.']"[40] without specifying that this word ultimately entered the Hebrew language via the Greek λάγηνος or λάγυνος, and has been considered by other scholars to be an additional Greek loanword (as we will see later).

1.2 *Milik 1962*

The "Préface" of DJD 3 (which has a copyright date in 1962) is signed by De Vaux in 1959, prior thus to the publication of Allegro's book in 1960. A curious note by the author on an "Addenda à 3Q15" indicates that he knew Allegro's book but that he decided to ignore it.[41] The fact is that the four Greek loanwords noted by Allegro, appear as such in the DJD edition. Milik recognises "cinq ou six emprunts grecs"[42] in the *Copper Scroll*. In practical terms, Milik adds one Greek loanword he considers certain and one he considers possible to Allegro's list.

Milik's notes add some precision to the summary identifications of Allegro. On the first (פרסטלין in 1:7, as read by Milik) he notes: "'petit péristyle', i 7 (D 64) reproduit fidèlement le diminutif grec περιστύλιον. Ni ce mot ni περίστυλον ne sont pas attestés par les écrits talmudiques; un seul exemple fort douteux, qui exige d'ailleurs une correction, est proposé par S. Krauss, *Griechische und lateinische Lehnwörter im Talmud, Midrasch und Targum*, ii, p. 496."[43] A little further, explaining the whole expression, he writes: "הצר פרסטלין de i 6 s.

---

[39] *Ibid.*, 33.
[40] *Ibid.*, 137. The reference to *kad* in 7:16 is based on a faulty reading of בכדין instead of ככרין.
[41] "J'ai ajouté aux épreuves un certain nombre de références aux études parues après l'envoi du mansucrit à l'éditeur. Je ne tiens pourtant pas compte du livre de J.M. Allegro, *The Treasure of the Copper Scroll*, Londres, 1960, et cela pour des raisons qu'on pourra deviner en lisant les remarques de R. de Vaux dans la *Revue Biblique*, lxviii, 1961, pp. 146 s." DJD, 3, 299.
[42] DJD, 3, 230 (B 14).
[43] DJD, 3, 248 (C 104).

n'est probablement pas la 'Cour des péristyles', pluriel sémitique de περίστυλον mais plutôt la simple traduction de περιστύλιον (prononcé même en grec *peristülin*) 'petit péristyle.'"[44] Both notes are, apparently, intended as a correction of the reading פרסטלון by Allegro and of the Greek word he proposed (περίστυλον), although, as already noted, Allegro is never mentioned.

On the second loanword noted by Allegro (אסתרין in 9:3, which Milik translates by "livres") he indicates: "(ן)אסתר de ix 3 est évidemment égal à mishnique et araméen (א)אסתר, emprunté au grec στατήρ 'statère, tétradrachme (ou didrachme)'. Mais ce poids est trop léger comparé à ceux des autres trésors du catalogue . . . Encore mieux, en partant de l'équivalence στατήρ = λίτρα (H.G. Liddell et R. Scott, *A Greek English Lexicon, s.v.* στατήρ), on songera à la livre romaine, dont le poids était assez proche de la mine."[45] Also here, Milik seems to dismiss Allegro's calculations, increasing the value of the hidden treasures.

Milik does not expend much time on the third loanword, אסטא στοά in 11:2. He translates the word by "portique," notes that the word exhibits the usual prosthetic vowel, keeps the hiatus (without replacing it by a consonant, as in some rabbinic texts which reproduce the word as אסטבא) and has probably a masculine form in *-an*.[46] As for its location, he identifies it with ἡ στοὰ τοῦ Σολομῶνος of the New Testament, and not with the αἱ μεγάλαι στοαί of Josephus *JW* 1, 401.

On האכסדרן in 11:3 which he translates by "vestibule" he notes: "אכסדרן, de xi 3 c'est encore une partie du monument des Bene Sadoq (D 40). Le terme *'aksadran* de 3Q15 est synonyme du mishnique *'aksadra* (voir B 14f), emprunté au grec ἐξέδρα 'réduit, salle, fermés de trois côtés et ouverts sur un des côtés longs'. Cette définition s'applique bien à un vestibule d'hypogée, peu profond et avec un pilier au milieu."[47] The second use of "exedra" found by Allegro on 11:5, is read differently (and more correctly) by Milik as בהבסה ראש.

To these four Greek loanwords Milik adds a fifth, reading לאה in 11:14 as a Greek loanword from ἀλόη. The line in question is fraught with difficulties, among other things the repetition of the word דמע which appears twice written as דם and is only corrected the second

[44] DJD, 3, 273 (D 64).
[45] DJD, 3, 253 (C 149).
[46] DJD, 3, 230 (B 14).
[47] DJD, 3, 246–247 (C 84).

time with an infralineal *'ayin*. For Milik לאה would be the complete form of the word, and explains the difference with the usual way the word is transcribed in Hebrew and Aramaic literature (אלוה, אלאן, or other forms, but always beginning with an *aleph*): "לאה de xi 14 cache, sur une graphie particulière (voir B 71 et 14a), le grec ἀλόη (synonyme: ἀγάλλοχον), nom du bois d'aloès dont les espèces les plus appreciées étaient l'Aloëxylon Agallochon Lour' et 'Aquilaria Agallocha Roxb.'"[48]

Milik's sixth possible Greek loanword is a fragmentary reading in 3:1 ⁰יאט[. The word comes from one of the isolated fragments that were detached from the scroll, and the original has been apparently lost.[49] Milik does not give his reasons for considering the word as a possible Greek loanword, but he is probably guided by the ending in אט-, and by the fact that חצר is used governing the word פרסטלין on other occasion, as we have already seen. This uncertainty does not stop him from identifying the structure to which it refers, and he translates the phrase בהצ[ר. .]⁰יאט "Dans le Parvi[s du *péri*]*bole*." He is equally assertive in his comments: "Le nom du péribole du sanctuaire, בהצ[ר. .]⁰יאט en iii 1, malheureusement incomplet, semble être d'origine grecque." and "Le nom du péribole du Temple יאט . . . iii 1 (D 55), malheureusement acéphale, est sans doute emprunté au grec, cf. B 14e."[50]

In practical terms, thus, Milik suggests that we change one of the Greek words recognised by Allegro to περιστύλιον instead of περίστυλον and adds a new word to the list ἀλόη.

Milik also identifies a Persian loanword in the Scroll, the already mentioned בלנין from 1:9. He translates the word as "bois de santal," and notes: "בלנין de i 9 désigne le bois aromatique de santal dont la plus importante espèce est le 'Santalum album L.' Le mot est emprunté au sanscrit *valgu*, qui reparaît en Syriaque sous la forme *'blwg*."[51] Precisely this loanword, however, is consider by J.C. Greenfield "as a particularly bad example of a methodological flaw in the lexicography used in this list" by Milik.[52] Greenfield concludes his analysis

---

[48] DJD, 3, 251 (C 128).
[49] DJD, 3, 287 and 212.
[50] DJD, 3, 274 (D 55) and 248 (C 103) respectively.
[51] DJD, 3, 251 (C 127).
[52] J.C. Greenfield, "The Small Caves from Qumran," *JAOS* 89 (1969) 128–141, p. 138 (reprinted in *'Al Kanfei Yonah. Collected Studies of Jonas C. Greenfield on Semitic Philology* (Leiden-Jerusalem, 2001) vol. II, 573–594, p. 589.

of Milik's discussion with the question: "What then is *blgyn* of 3Q15? The answer is *b* 'in' *lgyn*, a 'small flask or vessel' used during this period. The word is frequent in Mishnaic Hebrew and is borrowed from Greek *lágēnos*. Instead of a new aromatic to add to our list, we have simply 'in a flask.'"[53] The alternative suggestion by Allegro is here clearly stated and בלגין is considered as a Greek loanword from λάγηνος.

1.3 *Beyer 1994*

Although dedicated to the study of the Aramaic texts from the Dead Sea, the supplement to the *opus magnum* of K. Beyer also contains a new transcription and translation of the Hebrew letters of Bar Kokbah and of the *Copper Scroll*.[54] While the format of his book does not allow for explanations, Beyer's translations take care to mark the loanwords, writing them in Greek or in Latin (within brackets) after his German translation. In this way he also notes the resolution of the abbreviations of Greek letters with Greek names. As for the loanwords, a reading of his translation gives the following results:[55]

—"im Hof des kleinen Säulenganges (περιστύλιον)" (1:7)
—"Im (halbkreisförmigen?) Hof [des Laur]eatus (oder: [des Νικ]ίατος o.ä)" (3:1)
—"Kästen (αἱ χηλοί) (5:6)
—"Silberstater(στατῆρες)-Großbarren (9:3)
—"der Säulemnhalle" (ἡ στοά) (11:2)
—"der kleinen Vorhalle (τὸ ἐξέδριον) (11:3)
—"Priesterabgabe ('>'; *a'a* = *ā*) von Aloe" (11:14)

In practical terms, Beyer recognises the four loanwords common to Allegro and Milik, as well as the one proposed by Milik, ἀλόη (although offering a different explanation in order to account for the lack of the *aleph*), resolves the tentative proposal of Milik on 3:1 as a Greek personal name (similar to the Mannos of 1:13 which he also considers as a possible Greek personal name: "(Μάνες, Μένης, Μηνᾶς u.a.),"[56] opts for Milik's reading of περιστύλιον and suggest

---

[53] *Ibid.*, 138–139 [590].
[54] K. Beyer, *Ergänzungsbad* (Göttingen, 1994), 4: "Wegen ihres starken aramäischen Einschlags sind auch neuhebräische Briefe des Simon bar Kosiba (→ N 216) und wegen ihrer Angaben über die Essenerniederlassungen die neuhebräische Kupferrolle beigefügt (→ N 224)."
[55] *Ibid.*, 226–232.
[56] *Ibid.*, 226.

that אסתרין would represent the genitive form στατῆρες and not the plural. He does not mark בלנין ואפורה as loanwords but his translation "und zwar (Halbliter-)Flaschen und (25-Liter-)Amphoren" allows us to consider them as such. He likewise clearly adds a new loanword in 5:6: כאלין from χηλος, not considering the *aleph* as a simple *plene* form of the usual כלין (as it appears on 2:6.8 and 10:11) as Allegro,[57] nor as an exceptional effort of orthographically marking the full vowel *e* in medial position with an *alep* as Milik[58] or Thorion,[59] but as a completely different word.

1.4 *Puech 1997*

Although Puech has not yet published his final transcription and analysis of the *Copper Scroll*, performed on the occasion of the restoration of the scroll with the benefit of new x-ray photographs, direct examination of the original and a new galvanoplastic copy of the scroll in flattened form, he has already published some of his conclusions.[60] Although these publications focus the attention on palaeographical questions and on the discussion of the topographical features of the scroll, his notes show that he has recognised two other Greek loanwords in addition to those noted so far. Both are located in col. 3.

In 3:1 Puech recognises that no reconstruction can be certain because neither the shape nor the distance among the letters of the lost fragment have been recorded.[61] Nevertheless, he proposes that we read the unidentified consonant of Milik's transcription as a *dalet*. Puech calculates that the fragmentary word should consist of four or five letters and that it should be preceded either by the particle של or by the relative -ש (which in the scroll appears on about 31 occasions, mostly combined with the preposition ב in the form -שב

---

[57] Allegro, *The Treasure*, 148.

[58] DJD, 3, 228 (B 5a).

[59] Y. Thorion, "Beiträge zur Erforschung der Sprache der Kupfer-Rolle," *RevQ* 12/46 (1986) 163–1176, p. 168.

[60] E. Puech, "Quelques résultats d'un nouvel examen du Rouleau de Cuivre (3Q15)," *RevQ* 18 (1997) 163–190; *Id.*, "Some Results of the Restoration of the Copper Scroll by EDF Mécénat," in L. Schiffman et al. (eds.), *The Dead Sea Scrolls Fifty years After Their Discovery* (The Shrine of the Book: Jerusalem, 2000), 884–894; *Id.*, "Some Results of a New Examination of the Copper Scroll (3Q15), in *Copper Scroll Studies*, 58–89.

[61] Puech, "Quelques résultats," 171: "L'absence de tout relevé, faisant connaître les espacements et les traces de la lettre précédant le *yod*, interdit une quelconque décision." *Id.*, "Some Results of a New Examination," 67.

preceding a topographical feature), if the incomplete word designates, as assumed by Milik, a place name. Assuming also, for the same reasons as Milik, that the incomplete word should be of Greek origin, he proposes that we read the word as דיאט from the Greek δίαιτα (without any transcription of the vowel ending), which would mean "room, cell, seat of arbitration (or of judgment?)"[62] and reconstruct the sentence בחז]ר של/שב/ש[דיאט. Puech quotes a parallel to the use of this Greek loanword in *Esther Rabbah*, where it has apparently the meaning of "prison" and considers that it could mean "salle, cellule, siège d'arbitrage (ou de jugement?)"

The second loanword proposed by Puech originates in a different reading of a word in 3:9. Allegro has read the word in question as "wlbwhšyn," translated it as "garments,"[63] and noted that the *nun* was lost in the cutting of the segment.[64] Milik prefers to read it as לכושי, without the initial *waw* and the final *nun*. Puech prefers to read ולבישין (changing the *waw* from Allegro to a *yod*) and proposes that we understand the word as a loanword from the Greek λέβες, attested in Aramaic.[65] Puech suggests the meaning "cauldron, funeral urn" and proposes that we read the *waw* inserted before the *lamed* in an "explanatory sense" (in the English article) or "à sens explicatif" (in the French). He does not give a translation of the whole sentence, but if this "explanatory sense" of the copulative *waw* is taken seriously, it would imply that the *demaʿ* vessels in question are "cauldrons or funeral urns."[66]

In practical terms, Puech adds two new Greek loanwords to the list, both in column 3: δίαιτα in 3:1 and λέβες in 3:9. As for the other Greek or Latin loanwords mentioned so far, Peuch confirms Milik's readings of בלנין and ואפודת in 1:9, disapproving thus of Allegro's readings, but without any pronouncement on the meaning of the words or their origins. He does not comment on Beyer's reading כאלין and its interpretation on the basis of χηλος, nor on the other loanwords proposed by other scholars, except in the case of ἀλόη in 11:14. Here, Puech discusses several possibilities of reading

---

[62] *Ibid.*, 171 and 67 respectively.

[63] Allegro, *The Treasure*, 37. As his drawing and translation clearly show, the *he* is clearly a printing error, as is the omission of the *ayin* of the preceding word (*dm* for *dmʿ*).

[64] *Ibid.*, 142.

[65] Krauss, *Griechische und Lateinische Lehnwörter*, II, 303.

[66] Puech, "Quelques résultats," 172; "Some Results of a New Examination," 68.

and interpretation, but in the end he remains undecided, although with a slight preference for Milik's interpretation, but with Allegro's reading (unless we have here a typing error of the letters *he* and *ḥet* on which the readings of Allegro (לאה) and Milik (לאה) differ, as suggested by Puech's translation). I quote from the English version:[67]

> In line 14, one can envisage two possibilities for errors: either the passage of the sequence *mᶜ* to *ml* by haplography in the process of reading-engraving (notice the oblique stroke of the foot of the *lamedh*, which juts out), and one should therefore read *dm[[ᶜ m]]Ph*, 'imposi[tion of gr]ain', or, with the passing of the beginning of the *ayin* to the foot of the *lamedh* over the first downstroke of an *aleph*, the read *dm[[ᶜ ']]Ph*, 'spic(e of a)loe', which would appear materially better than Milik's proposal *dm[[ᶜ]]Ph*, which presupposes a phonetic haplography of *aleph*, and better than *dm[[ᶜ]]Ph*, 'liquid tithe' (with an unexpected spelling), of Allegro.

In summary: Our review of the scholarly literature has shown that nine words have been identified as loanwords from Greek[68] (of a total of 204 of word used on the *Copper Scroll*, excluding topographical and proper names, and the numerals according to the counting of Jiménez Bedman).[69] These are the nine words in the order in which they appeared in the Scroll: פרסטלין, περίστυλον or פרסטלין περιστύλιον in 1:7; לגין, λάγηνος or λάγυνος in 1:9; דיאט, δίαιτα in 3:1; לביש, λέβης in 3:9; כאלין, χηλός in 5:6; אסתרין, στατήρ in 9:3; אסטאנ, στοά in 11:2; אכסדרנ, εξεδρα in 11:3; לאה, ἀλόη in 11:14

2. SHIFTING THE EVIDENCE

Since scholars tend to disagree on the identification of several of these words, it is necessary to look carefully both at the arguments

---

[67] Puech, "Some Results of a New Examination," 76–77. The earlier French article ("Quelques résultats," 179) seems to give preference to the reading of Milik, while reconstructing the missing *'aleph* in the lacuna: "A la l. 14, on peut envisager deux possibilités d'erreurs: soit le passage de la séquence *mᶜ* à *ml* par haplographie dans les lecture-gravure, voir le trait oblique du pie du *lamed* qui dépasse, et on devrait alors lire *dm[[ᶜ m]]Ph* "impos[ition du gr]ain", soit le passage du début du *'aïn* au pied du *lamed* par dessus le premier jambage d'un *'alef* et lire alors *dm[[ᶜ ']]Ph* 'aroma[te d'a]loès', ce qui paraît matériellement meilleur que la proposition de l'édition *dm[[ᶜ]]Ph* qui suppose une haplographie phonétique du *'alef* ou que *dm[[ᶜ]]Ph* 'liquid tithe' (avec une orthographe inattendue) de Allegro."

[68] Together with two Latin loanwords, "amphora" and "via," which will remain outside of our discussion.

[69] F. Jiménez Bedman, *El misterio del Rollo de Cobre*, 229.

given and the different sets of drawings and photographs available
to us[70] in order to ascertain how many of these words can be considered real loanwords from Greek. Only when its presence has been
established with certainty can we attempt to extract some conclusions from this unique phenomenon.

לאה, ἀλόη in 11:14 presents problems both in terms of reading
and in terms of explaining the Hebrew form of the word if considered a Greek loanword. Since ἀλόη, in all other known cases, is
transcribed in Hebrew with an initial *aleph*, all the scholars who
recognise the presence of the word in the *Copper Scroll* are forced to
assume with Milik that the word is reproduced with a unique orthography (with the *aleph* elided), or to assume with Beyer and Puech
a chain of hypothesis: first the phonetic fusion of *ayin* and *aleph*, and
then the omission of the resulting unique letter (or the omission of
both if the fusion did not take place), because the preceding word
דמ has not been corrected by the inclusion of the missing *ayin* (as
has been done with the following דמע on the same line). Besides,
and this is more important, Milik himself recognises that the final
letter of לאה can be read both as a *he* and as a *ḥet*. Allegro reads
without hesitation a *ḥet*, a reading also adopted by Pixner and Lefkovits
among others.[71] In spite of the similarity of the two letters in many
occurrences on the Scroll, of the uncertainty of Puech's reading and
of his apparent preference for reading a *he* at this juncture, a careful examination of the photographs confirms, in my opinion without doubt, the reading of Allegro and deprives the reading לאה and
consequently (ἀ)λόη of any foundation[72]

דיאט, δίαιτα, proposed by Puech in 3:1 is, of course, purely hypothetical, as he himself recognises, since there are no drawings or
photographs which could prove or disprove the reading, and since

---

[70] Allegro's drawings, Baker's drawing as reproduced on the Plates volume of
DJD, 3, plate XLV, and Milik's corrected drawings as reproduced on the same
volume, the even plates from XLVIII to LXX. As for the photographs, I have used
those of Allegro, as reproduced in microfiche in *The Allegro Qumran Collection*, edited
by G. Brooke (Leiden, 1996), (frames 17–25, with 50 microfiches each), Starcky's
photographs as published in DJD, 3, and as reproduced both in Brill's *Microfiche
Edition* and in *The Dead Sea Scrolls Electronic Reference Library* (PAM 42,977–43.000),
some of the Zuckerman photographs (not all of them were available to me), and
the new photographs contained on a CD-ROM graciously offered by the EDF.
[71] Pixner, "Unravelling the Copper Scroll Code," 356; Lefkovits, *The Copper Scroll*,
384.
[72] Most recently, Lange, "The Meaning of *Demaʿ*," 136 has defended the reading of Milik and the presence of the Greek loanword ἀλόη here.

Milik, the only scholar who actually saw the fragments, was not able to ascertain the fragmentary first letter.[73] Besides, although the word δίαιτα[74] is indeed attested as a Greek loanword in rabbinic literature, mostly, if not always, it appears with a final *alep*, and the meaning given by Krauss varies from "Zimmer, Gemach, Stockwerk" to "Gefängenis,"[75] a meaning which does not seem adapted to a structure with a courtyard as required by the sentence in which the broken word appears, and which would be not exactly "comparable to a 'Roman praetorium, for which the existence of a square can be easily imagined" as Puech would like.[76]

ולבישין, λέβης in 3:9. This word also has been read in different ways, as already indicated. In this case, however, palaeography does not offer a completely satisfactory answer, since both *bet, kaph, waw* and *yod* can be easily confounded in this document. Nevertheless, the photographs assure us of the presence of the *waw* inserted below the *lamed* (not reproduced by Milik),[77] and show a clear distinction of the form of the medial *waw* and the final *yod*, making either the reading ולבושין or the reding ולכושין the most probable. This undermines Puech's reading. The strongest argument against the understanding of this word as a Greek loanword, however, is that in all the examples given by Krauss,[78] the word is always written in Aramaic with *samek*, not with *shin*, a fact not indicated by Puech. Although there are examples of transcription of the Greek *sigma*, be it in initial, medial, or final position, by ש or by צ, by far the commonest transcription is ס, as attested by the other Greek loanwords found in the *Copper Scroll*. Although it is true that in Qumran, and particularly

---

[73] There is also uncertainty as to the number of letters which may be fitted in the missing section. I fail to see, either in the drawings of in the photographs, traces of the *tsade*, reconstructed by Allegro, but transcribed as certain by Milik. Allegro, *The Treasure*, 141 asserts that "After a possible *ḥṣr*, there is room for 3 or 4 letters." Milik's transcription notes 3 letters before the ס (including the unidentified letter) and assumes two others in the lacuna in addition to the reconstructed *resh*, which gives a total of 5 letters for the same space.

[74] Liddell and R. Scott, *Greek-English Lexicon. With a Revised Supplement* (Oxford, 1996), 396, gives four different meanings to the word: (1) way of living, (2) dwelling, abode, room, (3) arbitration, (4) discussion, investigation.

[75] Krauss, *Griechische und Lateinische Lehnwörter*, II, 199.

[76] Puech, "Some Results of a New Examination," 68; *Id.*, "Quelques résultats," 172.

[77] Lange, "The Meaning of *Demaʿ*," 132 considers the stroke under the *lamed* as "a scribal error probably caused by a slip of the chisel" and not as a *waw*.

[78] Krauss, *Griechische und Lateinische Lehnwörter*, II, 303.

in the *Copper Scroll*, ס and שׁ are regularly confused,[79] it is mostly ס which replaces שׁ and not the contrary.[80] Since the alternative, and palaeographically the most probable, reading ולבושין makes perfect sense in Hebrew, there is no need to hypothesise a Greek loanword here.[81]

כאלין on 5:6 is recognised by Beyer as a loanword from χηλός. The reading is undisputed. The problem is posed by the *aleph*, since in all other cases in which the word כלי is used in the Scroll (כלי: 1:9; 3:2.9; 8:3; 11:1.4.10.14; 12:6; כלין: 2:6.8; 10:11; כליה: 1:3; 12:5) it is written without it, and this would thus be the only case in which the word (if identical) will have been written *plene*. Milik's explanation is rather convoluted: the *aleph* would have been used to indicate the full vowel *e* in medial position in order to distinguish it from the *shewa* of the construct state. He recognises that this orthography is exceptional and that in the other uses of the same plural כלין the writer has not differentiated the two vowels in this way[82] (nor has he thus marked the two uses of the word with the suffix כליה). Beyer takes the *aleph* seriously and considers it be a completely different word, proposing αἱ χηλοί, the plural form of χηλός.[83] This seems to the present author to be extremely problematic. Apparently,[84] he is forced to assume the introduction of the loanword in the plural form, in order to explain the Hebrew form, which does not reflect the -*s* ending of the Greek word. This would be most unusual. He is forced also to assume the equivalence of the Greek χ with the Hebrew כ, certainly not impossible, but less usual than its translation by the Hebrew ה. In addition, he is forced to accept Milik's conclusion that the *aleph* represents the vowel *e*. While these elements make Beyer's interpretation highly problematic, the element that definitively excludes this interpretation of כאלין for the present author lies in the fact that χηλός is attested as a Greek loanword in Hebrew clothing in another form. According to Krauss,[85] the word was imported in the singular, as expected, and appears both as חלוז (בחלוזך on *b. Pesah.* 113a)

---

[79] See F. Jiménez Bedman, *El misterio del Rollo de Cobre*, 157–158.

[80] Jiménez Bedman quotes ומעסר שני (1:10–11), לסמל (1:13), עסרא (2:8), and קסאות (3:4) as examples.

[81] This is also the conclusion of Lange, "The Meaning of *Demaʿ*," 133.

[82] DJD, 3, 228 (5 b).

[83] Beyer, *Ergänzungsbad*, 228.

[84] Due to the format of his book, Beyer does not explain his choices.

[85] Krauss, *Griechische und Lateinische Lehnwörter*, II, 251.

and חילש (בחילש in Tg. Zach 11:13). In both cases the vowel *e* is represented by *yod*, the χ is expressed with the Hebrew כ, and the *s* ending is reflected as *zayin* or *shin*. The most simple solution, thus, is to consider the word כאלין as a different orthographic version of כלין, in which the *aleph* has been introduced by error of the engraver (who was prone to use *aleph* in medial position to represent a *patah* or *qames* vowel (in אסטאנ, 11:2 and צהיאת, 11:15).

The reading of בלנין in 1:9 is assured. As we have already seen, Milik considered בלנין as a complete word, meaning "bois de santal," while Allegro proposed that we read it as formed by the preposition *b-* (which he considered as a *beth essentiae*, "consisting of")[86] and a plural form of the Biblical לנ. Lehmann[87] identified the word לנין with the Greek λάγυνος or Latin *lagoena*, though he proposed as alternative a reading of בלנין as פלנין "half-size" "because of the difficulty of translating the כ as 'consisting of.'"[88] Greenfield, who, as we have seen, forcefully insisted that the solution was in the *b* "in," considered לנין as a loanword from λάγηνος.[89] His translation "in a flask" is rather strange, however, when read in the sentence in which it is placed—בלנין כלי דמע and not in the abstract. Since Greenfield understands כלי דמע as "a particular type of jar used for the storage of *terumah* and other types of sacred gifts,"[90] he would have been forced to translate the phrase in question as "jars of *terumah* in a flask," which is certainly difficult to imagine.

Nevertheless, the identification of לנין as a Greek loanword has been widely accepted (most recently by Lange)[91] on the weight of its use in rabbinic literature in contexts dealing with sacred offerings, but apparently without realising the problem posed in this case by its singular form (in rabbinic literature attested both as a masculine form לנין and as a feminine לנינה). In the attested cases of use of the loanword in rabbinic literature the plural form is לנינין (for example *m. Kel.* 16:2, 30:4). Since the following word in the Scroll (be it

[86] Allegro, *The Treasure*, 137.
[87] M.R. Lehmann, "Identification of the *Copper Scroll* based on its technical terms," *RevQ* 5/17 (1964) 97–105, p. 98.
[88] *Ibid.*, p. 99
[89] Greenfield, "The Small Caves from Qumran," 138–139 [590].
[90] *Ibid.*, p. 139 [591]
[91] Lange, "The Meaning of *Demaʿ*," 129, on the basis of his conclusion that only vessels, gold, and silver are weighed in the Scroll. Lange subscribes to Allegro's interpretation of the *b-* as *bet essentiae*. For a complete overview of all the opinions on the matter, see Lefkovits, *The Copper Scrroll*, 518–525.

read as אפורה or as אפודה) is clearly plural and is joined by a *waw*, and the preceding כלי דמע is also plural, the reading of לנין as singular is less than evident, and even more problematic if the preposition *b-* governs both לנין and אפודה. This bring us back to the first suggestion of Allegro, reading לנין as the plural of the Biblical לנ. That the plural of לנ is not attested in Biblical Hebrew is not a difficulty, in view of other previously unattested plurals (like אפודה). The introduction of a Greek loanword does not seems to be required to explain the word. The same conclusion is reached by Lefkovits who translates "dedicated objects consisting of flasks and jars with handles."[92]

Pixner has proposed a different Greek loanword to explain לנין, considered as a singular preceded by a *b-* with a locative meaning "at": λόγιον "oracle."[93] He translates the whole sentence: "tithe vessels (KLY DEMʿ) at (the place) of the Logion (= breast plate) (LGYN) and the ephods (W'PWDOT)." His reasoning is rather convoluted: Josephus, when describing the garments of the high priest on *Ant.* 3. § 163, calls the breast plate ἐσσήν and gives as Greek equivalent of the word λόγιον. Pixner thus concludes that "the CS uses here possibly the Greek term for the highpriestly breast plate which was inserted into its ephod" and that "the tithe vessels were therefore to be looked for near the ephod with breast plate."[94] In my opinion, however, Josephus himself proves that λόγιον cannot be considered the Greek word behind לנין, because after having explained that ἐσσήν is called λόγιον in Greek (proving simply that he is using the LXX, which translates the Hebrew חשן by λογεῖον), he continues to use ἐσσήν and not λόγιον in the rest of his description of the high priest's ornaments (*Ant.* 3. §§ 166. 170. 171. 185). Neither λόγιον nor λάγυνος nor λάγηνος can be considered as established Greek loanwords on the *Copper Scroll*.

This leaves us only the four words recognised from the beginning both by Allegro and by Milik: פרסטלון, περίστυλον or פרסטלין περιστύλιον in 1:7; אסתרין, στατήρ in 9:3; אסטאנ, στοά in 11:2; אכסדרנ, εξεδρα in 11:3. Three of these words belong to the vocabulary of architecture: peristyle, stoa and exedra, and the fourth pertains to the economy: stater. Three of these words are attested as Greek loanwords in rab-

---

[92] *Ibid.*, 73 and 76, where he vocalises the word as *belagin* or *belugin*.
[93] Pixner, "Unravelling the Copper Scroll," 343.
[94] *Ibid.*, 343, note 8.

binic literature (אסטאנ, אכסדרנ and אסתרינ), the last one (פרסטלונ or
פרסטלינ) is not.

אכסדרנ is found often in rabbinic literature, under the feminine
forms אכסדרא or אכסדרה in the singular and אכסדראות in the plural,
and is registered as such in the Dictionaries.[95] The final *nun* (written in medial form) of the form in our manuscript has been diversely
explained. Milik, after having considered (and discarded) the possibility that it may reflect the genitive plural form of the Greek (-ων),
prefers to see it as "l'afformante sémitique *-an* ou *-on*, les deux très
fréquentes dans les emprunts talmudiques."[96] Beyer prefers to give
the *nun* a full value and proposes that we consider the diminutive
τὸ ἐξέδριον ("little exedra") as the Greek word from which the Hebrew
word has been formed. It seems to me easier to connect the addition of the *nun* with the well known phenomenon attested in Galilean
Aramaic and elsewhere of appending a final *nun* to a word which
ended in a vowel,[97] particularly since the same phenomenon seems
to apply to the word אסטאנ, from which no diminutive is at hand
(in this case, Beyer did use this explanation of the final *nun*).[98]

אסתרינ[99] is likewise attested in rabbinic literature, albeit in the
Aramaic singular forms איסתירא or אסתירא, but also איסטרא or איצטרא,
and in the Aramaic plural איסתירי or the Hebrew איצטראות. All these
forms exhibit the incorporation of the prosthetic *aleph* and the same
fusion of consonants which appear in our scroll. The word as used
in the Elephantine papyri (סתתרי, סתתרנ)[100] does not yet exhibit this
incorporation. The form in our manuscript is clearly masculine plural
(as required by the ארבע which follows) as in Elephantine, as opposed
to the feminine form of rabbinic literature.

---

[95] For example, Jastrow, *Hebrew Aramaic Dictionary*, 64; Clines, *The Dictionary of Classical Hebrew*, I, 249.

[96] DJD, 3, 230 (14f).

[97] See E.Y. Kutscher, *Studies in Galilean Aramaic* (Ramat Gan, 1976), 61, with the literature cited therein. Kutscher gives an example from an inscription from Jaffa in which a man is called Ἰουδα (= *ywdh*) in Greek and *ywdn* in Hebrew.

[98] Beyer, *Ergänzungsbad*, 231: Säulenhalle (ἡ στοά + *n*) with a reference to p.149 of the first volume of his work, where he gives many examples in order to prove that "spätestens vom 5. Jh. v. Chr. an wird drucklosen langen Auslautvokalen un Diphtongen teilweise *-n* angefügt."

[99] The reading איסתרינ of Allegro do not seems palaeographically possible; although the reading is somehow indistinct because a vertical fold in the metal, the assumed *yod* seems not to be anything other than the upper part of the *lamed* form the under line which joins the *samek*.

[100] See for the examples B. Porten – A. Yardeni, *Textbook of Aramaic Documents from Ancient Egypt*, I–III (Jerusalem, 1986–1993).

אסטא, as already indicated by Allegro, appears in rabbinic literature but under different forms (with or without *yod* after the *aleph*,
with *samek* or with *tsade* as second consonant, and always with a *beth*
or a *waw* to resolve the hiatus of the Greek word): אסטבא, אצטוא,
אצטבא, and several others, and has various meanings (from a portico
or roofed colonnade, to a balcony or a bench or even a platform).[101]
Although most of the lexicographers acknowledge the equivalence of
the form as attested in the *Copper Scroll* with the forms known from
rabbinic literature and with the Greek στοά, Lefkovits,[102] who summarises all interpretations, prefers to understand the word as related
to אסטן, which appears once in the tractate *Shemaḥot* 13:6 and which
would have the meaning of "ossuary." The rarity of this occurrence,
the uncertainty of its meaning and etymology (it has been derived
from Persian *astodan* "bone holder," or from Greek ὀστῶν "ossuaries"),[103] the fact that he is forced to read it as a plural form (but
translate it as a singular, because otherwise it would not serve as an
identifier), and the impossibility of conciliating this meaning with the
following indication of the place of burial of the cache (under the
pillar or column of Zaok's tomb), makes his suggestion unlikely.

The latest loanword (פרסטלין as read by Allegro or פרסטלין as
read by Milik) has been derived respectively from περίστυλον and
from its diminutive περιστύλιον. Scholars have generally followed the
reading of Milik, while adopting the translation of Allegro. Thorion
hesitates between the two readings[104] and Lefkovits clearly opts for
the reading of Allegro.[105] An examination of the photographs does
not help much in this case, since the engraver of this column does
not distinguish the two letters.[106] A decision should thus be taken on

---

[101] Krauss, *Griechische und Lateinische Lehnwörter*, II, 117–118. Krauss classifies the
different meanings of the word in Hebrew in no less than five different categories.
He also explains (in a long note, 253–254 of the first volume) the different explanations offered in order to explain the derivation of the Hebrew and Aramaic forms
of the word from the Greek

[102] Lefkovits, *Copper Scroll*, 364–366.

[103] See *ibid.*, 365 for references.

[104] Thorion, "Beiträge zur Erforschung der Sprache der Kupfer-Rolle," 169.

[105] Lefkovits, *Copper Scroll*, 64.

[106] In this column *waw/yod* are used 32 times. On 30 occasions the letter form
is exactly the same and can be read either as *waw* or as *yod*. In only two cases a
different form representing *waw* appears (the first *waw* of ואפדות on 1:9, and the
final *waw* of פתחו on 1:11).

other grounds. Neither Allegro nor Milik (nor indeed Beyer) offer explicit reasons for their preference. One reason might be the influence on the engraver of the large number of plural ending in ן־in the manuscript, but everybody recognises that the word here is singular not plural.[107] Since we do not have comparative material from rabbinic literature in this instance to fathom the way the word would have been imported into Hebrew, the only argument that can be used in my opinion is the likelihood of a foreign word being imported from its most often used form. In this case, therefore, the normal περίστυλον is a more likely candidate than its diminutive form περιστύλιον. I thus consider περίστυλον to be the most likely origin of the פרסטלון of our text.

3. Some Reflections on the Presence of Greek Loanwords on the Copper Scroll

What can we conclude from this review op the Greek loanwords used in the *Copper Scroll*? While the number of loanwords that have remained as such after having sifted through the evidence has certainly been reduced (only four), their presence in a manuscript found among others in one of the Qumran caves remains a unique phenomenon and one that needs to be explained.

Usually, the presence of the Greek loanwords in the *Copper Scroll* is considered as proof that the manuscript has nothing to do with the Qumran community; although for the matter more attention is given to the Greek letters than to the loanwords. For Jiménez Bedman, the loanwords in question point towards an urban context as the place of origin of the scroll.[108] This leads him in turn to consider the *Copper Scroll* as an Essene but non-Qumranic document.[109] He,

---

[107] Milik (DJD, 3, 230 [14e]) explicitly asserts that "la finale de פרסטלין n'est pas la désinence du pluriel sémitique mais la transcription de l'afformante diminutive -ιον."

[108] F. Jiménez Bedman, *El misterio del Rollo de Cobre*, 229: "La prolija presencia de préstamos griegos referidos recurrentemente a la descripción de elementos arquitectónicos nos indica un contexto sociolingüístico netamente urbano donde la influencia del griego debiera ser harto notable."

[109] *Ibid.*, 230: "Se trata de un documento esenio pero no qumránico. Las marcas de identidad, a modo de impronta lingüística legada por la comunidad que originó el documento, nos dibujan un cuadro urbano y esenio cuya ubicación más probable, así lo presumimos, sería la comunidad esenia de Jerusalén."

as the majority of scholars, see the absence of Greek loanwords in the rest of the Dead Sea Scrolls as a theologically motivated choice, a conscious refusal of interaction with a foreign culture.

In view of its strong opposition to all forms of Hellenism, of the closed character of the Qumran community and of the curtailing of contacts with outsiders attested in the Qumran manuscripts of sectarian origin, this explanation seems very appealing, at least at first sight. If the absence of Greek loanwords in the rest of the Qumran manuscripts was ideologically motivated, their presence in the *Copper Scroll* would be a clear indication of its different origin since it does not show the same ideological constraints. The fact, emphasised by Jiménez Bedman,[110] that our scroll uses the word פרסטלון in order to name an architectural element for which the author could easily have used a Hebrew word (פרור), as is done in the *Temple Scroll*, seems to conclusively establish the argument, since it would prove that the authors had the choice between a "Hebrew" and a "foreign" word.

Upon reflection, however, precisely this example leads us to reach a different conclusion, namely that the presence of Greek loanwords in the *Copper Scroll* cannot be used as an argument to prove or to disprove the Qumran origin of the composition.

Three of the four loanwords attested in the *Copper Scroll* pertain to the architectural domain and we dispose of two other compositions found at Qumran where architectural terms are very prominent, namely the *Temple Scroll* and the *New Jerusalem*. A detailed comparison of the architectural vocabulary of the *Copper Scroll* with the vocabulary of the *Temple Scroll* has already been done by L. Schiffman.[111] In his study Schiffman organises the evidence into three categories:— architectural terms used in both compositions (where he lists 15 words);—architectural terms used in the *Copper Scroll* but not in the *Temple Scroll* (a category in which he places 33 entries); and—archi-

---

[110] *Ibid.*, 230–231: "El uso del préstamo griego פרסטלון περιστύλιον '*peristilo*' para denominar el elemento arquitectónico que, presumimos, podría haber sido descrito perfectamente con términos hebreos פרור en *2 R 23,11* y/o פרבר en *1 Cr 26,18* nos conduce a profundizar más en el calado del aserto de Rabin. Este uso diferente cobra mayor importancia en tanto y cuanto documentos como el *Rollo del Templo*, con el que nuestro manuscrito ha compartido gran cantidad de léxico, sí muestra el término פרור en contextos semánticos idénticos al aportado por el término פרסטלון en el *Rollo de Cobre*."

[111] L.H. Schiffman, "The Architectural Vocabulary of the Copper Scroll and the Temple Scroll," in *Copper Scroll Studies*, 180–195.

tectural terms used in the *Temple Scroll* but not in the *Copper Scroll* (a category to which he assigns 22 words). The sheer number of architectural terms used in the *Copper Scroll* but not in the *Temple Scroll* and vice versa (55 as against 15 common words) seriously diminishes the weight of a single case of possible use of a different word for the same reality in both compositions, since it points rather (even after discounting the different subject matter of the two compositions) to a language that is evolving and does not represent the same period of history.[112] Besides, Schiffman relates both אכסדרן and פרסטלון to the פרור of the *Temple Scroll*. In his discussion of אכסדרן he notes that "it does not occur in the Temple Scroll, although the term פרור denotes a similar structure in several passages."[113] In his discussion of פרסטלון he also asserts that "no Greek words at all appear in the Temple Scroll, but the difficult word פרור is used for the same kind of colonnade or stoa."[114] Schiffman, surprisingly, does not include אסטאן in his lists (although it should have been considered as an architectural term, even according to the interpretation of Lefkovits, which he follows, as "ossuary"),[115] but this word would have provided him with a third equivalent of the פרור of the *Temple Scroll*, since Yadin in his edition of the manuscript describes the different פרורים which appear in the *Temple Scroll* as "סטווים" and "סטיו או פריסטיל."[116]

The comparison of the lexicon of the *Copper Scroll* with the vocabulary of the *New Jerusalem* text is more complicated because the latter text is written in Aramaic. The resulting general pattern, however, is similar to that discovered with respect to the *Temple Scroll*, with words common with the lexicon of the classical Hebrew appearing in the three documents (like סף "threshold" which appears in the *Temple Scroll* both in the biblical form used also by the *Copper Scroll* and in the Aramaic form of the *New Jerusalem*, אספא), with words previously only known from Mishnaic Hebrew (like אמה "canal or

---

[112] The dating of the *Temple Scroll* is a disputed matter, but 4Q524, the copy from cave 4 published by Puech in DJD, 25, 85–114, shows that it cannot be dated later than the 1st half of the second century B.C.E. As for the *Copper Scroll* the accepted date is not earlier than the 2nd half of the first century C.E. About two centuries thus separate the two compositions.

[113] L.H. Schiffman, "The Architectural Vocabulary," 187.

[114] *Ibid.*, 191.

[115] *Ibid.*, 181–182, note 9.

[116] Y. Yadin, מגילת-המקדש (Jerusalem, 1977), Vol. II, 16 and vol. I, 183 respectively.

aqueduct") absent from the *Temple Scroll* but frequently used in the *Copper Scroll* and in the *New Jerusalem*, and with the addition of the presence of at least another Persian loanword in it to express a measure of longitude equivalent to the stadium: רִיס, which is not used in either the *Temple Scroll* or in the *Copper Scroll*. We may even find a new synonym for פריסטיל in the שבק of the *New Jerusalem* text, if we follow Milik's interpretation of the term as "peristyle,"[117] although Greenfield prefers to translate it by "left open" in parallel to the meaning of "open areas" he gives to בריתא, translated by Milik by "galerie, portique longeant la rue."[118]

The weight of Jiménez Bedman's argument is thus less strong than it appears at first glance and its value is reduced even more when one considers that פרור is not an original Hebrew word, but rather a Persian loanword already introduced into Hebrew at the time of the composition of the biblical books of 2 Kings and 1 Chron.[119] In practical terms this means that the author/redactor of the *Temple Scroll* drew from the vocabulary that was current in his own time or present in the literary sources he was using and the author of the *Copper Scroll* did the same.

The use, thus, of Greek loanwords in the *Copper Scroll* cannot be employed as an argument for or against the sectarian origin of the composition. Their presence in the *Copper Scroll* is simply an indicator of the evolution of the language during the chronological span that separates the *Temple Scroll* and the *New Jerusalem* on the one hand and the *Copper Scroll* on the other. The conclusion of Schiffman's article can be endorsed in its entirety:

> All of this leads to an inescapable conclusion. The Temple Scroll is an older document and reflects an earlier stage in the development of the postbiblical Hebrew vocabulary. The Copper Scroll was composed at a later date, by which time this vocabulary had already replaced numerous terms.[120]

More than an indication of sectarian or non-sectarian origin, the Greek loanwords of *Copper Scroll* witness, as do other grammatical and syntactical phenomena, to a different phase of the Hebrew lan-

---

[117] DJD, 3, 188–189.
[118] Greenfield, "The Small Caves," 133–134 [582–583].
[119] See Koehler – Baumgartner, *Hebräisches und Aramäisches Lexicon* (Leiden, 1983), III, 905–906.
[120] Schiffman, "The Architectural Vocabulary," 195.

guage. The fact that its Greek loanwords evidently tend to be restricted for the most part to architectural vocabulary shows, as does the use of Greek loanwords for musical instruments in the book of Daniel,[121] that the peculiar vocabulary of crafts and arts are fast evolving sectors of the language and consequently the most likely to be adapted to new circumstances and a changing society.

If this conclusion is acceptable, it would provide a new proof (if proof were needed) that Greek and Hebrew were part of a cultural continuum in which interaction was always possible, even within closed systems such as that represented by the community of the Dead Sea Scrolls.

---

[121] Quoted in note 4.

BETWEEN OLD AND NEW:
THE PROBLEM OF ACCULTURATION
ILLUSTRATED BY THE EARLY CHRISTIAN
USE OF THE PHOENIX MOTIF

ANDERS KLOSTERGAARD PETERSEN*

SETTING THE STAGE

In current scholarship it is a truism that early Christianity emerged as a Jewish movement during the first century C.E. in an international atmosphere that encouraged cultural interaction and intensified religious syncretism. In a reconstruction of a plausible scenario reflecting the world of late antiquity the Hellenistic era is frequently depicted as a "meltingpot" embracing three distinct cultural and religious traditions, frequently epitomised—as in this *Festschrift*—by the grand cities of Jerusalem, Alexandria and Rome. The synedochal expression—patterned on Tertullian's famous remark in *De Praescriptione Haereticorum* 7:9–13—purports to represent the three decisive cultural entities that formed the most important stages of antiquity and eventually led to the birth of the modern occidental civilisation. To pay tribute to Ton Hilhorst who in his scholarly work has focused not least on the cultural interrelation and interaction of these three distinguished traditions of late antiquity I shall focus on one particular subject only: the problem of acculturation as illustrated by the early Christian use of the Phoenix motif.[1] In addition I shall reflect upon

---

* Aarhus.
[1] See for instance A. Hilhorst, *Sémitismes et latinismes dans le Pasteur d'Hermas* (Graecitas christianorum primaeva, 5; Nijmegen, 1976); *Id.*, "'Servir Dieu' dans la terminologie du judaïsme hellénistique et des premières génerations chrétiennes de langue grecque," in A.A.R. Bastiaensen, A. Hilhorst, C.H. Kneepkens (eds.), *Fructus Centesimus. Mélanges offerts à Gerard J.M. Bartelink à l'occasion de son soixsante-cinquième anniversaire* (Instrumenta Patristica, 19; Dordrecht, 1991), 177–192; *Id.*, "The Speech on Truth in 1 Esdras 4,34.41," in F. García Martínez, A. Hilhorst and C.J. Labuschagne (eds.), *The Scriptures and the Scrolls. Studies in Honour of A.S. van der Woude on the Occasion of his 65th Birthday* (VTSup, 49; Leiden, 1992), 135–151; *Id.*, "Was Philo Read by Pagans? The Statement on Heliodorus in Socrates *Hist. Eccl.* 5.22," *The Studia Philonica Annual* 4 (1992) 75–77; *Id.*, "The Cleansing of the Temple (John 2,13–25) in Juvencus and Nonnus," in J. den Boeft and A. Hilhorst (eds.) *Early Christian Poetry.*

some theoretical issues pertinent to the general debate on acculturation and cultural interaction.

BETWEEN OLD AND NEW

In the world in which Christianity originated a culturally pervasive
and universal idea was represented by the Greek sentiment: *Prebyteron
kreitton*, i.e. "the ancient is the better."[2] Traditions conceived to originate since the beginning of time were attributed a far greater value
than phenomena held to represent innovation and novelty. Similar
to the Greeks the Romans had their versions of the maxim. In *De
Bello Gallico* Caesar, for instance, is told to scorn the king of the
Celts, Dumnorix, for being a man hungering for novelties, a *cupidus
rerum novarum*.[3] The idea was also voiced by the well-known statement that the Roman state would endure only be means of its old
mores and citizens: *Moribus antiquis res stat Romana virisque*.[4]

A similar reasoning is also found in a Jewish context. A familiar
legend—known from its transmission by Christian writers—attributes
the following statement to the Pythagorean philosopher Numenius:
"For what is Plato, but an Attic-speaking Moses?"[5] An author of the
Jewish diaspora, Aristobul similarly argues that the wisdom of Homer,
Hesiod, Orpheus, Linus, Pythagoras, Socrates and Plato derives from

A Collection of Essays (VCSup, 22; Leiden, 1993), 61–76; *Id.*, "A Visit to Paradise:
Apocalypse of Paul 45 and Its Background," in G.P. Luttikhuizen (ed.), *Paradise Interpreted.
Representations of Biblical Paradise in Judaism and Christianity* (Themes in Biblical Narrative.
Jewish and Christian Traditions, 2; Leiden, 1999), 128–139.
   [2] The quotation is here represented in an Atticised version found in Timaios of
Locri, Περὶ φύσις κόσμου καὶ ψυχῆς, see T.H. Tobin, *Timaios of Locri, On the Nature
of the World and the Soul. Text, Translation and Notes* (SBLTT, 26; Atlanta, 1985), 34.
   [3] Caesar, *De Bello Gallico* 1:18,3. Cf. 5:6,1 and 1:9,3.
   [4] The quotation originates from Ennius Frg. 156 (Skutsch). Cicero (*De Re Publica*
5:1) and Augustin (*De Civitate Dei* 2:21) both relate to and discuss the Ennius-
quotation, which indicates its dissemination to the learned strata of the Roman society as well as its persistence as part of the cultural competence during the entire
Roman period. For an extensive discussion of the impact of the "proof of old age"
on the culture of antiquity, see P. Pilhofer, *Presbyteron Kreitton: der Altersbeweis der jüdischen und christlichen Apologeten und seine Vorgeschichte* (WUNT, 2,39; Tübingen, 1990).
   [5] The tradition has been transmitted by Clement of Alexandria, *Stromata* 1:22:150:4;
Eusebius, *Praeparatio Evangelica* 9:6,9; 9:7,1; 9:8,1–2; 11:10,14; 11:18,14; Theoderetus,
Graecarum Affectionum Curatio 2:114; Origen, *Contra Celsum* 1:15; 4:51; Pophyrius, *De
Antro Nympharum* 10; Lydus, *De Mensibus* 4:3. A convenient grouping as well as a
translation of the texts is provided by M. Stern, *Greek and Latin Authors on Jews and
Judaism, Volume Two, From Tacitus to Simplicius* (Jerusalem, 1980), 206–16.

the legislation of God transmitted by Moses.[6] Another Jewish author of the diaspora, Artapanus even identifies Moses with the legendary figure of Musaeus and makes Orpheus his disciple.[7]

The idea that the pagan world has acquired its wisdom from Torah serves at least three different purposes. First, the motif pacifies a potential threat from a competing world-view. Second, by the claim that the profundity of Athens derives from Jewish wisdom the Greek world is thrown upon the Torah as the true revelation of the wisdom of God. Third, by the argument that Torah is the sapiential progenitor of Greek intelligence Athens is depicted as a late-comer and a novel combatant in the dispute on representing the true manifestation of God's wisdom. In this manner the Greek traditions are relegated to the realm of religious novelty whereas the respective Judaisms can be claimed to represent traditions developed since the beginning of time and originating from God.

The rhetorical force of the criterion that "the ancient is the better" is vividly documented by Josephus. In *Contra Apionem*, for instance, he initiates a critique of Greek historiography by disavowing its purported antiquity. Contrary to the ancient world's general admiration Greek historiography enjoyed in the ancient world Josephus argues that Greek civilisation is a modern phenomenon with no respectable age and no traditions (τὰ μὲν γὰρ παρὰ τοῖς Ἕλλησιν ἅπαντα νέα καὶ χθὲς καὶ πρῶην, ὡς ἄν εἴποι τις, εὕροι γεγονότα). The gist of the argument is the more ironic because Josephus is relying on the view of the Egyptian priest depicted in debate with Solon in Plato's *Timaeus* (22B–C). The Egyptian priest claims that the Greeks are children (παῖδες) in whose midst no old man man (γέρων) could arise. The Hellenes are in fact nothing but newcomers, youthful souls, void of an ancient glory substantiated by the criterion of old age (δι' ἀρχαίαν ἀκοὴν) and without knowledge ensured by the greyness of time (χρόνῳ

---

[6] Aristobul, 13:12,1–4:13–16 according to A.-M. Denis, *Concordance Grecque de Pseudépigraphes d'Ancien Testament* (Louvain-la-Neuve, 1987). The impact of Aristobul on later Christian apologetics is documented by the fact that he has been exclusively transmitted by Christian authors, Clement of Alexandria (*Stomata* 1:148,1; 1:150,1–3; 5:107,1–108,1; 6:32,3–33) and Eusebius (*Praeparatio Evangelica* 8:10,1–17; 13:12,1–16; *Historia Ecclesiae* 7:32,17–18).

[7] Artapanus, 9,27,3f. according to A.-M. Denis, *Concordance Grecque de Pseudépigraphes d'Ancien Testament*. Parallel to the significance of Aristobul on early Christian apologetics also Artapanus has been transmitted by Christian authors only, Clement of Alexandria, *Stromata* 1:154,2f.; Eusebius, *Praeparatio Evangelica* 9:18,1; 9:23,1–4; 9:27,1–37.

πολιὸν) (22B). Based on this argument Josephus argues that the most novel and innovative part of Greek culture is historiography (1,6f.). By their indigenous inclination and preference for rhetoric, flattery and polemics at the expense of the endeavour "to discover the truth" the Greek historiographers have placed themselves at the margins of civilised culture (1,23–27). Jewish history, on the contrary, has been written by the prophets of old age. They have achieved "their knowledge of the most remote and ancient history (τὰ μὲν ἀνωτάτω καὶ παλαιότατα) through the inspiration which they owed to God, and they committed to write a clear account of the events of their own time just as they occurred" (1,37). In solemn reverence for their scriptures the Jews have neither ventured to add nor to remove a syllable from them (1,42). The allegation, of course, being that the Greeks neither refrain from adducing nor abstain from removing from their historical records (cf. 1,44–46). Rhetorically, Josephus' attempt to impale Greek historiography is embedded in an overwhelmingly polemical argument. His use of the proof of old age, however, is not limited to a polemical context only.

In his programmatic opening paragraph of the *Jewish Antiquities* he entreats his readers to focus their minds on God. If they carefully peruse the Jewish history as it is elaborated in the *Antiquities* they will realise that he who complies with the will of God and does not venture to transgress his holy laws will prosper in all things beyond belief and receive felicity (εὐδαιμονία) (1,14). Two things undergird the credibility and the *ethos* of the lawgiver Moses. First, Moses refrained from inventing mythological fictions about God. Second, he belongs to the distant past as he was born two thousand years ago. The dating of the birth of Moses intends to make a strong impression on the readers since "to that ancient date the poets never ventured to refer even the birth of their gods, much less the actions or the laws of mortals" (1,16).

What has all this to do, however, with acculturation and the motif of the Phoenix bird? With regard to the issue of acculturation the use of the criterion of old age in different traditions is an illustrative example of the cultural "meltingpot" in which individual authors drew from a reservoir of shared cultural and religious traditions. One may describe the situation synedochially as a fusion between Jerusalem, Alexandria and Rome. Martin Hengel has poignantly termed this nature of the Hellenistic world and epoch as a cultural and religious *koine*.[8] Before analysing some theoretical issues pertaining to this complex of problems I shall briefly suggest what this has to do with the motif of the Phoenix bird. My idea is that an important motive for the frequent occurrence of the Phoenix motif in early Christian texts—and possibly also in iconography—has to do with the embarrassment caused by the novelty of the Christian religion. In that very context the motif of the Phoenix bird could be used to "prove" the antiquity of Christianity and simultaneously to emphasise the radical novelty of the Christ-event. In order to substantiate this interpretation I shall look at early Christianity from the perspective of the dilemma between old and new.

EARLY CHRISTIANITY BETWEEN OLD AND NEW

Reading a number of early Christian writers it is obvious that issues pertaining to the ancestry and age of the Christian religion played a prominent part in the argument and fierce debates with contemporary Jewish and pagan writers who reproached Christianity for being a novel religion.[9] It follows from the previous reflections that during antiquity an ancient origin was considered a prime requisite in a religion which claimed to be true. No reproach was stronger than the reproach of novelty. This problem was intensified by the fact that an inherent and influential characteristic of early Christianity was the importance attributed to the idea of novelty. Since the Christ-event was understood to represent a radical change in the order of the world, a pivotal turning point of the human history,

---

[8] M. Hengel, "Zum Problem der 'Hellenisierung' Judäas," in *Judaica et Hellenistica. Kleine Schriften I* (WUNT, 90; Tübingen, 1996), 1–90, 82.

[9] In current scholarship it is of course a truism that Christianity from a historical point of view did not develop into an independent and in relation to Judaism separate religion before the second and third decade of the second century in which Greco-Roman authors as well as "Christian" and "Jewish" writers begin to look at Christianity as something different from Judaism. Even unto say 150 it is far from evident that Christianity should be conceived in relation to Judaism as an independent religion. Retrospectively one may, of course, argue that the early Christianities did represent something different from what at a later stage became rabbinic Judaism, but it is anachronistic to project back this situation unto the early Christianities. For a thorough discussion of the problem, see J.D.G. Dunn, *The Partings of the Ways. Between Christianity and Judaism and their Significance for the Character of Christianity* (London-Philadelphia, 1990).

early Christianity was caught in a quandary. The idea of the decisive *novum* was promulgated in a cultural context that favoured old age at the expense of the new and the innovative.

In 2 Cor 5:17, for instance, Paul emphatically claims that "if any one is in Christ, he is a new creature; the old has passed away, behold, the new has come." In the argumentative context the statement serves to legitimise Paul's preaching and, particularly, to gird his *ethos* as the true and rightful apostle of the Corinthian community. Simultaneously, however, the "innovative" nature of the Christ-event is underlined. In Gal 6:15 Paul emphasises that the distinction between circumcision and uncircumcision that divided "the old world" has fallen away. The differentiation has lost its *raison d'être* and has been replaced by a new creation. At the anthropological level the idea of a radical watershed is undergirded by the use of metaphors that thematise life and death. In baptism the Christ-believer is conceived to have died, to have been buried with Christ and to have been incorporated into a new realm of existence radically different from the one prior to the ritual enactment. He has definitively left the old Adamic life behind.[10]

Paul, however, is not the only one to emphasise the radical novelty of the Christ-event. In Matt 9:16f Jesus is told to have said that "no one puts a piece of unshrunk cloth on an old garment, for the patch tears away from the garment and a worse tear is made. Neither is new wine poured into old wineskins; if it is, the skins burst, and the wine is spilled, and the skins are destroyed; but new wine is poured into fresh wineskins, and so both are preserved." Contrary to the Pharisees and the disciples of John the Baptist who have not captured the euphoric character of the present time the disciples of Jesus—at this point representing the role of the intended readers in the text—are admonished to pay heed to his proclamation as a present manifestation of the mercy of God. His ministry does not only remove impurities, diseases and sins. It also tears apart the traditional understanding of what is truly good and holy.[11] The revelation of the grace of God in the proclamation of Jesus is conceived to represent a *novum* that tears apart and destroys the old laws in a

---

[10] See, A.K. Petersen, "Shedding New Light on Paul's Understanding of Baptism. A Ritual-Theoretical Approach to Romans 6," *StTh* 52 (1998) 1, 3–28.
[11] Cf. D. Patte, *The Gospel According to Matthew: A Structural Commentary on Matthew's Faith* (Philadelphia, 1987), 131.

period of time and a cultural context that favours elderly at the expense of novelty.[12]

Obviously, one may object to such an interpretation by claiming that it does not pay respect to the salvation-historical scheme in the light of which the idea of radical newness is to be identified with the true fulfilment of the promises made in the distant past. For some texts this is certainly true, but it does not solve the dilemma entirely. Granted that the motif of radical novelty can be interpreted in conformity with a salvation-historical scheme the idea of newness does nevertheless imply a deficiency. If the promises have not been fulfilled until the present day, then the old age is to be characterised as imperfect. A number of texts pay witness to this dilemma.

The argument for the antiquity of Christianity put forward by Theophilus of Antioch in his dialogue addressed to Autolyctus—app. 180—mirrors the embarrassment caused by the dilemma. The Christian doctrine is neither of a recent date, as insinuated by some, nor are the Christian tenets mythical and false. On the contrary, they are very ancient and true (3,29,1f.). Aristides (app. 150), on the other hand, emphasises the nature of novelty of the Christian religion. The Christians are a *nova gens* in whose midst the divine abides (16,4). The *Adversus Gentes* of Arnobius (app. 300) represents a considerable later stage of the development, but it is evident from the argument that the debate on the antiquity of Christianity has neither disappeared nor has it been brought to a conclusion. Arnobius attempts to impale the impact of the criterion of age. Although the Christians cannot refer their cultic practises to an ancient origin, their rites will eventually also be of an old age. A similar reasoning can be applied to the gentiles. Although their rites now appear to be of an impressive antiquity, previously they were also new. According to Arnobius, this shows the feebleness on which the criterion of age rests. In his opinion the credibility of a religion should not be determined by its age, but by its divinity. The gentiles, therefore, should stop considering when they began to worship and concentrate on what they

---

[12] In order to document the prominent role played by the idea of radical novelty some additional New Testament texts thematising the motif can be mentioned: Mark 1:27 (cf. 1:16); Luke 22:20 (cf. 1 Cor 11:25); 2 Cor 3:6; Romans 6:4; 7:6; 1 Cor 5:7; Eph 2:15; 4:24; Col 3:10; Hebrews 8:8; 12:24; John 13:34; 1 Peter 1:23; Acts 17:19; Apc 21:1f. Cf. also the *Epistle to Diognetus* 1:1; Ignatius *Eph* 19:2f.; *Kerygma Petrou* (Clement of Alexandria, *Stromata* 6:5,41).

worship (2,71,1f.). In spite of his devout and thoughtful attempt to eliminate the rhetorical ground on which the criterion of age rests Arnobius was not successful.[13]

In the *History of the Church* Eusebius chose the criterion of age as his programmatic point of departure. In the second chapter of the first book in which the double nature of Christ is taken as a literary scheme for the exposition of the history of the church Eusebius claims that his work: "will only be complete if we begin with the chief and lordliest events of all his (i.e. Christ) history. In this way will the antiquity and divinity of Christianity be shown to those who suppose it of recent and foreign origin (νέαν αὐτὴν καὶ ἐκτετοπ-ισμένην), and imagine that it appeared only yesterday." This brief survey of texts exemplify the dilemma of a religion caught in a tension between elderly and novelty in a world that reproached religious newness and adored excessive antiquity. It also suggests the deep embarrassment of belonging to a novel religion promulgating self-conscious thoughts of radical newness was felt among cultured Christians.

The Phoenix Motif: A "Signifiant Flottant" in the Ancient World?

It is far from evident that only one myth of the Phoenix bird ever existed. It seems more reasonable to talk about a cluster of motifs in which the focal point in some way or another was related to the Phoenix bird. Obviously the different uses of the motif do suggest some uniting and common characteristics,[14] but the semantic openness of the concept—as witnessed by the concept's history of reception—should make us hesitant about construing a distinct and monolithic Phoenix-myth. Indeed, it is far from certain that a seman-

---

[13] The earliest Christian uses of the proof of age are found in Justin, *Dialogue with Trypho* 7; Tatian, *Oratio* 31 (cf. 35); Tertullian, *Apologeticum* 6:9.

[14] That has been wonderfully documented in the two classical studies on the motif by J. Hubaux and M. Leroy, *Le Mythe du Phénix dans le littérature grecque et latine* (Bibl. de la Fac. de Philosophie et Lettres de l'Univ. de Liège, 82; Liège-Paris, 1939), as well as R. van den Broek, *The Myth of the Phoenix According to Classical and Early Christian Traditions* (EPRO, 24; Leiden, 1971). Both monographs, however, presuppose that a uniform myth can be identified. Although van den Broek is very well aware of the heterogeneous nature of the different uses of the motif he nevertheless continues to speak of *the myth* as if it exhibited a homogeneous and uniform nature.

tic core pertaining to the symbol of the Phoenix bird can be identified. Rather than defining the Phoenix motif in terms of content it may prove valuable to define it in terms of function.[15] In that case the nature of the motif should be sought not in a particular content from which all later applications are derivatives but rather in the manner in which it is used during its history of reception, i.e. as a specific discursive function of language. My point is neither that the motif did not and could not mean different things in different contexts, nor that its was entirely receptive or open to be attributed any kind of content. On the one hand it did not mean anything. On the other hand no fixed meaning could be established. As an alternative to understand the motif as a *signifiant flottant*, an undefined signifying,[16] I suggest that the ambiguity can be solved by the adoption of a functional definition.

If the use of the motif rather than its content is brought into focus one consistent characteristic does—in spite of different contents—unite the individual applications. The Phoenix motif is adopted in contexts in which a writer wants simultaneously to emphasise a break with the near past and a continuation from the distant past. In this manner different authors are capable of attributing very different meanings to the very same concept depending on their respective semantic universes. By the use of the Phoenix motif a writer is on the one hand able to indicate and to emphasise that a particular watershed has taken place, a *novum* in the human history. By the application of the very same motif the author simultaneously subscribes to a symbol that situates his identification of the epoch-making event in the remote and primordial, legitimising past. A few examples from the Greco-Roman context will suffice to make the point clear.[17]

---

[15] For a similar approach with regard to the definition of demonology, see A.K. Petersen, "The Notion of Daemon—Open Questions to a Diffuse Concept," in H. Lichtenberger and A. Lange (eds.), *Die Dämonologie der alttestamentlich-jüdischen und frühchristlichen Litteratur im Kontext ihrer Umwelt* (Tübingen, 2003), 129–147.

[16] The notion of *signifiant flottant* originates in C. Lévi-Strauss, *Introduction to the Work of Marcel Mauss* (London, 1987), 64. It is used also in J. van Baal and W.E.A. van Beek, *Symbols for Communication. An introduction to the anthropological study of religion* (Assen, 1985), 227. Cf. also M. Detienne, *De la pensée religieuse à la pensée philosophique: La Notion de Daïmôn dans le pythagorisme ancien* (Bibl. de la Fac. de Philosophie et Lettres de l'Univ. de Liège, 165; Paris, 1963), 13f., cf. 27.

[17] For a thorough discussion of the pre-Christian history of the motif, see van den Broek, *The Myth of the Phoenix*. Cf. A.K. Petersen, "Fønix mellem tradition og nybrud. Inkulturationsproblemet i den tidlige kristendom," *DTT* 64 (2001) 3, 189–212, 194–201.

156 ANDERS KLOSTERGAARD PETERSEN

When, for instance, Libanius characterises the short reign of government of the emperor Julian he compares it to the rare manifestations of the Phoenix bird in the world.[18] Aristides similarly adopts the motif in his *In Defence of Oratory* in order to emphasise that only a few true rhetoricians in fact exist: "For just as lions and all the nobler animals are naturally rarer than the others, so among men nothing is so rare as an orator worthy of the name. It is enough if one or two are born in a revolution of the sun, like the bird of India in Egypt."[19] In his *Epistle* no. 42 Seneca also applies the motif to document that only a genuine true Stoic wise men exist: "For one of the first class (the truly wise men) perhaps springs into existence, like the phoenix, only once in five hundred years."[20]

The motif of the rare manifestations of the Phoenix plays a prominent role in an influential strand of the tradition. When Aristides, for instance, claims that the Phoenix bird visits Egypt for every solar rotation only he presupposes a relationship between the appearance of the bird and a Sothic period.[21] A similar idea is found in Tacitus' *Annales* in which it is claimed that the usual interval between the Phoenix-manifestations in Egypt is 500 years. Some, says Tacitus, do, however, think that the interval equals 1461 years (6,28). In this manner the appearance of the Phoenix bird is thought to herald the dawning of a new golden age. In light of this it should come as no surprise that a number of emperors at the time of their accession to the throne embossed coins picturing a portrait of themselves along with an icon of the Phoenix.[22]

---

[18] Libanius, *Orationes* 17:10.

[19] Aristides, *Orationes* 144D:425f.

[20] Seneca, *Epistula* 42:1 quoted from the LCL-translation by R.M. Gummere. Cf. A.J. Malherbe, "Cynics" (*IDBSup*, 20), 202. See also Synesius, *Dion* 9:3.

[21] In the old Egyptian calendar a Sothic cycle is made up of 1461 years. The beginning of a Sothic period is determined by the fact that the 365 days of the normal calendar are congruent with the 365,25 days of the solar year. That occurs every 1461 normal years and 1460 solar years. The cycle has been named after Sirius (Sothis) which during the first four years of the period appears at the New Years day by the first flooding of the Nile in the month of Thot. The Sothic period was in the later period of antiquity related to ideas of the *Grand Year*, known from, for instance, Plato, *Timaeus* (39D) and Cicero, *De Natura* 2:51f. See further van den Broek, *The Myth of the Phoenix*, 98–112.

[22] Among the emperors are Hadrian, Antoninus Pius, Marcus Aurelius and Constantine the First. See H. Castritius, "Der Phoenix auf den Aurei Hadrians und Tacitus, 'Annalen VI,26'," *Jahrbuch für Numismatik und Geldgeschichte* 14 (1964) 89–95, and H. Mattingly, *Roman Coins from the Earliest Times to the Fall of the Western Empire* (London, 1927), 176.251.

The great number of Greco-Roman texts paying witness to the vivid fascination which the purported death and resuscitation of the Phoenix exerted on the people of the period point in one and the same direction: Phoenix as the triumphant conqueror of death symbolising renewal, immortality, eternity and recreation. In one of his *Epigrams* Martial compares the glorious rebuilding of Rome after a fire with the renewal of the Phoenix bird. He speaks of the fire that: "renews the Assyrian nests whenever one bird has lived its ten cycles, so has the new Rome shed her old age and put on herself the visage of her governor (*vultus praesidis ipsa sui*)" (5,7,1–4). In his panegyric *Phoenix* Claudian praises the bird:

> Happy bird, heir to thine own self! Death which proves our undoing restores thy strength. Thine ashes give thee life and though thou perish not thine old age dies. Thou hast beheld all that has been, hast witnessed the passing of the ages ... Yet did no destruction overwhelm thee; sole survivor thou livest to see the earth subdued; against thee the Fates gather not up their threads, powerless to do thee harm.[23]

This brief "Märchengang" through some of the Greco-Roman' applications of the Phoenix motif demonstrates that no fixed meaning pertained to the concept in antiquity. On the other hand, it does not follow from this observation that the concept was receptive to any meaning. One common characteristic does occur. The motif is used as an emphatic deictic marker in contexts in which a writer wants to emphasise an epoch-marking event and at the same time wishes to relate this event to the glorious past. We shall now consider how and why the early Christians adopted this motif commonly thought to be of a pagan origin.

Some Preliminary Modifications

Before looking at some early Christian texts in which the motif is applied I shall discuss two theoretical issues that relate to the subject of acculturation. I shall term the first one cultural fundamentalism or "thinking in terms of containers." The second one deals with the perspective from which the discussion is conducted: *emic* or *etic*.[24]

---

[23] Claudian, *Phoenix* 101–105.108–110. The translation is by M. Platnauer in the LCL-edition of Claudian.

[24] The distinction between an *emic* and an *etic* level of analysis is now frequently used in the humanities. It originates in K.L. Pike, *Language in Relation to a Unified*

When acculturation is discussed by scholars the problem is frequently posed in terms of pure cultural entities. The use of the Phoenix motif by Christian or Jewish authors is understood in terms of an adoption or a take-over of traditions that are commonly thought to be indigenously foreign to Judaism and early Christianity. This understanding presupposes the existence of pure cultural and religious entities which by a process of contamination—caused by borrowing and appropriation—have become "messy" affairs or syncretistic phenomena. At the individual level persons are conceived of as cultural or religious containers or carriers of cultural packages which they share with other members of their culture and religion. The German social-anthropologist Verena Stolcke has termed this hermeneutic manoeuvre cultural fundamentalism.[25] A culture which has never existed in reality is construed. Although individuals as cultural containers are mutually different they are nevertheless perceived as identical with regard to central elements. Thus a group of persons sharing a common cultural background is construed to partake in a common identity. A Jew is held to embody Judaism, and a Greek is thought to incarnate Greekness. This traditional model of interpreting acculturation is problematic because it is based on the assumption of a "meeting of cultures or religions" between separate and fundamentally different, but internally homogenous entities. Rather than ontologising or reifying cultural and religious identity I prefer—in line with a number of insights gained from current cultural anthropology—to apply a dynamic interpretation. Culture—and religion as part of the cultural construction—represents ways of interpreting the world, world-views. Culture represents what one does

---

Theory of the Structure of Human Behavior 1 (Glensdale, 1954). The distinction is often used synonymously with the difference between an insider- and an outsider perspective, for instance expressed in anthropology as the difference between the scholarly perspective and that of the informant. That, however, does not fully exploit the potential of the distinction in which both aspects refer to the analytical level of the scholar. An *emic* analysis is founded on concepts, thought structures, etc. familiar to the informants and is—ideally—worked out in a manner so that the "natives," i.e. those sharing the inside perspective, may recognise themselves in the analysis. The *etic* level of analysis, on the other hand, is founded on scholarly concepts and taxonomies. For further clarification of the distinction, see the excellent volume by T.N. Headland, K.L. Pike and M. Harris (eds.) *Emics and etics: the Insider/Outsider Debate* (Frontiers of Anthropology 7; Newbury Park, Cl., 1990).

[25] V. Stolcke, "Talking Culture: New Boundaries, New Rhetorics of Exclusion in Europe," *Current Anthropology* 36 (1995) 1, 1–13.

and not what one is.[26] In numerous publications the Dutch anthropologist Martijn van Beek has emphasised to what a great extent the talk about cultures is itself part of the cultural construction: "The point is not to deny that common features exist in particular fields but to document that the extrapolation from specific similarities and differences to homogenised, cultural and even civilising units is a creative process and not just a mapping of already existing facts."[27] Having modified the traditional concept of acculturation I shall focus on the intimately related problem of perspective.

I do not deny that cultural processes such as diffusion, reception, adaptation, assimilation, acculturation, etc. exist. It is a moot point only if they are conceived in terms of a presupposed idea of cultural purity which never did exist. Culture and religion are per se a "messy" affair. Analysing in terms of syncretism or cultural hybrids a conceptual distinction between already, existing "pure" cultures is presupposed. This is the assumption to be contested.[28]

At an *etic* level of analysis it does make sense to distinguish, for instance, between Judaism and Hellenism as "pure" conceptual abstractions useful in the taxonomic processing, i.e. the categorisation of the world. At an *emic* level it also makes sense to the extent that many texts themselves presuppose this distinction. One should, however, be careful not to attribute an ontological status to the distinction by a hermeneutic manoeuvre of reification. This is the problem of influential strands of contemporary scholarship. Groups and texts of early Judaism are compared from the perspective of their degree of cultural assimilation and religious acculturation. Philo and Josephus usually score high on a scale whose summit is identified as a prostration before Greco-Roman culture. But who knows that Philo or Josephus did not understand their own religiosity to embody the true Judaism? From an *etic* perspective of analysis it can reasonably be argued that Philo and Josephus are closer to what has been construed as Greco-Hellenistic culture than are say other voices of the

---

[26] Cf. M. van Beek, "Identiteternes møde, civilisationernes sammenstød?," *RvT* 40 (2002) 1–11, 4. Cf. Also "Beyond Identity Fetishism: 'Communal' Conflict in Ladakh and the Limitis of Autonomy," *Current Anthropology* 15 (2000) 4, 525–569.

[27] M. van Beek, "Identiteternes møde," 5f. [my translation]. Cf. the similar argument in the chapter "Census, Map, Museum," in Benedict Anderson, *Imagined Communities. Reflections on the Origin and Spread of Nationalism* (London-New York, 1996), 163–185.

[28] For a further elucidation of this point with regard to the Hellenism/Judaism-dichotomy, see A.K. Petersen, "Hellenisme og kristendom—en skæbnesvanger konstruktion" [to be published in *RvT* 2003].

late Second Temple period. But it is wrong to project this observation unto an *emic* level claiming that Josephus and Philo in their own
time were considered "cultural renegades." Some may obviously have
thought so, but did they represent Judaism in a more true or real
way than representatives of the cultural strata of a Philonic or
Josephean context? Only to the extent that it is denied or not fully
realised that culture and religion do exist only as cultural hybrids
and are developed in processes of Creolisation, can Philo and Josephus
be claimed to be less Jewish than say the Qumranites, for instance.

Numerous examples witness that in the culturally educated strata
of early Christianity representatives of the theology were fiercely
debating the extent to which a presupposed "pure" Christianity should
be receptive to influence from the Greco-Roman culture. The statement of Tertullian "What has Jerusalem in common with Athens"—
alluded to in the beginning of this essay—is an illustrative example.
In an allegorical exegesis of Ex 3:21f.; 11:2 and 12:35f. Origen argues
that similar to the Israelites who on their way out of Egypt by the
command of God captured the gold and silver jewels of the Egyptians
and robbed their clothes in order to decorate the Holy of Holies,
thus honouring God, so shall the Christians use the treasures of
paganism.[29] Clement of Alexandria similarly voices an understanding in which the inclusion of traditions thought[30] to embody paganism were perceived to represent a potential danger to Christianity.
The incorporation of "foreign good" was acceptable only to the
extent that it occurred on the premises of the Christian universe of
meaning. Clement compares it to the exchange of money (cf. 1 Thess
5:21) by arguing that the Christians should behave as money chang-
ers. Like the broker examining the coins, the Christian shall examine pagan philosophy. The coins are genuine if the obverse is stroked
with the portrait of the true king. The Christians may similarly keep
and exploit pagan traditions, if they are stroked with the portrait of
Christ.[31]

---

[29] Origen, *Epistle to Gregor Thaumatourgos* 2:19–44. The allegoresis is already known
from Irenaeus, *Adversus Haereses* 4:30,1–4 and is later found by authors such as
Gregor of Nyssa, *Vita Moysis* 67:9–69:3, Augustin, *De Doctrina Christiana* 2:40,60f.
and Casiodorus, *Institutiones* 1:28,4.
[30] Cyril of Jerusalem and the *Constitutiones Apostolorum* are the earliest Christian
texts in which the motif is perceived to be of a pagan origin.
[31] Clement of Alexandria, *Stromata* 6:81,2. Cf. 1:177,2; 2:15,4; 7:90,5. See also
Hieronymus, *Epistula* 70:2,5f. For these and other examples see the erudite work of
C. Gnilka, *ΧΡΗΣΙΣ. Die Methode der Kirchenväter im Umgang mit der antiken Kultur. Bd.
I. Der Begriff des "gerechten Gebrauchs"* (Basel-Stuttgart, 1984).

In the earliest Christian uses of the Phoenix motif, however, there is nothing to indicate any hesitation or scepticism towards the adoption of the motif on the part of the Christian writers. We should, in fact, refrain from talking about adoption and rather speak of uses. It is an important point because the preceding reflections suggest that the motif was not thought of as something foreign. Although the Phoenix motif in current research is understood to be of a pagan origin the earliest Christian writers did not think of it in that way. They simply used a symbol that was an inherent part of their own cultural and religious competence.

THE PHOENIX BIRD IN EARLY CHRISTIANITY

The first known example of a Christian use of the Phoenix motif is found in 1 Clement. In an argument that serves to enhance the probability of the resurrection of the dead Clement refers to the Phoenix bird. God has in different ways given signs that signify the resurrection. Day and night is such a sign: "The night sleeps, the day arises: the day departs, night comes on." Sowing and harvesting is another sign. "The seed falls on the ground, parched and bare, and suffer decay. From the decay, however, by the providence of the master the seed is raised, and from one grain more grow and bring forth fruit" (24:3–5). The Phoenix is another wondrous sign pointing towards the resurrection. At the time of its dissolution in death it makes a sepulchre of frankincense, myrrh and other spices, and when the time is fulfilled it enters into the sepulchre and dies. From the putrefied flesh, however, a worm springs forward that eventually develops into a new Phoenix bird which will carry the sepulchre of its predecessor from Arabia to Heliopolis (25:1–3).

In the period following Clement the motif is increasingly used polemically against the gentiles. In analogy with Clement Tertullian also exploits it as a symbol of resurrection. If the interchange of day and night and the alternation of the seasons do not represent a satisfactorily convincing argument because they symbolise cessation of being and not dying, renewal and not resuscitation, the gentile will have to accept the Phoenix as an indisputable proof of the hope of the resurrection. The Torah even proves it. In Scripture it is said the "the righteous shall blossom like Phoenix" (LXX Ps 91:13 ὡς φοίνιξ). Tertullian's interpretation—based on the homonym φοίνιξ date palm/Phoenix—is interesting because a similar tendency to read

Phoenix into the Bible can be detected in some Jewish texts.[32] Similarly to Clement Tertullian argues for the greater value of humans in comparison to the Phoenix: "The Lord has pronounced that we are superior to all sparrows (Matt 6:26). If that does not pertain to Phoenixes as well, it is of no great value (*nihil magnum*). But shall all humans die once and for all, while the birds of Arabia are secure about their resurrection?"[33]

Both Clement and Tertullian endorse Phoenix as a powerful symbol that enables them to render the idea of the resurrection probable. By subscribing to a tradition held to originate since the beginning of time they are capable of arguing simultaneously that a *novum* has occurred and that this epoch-making event is a fulfilment of some hidden paradigm of history. Some other texts point in the same direction but they take the understanding even further by identifying Phoenix with Christ. In the Greek *Physiologos*—the dating of which remains uncertain—the Phoenix symbolises Christ. After a period of 500 years the Indian bird leaves for the trees of Lebanon in order to collect aromates for its future immolation. It informs a priest of Heliopolis about its forthcoming arrival in the new month of Nissan. The rebirth of the bird is said to last three days. Both statements mirror a move towards an identification with Christ which is explicitly made in the final morale of the story. Phoenix has adopted the countenance of the saviour (πρόσωπον λαμβάνει τοῦ Σωτήρος)—an interpretation even further developed in the *Physiologos* of Pseudo-Basilius and the Syriac *Physiologos*.

In a number of texts from the third century and onwards Phoenix is used to symbolise the *vita angelica* of the Christian encratites. In one of his moral poems Gregory of Nazianzus asks how the ascetic shall flee the evil bonds of the flesh. He refers to the bird which despite dying renews itself. Those who in appearance seem to be dying are the truly eternally living, since they are burning by a flaming desire for Christ, the king.[34] The autogeny of the Phoenix

---

[32] See A.K. Petersen, "Fra opstandelsessymbol til messiansk dessert. Om den tidlige kristen- og jødedoms favntag med Fugl Fønix," *Fønix* 20 (1996) 4, 239–257, 254.

[33] Tertullian, *De Resurrectione Carnis* 13:14–16. Cf. Cyril of Jerusalem, *Mystagogical Cathecheses* 18:8; Ambrosius, *De Excessu Fratris Sui Satyri* 2:59 and *Constitutiones Apostolorum* 5:7.

[34] Gregory of Nazianzus, *Carmina* 1:2,525–533. Cf. also the allegoresis on the encratite life of the Christian ascetic by Lactanz in *De Ave Phoenice*.

has become a symbol of the ascetic's proleptic realisation of the heavenly life. Only the children of this world do marry. Those who are deemed worthy of the future world abstain from marriage. They can no longer die for they have become like angels. In the encratite circles of early Christianity the alleged non-sexuality and hermaphroditism of the Phoenix is developed in order to legitimise and to match the life of the ascetics. Phoenix symbolises the *vita angelica* and the Christian *virgo*.

In his burning defence for the ascetic life Pseudo-Titus reproaches the "spiritual marriage," an institution practised in encratite circles from the middle of the third century in which ascetics were living with virgins in a spiritual marriage simultaneously fulfilling Gen 2:18 "it is not good for man to live alone" and embodying the prelapsarian state. According to Pseudo-Titus he who has committed himself to a spiritual marriage has not yet understood the word of Jesus "Do not hold me, for I have not yet ascended to the Father." The true ascetics on the other hand are imitating the earthly Jesus. They are angels of God and virgins. To them the Phoenix has been given. It does not have a mate but lives alone in order to show that the youthful sexless state (*statum spadonis*) shall remain holy without blemish from women.[35] Two things are common to the use of the Phoenix motif among Christian ascetics. First, the bird symbolises the angelic life of the ascetic. Second, the privileged status which the Phoenix enjoyed in antiquity made it a powerful symbol which particular groups could subscribe to in order to claim that they represented the true traditions of the distant past. They were the true progeny of the Phoenix bird.

Epilogue

At the end of this "Zaubergang" it is evident that no definite, *a priori* meaning can be attributed to the Phoenix motif in antiquity. It meant different things in different contexts as witnessed by the concept's history of reception. On the other hand, it seems that one common

---

[35] Pseudo-Titus, *Epistula De Dispositione Sanctimonii* 336–339. On the spiritual marriage, see H. Achelis, *Virgines subintroductae. Ein Beitrag zu 1 Kor VII* (Leipzig, 1902) and E.A. Clark, "John Chrysostom and the *Subintroductae*," in *Ascetic Piety and Women's Faith: Essays on Late Ancient Christianity* (New York-Toronto, 1986), 265–290.

characteristic unites the different uses, i.e. Phoenix representing a discursive function by which claims can be made that a given tradition simultaneously represent a watershed and a conformity with the distant past. This duplicity was valuable in an age that favoured antiquity at the expense of novelty and innovation. For Christian writers in particular it solved a precarious dilemma. By the use of the Phoenix motif they were on the one hand able to argue that something decisively new had occurred in the Christ event, and on the other hand to maintain that this was a fulfilment of promises made in the distant past.

In a *Festschrift* devoted to the cultural interactions and interrelations in late antiquity it is interesting to see how Christian writers did not take over or adopt the Phoenix motif as a pagan symbol in need of adaptation. They simply utilised a powerful symbol which was an inherent part of their cultural and religious competence in order to make effective and persuasive statements. From this perspective the Phoenix bird was part of a common and shared stock of traditions uniting Jerusalem, Alexandria and Rome.

THE USE OF SCRIPTURE IN *1 ENOCH* 17–19*

Michael A. Knibb**

In an important monograph entitled *Asking for a Meaning*, Lars Hartman demonstrated that *1 Enoch* 1–5 had "grow[n] out of a soil consisting of an interpreted Old Testament,"[1] and he went on to show how the meaning of the text was bound up with recognition of it as interpretation of the biblical material on which it drew. What Lars Hartman showed in the case of *1 Enoch* 1–5 is of course more generally true of the Book of Enoch, namely that in many respects it represents a form of interpretation, and my purpose in what follows is to see what light is cast on the meaning of another passage in the book, chapters 17–19, by its use of scripture. In chapters 17–19, as elsewhere throughout *1 Enoch*, there are no explicit quotations from the Hebrew Bible, but it is not hard to recognise numerous allusions to passages in the Hebrew Bible and numerous parallel passages, and the commentaries are full of such references; the difficulty is to know whether we have to do with a conscious allusion, unconscious use of parallel phraseology, or merely an interesting parallel.[2] This problem is linked to the fact that it is hard to determine the extent to which we have exact quotation from the biblical text because for the most part we have to do only with a translation into Greek of the Aramaic original[3] or (for some three of the five sections of which the book was ultimately composed) with a daughter translation of the Greek, the Ethiopic version.[4] Notwithstanding these uncertainties,

---

* This brief study is offered in friendship to Ton Hilhorst, a respected and distinguished colleague, on his sixty-fifth birthday.

** London.

[1] L. Hartman, *Asking for a Meaning: A Study of 1 Enoch 1–5* (Coniectanea Biblica, NT Series 12; Lund, 1979), 37–38; see also his earlier study, *Prophecy Interpreted* (CB, NT Series 1; Lund, 1966).

[2] On the reasons for the lack of explicit quotation in *1 Enoch* and the difficulty of determining the level of dependence, see G.W.E. Nickelsburg, *1 Enoch 1: A Commentary on the Book of Enoch, Chapters 1–36; 81–108* (Hermeneia—a Critical and Historical Commentary on the Bible; Minneapolis, 2001), 57.

[3] I assume that the Parables were composed in Aramaic like the other parts of *1 Enoch*, although it is possible that the Parables were composed in Hebrew.

[4] For further discussion of this point, see Knibb, "Christian Adoption and Transmission of Jewish Pseudepigrapha: The Case of *1 Enoch*," *JSJ* 32 (2001) 396–415, esp., 400–405.

there seems to be a sufficient volume of evidence in *1 Enoch* 17–19 to justify an enquiry into its use of scripture.

1 Enoch 17–19 gives an account of Enoch's first journey through the cosmos and reaches its climax in the description of the mountain that reached to heaven, like the throne of God (18:8), and of the prison for the stars that transgressed the Lord's command and for the angels who were promiscuous with the women (18:12–19:2). The account of the journey has no introduction and is attached quite abruptly to the report of Enoch's ascent to the throne room of God and of the message of judgement on the watchers that he received there (chapters 14–16). This is one of several places within the Book of Watchers where there is an obvious literary seam, but the lack of any introduction or transitional passage means that the purpose of chapters 17–19 within the context of the Book of Watchers has to be inferred from their contents. I have argued elsewhere that the account of the journey is intended as a revelation of the true mysteries in contrast to the "worthless mystery" that the watchers had revealed to mankind, through which evil (τὰ κακά) had been introduced into the world (16:3).[5]

The abruptness of the transition between chapters (6)14–16 and chapters 17–19 is heightened by the fact that in the opening sentence (17:1) the subject is unspecified: "And they took and brought[6] me to a place where those who were there were like burning fire, and whenever they wished, they appeared as men." VanderKam has argued that the reference is to the winds and other natural phenomena that according to 14:8 carried Enoch up to heaven. He bases this view on the supposition that the same verb is used in 14:8 and 17:1, and on the fact that the angels lead Enoch, not lift him up, and he concludes that, if this view is right, "chapters 17–36 are meant to be the continuation of the action that begins in chapter 14."[7] This last point seems true, whether VanderKam's interpretation of 17:1 is right or not. But while the same verb (*naś'a*) is used

---

[5] See Knibb, "The Book of Enoch in the Light of the Qumran Wisdom Literature," in F. García Martínez (ed.), *Wisdom and Apocalypticism in the Dead Sea Scrolls and in the Biblical Tradition* (BETL 168; Leuven, 2003), 193–210.

[6] Eth does not have "and brought." The text could also be translated "I was taken and brought," but that still leaves open the question of the identity of those who escorted Enoch.

[7] J.C. VanderKam, *Enoch: A Man for All Generations* (Studies on Personalities of the Old Testament; Columbia, SC, 1995), 50.

in the Ethiopic of both 14:8 and 17:1, VanderKam has overlooked the fact that this verb can mean "to take" as well as "to raise" and corresponds to a number of different verbs in Greek; and that while the Greek of 14:8 has ἐπαίρω, in 17:1 it has παραλαμβάνω. One of the meanings of this latter verb is "to take somebody along" (so Gen 22:3; MT לקח, Eth *naś'a*), and it is surely this meaning that is intended here. It remains most likely that it is angels who are the unnamed subject in 17:1, not least because they are mentioned several times both before and after this passage: see 14:22–23; 14:25 (Greek); 18:14; 19:1.

The first part of the narrative (17:1–18:5) describes Enoch's journey through the cosmos to a group of seven mountains, the middle one of which reached to heaven like the throne of God (18:6–9a). The account of the journey is remarkable for the phenomena to which Enoch is led or which he sees, and these may be listed as follows:[8]

17:1 (i) [καὶ παραλάβοντες με εἴς τινα τόπον ἀπήγαγον] ἐν ᾧ οἱ ὄντες ἐκεῖ
γίνονται ὡς πῦρ φλέγον καί, ὅταν θέλωσιν, φαίνονται ὡσεὶ ἄνθρωποι

17:2 (ii) [καὶ ἀπήγαγόν με] εἰς ζοφώδη τόπον
(iii) καὶ εἰς ὄρος οὗ ἡ κεφαλὴ ἀφικνεῖτο εἰς τὸν οὐρανόν

17:3 (iv) [καὶ εἶδον] τόπον τῶν φωστήρων
(v) καὶ τοὺς θησαυροὺς τῶν ἀστέρων καὶ τῶν βροντῶν
(vi) καὶ εἰς τὰ ἀεροβαθῆ, ὅπου τόξον πυρὸς καὶ τὰ βέλη καὶ αἱ θῆκαι
αὐτῶν[9] καὶ αἱ ἀστραπαὶ πᾶσαι

17:4 (vii) [καὶ ἀπήγαγόν με] μέχρι ὑδάτων ζώντων
(viii) καὶ μέχρι πυρὸς δύσεως, ὅ ἐστιν καὶ παρέχον πάσας τὰς δύσεις
τοῦ ἡλίου

17:5 (ix) [καὶ ἤλθομεν][10] μέχρι ποταμοῦ πυρός, ἐν ᾧ κατατρέχει τὸ πῦρ ὡς
ὕδωρ καὶ ῥέει εἰς θάλασσαν μεγάλην δύσεως

17:6 (x) [ἴδον] τοὺς μεγάλους ποταμούς
(xi) καὶ μέχρι τοῦ μεγάλου ποταμοῦ
(xii) καὶ μέχρι τοῦ μεγάλου σκότους [κατήντησα]
(xiii) [καὶ ἀπῆλθον] ὅπου πᾶσα σὰρξ οὐ περιπατεῖ

17:7 (xiv) [ἴδον] τοὺς ἀνέμους τῶν γνόφων τοὺς χειμερινούς
(xv) καὶ τὴν ἔκχυσιν τῆς ἀβύσσου πάντων ὑδάτων

17:8 (xvi) [ἴδον] τὸ στόμα τῆς γῆς πάντων τῶν ποταμῶν
(xvii) καὶ τὸ στόμα τῆς ἀβύσσου

---

[8] Verbs of motion and of seeing have been included in the following list in square brackets for the sake of clarity.

[9] Eth has in addition "and a flaming sword," for which cf. the "flaming sword" of Gen 3:24 (LXX).

[10] Commonly emended to ἦλθον with Eth.

18:1 (xviii) [ἴδον] τοὺς θησαυροὺς τῶν ἀνέμων πάντων, [ἴδον] ὅτι ἐν αὐτοῖς
      ἐκόσμησεν πάσας τὰς κτίσεις
      (xix) καὶ τὸν θεμέλιον τῆς γῆς
18:2 (xx) καὶ τὸν λίθον [ἴδον] τῆς γωνίας τῆς γῆς
      (xxi) [ἴδον] τοὺς τέσσαρας ἀνέμους τὴν γῆν βαστάζοντας καὶ τὸ στε-
      ρέωμα τοῦ οὐρανοῦ.
18:3 [And I saw] how the winds stretch out the height of heaven,
      and they stand between earth and heaven; they are the pillars
      of heaven[11]
18:4 (xxii) [ἴδον] ἀνέμους τῶν οὐρανῶν στρέφοντας καὶ διανεύοντας[12] τὸν
      τροχὸν τοῦ ἡλίου, καὶ πάντας τοὺς ἀστέρας
18:5 (xxiii) [ἴδον] τοὺς ἐπὶ τῆς γῆς ἀνέμους βαστάζοντας ἐν νεφέλῃ
      (xxiv) [I saw] the paths of the angels[13]
      (xxv) [ἴδον] πέρατα τῆς γῆς, τὸ στήριγμα τοῦ οὐρανοῦ ἐπάνω

Enoch at this point has arrived at the ends of the earth, apparently
in the north-west (on this, see further below), and it is at this point
that he sees the group of seven mountains, the middle one of which
is like the throne of God (18:6–9a), and beyond that the prison for
the disobedient stars and the watchers (18:9b–19:2).

The account of Enoch's journey and the description of the seven
mountains and of the prison presuppose a geographical model which
it has often been assumed reflects the influence of non-Jewish—particularly Babylonian or Greek—conceptions. In recent years Grelot,[14]
followed by Milik,[15] has argued that the geographical ideas reflected
in chapters 17–19 (and in other section of 1 Enoch, particularly the
account of Enoch's second journey (chapters 21–36) and chapter 77)
are based on Babylonian, rather than Greek, conceptions, although
he suggests that they might have been mediated to the Jews via
Phoenicia. However, although some Babylonian ideas may ultimately
lie in the background of 1 Enoch, the suggestion of a major influence
from this source seems quite unlikely.[16] Much more plausible is the

[11] Greek omits the first and last clauses through homoioteleuton and for the
middle clause has: καὶ αὐτοὶ ἱστᾶσιν μεταξὺ γῆς καὶ οὐρανοῦ. Restoration is based
on Eth.
[12] Read δύνοντας (R.H. Charles, *The Book of Enoch*, Oxford, ²1912, 40).
[13] Greek omits through homoioteleuton ("I saw" . . . "I saw").
[14] P. Grelot, "La Géographie mythique d'Hénoch et ses sources orientales," *RB*
65 (1958) 33–69.
[15] J.T. Milik, *The Books of Enoch: Aramaic Fragments of Qumrân Cave 4* (Oxford:
Clarendon Press, 1976), 15–18, 29–30, 33–41.
[16] Grelot compared the geographical ideas reflected in Enoch with those of a
Late Babylonian World Map, and the phenomena that Enoch sees on his journey

assumption that the account of Enoch's journey reflects a number of ideas that were current in the popular geography of the day and derive from both Babylonian and, especially, Greek sources,[17] and in particular the river of fire (17:5, no. (ix) above) has long been compared with the Pyriphlegethon; the great rivers (17:6, no. [x]) with the Acheron, Styx, and Cocytus; and the great river (17:6, no. [xi]) with Oceanus, the Great Ocean Stream that encircled the earth. Beyond this, Nickelsburg, following the earlier suggestion of Glasson, has compared the account of Enoch's journey with a Nekyia, an account of a journey to the realm of the dead (cf. *Odyssey* x.504–540, esp. 508–514; xi), and this is helpful.[18] But perhaps of even greater importance is the influence of scripture in the composition of this material.

Enoch journeys first towards the west (17:4) and encounters fiery beings (17:1, no. [i]) as he is led towards a dark place and to a mountain whose summit reached heaven (17:2, nos. [ii]–[iii]). The significance of the fiery beings is not explained, but that they have some kind of semi-divine status is suggested by their fiery appearance, which may be compared with the appearance of the angel in Dan 10:5–6. Grelot has compared the fiery beings to the cherubim who are mentioned in Gen 3:24 as guarding the way to the tree of life.[19] The parallel is not exact but does point to the probable significance of the fiery beings as guardians of the way on which Enoch is journeying.

---

with those that, according to tablets 9 and 10 of the Gilgamesh Epic, Gilgamesh sees on his journey to Ut-Napishtim in search of the secret of immortality. However, VanderKam ("1 Enoch 77, 3 and a Babylonian Map of the World," *RevQ* 11/2 (1983) 271–78) has shown that Grelot's arguments were based on a reading of the textual evidence of the Babylonian World Map that is almost certainly wrong and on a false understanding of the ideas in *1 Enoch*. Nickelsburg (*1 Enoch 1*, 279–80) has further shown that there are significant differences between the phenomena seen by Enoch and those seen by Gilgamesh.

[17] M. Hengel, *Judaism and Hellenism: Studies in their Encounter In Palestine during the Early Hellenistic Period*. vol. 1 (London, 1974), 197–98; vol. 2. 132; Nickelsburg, *1 Enoch 1*, 279–80; cf. already A. Dieterich, NEKYIA: *Beiträge zur Erklärung der neuentdeckten Petrusapokalypse* (Leipzig, ²1913), 218–19.

[18] Nickelsburg, *1 Enoch 1*, 280; cf. T.F. Glasson, *Greek Influence in Jewish Eschatology* (London, 1961), 8–11.

[19] Grelot, "La Géographie mythique d'Hénoch," 38. Cf. also Ezek 28:14, 16. Nickelsburg (*1 Enoch 1*, 281 and n. 17) suggests that the author may be thinking of seraphim understood as "fiery beings," but this seems unlikely. The seraphim were serpentine beings, and any connection with the Hebrew root meaning 'to burn' is secondary.

The dark place and the mountain appear to be on the edge of the world in the west, where the sun has disappeared.[20] The mountain[21] is in the vicinity of the storehouses (θησαυροί) for the luminaries, the stars, the thunder, and the flashes of lightning, which are conceived to be on the edge of the world (17:3, nos. [iv]–[vi]). The word "storehouses" is not used in the Old Testament in relation to the luminaries and stars or the thunder and lightning, but the concept and the word are used in Job 38:22 (for snow and hail), in Ps 33:7 (LXX 32:7; for the deeps), and in Ps 135:7 (LXX 134:7); Jer 10:13; 51:16 (for the wind; but LXX Jer 10:13; 28:16, for the light). The elaboration of the description of the thunder and lightning in terms of God's bow, arrows, and quiver then draws on language used in theophanic passages that depict God appearing in a storm, for example Hab 3:9, 11; Ps 18:15 (LXX 17:15); 77:18–19 (LXX 76:18–19). Here we see for the first time a concern with natural phenomena, with the "secrets"—to use the term that is employed in the Parables (41:3; 59:1–3; 71:4)—of the cosmos, a concern that is characteristic generally of 17:5–18:5.

The significance of the living waters[22] and of the fire of the west (17:4, nos. [vii]–[viii]), to which Enoch is next led, is not entirely clear. The expression "living waters" is used in the Hebrew Bible to express the meaning "fresh water" (e.g. Gen 26:19), but that is hardly what is intended here. The expression is also used in Zech 14:8 in a context referring to life-giving water, and it is possible that this is what is in mind in *1 Enoch*, but if so, the idea is not developed. More is said about the fire of the west, which in the Greek is said to "provide," but in the Ethiopic, which should probably be preferred, to "receive" all the settings of the sun.[23] What may be in mind is the appearance of the sky at sunset. The relationship of this

[20] Cf. Milik, *The Books of Enoch*, 38.
[21] The description of the mountain in the Greek version of *1 En.* 17:2 ("whose top reached to heaven") corresponds exactly to what is said about Jacob's ladder in Gen 28:12. This is probably an instance of unconscious use of parallel phraseology.
[22] Eth "waters of life" is not a real variant, but merely represents the use of two nouns in a construct relationship to express Greek noun + adjective: cf. Zech 14:8 (Greek and Ethiopic); A. Dillmann, *Ethiopic Grammar* (London, ²1907), 462.
[23] Greek παρέχον is probably corrupt for παραδεχόμενον (so A. Dillmann, *SAB* 1892, 1045) or κατέχον (so M. Black, *The Book of Enoch or 1 Enoch: A New English Edition* [SVTP 7; Leiden, 1985], 156); contrast Nickelsburg, *1 Enoch 1*, 276.

fire to the fire described in chapter 23, to which Enoch goes during his second journey, is unclear.[24]

Enoch has now arrived at the extreme western edge of the world, but at this point he changes direction and goes towards the north, as the reference to the winter winds of darkness (17:7, no. [xiv]) indicates.[25] Milik suggests that Enoch at this point goes on a circular journey around the world,[26] but this has been questioned by Nickelsburg who points out that the verbs of motion and progression that typified 17:1–8 are missing in 18:1–5[27]—in fact there are no verbs of motion in 17:7–18:5. However, the reference to the four winds that support the earth and the firmament of heaven and are apparently situated at the edge of the world (18:2–3, no. [xxi]) does suggest that what is in mind is the four cardinal points of the compass (cf. Ezek 42:16–20; 1 Chron 9:24), and it is difficult to understand how Enoch would have seen the winds if he had not gone on a circuit of the world.

What is not in dispute is that 17:5–18:5 do have something of a different character from the surrounding material. On the one hand this section is not taken up in the account of Enoch's second journey except in so far as chapters 33–36 is also an account of a circular journey.[28] On the other a strong interest in natural phenomena is reflected in the material. In this connection it is of interest to observe, that after Enoch has visited the river of fire, the great rivers, and the great river (17:5–6, nos. [ix]–[xi]), which were discussed above, several of the items of natural phenomena that Enoch sees or visits are mentioned in the list of rhetorical questions with which Job is challenged (Job 38), or are mentioned in rhetorical questions in other wisdom passages, as the following list indicates. In Job 38, Job is asked whether he had any knowledge of, or power over, the objects that that are mentioned, and the answer implied is of course that he had no such knowledge or power—and was incapable of acquiring it.[29]

---

[24] Cf. Nickelsburg, *1 Enoch 1*, 282.
[25] Cf. Sir 43:17bLXX.
[26] Milik, *The Books of Enoch*, 39.
[27] Nickelsburg, *1 Enoch 1*, 284.
[28] Milik, *The Books of Enoch*, 38–39.
[29] Similarly the answer implied by the rhetorical question in Prov 30:4 is "God," and in Job 36:29; Sir 1:3 is "no one."

17:6   (xii) the great darkness: cf. Job 38:19, חשׁך/σκότος

17:7   (xv) the outflow of all the waters of the abyss: cf. Job 38:16,
חקר תהום/ἴχνη ἀβύσσου; Sir. 1:3, ἄβυσσος

18:1   (xviii) the storehouses of all the winds: cf. Ps 135:7 (LXX 134:7),
מוצא־רוח מאוצרותיו/ὁ ἐξάγων ἀνέμους ἐκ θησαυρῶν αὐτοῦ[30]
(xix) the foundation of the earth: cf. Job 38:4, איפה היית ביסדי־ארץ/
ποῦ ἦς ἐν τῷ θεμιλιοῦν με τὴν γῆν;

18:2   (xx) the corner stone of the earth: cf. Job 38:6, אבך פנתה/λίθον
γωνιαῖον
(xxi) the four winds that support the earth: cf. Job 38:24b,
אי־זה . . . יפץ קדים עלי־ארץ/πόθεν . . . διασκεδάννυται νότος εἰς τὴν
ὑπ᾽ οὐρανόν; Prov 30:4, מי אסף־רוח בחנפיו/τίς συνήγαγεν ἀνέμους
ἐν κόλπῳ;

18:3   (xxi) the height of heaven; cf. Sir. 1:3, ὕψος οὐρανοῦ; Prov 30:4,
מי עלה־שמים וירד/τίς ἀνέβη εἰς τὸν οὐρανὸν καὶ κατέβη;

18:4   (xxii) the winds of heaven that turn . . . the disk of the sun and
all the stars: cf. Job 38:33, הידעת חקות שמים/ἐπίστασαι δὲ τροπὰς
οὐρανοῦ;

18:5   (xxiii) the winds on the earth that support the clouds: cf. Job
36:29, אף אם־יביך מפרשי־עב/καὶ ἐὰν συνῇ ἀπεκτάσεις νεφέλης;

In addition, a comparison might be drawn between the statement
that Enoch reached the great darkness and went to a place where
no flesh walks (*1 En.* 17:6, nos. [xii]–[xiii]) and the question in Job
38:17: "Have the gates of death been revealed to you, or have you
seen the gate of deep darkness?"[31]

The fact that Enoch is said in *1 En.* 17:5–18:5 to have seen such
a variety of natural phenomena has rightly been regarded as evidence of the fact that the authors of apocalypses like the Book of
Enoch were concerned not only with eschatology, but also with the
cosmos, but the relevance of this passage at just this point in the
narrative does require further explanation.[32] However, the evidence

---

[30] Ps 135 (LXX 134) is not a wisdom psalm and does not employ rhetorical
questions, but the passage is listed here because of the similarity of the thought
(Yahweh as the one who [controls the forces of nature and] brings out the wind
from his storehouses) to that of *1 En.* 18:1 (Enoch sees the storehouses of the winds
with which God orders his creation).—Two of the objects seen by Enoch are not
mentioned in Job 38 or similar passages, but are mentioned in contexts referring
to God. For "firmament of heaven" (18:2–3, no. [xxi]; cf. 18:5, no. [xxv], with
στήριγμα for στερέωμα), cf. Gen 1:14–17; for "pillars of heaven" (18:2–3, no. [xxi]),
cf. Job 26:11.

[31] The parallel is not of course precise. Job is challenged whether he had visited
Sheol, in *1 Enoch* the claim is made that Enoch had visited a region—not, apparently, Sheol—inaccessible to other human beings.

[32] Cf. the comment of Nickelsburg (*1 Enoch 1*, 284): "Why these verses are inserted
here is not certain."

presented in the list above does suggest that there is some kind of connection with Job 38 in *1 En.* 17:5–18:5, and this may perhaps help in understanding the purpose of the passage. Enoch is presented here as gaining access to knowledge that, according to Job 38, was denied to Job and known only to God. The implication of this is that Enoch has access to secrets known otherwise only to God, and, as suggested above, that the mystery he reveals—unlike the worthless mystery revealed by the watchers (16:2–3)—is true.[33] In the light of this, we are then meant to understand that the further mysteries that Enoch reveals, concerning the fate of those who through the worthless mystery that they taught led men to commit sin and concerning the great judgement, are equally true.

The description of the seven mountains, the middle one of which resembled the throne of God, forms the climax of the account of Enoch's journey (18:6–9a). The fact that three of the mountains are said to lie towards the east and three towards the south indicates that the mountains were in the northwest, on the edge of the world (cf. 18:10 Greek).[34] Allusions in the narrative have long suggested that a deliberate link was intended by the author with traditions in the Hebrew Bible concerning the mountain of (the) god(s) and concerning other holy places.[35] Thus the location in the northwest suggests that the mountain in the middle (*1 En.* 18:8) was identified with the "mount of assembly" of the gods in the far recesses of the north that is mentioned in the mocking "lament" over the descent of an unnamed world-ruler into Sheol (Isa 14:4–21: see v. 13). Similarly, the fact that the mountains are made of precious stones suggests an allusion was intended to the description of the precious stones in the related tradition, also in the form of a lament, concerning the expulsion of the king of Tyre from the holy mountain

---

[33] It is impossible to know for certain whether or not the author of *1 Enoch* was making a conscious reference back to Job 38, but in a sense it does not matter because in any case quite remarkable claims are implicitly made here for the knowledge possessed by Enoch, a knowledge that Job was forced to admit he did not possess.—It may be noted that VanderKam (*Enoch: A Man for All Generations*, 91) has suggested a similar connection between the rhetorical questions in *1 En.* 93:11–14 and Job 38.

[34] According to 17:7, Enoch had already journeyed towards the north, and whether or not he had been on a circular journey around the world, it seems clear that he is now in the northwest.

[35] See, for example, the discussion of this material by Grelot ("La Géographie mythique d'Hénoch," 38–41).

of God (Ezek 28:11–19; see v. 13). But in Ezek 28, the mountain of God (vv. 14, 16) is described as paradise and is called "Eden, the garden of God" (v. 13), and this suggests a further allusion was intended by the author of *1 Enoch* to the paradise tradition of Gen 2–3. In his discussion of the account of Enoch's second journey (chapters 21–36), Grelot has suggested that the author has attempted to harmonise the conflicting biblical traditions concerning the location of paradise: of Gen 2, which places Eden in the east, of Isa 14, which places the residence of God on the mountain of the north, and that of Ezek 28, which identifies Eden as the mountain of God.[36] But whereas in *1 En.* 21–36, the harmonisation has been achieved by placing the mountain of God, which contains the tree of life, in the northwest (chapters 24–25) and the garden of righteousness, which contains the tree of knowledge, in the east (chapter 32), in chapters 17–19 the traditions are all associated with only one sacred place, and we should perhaps think in terms of a process of integration rather than of harmonisation. In any event the biblical traditions that lie in the background provide an indication of the significance of the mountain for the author as the holy mountain of God, identical with Eden.

More deserves to be said concerning the precious stones of which the seven mountains consist. In the first instance a deliberate allusion was no doubt intended to the list of precious stones of which the robe of the king of Tyre is said to consist in Ezek 28:13,[37] and thus to the idea that the mountain of God was also to be identified with Eden, the garden of God. But in detail there are few direct correspondences between the stones that are mentioned in *1 En.* 18 and those that are mentioned in Ezek 28, and it appears that the author also draws on the language of Isa 54:11–12,[38] where, significantly, the New Jerusalem is depicted as paradise restored, and of 1 Chron 29:2.

The seven mountains as a whole are said to be "of precious stones" (*1 En.* 18:6; ἀπὸ λίθων πολυτελῶν), and this seems obviously to be based on Ezek 28:13 (כל־אבן יקרה/πᾶν λίθον χρηστόν), but that is not the case for at least two of the three mountains that lay towards the

---

[36] Grelot, "La Géographie mythique d'Hénoch," 43.

[37] The fact that the list in Ezek 28:13 seems to have been secondarily inserted from Exod 28:17–20 is irrelevant to the point under discussion.

[38] It may be noted that Tobit 13:16 draws heavily on Isa 54:11–12.

east (*1 En.* 18:7). The first is "of coloured stone" (ἀπὸ λίθου χρώματος), perhaps the equivalent of the קרמה ... אבני (λίθους ... ποικίλους) of 1 Chron 29:2. The word for "pearl," of which the second mountain consists (ἀπὸ λίθου μαργαρίτου), does not occur in the Old Testament, but it is perhaps mentioned here as an example of a very precious gem. The third mountain on the east is said to be ἀπὸ λίθου ταθεν, probably corrupt for ἀπὸ λίθου ἰάσπιδος ("jasper"; cf. Ezek 28:13). Such a corruption seems not impossible at the uncial stage, while the Ethiopic "healing stone" is no doubt to be understood as an "etymological" translation of a Greek form that was corrupt or not totally intelligible.

The mountains that lay towards the south are all said to be "of red stone" (*1 En.* 18:7; ἀπὸ λίθου πυρροῦ, translated literally into Ethiopic as *'em'ebna qayyeḥ*). It may be suggested that this is the equivalent of ἄνθραξ ("carbuncle"; cf. Ezek 28:13, where Ethiopic translates as *yakent qayyeḥ* [literally "red jacinth"]).[39]

The mountain in the middle that reached to heaven, like the throne of God, is described as being "of antimony" (*1 En.* 18:8; ἀπὸ λίθου φουκά). In this case the Greek (followed by the Ethiopic) has transliterated the Hebrew פוך that is mentioned in Isa 54:11 and 1 Chron 29:2.[40] The summit of this mountain is, finally, said to be "of sapphire" (ἀπὸ λίθου σαφφείρου). Sapphire is one of the precious stones mentioned in Ezek 28:13 (and in Isa 54:11), but—apart from other occurrences in the Old Testament—it is also used in Ezek 1:26 of the "likeness of a throne" on which was seated "something like the appearance of a human form"; and in Exod 24:10 of the pavement under the feet of the God of Israel at the summit of Mount Sinai.[41] This last reference is perhaps the most significant as pointing to the identification of the mountain in the middle also with Sinai, which is mentioned in *1 En.* 1:4 as the mountain on which God will descend to exercise judgement.

The theme of judgement is certainly present in the account of the final part of Enoch's journey (*1 En.* 18:9b–19:2), in which he sees a

---

[39] The suggestion of Nickelsburg (*1 Enoch 1*, 286) that the "flame-coloured stones" (as he translates) correspond to "the stones of fire" of Ezek 28:14, 16 seems quite unlikely. On the latter, see W. Zimmerli, *Ezechiel*, 2. Teilband: *Ezechiel 25–48* (BKAT XIII/2; Neukirchen, 1969), 685–686.

[40] It is interesting to observe that the Septuagint does not transliterate in either case. In Isa 54:11 it uses ἄνθραξ, and in 1 Chron 29:2 λίθοι πολυτελεῖς.

[41] Cf. Grelot, "La Géographie mythique d'Hénoch," 40.

great chasm on the edge of the world in which pillars of heavenly
fire were falling (18:9b–11), and beyond this a desolate and terrible
place (18:12) that serves as the prison in which the stars that transgressed the Lord's command were to be kept until the time of the
consummation of their sin—ten thousand years (18:13–16), and in
which the angels who were promiscuous with the women were to
be kept until the great judgement (19:1–2). As has frequently been
observed, the location of this prison below the mountain of God was
no doubt suggested by the apparent location of the pit into which
the star Helel ben Šaḥar was cast below the mount of assembly of
the gods in the north (Isa 14:12–15) and of the place into which the
king of Tyre was cast below the mountain of God (Ezek 28:16–18).[42]
The importance of this passage in the context of the account of the
first journey as a whole is indicated by the fact that here for the
first time an angel (18:14; 19:1, here identified as Uriel) gives Enoch
an explanation of what he has seen,[43] and we should no doubt see
the message announcing the imprisonment of the watchers and the
limitation of the activity of the spirits "until the great judgement"
as crucial (19:1). But the interpretation of the passage is not without problems.

In the first place Nickelsburg has argued that 18:12–16 is a secondary addition: in his view the original text consisted of 18:9b–11
+ 19:1–2 and was concerned with the chasm beyond the edge of
the world that served as the prison for the watchers (cf. 21:7–10);
18:13–16 is a secondary intrusion that was concerned with the waste
and desolate place beyond the chasm that served as the prison for
the disobedient stars (cf. 21:1–6).[44] Nickelsburg, not entirely consistently,
then translates 18:13–16 *after* 18:9b–11 + 19:1–2 and interprets the
text as if it stood in this order.[45] However, as he notes, it is all but
certain that 18:12 followed immediately on 18:11 in 4QEn^c 1 viii.[46]
4QEn^c dates from the last third of the first century B.C.E., and thus

---

[42] Cf. e.g. Milik, *The Books of Enoch*, 39–40.
[43] Cf. Nickelsburg, *1 Enoch 1*, 286.
[44] Nickelsburg, *1 Enoch 1*, 287–88.
[45] Nickelsburg's comment (*1 Enoch 1*, 298) that in chapter 21 Enoch visits "in
reverse order" the prison for the disobedient stars and the prison for the watchers
that he had seen in the account of his first journey would only be valid if 18:12–16
did follow on 18:9b–11 + 19:1–2. But we have no evidence that such a text ever
existed.
[46] Cf. Milik, *The Books of Enoch*, 200.

if 18:13–16 is a secondary addition, it must have been inserted at a very early stage—but in this case it becomes questionable whether it makes sense to talk of a secondary addition. It seems much simpler to assume that 18:9b–19:2 has a different view from chapter 21 and thinks in terms of only one prison,[47] just as it also has a different view from 15:11–16:1 as to those who are responsible for the continuance of sin in the world. (In 15:11–16:1 it is the spirits of the giants, in 19:1 it is the spirits of the watchers themselves.)

A second problem concerns the significance of the stars in that the statement that the stars "transgressed the commandment of the Lord at the beginning of their rising . . . for they did not appear at their proper times" (18:15) stands in marked contrast to what is said in 2:1 about the obedience of the heavenly bodies to the order prescribed for them. It has long been suggested that the stars represent personified beings, that is angels, or rather the watchers that transgressed.[48] But the fact that there are said to be seven stars, and that the sin of which they are accused concerns their failure to appear at the right time, makes this suggestion unlikely, and we should think rather of the seven planets.[49] Elsewhere in the Enoch tradition there is a concern with the failure "in the last days" of the heavenly bodies to appear at the right time (80:2–6), and though the appearance of this theme in the Book of Watchers is unexpected, it was perhaps prompted by the reference to Helel ben Šaḥar in Isa 14:12 (a passage clearly in the mind of the author) and by the reference to the imprisonment of the host of heaven in a pit in Isa 24:21–22.

In view of what has been said above about Enoch as the recipient of mysteries otherwise known only to God, it is perhaps significant that the text ends with the statement: "I, Enoch, alone saw the visions, the ends of all things, and no human has seen what I have seen."

In conclusion, the account of Enoch's first journey is a densely-written narrative in which—in marked contrast to the account of the second journey—very little explanation is offered concerning the significance of the things that Enoch sees, and there are few explicit

---

[47] Cf. Milik, *The Books of Enoch*, 39.
[48] Cf. e.g. W. Bousset and H. Gressmann, *Die Religion des Judentums im späthellenistischen Zeitalter* (Tübingen, [4]1966), 323; Nickelsburg, *1 Enoch 1*, 288–89.
[49] Black, *The Book of Enoch*, 160.

clues as to the overall purpose of the material in the context of the Book of Watchers as a whole. However, consideration of the extent to which the material draws on, and represents an interpretation of, a range of interrelated biblical passages does cast light on its meaning.

THE INTERPRETATION OF METAPHORICAL LANGUAGE: A CHARACTERISTIC OF LXX-ISAIAH

ARIE VAN DER KOOIJ*

I

In this contribution in honour of Ton Hilhorst I would like to discuss a feature which is characteristic of the Aramaic versions of the Hebrew Bible, but not of the Old Greek version, the Septuagint (LXX). I have in mind the interpretative rendering of metaphorical language. Examples in Targum Jonathan to the Prophets (TJ) are: Isa 2:13, "Against all the cedars of Lebanon, lofty and lifted up, and against all the oaks of Bashan"; Targum Jonathan to the Prophets (TJ) has the following rendering: "And against all the kings of the peoples, strong and powerful, and against all the tyrants of the provinces." Isa 9:9, "The bricks are fallen"; TJ: "The chiefs were exiled." Zech 2:1 (E.V. 1:18), "and behold, four horns"; TJ: "and behold, four kingdoms."[1]

Generally speaking, metaphors have been rendered literally in the LXX. This does not necessarily mean that metaphors were taken literally,[2] but be that as it may, it was not part of the style of translation to render them in a non-literal way. There are, however, exceptions to this rule. Passages in LXX-Pentateuch, such as Gen 49 and Num 23–24, offer a few cases: The beginning of Gen. 49:10 ("The sceptre [שׁבט] shall not depart from Judah") has been rendered in Greek thus: "A ruler (ἄρχων) shall not fail from Juda." And as far the oracles in the book of Numbers are concerned, ch. 24:7a is an example in case: "Water shall flow from his buckets, and his seed shall be in many waters"; LXX: "There shall come a man out of his seed, and he shall rule over many nations." The underlying

---

* Leiden.

[1] See, e.g., P. Churgin, *Targum Jonathan to the Prophets* (Yale Oriental Series—Researches, XIV; New Haven, 1980) (reprint of 1907 [1927]), 86–87.

[2] For this phenomenon, see A. Hilhorst, "Biblical Metaphors Taken Literally," in: T. Baarda *et alii* (eds.), *Text and Testimony. Essays on New Testament and Apocryphal Literature in Honour of A.F.J. Klijn* (Kampen, 1988), 123–131.

interpretation may be reconstructed as follows: "water," that is "seed" understood here as "man"; "buckets," that is buckets containing the water, i.e. seed, here taken as referring to the people of Israel (cf. v. 5), and "many waters," that is "many nations" (for the latter, compare Isa 17:12).[3]

There is, however, one book in the LXX which displays a number of cases of this type of interpretation, LXX-Isaiah, as has been noted, some time ago, by J. Ziegler.[4] I will discuss some examples of an interpretative rendering of metaphors in this part of the LXX. For the sake of comparison between LXX-Isaiah and TJ-Isaiah, the rendering in TJ will also be given.

II

Isa 1:25

MT   ... I will smelt away your dross (סיגיך) as with lye
        and remove all your alloy (בדיליך)
LXX ... I will purge you into purity,
        but those who are disobedient (τοὺς δὲ ἀπειθοῦντας) will I destroy,
        and take away all the wicked ones (πάντας ἀνόμους) from you
        and will humble all the arrogant ones (πάντας ὑπερηφάνους).

This verse is part of a passage about divine judgement and renewal of Zion (vv. 21–27). MT contains the image of "the smelting away of your dross" and of "removing of your alloy" (see also v. 22: "your silver has become dross"). LXX, on the other hand, represents a text without metaphorical language: instead of "your dross" it offers the words, "those who are disobedient," introduced by the verbal form "I will destroy" (ἀπολέσω) which has no parallel in MT. Divergent from MT, where "your dross" is the object of "I will smelt away," LXX reflects a segmentation according to which "your dross" is taken as part of a new clause ("but those who are . . ."), while the previous one ("I will purge you into purity") constitutes a free rendering of the words in MT which in translation read, "I will smelt away" (ואצרף כבר). Regarding the second part of the verse ("I will

---

[3] See A. van der Kooij, "Perspectives on the Study of the Septuagint: Who are the Translators?" in F. García Martínez and E. Noort (eds.), *Perspectives in the Study of the Old Testament and Early Judaism* (VTSup, 73; Leiden, 1998), 214–229, esp. 224.

[4] See J. Ziegler, *Untersuchungen zur Septuaginta des Buches Isaias* (AA XII, 3; Münster, 1934), 80–91.

remove all your alloy"), LXX has two clauses: one about "the wicked ones" and one about "the arrogant ones."

Thus, unlike MT, LXX offers a text without metaphorical language: the image of "dross" seems to have been interpreted as "the disobedient ones," and that of "alloy" as "the wicked ones" and "the arrogant ones" as well. However, since the rendering of סִיגַיִךְ seems to be based on the association between the roots סִיג and סוּג, one could argue that this part of the LXX-text presupposes a different Vorlage, viz. סוּגַיִךְ, a reading which is actually attested by 1QIsaᵃ.[5] This may well have been the case, but it is also possible that both witnesses, LXX and 1QIsaᵃ, independently reflect a particular interpretation of the Hebrew סִיגַיִךְ, which, together with בְּדִילָיִךְ, actually attests the older text. The fact that the rendering of the latter (בְּדִילָיִךְ) in LXX clearly is a case of an interpretation of metaphorical language, favours the idea that, essentially, the same applies to the rendering of the former.

TJ offers a similar interpretation:

> I will separate, as those who purify with lye, all your wicked and I will remove all your sinners.

Isa 5:14b

MT and her dignity (הֲדָרָהּ) and her multitude (הֲמוֹנָהּ) go down, her uproar (שְׁאוֹנָהּ) and he who exults in her

LXX and the glorious (οἱ ἔνδοξοι), and great (οἱ μεγάλοι) and rich ones (οἱ πλούσιοι), and her pestilent ones, shall descend.

This verse is part of one of the woe-oracles in Isa 5 (vv. 11–17). Although in the Hebrew version, the feminine suffix is a bit strange, it must refer to the city, or, more likely, to the people of Israel. The best and finest of the people will go down, i.e., into the grave (cf. v. 14a). In LXX the three impersonal terms have been interpreted as referring to particular groups: "glorious ones" for "dignity," "great ones" for "multitude," and "rich ones" for "uproar." As to the rendering of the third item, one may compare Isa 32:9 and 33:20, where Hebrew שַׁאֲנָן has been rendered as πλούσιος. And for the notion of "richness" as interpretation of Hebrew שָׁאוֹן, see also Isa 24:8.

---

[5] See D.W. Parry and E. Qimron, *The Great Isaiah Scroll (1QIsaᵃ)* (STDJ, 32; Leiden, 1999), 3.

TJ has partly the same interpretation:

> and their honoured men and their multitudes go down,
> their throng and he who is strong among them.

Isa 10:33–34

MT   Behold the Lord, the Lord of Hosts, will lop the boughs (פֻּארה)
with terror, and the great in stature (רמי הקומה) will be cut off,
and the lofty (הנבהים) will be brought low.
He will cut down the thickets of the forest (סבכי היער) with iron
and Lebanon shall fall by (or: with?) a majestic one (באדיר).

LXX   For behold, the ruler, the Lord Sabaoth, will confound the glorious ones (τοὺς ἐνδόξους) with (his) power, and the haughty in
pride (οἱ ὑψηλοὶ τῇ ὕβρει) shall be crushed, and the lofty ones
(οἱ ὑψηλοί) shall be humbled.
The lofty ones (οἱ ὑψηλοί) shall fall by the sword, and the
Lebanon shall fall with his lofty ones (σὺν τοῖς ὑψηλοῖς).

In these verses God is portrayed as a forester who lops the boughs
of trees and cuts off tall trees. As conclusion of vv. 27–32, at least
as it stands now, the verses seem to suggest that the enemy approach-
ing Jerusalem, presumably the Assyrians (cf. 10:5ff.), portrayed here
as tall trees, will perish. The imagery of high trees and thickets has
been interpreted in LXX in terms of the glorious and the lofty ones.
The Old Greek is characterised by the repetition of the word ὑψηλός
(four times). The rendering "glorious" (ἐνδόξος) for Hebrew פֻּארה is
based on the association between this word and the noun פֻּאר.

TJ testifies to a similar interpretation:

> Behold, the master of the world, the Lord of Hosts casts slaughter
> among his armies as grapes trodden in the press; and the great in
> stature will be hewn down and the strong will be humbled. And he
> will slay the mighty men of his armies who make themselves mighty
> with iron, and his warriors will be cast on the land of Israel.

Isa 11:10

MT   In that day the root of Jesse shall stand as a signal (לנס) to the
peoples

LXX   In that day shall be the root of Jesse, he that stands up to rule
(ἄρχειν) the nations

This verse is the last one of the well known passage, 11:1–10, which
announces the righteous ruler in the person of a new Davidic king,
and his reign of peace. While at other places in Isaiah, LXX offers
a literal rendering of Hebrew נס (see, e.g., 5:26; 11:12; 13:2), in this

instance the image of standing as a "signal" has been interpreted as
standing up "to rule."

TJ has a literal rendering here ("to stand as an ensign to the
peoples").

Isa 22:22

MT   And I will place the key of the house of David (מפתח בית דוד)
        on his shoulder (על שכמו)
LXX   And I will give the glory of David (τὴν δόξαν Δαυιδ) unto him,
        and he shall rule (καὶ ἄρξει)

This verse, and the following ones (vv. 23–24, see below) as well, is
part of the passage about the promotion of Eliakim to the office
vacated by Shebna, and his glorious administration. Instead of the
phrase, "the key of the house of David," LXX offers a free rendering by taking the Hebrew as carrying the notion of power, or
glory. As a result of this free rendering, a literal rendering of what
follows ("on his shoulder") would not make sense. For the notion of
"ruling" in connection with "shoulder," one may compare Isa 9:6
("upon his shoulder was the government [LXX: ἡ ἀρχή]").

TJ offers, partly at least, a similar rendering:

> And I will place the key of the sanctuary and the authority of the
> house of David in his hand.

Isa 22:23

MT   And I will fix him as a peg (יתד) in a sure place
LXX   And I will set him as a ruler (ἄρχοντα) in a sure place

The image of the "peg" has been interpreted here as "ruler." Compare
also v. 25, where Hebrew "the peg" has been rendered as "the man"
(ὁ ἄνθρωπος).

This type of interpretation is also attested by TJ in both verses:
"And I will appoint him a faithful officer ministering in an endur-
ing place" (v. 23), and "a faithful officer" (v. 25).

Isa 22:24

MT   And they shall hang (תלו) on him
LXX   And on him shall every one trust (ἔσται πεποιθώς)

The expression used in the Hebrew text, "to hang on someone,"
has been explained in the sense of "to trust on someone."

In this case too, TJ testifies to the same interpretation: "And all
the glorious ones of his father's house will rely on him."

Isa 23:17

MT   and she (Tyre) shall play the harlot (וזנתה)
LXX   and she shall be a port of merchandise (καὶ ἔσται ἐμπόριον)

The imagery that Tyre will play again the harlot for the nations has
been interpreted as follows: she shall be a trading centre of the world.
The Hebrew זנה is taken in the sense of "to trade," or more specifically
"to be trade-station."

    Similarly, TJ: "and she will supply business."

Isa 31:9b

MT   says the Lord, whose fire (אור) is in Zion
       and whose furnace (תנור) is in Jerusalem
LXX   Thus says the Lord: Blessed is he that has seed (σπέρμα) in Sion
       and kinsmen (οἰκείους) in Jerusalem

While v.9b in MT forms the concluding passage of the whole of
31:1–9, in LXX it marks the beginning of a new section. MT is
about God who has his "fire" and "furnace" in Zion, which means
that Zion is the place where He has his home (his hearth). The Old
Greek is different: it is about "seed" and "kinsmen" in Sion/Jerusalem,
not of God, but of the "blessed." Seeligmann who speaks of a
"remarkable liberty"[6] of the translator, does not discuss the differences
in detail. Laberge is of the opinion that the *Vorlage* of the LXX might
have contained the reading שאר instead of אור. For this reading he
refers to passages in the book of Leviticus where it has been rendered as οἰκείος in LXX.[7] However, the differences regarding "fire"-
"seed" and "furnace"-"kinsmen" are more easily understood as an
interpretation in the same vein as the examples given above. Both
terms in Hebrew have been taken here as an image of seed and
family. As we know from other places in the Hebrew Bible, and
from Mesopotamian literature, the image of fire/furnace could carry
the notion of offspring. See for example 2 Sam 14:7: "Thus they
would quench my coal (נחלתי) which is left." The widow is referring
here to her last son, the only heir of the family. Like fire and furnace, the image of coal is clearly related to the hearth of the house.

---

[6] I.L. Seeligmann, *The Septuagint Version of Isaiah* (MEOL, 9; Leiden, 1948), 114.
[7] L. Laberge, *La Septante d'Isaïe 28–33* (Ottawa, 1978), 78f.

The domestic fireplace was regarded, as is also known from Babylonian texts,[8] as a symbol of the family.[9]

TJ offers a different interpretation of the text:

> says the Lord, whose splendour is in Zion for those who performs his law, and whose burning furnace of fire is in Jerusalem for those who transgress his Memra.

Interestingly, it seems that in the second part the "furnace" has been taken literally (in the sense of Gehenna).

III

So far some examples from LXX-Isaiah in order to show that this book of the Old Greek is characterised by a feature that is well known from the targums, viz., the interpretation of figurative language. It fits in with the interpretative character of LXX-Isaiah. It is also in line with the fact that LXX-Isaiah has its own, distinctive place in the LXX as a whole.

As becomes further clear from the examples discussed above, LXX-Isaiah contains renderings which are quite close to those in TJ-Isaiah. The interpretation of metaphorical language constitutes one of the aspects in which the Old Greek of Isaiah resembles the Aramaic version of the book (TJ-Isaiah).[10]

---

[8] A nice parallel is to be found in CAD Vol. 2: B, p. 73 (s.v. *balû*): "my assistant whose brazier (*kinunsu*) has gone out," i.e., who has no family.

[9] See K. van der Toorn, *Family Religion in Babylonia, Syria and Israel* (SHANE, VII; Leiden, 1996), 165.

[10] Other aspects are: the modernisation of geographical terms, and the actualisation of prophecies.

THE CRITICAL REWRITING OF GENESIS
IN THE GNOSTIC *APOCRYPHON OF JOHN*

In the second and last part of the Gnostic *Apocryphon* (or: *Secret Book*) *of John* (*Ap. John*)[1] we more than once come across the phrase, "It is not as Moses said (...) but (thereupon a Gnostic explanation of the primordial event in question is given)."[2] This formula is highly characteristic of the approach to Genesis traditions in *Ap. John* and in related early Christian Gnostic texts. In *Ap. John*, the corrections of the words of Moses are put into the mouth of Jesus Christ. The book claims to report an appearance of the exalted Christ to his disciple John on the Mount of Olives and to reveal the secret teachings given by the Saviour to John.

The first part of the revelation speaks of the eternal reality of the supreme God and his hypostasized thoughts or qualities (the aeons). Thereupon—in a transition to the second part of the revelation—the Gnostic Christ relates the tragic events that led to the coming into existence of an inferior Godhead, who is called Yaldabaoth. The second part, which deals with the creation and the early history of humankind, can be read as a critical revision of the first chapters of Genesis, from God's spirit moving upon the waters in Gen 1:2 down to the story of Noah and the Flood in Genesis chapters 6–8. The present essay focuses on the second part of *Ap. John*.

---

[1] We know *Ap. John* from four Coptic manuscripts. The Nag Hammadi collection includes three copies (II,1; III,1; IV,1). A fourth copy is contained in the so-called Berlin Codex (*BG*). The version of *BG* and Nag Hamm. Cod. III,1 is shorter than the text of II,1 and IV,1. As a rule I shall quote the *BG* text. An early Greek version of the first part of *Ap. John* is summarized by bishop Irenaeus of Lyons in his *Adversus Haereses* I 29 (*ca.* 180). This patristic source enables us to assume that the original Greek text was written at least some decades before the end of the second century. Synoptic text edition: M. Waldstein and F. Wisse, *The Apocryphon of John. Synopsis of Nag Hammadi Codices II,1; III,1; and IV,1 with BG 8502,2* (Nag Hammadi and Manichaean Studies 33; Leiden, 1995).

[2] *BG* 45,9; II 13,20 (God's Spirit moving upon the waters); *BG* 58,17; II 22,22; III 29,5 (Adam's sleep); *BG* 59,17; II 23,3; III 29,22 (Adam's rib); *BG* 73,4; II 29,6; III 37,23 (the redemption of Noah).

But it goes without saying that this last part of the text is fully understandable only in the light of what has been said in the preceding
sections.

A fundamental element of the preceding teaching is the distinction being made between the supreme God, the Invisible Spirit, and
the demiurgical God Yaldabaoth, and, furthermore, the identification
of the God of Genesis, the biblical Creator of heaven and earth,
with the inferior Demiurge.

The supreme God is conceived of as a hyper-cosmic entity who
because of his (its?) complete transcendence is unknowable to the
world. The Christ of *Ap. John* claims to reveal this previously unknown
God to John.[3] In a way, also the demiurgical God Yaldabaoth is
revealed by the Gnostic Christ. This allegedly cosmic God was known
long before, but Christ now explains to John who he really is:[4] he
speaks of his illegitimate descent (he is the fatherless son of Sophia,
which makes him an inferior being), of his "psychic" (rather than
spiritual) nature, of his residence in the cosmic world, his outward
appearance (he looked like a monster in the shape of a lion-faced
serpent with eyes shining with fire), his character traits (jealousy,
ignorance, arrogance), and his many treacherous actions.

The relationship between the Invisible Spirit and Yaldabaoth is
not hierarchical but antagonistic.[5] Note that according to *Ap. John*,
the coming into being of the demiurgical God was not caused by
the true God. Rather, this was the result of a trespass or an error
committed by Sophia on a lower level within the divine realm.[6] The
demiurgical God turned out to be the adversary of the true God
and the enemy of spiritual humanity. Of course, the identification
of the biblical God with this inferior figure had far-reaching consequences for the interpretation of Genesis traditions.

Why did Gnostic mythopoets emphasise this distinction between
a fully transcendent Divinity and an inferior Demiurge and ruler of

---

[3] It is implied that the true God was not revealed by Jesus in his pre-paschal
teaching. In the introductory frame story, John wonders who this God (the Father
of Jesus) is. Cf. my article, "The Evaluation of the Teaching of Jesus in Gnostic
Revelation Dialogues," *NovT* 30 (1988) 158–68.

[4] Cf. *BG* 36,16ff. and the discussion below.

[5] Yaldabaoth does not even know the supreme God, *BG* 46,2–6. Nevertheless
this radical theological dualism had a monistic background: the inferior God was
believed to be an abortive child of Sophia, one of the aeons of the supreme God.

[6] Sophia acted without the consent of the true God and without the knowledge
and collaboration of her divine male consort, *BG* 36, 16ff.

the world? And why did they identify the God of Genesis with the demiurgical God, and therefore feel the need to correct Moses' accounts of his actions? In my discussion of these questions I shall consider three aspects.

1. Intellectual Backgrounds of the Authors of *Ap. John*

Gnostics were not the first to distinguish between a purely transcendent divine principle and a cosmic God (or a plurality of cosmic gods). They may have adopted their theological dualism from Hellenistic philosophy.[7]

A few years ago, I proposed that some of the basic ideas underlying Gnostic mythological texts had developed in a non-Jewish environment permeated by some kind of Platonic thinking.[8] In my recent contribution to the volume in honour of Hans-Martin Schenke I tried to be more specific.[9] I focussed on the theological and anthropological ideas expressed in *Ap. John*'s version of the myth and argued that in these ideas we find features of a form of Platonism that was influenced by distinctly Aristotelian thought. First of all, I pointed to the idea of a hyper-cosmic God who has no dealings at all with the creation and the rule over the world. Whereas Plato, in his *Timaeus*, presented the Demiurge as an aspect or function of the divine principle itself, Aristotle insisted that the supreme God is not engaged in any practical activity and cannot be *causa efficiens* of motions and changes in the physical world. The discharge of the transcendent God from any responsibility for the rule over the lower world enabled Gnostic intellectuals to speak highly of their true God while at the same time uttering negative thoughts about the Demiurge and his powers.

The anthropological ideas of the authors of *Ap. John* become apparent in their rewriting of the stories of the creation of Adam and

---

[7] What made this distinction typically Gnostic was the idea that the creator and ruler of the world is not only a cosmic but also an incompetent and morally inferior figure. Cf. below, section II.

[8] "The Thought Pattern of Gnostic Mythologizers and Their Use of Biblical Traditions," in: J.D. Turner and A. McGuire, *The Nag Hammadi Library after Fifty Years* (Leiden, 1997), 89–101, 97.

[9] "Traces of Aristotelian Thought in the *Apocryphon of John*," in: H.-G. Bethge, S. Emmel, K.L. King, I. Schletterer, *For the Children, Perfect Instruction. Studies in Honor of Hans-Martin Schenke* (Leiden, 2002), 181–202.

Eve. *Ap. John* tells how the cosmic powers, the archons, moulded Adam's "psychic body" out of their own substance.[10] According to a widespread tradition in late antiquity, Aristotle taught that the human soul shares the fine-material ("ethereal") substance of the celestial gods.[11] *Ap. John*'s idea of a human soul-body composed by the archontic rulers out of themselves can be understood against this background. In addition, the pivotal Gnostic conviction that the spiritual centre of the soul is of divine origin and nature and, accordingly, that it was not created but received from above, may reflect Aristotelian teaching.[12] The same holds true of the belief that this divine element is given to human beings as a potential (δύναμις) that needs awakening and development.[13] In my contribution to the Festschrift Schenke I discuss these possible traces of Aristotelian thought in more detail.

While it is obvious that many vocabulary and narrative items of the Gnostic myth as it is told in *Ap. John* can be traced back to the first book of Moses and to other biblical and possibly also extra-biblical Jewish traditions, this does not apply to the underlying radical type of theological dualism nor to the idea of the human individual as a *compositum* of matter, fine-material soul, and divine "power." To a considerable extent, the critical interpretation of Genesis traditions in *Ap. John* and related Gnostic texts can be explained as the result of an adaptation of these traditions to the heterogeneous thought system outlined above.

---

[10] *BG* 48,14–49,2 and 49,9–51,1; the long version gives many more details about the creation of the psychic body and about the contributions of numerous cosmic powers (II, 15,5–19,15).

[11] In fact, Aristotle taught that the substance of the soul-body is "analogous" to ether, the substance of the celestial bodies, *De gener. animal.* II 3, 736b 39f. A.P. Bos, *The Soul and its Instrumental Body. A Reinterpretation of Aristotle's Philosophy of Living Nature* (Leiden, 2003), *passim*.

[12] *De gener. animal.* II 3, 736b 27–29: the *nous* alone is a divine element that comes into man additionally from outside. For later receptions of this idea see "Traces of Aristotelian Thought," 192f, n. 58.

[13] Particularly in codex III the Greek term δύναμις is used to denote the divine potential of the soul ("the power of the Mother"): III 15,24 (II 10,21); 18,14.18; 23,20; 24,6.10 (II 19,28); 25,2 (II 20,11); 34,7 (II 26,12f.); 34,14 (?). The other versions, notably *BG*, prefer the Coptic equivalent *kjom*.

II. THE NARRATIVE STRUCTURE OF THE
GNOSTIC MYTH OF ORIGINS

Our next step is to explain the specific narrative pattern and the story line of the Gnostic myth. Here a reference to the philosophical background of the authors is not of much help.[14] In the myth as it is related in *Ap. John*, the successive stages in the creation and the early history of humanity are presented as having resulted from actions and reactions alternately undertaken by good and evil forces (in their attempts to keep or to regain the divine light-power, see below).

I propose that this story is a variant of a myth which was current in a variety of forms in antiquity, in the Near East and Egypt as well as in the classical world. Its common pattern is designated in scholarly literature as the ancient combat myth.[15] According to Adela Yarbro Collins, the variants of the myth depict "a struggle between two divine beings and their allies for universal kingship. One of the combatants is usually a monster, very often a dragon. This monster represents chaos and sterility, while his opponent is associated with order and fertility. Thus their conflict is a cosmic battle whose outcome will constitute or abolish order in society and fertility in nature."[16]

The Gnostic variant of the myth is characterised by an utterly negative attitude towards the Demiurge, the Creator and ruler of the physical world. He is pictured as the source of all evil and indeed as the adversary of the true God. Note that the Gnostic myth never reports a direct confrontation of the two divine beings. What is at stake in their conflict is the spiritual power in humanity. It should also be noticed that in their attempts to appropriate this divine power, the two Gods resort to different methods.

---

[14] It will not be necessary to point to the differences between the overall purport of the Gnostic myth and the creation myth in Plato's *Timaeus*.

[15] J. Fontenrose, *Python. A Study of Delphic Myth and its Origins* (Berkeley and Los Angeles, 1959); N. Forsyth, *The Old Enemy. Satan and the Combat Myth* (Princeton, 1987), esp. 318–332.

[16] A. Yarbro Collins, *The Combat Myth in the Book of Revelation* (Harvard Dissertations in Religion, 9; Missoula, Mont., 1976), 57. Yarbro Collins does not refer to Gnostic variants of the myth. Cf. S. Giversen's observation in "The Apocryphon of John and Genesis," *ST* 17 (1963) 60–76, p. 74: "(. . .) there is a tendency to make it all a battle fought between spiritual forces."

The opening scene of *Ap. John*'s combat myth describes the appearance of the demiurgical God Yaldabaoth, the lion-faced monster whose coming into existence was due to an error committed by his mother Sophia.[17] Lest the immortal aeons see him, Sophia cast him away from the world above. Yet she placed him on a throne outside the realm of the divine world of light, and so installed him as the Chief Ruler of the lower world.[18]

The story begins to develop when it reports that this cosmic God wrongfully took away a portion of divine power from his Mother.[19] This compelled the Invisible Spirit to come into action (in spite of the absolute transcendence attributed to him in the earlier parts of *Ap. John*)[20] and to get his light-power back.[21] With a view to emptying Yaldabaoth of this spiritual power, the Invisible Spirit (or one of his emanations)[22] revealed himself in a human form to Yaldabaoth and his cosmic fellows.[23] When Yaldabaoth and his allies saw the form of God's image, they said to each other, "Let us create a man in the image of God and the likeness" (cf. Gen 1:27). But when they had fashioned their "psychic" creature after the image of the true God, it turned out to be an artefact rather than a living soul.[24]

At Sophia's request the true God ordered some of his light aeons to descend in the shape of cosmic angels and to suggest to Yaldabaoth that he breathe the power he had taken away from his Mother into Adam's face (cf. Gen 2:7b LXX). When the demiurgical God did what he was said to do, he lost his spiritual power to Adam.[25] In

---

[17] Cf. above, notes 4 and 6. Apparently Sophia is blamed for having yielded to "psychic" impulses.

[18] *BG* 38,1–10.

[19] *BG* 38,15–17; cf. 42, 15–18. After this first episode a long interlude follows in which we are informed of the creation of numerous cosmic powers and angels by Yaldabaoth, and in which Sophia's eventual repentance is related (*BG* 39,1–47,20).

[20] The transcendence of the supreme God is emphasized in the opening section of the book (*BG* 22,17–26,21). Above we explained this idea from the philosophical background of the authors. But cf. *BG* 31,11f.: "the Invisible Spirit wanted to make something."

[21] The editor of the long version seems to have realised that this initiative was at odds with the absolute transcendence of the Invisible Spirit (cf. the previous note), for in this version it is not the supreme God himself but one of his aeons (Pronoia, "Providence") who shows the cosmic archons a manlike form of God (II 14,18–24; IV 22,24–23,2).

[22] Cf. n. 21.

[23] *BG* 47,20–48,5.

[24] *BG* 48,6–51,1.

[25] *BG* 51,1–20. III 24,7f., "blow your spirit into his face," is preferable to *BG* 51,15f: "blow (something) of your spirit into his face."

this way Adam became an instrument by which the true God intended to redeem the lost divine substance from the lower world. However, Yaldabaoth and his forces tried to prevent this and made every effort to keep the spiritual substance which was now part of Adam's soul, in their dark world. Several Genesis stories are transformed into further episodes of a struggle over the divine power. I shall confine myself to summarising the more important narrative items.

The Demiurge realised that as a result of his breathing "the power of the Mother" into Adam, the intelligence of his creature was superior to that of himself and of all the cosmic rulers and angels. This prompted the archontic powers to seize Adam (i.e. Adam's soul-body with the divine potential in it) and to bring him deep down into the dark cosmos. Here they imprisoned him in a material body composed from the four sublunary elements.[26]

Due to its imprisonment in a physical body and its stay in the darkest regions of the cosmos, the spiritual core of Adam's soul was fully separated from the world above. But the true God "had mercy on the power of the Mother" in the first human being. Once again he came into action. He sent a female Spirit as a "helper" to Adam (cf. Gen 2:18 LXX) in order to inform him of his divine origin.[27] The sending of the Spirit to Adam provoked the cosmic rulers to make a counter-move. They created an "opposing Spirit,"[28] whose task it was to lead Adam astray so that he might not know "his perfection,"[29] to draw his soul to "the works of evil," and "to cast it into forgetfulness."[30]

---

[26] *BG* 55,2–6. 9–13.

[27] Eve, Adam's "helper" according to Gen 2:18 (LXX: βοηθός), is presented as a divine bringer of the Gnostic truth to Adam; Adam calls her Zoe, "Life" (Gen 3:21 LXX). *BG* 52,17–54,4.

[28] *BG* 74,6–10.

[29] *BG* 56,14–17.

[30] *BG* 69,1–5; cf. 63,8–9; 67,14–18. In the opposing spirit we can recognize features of the Devil or Satan as he appears in various ancient Jewish and Christian texts, in particular where he is described as a tempter or seducer of humankind; see e.g. Matt 4:3 (the Devil is introduced as "the Tempter"). The concept of two opposing spirits, the one guiding man to do "what God has desired," the other inciting him to sin is also found in the literature of Qumran; cf. 1QS III 17–IV 26 (text ed. with English translation in: F. García Martínez and E.J.C. Tigchelaar, *The Dead Sea Scrolls Study Edition* I [Leiden, 1997], 74–79). Similar ideas occur in *The Testaments of the Twelve Patriarchs* and in other early Jewish and Christian texts. In rabbinical literature, the two spirits developed into two internal tendencies in human beings, the inclinations to good and to evil.

But the fact remained that it was now Adam who possessed the divine power. Curiously enough, a detail of the story of the creation of Eve is supposed to show how the demiurgical God tried to take the spiritual power away from Adam in secret: "he (the Demiurge) wanted to bring out the power which had been given to him (Adam). And he cast a "trance" over Adam," etc. (cf. Gen 2:21).[31] But again his action was not entirely successful. What actually happened was that Adam gained a female consort with the same spiritual *ousia* as he had (cf. Gen 2:23). In the opinion of the Gnostic myth-makers this meant that the spiritual substance given to Adam was now divided over two creatures.

According to *Ap. John*, the creator God placed Adam in Paradise in order to delude him.[32] He forbade him to eat from the tree of knowledge lest he remembered who he really was and became aware of his present situation.[33] But the spiritual helper from above (or Christ himself) encouraged Adam (or both Adam and Eve) to eat. Then Yaldabaoth noticed that Adam and Eve "withdrew" from him. For this reason he cursed them, cast them out of Paradise, and "clothed them in gloomy darkness."[34] Later on Yaldabaoth is said to have defiled Eve and to have implanted sexual desire in her (and, through her, in her offspring).[35] The result of sexual intercourse was that the spiritual power was spread out over ever more human beings (cf. Gen 1:28) so that it became more difficult for it to return in its entirety to the world above.

Likewise the biblical traditions of the Great Deluge and the intercourse of sons of God with human females (Gen 6:5ff. and 6:1–4, respectively) are rewritten. The Flood story is interpreted allegorically as an attempt by the demiurgical God to cover humanity with darkness ("darkness was falling over everything upon earth").[36] But

---

[31] *BG* 58,10–14: Cf. my discussion of the slightly confused rewriting of the relevant Genesis story, "The Creation of Man and Woman in *The Secret Book of John*," in G.P. Luttikhuizen (ed.), *The Creation of Man and Woman. Interpretations of the Biblical Narratives in Jewish and Christian Traditions* (Themes in Biblical Narrative, 3; Leiden, 2000), 140–55, esp. 151–5.

[32] *BG* 55,18–56,3.

[33] *BG* 57,8–19.

[34] *BG* 61,7–62,3.

[35] In *Ap. John*, Cain and Abel are viewed as cosmic sons of Yaldabaoth. In contrast, Seth was a son of Adam. Through Seth, Adam's offspring received the divine power (*BG* 62,3–63,14). According to an earlier section it was the serpent in Paradise who taught Eve about sexual desire (*BG* 58,4–7).

[36] *BG* 73,16–18.

Noah and several others were saved in a luminous cloud by the spiritual helper who once more was sent from above. When the Demiurge and his allies found out that not all humans had been covered with darkness, they tried to *mix* the saved ones with darkness: "They sent their angels to the daughters of men, that they might raise offspring from them for their enjoyment."[37] Because this attempt failed, the angels resorted to a scheme: they changed their appearance into the likeness of the husbands of the women, "filling them with the spirit of darkness (. . .) and with evil."[38] But apparently this second attempt was not completely successful either. The subsequent context requires that the mythical ancestresses of the Gnostics did not fall victim to these temptations. They must have kept their spiritual nature free from the darkness of the demonic angels.

In *Ap. John*, one of the main charges brought against the demiurgical God and his allies is their alleged transference of the divine power in Adam's soul to the darkest regions of the cosmos and its subsequent imprisonment in a material body. Later on in the mythical narrative, several frauds and acts of violence are attributed to Yaldabaoth and his evil forces. Yaldabaoth is said to have deceived Adam, raped Eve, covered humanity with a flood of darkness, et cetera. Otherwise, the stories are not devoid of irony where they expose the ignorance and the unwarranted pride of the Demiurge (see also below) and point to the failures resulting from his incompetence. The Invisible Spirit and his representatives could take advantage of the blindness of the adversary party. The true God is portrayed as a merciful Father, whose interventions disclose his unremitting care for the light-power in humanity.

In conclusion, the Gnostic myth describes primeval history as the scene of a battle over a portion of divine spirit that supposedly was usurped by the inferior cosmic God Yaldabaoth and, by the agency of the true God, came to dwell in the souls of human beings. The true God and the demiurgical God Yaldabaoth are contrasted as the redeemer and the oppressor of spiritual humanity.

---

[37] *BG* 73,18–74,5.
[38] II 29,28–30 and IV 45,30–46,2 (cf. *BG* 74,13–16). The version contained in II and IV adds that "they (those who were descended from this illegitimate union) died without having found truth and without knowing the God of truth" (II 30,3–4; IV 46,11–13).

III. HISTORICAL CONTEXT AND FUNCTION OF THE
GNOSTIC GENESIS INTERPRETATION

The Gnostic mythologizers used a variant of an ancient myth to give expression to their distinct ideas of the origin and the salvation of humankind. But what prompted them to use and re-interpret biblical concepts and narrative materials?[39] A closer examination of the possible function and the historical context of *Ap. John*'s Genesis interpretation might help us to answer this question.

I have to begin with a literary-critical issue. It is usual in scholarly literature to distinguish the actual mythical teaching of our text from its narrative frame story speaking about a revelation of the exalted Christ to his disciple John.[40] I do not doubt that this distinction makes sense (although in some cases it might be difficult to determine where the earlier teaching ends and where the secondary frame story begins).[41] My doubts begin, however, where scholars argue that while the frame story is obviously Christian, the actual teaching of the myth is pre-Christian Jewish.[42] This argument is based on the questionable assumption that in the body of the text we do not find Christian features.[43] I surmise that this reasoning ignores

---

[39] Cf. I. Gruenwald, "Aspects of the Jewish-Gnostic Controversy," in B. Layton (ed.), *The Rediscovery of Gnosticism*, II (Leiden, 1981), 713–23, esp. 717–19.

[40] The frame story consists of the opening and concluding parts of the text and, furthermore, of those passages where questions posed by John seem to interrupt the discourse: *BG* 45,5–11 (question and answer about Gen 1:2, the moving of the Spirit/Sophia); 58,1–7 (question and answer about Gen 3, the role of the serpent in Paradise); 58,14–20 (question and answer about Adam's sleep/oblivion); 64,13–71,2 and 71,2–5 (dialogue about the redemption of the souls and John's question about the origin of the adversary spirit). Irenaeus, who summarized the first part of *Ap. John* (above, n. 1) apparently was not yet familiar with the opening frame story.

[41] This applies e.g. to the formula, "It is not as Moses said (. . .)." Do all four occurrences (cf. above n. 2) belong to the frame story?

[42] For the challenged view see in particular the many pertinent studies by B.A. Pearson, e.g. "Jewish Sources in Gnostic Literature," in M. Stone (ed.), *Jewish Writings of the Second Temple Period* (Philadelphia-Assen, 1984), 443–81, esp. 461f.; "*Apocryphon Johannis* Revisited," in P. Bilde, H.K. Nielsen and J.P. Sørensen (eds.), *Apocryphon Severini presented to Søren Giversen* (Århus, 1993), 155–65. Cf. also M. Waldstein's recent introduction to his German translation of *Ap. John*, in: H.-M. Schenke, H.-G. Bethge, U. Kaiser, *Nag Hammadi Deutsch*, vol. I (Berlin, 2001), 96–101.

[43] Cf. B.A. Pearson, "Jewish Sources," 461: when one removes the framework, "one is left with material in which nothing 'Christian' remains"; "the basic material is a product of Jewish Gnosticism"; Ph. Perkins, *The Gnostic Dialogue* (New York, 1980), 93: *Ap. John* "is not yet involved in debating specific points of Christian teaching"; H.-M. Schenke, "The Phenomenon and Significance of Gnostic Sethianism,"

the very function and the *Sitz im Leben* of the critical Genesis interpretation of *Ap. John*.

Let us first give attention to the function and the purpose of the
frame story. It is evident indeed that in these passages the Gnostic
Christ rejects particular literal interpretations of Moses' accounts of
what happened in primordial times (if not Moses' accounts themselves). As is well-known, this literal understanding of the relevant
biblical texts was quite common in early Christianity. It is not far-
fetched, therefore, to assume that this Gnostic appeal to Christ had
its background in a controversy with non-Gnostic Christians over
the proper exegesis of certain Genesis traditions.[44]

My hypothesis, which will be argued in more detail below, is that
as far as this specific attitude towards biblical traditions and the biblical God is concerned, the frame story does not differ substantially
from the teaching it conveys. In other words, not only the appeal
to Christ of the frame story but also the critical rewriting of Genesis
accounts had its *Sitz im Leben* in debates among Christians,—disagreements, that is, about the value of the Old Testament as a source
of divine revelation and about the identity of the biblical creator-
God. This assumption means that *Ap. John*'s critical use of the books
of Moses is *a Christian element*. A closer look at some passages may
help to substantiate this hypothesis.

Shortly before the story of the creation of Adam, we are told how
the demiurgical God engendered or created a host of cosmic powers, and how he enjoyed the view of so many angels below him.
According to *Ap. John*, it was on this occasion that he said: "I am
a jealous God, there is none beside me" (cf. esp. Exod 20:5 and Isa
45:5). These quotations of the biblical God are commented in the
following way: "So he already indicated to the angels who attended
him that there exists another God. For if there were no other one,
of whom would he be jealous?" Apparently the ironical remark about
God's jealousy was meant to defy the belief in the Creator of the
world as the only God. Was this polemical comment originally worded

---

in B. Layton (ed.), *The Rediscovery of Gnosticism*, vol. II (Leiden, 1981), 588–616,
p. 611: "no specifically Christian traits" in the interior of the writing; Waldstein,
Nag Hammadi Deutsch, 98: the organizing principle is Hellenistic-Jewish, not specifically
Christian.

[44] *Ap. John* presents itself as an esoteric writing (it does not directly address non-
Gnostic Christians). This does not preclude that the polemical Genesis interpretation developed in discussions with non-Gnostics.

by Jews (Jews who had dissociated themselves from their traditional faith)?[45] The more plausible assumption, in my opinion, is that we are dealing with an attack worded by Gnostic Christians (Gnostic Christians with a background in Greek-Hellenistic philosophy, see above) against other Christians (representatives of emerging ortho-dox Christianity and/or Christians sympathising with Judaism) who claimed that the God revealed by Jesus was none other than the biblical Creator of heaven and earth.

We are facing a similar alternative in the rewritten story of the creation of Eve.[46] This story denies that the creator-God caused just a physical sleep to fall over Adam. He allegedly did something more serious: he laid a veil over Adam's "perception" so that the first human could not see and understand what happened to him. Thereupon Isaiah 6:10 is quoted: "for he (the creator-God) also said through the prophet, 'I will make the ears of their hearts heavy that they may not understand and may not see.'" The obvious sugges-tion is that such a treatment of Adam could be expected from this God. The reference to a proof-text from Scripture made sense in a debate with opponents who held Moses and the biblical prophets in high esteem.[47] They are being fought with their own weapons: in spite of the allegedly clear warning of the prophet, these people con-tinued to worship the demiurgical God and thus to live in igno-rance. I do not recognise in this passage the hand of an early Jewish exegete.[48] Rather this polemical use of biblical texts originated in debates among second century Christians about the status of the Old Testament and the identity of the biblical creator-God. The frame story did not make a pre-Christian Jewish text into a revelation by the Christian Saviour. It merely added the authority of Christ to a Gnostic-Christian text.

---

[45] Cf. B.A. Pearson, "Jewish Elements in Gnosticism and the Development of Gnostic Self-Definition," in Id., *Gnosticism, Judaism, and Egyptian Christianity* (Minneapolis, 1990), 124–135, 133: "it seems most plausible to conclude that the earliest Gnostics were Jewish intellectuals eager to redefine their own religious self-understanding, convinced of the bankruptcy of traditional verities."

[46] Cf. above, section II.

[47] Cf. O. Wintermute, "A Study of Gnostic Exegesis of the Old Testament," in J.M. Efird (ed.), *The Use of the Old Testament in the New and Other Essays* (Durham, NC., 1972), 241–70, 250.

[48] *Pace* G.A. Stroumsa, *Another Seed, Studies in Gnostic Mythology* (Leiden, 1984), who explains the emergence of Gnosticism from Jewish exegetical problem solving, espe-cially problems of the first chapters of Genesis. Cf. also M.A. Williams, *Rethinking "Gnosticism"* (Princeton, 1996), 64–79.

Various early sources inform us about uncertainties, differences of opinion and quite fundamental discussions in second century Christianity concerning the proper understanding of the ancient Scriptures.[49] It is here that we find the historical context of *Ap. John*'s critical attitude towards Moses and the prophets.[50] It would be recommendable therefore to continue the present analysis of *Ap. John*'s Genesis rewriting with a comparative study of the biblical hermeneutics of contemporary Christians. Such an investigation, however, is bound to go beyond the scope of this essay and must await another occasion.[51]

Conclusion

Our answers to the questions posed in the introductory section can be summarised in the following way. The authors of *Ap. John* were second-century Christians with an intellectual background in popular Greek-Hellenistic philosophy.[52] Their theological dualism and their anthropological ideas remind us of a form of Middle Platonism that was influenced by Aristotelian thought.

Just as Greek philosophers (notably Plato) had done before, the composers of *Ap. John* used mythical narratives to give expression to

---

[49] Cf. apart from related demiurgical Gnostic texts, the so-called *Epistle of Barnabas*, Ignatius' Letters (cf. Phil. 8,2); Justin's *Dialogue with Trypho*, Marcion and Apelles, the Letter of the Valentinian teacher Ptolemy to Flora, hypothetical early sources or versions of the pseudo-Clementine writings, and, last but not least, Irenaeus, *Adversus Haereses*, esp. I 10 and III.

[50] It should be clear that this solution does not deny that Christians of the second century could be engaged in controversies with Jews about the meaning of biblical texts (cf. R. Hvalvik, *The Struggle for Scripture and Covenant* (Tübingen, 1996), esp. part III: "Judaism as a Challenge to the Early Church"). But there is no special reason to assume that the polemics of *Ap. John* were originally addressed to Jews.

[51] Cf. the pertinent studies by H. von Campenhausen, *Die Entstehung der christlichen Bible* (Tübingen, 1968), 76–122 (English transl.: *The Formation of the Christian Bible*, Philadelphia 1972, 62–102); Hvalvik (above, n. 50), Williams, *Rethinking "Gnosticism,"* (above, n. 48), 64–7.

[52] Unlike S. Pétrement, *Le Dieu séparé: les origines du gnosticisme* (Paris, 1984) (English transl.: *A Separate God. The Origins and Teachings of Gnosticism* [San Francisco, 1994]) and A.H.B. Logan, *Gnostic Truth and Christian Heresy, A Study in the History of Gnosticism* (Edinburgh, 1996) (p. 22: the world-view of "Sethian" Gnostics "reflects Christian ideas and ways of interpreting the Old Testament in the light of the message of Paul and John") I do not associate the ideas expressed in *Ap. John* with Pauline or Johannine currents of thought. Anyhow, early Christianity was a much more diverse phenomenon than the contents of the canonized texts lead us to suspect. Cf. my *De veelvormigheid van het vroegste christendom* (Delft, 2002).

their religious-philosophical convictions. In *Ap. John*'s myth of origins we are able to detect features of an ancient combat myth. The present variant of this myth describes a primordial struggle between the true God, the Invisible Spirit, and the demiurgical God Yaldabaoth about a portion of divine light in the lower world.

In the biblical Creator and ruler of heaven and earth the Gnostic myth-makers could not recognise the fully transcendent God of their own tradition. Instead, the God of Genesis reminded them of their demiurgical God. They were convinced that Jesus Christ had revealed the previously unknown supreme God. This is one of the ideas that brought them into conflict with other Christians, notably representatives of emerging orthodox Christianity. In their debates with these Christians they adopted and adapted biblical concepts and narrative traditions with a view to exposing the inferiority of the Old Testament God and the ignorance of those Christians who continued to worship this God. Not only does their critical rewriting of Genesis show how they evaluated the traditions in question, it also shows how they judged the biblical interpretations of other Christians.[53]

---

[53] For the first time in many years I did not put my article to the severe test of Ton Hilhorst's critical judgement before sending it in for publication. Still I profited from earlier discussions with Hilhorst about important aspects of this study.

THE IRISH LEGEND OF ANTICHRIST

Martin McNamara*

1. Introduction

I am very grateful to Professors F. García Martínez and G.P. Luttikhuizen, the editors of this volume in honour of A. Hilhorst, for the
kind invitation to contribute an essay. This I consider a great honour indeed. The wide range of Anthony's interests, learning and
expertise will be evident from the variety of papers here brought
together. My contribution will be on one of these areas of interest,
namely New Testament apocrypha, to which Dr. Hilhorst has made
such lasting contribution, not least by his edition of texts of the
Apocalypse of Paul (*Visio Pauli*).

I chose to write on an item of Irish New Testament apocrypha.
Over the past four decades or so interest has been growing in Irish
biblical apocrypha, especially in those dealing with New Testament
themes. In conjunction with AELAC (Association pour l'Étude de la
Littérature Apocryphe Chrétienne) the Irish Biblical Association is
attending to the critical edition of Irish New Testament apocrypha.
The first volume, with Irish Infancy Narratives, has already appeared.
In this we have two independent Irish texts which contain an infancy
narrative closely related to the Latin Infancy Gospels published by
M.R. James in 1927. While the Irish vernacular translations can be
dated to the twelfth century or so, the Latin form of the narrative
they contain must have reached Ireland before the year 800. The
second volume in the series will carry Irish apocryphal texts of an
apocalyptic and eschatological nature. It should contain about twenty-
eight distinct items. One of these is the Irish Antichrist legend.

Part of the task of critical editions of these texts will be to identify as far as possible the sources of the individual items and to situate them within the larger context of western and eastern tradition.

The Antichrist tradition has been growing since biblical times. The
oldest work known to us on this developing Antichrist legend is to

* Dublin.

be found in the commentary on Daniel by Hippolytus, a presbyter in Rome (died *ca.* 236), who in this work refers to an earlier writing of his own *On Antichrist*. About 399 Jerome composed a work on "Antichrist in the Book of Daniel" which he later inserted into his commentary on the book of Daniel (composed probably in 407). Among the Latin texts that treat of Antichrist from the first millennium we may also mention the sermon on the end of the world, transmitted under the name of Ephrem (and occasionally under that of Isidore): *Scarpsum de dictis S. Efrem prope fine mundi et consummatione saeculi et conturbatione gentium* (PLS 4, 608), which may have been composed between the fifth and seventh centuries, although some opt for an earlier and fourth century date of composition. In the west the best known writings on Antichrist date from the tenth century and some centuries later. The classic work here is *De ortu et tempore Antichristi* by the monk Adso (between 949 and 954), later abbot of Montier-en-Der.[1] Adso's work was highly influential and occasioned a whole series of similar writings on the subject between the tenth and the twelfth century. It is not easy to say how original Adso's work was. It was probably a compilation which consigned to writing some of the views current on the subject at his time; other current forms of the legend Adso probably rejected, some of which would resurface in one or other of the adaptations of his work. It is likely that during the first millennium and in the later Middle Ages many more forms of the legend circulated than are registered in the better known writings on the subject. This is a point to be borne in mind in an examination of the Irish material.

In his edition of a poem on "The Conception and Characteristics of Antichrist" (a composition hard to date but which in general has the appearance of a very late Middle Irish composition [*ca.* 1200?]) Brian Ó Cuív has listed practically all the vernacular Irish texts with descriptions of, or reference to, Antichrist.[2] We have six such in verse compositions and seven in prose compositions. Ó Cuív also notes that there is a certain unity of presentation in these texts. In so far as the Irish text he edits is intelligible, he remarks, the Antichrist

---

[1] Edited by D. Verhelst, *Adso Dervensis, De Ortu et tempore Antichristi, necnon et tractatus qui ab eo dependunt* (Corpus Christianorum Continuatio Mediaevalis, 45; Turnhout, 1976).

[2] B. Ó Cuív, "Two Items from Apocryphal Tradition," *Celtica* 10 (1973) 87–113, at 88.

story given there has the following elements: (1) Antichrist is the son of his own sister who conceives him when her father, a bishop in Jerusalem, lies with her on the Friday before Easter at the instigation of the devil (§§ 16–19); (2) in appearance Antichrist has a face with one eye (§ 20); (3) he has miraculous powers: he can make gold out of grass and anise (?) and wine out of water, he can cause disease and cure the sick, he can create a moon, sun and elements (?), he can do anything that Christ did on earth except restore people to life (§§ 21–26); he has a thousand fair women in his company. Ó Cuív also notes that comparison with other texts of the list he has given shows several correspondences.

In our study of the subject we shall follow Ó Cuív's list of vernacular texts, adding information from Latin compositions as required—however, following chronological order as far as possible.

2. The Texts

(1) The Poems of Blathmac (A.D. 750).

Blathmac, writing about 750, ends his two poems in honour of the Virgin Mary, with mention of the crucifixion of Christ and the death of those who shed, or will shed, their blood for him. The final martyrdom is that of Elias and Enoch. The final verse (quatrain 259) is on the slaying of Antichrist by Michael:[3]

> (258) Since Abel's blood went beneath the sod until the martyrdom of Elias and Enoch (*co martraí Elí Enóch*)—it is by your son, sun of women, that the blood of every saint will be avenged.
> 259. It is Michael, your son's warrior, who will take a smiting sword to the body of impious Anti-Christ who shall be born of a great sin. (*Is he Michél, míl do maic, / gébas claideb comairt/ do chorp Antchríst nád etal, / génathar do mórphecath.*)

Even from this brief poetic text we can gather that Blathmac knew of a rather developed Antichrist legend, a legend that he draws on rather than give in any detail. He must have known the tradition of the advent of Elias and Enoch, their slaying by Antichrist and the slaying of Antichrist by Michael. Very significantly, Blathmac's

---

[3] James Carney (ed.), *The Poems of Blathmac Son of Cú Brettan together with The Irish Gospel of Thomas and A Poem on the Virgin Mary* (Irish Texts Society, 47; Dublin, 1964), 86–88.

Antichrist tradition also contained the element of his birth "of a
great sin." This seems proper to the Irish form of the legend, as we
shall see in consideration of the next item and in some of those that
follow.

(2) The Hiberno-Latin *Liber de Numeris* (*ca.* A.D. 750).

This composition is extant in a number of manuscripts. Indications
point to the area of Salzburg, and the later eighth century, as the
place and date of composition. The work is as yet unpublished, but
the late Robert E. McNally has made a transcript of it. McNally
has made a detailed examination of its contents,[4] and considered the
work as emanating from Hiberno-Latin circles of the Irish monk and
bishop Virgilius of Salzburg. A critical edition is in preparation. The
author arranges his subject according to numbers. The number four
has him consider the four beasts of the Book of Daniel, in the examination of which he inserts the section on Antichrist. McNally has
been able to identify the sources of (or parallels to) many of the
items. The belief that Antichrist is to come on earth as a mortal
and from the tribe of Dan was widespread. The belief that his birth
would be the result of an unnatural union was also known; thus
Pseudo-Ephrem (PLS 4, 608): *Ex semine viri et ex immunda turpissima
virgine, malo spiritu.* . . . The *Liber de numeris* text, however, presents the
union as incest: *Pater in filia propria peccans maledictum infantem maledicta
in sua filia et nefando facit.* Such a presentation of the birth of Antichrist,
McNally noted, occurs nowhere else.[5] We now know that it is a
specific feature of the Irish Antichrist tradition which was, it would
appear, already known by Blathmac. I here give the relevant section of this text, and the entire entry on Antichrist in a footnote.[6]

---

[4] R. McNally, *Der irische Liber de numeris. Eine Quellenanalyse des pseudo-isidorischen
Liber de numeris* (Doctoral Dissertation Ludwig-Maximilians-Universität zu München,
1957).

[5] "Diese Auffassung von der Geburt des Antichrist kommt sonst nirgends vor,"
McNally, *Der irische Liber de numeris*, 90.

[6] The full text on Antichrist in the *Liber de Numeris* (according to a transcript
made by Robert E. McNally) reads: <44> Antechristus itaque quis est aut unde
est? De qua gente oritur et nascitur? Quomodo nasciturus et regnaturus et interfectus moriturus? A quo interficitur, et in quo loco peribit interfectus? Haec omnia
breviter dicamus. quia ad alia festinamus. Antecristus ergo est qui in principio
Lucifer dicebatur et quasi signaculum Dei vivi videbatur. In tali gloria superbae
aegit. Superbiendo in perditionem cecidit, quem Deus de caelo deiecit. Ille deiec-
tus In terram primum hominem seduxit. Et in mundo usque adventurn Christi

Before the judgement he (i.e. Antichrist) will be set loose for a short while so that he may come and dishonestly and illicitly assume flesh, to test the saints and deceive his own, and so that with his own and the impious he may perish all the worse later. From the tribe of Dan he, cruel flesh, takes flesh, and a father sinning in his own daughter makes a cursed child . . ., so that his (i.e. Antichrist's) father appears as his grandfather and his mother as his sister.

Ante iudicium tamen breviter solvitur, ut veniat et carnem inhoneste et inlicite suscipiat, ut sanctos probat et suos decipiat, et cum suis et impiis postea peius pereat. De tribu autem Dan caro crudilis carnem sumit, et pater in filia propria pecans maledictum infantem maledicta in sua filia et nefanda facit, ita tamen ut pater eius avus esse videatur, et mater eius soror eius esse intellegatur.

(3) The Martyrology of Oengus Céile Dé (*ca.* 800).

In this text Michael's victory over Antichrist is foretold by Oengus Céile Dé: "At the fight with the multitudinous Dragon by Michael the strong, victorious, the whitesided hostful soldier will slay wrathful Antichrist" (*Ancrist*).[7]

(4) Poem on St Michael by Maél Ísu ua Brolcháin (died 1086).

This has a mere reference to Antichrist. In this poem Michael is referred to as "the slayer of Antichrist" (*marbaid Ainchrist*).[8]

---

crudeliter regnavit. cui Dominus infernum praeparavit. quem Dominus, crucem sustenans, superavit. Et inferna penetrans draconem tortuosum tenuit et prostravit. Tunc ibi leo leonem ligavit. Ibi ligatus ardet, et sine fine ardebit. Ante iudicium tamen breviter solvitur, ut veniat et carnem inhoneste et inlicite suscipiat, ut sanctos probat et suos decipiat, et cum suis et impiis postea peius pereat. De tribu autem Dan caro crudilis carnem sumit. et pater in filia propria pecans maledictum infantem maledicta in sua filia et nefanda facit, ita tamen ut pater eius avus esse videatur, et mater eius soror eius esse intellegatur. Tunc cre scit draco crudilis. Christianis regnat autem sex me nsibus et tribus annis. Ideo ergo antechristus nominatur, quia ante adventum Christi ad iudicium ille venire et multos seducere non dubitatur, quia quando tunc finis proximat, anticristus ipse ab omni gente impia impios multos congregat, et contra Enoc et Heliam, qui tunc sunt sancti Dei principes, pugnat. Talis pugna crudelis et terribilis erit, ut nullatenus antea ei pugna alia aequalis fuit. In illo ergo horribili et crudeli certamine Enoc et Helias, milites Christi, coronam martirii tenebunt et postea cum omnibus sanctis in caelo coram Deo gloriosae gaudebunt. Tunc Mihahel, milis maximus, terribiliter supervenit, et in monte Oliveti durissimum draconem gladio igneo interficit in illo loco, ubi Christus ascendit in caelis.

[7] *Félire of Oengus* for September 29; Whitley Stokes (ed.), *Félire Óengusso Céli Dé The Martyrology of Oengus the Culdee* (Henry Bradshaw Society, 29; London, 1905), 197.
[8] The poem has been edited with English translation by C. Plummer, *Irish Litanies* (Henry Bradshaw Society, 62; London, 1925), 88–89.

(5) The Two Sorrows of the Kingdom of Heaven (Dá Brón Ftatha Nime (11th century).

The opening words of this Irish apocryphal writing inform us that the Two Sorrows in heaven are Elias and Enoch. The writing presents them as being in Paradise where Elias preaches repentance to the souls of the just. He tells of the judgement to come. At the end of the text we are told that Elias and Enoch await their return to earth, and martyrdom. This leads to description of Antichrist. I give this ending here (in the translation of M. Herbert).[9]

> 8   Now this Elijah and Enoch, of whom we have been speaking, await their slaying and martyrdom in fulfillment of the prophecy of the Lord, uttered through the mouth of the prophet: *Quis est homo qui uiuit et non uidebit mortem?* "Who has tasted of life who will not taste death?" At the end of the world they will oppose Antichrist, who will be put to the sword by them. A demon in human form is this Antichrist, in the guise of one who comes to spread faith. A bishop will beget him on his daughter on a Friday. It is said that there is no miracle performed by Christ on earth that he will not perform, except for the raising of the dead. However, he will be full of lust and falsehood. He will be thirty-three and a half years old, the same age as that of Christ. The inversion of his writing-tablet in front of him is a sign by which he will be recognized. He will put to the sword everyone who does not believe in him, for he will declare himself to be the son of God, one who was foretold by prophets. It is Michael who will descend from the heavens to crush him, and it is he who will set upon him with the sword. And, finally, there are the two sorrows of the kingdom of heaven, Elijah and Enoch, in their earthly bodies among the angels of heaven, awaiting their encounter with Antichrist.

(6) Leabhar Breac Homily (11th–12th century?).

In a homily on the archangels, particularly Michael, for the Feast of St Michael, in the *Leabhar Breac*, one of the five victories attributed to Michael is that "he will fight against Antichrist (*fri hAncrist*) on Mount Sion in the end of the world, and will gain the victory and triumph over him."[10]

---

[9] Ed. G. Dottin, "Les deux chagrins du royaume du ciel," *Revue Celtique* 21 (1900) 349–387, at 385–387; English translation by Máire Herbert in M. Herbert and M. McNamara, *Irish Biblical Apocrypha* (Edinburgh, 1989), 191–21, at 21.

[10] Ed. in R. Atkinson (ed.), *The Passions and the Homilies from the Leabhar Breac* (Dublin, 1887), lines 6273–6275 (p. 216); English translation, p. 453.

(7) Leabhar Breac Homily (11th–12th century?).

At the end of another *Leabhar Breac* homily on St Michael and his victory over the beast on Mount Garganus, a full legend on Antichrist is given. It is as follows:[11]

> Be it known to you that Michael will come again to the help of the human race. For a man named Antichrist shall be born in the end of the world, his mother being his own sister. There is a grey protuberance in the exact middle of his forehead, in the centre of which is the one eye in his head; he has one eyebrow, which stretches from one ear to the other, beneath his eye; his whole body is one flat surface, as are also his feet: He pulls trees up from the roots, thrusts them upside down into the ground, and puts leaves and fruit on the roots and bottoms of the trees. He will make gold and silver out of the manure and dung of horses and camels, and from every useless thing besides; and he will sow disbelief throughout the world. Water will not drown him, nor fire burn him, nor iron touch him. Now Eli and Enoch are still alive in paradise: great jealousy shall seize them, so that they will come to battle with Antichrist; but they shall have no success, for they will be slain. Then Michael will come from heaven, with his red, fiery sword in his hand, and he will slay Antichrist. Thus he will get rid of that plague. After that the day of judgment shall draw nigh. Michael will blow his trumpet, so that all will rise from their graves. The Judge will come to judge the human race; He will put the accursed children on His left into everlasting fire; but the holy and righteous children, i.e. the folk of charity and mercy, He will place on His right, to go to the kingdom of God, to partake of the feast prepared for them from the beginning of the world, in the unity of the almighty Trinity, Father, Son, and Holy Spirit.

(8) Prose and Verse Tract on the Canonical Hours (11th–12th century).

In both prose and verse texts on the canonical hours, Elias takes part in the conflict with Antichrist: At none Elias will come to fight against Antichrist (*fri hAncrist*).[12]

(9) Late Middle Irish Poem on the Conception and Characteristics of Antichrist (12th century?)

---

[11] In ed. R. Atkinson, *The Passions and Homilies*, lines 7268–7289 (p. 244); translation pp. 477–478. The *Leabhar Breac* text is given and commented on by W.W. Heist in *The Fifteen Signs Before Doomsday* (East Lansing, 1952), 94.

[12] Ed. R. Best, "The Lebar Breac Tractate on the Canonical Hours," in *Miscellany Presented to Kuno Meyer* (Halle, 1912), 142–166, at 144, 150.

This poem has been published by Brian Ó Cuív.[13] He notes that
there is nothing in the language of the poem, which in general has
the appearance of a very late Middle Irish composition [*ca.* 1200?],
to determine its date exactly.[14] The composition first (in quatrains
1–15) describes four kinds of conception "whereby through which
the will of God who is powerful here on earth, bright-formed offspring
are produced." With these the conception of Antichrist is contrasted;
"It is not through any of these conceptions that Antichrist is formed,
but through . . . (*mar charas*, meaning of words in context uncertain),
since it is his fit covenant" (quatrain 16). A description of Antichrist's
conception, characteristics and powers follows. It is in the Irish tradition. I cite the relevant section in B. Ó Cuív's translation.

> 17. A bishop in Jerusalem, great evil does he contemplate, it is from
> this that he begets the male child on Friday with his daughter.
> 18. On the Friday before Easter he performs the wicked deed: lying
> shamefully with his daughter between the altar and the wall.
> 19. Through Lucifer's wicked inspiration comes the furious assaulting
> of a body—long are his course and his time before death to take each
> one (of us) on an evil path.
> 20. His face is as one level unbroken (lit. 'unblemished') surface, there
> is a single eye [protruding] out of his forehead; these are the signs of
> his hard body . . . evil at every time.
> 21. He will, if he wishes, make gold out of the green grass [and] out
> of anise; the vilest water which is dispensed by you [he will make]
> into intoxicating wine for his people.
> 22. Everyone who will firmly believe in him will obtain [the torment
> of] hell; everyone who will not believe in him will be welcomed by
> the angels.
> 23. He causes disease to every healthy person, he cures every ill per-
> son, to each misshapen one he gives whatever form he chooses.
> 24. He makes the moon, he makes the sun, he makes the elements
> without good intent, through hardness on earth he occasions the eyes
> to be continually giving warning of him (?).
> 25. The floodtide of the great sea is lacking from one time of day to
> the next—it is abnormal—the testimony of the sea—joyful appear-
> ance—he does not let go from him in many shapes.
> 26. Everything that fair Christ did while He was on earth Antichrist
> does without difficulty except raise people from the dead.
> 27. A thousand beautiful women—it is true—Antichrist has in his com-
> pany, . . . (ends imperfect).

[13] B. Ó Cuív, "Two Items from Apocryphal Tradition," *Celtica* 10 (1973) 87–113,
at 87–102.
[14] B. Ó Cuív, "Two Items," 91.

(10) Poem on the end of the World ascribed to Colum Cille.

In the early sixteenth-century MS Bodleian Laud Misc. 615 we have a selection of poems associated with Colum Cille. One of these is on the end of the world.[15] The ending is on Antichrist, even though he is not named. The text breaks off in the middle of a quatrain, with a space left after the last half-quatrain. I reproduce Ó Cuív's translation (which he himself describes as tentative).

> A *macu* will come to the world with great strength, a powerful cunning man; a sister of his own will be his mother.
> A daughter will conceive him by her own father like a serpent; very beastlike (?) will be the son who will be born in the city.
> His teeth will form one surface—certain according to my tidings—a host behind ramparts (?); his slender feet will have six toes according to the mysteries.
> A sour resolute man, a scourge from hell, what I say is true, a black hard deceiver with a grey bush protruding from his brow.
> He makes (*recte* will make) gold from biestings of the plain, what is more gloomy?

(11) A Poem attributed to Bécán Bec mac Dé (not much later than 1150).

In a poem of prophecies attributed to Bécán mac Dé Antichrist is associated with the end of the world: "After that the signs of Antichrist (*airde Anticrist*) will come over there towards the end of the world."[16]

(12) Fragment of an Apocalypse of John in "A Life of John, the Beloved Disciple" in the Liber Flavus Fergusiorum (translated from the Latin *ca.* 1400).

This fragment of an apocalypse occurs in a composite Irish text containing episodes from the Life of John, the Beloved Disciple. It is headed: *Beatha Eoin Bruinne*, "The Life of John the Beloved Disciple" (literally "of John of the Breast"). The beginning of text is lost. It contains two distinct texts on the life of John and this fragment of

---

[15] The poem beginning: *Do fil aimser laithe mbratha*; ed. K. Meyer in "Mitteilungen aus irischen Handschriften. Ein altirisches Gedicht über das Ende der Welt. Aus Laud 615, SS. 132–4," *Zeitschrift für celtische Philologie* 8 (1911), 195–196 (text only). Text of relevant section, with translation, in B. Ó Cuív, "Two Items," 90.

[16] Ed. Eleanor Knott, "A Poem of Prophecies," *Ériu* 18 (1958) 55–84, at 72, § 68. Knott considered that the poem could not be dated to much later than 1150.

what appears to be an apocalypse of John. The composite text was translated from the Latin into Irish by Uighisdin Mac Raighin (of the Canons Regular of St Augustine), who died in 1405. The source of one of the sections on the Life of John is the Latin text of Pseudo-Abdias (or Pseudo-Mellitus), of another a text attested only in a very old Greek witness of the *Acta of John* preserved in a fourth-century Oxyrhynchus Papyrus.[17] The sources behind the text that interests us have not been identified. We may note that the piece mentions Antichrist only in relation to his descent on Mount Garganus (in the fourth century), even though the context seems to require an end of time reference. Since a description of the Archangel Michael is given, one would also expect a description of Antichrist. The original of this fragment may have contained more on Antichrist. It is worth noting that the text on Antichrist and on the end of the world are both explicitly indicated as having been received by John in revelations from God, i.e. as apocalypses. I give the text here in the translation of Máire Herbert.[18]

> Then Christ sent the divine helper, the splendid holy angel Michael to fight against arrogant Antichrist as he had fought against Lucifer. And Antichrist came in the form of a dragon to the summit of Mount Garganus to harm and attack the Christians. But Michael killed the dragon, and as a result, God and Michael were greatly glorified in heaven and on earth.
>
> 3   This is the manner of Michael's appearance as he comes to fight Antichrist. He is radiant, fair of countenance, red-cheeked, with gentle steady long-lashed eyes, with eloquent red lips, and a white throat. He is shining with zeal, light-footed, angry, furious, aggressive, with his beautiful four wings spread around him, with a protecting sharp-edged splendid sharp ornamented slender sword firmly in his strong hand, to smite Antichrist in a manner befitting a noble angelic heavenly personage.
>
> 4   With harshness, deep anger, bravery and strength, with swiftness and severity, strongly, fearlessly and terribly, he strikes Antichrist on the crown of the head, halving him on the spot in two splendid broad halves from the top of his head down to the ground. "And that is the evil strange tale of Antichrist up to the present, as God confirmed to me," said John, the eloquent Beloved Disciple.
>
> 5   The world will have three years of peace.

---

[17] See M. McNamara, *The Apocrypha in the Irish Church* (Dublin, 1975), 95–98.
[18] Herbert, in M. Herbert and M. McNamara, *Irish Biblical Apocrypha*, 95–96.

6   And after all that, there will be a great silence throughout the whole universe, so that neither the sound of the sea, nor the roar of the wave, nor the cry of the wind, nor bird-song, nor the sound of any created thing in the whole world will be heard for forty days and forty nights. Then the signs of Doomsday will appear, on the fifteen days before the Judgement.

7   After these have come, four angels rise up from the four cardinal points of the world, and they call out loudly and impressively: "Arise! Arise! Arise! Arise!"

8   Then the beautiful pure souls of heaven and the many evil souls from hell will go jointly with their bodies from the earthly graves in which they were buried to the judgement of Doomsday.

9   "And that is a brief account of the end of this bad world, as was narrated to me by the Creator, the good Lord," said John, the eloquent Beloved Disciple.

(13) A Life of St Maighneann, an Irish saint of the seventh century (in 15th cent. MS).

The Irish Life of St Magniu or Maignenn of Kilmainham, Dublin, ends with a brief summary of the Irish Antichrist legend. This text itself is not strictly a life of the saint, but rather a homiletic collection of his sayings on matters of discipline, eschatology and such like, chiefly provoked by questions from other saints visited by him on a "devotional round" which he made. The MS containing it (British Library Egerton 91) is by Uilliam Mac an Lega, 15th century. The final item in this homiletic collection is on Antichrist; the text ends imperfectly (fol. 51b), the greater part of the page being left blank for its continuation.[19]

I give the text in O'Grady's rendering, including his explanatory glosses, within square brackets. (The "Rowing Wheel" referred to is the machine constructed by Simon Magus and the Irish druid, Mog Ruith.) The text reads:[20]

---

[19] The text has been edited and translated by Standish O'Grady, *Silva Gadelica (I–XXXI). A Collection of Tales in Irish with Extracts illustrating Persons and Places.* (I) Irish Text (London and Edinburgh, 1892; reprint, Dublin, 1935), 37–49, at 48–49 (introduction to text p. vii); English translation of ending *Silva Gadelica* II, 49. See also R. Flower, *Catalogue of Irish Manuscripts in the British Library [formerly British Museum]* (Dublin, 1992; original London, 1927), 438, 446–447.

[20] S. O'Grady (ed.) *Silva Gadelica. II. Translation and Notes* (London: William and Norgate, 1892), 35–49, at 49. The Irish text reads: In fetarais a Mignenn ar Mochuta cuin [tic in] roth rámhach ac tarrngaire in tsáebaigteoir indErinn. is amlaid tic

Magnenn said: "Knowest thou, Mochutu, at what time comes the *roth ramhach* ['the Rowing Wheel'] prognosticating the Perverter's advent in Ireland?" "Thus Antichrist shall come: as one that is mighty and wise, yet foolish: foolish namely towards God, but wise to work out his own proper detriment; one whose mother (for he is a daughter's progeny of his father) is a sister of his own; one whose entire face is but one flat surface, and he having on each foot six toes; and the manner of him is besides that he is a judge violent and black [i.e. pitiless and unjust] having in his forehead a light grey tuft; out of all metals he makes gold [i.e. transmutes them] and raises up the dead. In whose time mercy shall not be until that Eli come and Enoch...

(14) A Text headed "Sgél Ainnte Crisd" ("The Story of Antichrist"), in the Book of Lismore.

The Book of Lismore is a work written in the latter part of the fifteenth century. The Antichrist legend it contains has been edited and translated by Douglas Hyde;[21] it has been translated anew by Máire Herbert,[22] whose text is here reproduced.

1   The Lord said that Antichrist would be the devil who would come in human form, and that he would perform great signs among the people. He would say that he was the true son of God, the one who had always been prophesied, and that no one should presume to assert that Christ had come before him to succour the human race. John the Evangelist said to Jesus: "O Lord, in what manner will that man appear? We should have a written description, so that he may be recognized by his evil deeds, so that, thus recognized, allegiance would not be given him."

2   The Lord said that he would be born in Bethlehem, of a harlot of the tribe of Daniel, that he would be reared in the Carbuban (sic), and that he would live in the city called Besasta. His body will be six hundred lengths high, and forty in width. He will have a single eye protruding from his forehead, with a flat-surfaced face, and a mouth extending as far as his chest. He will have no upper teeth, nor will

---

Anticríst: fer trén glicc aimglicc .i. aimglicc fri dia ocus glic fri dénum a aimlesa féin .ocus deirbshiur dó féin a máthair ocus ingen doghní /49/ rena hathair é .ocus aenclár a édan uile ocus sé meoir ar cach coiss dó .ocus is amlaid bíos ina breithem diandub ocus tomm gléliath ina édan. ocus doghní ór do cach mitain ocus tódúiscid mairb .ocus ní bí trócaire ina aimsir sin no co tic Elí ocus Enócc.

[21] D. Hyde, "A Medieval Account of Antichrist," in *Medieval Studies in Memory of Gertrude Schoepperle Loomis*, edited by R. Sherman Loomis (Paris-New York, 1927), 391–398.

[22] M. Herbert, in M. Herbert and M. McNamara, *Irish Biblical Apocrypha*, 149–150. See also W.W. Heist, *The Fifteen Signs before Doomsday*, 64.

he have knees, and the soles of his feet will be rounded like a cart-wheel. He will have fearsome black hair, and three fiery vapours from his nose and mouth which will rise in the air like flames of fire.

3   Nobody in the world will be able to hide himself from him. With red-hot iron he will brand a mark on the forehead of every person who believes in him, and no one in the world can ever conceal that mark even till Doomsday. He will kill all who will not believe in him, and these will be among God's elect. He will raise the dead in imitation of Christ, with sinners being the ones who are raised thus. He will tear, trees up by the roots, setting the roots uppermost, and causing the fruit to come up through the roots, by the powers of the devil.

4   In that man's time, rivers will turn and face up heights. Father will kill son, and son father. Kinsman will kill kinsman, and there will be neither faith nor honour at that time. Churches will be destroyed, and priests will flee, unmindful of the relics of the saints who had preceded them, or of the churches where the saints had dwelt. The women serving in church will be without modesty, flaunting their shame and nakedness.

5   On the day of the birth of Antichrist, there will be someone dead in every house throughout the four corners of the world. Later on, the two prophets now in Paradise, Elijah and Enoch, will come to do battle with him. They will fight together for three hundred and forty days, and thereafter he will slay them both in the Plati, that is, in the palace of the city of Jerusalem. They will lie dead for three and a half days, during which time nobody will dare to bury them for fear of Antichrist. Then, at midday, they will arise in the presence of all. And an angel will descend from heaven, and will say to them: "O Elijah and Enoch, enter into eternal life from henceforth." And they will ascend then in the sight of all the people.

6   Then there will be an earthquake and terrible fiery thunder upon the hosts. Everyone in the company of Antichrist will be burnt and killed by the power of God. Thereafter, to save the people, almighty God will send the archangel Michael, carrying a naked sword. He will slay Antichrist with a single blow, splitting him in two halves from the crown of his head down to the ground. Michael did not deliver that blow simply to destroy Antichrist, but to return the world to a better state. Then every pagan, Jew, and foreigner will convert to the Catholic faith. Only three and a half years will remain after that until the Day of Judgement.

(15) Expanded version of the Legend with Latin phrases in two eighteenth-century Manuscripts (RIA 23 N 15; NLI G 411).

Texts bearing on Antichrist and with the Antichrist legend were still being copied in Irish manuscripts in the eighteenth and nineteenth

centuries. We have one example in the manuscript 23 N 15 (490)
of the Royal Irish Academy. This manuscript with miscellaneous
material was written by the scribe Micheál Mac Peadair Uí Longáin.
It has an item on the coming of the Last Judgment, given as a
response to a query of John the Evangelist concerning the end of
the world. This appears to end incomplete with the phrase: ". . . At
that time Enoch the son of Methusalem will go forth in his human
body from the places of the great light of Paradise to encounter the
Antichrist." After this sentence Micheál Óg Ó Longáin, the scribe's
son, has appended a text on Antichrist, under the heading *Sgél
Ainntecrisd*, "the Story of Antechrist." This is followed by the colophon:
"It is now 50 years since my father wrote the beginning of this story
of Antechrist, and it is now in the year 1816 that I myself have
finished it in Cork, having drawn it from an old vellum book (*sein-
leabhar meamruim*) that was written 900 years ago." Gerard Murphy
was of the opinion that while the tract on the last judgment (of
Micheál Mac Peadair Uí Longáin), though mainly concerned with
Antichrist, is very different from the Book of Lismore, there can be
little doubt that the "ancient vellum book" from which Micheál Óg
copied was the Book of Lismore.[23] If Micheál Óg's text is a copy
of Lismore, some explanation is required for the Latin phrases embedded in the Irish, indicating, it would appear, translation from a Latin
original. The interrelationships of these Irish Antichrist texts is a
matter to be considered by future study. In the present state of
research what seems indicated is that they be presented in translation. The text of MS 23 N 15 has not been edited, but a French
translation has been published by G. Dottin in the introduction to

---

[23] Gerard Murphy in his description of MS 23 N 15 in *Catalogue of Irish Manuscripts
of the Royal Irish Academy*, fascicle XI (Dublin: Royal Irish Academy), 1358. There
is another copy of this text, including Micheál Óg's colophon, in the nineteenth-
century Royal Irish Academy MS 23 B 25 (500), written by Uilliam Mac Dhómhnuil
Uí Dhuinnin, Co. Cork. Brian Ó Cuív ("Two Items," 88, n. 13) says that the oldest manuscript with this form of the text that he has seen is National Library of
Ireland G 441, written by Henri Ó Muircheartaigh in 1724. There are some inac-
curacies in this description: the MS in question is G 411 (pp. 61–71; not 441), a
manuscript written by Henri Mac (not Ó) Muircheartaigh, this section of it in 1724.
The scribe may have been from Co. Meath. (I wish to thank Pádraig Ó Meacháin
of the Dublin Institute for Advanced Studies and Elizabeth Kirwin of the National
Library of Ireland for their help in tracing the exact reference to this item.)

his edition of the *Two Sorrows of the Kingdom of Heaven*.[24] The relevant section of his rendering is reproduced here.

L'Antechrist .i. *diabolus faciet magna prodigia in populo* et alors il y aura un seigneur malheureusement fort, très horrible et le regne et la règle de l'Antechrist seront comme une herse sur le monde et il ferait des signes contraires, extrêmement merveilleux chez les peuples, et il dirait qu'il est le fils chéri de Dieu et que c'est lui qui est dans la prophétie universelle et personne n'osera dire que le Christ est venu délivrer la race humaine. Alors Jean demanda au Seigneur quelle sorte de forme ou d'apparence il aura, ou à quoi il ressemblera pour qu'on le reconnaisse, dans l'espoir qu'ensuite nous ne croirons pas en lui. *Dixit Dominus: de muliere meritrici nascetur* .i. le Seigneur a dit que ce serait d'une courtisane de race juive qu'il naîtrait et que ce serait à Babylone qu'il serait mis au monde et que ce serait dans cette ville-là qu'il demeurerait. C'est lui le père des quatre personnages les plus mauvais qui naquirent jamais .i.e. Cain, Jerosopilat, Simon Magus. L'Antechrist sera le grand bannisseur des justes et le destructeur des chrétiens et le proclamateur dc l'incrédulité, et le négateur de l'humanité, et le fils chéri du diable et malheur à qui vivra dans le temps de cette naissancc maudite, c'est-à-dire de l'Antechrist. *Sexcentum cubitos in longitudinem corporis sui.* Ainsi sera cet homme-là: six cents toises la hauteur de son corps et quarante toises la largeur; et il est grand, effroyable, hideux. Une chevelure douce, lisse, sombre, épaisse sur sa tete. *Oculum unum in fronte ejus.* Il aura un oeil dans la tête et un masque noir diabolique sur lui, et des sourcils louables, mouchetés comme une crinière. One seule oreille dans sa tête; et le grand oeil qu'il aura sera rapide, brillant. *Et fumus de naribus.* Et de la fumée de feu sinistre, puante, sortira des narines de son nez et des flammes de feu de l'unique oreille qui est dans sa tête noire et horrible; une seule surface plane forte, diabolique, de couleur horrible dans sa mâchoire; pas de dents il a la mâchoire supérieure; une côte haute et grande, étonnante, dans son sein. Deux côtes larges et grandes dans son côté gauche. *Nec genua habebit*, et il n'aura pas de genoux; les plantes de ses pieds seront aussi unies et aussi rondes que des roues de charrette. Il aura une chevelure noire effrayante et il ne souffrirait pas que personne au monde se cachât à lui et à quiconque croira en lui il mettra sur le front un signe avec un fer rouge et personne au monde ne pourra cacher ce signe jusqu'au jour du Jugement et quiconque ne croira pas en lui il le tuera et ce sera d'après le choix de Dieu. Jean l'evangéliste dit qu'il n'est pas le diable lui-meme, mais le fils chéri du diable après son accomplissemeut désormais.

---

[24] G. Dottin, "Les deux chagrins du royaume de ciel," *Revue Celtique* 21 (1900) 349–387, at 353–356.

3. SOURCES AND DEVELOPMENT OF THE IRISH LEGEND

There are at least three questions which merit examination with regard to the Irish legend of Antichrist. One is its source, whether it can be traced to a known apocryphal text. In three of the texts presented above (the *Liber Flavus* text, the text of the *Book of Lismore* and the related text of the Royal Irish Academy manuscript) the "strange story of Antichrist" is said to have been revealed to John (John the Evangelist, John the Beloved Disciple). In the last two texts John requests of the Lord a description of Antichrist so that he could be recognised. A natural source for this and other elements of the Irish Antichrist legend might be the apocryphal *Apocalypse of John*. In this work John is told of the coming of the denier, who is called Antichrist. In the heavenly reply to the seer's question, "Lord, reveal to me what he is like," the appearance of Antichrist is given as follows:[25]

> The appearance of his face is dusky (or: gloomy); the hairs of his head are sharp, like darts; his eyebrows like a wild beast's; his right eye like the star which rises in the morning, and the other like a lion's; his mouth about one cubit; his teeth span long; his fingers like scythes; the print of his feet of two spans; and on his face is an inscription. Antichrist.

A text of this apocryphal work has been published by C. Tischendorf.[26] The composition is often dated to the fifth century, but may be considerably earlier. It has been little studied.[27] The present state of research scarcely permits us to draw any conclusions as to its connection with the origins of the Irish Antichrist legend. There may well have been many such apocryphal apocalypses attributed to John, author of the canonical book of this name.

The earliest Irish (eighth-century) texts speak of the immoral, even incestuous, origins of Antichrist, a feature retained right through the following eleven hundred years.

Another feature of the Irish texts is the treatment of the physical

---

[25] English translation, by A. Walker, in *Apocryphal Gospels, Acts and Revelations* (Ante-Nicene Christian Library vol. 16; Edinburgh, 1870), 493–505: 494.

[26] C. Tischendorf, *Apocalypses apocryphae* (Leipzig, 1866; reprint Hildesheim, 1966), 70–93, found in Armenian, Arabic and Old Slavonic translations; English translation by A. Walker, in *Apocryphal Gospels, Acts and Revelations*, 493–505.

[27] See comments on it by Adela Yarbro Collins, *Early Christian Apocalypticism: Genre and Social Setting* (Semeia 36; Decatur, GA, 1986), 76–77.

features of Antichrist, the Antichrist physiognomy. In this, and in other aspects of the Antichrist legend we are fortunate that the entire subject has been the subject of intense research, particularly in recent years.[28] Bernard McGinn has traced the development of the tradition from the beginnings, down through patristic, early and later medieval times to our own day. In his study of the figure of Antichrist in the period of development (A.D. 100–500) McGinn devotes a section to Antichrist's physical appearance. For him the second important theme of this period (whose earliest written evidence comes from the third century) is that of the Antichrist physiognomies, the physical descriptions of his unusual appearance. These are Eastern, rather than Western; indeed, McGinn notes, it is curious that they had so little effect on Latin Antichrist beliefs. It is possible that those texts had Jewish roots, but it is also clear that fascination with how physical features reveal character was widespread in the ancient world.[29] The Antichrist physiognomies currently known to us are found in texts that are not critically edited and that are difficult to date. Almost every important apocalyptic revealer (Elijah, Ezra, Daniel, John, and even the Sibyl) was eventually credited with providing a physical description of Antichrist, as the chart McGinn gives detailing fourteen examples shows. Of these fourteen most are eastern, two are Latin, two Irish (*Leabhar Breac, Book of Lismore*).[30]

The classical text on Antichrist in the West comes from around A.D. 950, in *De ortu et tempore Antichristi* of Adso, later abbot of Montier-en-Der. The Irish tradition does not belong to this. It is independent of it. As McGinn writes:[31]

---

[28] See in particular Bernard McGinn, "Portraying the Antichrist in the Middle Ages," in W. Verbeke, D. Verhelst and W. Welkernhuysen (eds.), *Use and Abuse of Eschatology in the Middle Ages* (Mediaevalia Lovaniensia 1,15; Leuven, 1988), esp. 3–13; B. McGinn, *Antichrist. Two Thousand Years of the Human fascination with Evil* (New York, 2000). See also J.M. Ford, "The Physical features of the Antichrist," *JSP* 14 (1996) 23–41. From the earlier works on the subject we may note: Willhelm Bousset, *Der Antichrist in der Überlieferung des Judentums, des Neuen Testament und in der alten Kirche: Ein Beitrag zur Auslegung der Apokalypse* (Göttingen, 1895); English translation by A.H. Keane under the title *The Antichrist Legend: A Chapter in Christian and Jewish Folklore* (London: Hutchinson, 1896); Horst Dieter Rauh, *Das Bild des Antichrist im Mittelalter: Von Tyconius zum Deutschen Symbolismus* (Beiträge zur Geschichte der Philosophie und Theologie des Mittelalters, N.F. 9; Münster, 1973).

[29] McGinn, *The Antichrist*, 68.

[30] Charts in McGinn, *The Antichrist*, 72–73.

[31] McGinn, *The Antichrist*, 97–98.

Antichrist physiognomies accompanied by unusual legendary accretions belonged to the Eastern imagination at this time [950–1000]. Yet they became prevalent in one place in western Europe—Ireland, at least from the tenth century on. The native imagination, coupled with Irish predilection for apocryphal literature suspect in other parts of Latin Christendom, seems to have had much to do with this unexpected turn of events.

McGinn then draws attention to a tenth-century Latin text edited by Bernhard Bischoff, containing what Bischoff believes to be the oldest text on Antichrist in the West.[32] The text, now in Avranches, Bibliothèque municipale as MS 108, was from the 12th century at the latest, in the famous monastery of Mont St. Michel (Brittany) and Bischoff believes the legend originated there. Bischoff notes that this description of the Antichrist should be compared with a Latin-Irish text given in translation by G. Dottin in the introduction of his edition of "The Two Sorrows of the Kingdom of Heaven," of which there is an almost identical description in the *Book of Lismore*.[33] There are some Latin phrases retained in the Irish text, an indication that the work is translated from Latin. The Latin text published by Bischoff has many irregular Latin forms which makes understanding and translation difficult. The general sense, however, is clear. The text begins by reference to the phoenix, destroyed by fire from heaven. The fire is extinguished by rain from Africa. The text continues:[34]

> From the ash and the rain will be born the girl from whom Antichrist will come. Two young virgin girls will stand there, called Abilia and Lapidia, from whose breasts will pour the milk by which they will nourish him for five years. When the five years are over, he will begin to reign.
>
> His disciples said to Jesus: "Lord, tell us what he will be like." And Jesus said to them: "His stature will be nine cubits. He will have black hair pulled up[?] like an iron chain. In his forehead he will have one eye shining like the dawn. His lower lips will be large, he will have no upper lips. On his hand the little finger will be the longer; his left foot will be wider. His stancewill be similar [?]. He will come to the sea, say "Dry up," and it will be dried. "Become dark," and it will be darkened. And the stars will fall from heaven.

---

[32] See B. Bischoff, "Vom Ende der Welt und vom Antichrist (I); Fragment einer Jenseitsvision (II) (Zehntes Jahrhundert)," *Anecdota Novissima: Texte des vierten bis sechzehnten Jahrhunderts* (Stuttgart, 1984), 80–84; 82 for Latin text cited.

[33] G. Dottin, "Les deux Chagrins du royaume du Ciel," 349–387: 353–536, from MS Royal Irish Academy 23 N 15 (490).

[34] In the translation of McGinn, *The Antichrist*, 98.

(. . . ex ipsa pulvera et pluia erit gerata puella, unde ortus erit antechristus. In illo loco stabunt duas puella virginis, quis apellatur Abilia et Lapidia, unde mamellas eorum lactus fundebatur et nutrierunt eum V annos. Quod fuerat annorum quinque, sic inciperat regnare. Et dixerunt ad Iesum discipuli eius: 'Domine, dic nobis, quod similia tenebatur.' Et dixit eis Iesus: 'Similia tenebatur status eius cubitorum novem. Habet capillum nigrum in tortorio sicut catena ferrea. In medio frontem habet oculum unum et lucebit sicut aurora. Labia subteriores grande habet, superiores non habet. In manus eius digitus minor longior erit. Pedes sinistro latior erit. Status eius in similitudinem. Venit ad mare, dicit: "Sica," et sicabitur, et dicit ad sol: "Sta" , et stetit, et dixit ad luna: "Tenebriscare," et tenebricabitur, et stellae cadent de celo.)

CONCLUSION

In this essay I have given the relevant texts and outlined the state of research on the Irish Antichrist legend as best I can. The times now seems ripe for a thorough examination of this material, through critical editions of all the Irish texts, accompanied with an attempt to situate these in the general history of the Antichrist legend, at the same time tracing developments within the Irish tradition itself over the eleven hundred years between the earliest (*ca.* A.D. 750) and latest texts.

Βεθαβαρα τὸ τοῦ ἁγίου Ἰωάννου τοῦ Βαπτίσματος
REMARKS ABOUT STORIED PLACES AT THE JORDAN, JOHN THE BAPTIST AND THE MADABA MOSAIC MAP

Ed Noort*

I. The Prayer of Pope John Paul II

During his visit to the Holy Land in the year 2000 Pope John Paul II prayed at the east bank of the river Jordan at Wadi al-Kharrar. The pope said: "Here, at the River Jordan, where *both banks* are visited by hosts of pilgrims honouring the Baptism of the Lord, I too lift up my heart in prayer: . . . On the *banks* of the River Jordan, you raised up John the Baptist, a voice crying in the wilderness. . . ."[1] It was a wise prayer, because no one was excluded. And it was a cautious prayer, because it left in the middle whether the baptism of Jesus was believed to have taken place on the western or on the eastern bank of the river. The location of the prayer, however, was taken as an implicit confirmation of the Jordanian claims, but the Vatican has officially not taken a position on either side's claim. The papal visit to wadi al-Kharrar was an enormous stimulus for politics and all churches in Jordan. Tourist facilities are planned and on Friday, January 17, 2003 the cornerstone of a new Greek Orthodox church in honour of John the Baptist was laid.[2] This renewed interest in a wadi outside the usual tourist patterns is due to new surveys and excavations. Since 1995/1997 important material remains are discovered here. First it looked that the western bank would take the lead after the peace treaty between Israel and Jordan enabled pilgrims again to visit the holy sites at the Jordan. For the moment, however, the eastern side leads the way in the centuries-old fight about *hic est locus* . . . And a papal visit is a mighty weapon.

But there is more at stake than either the western or the eastern side of the river. In recent research a new proposal has even included

---

* Groningen.

[1] Catholic Information Network: http://www.cin.org/jp2/jp00321b.html.

[2] http://www.holytrinityaugusta.org: "Greek Orthodox Archimandrite Christofios Hanna held mass at the site where the new church's cornerstone was laid. The Byzantine-styled Church of St. John is expected to be finished early 2004."

the Batanea in the Northeast of Palestine as a place of John's ministry. In this part of the Near East, however, archaeology is always
a part of religious and political interests. So the different claims may
spark cross-border disputes again.

Intrigued by the revival of the old claims, the excavations and the
prayer of the Pope, the underlying question seemed to be a nice
theme for an article honouring our friend and colleague Ton Hilhorst
at the occasion of his retirement. He was travelling a lot during his
stay at the École Biblique in Jerusalem. My own commitment goes
back to the days when I was conducting the "Lehrkurse" of the
"Deutschen Evangelischen Institutes für Altertumswissenschaft des
Heiligen Landes" in Jerusalem, a (protestant) way of connecting his-
torical-critical exegesis and the material culture of Palestine. So, it
is a kind of ecumenical contribution, which is offered here.

The aim of this article will not be a statement whether and where
Jesus was baptised. As a historical question this is out of reach. What
is fascinating, however, is to look for the different traces in the history of reception. Where were traditions located and why and how
did they change? And when they changed, which loss or enrichment
was reached?

I want to argue that in the case of John the Baptist the traditions
crossed the Jordan from east to west and that this geographical shift
caused differentiation in the focus of those traditions. To follow those
traces we have to return to the river itself, the basis of all the
reflections.

II. THE RIVER JORDAN

In his informative article about the Jordan in *TDOT*, Manfred Görg
deals with the problems of the narrative of Josh 3f.: the miraculous
crossing of the river by Israel.[3] He outlines the most familiar theo-
ries of the literary-critical approach and concludes that the parallel
of the miracle at the Reed Sea (Exod 15:8.10) and Josh 3:23 "has
reached a stage at which, in line with Deuteronomic usage, the 'crossing' has simply become a theologoumenon."[4] No doubt, he is right.
The river Jordan and its banks have functioned many times as a

---

[3] M. Görg, s.v ירדן, *TDOT* VI (1990) 322–330.
[4] Görg, 330.

theologoumenon in the tradition history of the biblical writings and
their afterlife. But there is something particular with the river Jordan.
In contrast with the great rivers of the Ancient Near East: Nile,
Euphrates and Tigris, the physical size and shape of the Jordan[5]
never allowed to use it as a means of transport. The river's tortuous
course with numerous windings, its shallowness and the partly inac-
cessibility of its banks makes the Jordan to a non navigable stream,
commercially of no interest. The Jordan is a river to be crossed, not
to be sailed.

Until the last century there was a wide gap between the real,
physical knowledge, the use of the river and its religious meaning.
Subtracting some exaggeration, the judgement of F. Vigouroux is
correct: "Aucun autre fleuve du monde n'est sacré comme lui pour
les Juifs et les chrétiens et, sur toute la surface du globe, aucun cours
d'eau ne présente des caractères aussi extraordinaires et aussi singuliers. Cependant, jusqu'au xixe siècle, il est resté unes des rivières les
plus mal connues, quoique son nom fût dans toutes les bouches et
que des milliers de pieux pèlerins se fussent baignés dans ses eaux."[6]

The historical role of the Jordan as a boundary does not interest
us here. Important are the possibilities for crossing the river. They
are points deeply rooted in history, legend and myth. In history for
their necessity to connect the main routes from south to north: the
so called *via maris* in Cis-Jordan, the King's Highway in Trans-Jordan
and the subdominant roads of the water-parting route through the
western highlands and the Jordan Valley roads, following the foot
of the mountains on either side of the river. These south-north routes
ask for east-west connections and this means crossing the Jordan.
From ancient times on, many fords (מעברה מעבר), ferries[7] and bridges
(נשר)[8] are known.[9] At the same time these physical demonstrable

---

[5] Th. Fast, "Verkehrswege zwischen dem südlichen West- und Ostjordanland,"
ZDPV 72 (1956) 149–151; M. Noth, "Der Jordan in der alten Geschichte Palästinas,"
ZDPV 72 (1956) 123–148; W. Wiefel, "Bethabara jenseits des Jordan," *ZDPV* 83
(1967) 72–81.

[6] F. Vigouroux, s.v. Jourdain, *DB* III (1903) 1704–1749 (1706).

[7] Cf. the ships for crossing the Jordan: H. Donner, H. Cüppers, *Die Mosaikkarte
von Madeba*. Tafelband (ADPV; Wiesbaden, 1977), Plates 98,100; 91,45, XV.

[8] Noth 1956, 136 argues that the classical Hebrew does not know a word for
"bridge." Only late Hebrew knows it as a loanword from akkadian *gišru*. It is, however, already known in Qumran in the 2nd century B.C. (4Q521 Fragm. 7:12—
private communication F. García Martínez).

[9] E. Noort, "Klio und die Welt des Alten Testaments. Überlegungen zur Benutzung
literarischer und feldarchäologischer Quellen bei der Darstellung einer Geschichte

crossing points attracted (legendary) narratives. Even, if there is no historical background, the *location* is important. Space and place are an indispensable part of the possibilities of explanation. In the traditions about the Jordan, fords are used for crossing as part of a conquest, a migration, or as a route of escape. Even the places of baptism are located at places where the river easily can be crossed, with enough water and where the banks are not too steep to endanger the people. Here is storied place.[10] Even mythological aspects are in need of location. Their spectrum reaches from local points at the Jordan to the river *in toto*: Water of Life and River of Death.

Where can those points be found? Looking for crossing points of the southern part of the river and going from south to north, we meet Jisr Abdallah (201134).[11] Its role is not important, because road and bridge are only constructed in the fifties of the last century.[12] The most southern ford is al-Henu. About two kilometres to the north the ford Makhadat Hajla (201136),[13] south of the mouth of Wadi Qilt, can be found. Two kilometres to the north again one encounters the ford Al Maghtas (201138), near Deir Mar Yuḥanna, one of the most important crossing points in the history of reception. Following the meandering Jordan to the north the Allenby bridge comes into sight (201142). At the moment this bridge is the most important connection between Jerusalem and Amman.[14] The next ford is Makhadat Umm an Nakhla at a distance of about one kilometre (200144). Passing it the next possibility is the ford Makhadat al Mundassa (200147). This first view results in six possible crossing points within 13 kilometres.[15] They all can easily be reached from Jericho (Tell es Sultan-191141). Of course one has to be careful with

---

Israels," in: D.R. Daniels, U. Glessmer, M. Rösel (Hrg.), *Ernten was man sät. Festschrift für Klaus Koch* (Neukirchen-Vluyn, 1991), 533–560 (548ff.).

[10] W. Brueggemann, *The Land. Place as Gift, Promise and Challenge in Biblical Faith* (OBT, 1; Philadelphia, 1977).

[11] *Survey of Israel* 1:100.000 (1988) Sheet 9 (Palestine Grid).

[12] The Abdallah Bridge was closed after 1967 and officially opened again after the peace treaty between Jordan and Israel in 1994.

[13] GSGS Palestine 1:100.000 (1955) Sheet 10 (Jerusalem).

[14] "Sie ist 8 km von Jericho entfernt und löste die roranije-Furt ab, die immer die wichtigste Verbindung zwischen dem Ost- und Westjordanland am unteren Jordan war" (Cl. Knopp, *Die heiligen Stätten der Evangelien* [Regensburg, 1959]), 143.

[15] The next ford is Makhadat Umm ash Shurat (201153). The distance is about 7 km further to the north.

geographical items taken from recent data. Current and erosion may have brought changes, wadi's take different courses, the marl hills around the southern part of the Jordan with a height of 40–60 metres change their shape due to rough weather circumstances.[16] That the Hebrew Bible, however, speaks about fords in the plural is significant (Josh 2:7; Judg 3:28). The ancient authors knew about many fords in the neighbourhood of Jericho. Edward Robinson, the great geographer of the biblical lands, knew in 1838 both the southern fords and the crossing place at Wadi Nimrin, north of the present Allenby Bridge.[17] Going back in time the crusaders were aware of the possibilities of crossing the Jordan in the neighbourhood of the present Allenby Bridge and at Al Maghtas (201138). Al Maghtas connected in Roman and Byzantine times Jerusalem-Jericho with Livias on the road to Heshbon.

Crossing the Jordan at one of the fords was sometimes a difficult, but never an impossible job. In 1867 a crossing with horses, mules loaded with baggage, tents and expedition materials did not take more than one and an half hours.[18] From the mid sixties of the 19th century there are photographs of Jordan crossings where men and animals easily reach the other side. From here it is understandable that the Jordan could be a political boundary but never was a serious obstacle.[19]

Summing up:

—Until modern times several crossing points in the southern part of the Jordan are known. Al Maghtas was the most important connection between west and east.

—Traditions, legends and stories connected with the Jordan were centred on those crossing points and play an important role here.

---

[16] Knopp 1959, 143 refers to differences in the outer shape of the Jordan in the 19th and 20th century.

[17] E. Robinson, E. Smith, *Palästina und die südlich angrenzenden Länder II* (1841) 494–496.

[18] Ch. Warren, C.R. Conder, *The Survey of Western Palestine: Jerusalem* (London, 1884), 454:—"July 18th Ain as Sultan. Started at 6.30 a.m., and arrived at en Nwaimeh ford at 8.30 . . . The Jordan just now was very low, and there was little danger in crossing; for about 30 feet the depth was 7 feet or more, and for the remainder it was only 2 to 4 feet."

[19] Knopp 1959, 143, however argues that in the fifties of the 20th century, the Lower Jordan could only be crossed by boat or bridge.

III. The Gospels about John the Baptist
and the Geographical Setting

With these points in mind we ask for the geographical settings of the traditions concerning John the Baptist. The Synoptic Gospels locate John and his ministry in the south without clear specification. ἐγένετο Ἰωάννης [ὁ] βαπτίζων ἐν τῇ ἐρήμῳ tells Mark 1:4, but the setting of his gospel and the public πᾶσα ἡ Ἰουδαία χώρα καὶ οἱ Ἱεροσολυμῖται πάντες (Mark 1:5; Matt 3:5 with widening circles: Jerusalem—all Judea, and πᾶσα ἡ περίχωρος τοῦ Ἰορδάνου; Luke 3:3 πᾶσαν [τὴν] περίχωρον τοῦ Ἰορδάνου) enables Matt 3:1 to add ἐν τῇ ἐρήμῳ τῆς Ἰουδαίας.

Even the scenes of the baptism of Jesus are not a great help. After Mark 1:9 Jesus "comes from Nazareth of Galilee" to be baptised. Matt 3:13 omits Nazareth and states more in general that Jesus covers the distance from Galilee to the Jordan. The specific localization may be unclear, but two traditio-historical building-stones are not. Mark, Matthew and Luke as well, refer to Isa 40:3 קוֹל קוֹרֵא בַמִּדְבָּר פַּנּוּ דֶּרֶךְ יהוה, LXX: φωνὴ βοῶντος ἐν τῇ ἐρήμῳ ἑτοιμάσατε τὴν ὁδὸν κυρίου. The strong relation of John with the desert is stressed by the change of the role of the desert in the Old Testament quotation. Isa 40:3—in the context of the Babylonian exile—undoubtedly wants to say: "a (heavenly) voice cries out: 'Prepare *in the wilderness* the way of YHWH.'" The gospels, including John, take it up as: "The voice of one crying out *in the wilderness*: 'Prepare the way of the Kyrios . . .'" (Mark 1:3; Matt 3:3; Luke 3:4 [add Isa 40:4*.5*]; John 1:23 I-Speech: ἔφη· ἐγὼ φωνὴ βοῶντος ἐν τῇ ἐρήμῳ·). This last increase of the connection between John and Isa 40:3 serves in the Gospel of John as a denial of his being Elijah (John 1:21), the second traditio-historical link. For Mark 1:2 opens with the varied quote from Mal 3:1 הִנְנִי שֹׁלֵחַ מַלְאָכִי וּפִנָּה־דֶרֶךְ לְפָנָי understood as the prophet Elijah, whom YHWH will send "before the great and terrible day of YHWH comes" (Mal 3:23). The strong relations between Elijah and John are stressed here right at the beginning of the gospel. The gospels may differ about the exact function and role of John, but the relation with Elijah is a theme. According to Mark 9:11–13 Jesus himself believed that John was Elijah. The same is stated in Matt 11:9–14, but the role of John/Elijah as the prophet preparing the coming of Jesus as Messiah is stressed. In the Jesus-speech John/Elijah is the greatest human being up till now (Matt 11:11.14). For Luke the portrait of John in relation to Elijah is summarized in the message of the angel to Zechariah: "John shall go before the Lord ἐν πνεύματι καὶ δυνάμει Ἡλίου to turn the hearts of parents to their children, and the disobedient to the wisdom of the righteous, to make ready a people prepared for the Lord" (Luke 1:17). The gospel of John uses the self-denial of John that he is *not* Elijah (1:21) for stressing his role as forerunner of the "Son of God" (1:34). Summing up: Mark and Matt use the highest authority for the statement that John is Elijah, Luke sees him as a prophet working in the spirit and in the power of Elijah, the gospel of John denies an Elijah role for John in favor of an even higher calling.

If we did not have the fourth gospel, John, his appearance as the second Elijah, his wilderness and his baptisms would be located somewhere at the fords or some other fitting locations at the Jordan roughly between Jericho and the Dead Sea. The gospel of John, however, fills in some geographic details. John is baptizing in "Bethany across the Jordan" (ἐν Βηθανίᾳ . . . πέραν τοῦ Ἰορδάνου John 1:28). Referring to contacts between rivalling disciples of Jesus and John it is told that Ἦν δὲ καὶ ὁ Ἰωάννης βαπτίζων ἐν Αἰνὼν ἐγγὺς τοῦ Σαλείμ, ὅτι ὕδατα πολλὰ ἦν ἐκεῖ (3:23). This Ainon near Salem is qualified by an abundance of water. The third important reference is John 10:40. Jesus escapes from the hands of the Jews of Jerusalem and goes πέραν τοῦ Ἰορδάνου εἰς τὸν τόπον ὅπου ἦν Ἰωάννης τὸ πρῶτον βαπτίζων. The expression "across the Jordan" used here can only mean the same place as in John 1:28.

John burdens us with two topographical riddles. The first topic is the location of Ainon near Salem (3:23). The second one and the main problem is the "Bethany across the Jordan" (1:28).

It is a cold comfort that "Bethany across the Jordan" is already a very old riddle. Although the as text adopted ({C}) reading ἐν Βηθανίᾳ has strong support (ABC*WN, p[66], p[75] a.o.) and reaches back until about 200, there are other variants,[20] the most important being ἐν Βηθαραβᾷ or ἐν Βηθαβαρᾷ. The former one can be easily explained as an adaptation to the town of Betharabah (Jos 15:6.61)[21] or to the Arabah as the well known name for the Jordan Valley,[22]

---

[20] Wiefel 1967, 72f.

[21] J.C. de Vos, *Das Los Judas. Über Entstehung und Ziele der Landbeschreibung in Josua 15*, (Diss. Groningen, 2002), 193ff.

[22] Deut 3:17; 4:49; [11:30] Josh 3:16 (crossing the Jordan); 11:2; 12:3; 18:18; 1 Sam 23:24; 2 Sam 2:29 etc.

especially the southern part of it. The change of Bethania into Betha-
raba can be explained, the other way around not. The second variant Bethabara, however, has got an impressive place in the history
of exegesis. It is important that already Origen chose for the reading Βηθαβαρα,[23] followed by Eusebius[24] and Jerome, the early giants
in biblical topography. So did the marvelous Madaba mosaic map
from the 6th century as well, where Βεθαβαρα is the most southern
place-name before the Jordan flows into the Dead Sea. The Hebrew
root behind it, עבר, has many aspects,[25] but it functions in many
texts of the Hebrew bible as a deuteronomistic terminus technicus
for the settlement narratives and as a signal word in Josh 3f. for
crossing the Jordan (22x).

IV. The Gospel of John and its two Topographical Riddles

What can be said about the two topographical problems with which
the Gospel of John burdens us?

The first point is the Ainon of John 3:23. Here are some more
data as usual at present. The Madaba map refers to two Ainon's.
Opposite Bethabara on the east bank is written: ΑΙΝΩΝ ΕΝΘΑ ΝΥΝ
Ο ΣΑΠΣΑΦΑΣ. This "Ainon, where now is Sapsaphas," however, is
not the Ainon near Salem from John 3:23. A second Ainon on the
west bank is mapped near the second ferry on the mosaic, about 8
miles in the south of Beth Shean: ΑΥΝΩΝ Η ΕΓΓΥΣ ΤΟΥ ΣΑΛΗΜ,
located in the vicinity of Salumias. "Ainon near Salem" is a direct
quotation from John 3:23. This Ainon is referred to by Eusebius[26]
and about 400 it is described by the amazing pilgrim Egeria: *Tunc
ergo quia retinebam scriptum esse baptizasse sanctum Iohannem in Enon iuxta
Salem . . . ubi ostendit (sanctus presbyter) nobis in medio fontem aquae optimae
satis et purae, qui a semel integrum fluvium dimittebat. Habebat autem ante se
ipse fons quasi lacum, ubi parebat fuisse operatum sanctum Iohannem baptis-
tam.*[27] The twofold mentioning on the map leaves some questions
open. Where does the Ainon opposite Bethabara come from? Is the

[23] *Comm. in Ioann.* VI 205, GCS 4, 149f.; VI 221, GCS 4,152.
[24] Eusebius, *Onomasticon*, 58,18–20.
[25] H.F. Fuhs, עבר, *ThWAT* V (1986) 1015–1033.
[26] *Onom* 40,1–4; 152,4ff.
[27] *CSEL* 39, 15.1–3*.

southern Ainon secondary to the original Ainon in the north so that the concentration of all the important Jordan crossings in the south could claim a place of Johannine baptism too? Or did the Ainon in the north grow out of the southern tradition as an independent place of baptism?[28] In favor of the last possibility can be mentioned that John 3:23 is not an isolated topographical remark, but a contrast to the communication that Jesus and his disciples went εἰς τὴν Ἰουδαίαν γῆν . . . καὶ ἐκεῖ . . . ἐβάπτιζεν. So it could be argued that the northern location Ainon (Tall ar-Ridga 199/200) represents a construction to separate the baptisms of Jesus and John. Secondly the wonderful description of Egeria about the northern place of baptism sounds more like paradise than a real existing place. This *fons* and *lacus* in the midst of a *hortus pommarium* flowing into one river and fed by *aquae optimae et purae* remember of the idealized topography of Gen 2:10–14.

In favor, however, of an original northern location as mentioned by John 3:23 two positive arguments can be called. The ἐν Αἰνὼν ἐγγὺς τοῦ Σαλείμ of John 3:23 tries to give an exact location in contrast to other places called Ainon and locates it in the vicinity of Salumias, partly represented on the Madaba map.[29] This Salumias is well known in the tradition and can be identified.[30] There are abundant springs in the vicinity. The distance of 8 miles to Skythopolis (Beth Shean) mentioned by Eusebius[31] fits perfectly. Secondly: until now the old name Salem has partly survived.[32] This means, John provides us here with a topographical detail which can be checked in the later material.

---

[28] The Madaba Map itself is not a help at all. There are more examples of contradicting traditions which both found a place on the map as in the case of the famous double location of Ebal and Gerizim.

[29] The famous drawing of the map by Palmer & Guthe (P. Palmer, H. Guthe, *Die Mosaikkarte von Madeba*: I: Tafeln, Leipzig, 1906) is re-used by many influential studies, the most important being M. Avi-Yonah, *The Madaba Mosaic Map. With Introduction and Commentary* (Jerusalem, 1954). The map is inaccurate about Ainon. The last letters to be read are ΣΑ-ΛΗΜ. The accurate photographs of Donner/Cüppers 1977 before and after restauration of the map read under Salem the first two letters a second ΣΑ . . . representing Σα[λουμιας] (Donner/Cüppers 1977, Pl. 45 [before)] and Pl. 97 [after]).

[30] Donner 1992, 37.

[31] Eusebius, *Das Onomastikon der biblischen Ortsnamen*, 40,1–4, hrsg. E. Klostermann, GCS III 1, Leipzig, 1904.

[32] R. Riesner, *Bethanien jenseits des Jordan. Topographie und Theologie im Johannes-Evangelium* (Giessen, 2002), 145 with a reference to F.M. Abel (1913).

Probably the Gospel of John is right, John was baptising *too* in the vicinity of Beth Shean, one of the cities of the Dekapolis. Doing so he escaped for a while the power of Herod Antipas whose jurisdiction was limited to Galilee and Perea. His roots were in the south in the vicinity of the well-known fords. There he could have both: desert and audience. Outside the reach of Herod Antipas he worked in the north and again in the vicinity of one of the most important fords between west and east: the ancient road between Beth Shean and Pella. The name Ainon (> *ʿayn*, "spring"), is a general one. When the Madaba Mosaicists and the learned tradition behind it knew both: an original location for John's working in the south and a temporal working at Ainon near Salem, the southern Ainon on the map could be a move from north to south. In the time of the map Sapsas had to be replaced and the name Ainon fits for Wadi al-Kharrar, the traditional place of baptism.

The second point is the location ἐν Βηθανίᾳ . . . πέραν τοῦ Ἰορδάνου (John 1:28). The strange thing about this Bethany is that the name could not ever be traced anywhere. The NT text is—in spite of the variants ἐν Βηθαραβᾷ or ἐν Βηθαβαρᾷ well attested. But neither pilgrim texts nor material remains have ever revealed a Bethany beyond the Jordan. The most challenging thesis about Bethany comes from Rainer Riesner, who defends in his last monograph[33] that Bethany beyond the Jordan is an adaptation from the Batanea, the territory in the north-east of Palestine. Riesner argues that the chronology in the gospel of John, the eschatological messianic expectations related to the north of Palestine, the boundaries of the territories, the use of "beyond the Jordan" and the failure of solutions up till now make it possible to understand Bethany as the Batanea. The thesis is attractive, but based on many presuppositions. John is understood as an entity of its own, even in the geographical domain. By this I mean that the locations of Mark and Matt cannot be combined with those of John if Bethany is Batanea. After Riesner, John's proclamation of Jesus as "the Lamb of God" (1:29) took place in Batanea. Then you

---

[33] R. Riesner 2002. Riesner defended his thesis earlier: "Bethany beyond the Jordan (John 1:28)," *Tyndale Bulletin* 38 (1987) 29–63. Bargil Pixner was involved in the first stadium: B. Pixner, *With Jesus through Galilee According to the Fifth Gospel* (Rosh Pina, 1992). The same idea was brought up by W.W. Winter, "Bethany beyond Jordan: John the Baptist in the Decapolis," *Evangelical Theological Society Papers* (1990) 1–16. He, however, depends on Riesner 1987 and is not precise enough in his territorial analyses.

must be able to prove that the Batanea in the NT was geographically covered by the Basan from the Hebrew bible and included both sides of the Yarmuk. The normal geographical understanding, however, locates the Batanea further to the northeast. There must be proof that those territories like the Batanea, Trachonitis, Gaulanitis were entitled as "beyond the Jordan." Riesner has gathered a lot of messianic, or eschatological interpreted texts related to the north, but as in the case of some psalm texts there is a lot of uncertainty. Riesner's thesis should get careful consideration, but it needs a detailed examination and it must be supported by more arguments than could be given in his overview. Nevertheless it seems fair to keep open the possibility that John worked in the north of Transjordan too.

Summing up:

—The synoptic gospels locate the baptism somewhere in the southern part of the Lower Jordan, roughly between Jericho and the Dead Sea. A location near one of the important fords makes sense.
—The gospel of John brings in a place further to the north: Ainon near Salem. This Ainon can be located and is brought in on the Madaba map two times. One time at the "real" location, one time for concentrating all the important traditions in the south.
—The gospel of John knows a Βηθανία ... πέραν τοῦ Ἰορδάνου, a place never identified by one of the ancient topographers and commentators. A recent proposal thinks the Batanea is meant.
—The toponym Βη/εθαβαρα is wellknown however. It is both a functional name and a reminder of ancient traditions about famous Jordan crossings.

V. The Traditions of the Western Bank of the Jordan

How strong are the roots of Βη/εθαβαρα in tradition? We have already seen that the NT manuscripts do not favor a reading Βηθαβαρα. With this uncertainty in mind we start with the most informative source, the Madaba Mosaic Map from the sixth century. Around the southernmost church on the banks of the Jordan Βεθαβαρα τὸ τοῦ ἁγίου Ἰωάννου τοῦ βαπτίσματος, "Bethabara, (the sanctuary) of the Baptism of St. John" can be read.[34] This Bethabara is closely related to the baptism of John, no Bethany emerges. The location,

---

[34] M. Avi-Yonah, *The Madaba Mosaic Map: With Introduction and Commentary* (Jerusalem, 1954), 38f., Plate 2; Donner/Cüppers 1977, Abb. 98, 100; H. Donner, *The Madaba Mosaic Map* (Palaestina Antiqua 7; Kampen, 1992), 38 nr. 6.

however, is at the west side of the Jordan, not at the eastern side, which would be expected after πέραν τοῦ Ἰορδάνου. To the south a wadi flows into the Jordan, really near to the Dead Sea. Probably it is Wadi el Qilt.[35] Only the names of the arms of the Nile are written in the water, otherwise there is no writing in the rivers. So it could be possible that Wadi el Qilt emerges so far to the south because of the needed space for Bethabara in its right location,[36] its connection with John the Baptist and Beth Hagla, here identified with the threshing-floor of Atad, the place of "the great and sorrowful lamentation" for Jacob (Gen 50:10). Here too the location appears in a surprising way at the western side of the Jordan. It is brought "home westwards" in opposition to the biblical text which reads האטד אשר בעבר הירדן.[37] North of the church of John the Baptist and Bethabara is a watchtower and a ferry, the first for the protection of the latter. The ferry itself is moved by means of a construction built up across the river between the two banks.[38] An exact localization is difficult but by calculating the proportions between this ferry and the second one, in the neighborhood of Beth Shean, it may be localized as the ford in the north of the present Allenby-Bridge (200144).

Bethabara itself can be localized because of the continuity of tradition at this very place. It is the present Deir Mar Yuḥanna/Qasr al Yahud near Al Maghtas (201138). With the eyes of the tradition it is one and the same. It was here that John had baptized and that Jesus was baptized. But even the present name Qasr al Yahud demonstrates that here was a Jewish site too. Here Elijah and the crossing of the Jordan under Joshua (Josh 3f.) come in. The site on the right bank of the Jordan therefore is often mentioned in the early Pilgrim texts.[39] In the 6th century, around 570, the Piacenza pilgrim knows the spot on the west bank of the Jordan: *super Iordane non mul-*

---

[35] This southern position makes it impossible for Avi-Yonah 1954, 38 n. 15 to recognise here Wadi el Qilt. His argument does not fit geographically.

[36] There is open space on the map between Bethabara and the watchtower.

[37] Threshing-floors and the land east of the Jordan, play a role in the cult of the dead. A location west of the Jordan for the most important patriarch Jacob could be a try to get the lamentation for him out of this context.

[38] For a discussion of the construction, see Noort 1991, 550, n. 46.

[39] Kopp 1959, 153–172; J. Wilkinson, *Jerusalem Pilgrims Before the Crusades* (Warminster, 1977); H. Donner, *Pilgerfahrt ins Heilige Land. Die ältesten Berichte christlicher Palästinapilger (4.–7. Jahrhundert)* (Stuttgart, 1979).

tum longe <a loco>, ubi baptizatus est Dominus, monasterium est sancti Iohannis grande valde, in quo sunt xenodochia duo.[40] This pilgrim, however, knows perfectly the important places on the eastern bank of the river, to which we will return later. There is a detailed description in 9:46–49 and 10:50. Although he tells about the journey from Galilee to the Lower Jordan, the other location of John's baptism, Ainon near Salem (John 3:23), is missing. He only refers to the wonders John did in Beth Shean (Scythopolis): *venimus in civitate metropoli Galilaeae, quae vocatur Scitopolis, in monte posita, ubi sanctus Iohannes multas virtutes operatur* (8:7–9). Baptism is not mentioned. This means the Piacenza pilgrim localizes the baptism of John and Jesus at Al Maghtas/Betha-bara. But there is more. Adomnan, the abbot of Iona, describes the travel of bishop Arculf of Gaul around 680. Here also are references to the place of baptism of John and Jesus and to the church of John within the monastery on the westbank of the Jordan: *ibidemque et eccle-sia in honorem sancti baptizatoris Iohannis fundata eodem monasterii circum-datur muro quadratus constructo lapidibus.*[41] The next witness is Epiphanius the Monk.[42] Although the source itself is difficult to date, the core—document from about 675 is a kind of itinerary or guide among oth-ers to the Jordan and the place of Baptism. Coming from Jericho the distance to the Jordan is eight miles. A fort contains the Holy Trinity Church. On the bank of the river you find the church of John the Forerunner and even in the apse you see the stone on which John stood when he baptized Jesus.[43] Without any doubt Epiphanius is speaking about the west bank of the Jordan. But after this we get further information. John himself lived across the river, there the cave of the Forerunner can be found.[44] (And the pillar of salt with the wife of Lot!). Here the east side of the Jordan is taken into account and we have a division: John baptized (at least Jesus) at the *west* side of the Jordan, he himself lived, however, in a cav-ern on the *east* bank of the river.

From 724 until 727 Willibald, the later Bishop of Eichstätt (741), spent four years in the Holy Land and stayed overnight in the

---

[40] *Antonini Placentini Itinerarium* 12:7–9, in: P. Geyer, *Itinera Hierosolymitana Saeculi IV–VIII* (CSEL, 39; Praag-Wenen-Leipzig, 1898) (Further *CSEL*, 39).
[41] *Adamnani de locis sanctis libri tres, CSEL, 39,* II xvi, 14–15.
[42] Edition of the text by H. Donner, "Die Palästinabeschreibung des Epiphanius Monachus Hagiopolita," *ŽDPV* 87 (1971) 42–91. See too: Wilkinson 1977, 117–121.
[43] Epiphanius XI, 19–20.
[44] Epiphanius XI, 20–22.

monastery of John the Baptist on the west bank of the Jordan. He encountered about 20 monks and describes the distance to the place of baptism as about one mile.[45] Interesting is his observation that on the spot "where is baptized now" a rope between the riverbanks is fixed as a help for the people who want to immerse themselves.[46] One and a half centuries later (870) Bernard, the Monk, still mentions the monastery of John the Baptist.[47] The last mentioning of a chapel of baptism comes from the abbot Daniel in the year 1106. After the crusades, memory is not longer sustained by existing monuments, only a general location is transmitted.

The maps from the Middle Ages, collected by W. Wiefel show different locations.[48] R. Röhricht published in 1891 a map dating back from c. 1300 (now in Firenze). In the east of Jericho there is a small stronghold with the legend: "*baptismus Christi, ubi est capella Johannes baptistae.*" The stronghold/chapel is found clearly on the west side of the Jordan. Northern of the building opposite Gilgal 1 (Gagala) the spot is marked where Israel crossed the Jordan: *transitus filiorum Israel per Jordanem.*[49] A map from Firenze from the 12th century overwrites the Jordan in the south of Jericho "*Christi baptisma.*" West or east can not be determined, because the writing covers both banks of the river. An interesting building—northern of Jericho, but still closer to Jericho than to Beth Shean/Scitopolis—at the east side of the Jordan, called Bethabra, is marked with "*ubi erat Johannes baptizans.*"[50] A map from the Oxford Bodleian (13th century) locates both: the baptism of Jesus and the church of John the Baptist on the east bank: "*ubi baptizatus est Dominus ecclesia (Johannis) baptiste.*"[51]

Marino Sanudo from Venice (14th century) allocates an Eccl. Joh. Bapt. to a spot eastern of Jericho but on the west bank of the Jordan.[52] A later map, based on Sanudo[53] writes on the westbank north-

[45] The present distance is about 600 meters.

[46] Hugeburc, *The Life of Willibald* (Monumenta Germanicae Historiae XV; 1887, xvi 15f., 20–22.

[47] Wilkinson 1977, 144: 318,18–19.

[48] W. Wiefel 1967, 79f.

[49] R. Röhricht, "Karte und Pläne zur Palästinakunde aus dem 7. bis 16. Jahrhundert I," *ZDPV* 14 (1891), 8–11, Pl. 1.

[50] R. Röhricht, "Karten und Pläne zur Palästinakunde aus dem 7.–16. Jahrhundert VI," *ZDPV* 18 (1895), 173–182, Pl. V.

[51] Röhricht 1895, 177, Pl. VI.

[52] 18ᵉ Palästinakarte des Marino Sanudo aus dem Londoner Codex 27376. R. Röhricht, "Marino Sanudo sen. als Kartograph Palästinas," *ZDPV* 21 (1898) 84–126, Pl. 2.

[53] Florenz Bibl. Laurent., plut. XXIX, 26 fol. 58b–59a; Röhricht 1898, Pl. 6.

east of Jericho "*Hic Christus baptizatus est*," but gives a legend "*Ecclesia S. Johannes*" on the east bank of the river. Here we find the clear topographical division, west and east, back on the maps. Going east is offered by Florenz Bibl. Laurent plut. LXXXVI, 56, fol. 97+98. Opposite Jericho the desert of the temptation of Jesus can be seen. But the place of baptism is to be found on the east bank: "*Hic battiçatus fuit Christus.*"[54] An alternative, made possible by John 3:23, is noticed in the Prologus Arminensis from Lübeck (1478). Here, the northern location is chosen. On the west bank of the Jordan Galgala and Jericho are drawn. On the east side, however, to the north, but nearer to Jericho than to Beth Shean, Salem is noticed, and written to it "*In Iordane Christus hic baptisatus.*"[55] Salem is mentioned here not as the general place of baptism, but as the specific place of the baptism of Jesus by John.

Summing up: Starting with the monumental remains on the west bank of the Jordan it can be said that most of the pilgrims texts and the Madaba Mosaic Map locate the place of John's baptism there. The earliest texts supporting the west side date back to the middle of the 6th century. The focus is not on the work of John the Baptist *in toto*, but on John as the instrument by which Jesus is baptized. His function as Forerunner is enlightened. The textual and iconographical evidence sees him as a means, as a stage in the mission of Jesus. Where his own mission is stressed the eastern side of the Jordan comes into sight. From the middle of the 6th century until the crusades the monastery of John on the west bank is the center of pious activities. If we can trust Procopius of Caesarea and his hymn on the deeds of Emperor Justinian, Justinian had constructed "a well in the monastery of Holy John on the Jordan."[56] This would make the monastery of John date back to the first half of the 6th century. Going further back is connected with uncertainty and speculation. The "Bethany . . . across the Jordan" from John 1:28 could not be located by the ancient topographers and pilgrims. The minority reading "Bethabara," however, adopted by Origen, Eusebius and Jerome got a prominent place on the Madaba Mosaic Map in the 6th century.

---

[54] Röhricht 1898, Pl. 7.
[55] Röhricht 1898, Pl. 11.
[56] H.B. Dewing, G. Downey, *Procopius of Caesarea* (Loeb Classical Library, 7; London, 1961), V ix 19; Wilkinson 1977, 77.

In spite of the stress on the west bank several texts and some maps from the Middle Ages demonstrate that the traditions of the eastern side of the river have not been silenced totally. In one case there was a northern Salem at the east side, based on John 3:23.

VI. The Traditions of the Eastern Bank of the Jordan

But how about the southern and eastern Ainon? Here the tradition starts earlier than on the west bank. The unknown Bordeaux traveler, the earliest pilgrim to the Holy Land in the Christian tradition, wrote about 330 that the distance from the Dead Sea *"ad Iordane ubi dominus a Iohanne baptizatus est milia quinque."* These five miles bring us to Al Maghtas.

But the Bordeaux pilgrim does not aim at the later famous west bank of the Jordan, but at the east side of the river. For him the location of baptism is connected with the ascension of Elijah (2 Kgs 2:11f.), he even knows the *monticulus* where this happened. After a gap of about two hundred years it is Theodosius, who tells it more precisely: "At the place where my Lord was baptized is a marble column, and on top of it has been set an iron cross. There (*ibi*)[57] is also the church of Saint John the Baptist, which was constructed by the emperor Anastasius[58] . . . Where my Lord was baptized there is on the far side of the Jordan a *mons modicus* called Armona[59] . . . where Saint Elijah was taken up. The tomb of Saint Elisha is there. . . . It is five miles. . . ."[60] The place attracts even more saints and more details. About 570 the Piacenza pilgrim locates the baptism of Jesus, Israel's crossing the Jordan (Josh 3f.), the axe-head of Elisha (2 Kgs 6) at the same spot. Even the brook Krith (1 Kgs 17) and the ascension of Elijah (2 Kgs 2:11f.) with an explicit reference to the psalm text of the "little Hermon" can be found here according to the Piacenza pilgrim.[61] The baptism of John and Elijah traditions are interwoven here.

---

[57] The here used *ibi* troubled the exegetes. Most probably the east side of the Jordan is meant.

[58] Anastasius I, 491–518.

[59] A gloss in the text explains Armona as Mount Tabor in Galilee, trying to connect this Armona with the mount of transfiguration of Matt 17: Theodosius, *CSEL*, 39, 20 (Geyer 146, r. 5). The direct reference is Ps 42:7 "the land of the Jordan and the Hermonim."

[60] Theodosius, *De situ terrae sanctae*, *CSEL*, 39, 20.

[61] Antoninus, *CSEL*, 39, 9 (Geyer 165, 20).

The learned tradition seeks this location for the greater part in
Wādī al-Kharrār. Donner searched the wadi in 1963,[62] was skepti-
cal about a *Jebel mar elyas*, [63] did not find traces of the church of
Anastasius, but he found a lot of caves of hermits, already mentioned by the Piacenza pilgrim. At least those caves confirmed the
important status of the wadi in early Byzantine times. But more can
be said. Abel saw in 1932 architectural rests about 50 meters from
the Jordan.[64] And M. Piccirillo tells about photographs (dating back
to 1899) of a small chapel built on arches which Father Féderlin of
the White Fathers at St. Anne (Jerusalem) made on the east bank
of the river.[65] Those half-forgotten memories combined with occasional remarks by the professional travelers of the 19th century grew
more important after the surveys and excavations a few years ago.[66]
Wādī al-Kharrār booms again!

After fifty years of war threat and political tension, the peace treaty
between Jordan and Israel made it possible to visit the traditional
sites on both banks of the river again. In 1995 Wādī al-Kharrār was
visited by a group of archaeologists and in 1997 King Hussein set
up a commission to develop the Park of the Baptism of Christ.
Surveys and excavations directed by Mohammad Waheeb started.[67]
Along Wādī al-Kharrār 21 sites were located. Early to Late Roman
and Early to Late Byzantine remains dominated: "the periods between
the first century B.C. and the seventh century A.D. mark the 'high
point' of human occupation and exploration of the limited resources
of the area."[68]

The most important discoveries relating to the question under discussion, were a church immediately adjacent to the east of the Jordan.
The place of the remains of this church are surrounded by lissan
marl cliffs. The distant to the east side of the river is about 300
meters. There is a high probability that this is the church built by
Anastasius. The ongoing excavations revealed the foundations of three

---

[62] Donner 1992, 38 repeats that Ainon can be found in Wādī al-Kharrār.
[63] Antoninus, *CSEL*, 39, 9 (Geyer 165, 20).
[64] F.M. Abel, *RB* 41 (1932), 240.
[65] M. Piccirillo, *The Mada Map Centenary* (Jerusalem, 1999), 218–221 and http://
198.62.75.1?www1/ofm/mad/articles/piccirillosapsaphas.html.
[66] R. Riesner, *Bethanien jenseits des Jordan. Topographie und Theologie im Johannes-
Evangelium* (Giessen, 2002), 29–33.
[67] M. Waheeb, Wādī al-Kharrār Archaeological Project (al-Maghtas), *ADAJ* 42
(1998), 635–638; M. Waheeb, Wādī al-Kharrār Archaeological Project (al-Maghtas),
Studies in the History and Archaeology of Jordan VII (Amman, 2001), 591–600.
[68] Waheeb 2001, 594.

succeeding churches. The first being the one built by Anasastasius, the last one could be the famous Trinity-Church.[69]

The second important item, are the now excavated buildings and structures on or near Tall al-Kharrar, two kilometers east of the river. This hill was protected by a wall around it. It was occupied during Roman and Byzantine times. Three churches, three caves and three (baptism?) pools were found. This massive Christian presence supports the theory that here the *mar elyas* could be located. Of course one needs to be cautious. All the now published facts and interpretations do come from interim reports and they are definitely not free from religious-economic motives.[70] On the other hand, we have now a situation where the literary witnesses about the traditions on the east bank of the Jordan are accompanied by material remains dating back to Roman and Early-Byzantine times. The mentioning on the Madaba Map "Ainon where now is Sapsaphas" supports the ancient traditions on the eastern bank of the river. The reference aims at the Sapsas Monastery, built at the end of the 5th century and referred to by John Moschus about 615 A.D. There is still an historical argument for the eastern bank of the Jordan. The dispute between John and Herod Antipas ends with the execution of the latter at Macharaeus in Perea. John felt under Herod's jurisdiction. The east side of the Jordan belonged to the tetrarchy of Galilee and Perea under Herod Antipas, while the west side belonged to Judea, reigned by Roman procurators from 6 A.D. on.

VII. The Shift from East to West

The walk along the literary and material remains about John the Baptist can now be evaluated. The surveyed material demonstrated that the tradition of the western bank starts in the sixth century and continues through the 12th century. At the same time there were references to the eastern bank too. Some authors located the baptism of Jesus on the western bank but John himself lived east of the river (Epiphanius). Some maps did the same thing. They located the baptism of Jesus by John on the west side but refer at the same

---

[69] Riesner 2002, 31 "Von einem vor der Kirchenanlage liegenden gepflasterten Hof führten 22 Marmorstufen zu einem Seitenarm des Jordan hinab, der etwa 70 meter vom Hauptstrom entfernt verläuft."

[70] http://www.elmaghtas.com.

time to the church of St. John at the eastern side. One map refused to cut the Gordian knot and located the baptism in the middle of the river, neither west nor east. The material about the eastern traditions clearly preceded that of the western bank. That could already be said of the written sources. The new archaeological material supports this in a most welcome way. That can even be said in a situation where the dating and the material to be checked cannot be so exactly evaluated as we wished we could. It seems to be without doubt that the material remains of a Christian presence in and around Wādī al-Kharrār goes back to Early Byzantine and probably Roman times. The conclusion is clear. At some date in history, probably in the last half of the 6th century, the baptism of John and the baptism of Jesus were moved from east to west. The historians do have several reasons for that. It is argued that the eastern bank of the Jordan was difficult to reach. After the conquest of Palestine by the Moslems the access would be even more difficult. For both reasons individual literary witnesses exist. The western bank however, could easily be reached by the stream of pilgrims who were visiting holy places as Bethlehem and Jerusalem on the western side of the Jordan. A liturgical solution is offered by Wiefel.[71] He argues that the shift from east to west was due to the realization of a separate Christmas Feast. As long as birth and baptism were not separated, but celebrated as the Epiphany on January 6th, the Jordan did not play a role in the liturgical setting. As soon as, in the sixth century, a separate Christmas Feast was celebrated,[72] time and space were available for the Christians to pilgrimage to the Jordan and to celebrate the baptism of Jesus in a liturgical setting. Probably this liturgical argument was supported by political reasons too.

VIII. The Different Roles of John the Baptist

The really interesting point is neither the date nor the direct reason for the shift from east to west. It is the shift in the role of John the Baptist. Almost all sources locating John on the eastern bank relate him to Elijah. John enters the stage following the footprints of Elijah. That makes sense, for the ascension of Elijah is told as

[71] Wiefel 1967, 77–79.
[72] Wiefel 1967, 78.

happening at the eastern side of the Jordan. And it is this ascension that creates the possibility of an Elijah *redivivus*. It does not mean that the baptism of Jesus by John is out of the picture, but the focus is on John as a revived Elijah with the same strength, the same radicality, the same 'no' to the existing religious structures. The Baptist not the baptism is in the center. This changes after the shift from east to west. Here the role of John is important, but only as the instrument by which Jesus is baptized. The baptism of Jesus is in the center of memory and liturgy. And when the liturgical background for the shift makes sense, it is clear why this happens. When the western bank is the place of Epiphany the relation between John, his radical movement and Elijah must fade. In the center is now the baptism of Jesus as the beloved Son of God.

This does not mean, however, that the other elements of the drama of salvation history as experienced by the pilgrims disappeared. The Piacenza pilgrim tells what happens at Epiphany: *Tenui autem theophaniam in Iordane, ubi talia fiunt mirabilia in illa nocte in loco, ubi baptizatus est Dominus . . . et tenentes diaconi descendit sacerdos in fluvium et hora, qua coeperit benedicere aquam, mox Iordanis cum rugitu redit post se et stat aqua usque dum baptismus perficiatur.*[73] As soon as the priest descends into the water of the Jordan and pronounces the blessing, de river does, what it did in Josh 3: it turns back, flees and stops the water!

Hundred and seventy years before, Jerome described in his letter to Eustochium the experiences of her mother, the pious Paula, who had died on 26 January, 404: "Night was hardly over when, with burning devotion, she reached the Jordan. As she stood on the (western) river-bank she saw the sun rise, and remembered the *Sun of Righteousness*; and how the priests dry-shod across the river-bed; and how the waters made way, and stood to the right and left at the command of Elijah and Elisha; and how by his Baptism, the Lord cleansed the waters which had been fouled by the flood and stained by the extermination of the human race."[74] Beyond all details about the geographical settings, a centripetal move connects every known part of the tradition with each other. Israel's crossing of the river, the crossing of Elijah and Elisha, the ascension of Elijah, John's baptizing and the baptism of Jesus come dramatically together. Even

---

[73] Antoninus, *CSEL*, 39, 11 (Geyer, 166, 17ff.).

[74] Epitaphium S. Paulae, *epistula 108 ad Eustochium*, *CSEL*, 55, 12 in the translation of J. Wilkinson, *Jerusalem Pilgrims before the Crusades* (Warminster, 1977), 51.

the interpretation of the baptism of Jesus is renewed. With his baptism Jesus *cleans* the Jordan. What Paul does with a first and second Adam typology happens here with the Jordan. Its water, fouled by the floods of Gen 6–9, is now cleansed by Jesus. That is storied place!

THE THREE NETS OF BELIAL FROM QUMRAN TO THE *OPUS IMPERFECTUM IN MATTHAEUM*

Monika Pesthy*

Introduction

The three nets of Belial are mentioned in the *Damascus Document* (CD 4:12–19) in connection with Isa 24:17: "Panic, pit and net against you, earthdweller." The explanation of this quotation runs as follows: "They [the three expressions used by Isaiah] are the three nets, about which Levi, son of Jacob spoke, by which he [Belial] catches Israel and makes them appear before them as three types of justice. The first is fornication (הזנות); the second, wealth (ההון); the third defilement of the temple (טמאה מקדש). He who eludes one is caught in another, and he who is freed from that, is caught in another."[1]

It is generally held that the whole passage is an accusation against Israel and its purpose is "to reinforce the central assertion of the first columns of the *Damascus Document* that God has abandoned Israel and now deals only with the community."[2] The three sins mentioned are those by which Belial led astray the sons of Israel, so that they consider them as three kinds of "justice." The meaning of the first and second sin is clear, but the third is rather difficult to interpret. The continuation of the text suggests that it has to do with sexual impurity: according to 5:6–8 those (the adversaries) defile the sanctuary by lying with a woman who sees the blood of her menstrual flow, or by marrying their niece. It is not quite clear what is the connection between sexual impurity and defilement of the temple. According to Kosmala מקדש denotes here "the purity and holiness of the people, that is, of every individual member as well as of the community of the New Covenant as a whole."[3]

---

* Budapest.
[1] DSSSE, 557.
[2] F. García Martínez, "Man and Woman: Halakha Based upon Eden in the Dead Sea Scrolls," in G.P. Luttikhuizen (ed.), *Paradise Interpreted. Representations of Biblical Paradise in Judaism and Christianity* (Themes in Biblical Narrative, 2; Leiden, 1999), 101.
[3] H. Kosmala, "The Three Nets of Belial. A Study in the Terminology of Qumran and the New Testament," *ASTI* 4 (1965) 103.

Even if we accept that the midrash of the three nets is directed against Israel, and the sanctuary must be understood as the temple of Jerusalem, defilement of the temple has probably not to be taken in a very strict sense, as the examples given in 5:6–8 prove, because neither of them has anything to do with the temple. The essence of it seems to me expressed in 5:6: וגם מטמאים הם את המקדש אשר אין הם מבדיל כתורה "they defiled the sanctuary because they made no distinction according to the Law," and Kosmala might be right when explaining defilement of the sanctuary as the transgression of God's will.

The *Damascus Document* refers to Levi as its source, which of course brings to mind the *Testament of Levi*, but the quotation is not to be found there, nor anywhere else in the *Testaments of the Twelve Patriarchs*. It is true that the *Testaments* concentrate on the different kinds of temptations by which men are ruined, and even speak of the nets of deceit (τὰ δίκτυα τῆς πλάνης, *TestDan* 2:4), but they nowhere mention any three major kinds of temptations. The symbolical use of "net" (פח in Hebrew, translated in Greek generally by παγίς) goes back to the OT.[4]

An interesting parallel to our text is found in the *Book of Jubilees*.[5] In 7:20–21 Noah warns his descendants "from fornication, uncleanness and from all injustice. For it was on account of these three things that the flood was on earth."[6] According to *Jubilees* the Watchers who married the daughters of men, committed not only the sin of fornication but that of uncleanness, too. The injustice Noah speaks about was committed by the descendants of the fallen angels, when they killed one another and the humans as well. Following them mankind also began to kill one another.[7]

In Christianity we very often meet with the idea according to which there are three principal temptations containing all the rest, or being the source of all the rest. In this paper I shall examine this idea as it appears in various forms as well as its relation to the three nets mentioned in the *Damascus Document*.

---

[4] Cf. D. Kellermann, פח, *TWAT*, 6 (Stuttgart, 1989), col. 547–552 ; J. Schneider, παγιδεύω, παγίς, *TWNT*, 5 (Stuttgart, 1954), 593–596.

[5] Cf. Kosmala, 95 note 6.

[6] Transl. by J.C. VanderKam (CSCO, 511; Louvain, 1989), 47.

[7] *Jub* 7:21–22.

THE THREE NETS OF BELIAL IN THE NT?

Kosmala collects several passages from the NT where, according to him, the same three cardinal sins can be found (none of the passages makes use of the symbolism of the nets):

> Eph 5:3: πορνεία δὲ καὶ ἀκαθαρσία πᾶσα ἢ πλεονεξία (Cf. Eph 5:5)
> Eph 4:19: . . . ἑαυτοὺς παρέδωκαν τῇ ἀσελγείᾳ εἰς ἐργασίαν ἀκαθαρσίας πάσης ἐν πλεονεξίᾳ;
> Col 3:5 where πορνεία ἀκαθαρσία and πλεονεξία are enumerated along with other sins
> Mark 4:18f. with its parallels Luke 8:14 and Matt 13:22.

Explaining the parable of the sower Jesus mentions three reasons which hinder the development of the seed: αἱ μέριμναι τοῦ αἰῶνος καὶ ἡ ἀπάτη τοῦ πλούτου καὶ αἱ περὶ τὰ λοιπὰ ἐπιθυμίαι (Mark 4:18), Matt 13:22 has only ἡ μέριμνα τοῦ αἰῶνος καὶ ἡ ἀπάτη τοῦ πλούτου, and according to Luke 8:14 they are: μέριμναι, πλοῦτος, ἡδοναὶ τοῦ βίου.

In my opinion, there is another very important passage (not mentioned by Kosmala) containing the three kinds of temptations:

> πᾶν τὸ ἐν τῷ κόσμῳ, ἡ ἐπιθυμία τῆς σαρκὸς καὶ ἡ ἐπιθυμία τῶν ὀφθαλμῶν καὶ ἡ ἀλαζονεία τοῦ βίου, οὐκ ἔστιν ἐκ τοῦ πατρός, ἀλλὰ ἐκ τοῦ κόσμου ἐστίν (1 John 2:16)

The "desire of the flesh" can mean sexuality, but also eating and drinking. The "desire of the eyes" "hat man seit alters mit der zweiten verführerischen Macht des Besitzes in Verbindung gebracht."[8] The meaning of ἀλαζονεία τοῦ βίου is not quite clear. According to Herder's Commentary to the NT it is self-confidence caused by wealth which makes us forget God and despise our brother. I am not convinced that we should translate here βίος as "wealth" (a meaning attested in the NT, but only in very few cases). I think it means simply "life" (as it was the case with ἡδοναὶ τοῦ βίου in Luke 8:14), and I agree with Delling who interprets it in the following way: "1 J 2,16 ist damit die Haltung des kosmischen Menschen gekennzeichnet, der nicht nach dem Willen des 'Vaters' fragt, sondern sich den Anschein gibt, als ob er souverän die Entscheidung über seine Lebensgestaltung hätte, die in Wirklichkeit Gott hat, was

---

[8] *Herders Theologischer Kommentar zum Neuen Testament* 13/3: *Die Johannesbriefe*. Auslegung von R. Schnackenburg (Freiburg, 1984), 130.

sich in der Vernichtung der 'Welt' zeigt (v. 17)."[9] The Vulgate seems
to understand it this way, since it has "superbia vitae."

Now we can ask the question whether in 1 John 2:16 we have
to do with the three nets of Belial. It is sure that here we have to
do with three temptations which imprison us in the world and which
hinder us in doing the will of the Father. The first two can be easily identified with the first two nets mentioned in the *Damascus
Document*, even if "desire of the flesh" has a broader meaning than
fornication. The "confidence in one's own life" and "defilement of
the sanctuary" are not the same, but they both mean a revolt against
the will of God.

Finally, examining the NT, we cannot avoid to speak about the
threefold temptation of the Lord. Interpreting this scene, Kelly mentions CD 4:12–19 as a parallel to it and gives the following explanation:
"In comparing it with the accounts of Luke, we may correlate the
net of lust with the invitation to make bread out of the stones; the
net of riches with the offer of the authority and glory of all kingdoms
of the world; the net of defilement of the Sanctuary with the temptation to tempt God by leaping from the pinnacle of the temple."[10]

CHRISTIAN TRADITION

In Christian tradition the notion of the three principal sins or temptations appears under different forms:

1. *The three capital sins*

Tertullian is the first Christian author to speak about three capital
sins: in his treaty *De pudicitia* he considers fornication, idolatry and
murder as irremissible.[11] As this work was written in his montanis-
tic period, we could think that it reflects only the moral severity of
its author. But as a matter of fact, we find by Origen very similar
ideas. In *De oratione* 28,9–10 he interprets John 20:22–23 saying that
certain sins, such as adultery, idolatry and wilful murder cannot be
remitted, and to support his opinion he refers to the OT where it
was prohibited for the priests to present offerings for certain sins.

---

[9] ἀλαζών, ἀλαζονεία, *TWNT*, 1, 227–228.
[10] H.A. Kelly, "The Devil in the Desert," *CBQ* 26 (1964) 212.
[11] *De pudicitia* 5.

We can remark that the three capital sins are practically the same mentioned by *Jubilees*.

2. *The three major temptations man has to avoid*

In the *Acts of Thomas* (ch. 28) Thomas warns his listeners "from fornication and avarice and the service of the belly; for in these three heads all lawlessness is comprised." Then the Apostle goes on to describe them one by one and so it becomes clear that he is not speaking about sins actually committed, but about the desire of fornication, riches and eating. He closes his exhortations with the following words: "If you escape from these, you become free from care and sorrow and fear," which suggests that Satan (not mentioned in this passage) tries to catch us by these three desires. The speech of the Apostle does not follow from the preceding (the baptism of the king Gundaphor and his brother), rather, it seems that the "three heads" of lawlessness he mentions represent a well-known scheme.

The same tradition appears perhaps in the *Shepherd* of Hermas where "bad desire" (ἡ πονηρὰ ἐπιθυμία) is explained as ἐπιθυμία γυναικὸς ἀλοτρίας ἢ ἀνδρὸς καὶ πολυτελείας πλούτου καὶ ἐδεσμάτων πολλῶν καὶ μεθυσμάτων καὶ ἑτέρων τρυφῶν καὶ μωρῶν (Mand 12.1,1–2); the desires here enumerated correspond quite well to the three "heads" mentioned by Thomas.

3. *Connected to the temptation of Christ*

The temptation of Christ is very soon considered as the prototype and summary of all temptations. Irenaeus sees in it an example for us: when we are hungry we have to ask God for food; when we are on high we have to remain humble and not become haughty; and we must resist the wealth and the glory of the world (the order of the temptations of the Lord as discussed by Irenaeus is that of Matthew). Irenaeus does not say explicitly that all the possible temptations are included in these three, but the idea is often expressed by later writers, as for example in the pseudo-Athanasian homily *Sermo in Sanctum Pascha*. Interpreting the temptation of the Lord it continues: "But you think probably that there are three types of temptation. In reality, the whole race of the temptations is included in these three, for he [the Devil] would not have stopped tempting, if he had not emptied all the arrows of his quiver." The three "arrows" are: gluttony (ἡ περὶ τὴν βρῶσιν ἐπιθυμία), arrogance (μεγαλαυχία) and

avarice (φιλαργυρία).¹² As we can see, the text makes use of hunting symbolism, though the devil's arms are arrows instead of nets.

For Ambrosius the temptation of the Christ demonstrates that "the
Devil is armed with three main lances by which he wants to wound
the human souls: the first is gluttony, the other vanity, the third
ambition."¹³ According to Evagre the Devil presented to Jesus the
three main passions, gluttony, avarice and vainglory, through which
the demons besiege us and open the way before all the others.¹⁴ In
his treaty *De diversis malignis cogitationibus*, ch. 24,¹⁵ Evagre speaks of
the same three principal passions (γαστριμαργία, φιλαργυρία and ἡ
τῶν ἀνθρώπων δόξα), without connecting them with the temptation
of the Lord, and calls their demons front-rank chiefs (ἄρχοντες πρω-
τοστάται) in the battle led against us. In the first chapter of the same
work he explains that nobody can fall to the other five demons without having fallen previously to these.¹⁶

4. *Adam and Christ*

The temptation of the Lord was in general considered as a counterpart of the temptation of Adam: where the first man failed, the
second Adam triumphed. The majority of authors saw in the first
temptation of Christ a parallel to Adam's eating from the forbidden
fruit. However, Irenaeus goes further: for him the temptation of
Christ is a recapitulation of the Fall. In the first temptation Christ
who was hungry remained strong, whereas Adam who was not hungry failed, in the second, the humility of Christ destroyed the arrogance (ὑπερφρόνησις) which had been in the serpent and, in the
third, Christ denounced the devil as apostate (by naming him Satan).¹⁷
Thus the three primordial sins remedied by Christ are: gluttony,
arrogance and apostasy. However, the parallel between Adam and
Christ is not complete: the sin of gluttony was committed by Adam,
while the other two by the serpent or the Devil. But later it was

¹² *Sermo in Sanctum Pascha* 6–7, PG, 28, col. 1088–1089.
¹³ "Tria praecipue tela diaboli, quibus ad conuulnerendam mentem hominis con-
suerit armari, gulae unum, aliud iactantiae, ambitionis tertium," *ComLc* IV,17.
¹⁴ *Letter* 6, W. Frankenberg, *Evagrius Ponticus*, (Abhandlungen der königlichen
Gesellschaft der Wissenschaften zu Göttingen, Philol.-hist. Klasse, Neue Folge, Bd.
XIII, 2; Berlin, 1912), 570.
¹⁵ PG, 79, col. 1228.
¹⁶ PG, 79, col. 1200–1201.
¹⁷ *AdvHaer* V,21,2.

understood that, as Christ was tempted in a three-fold way, so Adam also was subject to three temptations.[18] As Cassian says, Christ could be tempted only by the passions Adam had had before the Fall, the primeval passions: gluttony, vanity and arrogance.[19]

Ambrosius connects beautifully the temptation of Adam, Christ and the believer:

> *Ceterum quod ad mysticum ordinem spectat, cernis uetusti erroris uincula suis resoluta uestigiis, ut primo gulae, secundo facilitatis, tertio ambitionis laqueus solueretur. Perlectus est enim Adam cibo in locum interdictae arboris sententiae facilitate transgressus temerariae quoque ambitionis crimen incurrit, dum similitudinem diuinitatis adfectat. Et ideo prius dominus ueteris nexus soluit iniuriae, ut nos iugo captiuitatis excusso uincere crimina scripturarum praesidio disceremus.*[20]

The symbolism of fighting and hunting is very often used to describe the schemes of the Devil against us, while also the "nets" of the Devil is quite a common image to represent the insidious, treacherous character of his dealings.[21] Ambrosius even calls "nets" the three principal temptations, which evokes naturally the *Damascus Document*, but the similarity between the two texts is not strong enough to suppose any direct connection between them. It is the more surprising to find a passage in a late (5th or 6th century) Latin pseudo-Chrysostomian work showing a very remarkable resemblance to CD 4:12–19.

5. *The Opus imperfectum in Matthaeum*

In the fifth homily the temptation of the Lord is presented from the Devil's point of view: his aim is to discover whether Christ is God or man. Having failed twice and still not knowing anything he says to himself:

> *Tria haec retia habeo extensa super omnem mundum, ut quisquis evaserit de retibus gulae, incurrat in retia vanae gloriae: qui evaserit de retibus vanae gloriae, incidat in retia avaritiae. De his autem tribus retibus nullus hominum ad perfectum evasit: et si evasit, non integer, sed contritus evasit. Hic autem jam retia ventris dirupit, retia vanae gloriae transivit. Ponam ei nunc retia avaritiae, et ostendam illi omnia*

---

[18] Concerning the patristic interpretation of Adam's sin cf. E. Testa, *Il peccato di Adamo nella Patristica* (Gen III) (Studii Biblici Franciscani Analecta 3; Gerusalemme, 1970).
[19] *Collationes* 22,10–12.
[20] *ComLc* IV,33.
[21] παγίς, PGL, 991.

regna mundi. Si concupierit ea, scio quia homo est. Nam omnes homines propter
gulam, et propter pecuniarum avaritiam, et propter vanos honores serviunt mihi: si
autem contempserit ea, scio quia Filius Dei est.[22]

The first phrase looks almost as a quotation from the *Damascus
Document*. It was pointed out that this Qumranic writing looks at sin
and temptation in a fatalistic way: man cannot escape from the nets
and if he is freed from one, he will fall into another.[23] The Christian
point of view was quite different: man has to be vigilant in order
to triumph over these temptations exactly as Christ has done. The
Opus imperfectum presents again the fatalistic way of seeing: as all the
humans are caught in these nets, he who escapes them cannot be
human.

Now one may ask the question, how these ideas found their way
into the *Opus imperfectum*. The similarities with the *Damascus Document*
are so striking that to assume a mere coincidence is out of question.
However, to claim that the author of the *Opus imperfectum* knew the
Qumranic writings would be somewhat audacious. The only solution I can think of is that he knew other early Jewish or Jewish-
Christian apocrypha which contained our passage, perhaps the
Levi-apocryphon quoted by the *Damascus Document*. This is quite possible, because there are also other instances in which the *Opus imperfectum* presents ancient material coming from early apocrypha, such
as the *Ascension of Isaiah*.[24]

We have now passed in review the different forms in which the
three principal temptations or sins appear in early Christian writings. We started our investigations from the *Damascus Document*, but
the origins of this tradition probably reach further back. This is indicated, on the one hand, by the fact that the CD itself refers to an
earlier source, and on the other hand, by the list of sins found in
Jubilees. In my opinion, a tradition about the three principal sins (sins
and not temptations), or rather of three principal categories of sins,
must have originally existed in the intertestamental period, approximately as we have them in *Jubilees*. The first was probably forni-

---

[22] PG, 56, col. 667.
[23] Kosmala, 98.
[24] Concerning the much debated question about the relations of the *Ascension of
Isaiah* and the *Opus imperfectum* see E. Norelli, "AI 1 et l'*Opus imprefectum in Matthaeum*"
in *Id.*, *L'Ascensione di Isaia. Studi su un apocrifo al crocevia dei cristianesimi* (Origini. Nuova
serie 1; Bologna, 1994).

cation, the second an affront against the divinity (which can range from ritual negligence to idolatry and apostasy), the third violence against other human beings (called "injustice" by *Jubilees*, but meaning in reality murder). In fact, they are the three (quite large categories) of sins punished by death according to veterotestamental legislation. In Christianity we discover them in the three capital sins.

The *Damascus Document* (following probably the Levi-apocryphon) omits violence and inserts wealth. This can be explained by the special interests and the situation of the community: greed constituted for them a greater problem than murder. Further on, there is an important change in the point of view: instead of sins, we have to do with temptations. This reflects a new way of thinking: whereas the OT does not meditate much about the mechanism of sin, and the existence of evil is not attributed to Satan, intertestamental writings are very much concerned with the origin of evil in the world and in the human soul, and they find it in the malignity or jealousy of Satan. The emphasis has now shifted from the sins actually committed to the procedure which leads to sin, i.e. temptation. As we have seen, the three major temptations play a very important role in Christian theology, and the *Damascus Document* is the first writing known to us to mention them.

In the NT these ideas are developed along different lines. The most characteristic form of their appearance is naturally the temptation of Christ. I do not claim that the description depends directly on the *Damascus Document*, I would rather say, that by its time the ideas in question were quite well-known, as their presence in different writings of the NT suggests. Kelly, when treating the similarities between Luke 4:1–13 and CD 4:12–19 sees here only "a resemblance of form but not of content," because, according to him, the importance of the temptation of the Lord is quite different from that of the sins described in the CD.[25] This may be true, but in the evangelist's mind the Lord had to affront these three temptations exactly because all humans are caught in them. Most of the NT scholars are convinced that the temptation-story of Matthew and Luke does not go back to Christ (which does not mean that the temptation itself was not real). If we accept this, it seems quite probable, that the descriptions given by Matthew and Luke are arranged according

[25] Kelly, 212 note 62.

to an already existing pattern. The little phrase in Luke "having
finished all the temptation" (4:13) seems to make allusion to it: in
Luke's mind Satan had probably three kinds of temptation, and he
tried them all against Christ. But again a change took place: instead
of fornication (which would be unthinkable in the case of Christ) we
have gluttony. They have in common that they are both "desires of
the flesh" mentioned in 1 John. The approach of this letter is again
different: the three temptations are not attributed to Satan, but to
ἐπιθυμία. Psychological reflections as to the origin of sin are quite
alien to the OT and the idea that temptation comes from desire,
i.e. from inside, appears only in the deuterocanonical *Book of Wisdom*:
ῥεμβασμὸς ἐπιθυμίας μεταλλεύει νοῦν ἄκακον (4:12). In the NT it is
expressed most clearly in James 1:13–15. 1 John 2:16–17 connects
this tradition with the idea of the three principal temptations and
has in mind probably the temptation of the Lord also. The first
temptation, that of food, corresponds very well to the "desire of the
flesh." The second (following the order of Luke), when Satan shows
the Lord all the wealth and glory of the world seems almost as a
demonstration of the "desire of the eyes" and the third (to throw
himself down from the temple) is a kind of ἀλαζονεία.[26]

In early Christianity, we have a few lists of temptations (not connected with the temptation of Christ) where fornication is still present (as in the *ATh* and the *Shepherd* of Hermas), and it remains as
one of the capital sins, but, under the influence of the temptation
of the Lord, it is soon eliminated, and the three main temptations
or passions are definitively established as gluttony, avarice and vainglory.[27] They get even connected with Adam's fall. Here again we
can remark that, whereas early Apocrypha and also some Christian
writers identified Adam's sin as sexuality, in this pattern where Adam's
sin is put in parallel with the temptation of Christ, it is first of all
gluttony, while sexuality becomes just the consequence of the fall.
Finally, to complete the parallel between Christ and Adam, it was
established that the Devil tempted Adam with the three main passions.

---

[26] Later Christian writers identified the three temptations of the Lord with the
three desires of 1 John 2:16–17.
[27] There can be some divergencies in this list.

Conclusions

The tradition of the three main temptations as they appear in the CD is a determining factor of early Christian thought. Notwithstanding this fact, Christian authors do not seem to know directly CD 4:12–19, and the only text which shows to it great similarities is the passage quoted from the *Opus imperfectum*.

Fornication, surely present in the original list, is replaced, under the influence of the temptation of the Lord, by gluttony.

As a parallel is established between Adam, Christ and the believer, the three main temptations seem to determine the entire earthly existence and they run through the whole story of salvation: Adam's fall was caused by them, man is caught in them and Christ, through his example, shows the way to escape them.

ERASMUS' NOTE ON GAL 4:25:
THE CONNECTION BETWEEN MOUNT SINAI
AND JERUSALEM

MIEKSKE L. VAN POLL-VAN DE LISDONK*

ERASMUS' NEW TESTAMENT EDITION

Erasmus' edition of the New Testament, the *Novum Instrumentum*, containing the *editio princeps* of the Greek text, his own Latin version and his notes, appeared in 1516. The genesis and the nature of this edition have been objects of study.[1] The improved versions of the New Testament, which Erasmus no longer entitled *Novum Instrumentum*, but *Novum Testamentum*, were published in 1519, 1522, 1527, 1535; the notes, the *Annotationes*, appeared after 1516 separate from the successive editions of the Greek of the New Testament more accurately than the existing Latin Vulgate version(s) of his time; he wished to ameliorate the style of the Vulgate: a more elegant classical Latin was the object he had in view.[2]

---

* Vierpolders. I would like to thank Marion van Assendelft for reading and correcting my English text.

[1] See e.g.: E. Rummel, *Erasmus Annotations on the New Testament. From Philologist to Theologian* (Toronto, 1986); H.J. de Jonge, "Novum Testamentum a nobis versum: The essence of Erasmus' edition of the New Testament," *JTS* 35 (1984) 394–413; *Id.*, "The date and Purpose of Erasmus's Castigatio Novi Testamenti: a note on the origins of the Novum Instrumentum," in A.C. Dionisotti *et al.* (eds.), *The Uses of Greek and Latin, Historical Essays* (London, 1988), 97–110; *Id.*, "Wann ist Erasmus Übersetzung des Neuen Testaments entstanden?," in J. Sperna Weiland and W.Th. Frijhoff (eds.), *Erasmus of Rotterdam, The Man and the Scholar* (Leiden, 1988), 151–157; J.H. Bentley, *Humanists and Holy Writ, New Testament Scholarship in the Renaissance* (Princeton, 1983); A.J. Brown, "The Date of Erasmus' Latin Translation of the New Testament," *Transactions of the Cambridge Bibliographical Society* VIII (1984) 351–380.

[2] See the Introduction to the critical edition of Erasmus' Greek and Latin version of John and Acts in the Amsterdam edition of *Erasmi Opera Omnia*, A.J. Brown (ed.), *Novum Testamentum ab Erasmo recognitum* (Ioh., Act.) (ASD VI, 2; Amsterdam, 2001), 1–9.

The Annotationes

The notes (*annotatiunculae*, cf. Allen, *Ep*. 373, l.4) were meant to justify the changes in the Latin text of the New Testament made by Erasmus and to explain a number of difficulties in the Bible. Erasmus also tried to anticipate criticism. He continued to revise and expand his *Annotationes* in the successive editions because the critical reception of his work forced him to defend his opinions and to justify his emendations. The revised editions also reflect Erasmus' increasing biblical scholarship.

In his *Annotationes* Erasmus discussed questions of grammar and syntax, and of content; he examined (possible) errors of the interpreter(s) of the Vulgate and of the transcribers; in a large number of notes he dealt with the meaning of individual words as well.[3] He wished the Latin version to render the meaning of the original Greek expression precisely. He expanded the history of an individual word in view of a better understanding of the word (or extract) in question. The phrases περίψημα, peripsema, καθάρματα, for instance, are discussed in the note on 1 Cor 4:13 (*LB* VI, coll. 675 E–676 E). Erasmus referred to Church Fathers such as Chrysostom, Ambrose, to commentators of the Bible such as Ps. Oecomenius and Theophylact,[4] to the lexicographers Hesychius and Suidas, to the scholiast on Aristophanes; in the discussion he also mentions classical authors, viz. Vergil (and Servius), Curtius Rufus, Petronius, Terence. Completing his discourse he says: *Scholiastae sum functus officio, iudicium penes lectorem esto*: "I have performed the task of the scholiast; it is up to the reader to evaluate."

Sepulveda on Gal 4:25

Erasmus' note on Gal 4:25 was added in the last authorized edition of the *Annotationes* (1535). This addition was closely connected with Allen, *Ep*. 2873, dated 23 October 1533, which Erasmus received

---

[3] Rummel, *Erasmus Annotations*, 89–121.

[4] The Ps. Oecomenius commentary is an anonymous catena-like commentary on Paul, wrongly ascribed to Oecomenius. The reader is referred to H.J. de Jonge (ed.), *Apologia respondens ad ea quae Iacobus Lopis Stunica taxaverat in prima duntaxat Novi Testamenti aeditione* (ASD IX, 2; Amsterdam, 1983), 195, n.l. 539. Theophylact, the bishop of Ochrida (now Ohrid in Macedonia), wrote a commentary on the Pauline Epistles. He died c. 1108. Erasmus used the commentary of the latter intensively.

from Sepulveda. Juan Ginés de Sepúlveda/Johannes Genesius Sepulveda (c. 1490–1573) studied theology between 1510–1523 in Alcalá,
Sigüenza and Bologna and as a friend of Alberto Pio, prince of
Carpi, he spent two years in Carpi and Rome. When Rome was
sacked he took refuge in Naples, and later returned to Rome. Erasmus
first heard of him sometime during 1526–1528 and they exchanged
letters dealing (among others) with exegetic and philological questions about the Scriptures.[5] Three letters, viz. Allen, *Ep.* 2873, 2905,
2938, are of particular interest to Erasmus' note on Gal 4:25.

Sepulveda tells about the famous Vatican manuscript B of the
Bible (Gr. 1209)[6] in Allen, *Ep.* 2873, ll. 19–22:

> *Est enim Graecum exemplar antiquissimum in bibliotheca Vaticana, in quo dili-
> gentissime et accuratissime literis maiusculis conscriptum utrumque Testamentum
> continetur, longe diversum a vulgaribus exemplaribus;*

> There is a very old Greek copy in the Vatican Library which includes
> the Old and New Testaments. This copy was very diligently and accu-
> rately transcribed in majuscule and varies greatly from the standard
> copies.

Next Sepulveda discusses Gal 4:25 (Allen, *Ep.* 2873, ll. 35–74). He
quotes the *vetus translatio*, the Vulgate:

> *Sina mons est in Arabia, qui coniunctus est* (bordering on) *ei quae nunc est
> Hierusalem,*

and mentions Erasmus' translation without quoting the text in question word for word. Erasmus reads in *Novum Testamentum* as follows:

> *Sina mons est in Arabia, confinis* (adjacent) *est autem ei, quae nunc vocatur
> Hierusalem.*

Sepulveda, seeing the great distance between Mount Sinai and
Jerusalem, wonders about both translations. He refers to Thomas

---

[5] See P.G. Bietenholz and Th.B. Deutscher (eds.), *Contemporaries of Erasmus. A
Biographical Register of the Renaissance and Reformation* (Toronto, 1985–1987) vol. III,
240–242 s.v. (Juan Ginés) de Sepúlveda.

[6] See: Allen, Introduction to Ep. 2873, in Desiderius Erasmus, *Opus Epistolarum.*
Denuo recognitum et auctum per P.S. Allen, H.M. Allen and H.W. Garrod (Oxonii,
1906–1908); E. Rummel, *Erasmus and his Catholic Critics I, II* (Nieuwkoop, 1989) vol.
II, 127–128 (cf. vol. I, 201, n. 31); P.F. Hovingh (ed.), *Annotationes in Novum Testamentum*
(Matth., Mc., Lc.) (ASD VI, 5; Amsterdam, 2000), 355, ll. 77–92. The manuscript
in question figures in Erasmus' texts, see e.g. *Annotationes in Mc.* 1, 2, ASD VI, 5,
354, ll. 77–78: "Sunt qui indicent in bibliotheca Vaticana haberi codicem Graecum
maiusculis descriptum." *Annotationes in Lc.* 10, 1, ASD VI, 5, 534, ll. 342–347.

Aquinas, who states that the distance between the two places requires a twenty days' journey. Meanwhile Sepulveda rejects Thomas' interpretation of the present Bible passage, viz. that Mount Sinai is connected with Jerusalem because of the unbroken journey of the Jews from the former to the latter.[7] Then he says that both translations (Vulgate and Erasmus' *Novum Testamentum*) do not reflect Paul's line of thought. He goes on to say that the Greek text of Gal 4:25 solves the problem of interpretation. The verb form συστοιχεῖ is the key word in this matter.

Sepulveda cites the Greek text—possibly the text he found in Ms. gr. 1209—in Allen, *Ep.* 2873, ll. 54–55:

Τὸ γὰρ Ἄγαρ Σινᾶ ὄρος ἐστὶν ἐν τῇ Ἀραβίᾳ συστοιχεῖ δὲ τῇ νῦν Ἱερουσαλήμ,[8]

and adds, ll. 57–59:

Nam verbum συστοιχεῖ neque "coniuncta" esse significat, neque "confinia," quemadmodum te miror convertisse,

The verb form συστοιχεῖ indeed does not mean "bordering on," neither "is adjacent," as I was amazed to read in your translation.

He goes on to discuss the meaning of σύστοιχος[9] and, referring to Suidas and Aristotle, he specifies the phrase σύστοιχος (σύστοιχα) as follows *quae quandam inter se proportionem ordinemve habent* "which to a point correlate or correspond." Sepulveda suggests the following translation of the Bible passage in question, ll. 68–69:

Agar enim Sina mons est in Arabia. Est autem eiusdem rationis atque ea quae nunc est Hierusalem,

---

[7] Thomas Aquinas, *Super Epistolas S. Pauli lectura*, ed. by Raphaelis Cai (editio viii revisa, vol. I, Roma, 1953) cf. lectio VIII, 261, p. 622: *Ubi primo oritur dubitatio, quia cum Sina distet a Ierusalem per viginti fere dietas, videtur falsum quod Sina iunctus sit Ierusalem, ut hic Apostolus dicit,* and VIII, 262: *Ierusalem enim etiam generat filios servitutis, et ideo quantum ad hoc coniungitur mons Sina cum illa. Et hoc est quod dicit "qui coniunctus est ei," scilicet per continuationem itineris euntium in Ierusalem.* Note that Sepulveda oversimplifies Thomas' words in Allen, *Ep.* 2873, ll. 50–51: *eadem [loca, viz. Sina; Ierusalem] tamen propter itineris Iudaeorum continuationem coniuncta dici interpretatur.*

[8] Modern editions read as follows: Tischendorf: Τὸ γὰρ Σινᾶ ὄρος ἐστὶν ἐν τῇ Ἀραβίᾳ· συνστοχεῖ δὲ τῇ νῦν Ἱερουσαλήμ. Nestle-Aland: Τὸ δὲ Ἄγαρ Σινᾶ ὄρος ἐστὶν ἐν τῇ Ἀραβίᾳ· συστοιχεῖ δὲ τῇ νῦν Ἱερουσαλήμ. See the variant readings in respectively the apparatus of Tischendorf (*Novum Testamentum Graece*, editio octava critica maior, Lipsiae 1872), and Nestle-Aland (*Greek-English New Testament*, 8th ed., Stuttgart, 1998). Erasmus (*Novum Testamentum*) and Sepulveda follow the same Greek reading.

[9] According to H.G. Liddell, R. Scott, *A Greek-English Lexicon*. Rev. and augm. by H.S. Jones (Oxford, 1940; Supplement 1968. With a revised supplement 1996) "correspondent," "coordinate," "congruous."

which does not differ much from the Revised Standard Version:[10] "Hagar is Mount Sinai in Arabia; she corresponds to the present Jerusalem."

ERASMUS' ANSWER

Erasmus explicitly replied to Sepulveda's letter in Allen, *Ep.* 2905 of 17 February 1534, but implicitly by his addition to the *Annotationes* (1535). See Allen, *Ep.* 2905, ll. 16–30, which I recapitulate here: Erasmus' translation *confinis est* is founded on Jerome's commentary ad loc.; Chrysostom and Theophylact interpret συστοιχεῖ as *vicinus est*. Given the unbroken journey of the Jews to Jerusalem, and the fact that the Law also came to Jerusalem from Mount Sinai, why did Sepulveda reject Thomas Aquinas' explanation that Mount Sinai is connected with Jerusalem?[11] Then Erasmus refers to Budaeus (cf. Allen, *Ep.* 2905, n. 29), observing: *Ipse tamen miror cur in annotationibus non senserim scrupulum* "I aks myself why I did not notice the difficulty in the *Annotationes.*"

This observation is remarkable, because Erasmus was not receptive to criticism. Erasmus made good use of Sepulveda's findings, as we will see, when he added his annotation on Gal 4:25 for the 1535 improved edition of the *Annotationes.* He does not, however, mention Sepulveda's name.

THE ANNOTATIONES ON GAL 4:25

The annotation which accompanies the text "*qui coniunctus est ei quae nunc est Jerusalem*" was, as I mentioned above, added in the 1535 edition of the *Annotationes* and reflects Sepulveda's observations. Erasmus' answer in Allen, *Ep.* 2905, ll. 16–30 and the present annotation partly overlap. The text concerned is easily available in the Leiden edition, vol. VI from 1705, reprinted Hildesheim 1962, coll. 820 F–821 E, and in the facsimile edition from Reeve-Screech,[12] 584, but

---

[10] This translation is reproduced in Nestle-Aland, *Greek-English New Testament.*

[11] See Allen, Ep. 2938 (23 May 1534), ll. 31–35, in which Sepulveda elucidates his objections to Thomas' explanation: first his explanation does not describe what Paul meant and in the second place the journey of the Jews was not unbroken: they dwelled years and years in the desert.

[12] H.J. de Jonge in *Nederlands Archief voor Kerkgeschiedenis* 71 (1991) 111–113 reviewed

a critical edition of this part of the *Annotationes* does not yet exist.[13] I will follow the reading of the 1535 edition (Reeve-Screech, 584).

Erasmus defends his translation by saying that he relied on Jerome's rendering "*confinis est*."[14] He goes on to tell us that Paul did not mean "*coniunctus est*" in a litteral sense, but that he took the phrase metaphorically, as the use of the expression συστοιχεῖν ("stand in the same rank," "correspond") proves. He then states that "*confinis*" and "*vicinus*" have the same meaning as σύστοιχος/συστοιχέω and proceeds to discuss the key word σύστοιχεῖν in his usual manner (see above: περίψημα etc.). He examines the etymology of the expression and traces the words στοιχεία ("letters"[15] as Erasmus says; "elements," "components") and στίχοι ("lines of poetry," "row of soldiers")[16] to στείχειν ("march in line or order"). He then explains that Mount Sinai and Jerusalem lie far apart, but that they are connected—"lie in one line"—through analogy and that the point of similarity is the Law: the Mosaic Law given on Mount Sinai and the Law of Sion, Jerusalem (in his opinion the same Law). He cites in this context Isaiah 2:3: *De Sion exibit lex et verbum Domini de Hierusalem.*

One finds the meaning of συστοιχεῖν he had in view, as Erasmus

---

the facsimile edition of the *Annotationes* on Acts, Romans and both letters to the Corinthians by Reeve-Screech (*Erasmus' Annotations on the New Testament, Acts—Romans— I and II Corinthians*, Facsimile of the final Latin text with all earlier variants, edited by Anne Reeve and M.A. Screech, Leiden, 1990). He states: "Until a really critical edition appears, the present work can help the user in many cases to see quickly in which stage of the development of the *Annotations* a particular portion of the text originated," but after collating a chapter he concludes "that in my view the result of this comparison makes the Reeve-Screech edition unusable for *critical* purposes." The same judgement—in my opinion—goes for the present facsimile edition by Reeve-Screech.

[13] The critical edition of the *Annotationes* on Matthew, Mark and Luke in the Amsterdam edition of *Erasmi Opera Omnia* appeared in 2000 (ASD VI, 5, ed. by P.F. Hovingh); the *Annotationes* on the Gospel of John, Acts and on Corinthians 1 and 2 are in preparation (ASD VI, 6, and 8); the publication of the *Annotationes* on Rom. (ASD VI, 7), on Gal—1 Thess (ASD VI, 9) and on 1 Tim—Apocalypse (ASD VI, 10) are scheduled for 2006 and the years after.

[14] See Jerome, *Commentarii in iv epistolas Paulinas*, lib. II, cap. iv, Migne *PL* 26, 417 B: "*in monte Sina, qui . . . confinis est*," but compare 417 A: "*qui conterminus est*."

[15] See Liddell-Scott s.v. στοιχεῖον II.1: "a simple sound of speech, as the first component of the syllable . . . στοιχεία therefore, strictly, were different form letters (γράμματα) . . . but are frequently not clearly distinguished from them." Note that the translations of στοιχεία, συστοιχεῖν etc., here given, originate from Liddell-Scott.

[16] Erasmus distinguishes στίχοι (*versus* "lines of poetry") and στίχαι (*acies ordine compositae* "armies drawn up in order of battle"). One does not find this distinction in Liddell-Scott, but see W. Pape, *Handwörterbuch der griechischen Sprache*. 3. Aufl., bearbeitet von M. Sengebusch (Hannover, 1880) s.v.: στίχη = στίχος.

says, in Theophrastus' *De causis*[17] and in the *Metaphysics* of Aristotle. Actually, in *De causis* only συστοιχία ("column" or "series"; "a series of co-ordinate pairs") and σύστοιχος are mentioned, in Aristotle's *Metaphysics* only συστοιχία.[18] Sepulveda also refers to Aristotle (Allen, *Ep.* 2873, ll. 59–63). Erasmus mentions Suidas,[19] as Sepulveda does, and gives examples of συστοιχία: the three sharp consonants π, κ, τ form a συστοιχία (the three aspirates φ, χ, θ form a συστοιχία too, but being the opposites of the *tenues* π, κ, τ they are ἀντίστοιχα).

Erasmus then cites a number of Christian commentators to corroborate his interpretation: Chrysostom,[20] Theophylact,[21] (the authors of the) Glossa Ordinaria[22] and Thomas Aquinas. Originally in Allen, *Ep.* 2905, Erasmus defended Thomas' interpretation of Gal 4:25 (that, because of the unbroken journey of the Jews, Mount Sinai and Jerusalem are connected). In the present *annotatio*, however, he rejects Thomas' explanation. Referring to Ambrosius/Ambrosiaster,[23] he says that the verb form συστοιχεῖ cannot be linked with the history of the Jews of many years ago, because it is in the present tense.[24] Finally he refers to the commentary of Pelagius,[25] whose opinion he summarises in a few words.

---

[17] Theophrastus: συστοιχία in *De causis* VI, 5, 6; VI, 6, 10 (Wimmer, *Theophrasti Eresii opera* ... Graeca recensuit, Latine interpretatus est Fridericus Wimmer, Parisiis, 1866), 295; 297; σύστοιχος in *De causis* VI, 4, 2 (Wimmer, 293).

[18] Aristot. *Metaphysica*, συστοιχία: 986 a 23; 1004 b 27; 1054 b 35; 1058 a 13; 1066 a 15; 1072 a 31; 1072 a 35; 1093 b 12.

[19] Suidas (the *Suda*): συστοιχα 1691, A. Adler (ed.), *Suidae Lexicon* (Lipsiae, 1928–1938) vol. IV, 482, partly quoted by Sepulveda in *Ep.* 2873, ll. 66–67.

[20] Chrysostom, *In epistulam ad Galatas commentarius*, Migne *PG* 61, 662: Συστοιχεῖ ... τουτέστι, γειτνιάζει, ἅπτεται.

[21] Theophylact, *Expositio in epistulam ad Galatas*, Migne *PG* 124, 1005 C: συστοιχεῖ ... τουτέστι γειτνιάζει, ἅπτεται. ἢ ὅτι ἀπεικάζεται ... καὶ ἀναλογεῖ.

[22] See for the Glossa Ordinaria: H.J. de Jonge (ed.), *Apologia respondens ad ea quae Iacobus Lopis Stunica taxaverat in prima duntaxat Novi Testamenti aedition* (ASD IX, 2; Amsterdam, 1983) 79, n. 379: "Glossa Ordinaria. The standard medieval commentary on the bible, begun by Anselm of Laon (c. 1100) and completed by others by c. 1150." See the editio princeps, Adolph Rusch of Strasburg 1480/1481, reprinted, Turnhout, 1992, Gal 4:25: the interlinear glossa describes *coniunctus: similis*.

[23] Erasmus calls Ambrosiaster "Ambrosius." See R. Hoven, "Notes sur Érasme et les auteurs anciens," *L'Antiquité classique* 38 (1969) 169–174. Cf. Ambrosiaster, *CSEL* 81, 3, 51: *Sina autem mons est in Arabia, quae coniungitur huic quae nunc est Hierusalem.*

[24] Sepulveda's letter of 23 May 1534, *Ep.* 2938, ll. 31–36 may have convinced Erasmus of the inaccuracy of Thomas' interpretation. See n. 11.

[25] Erasmus used an anonymous commentary that proved to be compiled by Pelagius: see A. Souter, *Pelagius's Expositions of Thirteen Epistles of St Paul*, vol. I–III (Cambridge, 1922–1931) vol. I, Souter I, 6. 265–282. The passage to which Erasmus refers is Souter II, 330 (= Migne *PLS* I, 1282).

Erasmus ends his annotation of Gal 4:25 by adding his own interpretation. Paul, he says, equates the Jews from Mount Sinai (*Iudaeos
Arabes*) with those from Jerusalem because both obey the Law and
belong to the Synagogue, not to the Church. He contrasts temporal Jerusalem with the New Jerusalem which is the Church. He
expresses surprise about the fact that neither Jerome nor "Ambrosius"
(viz. Ambrosiaster) discusses the problem of the distance between
Mount Sinai and Jerusalem.[26]

Conclusion

Sepulveda provided Erasmus with substantial information about Gal
4:25, viz. the significance of the Greek text and particularly of the
verb συστοιχεῖν. In this context Sepulveda mentions Suidas and
Aristotle, and explains and translates the difficult Bible passage Gal
4:25. Erasmus used and completed this material in his addition to
the 1535 edition without naming his source.[27] He often treats his
sources in this way, e.g. Lorenzo Valla.[28] Moreover, the additions
he makes are not always fundamental. The large range of his investigations, however, and his method of inquiry into a word such as
on συστοιχεῖν have a modern touch and are comparable with the
twentieth century studies as published by the scholars of the "École
de Nimègue."[29] Erasmus' brilliant style and his inspired personality
are reflected in his texts and are always captivating. The present
annotatio is certainly a case in point.

---

[26] See the annotation on Gal 4: 25 (edition 1535): *Mihi Paulus aequare videtur Iudaeos
Arabes et Hierosolymitanos, quod utrique pariter servirent legi et ad synagogam pertinerent, non
ad ecclesiam. Hierosolymae vero terrenae, quam non discernit a monte Sina, opponit coelestem
Hierosolymam, quae est ecclesia. Mirum est autem nec Hieronymum nec Ambrosium hunc de
vicinia scrupulum attingere.*

[27] See, however, *Epist.* 2951 (3 July 1534), ll. 14–15: *Locum de* συστοιχεῖ *tuo
admonitu tractaui attentius*, und *Epist.* 3096 (from Sepulveda, 13 February 1536), ll. 13–15:
*tuque meam sententiam non solum rescripta epistola (*Epist.* 2951) probasti, sed etiam editis pro-
xime commentariis caeteris omnibus, quod nuper non sine iucunditate perspexi, praetulisti*, etc.

[28] See M.L. van Poll-van de Lisdonk, "Erasmus' *Annotationes* on 1. Cor. 15, 51:
'We shall indeed all rise or We shall not all sleep?'" in C. Kroon and D. den
Hengst (eds.), *Ultima Aetas, Time, Tense and Transience in the Ancient World, Studies in
Honour of Jan den Boeft* (Amsterdam, 2000), 163–174.

[29] See Christine Mohrmann, *Études sur le latin des chrétiens*, vol. I–III (Roma,
1961–1065), *passim*, esp., vol. I, 3–19.

THE FOUR RIVERS OF EDEN IN THE
APOCALYPSE OF PAUL (VISIO PAULI):
THE INTERTEXTUAL RELATIONSHIP OF
GEN 2:10–14 AND THE *APOCALYPSE OF PAUL* 23

JACQUES T.A.G.M. VAN RUITEN*

The influence of the Old Testament and early Jewish literature on the *Visio Pauli* is enormous. However, it is not always clear whether this influence has come directly from early Jewish sources or, indirectly, via Christian mediation.[1] In this paper, I have restricted myself to one aspect of this influence, i.e. the biblical book of Genesis. In the *Apocalypse of Paul* 3–10; 45, in particular, elements of Genesis 1–3, the creation story and the story of Paradise are easy to determine. Moreover, in the intervening chapters, references to the story of Paradise can also be picked out, while echoes of other texts from Genesis can also be found throughout the *Apocalypse*. Therefore, I will narrow the subject down further and focus on the four rivers of Eden (Gen 2:10–14). I intend to explore the inter-textual relationship between Genesis 2:10–14 and the *Apocalypse of Paul 23*, and answer the questions: in which form does the text of Genesis occur in the *Vis. Paul* 23, and how can the differences between both texts be explained?

---

* Groningen.
[1] See A. Hilhorst, "A Visit to Paradise. Apocalypse of Paul 45 and Its Background," in: G.P. Luttikhuizen (ed.), *Paradise Interpreted. Representations of Biblical Paradise in Judaism and Christianity* (TBN, 2; Leiden, 1999), 128–139. In this article he shows how much the author of the *Apocalypse of Paul* owes to the conceptual universe of early Judaism, viz. with regard to the location and inhabitants of Paradise. In the notes to the edition of three Latin texts of the *Visio Pauli*, Hilhorst and Silverstein refer profusely not only to the New, but also to the Old Testament. However, they restrict themselves to evident quotations of biblical texts. Broader allusions to and echoes of biblical texts are not mentioned, neither are quotations of and allusions to para-biblical texts. Cf. T. Silverstein – A. Hilhorst, *Apocalypse of Paul. A New Critical Edition of Three Long Latin Versions* (Cahiers d'Orientalisme, 21; Geneva, 1997).

GENESIS 2:10–14

The second creation story of the Hebrew Bible (Gen 2:4b–25) describes the creation of man, the garden, and man's helpers (first the animals and then the woman). In this story, the man who has been given access to the Garden is prohibited from eating from the tree of knowledge of good and evil. Within the framework of this contribution, I shall confine myself to the part of the creation story that describes the four rivers of the Garden (Gen 2:10–14). According to some, this description interrupts the narrative of the creation story, and therefore these verses reflect a different (older) source than the rest of the chapter.[2] According to others, the enumeration of the rivers can be compared to the genealogies of Genesis 1–11. It need not be secondary in the narrative.[3] It relates the present reality to its ultimate source in primeval history.

I consider the Masoretic text of Gen 2:10–14 hypothetically as the original text of the last redaction. This text runs, in translation, as follows:

Genesis 2:10–14 *(RSV, with some slight alterations)*

10a	A river flowed out of Eden to water the garden,
b	and from there it divided
c	and became four rivers.
11a	The name of the first is Pison;
b	it is the one which flows around the whole land of Havilah,
c	where there is gold;
12a	and the gold of that land is good;
b	bdellium and onyx stone are there.
13a	And the name of the second river is Gihon;
b	it is the one which flows around the whole land of Cush.
14a	And the name of the third river is Tigris,
b	which flows east of Assyria.
c	And the fourth river is the Euphrates.

---

[2] Cf. G.J. Wenham, *Genesis 1–15* (WBC, 1; Waco, Texas, 1987), 64. See already J. Wellhausen, *Die Composition des Hexateuchs und der historischen Bücher des Alten Testaments* (Berlin 1899³; 1963⁴); K. Budde, *Die biblische Urgeschichte (Gen 1–12:5) untersucht* (Giessen, 1883), 46–88 (esp. 82–83); Id., *Die biblische Paradiesgeschichte* (BZAW, 60; Giessen, 1932), 24–27.

[3] C. Westermann, *Genesis 1–11* (BKAT I,1; Neukirchen, 1999⁴), 293–295; cf. G.W. Coats, *Genesis with an Introduction to Narrative Literature* (FOTL, 1; Grand Rapids, MI, 1983), 52.

The text of Gen 2:10 seems to speak about one common source river that flows out of some place in Eden (ונהר יצא מעדן), then enters the garden to water it (להשקות את הגן).[4] However, if Eden and the garden are conterminous, the river must have risen in the garden.[5] The verb יצא can be used here not so much in the sense of "to flow out," but as the welling of a stream at its source (cf. Exod 17:6; Num 20:11; Judg 15:19; Ezek 47:1; Zech 14:8; Joel 4:18).[6] "From there" (משם) should probably be understood in the sense of "thereafter." After it had left the garden, it divided into four rivers.[7] The text speaks about ארבעה ראשים, which literally means "four heads." It could mean four elevations, higher places within the river,[8] but also "four beginnings,"[9] or "four branches."[10] There is one common source river in the Garden of Eden for the four rivers that stream out of Eden. Moreover, three of the rivers are connected with specific countries. The Pison is connected with the land of Havila, and the Tigris with Assyria, be it the land, the capital, or the inhabitants. The Gihon surrounds the whole land of Cush. In the Bible, the name Cush is usually reserved for the area south of Egypt, i.e. Nubia and Ethiopia.[11] Egypt and the Nile seem to fall outside the scope of the text.[12]

It is by no means sure to which text form the author of the *Apocalypse* had access. Therefore, we should also take into account

---

[4] E.g., Budde, *Paradiesgeschichte*, 27.

[5] Wenham, *Genesis*, 64.

[6] Cf. J. Skinner, *A Critical and Exegetical Commentary on Genesis* (ICC; Edinburgh, 1910), 59.

[7] Cf. Skinner, *Genesis*, 59; Westermann, *Genesis*, 295; Wenham, *Genesis*, 64. According to Renckens the division should be placed *inside* the garden. Cf. H. Renckens, *Israëls visie op het verleden. Over Genesis 1–3* (Woord en beleving, 4; Tielt, 1956), 155.

[8] *ThWAT VII*, 279.

[9] Cf. the translation of the Septuaginta (ἀρχαι).This is interpreted by Philo in the sense of "four principles." There is also one reading in Old Latin, which has "in quator initia."

[10] Cf. Skinner, *Genesis*, 59; Westermann, *Genesis*, 295; Wenham, *Genesis*, 64–65. So also *ThWAT, II*, 707.

[11] Cf. Esther 1:1; Isa 11:11; 18:1; Zeph 2:1; 2:12. Some differentiate between African Cush and Arabian Cush. Because of the reference to the Euphrates and the Tigris, some think that Cush in Gen 2:13 refers to some area in Mesopotamia. C.H. Fleder, *Troubling Biblical Waters* (Maryknoll, 1989); E. Ullendorff, *The Ethiopians* (Oxford, 1973³).

[12] Only later are the Gihon and the Nile identified. See LXX Jer 2:18; Ben Sira 24:27; *Jub* 8:15; Josephus, *Ant.* I:39. For the mythical world view of the author of Genesis 2, see G. Hölscher, *Drei Erdkarten* (Sitzungsberichte der Heidelberger Akademie der Wissenschaften, Philosophisch-historische Klasse, 1944–48, 3; Heidelberg, 1949), 35–44.

the Septuagint Gen 2:10–14 insofar as it deviates from the Hebrew
text.[13] In general, the Septuagint translates its *Vorlage* of Gen 2:10–14
quite literally. With regard to Gen 2:10 ("A river flowed out of Eden
to water the garden, and from there it divided into four beginnings"),
there are some minor deviations. Firstly, the participle form of יצא
is replaced by a finite form of the verb (ἐκτορεύεται). Secondly, the
two phrases of the Hebrew והיה ל יפרד ("it divided and became") are
replaced by one phrase ἀφορίζεται εἰς ("It divided into"). The translation of ראשים, which probably means "branches," is translated as ἀρχάς
("beginnings"). The river divides itself into four beginnings, probably
in the sense of four branches.[14] With regard to Gen 2:11–14, I shall
refer first to the names of the rivers. Φισών (Phison) may be considered a transcription of the Hebrew פישון. The same can be said
of Γηών (Geon), which is a transcription of the Hebrew גיחון. With
regard to the Hebrew חדקל the Septuagint offers the geographical
meaning of the word, i.e., Τίγρις (Tigris), as is the case with the
Hebrew פרת, which is translated as Εὐφράτης (Euphrates). With
regard to the countries the rivers surround, some observations can
be made. The land of החוילה is transcribed as Εὐιλάτ, probably
because the author could not identify it. The land of כוש, is translated as Αἰθιοπίας. This is in line with the Hebrew Bible, where the
name Cush is usually reserved for the area south of Egypt, i.e. Nubia
and Ethiopia.[15] It supports the identification of Gihon with the Nile.
In the Hebrew text, it is not quite clear whether Assyria means the
land or the capital,[16] whereas the Septuagint links the Tigris not to
the land or the country but to the inhabitants (κατέναντι Ἀσσυρίων).[17]

---

[13] The preserved readings of the Old Latin texts of Gen 2:10–14 more or less
follow the Septuagint.

[14] M. Rösel, *Übersetzung als Vollendung der Auslegung. Studien zur Genesis-Septuaginta*
(BZAW, 223; Berlin, 1993), 64; M. Alexandre, *Le Commencement du Livre Genèse I–V.
La version grecque de la Septante et sa réception* (Christianisme antique, 3; Paris, 1988),
262. The four ἀρχάς are interpreted by Philo in the sense of "four principles."

[15] See note 10.

[16] Westermann, *Genesis*, 298.

[17] According to Rösel, this might reflect the translator hinting at the fact that
the city of Assur after the destruction by the Medes was without meaning. Cf.
Rösel, *Übersetzung*, 66.

APOCALYPSE OF PAUL 23

In the *Apocalypse of Paul*, four rivers appear for the first time in the description of Paul's first visit to Paradise (*Vis. Paul* 19–30). In *Vis. Paul* 23 the rivers surround the City of Christ: "And there were twelve gates in the circuit of the city, of great beauty, and four rivers which encircled it. There was a river of honey, and a river of milk, and a river of wine, and a river of oil."[18] They all flow for those who are in this land of Promise. These four rivers are identified with the four rivers of Gen 2:10–14, as it is said: "the river of honey is called Pison, and the river of milk Euphrates, and the river of oil Gihon, and the river of wine Tigris."

The reference to the rivers establishes an explicit connection between *Vis. Paul* 23 and Gen 2:10–14. Nevertheless, the differences between both texts are obvious. Firstly, the order in which the four rivers are mentioned is different, in that the Euphrates, which is the fourth river in Gen 2:10–14, is relocated to second place in the *Apocalypse of Paul*, between the Pison and the Gihon. The order of their qualities seems to be more important than the exact reproduction of the order of these rivers in Genesis.

Secondly, it does not speak about a common source river for the four rivers. It is not clear where the rivers come from. They do not enter the garden, nor do they divide themselves afterwards. In the direct context, the *Apocalypse* speaks of a river which forms the base of the beginning of the foundation of the firmament, or the gates of heaven, a river which waters all the earth, which is the ocean that surrounds the whole earth (*Vis. Paul* 21; 31). However, there is no direct connection in the text between this river and the four rivers.

Thirdly, the countries that the rivers surround (Havila, Cush, Assyria) are not mentioned either. Instead, they surround the City of Christ. The location of this city can be derived from the context. It is situated close to the Acherusian Lake, probably inside it (cp. 22: "This is the Acherusian Lake where is the City of Christ"; cp. 23: "And he was standing on the Acherusian Lake and he put me into a golden ship and about three thousand angels were singing a

---

[18] All translations are taken from J.K. Elliott, *The Apocryphal New Testament. A Collection of Apocryphal Christian Literature in an English Translation* (Oxford, 1993), 616–644.

hymn before me till I arrived at the City of Christ"). According to
Vis. Paul 24, twelve gates surround the city and there is some space
between these gates and the entrance to the city. In between there
are trees. The Acherusian Lake in its turn is situated in "the land
of promise." This land, including the Acherusian Lake and the city
of Christ, is clearly situated outside the heavens. The angels lead
Paul upwards to the third heaven (*Vis. Paul* 19), then through a gate
into Paradise (*Vis. Paul* 20), from Paradise back to the third heaven,
and from the third heaven down to the second heaven, from this
heaven to the firmament, to the gates of the heavens. The fundament of these gates is above the river that waters the whole earth,
and it is called the ocean. Paul comes *out* of the heavens, and enters
the land of promise. This land will be disclosed only when Christ
has come to reign there for a thousand years, after which the first
earth will disintegrate. Paradise is clearly located above the third
heaven. The Land of Promise, with the Acherusian Lake and the
City of Christ inside, is located outside the heavens, but is not visible. It is not part of the first earth. The location seems to be outside "normal" space and time.

Finally, the four rivers of Paradise are identified with four qualities, or substances (honey, milk, wine and oil), meant for various
groups of righteous people who, having passed away, are now living in the City of Christ. In the ensuing chapters (*Vis. Paul* 25–28),
the author elaborates on these rivers in a slightly different order.
The river of honey is the place where the minor and major prophets
of the Old Testament reside. It is meant for "everyone who shall
have afflicted his soul and not done his own will because of God"
(*Vis. Paul* 25). The river of milk is the place where all the infants
whom Herod slew in the name of Christ dwell. It is meant for "all
who keep their chastity and purity" (*Vis. Paul* 26). The river of wine
is the place of Abraham, Isaac, Jacob, Lot and Job. It is meant for
"all who have given hospitality to strangers" (*Vis. Paul* 27). Finally,
the river of oil is the place where men rejoice and sing psalms; to
this river "all those who rejoice in the Lord God and sing psalms
to the Lord" are brought (*Vis. Paul* 28).

Elsewhere, the *Apocalypse* also speaks about "milk and honey" in
relation to rivers. *Vis. Paul* 22 speaks about only one river (in that
land), "flowing with *milk and honey*, and there were trees planted by
the bank of that river, full of fruit; moreover, each single tree bore
twelve fruits in the year." In *Vis. Paul* 31 Paul was brought outside
the city through the midst of trees and far from the places of the

land of the good, and he was taken across the river of *milk and honey*. Moreover, the text also speaks about a river, whiter than *milk*, which is called the Acherusian Lake, where the City of Christ is, into which not everyone is permitted to enter (*Vis. Paul* 22). Although rivers appear in more places throughout the *Apocalypse of Paul*, the four rivers of Paradise from Gen 2:10–14, besides *Vis. Paul* 23, only appear in *Vis. Paul* 45. However, except for the names of the rivers, there is considerable discrepancy between the descriptions of the rivers in both chapters. *Vis. Paul* 45 is much closer to the biblical text. The sources of the four rivers are connected with Paradise, the place where Adam and his wife erred. They are said to surround the land of Evila, the land of Egypt and Ethiopia, the land of the Assyrians and the land of Mesopotamia. In *Vis. Paul* 45 the rivers do not have specific qualities (honey, milk, wine and oil), meant for those who are in the land of promise. Moreover, the order in which the rivers are mentioned is different: *Vis. Paul* 45 follows the biblical order, whereas *Vis. Paul* 23 deviates from it. When the qualities of the rivers are also included, the author of the *Apocalypse of Paul* provides a different picture with regard to the order of the rivers.[19] Finally, in *Vis. Paul* 23 nothing is said about the sources of the four rivers, whereas in *Vis. Paul* 45 Paul "saw the beginning of the waters," and he "saw a tree planted from whose roots water flowed out, and from this beginning there were four rivers." The waters of the river flow forth from the tree, "when the Spirit of God, who is resting on the tree, blows."

THE BACKGROUND TO THE DIFFERENCES

I now would like to go into the question of how the differences between the descriptions of the four rivers in Genesis 2:10–14 and in *Vis. Paul* 23 can be explained. Are there texts or traditions that

---

[19] The following table summarises the different orders of the rivers:

Vis. Paul 23 (line 24)	*Apc Pl 23* (line 30–33)	*Apc Pl 25–28*	*Apc Pl 45* (cf. Gen 2:10–14)
1. river of honey	1. Pison, river of honey	1. river of honey (25)	1. Pison
2. river of milk	2. *Euphrates*, river of milk	2. river of milk (26)	2. Gihon
3. river of wine	3. Gihon, river of oil	3. river of wine (27)	3. Tigris
4. river of oil	4. Tigris, *river of wine*	4. river of oil (28)	4. Euphrates

may have influenced the author of the *Apocalypse* when he used the biblical text of Gen 2:10–14? I shall confine myself to two aspects of these differences. Firstly, the connection between the four rivers of Paradise and the city, and secondly, the different qualities which are attributed to the rivers. I will look in the Old Testament, in the Apocrypha and the Pseudepigrapha of the Old Testament to discover whether we can find a proper Jewish background for these aspects of the *Apocalypse of Paul.*

THE FOUR RIVERS AND THE CITY OF CHRIST

In *Vis. Paul* 23, a paradisiacal motif (the four rivers) is connected with the motif of a city ("City of Christ"). This should not cause much surprise since the connection is an old one. Although the four rivers of Paradise are not mentioned outside Genesis 2 in the Hebrew Bible,[20] texts occur in which rivers are connected with a city, usually the abode of YHWH, i.e., Jerusalem, or Sion. I refer to the following texts: Ps 36:9–10 ("They feast on the abundance of *thy house* (ביתך), *and thou givest them drink from the river of thy delights* [ונחל עדניך תשקם]. For with thee is *the fountain of life* [מקור חיים]; in thy light so we see light"); 46:5 ("*There is a river whose streams make glad the city of God* [נהר פלגיו ישמחו עיר אלהים], the holy habitation of the Most High"); 65:10 ("*The river of God is full of water*" [פלג אלהים מלא מים]);[21] 87:7 ("All my springs are in you" [כל מעיני בך]);[22] Isa 33:21 ("There, rather, YHWH will be mighty for us; it is *a place of rivers, broad streams* [מקום נהרים יארים רחבי ידים], where no galley with oars can go, no stately ship can pass");[23] Ezek 47:1 ("Then he brought me back to the door of the temple; *and behold, water was issuing from below the threshold of the temple* [והנה מים יצאים מתחת מפתן הבית] toward the east—

---

[20] The Septuagint of Jeremiah 2:18 mentions the Gihon.

[21] According to some the river of God reflects here the idea of a conduit for rainwater from reservoirs above the heavens down to earth (cf. Job 38:25; Deut 11:11). It is also possible, however, that it is an allusion to the motif of the fountain in the temple. Cf. H.-J. Krauss, *Psalmen. 2. Teilband. Psalmen 60–150* (BKAT, XV/2; Neukirchen-Vluyn, 1978⁵), 613; M.E. Tate, *Psalms 51–100* (WBC, 20; Waco, Tex, 1990), 143; F.-L. Hossfeld – E. Zenger, *Psalmen 51–100* (HTKAT; Freiburg, 2000), 218.

[22] The addressed one is Zion (cf. Ps 87:5).

[23] We consider "place" (מקום) to be in apposition to "there" (שם) rather than to YHWH. Thus, the imagery presents Jerusalem as surrounded by water but protected from attack from any hostile fleet.

for the temple faced east—*and the water was flowing down* [והמים ירדים]
from below the south end of the threshold of the temple, south of
the altar"); Joel 4:18b (*"And a fountain shall come forth from the house of
YHWH and water the valley of Shittim"* [ומעין מבית יהוה יצא והשקה את
נחל השטים]); Zech 14:8 (*"On that day living water shall flow out from
Jerusalem* [יצאו מים חיים מירושלם]], half of them to the eastern sea and
half of them to the western sea; it shall continue in summer and in
winter"). These texts reflect the motif of *the fountain of the Temple.*
According to this motif, living waters will go forth from the abode
of God, guaranteeing the survival of nature and society.

The motif of a fountain that flows out from the abode of a God
occurs in the whole of the Ancient Near East.[24] Several mythological
conceptions seems to play a role, for example, the king of the gods
who resides at the mountain of the gods, and from there keeps away
chaos and creates the cosmos. At the mountain of the gods, the
fountains of life that make a paradisiacal life possible, rise.[25] Ugaritic
texts describe the dwelling of El at the "sources of the Two Rivers,
in the midst of the pools of the Double Deep."[26] The four streams
leaving Paradise can also be compared with the four streams that
often appear in Mesopotamian art,[27] for example, the images of a god
with an overflowing vase, and of a god from whose body streams flow.[28]

The background to the motif of the fountain of the Temple in
the Hebrew Bible is the identification of the Temple with Eden. The
consequence of this identification is an exchange of several motifs
(e.g., the holy mountain, the residence of God, fruitful rivers). It is
nevertheless difficult to find a place in the Hebrew Bible where Eden
is *explicitly* related to the Temple. Nowhere is the word "temple,"
the "Holy of Holies," or the "dwelling-place of the Lord" used in
connection with Eden. Only once is Eden related to a restored "Zion"

---

[24] The material is collected by M. Metzger, "Gottheit, Berg und Vegetation in
der vorderorientalischen Bildtradition," *ZDPV* 99 (1983) 54–94. See also I. Cornelius,
"Paradise Motifs in the Eschatology of the Minor Prophets and the Iconography
of the Ancient Near East. The Concepts of Fertility, Water, Trees, and 'Tierfireden'
and Genesis 2–3," *JNSL* 14 (1988) 41–83.

[25] Cf. R.J. Clifford, *The Cosmic Mountain in Canaan and the Old Testament* (Cambridge,
Ma, 1972).

[26] *CTA* 17; vi 47. Cf., e.g., Clifford, *Cosmic Mountain,* 48, 159.

[27] Cf. Clifford, *Cosmic Mountain,* 100–103.

[28] See O. Keel, *Die Welt der altorientalischen Bildsymbolik und das Alte Testament. Am
Beispiel der Psalmen* (Neukirchen-Vluyn, 1977²), 104, 122; Metzger, "Gottheit," 78;
Hossfeld-Zenger, *Psalmen 51–100,* 559.

(Isa 51:3a), and once to the "holy mountain" (Ezek 28:13–14); Eden is related a few times to the "land" (Ezek 36:35; Joel 2:3). With regard to the motif of the fountain of the Temple, the texts above show an *implicit* connection between Zion and Eden, in that fruitful rivers are related to the city. Textual similarities between these texts and Gen 2:10–14 are restricted by the occurrence of the verb יצא (Ezek 47:1; Joel 4:18; Zech 14:8), the *hif'il* form of the verb שקה (Ps 36:9; Joel 4:18), a word for "river" (נהר in Ps 46:5; cf. Isa 33:21; or a parallel word נחל in Ps 36:9; מעין in Joel 4:18; Ps 87:7; מים in Ezek 47:1; מים חיים in Zech 14:8), and the theme of general fertility (Ps 36:9; 65:10–11; Joel 4:18; Ezek 47:1–12).

At several points in early Jewish literature, there is a relation between the Garden of Eden and the Temple. In *1 Enoch* 24–27 is a section about the tree of life and the middle of the earth. It describes Jerusalem. In 25:3 "the throne of the Lord" is mentioned, in 25:5 "the house of the Lord, the eternal King," and in 26:1 "the middle of the earth."[29] The passage probably describes the new Jerusalem. In the description, much Edenic imagery from Genesis 2–3 and Ezek 28:11–19 is used.[30] In 24:1, the mountain of fire is reminiscent of Ezek 28:14; the precious and beautiful stones in 24:2 refer to Ezek 28:13. The description of the tree in 24:5 is very similar to Gen 2:9; 3:6. In 25:4–5 the tree of life appears, but with a remarkable difference to Genesis 2–3. Finally, the place is well watered: "And there I saw a holy mountain; underneath the mountain . . . there was a stream which was flowing in the direction of the north." In this passage we have a clear example of a connection between the Garden of Eden and the Temple. It is curious, however, that neither the words "Zion" nor "Jerusalem" are mentioned, nor the word "(Garden of) Eden." *T. Levi* 18:6 speaks about the heavenly Temple where God resides: "The heavens will be opened, and from the Temple the glory there will come on him." The new priesthood of this Temple is related to Eden (18:10). Also, in *T. Dan* 5:12 there is a connection between a future Jerusalem and Eden: "And the saints will rest in Eden and the righteous will rejoice in the new Jerusalem which will be the glory of God for ever."[31] The connection with the new Jerusalem

---

[29] The last expression is borrowed from Ezek 5:5; 38:12, which refers to Jerusalem as the navel of the earth (cf. *Jub* 8:12, 19).

[30] See J.C. VanderKam, *Enoch. A Man for All Generations* (Studies on the Personalities of the Old Testament;, Columbia, S.C.), 55–58.

[31] Cf. also *4 Ezra* 8:52 ("Because it is for you that *Paradise* is opened, the tree

points to the identification of both with Eden. In *Greek Life of Adam and Eve* 29:1–6, Adam asked the angels to take fragrances from Paradise, so that after he had been driven out of Paradise he could continue to bring offerings to God. In all these passages in early Jewish literature, Eden is associated with the *future* temple. This is also the case in some Qumran texts where the expression מקדש אדם is used (*4Q174; 4Q265; 4Q421*). The expression could mean a sanctuary built by men, or a sanctuary consisting of men.[32] According to some, however, this should be identified as Eden, that is to say, it is an epithet for the Garden of Eden.[33]

Also, in Apoc 22:1–2 the new Jerusalem is described with imagery associated with the Garden of Eden: "Then he showed me the river of the water of life, bright as crystal, flowing from the throne of God and of the Lamb through the middle of the street of the city; also on either side of the river, the tree of life with its twelve kinds of fruit, yielding its fruit each month." The river of living water flowing from the throne fits very well with the motif of the source of the Temple which was pointed out in the Hebrew Bible. In particular, the influence of Ezek 47:1–12 can be detected in the passage from Apoc 22:1–2.

THE RIVERS AND THEIR QUALITIES

In the Old Testament there is no explicit relationship between the four Rivers of Eden and the qualities mentioned. However, sometimes rivers, or streams, are mentioned in relation to the substances honey, milk, and wine. Firstly, consider Joel 4:18, which describes an abundance of wine, milk and water. At the end of the book this announces

---

of life is planted, the age to come is prepared, plenty provided, *a city* is built, rest is appointed, goodness is established and wisdom is perfected beforehand"). The new Jerusalem and Paradise also appears connected in *2 Bar* 4:3–7.

[32] Cf. D. Dimant, "4QFlorilegium and the Idea of the Community as Temple," in: A. Caquot, M. Hadas-Lebel, J. Riaud (eds.), *Hellenica et Judaica. Hommage à Valentin Nikipowezky* (Leuven, 1986), 165–189; G.J. Brooke, "Miqdash Adam, Eden and the Qumran Community," in B. Ego, A. Lange, P. Pilhofer (eds.), *Gemeinde ohne Tempel. Community without Temple* (WUNT, 118; Tübingen, 1999), 285–301.

[33] J.C. Baumgarten, "Purification after Childbirth and the Sacred Garden in 4Q265 and Jubilees," in G.J. Brooke, F. García Martínez (eds.), *New Qumran Texts and Studies. Proceedings of the First Meeting of the International Organization for Qumran Studies, Paris 1992* (Leiden, 1994), 3–10 (esp. 8–10); M.O. Wise, "4QFlorilegium and the Temple of Adam," *RevQ* 15 (1991–92) 103–132.

a new future, which should be considered as the opposite of the drought and thirst during the catastrophe described at the beginning of the book.[34] The text of Joel 4:18 reads as follows:

Joel 4:18

18a	And in that day
b	the mountains shall drip sweet wine,
c	and the hills shall flow with milk,
d	and all the stream beds of Judah
e	shall flow with water;
f	and a fountain shall come forth from the house YHWH
g	and water the valley of Shittim.

Strictly speaking, the combination of the four rivers of Paradise and their four qualities does not occur in this text, nor the attribution of one of these four substances to a river. The dripping (נטף) of young wine and the flowing (הלך = "to go") of milk are to be considered, in any case, as metaphors for fruitful vineyards and milking stock. The first promise (Joel 4:18b) refers to vineyards growing on mountain slopes and bearing fruit abundantly. The abundance of wine is contrary to the beginning of the book of Joel, where it is said that young wine is cut off from the mouths of drinkers of wine (Joel 1:5), and that wine fails (Joel 1:10). The second promise (Joel 4:18c) refers to the large flocks that could again give milk abundantly because they had sufficient grass. Also, this promise contrasts with the judgement at the beginning of the book, where it is said that "the beasts groan! The herds of cattle are perplexed because there is no pasture for them; even the flocks of sheep are dismayed" (Joel 1:18). The third promise (Joel 4:18de) functions as the cause of the first and second promises, in that plentiful water is conditional for the growth of the vineyards and the pasture. The abundance of water is also in contrast with the beginning of the book, which speaks of an extreme drought (cf. Joel 1:20). The motif of the streams full of water that results in new fertility, and an abundance of wine and milk, is connected with the motif of the fountain of the Temple, as

[34] Cf. W. Rudolph, *Joel, Amos, Obadja, Jona* (BKAT, XIII, 2; Gütersloh, 1971), 86; H.W. Wolff, *Dodekapropheton 2. Joel und Amos* (BK, XIV 2; Neukirchen-Vluyn, 1975²); W. van der Meer, *Oude woorden worden nieuw. De opbouw van het boek Joël* (Kampen, 1989), 238–241; C. van Leeuwen, *Joël* (POT; Nijkerk, 1993), 206–212; J.L. Crenshaw, *Joel* (AB, 24C; New York, 1995), 198–199.

seen above. On the one hand, the fountain that comes forth from
the house of YHWH is the guarantee of the fruitfulness of the land
(cf. Joel 4:18a–e), and on the other, the fountain gives water to the
valley of Shittim.[35]

Secondly, consider Amos 9:13, which describes the abundance in
the New Age with relation to the restoration of the people and the
renewal of the land.

Amos 9:13

13a	Behold, the days are coming
b	says YHWH
c	when the ploughman shall overtake the reaper,
d	and the treader of grapes him who sows the seed;
e	the mountains shall drip sweet wine,
f	and the hills shall flow with it.

A combination of a river and one of the four substances does not
occur in this text. Only the dripping (נטף) of young wine and the
flowing (מוג) of it. Amos 9:13e is nearly identical to Joel 4:18b, with
the exception of the form of the verb (והטיפו instead of יטפו). The
situation described is in sharp contrast to its treatment in the oracles of judgement earlier in the book of Amos. There the relationship with vineyards bearing abundant fruit is made explicit in 9:14
("They shall plant vineyards and drink their wine"). The texts focus
on the last days, in which "the booth of David that is fallen" will
be raised up (9:11).

Furthermore, two texts from the Book of Job refer to some sort
of relationship between rivers and their specific qualities, Job 20:17
and 29:6. Job 20:17 is very difficult from a text critical point of view.
The Hebrew text runs as follows: אל ירא בפלגות נהרי/נחלי דבש וחמאה.
The translation in the RSV is as follows: "He will not look upon
the rivers/the streams flowing with honey and curds." In this translation the verb ראה followed by the preposition ב is translated as
"look upon." According to others the construction sometimes means
"look at with pleasure." According to Blommerde, "to enjoy" better
describes its meaning.[36] Others seem to treat ראה as an equivalent

---

[35] This could refer to the wood that was needed for the Temple, see Van der
Meer, *Oude woorden*, 239–240.
[36] A.C.M. Blommerde, *North Semitic Grammar and Job* (Biblica et Orientalia, 22;
Rome, 1969), 90; D.J.A. Clines, *Job 1–20* (WBC, 17; Dallas, Tx, 1989), 475, 490.

of the verb רוה "saturate."[37] The sequence of the words פלנות נהרי
נחלי דבש ("rivers of streams of brooks of honey") forms an unusu-
ally long chain of *status constructus* connections. The Masoretic accentuation distinguishes between פלנות and נהרי. The BHS, as well as
the translation in the RSV, follows this accentuation in the division
of the lines. In this way, the verse is irregularly divided into two
lines (i.e., two stresses in the first line, and four in the second colon).
The second line seems to be interpreted as an apposition to פלנות
("He will not look upon rivers, streams of brooks of honey").

In my opinion, it is better to divide the verse into two regular
lines of three stresses each: אל ירא בפלנות נהרי / נחלי דבש וחמאה.
The meaning of פלנות נהרי ("channels of streams") however, remains
problematic in this pattern of division. Several exegetes have emended
נהרי ("streams") into יצהר ("oil").[38] The meaning of the construction
פלנות יצהר is in that case "rivers of oil." From the point of view of
textual criticism, the proposed emendation is not attractive because
of the substantial graphic alteration that is necessary in order to
change נהרי into יצהר. However, it may be possible to read נהר as
a noun, meaning "oil," being derived from the root נהר ("to shine").[39]
The final י could be read as a ו and connected with the next word.
Therefore, I propose the following translation: "He will enjoy no
streams of oil, nor torrents of honey and cream."

In this interpretation of the partly reconstructed version of MT
Job 20:17, one finds three of the four relevant substances: "oil,"
"honey" and "cream." The Hebrew vocabulary differs somewhat
from more commonly used words. I refer to נהר ("oil") instead of
שמן and חמאה ("cream, fat milk") instead of חלב ("milk"). It is true
that the text does not mention the four rivers of paradise, but the
connection of streams and rivers with the substances does occur.
That honey also flows is considered by some as quite exceptional.[40]
However, the liquidity of honey could be one of its qualities.[41]

---

[37] E.g., N.H. Tur-Sinai, *The Book of Job. A New Commentary* (Jerusalem, revised
edition 1967) 314: "He shall not drink his fill from . . ."

[38] So, e.g., H.H. Rowley, *Job* (The Century Bible; London, 1970), 179; J.H.
Kroeze, *Het Boek Job* (COT; Kampen, 1961), 233; P. van der Lught, *Rhetorical
Criticism and Poetry in the Book of Job* (OTS, 32; Leiden, 1999), 231.

[39] So also Blommerde, *Grammar*, 90; R. Gordis, *The Book of Job* (New York, 1978),
217.

[40] Cf. Clines, *Job*, 491.

[41] Cf. N. Hareuveni, *Nature in Our Biblical Heritage* (Kiryat Ono, 1980).

Although a word for "river" is used in the original text of Job 20:17, it seems that it does not refer to concrete, geographic rivers, but to the river as an image of abundance.

A direct influence of Job 20:17 on the *Apocalypse of Paul* is unlikely. Apart from the fact that Job 20:17 does not refer to the rivers of Paradise, nor to the rivers of a city, the translation of the LXX deviates somewhat from the Hebrew Text. The LXX Job 20:17 runs as follows: "May he not see the milking of the cattle, nor the distribution of honey and cream").[42] The Old Latin of Job 20:17 follows more or less the Septuagint: "He did not see milk of the cattle, nor food, honey and cream" (*Et non videat mulcturam pecorum, neque pabula, mellis & butyri*).[43]

Finally, the Hebrew text of Job 29:6 reads as follows: ברחץ הליכי בחמה/וצור יצוק עמדי פלני שמן. The translation in the RSV is as follows: "When my steps were washed with milk,/and the rocks poured out for me streams of oil!" The division of this verse into the cola found in the BHS and the RSV is in accordance with the most obvious syntactical structure. The Masoretic accentuation points also to this division. The parallelism between both cola (ברחץ//יצוק; פלני שמן//בחמה;עמדי//הליכי) seems to confirm the division. However, the spread of words over the cola of the verse is rather unbalanced. There are three stresses in the first colon and five in the second. Because of this irregular rhythm, many exegetes consider עמדי (29:6b) as an explanatory gloss, which slipped into the text of 29:6 because of its occurrence in 29:5.[44] However, some reference to Job in the first person is needed. It occurs in all the other seven cola (29:2–6a).[45] Others delete וצור and translate 29:6b as follows: "Where I stood, were flowing streams of oil."[46] In this reading, עמדי ("where I stood," translated in the RSV as "for me") is considered as parallel to הליכי ("my steps").[47] Although this emendation is attractive, it remains difficult to explain how וצור was inserted in the Masoretic transmission.

---

[42] I translate νομάς as "roaming," and νομη as "distribution." Cf. *LS*, 1178.

[43] Cf. P. Sabatier's edition of the *Vetus Latina*, 867. The Vulgate of Job 20:17 does read some words for river in this context of milk and honey (*non videat rivulos fluminis torrentes mellis et butyri*).

[44] G. Fohrer, *Das Buch Hiob* (KAT, 16; Gütersloh, 1963), 406; Rowley, *Job*, 236; H. Stauss, *Hiob 2. Teilband 19,1–42,17* (BKAT, XVI/2; Neukirchen-Vluyn, 2002), 186.

[45] Cf. Gordis, *Job*, 319.

[46] Cf. P. van der Lught, *Rhetorical criticism*, 286–287.

[47] Cf. Tur-Sinai, *Job*, 411.

Moreover, the Septuagint probably had צורי in its *Vorlage* (τὰ ὄρη μου, "my mountains"). Also attractive is Dahood's proposal to read 29:6 as follows: ברחץ הליכי בחמה וצורי/צוק עמדי פלני שמן ("My steps were bathed in butter *and mastic*/streams of oil were flowing over my legs"). It is not clear, however, whether צרי (mastic, resin of *Pistacia mutica*, used for medicinal purposes, or for incense; cf. Jer 8:22; 46:11; 51:8) was suited to the bathing of feet.[48] Despite the problems with regard to the rhythm, I propose the retention of the Masoretic text, including the accentuation. The longer colon (29:6b) could perhaps be explained by the fact that it is the last colon of the section 29:2–6, and therefore functions as an end. As far as the content of Job 29:6 is concerned, the just Job is speaking metaphorically in saying that he shares completely the blessings of God.[49] The images used are analogous to the portrayal of abundance elsewhere (cf. Job 20:17; Gen 49:11; Exod 3:8; Deut 32:13–14; 33:24; Ps 81:17).[50] There is no clear connection with *Vis. Paul* 23 nor with the rivers of Paradise. The only objection that can be made is that the image of the flowing of oil and milk had probably become part of the stock metaphorical language of ancient Israel for describing well-being.

In the Apocrypha and Pseudepigrapha of the Old Testament there are two texts that might be relevant in this respect, i.e., Ben Sira (Ecclesiasticus) 24:25–27 and *2 (Slavonic) Enoch* 8:5–6.[51]

I shall start with the text of Ben Sira.[52]

---

[48] Cf. OTS on Job.

[49] Cf. Fohrer, *Hiob*, 406; Strauss, *Hiob*, 186.

[50] In addition, there is the metaphor used in the Song of Songs 5:12 ("His eyes are like doves beside springs of water, bathed in milk, fitly set") which is used in the sense of pure pleasantness and well-being.

[51] *5 Ezra* 2:18–19 may also be relevant in this respect: "I will send you help, my servants Isaiah and Jeremiah. According to their counsel I have consecrated and prepared for you *twelve trees loaded with various fruits and the same number of springs flowing with milk and honey*, and seventy mighty mountains on which roses and lilies grow; by these I will fill your children with joy." However, it is not certain that *5 Ezra* 2:18–19 preceded the *Apocalypse of Paul*, since it should be dated to the second half of the third century. Moreover, it seems to be of Christian origin. In the *New Testament* there is no connection between the four rivers and the substances. According to Ginzberg, the four rivers should occur in *Rabbinic Literature*, i.e., in *Pesikta Rabbati* 38 (163a), a text that is much later than the *Apocalypse of Paul*. When the passage in Pesikta Rabbati 38 is examined, there is no reference to four rivers whatsoever.

[52] For an analysis of Ben Sira 24:23–29, see J. Marböck, *Weisheit im Wandel. Untersuchungen zur Weisheitstheologie bei Ben Sira* (BBB, 37; Bonn, 1971), 77–81; M. Gilbert, "L'éloge de la Sagesse (Siracide 24)," *RTL* 5 (1974) 326–348 (esp. 336–341);

Ben Sira (Ecclesiasticus) 24:23–30 (tr. NEB, with some slight alterations)

23a	All this is the covenant-book of God Most-High,
b	the law which Moses enacted to be the heritage of the assemblies of Jacob.
25a	He sends out wisdom in full flood like *the river Pison*
b	or like *the Tigris* at the time of the first-fruits;
26a	he overflows with understanding like *the Euphrates*
b	or like the Jordan at the time of harvest.
27a	He pours forth instruction like the Nile,
b	like *the Gihon* at the time of the vintage.
28a	The first human never knew fully wisdom;
bf	from first to last no one has fathomed her;
29a	for her thoughts are vaster than the ocean
b	and her purpose deeper than the great abyss.
30a	As for me, I was like a canal leading from a river,
b	a watercourse into a pleasure-garden . . .

In this passage about wisdom, the names of the four rivers of Paradise are mentioned (Pison, Tigris, Euphrates, Gihon) together with the names of some other rivers (Jordan, Nile),[53] and with some other terminology that refers to the story of Eden, for example "the first man" in v. 28, and the "pleasure-garden" in v. 30.[54] Wisdom is connected with *nomos*, the Law of Moses, which seems to be the law as a literary entity, namely the Pentateuch.[55] There is a connection between Law and Wisdom, although they are not identified.[56] The

---

H. Stadelmann, *Ben Sira als Schriftgelehrter. Eine Untersuchung zum Berufsbild des vormakkabäischen Sofer unter Berücksichtigung seines Verhältnisses zu Priester-, Propheten- und Weisheitslehrertum* (WUNT, 2.6; Tübingen, 1980), 247–252; B. Ego, "Der Strom der Tora. Zur Rezeption eines tempeltheologischen Motivs in frühjüdischer Zeit," in B. Ego, A. Lange, P. Pilhofer (eds.), *Gemeinde ohne Tempel. Community without Temple. Zur Substituierung und Transformation des Jerusalemer Tempels und seines Kults im Alten Testament, antiken Judentum und frühen Christentum* (WUNT, 118; Tübingen, 1999), 205–214 (esp. 206–208).

[53] The order of the rivers is different from Gen. 2:10–14 in that the second river (Gihon) is placed at the end of the passage. It could function as a sort of inclusion. The first and the last river bracket the rest of the rivers to make them appear as additional streams of paradise. Cf. G.T. Sheppard, *Wisdom as a Hermeneutical Construct. A Study in Sapientializing of the Old Testament* (BZAW, 151; Berlin, 1981), 68–71. The Jordan is used probably because of Gen. 13:10, where the plain of the Jordan is compared to the Garden of Eden ("And Lot lifted up his eyes, and saw that the Jordan valley was well watered everywhere like the garden of YHWH"). The Nile is introduced, probably because of the double association of the Gihon. This river is identified either with the Nile, or with a river in the neighbourhood of Jerusalem.

[54] Cf. also 24:31 "I will water my garden."

[55] Marböck, *Weisheit*, 77; Stadelmann, *Ben Sira*, 250; Cf. 24:23a: "the covenant-book of God Most-High"; 24:23b is nearly a verbatim quotation of Deut 33:4.

[56] Ego, "Strom," 207.

Law is presented as the source of Wisdom. This is elaborated in the use of the rivers. Wisdom, understanding, and instruction come forth from the source (i.e., the Law) and now flow abundantly like the rivers of Paradise. The rivers, used as an image of abundance, are not identified themselves as rivers of wine, or any other substance. It is only *in the time* of the harvest that they are full of water: Pison and Tigris are full in the days of the first-fruits (24:25); Euphrates and Jordan overflow in the days of the harvest (24:26); Nile and Gihon pour out in the days of the vintage (24:27). Although the author of Ben Sira uses metaphorical language, it is nevertheless the first time that the four rivers of paradise are explicitly related to fruit, especially to the first-fruits and to wine. The Gihon itself is connected here with the vintage, whereas in the *Apocalypse of Paul*, it is connected with oil while the river of wine is the Tigris.

In *Ben Sira* 24:25–29, Wisdom is identified with the Torah and compared to the rivers of Paradise. In 24:30–34, the instruction of Wisdom by Ben Sira is described by using metaphors of water and rivers. Wisdom is localised on Mount Sion (24:10–11). Moreover, Ben Sira 24:30–31 is alluding to Ezek 47:1–12, according to which the source of the waters is in the Temple.[57] In this way, Ben Sira combines the motif of the rivers of paradise (24:23–29) with the motif of the water that flows out from the city of God and the Temple (24:30–34). One might suggest that Ben Sira identifies Jerusalem and the Temple with the Garden of Eden.[58]

The text of the longer recension of *2 (Slavonic) Enoch 8:4–6* runs in translation as follows:[59]

2 (Slavonic) Enoch 8:4–6

4b	And it [= the Tree of Life in the midst of the garden] covers the whole of Paradise.
c	And it has something of every orchard tree and every fruit.
d	And its root is in Paradise at the exit that leads to the earth.
5a	And Paradise is in between the corruptible and the incorruptible.
b	And two streams come forth, one a source of honey and milk, and a source which produces oil and wine.

---

[57] See, e.g., O. Rickenbacher, *Weisheitsperikopen bei Ben Sira* (OBO 1; Freiburg, 1973), 168–169; Gilbert, "L'éloge," 340; Ego, "Strom," 209.

[58] Cf. Zimmerli, *Ezechiel*, 2, 1192f.; Görg., *Eden*, NBL I, 467.

[59] The translation of the longer recension is taken from M. Pravednou, "2 (Slavonic Apocalypse of) Enoch," in: J.H. Charlesworth (ed.), *The Old Testament Pseudepigrapha*, I, (London, 1983), 91–213 (esp. 114–116).

c	And it is divided into 4 parts,
d	and they go around with a quiet movement
6a	And they come out into the Paradise of Eden, between the corruptible and the incorruptible.
b	And from there they pass along
c	and they divide into 40 parts.
d	And it proceeds in descent along the earth,
e	and they have a revolution in their cycle, just like the other atmospheric elements.

This is the first text in which rivers are explicitly connected and identified with the four substances mentioned in the *Apocalypse of Paul* (honey and milk, oil and wine). Although the rivers are not mentioned by name, it is clear from the context that the four rivers of Paradise are meant. Enoch is sitting in the Third Heaven, and he is looking down at Paradise (8:1). It seems as if the text gives a picture of a double paradise.[60] A tree is rooted in the earthly garden and rises to the Third Heaven, where it covers Heavenly Paradise. The exit that leads to earth is probably the root of the tree in the Garden of Eden (cf. 8:4: "And its root is in Paradise at the exit that leads to the earth"). The geography of these rivers, however, is somewhat different from the biblical text of Genesis, as well as from the text of the Apocalypse. The four rivers come from two sources, two streams. In Genesis only one river is the source of the four rivers, in *Vis. Paul* 23 no common source of the four rivers is mentioned. In *Vis. Paul* 45 there is a beginning of the four rivers at the roots of the tree. Also, in *2 Enoch* there is a strong connection between the sources of the rivers and a tree, although it is not the same tree as in *Vis. Paul* 45, where it is not the Tree of Life, nor the Tree of Knowledge, but a third kind of tree. In *2 Enoch*, the rivers seem to be already divided before they enter Paradise,[61] and from there, when they leave Paradise and descend to the earth, they are divided again into 40 rivers. In the end they evaporate, and apparently return to Paradise in the form of rain, or perhaps mist. Despite these differences, *2 Enoch* is the first text where there is an explicit identification of the substances with the four rivers of Paradise.

---

[60] Cf. C. Böttrich, *Das slavische Henochbuch* (JSHRZ, V/7; Gütersloh, 1996), 848.
[61] Cf. LXX Gen 2:8.

The Four Substances (Honey, Milk, Oil, and Wine)

In the Old Testament, the word-pair "milk and honey" is a formula to designate the fertility and abundance of the promised land (e.g., Exod 3:8, 17; 13:5; 33:3; Lev 20:24; Num 13:27). These aspects of the promised land are eschatologically interpreted by the author of Paul as aspects of the heavenly paradise. The reversed word order "honey and milk" occurs for the first time in *2 Enoch* 8:5. As far as the "oil" and "wine" are concerned, they are also gifts of the land, and mentioned either together (cf. Deut 7:13) or apart. There are, however, more gifts of the land, which have not been selected for inclusion by the author of the *Apocalypse*. Also, in early Jewish and Rabbinical literature, "oil" and "wine" are connected with Paradise. In the *Greek Life of Adam and Eve*, Seth looked for *oil* for his father Adam in Paradise. In rabbinical literature the streams of oil are not mentioned directly in connection with Eden, but rather as a reward for the righteous just before dying. I refer to *Gen. Rab.* 62:2: "When R. Abbahu was dying he was shown thirteen streams of balsam. Said he to them: For whom are these? They are yours, he was assured. All these are for Abbahu, he exclaimed. "Yet I had thought, I have laboured in vain, I have spent my strength for nought and vanity; yet surely, my right is with the Lord, and my recompense with my God" (Isa 49:4) "This proves that when the righteous are departing from the world the Holy One, blessed be He, shows their reward." Ben Azzai expounded: It is written: "Precious in the sight of the Lord is the death of His saints" (Ps 116:15): when does God show them the reward he prepared for them? Just before their death, wherefore it is written: Is the death of his saints."

The same can be said of *wine*. It is a reward for the righteous just before dying (cf. *b. Sanh* 99a). One can also refer to Matthew 26:29: "I tell you I shall not drink again of this fruit of wine, until that day when I drink it new with you in my Father's kingdom." There are some points in rabbinical literature where wine is explicitly related to the Garden of Eden. Targum Pseudo-Jonathan Gen 9:20 recounts that Noah "found *a vine which the river* had brought from the Garden of Eden." See also *Gen. Rab.* 36:3, according to which Noah took with him "into the ark shoots from vines ready for planting as well as shoots from figs and olives."

Wine is not always related to Paradise in a positive way. There is a rabbinical tradition according to which the tree from which Adam ate was a vine: "R. Hisda said in the name of R. Uqba (though others say it was Mar Uqba in the name of R. Zakkai): The Holy One, blessed be He, said to Noah: Noah, why did you fail to take a warning from Adam, whose offence was caused by wine? This follows the opinion that the tree from which Adam ate was the vine, as it has been taught: R. Meir said: That tree from which Adam ate was a vine, because only wine brings grief to a man" (*b. Sanh* 70ab).

CONCLUSION

The connection of the four rivers of Paradise to the City of Christ in the *Apocalypse of Paul* was prepared long beforehand. We have referred to texts in the Hebrew Bible in which rivers are mentioned in connection to a city, i.e. the abode of YHWH, Jerusalem or the Temple. These texts, which reflect the motif of the fountain of the Temple according to which living waters spring forth from the residence of God, guaranteeing the survival of nature, have, in fact, deep roots in the literature of the Ancient Near East. Moreover, these texts show an implicit identification of the Temple with the Garden of Eden through which the co-relation of several motifs, in particular that of the fruitful rivers, was made possible. At several points in the early literature and the New Testament, there is a strong connection between the *future* Jerusalem and the Garden of Eden. The connection of the rivers with the substances in *Vis. Paul* 23 shows considerable similarity to *2 Henoch* 8:4–6. However, this motif was prepared long beforehand in the Hebrew Bible, where rivers are placed in relation to several of the substances. The nature of the four substances (i.e., liquids) means that they could flow. The river is a metaphor for abundance. Moreover, oil and wine are gifts which in Jewish tradition are connected with the Garden of Eden, and this Garden is eschatologically interpreted in the *Apocalypse of Paul*, whereas the Land of milk and honey is also used to refer to the abundance waiting for the righteous in the future paradise.

"MOSES RECEIVED TORAH . . ." (*M. AVOT* 1,1): RABBINIC CONCEPTIONS OF REVELATION

GÜNTER STEMBERGER*

The perhaps best known passage of the entire rabbinic literature is the beginning of *Mishnah Avot*: "Moses received Torah from Sinai and handed it on to Joshua, and Joshua to the elders, and the elders to the prophets, and the prophets handed it on to the men of the Great Assembly." Thus it is highly astonishing that in rabbinic literature this text is hardly ever quoted. There are only two passages where it occurs,[1] both times without a quotation formula. We first encounter it in *y. San* 10,1,28a, commenting on Qoh 12:11: "The sayings of the wise are like goads" (כדרבנות): "That is, like this ball (כדור) between girls (בנות). Just as this ball goes from hand to hand, but in the end comes to rest in one hand, so *Moses received Torah from Sinai and handed it on to Joshua, Joshua to the elders, the elders to the prophets, and the prophets handed it on to the Men of the Great Assembly.*"

If we did not know the passage by heart, we would not recognize it as a quotation. Neither does *Qoh. Rab.* 12,11, commenting on the same verse, introduce the passage as part of the Mishnah: "Just as this ball goes from hand to hand and does not fall on the ground, so *Moses received Torah from Sinai and handed it on to Joshua, Joshua to the elders.*"[2]

---

* Wien.

[1] Apart from *Avot deR. Natan*, of course, which builds on *Avot*. But even there the passage is not as central as one might expect. Version A quotes it at the very beginning (ed. Schechter 1): "Moses was sanctified in the cloud and received Torah from Sinai"; a few lines later the text continues: "By the hands of Moses was the Torah given at Sinai . . . The Torah which the Holy One, blessed be He, gave to Israel was given by the hands of Moses only . . . Moses merited becoming God's messenger to the children of Israel." Version B quotes the text of *Avot* 1,1 only a little later (ed. Schechter 2), first with an enlarged chain of tradition, then again with a brief commentary: "Moses received Torah from Sinai. Not from the mouth of an angel and not from the mouth of a Seraph, but from the mouth of the King over the kings of kings, blessed be He." The passage does not seem central at all; apart from this quotation of *Avot* 1,1, the formula "to receive Torah" occurs also in *ARN* A 2 and B 2 (ed. Schechter 9–10): Israel receives the Torah in purity.

[2] MS Vatican stops here; the Wilna edition continues: "*the elders to the prophets, and the prophets handed it on to the Men of the Great Assembly etc.,*" thus indicating that a well known text is being quoted.

In order better to understand the position of the beginning of
tractate *Avot* within the context of rabbinic tradition, I propose to
analyze the characteristic formula of this passage, לקבל תורה (and its
variants), as it is used in rabbinic literature.[3]

1. MISHNAH, TOSEFTA, HALAKHIC MIDRASHIM

In the *Mishnah*, the phrase occurs only twice outside of *Avot*. During
the service of Yom Kippur, "the beadle of the community takes the
scroll of the Torah and gives it to the head of the community, and
the head of the community gives it to the prefect [of the priests],
and the prefect gives it to the high priest. The high priest rises and
receives it and reads . . ." (*m. Yoma* 7,1; parallel *m. Sotah* 7,7). It is
the physical scroll of the Torah, not Torah as such, which goes from
hand to hand (comparable to the chain of tradition) until the high
priest receives it. The verb used for handing on the scroll is not מסר
as in *Avot*, but נותן. In *Avot*, לקבל is used once more in connection
with the Torah (3,6): "Every one who takes upon himself the yoke
of the Torah . . ." (מקבל עליו עול תורה), a phrase which in this or
similar forms (with or without "yoke") is frequent in rabbinic literature. In the *Tosefta* we encounter only the similar phrase: "A pros-
elyte who takes upon himself all words of the Torah" (*t. Dem* 2,4.5:
גר שקיבל עליו כל דברי תורה).

One could argue that because of the subject matter of Mishnah
and Tosefta we cannot expect more attestations of the phrase לקבל
תורה. But we do find מתן תורה (*m. Taan* 4,8; *m. Neg* 7,1; *t. Hul* 7,8;
t. Parah 4,5) or a threat against those who say that "the Torah is
not from Heaven" (*m. San* 10,1); *t. Qid* 5,21 says that Abraham "kept
the entire Torah before it had come" (עד שלא באת); according to *t.
San* 4,7 "Ezra was worthy for the Torah to have been given by him
(שנתתן תורה על ידו), had not Moses come before him"; in the same
passage, the rabbis discuss in what form of writing "the Torah was
given (ניתנה) to Israel" (4,7.8).

We thus see that Mishnah and Tosefta prefer to speak of the giving (ניתנה ,מתן) or coming (באת) of the Torah; the Torah is the sub-

---

[3] S. Abramson, "Expressions concerning the Giving of the Torah: מעמד הר סיני
מתן תורה ,יום סיני" (in Hebrew), *Lešonenu* 58,4 (1994–95) 317–322, deals mainly with
the linguistic usage in the Middle Ages, above all the phrase "standing at Sinai."
The formula לקבל תורה does not occur in his discussion.

ject, not an object which Moses received. The preferred passive form
ניתנה, נתן may be understood as *passivum divinum*: God gives the
Torah;[4] Moses intervenes only as an instrument, as Ezra would have,
but the agent is always God alone. *m. Avot* 1,1 is the only text in
Mishnah and Tosefta where Moses is active in the giving of the
Torah. Theologically this passage is different from the other texts.

In the *halakhic midrashim*, phrases with לקבל תורה do occur, but
not in the meaning "to receive the Torah," but "to accept the Torah,
to take it upon oneself." In the *Mekhilta*, it is said seven times of
Israel (e.g. *Beshallah* 6, ed. Horovitz-Rabin 112 בזכות תורה שעתידין
לקבל; further occurrences Horovitz-Rabin 138, 146, 219, 235), three
times of the nations of the world who are offered the Torah and
do not accept it because of its contents (ed. Horovitz-Rabin 221).
The phrase ניתנה תורה occurs ten times (ed. Horovitz-Rabin 76, 159,
161, 188, 205, 212, 222), מתן תורה nine times (188, 207, 236, 263,
337); ליתן את התורה, said of God, twice (77, 206).

Sifra has only (three times) the phrase קיבל עליו כל דברי תורה
(*Shemini Mekhilta de Milluim*, ed. Weiss 45d, and *Qedoshim* Pereq 8,
Weiss 91a, a quotation of *t. Dem* 2,4.5, already referred to)—somebody who "took upon himself all words of the Torah"; in *Behuqqotai* Pereq 8 (ed. Weiss 112c) it comments on Lev 26:46 "on mount
Sinai by the hand (ביד) of Moses": "This teaches that the Torah
was given (ניתנה) ... through (על ידי) Moses from Sinai": Thus the
single text which speaks of the revelation of the Torah, uses the traditional passive formula, Moses is only the instrument.

In *Sifre Num.* § 112 (ed. Horovitz 121) we read: "Somebody who says:
I take upon myself the whole Torah save this one matter..." (כל
התורה כולה אני מקבל עלי); regarding the revelation of the Torah, the
passive form ניתנה תורה is used (*Sifre Num.* § 115, ed. Horovitz 126).

Sifre Deut. uses the phrase "you have taken upon yourself the
Torah" (קבלתם עליכם את התורה: § 5, ed. Finkelstein 13), but also
"after they accepted the Torah" (קבלו תורה: § 76, ed. Finkelstein
141, here directly preceded by מתן תורה which occurs also in § 343,
ed. Finkelstein 397.398); in the same paragraph, the Midrash also
speaks of "every commandment which they accepted" (כל מצוה
שקבלו אותה), thus making it clear that with regard to the Torah, too,
its acceptance and not its revelation is meant. In the same way the

---

[4] See also *m. Yad* 3,5: "the Song of Songs was given (ניתנה) to Israel."

phrase is to be understood in § 306 (ed. Finkelstein 335), where
Moses is afraid that after his death Israel might say: "we have not
accepted the Torah" (לא קבלנו את התורה). In § 311 (ed. Finkelstein
352) we read: "When the Holy One, blessed be He, gave Torah
(כשנתן . . . תורה) to Israel . . . no nation among the nations was suitable to receive/accept the Torah (לקבל את התורה) except for Israel."
Here one might hesitate what the primary meaning of לקבל is; but
even if we translate "receive the Torah," it is in view of keeping its
commandments.

That God gives the Torah to Israel (and not only the passive formulation "the Torah is given to Israel") is to be found also in § 305
(ed. Finkelstein 324): When Joshua started teaching the Torah, he
began with the benediction "Blessed is the Lord, who has given
Torah to Israel through (על ידי) Moses, our master." Here we may
also quote § 313, ed. Finkelstein 356: "when the Holy One, blessed
be He, revealed himself to give Tora—ליתן תורה—to Israel." We
encounter the same phrase three times in § 343 (ed. Finkelstein 395).
There we also find the well known story how God turns to the
different nations: "will you accept the Torah?" (מקבלים אתם את התורה),
and none accepts the Torah; even the seven Noachide commandments which they had taken on themselves (שקיבלו עליהם), they threw
off again. Israel alone "accepted the Torah" (קבלו את התורה) with
all its interpretations and details (Finkelstein 396–7).

There is only one passage which casts Moses in an active role in
the giving of the Torah. § 357 (ed. Finkelstein 427) asks how Moses
could have written about his own death. An answer is: "Is it possible that Moses gave the Torah (שנתן משה את התורה) when it was
lacking even a single letter? But this teaches that Moses wrote what
the Holy One, blessed be He, told him, in line with this verse, 'And
Baruch said to them, By his own mouth he dictated me' (Jer 36:18)."
It is obvious that the saying about Moses giving the Torah is not
equivalent to God giving the Torah; as to Moses, the phrase is to
say that he did not hand over the Torah to the people before its
writing was completed.

If we summarize the outcome of the oldest stratum of rabbinic
literature, we see that apart from m. Avot 1,1, no text speaks of a
single person receiving the Torah. The subject is Israel who accept
the Torah contrary to the nations of the world who are not prepared to accept it. This meaning of קיבלו is different from that in
m. Avot 1,1 where Moses received the Torah in order to hand it on

(קיבל/מסר) whereas of Israel one obviously cannot say that they handed on the Torah—they accepted it as an obligation. The phrase about Moses receiving the Torah, on the other hand, may be compared to the high priest receiving the scroll of the Torah in order to read from it, i.e. the object of the Torah scroll and not the Torah as ideal entity. When Moses is spoken of as receiving the Torah, he is pictured as God's messenger, as the mediator between God and the people, an aspect not at all common in early rabbinic literature.[5] Here the immediacy between God and the people is paramount.

2. Yerushalmi and Contemporary Midrashim

In the *Yerushalmi*, the phrase does not become more important. Apart from the quotation of *m. Yoma* 7,1 and *m. Sotah* 7,6 (the high priest receives the scroll of the Torah in the liturgy of the Yom Kippur), it occurs only three times. In *y. RH* 4,8,59c Israel is praised for having taken upon itself the yoke of the Torah (קיבלתם עליכם עול התורה); in *y. Shab* 9,3,12a it is said that Israel received the Torah in the state of *tevul yom* (כלם טבולי יום קבלו ישראל את התורה); the last text, *y. San* 10,1,28a, has already been referred to in the introduction to this essay: it is the only early parallel to *m. Avot* 1,1, without any indication that it quotes a Mishnaic text. Whereas with regard to Israel, the meaning of the phrase is clearly that Israel receives the Torah in order to take its commandments upon themselves, in the case of Moses it is, as in *m. Avot*, as a mediator, שליח.

---

[5] *Sifra Behuqqotai* Pereq 8,12 (ed. Weiss 112c), i.e. the end of the midrash on Lev 26, comments on Lev 26:46 "These are the statutes and ordinances and laws, which the Lord made between Him and the children of Israel on mount Sinai by the hand of Moses": "Mose was worthy to be made shaliah between Israel and their father in heaven." At the end of the whole midrash (*Behuqqotai* Pereq 13,7, Weiss 115d), it comments on Lev 27:34 "These are the commandments, which the Lord commanded Moses for the children of Israel on mount Sinai": "Worthy is the messenger (שליח) of the one who sent him . . . the messenger is worthy of those to whom he is sent, and those to whom the messenger is sent are worthy of the messenger." A similar phrase is to be found at the end of *Sav*, part of the *Mekhilta de Milluim* (ed. Weiss 43b), commenting on Lev 8:36 "And Aaron and his sons did all the things which the Lord commanded by the hand of Moses": "The messenger is worthy of the one who sent him." As is known, the *Mekhilta de Milluim* is not part of the original *Sifra*, but is closely related to *Sifra Behuqqotai*, the only other passage in this midrash which calls Moses a messenger. Apart from these passages, this notion is to be found only in much later texts, as *ARN* A 1,1 (Schechter 1), a close parallel to *Sifra* on Lev 26:46, *Shir. Rab.* 1,14 etc.

Apart from the single passage in *y. San*, Moses is never described as active in the reception and transmission of the Torah. In *y. Sheq* 6,1,49d God gives the Torah to Moses ("when the Holy One, blessed be He, gave the Torah to Moses, he gave it to him as white fire engraved on black fire"), and in *y. Hor* 3,7,48b it is said that during the forty days on Sinai Moses learned the Torah but kept forgetting it until "in the end it was given to him as a gift." The normal way to express the revelation of the Torah is for the Yerushalmi as for all earlier texts the passive formula "the Torah was given" (תורה ניתנה), used as a *passivum divinum* (as is clear from the passage against those who say "that the Torah was not given from heaven," לא ניתנה תורה מן השמים: *y. Peah* 1,1,16b).

The same picture prevails in *Genesis Rabbah*. לקבל את התורה is never said of a single person: It is Israel as a people who are to receive, i.e. to take upon themselves the Torah. "All of the flocks of Israel had to be present, for if any one of them had been lacking, they would not have been worthy of receiving the Torah" (*Gen. Rab.* 70,9, ed. Theodor-Albeck 808; cf. 1,4, p. 7; 21,9, p. 204). The righteous have received/accepted the Torah which was given from the mountains of God (Ps 36:7), in contrast with the wicked who have not accepted the Torah which was given from the mountains of God (*Gen. Rab.* 33,1, Theodor-Albeck 298; the parallels *Lev. Rab.* 27,1, ed. Margulies 613, and *PesK* 9,1, ed. Mandelbaum 146, read both times עושין instead of קיבלו; another reading is קיימו). לקבל תורה always refers to a community which receives the Torah as a gift and accepts it with all the obligations deriving from it.

The act of the revelation of the Torah and its transmission to Israel is always formulated in a passive phrase, ניתנה התורה, "the Torah was given (by God)" (e.g. *Gen. Rab.* 18,4, Theodor-Albeck 164; 31,8, p. 281; 32,5, p. 292). A single person never plays an active role in this event, he can only be an instrument, as in *Gen. Rab.* 24,5 (Theodor-Albeck 234): "The first man (Adam) was worthy to have the Torah given through him" (שתנתן התורה על ידו), but God decided not to do so: Adam had not been able to keep the six commandments which he was given; how could he have stood by the 613 positive and negative commandments?! Here again it is clear that the individual is no more than God's instrument and *shaliaḥ*, and that to receive the Torah always implies the obligation to live by it.

Leviticus Rabbah, redacted at about the same time as *Gen. Rab.*, offers the same results. In contrast with "the nations of the world who did not carry out the teachings of the Torah (קיימו את התורה) which was given out of darkness," Israel "has kept the teachings of the Torah which was given out of darkness" (6,6, ed. Margulies 146; the first edition and two Oxford manuscripts as well as the parallel in *PesK* 7,12, Mandelbaum 134, read קיבלו instead of קיימו—the two terms are roughly equivalent in this context).

No nation but Israel and no generation but the generation of the wilderness was worthy to receive the Torah (לקבל את התורה). The printed editions continue: God "found no mountain but Sinai on which the Torah should be given (שתנתן בו את התורה); the edition Margulies reads instead: "no mountain but Mount Moriah that was truly worthy for the presence of God to come to rest upon it" (*Lev. Rab.* 13,2, Margulies 273). "The Torah had been given to Israel at Sinai as a fence" (ניתנה תורה סיני), thus emphasizing again the obligations connected with the giving of the Torah (*Lev. Rab.* 1,10, Margulies 24).

The only passage which uses the phrase לקבל תורה of an individual, is 3,6 (Margulies 70). J. Neusner[6] paraphrases: Aaron "accepted upon himself the discipline of the teachings of the Torah (קבל עליו כל דברי תורה) in a spirit of fear, awe, trembling and quaking"; compared with sayings concerning the people of Israel, the wording differs significantly.

Of special interest is *Lev. Rab.* 1,3 (Margulies 12) because of its textual variants. The passage interprets the names in 1 Chron 4:17 allegorically as referring to Moses and his merits: "[Moses was called] 'the son of Nethanel' because he was the son to whom the Torah was given from Hand to hand" (שניתנה לו תורה מיד ליד). MS Oxford 147 reads instead: שנתן הקדוש ברוך הוא על ידו; the *Yalqut* replaces מיד ליד with מיד אל. The manuscript of the British Museum which served as the basis for Margulies' critical edition, introduces the idea of handing on the Torah from God's hand to the hand of Moses, thus speaking of the material copy of the Torah, perhaps even implying the beginning of a chain of transmission, somehow similar to *m. Avot* 1,1, but with the important difference that Moses is not the active subject of the sentence, but the passive recipient of the Torah which is handed over to him. The version of MS Oxford depicts

---

[6] J. Neusner, *The Components of the Rabbinic Documents X. Leviticus Rabbah* (Atlanta, 1997), I 38. Where available, Neusner's translations have been used throughout, adapting them to the context where necessary. In other places the Soncino translations have been used.

Moses as a mere instrument in the giving of the Torah; the reading of the *Yalqut* eliminates the symmetry מיד ליד, emphasizing the
only important hand of God, thus explaining the full name Nethanel.
This is not to suggest that the reading of the *Yalqut* has to be the
"original" and correct reading; important in our context is only the
fact that the scribes of *Lev. Rb.* are still very careful to limit Moses'
role in the giving of the Torah.

The overall picture does not change in the roughly contemporary
Pesiqta deRav Kahana. It is never an individual, but always Israel as
such which receives/accepts the Torah (e.g. 1,2, ed. Mandelbaum
3; 12,1.3, pp. 204–6), whereas the nations of the world do not accept
it (5,2, Mandelbaum 81; 7,12, p. 134). God's act of giving the Torah
is frequently formulated in the passive form (e.g. 5,9, p. 94 זמנה של
תורה שתנתן, "the time for the Torah to be given") or in the abstract
מתן תורה (e.g. 12,11, p. 211: "You should count my reign from the
time of the giving of the Torah," למתן תורה), but also said directly
of God himself (e.g. 12,17, p. 216: "I shall give them the Torah"):
He gives the Torah to Israel, not to Moses or another individual.
Particularly relevant is 12,11 (Mandelbaum 211): "So said the Holy
One, blessed be He, to Moses, 'So that the Israelites should not say,
if it were not for the fact that Jethro came and taught you the laws,
you would not have had the power to give the Torah to us. Therefore
I shall give them the Torah, wholly made up of laws. . . .'" God, not
Moses, gives the Torah to Israel.

There are only two passages which do not fit the pattern observed
until now. In a text published by Mandelbaum as Supplement 1 to
PesK, we read: "In the hour when Moses had the privilege of receiving
the Torah from the hand of the Holy One, blessed be He (שזכה
לקבל את התורה מידו של ברוך הוא), he first said the blessing over the
Torah and then read" (p. 439). At the end of the chapter it is said of
Moses: "His hand received the Torah" (p. 451 שידו קיבל את התורה).
These phrases fit the saying of *m. Avot* 1,1, thus far encountered only
once in all rabbinical texts of the classical period (*y. Sanh*): Here it
is Moses as the chosen leader of God's people and their *shaliaḥ* who
receives the Torah from God's hand in order to hand it on to the
people. But the whole chapter does not belong to the original *Pesiqta
deRav Kahana*, but is a *Yelammedenu*-homily and should not be taken
into account here.

3. The Babylonian Talmud

In the Bavli, most texts speaking of the receiving of the Torah refer to the people of Israel; a number of texts also use the phrase "to accept the Torah" (לקבל עליו/עליהם את התורה). But there are also several passages where Moses is the recipient of the Torah. Thus we read in *b. Er* 18b that a man who "counts out coins into a woman's hand from his own in order to have a chance to stare at her, even if he is like Moses, our master, who received the Torah from Mount Sinai, will not be quit of the judgment of the Gehenna" (cf. *b. Sotah* 4b; another passage where Moses receiving the Torah is mentioned in passing, is *b. Men* 53b). In the midrash on the first chapters of Exodus inserted into *b. Sotah*, the rabbis discuss on which day the child Moses was saved from the Nile. One rabbi suggests that it was the sixth of Sivan and the ministering angels pleaded for Moses before God: "Should he who is destined to receive the Torah at Mount Sinai on this very day be smitten on this very same day?" (*b. Sotah* 12b, cf. *Exod Rab.* 1,24, ed. Shinan 79).

Only two passages offer more than just the formula that Moses received the Torah, and give some details as to the revelation of the Torah. In *b. Shab* 88b, we read: "And said R. Joshua b. Levi: 'When Moses came up on high, the ministering angels said before the Holy One, blessed be He, 'Lord of the world, what is one born of woman doing among us?' He said to them, 'He has come to receive the Torah' (לקבל תורה בא)." When the angels object against giving the Torah to a mortal, Moses is commanded by God to answer them. Moses asks God: "Lord of the world, the Torah that you are giving me (תורה שאתה נותן לי)—what is written in it?" By the contents of the Torah he can convince the angels that it is not for them, but for man. Several times the text repeats "the Torah that you are giving me," and even Satan in search of the Torah asks Moses: "The Torah that the Holy One, blessed be He, gave you—where is it?" (*b. Shab* 89a). To say that the Torah is given to Moses, is the reverse of the phrase that Moses receives the Torah. Both phrases are rather rare in rabbinic texts which prefer to speak of Israel as the recipient of the Torah.

This rather mythological description of Moses receiving the Torah in heaven against the protests of the angels may be compared with the more sober discussion of *b. Yoma* 4a–b. The text states in the name of Resh Laqish: "Moses ascended in a cloud, was covered by a cloud, was sanctified by a cloud, so as to receive the Torah for Israel in sanctity." But after having underlined the role of Moses, the text continues commenting on Exod 24:16: "'Then he called Moses on the seventh day'. Moses and all Israel were standing there. But the purpose of the Scripture is solely to pay respect to Moses." Already before, the Ten Commandments had been given to Israel. Thus when God called to Moses on the seventh day, it was only "to receive the rest of the Torah (Aramaic לקבולי שאר תורה). For if it should enter your mind to suppose that the sense is . . . so as to receive (לקבולי) the Ten Commandments, surely they had already received them on the sixth day and the cloud had departed on the sixth day!" For the present context, there is no need to enter into the details of the talmudic discussion regarding the exact sequence of the revelation of the Torah. What matters, is the fact that the text here attributes to Moses a special role in receiving the Torah, but at the same time tries to maintain the role of the whole people of Israel—if Moses is mentioned separately, it is only to pay him special honor. In agreement with the text of the Bible, one has to accept Moses' special role, but at the same time insists on the fundamental role of Israel as such at Sinai.

4. THE TANHUMA TRADITION

In the *Tanhuma* midrashim the traditional expressions of giving and receiving the Torah are continued, but a new element appears: it is now much more frequent that not only Israel receives the Torah (or the nations refuse to receive/accept it), but Moses as an individual is the receiver. "Our teacher Moses merited receiving the Torah (זכה משה רבינו וקיבלה), for the sole of the Torah is humility and its crown is fear" (*Bereshit* 1). When "Moses and Aaron went up to Mount Sinai with the elders to receive the Torah (לקבל את התורה), the Holy One, blessed be He, kept the elders away" (*Shemot* 24; *TanB Shemot* 21; cf. *Tan Beha'alotkha* 14, *TanB Beha'alotkha* 24; *Exod Rab.* 5,14, ed. Shinan 168; *Num. Rab.* 15,21). Moses had to fast a hundred and twenty days "so that he might receive the Torah" (*Exod Rab.* 47,7); "while Moses was on Sinai receiving the Torah," the people asked Aaron to make them a god (*Exod Rab.* 51,8). *Deut. Rab.* 11,6 gives as the reason for reciting a blessing before the reading of the Torah that "Moses when he had the privilege of receiving the Torah, first recited a blessing and then he read it."

Deut. Rab. 7,8 (*Deut. Rab.* ed. Lieberman 111) even states that the minimum of three verses which the reader of the Torah has to recite, corresponds "to Moses, Aaron and Miriam, through whom the Torah was given" (שניתנה על ידיהן)—no other texts associate Aaron and Miriam with the giving of the Torah! A little later in the same passage we read: "You find that when God gave the Torah to Moses, He gave it to him after 'calling' . . . Also Moses our teacher, when he came to repeat the Torah to Israel, said to them: 'Just as I received the Torah with 'calling,' so too will I hand it over to his children with 'calling'" (כשם שקיבלתי . . . אני מוסר). Here, God gives the Torah to Moses, Moses receives it and hands it over to Israel. The wording of this passage comes very close to that in *m. Avot* 1,1, but here it is still explicitly God who initiates the process.

The tendency encountered in *b. Yoma* 4a-b to acknowledge Moses' special role at the giving of the Torah, but at the same time to limit is as much as possible, is to be seen again in *Exod Rab.* 28. Commenting on Ps 68:19 "Thou hast ascended on high, thou hast led captivity captive. Thou hast received gifts among men," the Midrash speaks of Moses who ascended on high and took away the Torah against the will of the angels; Moses receives it as a gift, but God tells him: "It is only for the sake of Abraham that the Torah is given to you" (28,1). The tension is heightened in 28,3 on Exod 19:8: "God wished at the moment to give them the Torah and to speak with them, but Moses was still standing and God said: 'What can I do because of Moses?'" God does not want that the people mistake his revelation for the word of Moses. "Let Moses, therefore, descend and then I will proclaim: 'I am the Lord thy God' . . . and as Moses descended, God revealed himself, for immediately after it says, So Moses went down unto the people, we are told that God spoke."[7]

It is mainly in the context of Moses' death that his role in receiving the Torah is expanded upon. When Moses went up to the firmament, he was like the angels and spoke with God from face to face "and received the Torah from the hand of the Holy One, blessed be He"; and when the time came that he was to die, he

---

[7] For this passage see C. Thoma – H. Ernst, *Die Gleichnisse der Rabbinen. Vierter Teil: Vom Lied des Mose bis zum Bundesbuch: ShemR 23–30* (Bern, 2000), 105–107.

wanted to be spared this fate: Should the hands which received the Torah from God's hands rot in the dust (cf. *Midrash Mishle* 14,5, ed. Visotzky 120)? The people would say that Moses who went up to heaven and received the Torah from God's hand, had nothing he could answer God (*Tan Wa-ethanan* 6). Five times in this sole chapter (and equally in *TanB Wa-ethanan* 6, twice in *Deut. Rab.* Lieberman *Wa-ethanan* 38–40, and once more in *TanB* Supplement to *Wa-ethanan*) the fact is mentioned that Moses received the Torah from God.

Facing death, Moses pleads: "when I was three months old I prophesied and declared that I was destined to receive the law from the midst of flames of fire . . . and when I was eighty years old . . . I ascended to heaven . . . and engaged in battle with the angels, and received the law of fire . . . and received the Law from the right hand of God, and taught it to Israel," but all this cannot save Moses from death (*Deut. Rab.* 11,6). This last passage is part of the medieval Ashkenazic expansion of the story of Moses' death, not yet present in the Spanish version of Lieberman's edition, but very popular in the different versions of the Midrash *Petirat Mosheh*.

5. OTHER LATE MIDRASHIM

Pesiqta Rabbati 20 is a homily completely dedicated to the revelation of the Torah at Sinai. It may seem astonishing to see that in the first half of this homily Moses is not mentioned even once. The text speaks several times of "the Torah which was given to Israel" (כשניתנה תורה לישראל) or of "God who appeared to give the Torah to his people" (לתת לעמו תורה), but never of Moses. Moses enters the scene only in the second half in a text which vastly expands the description of Moses' heavenly journey in *b. Shab* 88b mentioned above.[8] Moses answers the angel who tries to turn him back: "I am Moses, the son of Amram, who has come to receive the Torah for Israel" (20,11, ed. Ulmer 422). God reminds the angels that they had opposed the creation of man (Ps. 8:5); "now again you rise in quarrelsomeness, and do not let him (mss. Dropsie and Casanata: Me) give the Torah to Israel. But if Israel do not receive the Torah, there shall be no abiding place—neither for Me nor for you" (20,13, Ulmer

---

[8] For this text see the commentary in K.-E. Grözinger, *Ich bin der Herr, dein Gott. Eine rabbinische Homilie zum Ersten Gebot (PesR 20)* (Frankfurt, 1976), 130ff.

424). The difference between the manuscripts is revealing: Ms. Parma and the *editio princeps* attribute the giving of the Torah to Moses (unless we consider the reading לו as a mistake for לי, the other manuscripts to God. But after describing Moses' heavenly visions, the text does not go on to say how he received the Torah and handed it over to Israel, but ends: "Thereupon the Holy One, blessed be He, opened the portals of the seven firmaments and appeared over them and over Israel—eye to eye, in His beauty, in His glory, in the fullness of his stature, with His crown, and upon His throne of glory." In spite of the statement that Moses had gone up to heaven to receive the Torah for Israel, in the end it is God himself who reveals himself to Israel, without the need of a mediator.

PesR 21, a homily dedicated to the revelation of the Ten Commandments, again insists on God directly giving the Torah to Israel and on Israel accepting the Torah whereas the nations of the world refuse it. Only once it is said in the name of R. Yannai: "The Torah which the Holy One gave to Moses, was given to him with forty-nine arguments by which a thing may be proved clean, and forty-nine other arguments by which a thing may be proved unclean" (21,15, Ulmer 452). But here again, Moses plays no particular role.

Midrash Qohelet which may be dated in the late eighth century, has already been referred to in the introduction to this paper. *Qoh. Rab* 12,1 is the only second clear parallel to (quotation from?) *m. Avot* 1,1 after *y. San* 10,1. Apart from this passage, Moses receiving the Torah is mentioned only once in this midrash: Ps 105:8 "The word which He commanded to a thousand generations" teaches "that the Holy One, blessed be He, examined all the vessels but found none so well pitched as that of Moses who stretched forth his hand and received the Torah" (*Qoh. Rab.* 7,41).

Two other texts dating perhaps to the same period are *PRE* 2 which says that a person who resembles a full flowing spring "is able to say more words of Torah than what Moses received from Sinai," and *Seder Eliyahu Zutta* 24,2 (Friedmann Appendix 44): "Even our teacher Moses in his wisdom, although he ascended on high where he received the Torah, was not spared death." A similar statement occurs in *Midrash Psalms* 106:2 (Buber 453): "Not even Moses who went up into heaven and received the Torah from God's hand into his own, could fathom heaven's depth."

6. Conclusions

In this brief survey, we have covered all rabbinic texts from the early and classical period as well as most late midrashic texts which speak of Moses receiving the Torah. The main outcome is the strange isolation of the statement of *m. Avot* 1,1 in the context of rabbinic literature. It is not only the fact that this famous passage about Moses who received Torah from Sinai, is never directly quoted as Mishnah and that its wording is paralleled only twice, first in *y. San* and then, hundreds of years later, again in *Qohelet Rabbah*. More important is the fact that the whole idea expressed by this formula, runs counter to how most rabbinic texts present the revelation of the Torah. All early texts emphasize God's exclusive role in giving the Torah and insist on Israel as people which receives the Torah and to whom it is given by God. Moses is kept in the background.

Moses' role in the scene of the revelation of the Torah becomes more important only rather late, in some texts of the Babylonian Talmud and in texts belonging to the *Tanḥuma* tradition, mainly in the context of the story of Moses' death. This scene has been popular from the earliest period, but it has been changed considerably over the centuries; in the form it has come down to us in the normal text of *Deuteronomy Rabbah* and in the various recensions of the midrash *Petirat Mosheh*, it is clearly medieval. In this mythologically charged story, the role of Moses in receiving the Torah is emphasized as never before; it is mainly in this context that Moses claims in the first person: "I have received the Torah" or "my hands have received the Torah."

Earlier texts seem to be afraid of emphasizing too strongly the role of the mediator Moses. This may be considered a reaction against some conceptions of Moses in Hellenistic and generally Second Temple Judaism; one might also think of Christian ideas as, for example, Paul's epistle to the Galatians 3:19–20 that the law (or Torah) "was ordained by angels through an intermediary. Now an intermediary implies more than one: but God is one." Against such ideas, the *Mekhilta* insists: "'God spoke to Moses' (Exod 31:12)— (directly and) not through an angel or through an intermediary" (*Shabbeta* 1, ed. Horovitz-Rabin 240.)[9] But rabbinic texts do no stop

---

[9] For the larger context of this formula, popular because of its quotation in the Passover Haggadah, see M. Pesce, *Dio senza mediatori. Una tradizione teologica dal giudaismo al cristianesimo* (Brescia, 1979).

here: Moses himself as an intermediary between God and his people has to recede into the background and regains his earlier prominence only centuries later.

But it is not only the role of Moses in *m. Avot* 1,1 which is problematic in early rabbinic thought. The terminology of receiving and handing on the Torah (קיבל/מסר) is frequently regarded as characteristic of the Pharisees to whom some authors would attribute the tractate *Avot* or at least its introductory chain of tradition. Paul's statement in 1 Corinthians 11:23: "For I *received* from the Lord what I also *delivered* to you" is frequently explained on the basis of the word-pair קיבל/מסר in *m. Avot* 1,1.[10] As we have seen, the terminology קיבל/מסר is hardly ever used (apart from *m. Avot*) for the reception and transmission of the Torah or of tradition as such. There are texts like *m. Peah* 2,6 where a chain of tradition is built with forms of קיבל: "I have a tradition from R. Me'asha who received it from his father who received it from the pairs . . ." (שקובל אני . . . שקיבל . . . . . . שקיבל); מסר, however, is not used of handing on the tradition or the Torah, but for delivering material objects or persons.

The linguistic argument is, of course, no absolute evidence for a late dating of this passage and the conceptions it contains. One might still argue that it is early and that it is only by accident that no earlier quotations of the passage are preserved. But such an argument is very precarious; it is much more likely that the text of *m. Avot* 1,1 not only became popular rather late, but that the text *is* late. Already A. Guttmann argued for a late date of the chain of tradition in *m. Avot*;[11] much points to a rather late date of other parts of this tractate as well. One should, therefore, be very careful before using this text as a product of Pharisaic thought and for the interpretation of the New Testament.

---

[10] Many commentators simply rely on (H.L. Strack-) P. Billerbeck, *Kommentar zum Neuen Testament aus Talmud und Midrasch* III, München 1926 (= 9th ed. 1994), 444.

[11] A. Guttmann, "Tractate Abot—Its Place in Rabbinic Literature," *JQR* 41 (1950f) 181–193 (= idem, *Studies in Rabbinic Judaism* [New York, 1976], 102–114), p. 190. He dated it to the post-Talmudic period and understood it in the context of Islam. See also G. Stemberger, "Die innerrabbinische Überlieferung von Mischna Abot," in: H. Cancik, H. Lichtenberger, P. Schäfer (eds.), *Geschichte—Tradition—Reflexion. Festschrift für M. Hengel.* I (Tübingen, 1996), 511–527.

THE WHITE DRESS OF THE ESSENES
AND THE PYTHAGOREANS

Eibert J.C. Tigchelaar*

Dress communicates characteristics of groups and individuals such as, for example, gender, age, ethnicity, social status, sexual availability, occupation, or religious affiliation.[1] In other words, dress is also a code system of non-verbal communication.[2] As with all codes and communications, one should distinguish between the intended meanings of symbols and signs and their perceptions.

In the description of the Essenes in the *Jewish War* (2.119–161), Josephus refers twice to their white dress: they made a point of being always dressed in white (2.123: λευχειμονεῖν διαπαντός), and an axe (or hatchet), a loincloth and white clothing (2.137: λευκὴ ἐσθής) were given to candidates. The loincloth should, of course, also be considered as part of their dress, but I shall mainly focus on the third item, the white dress.

White clothing is, of course, in itself not special, and is found in many cultures and texts.[3] It is interesting, however, that in this case

---

* Groningen.

[1] This first essay of a planned series on the body is dedicated to Ton Hilhorst who on separate occasions expressed to me both his interest in the Essenes, and in clothing in biblical and parabiblical literature. The second part of this contribution was presented as a lecture at the 2002 SBL International Meeting in Berlin. At the final stage of preparing this article I read Jodi Magness's section on "Sectarian clothing," which in several respects agrees with my own conclusions, though we emphasize different aspects.

[2] See, for example, Joanne B. Eicher, "Introduction: Dress as Expression of Ethnic Identity," in *eadem* (ed.) *Dress and Ethnicity. Change Across Space and Time* (Oxford-Washington, D.C., 1995), 1–5 at 1.

[3] See, for example, the Mandaean *rasta*, a white ritual dress worn by priests and laymen, made of a natural fibre, usually cotton or muslin, although silk is allowed. See E.S. Drower, *The Mandaeans of Iraq and Iran. Their Cults, Customs, Magic, Legends, and Folklore* (Oxford, 1937), 30–39. For photographs of the *rasta* see *ASUTA. The Journal for the Study and Research into the Mandaean Culture, Religion, and Language* vol. 2 (http://www.geocities.com/mandaeans/). Or see the descriptions of the Bardesanites: "They all dress in white, with the idea that everyone who wears white belongs to the followers of the Good One, and whoever wears black to those of the Evil One." See H.J.W. Drijvers, *Bardaisan of Edessa* (Assen, 1966), 104, 106–7, 111.

members of a group distinguished themselves from others by the colour of their dress. Texts often refer to white clothes when describing special occasions, such as sacrifices, festivals or processions.[4] It is therefore important that Josephus tells that the Essenes were "always" dressed in white. In this respect they may perhaps be likened to the Pythagoreans. Several sources refer to the whiteness of the clothes of Pythagoras and the Pythagoreans, a group that has been compared, both by Josephus (*Ant.* 15.371), and by modern scholars, with the Essenes.[5] Why were the Pythagoreans dressed in white? Did the Essenes have similar reasons for wearing white clothes?

The Dead Sea Scrolls are the library of a sect that was somehow related to the Essenes.[6] However, none of the preserved texts from these finds describes or prescribes the wearing of white clothes. Nonetheless, one may search for other clues in the scrolls that may relate to the white dress of the Essenes.

THE WHITE DRESS OF THE PYTHAGOREANS

There are many attestations that Pythagoras or the Pythagoreans dressed in white. Aelian (*ca.* 170–235 A.D.) has the anecdotal remark that Pythagoras was dressed in white clothes and wore a golden wreath and trousers.[7] Neo-Pythagorean sources tell that Pythagoras,

---

[4] See, for example, Christopher Jones, "Processional Colors," in Bettina Bergmann, Christine Kondoleon (eds.), *The Art of Ancient Spectacle* (Studies in the History of Art 56; Center for the Advanced Study in the Visual Arts Symposium Papers 34; Washington, 1999), 247–57 on the colours worn in Greek processions, 200 B.C. to 200 A.D.

[5] For a short discussion and bibliography, see John T. Fitzgerald, "Pythagoreans," in Lawrence H. Schiffman, James C. VanderKam (eds.), *Encyclopedia of the Dead Sea Scrolls* (Oxford, 2000), 728–9.

[6] For a succinct overview of scholarship, see Charlotte Hempel, "The Essenes," in Dan Cohn-Sherbok, John M. Court (eds.), *Religious Diversity in the Graeco-Roman World. A Survey of Recent Scholarship* (The Biblical Seminar 79; Sheffield, 2001), 65–80.

[7] Aelian, *Historical Miscellany* 12.32. The topic of the "golden wreath" is related to the idea that Pythagoras was a reincarnation of Euphorbus (Iamblichus, *Pythagorean Life* 63; Ovid, *Metamorphoses* 15.160–165), whose locks were bound in bands of silver and gold (Homer, *Iliad* XVII 66–7). The reference to the trousers seems to be related to his connection with Orpheus from Thracia, a region where people wore trousers. See Walter Burkert, *Lore and Science in Ancient Pythagoreanism* (Cambridge, Ma,, 1972), 165; Christoph Riedweg, *Pythagoras. Leben, Lehre, Nachwirkung. Eine Einführung* (München, 2002), 14, 17. A general study on the study of the symbolism of the colour "white" in Ancient Greece is Gerhard Radke, *Die Bedeutung der weissen und der schwarzen Farbe in Kult und Brauch der Griechen und Römer* (Jena, 1936). See espe-

or his followers, wore a clean or pure (καθαρός) white dress and used clean (or pure) white bed clothes, made of linen, not of skins of animals.[8] These texts do not explicitly give a motivation for this preference for white clothes, nor do they specify what is meant here by καθαρός. Were the dress and bed clothes physically pure, that is, spotless, or were they ritually clean? Both Diogenes Laertius (ca. middle 3rd c. A.D.) and Iamblichus (ca. 240–325 A.D.) rarely use καθαρός or its cognates as "clean" in a physical sense.[9] In the introduction to the *Life of Apollonius of Tyana*, Philostratus (ca. 170–244/249 A.D.) states that Pythagoras "declined to wear apparel made from dead animal products and, to guard his purity, abstained from all flesh diet, and from the offering of animals in sacrifice" (1.1).[10] In his description of the life of Apollonius, which often runs parallel to that of Pythagoras, Philostratus reports that Apollonius declared garments which were made of the hides of dead animals to be impure. Therefore, Apollonius dressed in linen.[11] However, it is not clear to what extent Apollonius' life has been modelled on that of Pythagoras, or the other way around. It is clear, though, that we have here a third-century perception of Pythagoras.

Other "Pythagorean" references to white clothes are found in specific prescriptions attributed to Pythagoras, such as that one should worship the Gods or attend funerals dressed in white or clean/pure clothes.[12] The same terms ("white"; "clean"/"pure") are used, and one may consider the possibility that the Pythagorean way of life is

cially pp. 38–44 on white dress, in particular white funeral dress, and pp. 58–62 on the white dress of priests and worshipers.

[8] Iamblichus, *Pythagorean Life* 100, 149; Apuleius, *Apology* 56 on linen *versus* wool. However, Diogenes Laertius 8.19 says that Pythagoras' bedclothes were of wool, because linen was not yet known in his time. Also Ovid, *Metamorphoses* 15.118–119 indicates that Pythagoras allowed for the use of wool. Perhaps contrast the white bedclothes to the purple-dyed, with gold interwoven, coverlets described by Philo, *On a Contemplative Life* 49.

[9] One of the few exceptions is Diogenes Laertius 5.67, according to whom Lyco kept his dress immaculately clean. See also the designation *toga pura* or *toga virilis* for the woollen white toga of ordinary male Roman citizens.

[10] Translation by F.C. Conybeare, *Philostratus. Life of Apollonius of Tyana* (LCL; Cambridge, Ma., 1912). See also 1.32.

[11] Philostratus, *Life of Apollonius*, 8.7.4. See also 1.8; 6.11.

[12] Diodorus Siculus 10.9.6: one should bring offerings to the Gods, not dressed in expensive, but in bright (λαμπρός), clean clothes; Diogenes Laertius 8.33: one should worship the Gods dressed in white and after purification; Iamblichus, *Life* 153: entering a sanctuary in clean clothes; 155: attending funerals in white dress.

an extension of ritual; it reflects, to some extent, a sacralisation of everyday life. Hence, it may be the case that the Pythagoreans were dressed in white because (at least according to the late *vitae*) they attempted to live in a continuous state of purity.[13]

Several pseudepigraphic neo-Pythagorean writings prescribe that women should be chaste and modest. They should wear white and simple clothes, and refrain from using rouge or ornaments. Thus, for example, the treatise "On the Conduct of a Woman" that is attributed to Phintys, a female member of the Pythagorean community in Croton, and transmitted in Stobaeus' *Anthology* (5th *c.*? A.D.), prescribes that a woman should be dressed in white, natural, and plain clothes (δεῖ λευχείμονα εἶναι καὶ ἁπλοϊκὰν καὶ ἀπερίσσευτον).[14] These should not be transparent, with adornments, or silken, but they should be moderate and white-coloured.[15] This prescription corresponds with the legend that Pythagoras' words to the women of Croton resulted in their putting away of their expensive clothes and adornments, and dedicating them to the temple of Hera Lacinia, of which the excavated treasures show its one-time wealth.[16] Here, white clothes seem to be equivalent to simple clothes, as opposed to expensive or luxurious clothes.

The same concept, namely that Pythagoreans dress in plain clothing, may be found in comedy that ridiculed the Pythagoreans. Aristophon (fr. 12 Kassel-Austin) mocked them for their lice, their worn out garments, and their being unwashed.[17] Likewise, Theocritus'

---

[13] See Riedweg, *Pythagoras*, 90 citing Maurizio Giangiulio, *Ricerche su Crotone arcaica* (Pisa, 1989), 149: "[u]na sorta di ossessione per la purezza rituale."

[14] Text in Holger Thesleff, *The Pythagorean Texts of the Hellenistic Period Collected and Edited* (Acta Academia Aboensis, Ser. A Humaniora 30.1; Åbo, 1965), 151–4.

[15] See also Pseudo-Melissa's *Letter to Kleareta* (2nd *c.* A.D.): the temperate woman should be "clad in neat, simple, white dress without extravagance or excess," "avoid clothing that is either entirely purple, or streaked with purple and gold," and "must not have her heart set on expensive clothing." Text: Thesleff, *The Pythagorean Texts*, 115–16. Text, translation and commentary: Alfons Städele, *Die Briefe des Pythagoras und der Pythagoreer* (Beiträge zur Klassischen Philologie 115; Meisenheim am Glan, 1980), 160–63 and 253–66. Translation: Abraham J. Malherbe, *Moral Exhortation. A Greco-Roman Sourcebook* (Philadelphia, 1986), 83.

[16] Iamblichus, *Life* 56, 187, 205 (on "luxurious clothes"). See also Giangiulio, *Ricerche*, 305–6; Roberto Spadea, "Il tesoro di Hera," *Bolletino d'Arte* 79 (1994 [1996]) 1–34; idem, *Il tesoro di Hera. Scoperto nel santuario di Hera Lacinia a Capo Colonna di Crotone: catalogo* (Milan: ET, 1996); Id., "Santuari di Crotone," in J. de la Genière (ed.), *Héra. Images, espaces, cultes* (Collection du centre Jean Bérard 15; Naples, 1997), 235–59.

[17] But note that in later times the τρίβων, the "threadbare cloak," is almost a

Idyllia (14.5–6) describes the Pythagoreans as "pale" and "unshod."

These statements about the clothing of the Pythagoreans stem from diverse sources from different periods. There is no early evidence that Pythagoras himself dressed in whatever manner, but if Pythagoras really was dressed in white, this might reflect an aristocratic appearance. The Pythagorean prescription that one should wear white when sacrificing might be relatively old. The fragments of Middle Comedy ridicule the poor dress of the later Pythagoreans on two occasions. It is, however, only in neo-Pythagorean texts from Hellenistic and later times that one finds statements that Pythagoras and Pythagoreans wore white. Pseudepigraphic Pythagorean writings like those of Phintys and Melissa prescribe that women are chaste, modest, and dressed in white. The late Pythagorean *vitae* comment on several aspects of dress, namely its colour (white), purity, plainness, and material (linen). According to the different sources the simple white pure linen dress reflects asceticism and frugality, religious purity, or a veganism, which even excluded the use of animal products for clothing.[18] In some cases, these different concepts may have been combined.

The white dress of the Pythagoreans may be contrasted to other dress. Implicitly, the prescription to wear white at funerals is opposed to being normally dressed in black.[19] One should enter a sanctuary blessed in pure (white?) clothes, since black and red are colours of inertia. In neo-Pythagorean prescriptions for women, white clothes are contrasted to expensive clothes in general, whereas especially the colours red and purple, as well as dresses streaked with gold, are frowned upon, since that kind of dress was regarded as the dress of hetaerae.[20] Of course, purple clothes were not only worn by hetaerae. Plato is reported to have refused to dress in purple, because

---

technical term for the Cynics' cloak (although comedy also uses it for Socrates' dress).

[18] In ancient as well as modern vegetarianism and veganism there are several degrees of strictness. For example, according to Chaeremon (Fr. 11 Van der Horst), the ancient priests of Egypt abstained from egg, as if it is meat, and from milk, but nowhere does he refer to the issue of clothes made from animal products.

[19] Iamblichus, *Life* 155.

[20] See Melissa's *Letter to Kleareta*, as well as the laws of Zaleukos at Diodorus Siculus 12.21.1 (forbidding garments with purpled hems unless one is a hetaera). On the dress of hetaerae, see Andrew Dalby, "Levels of Concealment: The Dress of *Hetairai* and *Pornai* in Greek Texts," in Lloyd Llewellyn-Jones (ed.), *Women's Dress in the Ancient Greek World* (London, 2002), 111–24.

that belonged to women's dress.[21] In the neo-Pythagorean *vitae* the linen or white dress and bedclothes are opposed to clothes made of animal skin or even wool. In these late texts wearing white dress implied wearing linen or cotton.

The late neo-Pythagorean texts thus reflect several oppositions: white *versus* coloured, especially red, purple, and gold-coloured; pure *versus* non-pure; simple *versus* expensive and adorned; linen, that is non-animal, *versus* animal skin. Some confusion may arise from the terminology. λευκός may refer to different shades of white, either "un-dyed," or "shining white." In the latter case, often λαμπρός, or another specification is used instead. This distinction more or less corresponds to Latin *albus* and *candidus*. Likewise καθαρός, which may be "spotless," or "pure," largely corresponds to Latin *purus*, "pure," "clean," which in reference to clothes or other textiles often means "simple," "unadorned."

THE DRESS OF THE ESSENES[22]

Philo, the oldest author on the Essenes, described their communal life as well as their frugality and asceticism. He told that "they have clothes and food in common, and that they eat together."[23] These clothes consisted of thick coats (στιφραὶ χλαῖναι) for winter, and cheap tunics (ἐξωμίδες εὐτελεῖς) for summer.[24] In *On A Contemplative Life*, he described the so-called Therapeutes, of which it is a moot point whether they were fictional or really existed, perhaps even as an Egyptian branch of Essenism.[25] Whatever the case, Philo's description of the Therapeutes is often reminiscent of both his own and Josephus' descriptions of the Essenes. The Therapeutes, too, were dressed in extremely cheap (εὐτελεστάτη) clothes, whose only function was to protect against heat and cold: they wore a thick coat

---

[21] Diogenes Laertius 2.78.

[22] The most extensive discussion of the dress of the Essenes appeared just before I finished this article. See now Jodi Magness, *The Archaeology of Qumran and the Dead Sea Scrolls* (Studies in the Dead Sea Scrolls and Related Literature; Grand Rapids MI, 2002), 193–209.

[23] *Prob.* 85–88; *Apology for the Jews* 12.

[24] *Apology for the Jews* 12.

[25] See most recently Troels Engberg-Pedersen, "Philo's *De Vita Contemplativa* as a Philosopher's Dream," *JSJ* 30 (1999) 40–64 with some references to recent discussions; see also Hempel, "The Essenes," 67–8.

(χλαῖνα παχεῖα) in the winter,[26] and a linen tunic (ἐξωμίς ὀθόνη) in the summer.[27] Note that here he refers to the material the clothes are made of, but makes no mention of their colour. This is mentioned only when Philo tells that the Therapeutes gather for their festival meals in shining white garments.[28]

Josephus is more informative about the clothes of the Essenes, but not in a systematic manner. Throughout his account in the second book of the *Jewish War* he touches some ten times upon their clothing. The Essenes made a point of wearing white clothes (λευχειμονεῖν) all the time (*JW* 2.123). Each city had an Essene supervisor who provided (Essene) guests with clothes (ἐσθής) and food (125). With regard to clothes (καταστολή) and attitude they behaved like children that are afraid of their tutors (126). They did not change clothes (ἐσθής) or shoes unless these were entirely worn out (126). In the ritual bath preceding the noon-meal, they covered themselves with linen coverings (σκεπάσματα λινᾶ; 129). After the meal they put their clothes (ἐσθής) away as if they were holy (131). A candidate who wanted to become a member received an axe, a loincloth (περίζωμα) and white clothing (λευκὴ ἐσθής; 137). Their initiation oath contained a clause stating that if one achieve some kind of authority, one should not try to distinguish oneself by means of dress (ἐσθής) or adornments (κόσμος; 140). When defecating into a hole, they wrapped their mantles (ἱμάτιον) around themselves, in order that the excrements could not be seen (148). With regard to the so-called other branch of the Essenes (160–161), who only distinguished

---

[26] *On A Contemplative Life* 38. Here we have a textual problem. The words in between can be read with most MSS ἀπὸ λασίου δορᾶς, "made of hairy skin," the reading of the editio maior of L. Cohn, S. Reiter (eds.), *Philonis Alexandrini Opera quae supersunt VI* (Berlin; 1915) which is adopted by A. Adam, C. Burchard (eds.), *Antike Berichte über die Essener* (Berlin, 1972). On the other hand, F. Daumas, P. Miquel (eds.), *De vita contemplativa* (PAPM, 29; Paris, 1963), 107–8, argue for the *lectio difficilior* ἀντὶ λασίου δορᾶς, "instead of hairy skin." Daumas and Miquel specify χλαῖνα or λαίνα as a coat made either of the fur of an animal, or the skin itself. However, in LXX Prov 31:22 δισσὰς χλαίνας renders מרבדים made of βύσσος, "fine linen."

[27] These are the only two times Philo uses ἐξωμίς. Daumas, Miquel, 108, explain ἐξωμίς as "une tunique courte qui ne comportait qu'une seule manche, et laissait une épaule nue. Elle était portée par des esclaves ou des acteurs tenant leur rôle."

[28] *On A Contemplative Life* 66: λευχειμονοῦντες φαιδροί. This short statement may serve as a contrast to the long description of the extricate and dazzling white dress of the "pretty boys" attending at Italian and Greek banquets in *On A Contemplative Life* 51–52.

themselves from the main branch by marrying and getting children, the women wore a dress (ἔνδυμα), and the men a loincloth (περίζωμα) while bathing (161).

Most of these terms are rather general: ἐσθής, καταστολή, σκεπάσματα, ἱμάτιον, and ἔνδυμα. The only specific word is περίζωμα, "girdle" or "loincloth." The adjective "linen" is used once with regard to the "coverings" with which the Essenes covered themselves in the bath. The colour "white" is mentioned twice: in the general remark that they always wear white clothes, and in the list of things given to the candidate: axe, loincloth, white dress.

The Slavonic version of Josephus' *Jewish War*, and Hippolytus' reworking of Josephus' account, have several explanatory, and therefore probably secondary, variants with regard to the clothes.[29] The most important are the following: both the Slavonic version and Hippolytus describe the loincloth as being linen, and Hippolytus tells that the Essenes cover themselves in the ritual bath with "linen loincloths" (περιζώματα).[30] The Slavonic version describes the clothes worn during the meal as white, whereas Hippolytus identifies these as linen (εἰσι δὲ λιναῖ). The Slavonic version does not refer to a mantle in the account of the toilet practice. In the text corresponding to *JW* 2.126, Hippolytus states that the Essenes did not own two tunics or two pairs of sandals.

Broshi used these data in his fictional "A Day in the Life of Hananiah Nothos. A Story."[31] I quote the sections dealing with dress:

> they wore the same clothes day and night . . . dressed in tattered sandals and ragged clothes, white garb that had known better times . . .
> Squatting, he took care to cover his lower body with his mantle, which he had with him at all times, even on hot days, when he brought it

---

[29] For a synoptic comparison of the Greek texts of Josephus, *JW* 2.119–161 and Hippolytus, *Ref.* 9.18.2–28 see C. Burchard, "Die Essener bei Hippolyt," *JSJ* 8 (1977) 1–41.

[30] This seems to be implied in Josephus' description. The Essenes covered themselves with linen coverings in the purificatory bath (2.129). Later on, in 2.138, Josephus refers to the *"already mentioned* loincloth," even though this is the first time he uses the word περίζωμα in his account. Since 2.161 states that the men of the other branch of the Essenes wore loincloths in bath, the identification of the "linen coverings" with the "loincloth" seems evident.

[31] Magen Broshi, "A Day in the Life of Hananiah Nothos," in A. Roitman (ed.), *A Day at Qumran: The Dead Sea Sect and Its Scrolls* (Jerusalem, 1997), 61–70, incorporated in Magen Broshi, *Bread, Wine, Walls and Scrolls* (JSPSS, 36; Sheffield, 2001), 284–95. Note that Broshi transposes the account of the Essenes to the Qumran Community.

along expressly for this purpose.... After bathing, naked except for
loincloths, they changed into neat, white dress ... After the meal, everyone changed back into shabby dress and returned to work ... In the
evening ... they immersed themselves once again, changed into white
garments, and set down for the evening meal.

Apart from the sandals, this story distinguishes four items of dress:
a shabby everyday garment (ἐσθής) that was white and ragged; a
mantle (ἱμάτιον) against the cold, that was also used for covering
one's lower body if one had to move one's bowels; a loincloth
(περίζωμα) to be used while bathing and a neat white dress (ἐσθής)
for use during the communal meals.[32] Strictly speaking, the different
terms ἐσθής *versus* ἱμάτιον need not imply that the Essenes possessed
both a garment and a mantle. Like Cynics and other ascetics, they
might have possessed only one single garment.[33]

Josephus does not elaborate on the dress worn during the meal,
and only states that they were put away as if they were holy (2.131),
which reflects the description of the priests' linen clothes in Ezek.
44:17–19. Since the Essenes preferred to dress always in white, Broshi
assumes (with the Slavonic version) that the dresses are white and
neat. Many scholars assume that they are made of linen,[34] because
they identify these clothes with the "linen coverings,"[35] because of
Hippolytus' identification, because of Philo's remark on the Therapeutes,
or because of the correspondence to Ezek. 44:17–19.[36]

What was the white dress (λευκὴ ἐσθής) given to the candidates?
The Greek expression, grammatically singular, need not indicate one
single item of clothing, "a white garment,"[37] since ἐσθής often serves
as a general term for clothing.[38] Some have surmised that the white

---

[32] Magness, *Archaeology*, 194, 201–2, does not distinguish between the everyday
garment and the communal dress, and merely refers to tunic, mantle, and loincloth.

[33] Data on the phenomenon of wearing only one single garment or cloak are
gathered in J.N. Bremmer, "Symbols of Marginality from Early Pythagoreans to
Late Antique Monks," *Greece & Rome* 39 (1992) 205–14 at 206–7. See also Hippolytus's
statement that the Essenes did not own two tunics.

[34] For example, Catherine M. Murphy, *Wealth in the DSS and in the Qumran
Community*, 432: "the white linen garment worn during the meal."

[35] Todd Beall, *Josephus' Description of the Essenes Illustrated by the Dead Sea Scrolls*
(SNTSMS, 58; Cambridge, 1988), 46: "And in *JW* 2 § 131 the Essenes' linen (2
§ 129) garments are laid down after breakfast 'as holy things.'" But see also p. 75
where he identifies the "wraps" with the "loincloth."

[36] Magness, *Archaeology*, 201–2.

[37] As, for example, Beall, *Josephus' Description*, 17.

[38] This certainly goes for Josephus, where ἐσθής is the common word for cloth-

dress given to the novices was the garment worn at the communal meal.[39] However, since Josephus explicitly mentions that the Essenes were always dressed in white, the white clothing given to the novices probably included the daily tunic.[40]

WHY WEAR WHITE CLOTHES?

Why did the Essenes always wear white? The meaning of the terms λευκός and לבן, and the codes in Antiquity and Early Judaism relating to the colour white, have been discussed comprehensively.[41]

An association between whiteness and purity is not only attested in Greek society, but also in the Hebrew Bible and later Jewish sources. Hence, ritual purity may have been behind the Essene preference for white garments,[42] but one would like to know the precise relation. White clothes make it easy to detect spots, which would help to determine whether one has been stained or polluted in some manner.[43] The Mishnah gives suggestions about how to ascertain whether a stain is blood or dye,[44] a procedure, which would not be necessary if clothes were white and hence un-dyed. However, not

---

ing. On the other hand, in the LXX and the NT, ἐσθής is much less common, and usually refers to a robe. In those corpora ἱμάτιον is the more common word.

[39] Alfred Edersheim, *The Life and Times of Jesus the Messiah Vol. 1* (London, 1887⁴), 327: "a white dress, which was always worn, the festive garment at meals being of linen"; Pieter Willem van der Horst, *Bronnen voor de studie van de wereld van het vroege Christendom. 1. Joodse Bronnen* (Kampen, 1997), 158 n. 744 and 159 n. 753; A.I. Baumgarten, "He Knew that He Knew that He Knew that He was an Essene," *JJS* 48 (1997) 53–61 at 55.

[40] Beall, *Josephus' Description*, 75.

[41] See, for example, W. Michaelis, "λευκός, λευκαίνω," in *TDNT* IV, 241–50; H. Ringgren, "לבן," in *TWAT* IV, 451–4; Athalya Brenner, *Colour Terms in the Old Testament* (JSOTSS, 21; Sheffield, 1982), 81–94.148–9.180; Gildas Hamel, *Poverty and Charity in Roman Palestine, First Three Centuries C.E.* (University of California Publications: Near Eastern Studies 23; Berkeley, 1989) 82–6. Many references to white clothes are found in Ulrich H.J. Körtner and Martin Leutzsch, *Papiasfragmente. Hirt des Hermas* (Schriften des Urchristentums 3; Darmstadt, 1998), 386 n. 71 and 480 n. 202.

[42] Beall, *Josephus' Description*, 46.

[43] See Hamel, *Poverty and Charity*, 83–4; Yigael Yadin, *The Finds from the Bar Kokhba Period in the Cave of Letters* (Jerusalem, 1963), 229: wearing white clothes would "facilitate the keeping of the various *halakhoth*, especially those of cleanness." The problem with this explanation is that white clothes may remain ritually clean, even if they become dirty. Thus, for example, the Mandaean *rasta* may not be washed with soap and becomes stained due to the mud of the river. See Drower, *Mandaeans*, 32.

[44] *m. Nid.* 9:6.

all spots render one impure, and physical stains need not accompany impurity. Since Josephus (*JW* 2.123) mentions the preference for white clothes together with their avoidance of oil, there may be a connection: "the Essenes attached importance to white garments out of fear of contact with oil."[45] White clothes would enable one to easily detect whether one had been defiled with a drop of oil. However, the idea that the Essenes dressed in white merely in order to be able to detect spots of oil looks somewhat far-fetched. Also, one wonders to what extent such a functionalist explanation is compatible with the statement that clothes were worn until they were rags (*JW* 2.126).

The Essene white dress might have been a symbol of purity, just like the white priestly clothes. This could apply to the dress worn during the communal meals, which Josephus describes as a sacred meal. After their meals they put down the clothes worn during the meal "as sacred" (ὡς ἱεράς). "Sacred clothes" are used only with regard to the priests, who indeed put down their sacred clothes before leaving the sanctuary.[46] Yet, "white garb" was only one of the dresses of priests,[47] who dressed on other occasions in coloured vestments. More importantly, this explanation of the white clothes during meals does not explain why white dresses were worn everyday.[48]

---

[45] Lutz Doering, "Purity Regulations Concerning the Sabbath in the Dead Sea Scrolls and Related Literature," in Lawrence H. Schiffman, Emanuel Tov, and James C. VanderKam (eds.), *The Dead Sea Scrolls: Fifty Years after Their Discovery. Proceedings of the Jerusalem Congress, July 20–25, 1997* (Jerusalem, 2000), 600–609 at 603.

[46] See Ezek 42:14; 44:19 and Lev 16:23.

[47] The high-priest wore white garments on the Day of Atonement. See *m. Yoma* 3:6; 7:1.4.

[48] Magness, *Archaeology*, 200–202, does not distinguish between the everyday white dress of the Essenes ("sectarian men") and the linen "sacred" dress worn during communal meals. I agree with her argument that "white" should be equated with "undyed," but her equation "white" is "undyed" is "linen" is problematic. First, Magness claims (194–5) that Josephus "made a special point of describing their loincloths as linen." However, Josephus uses the adjective λίνον only once without any special emphasis. Moreover, none of our sources claims that the everyday white dress was linen. All these texts, implicitly or explicitly, regard the loincloth and the communal "sacred" attire as linen. Second, other Jewish texts (see below) contrast "white" to "coloured," and not "linen" to "wool." Third, Magness's argument that linen was difficult to dye, "especially with colors of decorative patterns," does not mean that undyed clothes as such were linen. There were also white woollen clothes and dyed linen clothes. Fourth, though tunics could be linen, this is much less to be expected of mantles (see also Philo). Magness, 200, poses the question: "Was the white clothing a result of wearing linen or was linen chosen because it is white?"

Alternatively, there might have been a connection between the white dress of the Essenes and the bright dress that is sometimes worn by angels.[49] For example, the white *rasta* of the Mandaeans, also called the "garment of splendour" (עוצטלא דזיוא), is symbolic of the heavenly dress of light which is worn by the angels.[50] Similarly, Adam's "garments of light" are associated with paradise and priesthood.[51] Josephus does not refer explicitly to a correspondence between angels and Essenes. However, the Dead Sea Scrolls show that there were groups related to the Essenes who wanted to imitate the angels in as many respects as possible. The wearing of white clothes may therefore have been part of an *imitatio vitae angelicae*. This, in fact, would explain διαπαντός "all the time." That is, the Essenes always wore white clothes, not only during meals.[52]

Later Rabbinic texts connect whiteness and purity to nobility. Only the noble and well to do could afford dressing in shining white. Moreover, it was a symbol of exemption from manual labour. However, it is hard to reconcile the image of noble Essenes clad in shining white dress, with that of the same Essenes dressed in rags.[53]

In his study of Jewish sects, Albert Baumgarten touches upon the dress of John the Baptist, Bannus and the Essenes, but does not discuss the whiteness of the Essenes' dress. Instead, he departs from the other aspects given by Josephus and Philo: the cheapness and plainness of their dress, without marks of distinctions, and worn until rags. With regard to dress, Bannus and the Essenes openly displayed disdain towards modern tastes, and adopted "particular forms of dress" as "a means of expressing opposition to contemporary prac-

---

My answer is that undyed linen, as well as undyed wool, could have been chosen because they were "white."

[49] Often the appearance and dress of angels is described as shining white. See, for example, *TestLevi* 8:2; *1 Enoch* 71:1; Matth 28:3 (Mark 16:5; Luke 24:4); John 20:12; Acts 1:10; 10:30; part of the transfiguration of Jesus is the whitening of his clothes (Matth 17:2; Mark 9:3; Luke 9:29).

[50] F.M. Braun, "Le Mandéisme et la secte essénienne de Qumrân," in *L'Ancien Testament et l'Orient. Études présentées aux VIes Journées Bibliques de Louvain (11–13 septembre 1954)* (Orientalia et Biblica Lovaniensia, 1; Louvain, 1957), 193–230 argues for a connection between Essenes and Mandaeans, and refers, *inter alia*, to the white dress (at 217).

[51] The colour white as the colour of the future life of the elect in Rev 3:4–5, and *Hermas*, Vis. IV 3.

[52] See Drower, *Mandaeans*, 36: "Mandaeans are fond of telling me that at one time they always wore white, and that it was a sin to wear a colour."

[53] Hamel, *Poverty and Charity*, 69 n. 88, refers to this "apparent contradiction."

tices" such as nudity in the gymnasium, and new fashions such as wearing a Greek hat.[54]

The whiteness of the Essenes' dress should also be regarded as a statement regarding contemporary practices. One of those practices which seems to have raised controversy is touched upon in the *Epistle of Enoch*:

> For men will put on adornments as women,
>   and fair colours more than virgins.[55]

This section describes the "extravagant behavior of the rich . . . include extraordinary dress and adornment, with men exceeding what is proper for their sex and status. . . ."[56] Also other Jewish texts attest that, in Hellenistic and Roman times, some men wore multi-coloured garments, a dress thought to be typical of women.[57] A late third- or early second-century B.C. opposition against dyed garments is to be found in the story of the Watchers in *1 Enoch* 8, according to which Asael taught men "concerning antimony and eye paint and all manner of precious stones and dyes." Therefore, one can read the "white garments" of the Essenes as a social, and perhaps also political, statement: the Essenes opposed the dress of the rich who followed modern fashion by wearing expensive coloured garments.

This interpretation goes well with the other aspects of Essene dress, all of which may be read as a political statement or conservative reaction against contemporary society. First, the Essenes wore standard uniform clothes: the "sense of equality of the group . . . was thus reinforced." At the same time this was a criticism of a society with a high degree of inequality. Second, their dress was distinctive for its simplicity and plainness (Philo), a statement against extravagance

---

[54] A. Baumgarten, *The Flourishing of Jewish Sects in the Maccabean Era: An Interpretation* (JSJS 55; Leiden, 1997), 100–101; "He Knew that He Knew," 56; Likewise, Magness, *Archaeology*, 203–4, relates the Essenes' dress to an 'anti-Hellenizing sentiment."

[55] *1 Enoch* 98:2, translation of G.W.E. Nickelsburg, *1 Enoch 1: A Commentary on the Book of 1 Enoch Chapters 1–36, 81–108* (Hermeneia; Philadelphia, 2001).

[56] Nickelsburg, *Enoch*, 475.

[57] See Josephus *BJ* 4.561–565: the Zealots dressed themselves in "women's dress," that is, multi-coloured garments. The *Book of the Laws of Countries* describes the Laws of the Geli, according to which women do not wear colourful clothes or shoes, and do not use fragrant oils, whilst their husbands wear colourful clothing, adorn themselves and use oils. However, the point is that they do things different from other nations. See text in H.J.W. Drijvers, *The Book of the Laws of Countries. Dialogue on Fate of Bardaisan of Edessa* (Semitic Texts with Translations, 3; Assen, 1965), 44–5.

of the rich. Third, the Essenes displayed an open disdain for clothing, expressed by wearing clothes until they were rags, thereby pro-
claiming "their devotion to a higher way of life."[58]

One may add to this list the strict avoidance of unnecessary nudity,
possibly as a reaction to the Hellenistic practice of nude exercises
in the gymnasium. The loincloth ("a distinctively Essene article of
dress")[59] by which one should cover one-self, even during a bath, is
an expression of resistance towards gentile uncovering.

Josephus discusses the avoidance of oil and the preference for
white clothes in the same section, and partly even in the same clause.
He writes:

> Oil they consider staining, and anyone who is accidentally anointed
> with it scours his body; for they think it good to keep a dry skin and
> to be always dressed in white.

Is there any connection between the two, either in the eyes of the
beholder, or in the mind of the Essenes? The verb generally translated "to keep a dry skin" is αὐχμεῖν, "to be squalid, dirty or
unwashed." In view of the Essenes' daily ritual baths this probably
does not mean that the Essenes made a point of being unwashed
or dirty, but apparently that they did not want to use oil on their
skin. In the eyes of Roman beholders, who used oil in their bath-
houses, this may have been the same as being unwashed. In earlier
scholarly literature the avoidance of oil was related to the frugality
or asceticism or the Essenes; the use of perfumed oil would be an
extravagance to be avoided.[60] At the same time, the open avoidance
of oil would express opposition towards the rich. One may note that
the exact opposite of the Essenes is found in the Zealots, who, according to Josephus, dressed in multi-coloured garments, and drenched
themselves in perfumed oil.[61]

The avoidance of oil may have been related to halakhic concerns
about the purity and impurity of oils.[62] The issue is not easy to
understand for those uninitiated in halakha, but it boils down to the
fact that oil is not in itself impure, but can easily transmit impurity:

---

[58] Citations in this section are from Baumgarten, *Flourishing of Jewish Sects*, 101.
[59] Magness, *Archaeology*, 201.
[60] See also John 12:3–5.
[61] Josephus *JW* 4.561.
[62] J. Baumgarten, "The Essene Avoidance of Oil and the Laws of Purity," *RevQ*
4 (1967) 183–93.

the Essenes avoided oil because of the risks of the transmission of impurity. This halakhic background of the avoidance of oil raises the question whether one should not also consider the possibility of a halakhic background for the wearing of white clothes. In this connection one should be aware that Josephus writes for a Greek audience, and does not elaborate all the reasons for the Essenes' behaviour.

A possible halakhic background for the preference for white clothing stems from the interpretation of Deut 22:5 which prohibits transvestism:

> No woman shall wear an article of man's clothing (כלי גבר), nor shall a man put on a woman's dress (שמלת אשה); for those who do these things are abominable to the Lord your God.

In parts of modern Judaism and Christianity this is taken to mean that a woman should not wear pants or trousers, but *Sifre Deuteronomy* § 226 shows that in Antiquity some people thought that this meant

> that a woman shall not wear white clothes (כלי לבנים), and that a man shall not cover himself with coloured clothes (כלי צבעונים).[63]

Indeed, both *1 Enoch* 98:2 and Josephus' description of the Zealots qualify brightly coloured garments as women's dress, a point which was more or less substantiated by Yadin's study of the garments of the Cave of Letters. In reality, this difference was a matter of degree: "the ground of men's civilian cloth was typically white, or undyed, while that of women was often coloured."[64] It is plausible that the Essenes, who in many respects seem to have been rather strict, interpreted this to mean that they should wear white.

However, the preference for white clothes might perhaps also have been related to an entirely different halakhic concern, namely the origin of the dyes. The Mishna explicitly forbids the use of dyes made from the rinds of fruits, such as nuts or pomegranates, which were still *orlah*.[65] According to Lev 19:23–25 one may not use the

---

[63] In general, the distinction is between undyed white clothes and dyed coloured clothes. See Samuel Krauss, *Talmudische Archäologie I* (Hildesheim, 1966 reprint), 145.

[64] A. Sheffer, H. Granger-Taylor, "Textiles from Masada: A Preliminary Selection," in *Masada IV: The Yigael Yadin Excavations 1963–1965; Final Reports* (Jerusalem, 1994), 260.

[65] See *m. Orlah* 3.1: a garment which one dyed with rinds of *orlah* has to be burned. See also the case in 3.2 about the thread dyed with rinds of *orlah* woven into a garment. Some textiles found at Masada were dyed with dyes made of pomegranates (see *Masada IV*, 260). On the use of nuts and pomegranates for brown and yellow dyes, see R.J. Forbes, *Studies in Ancient Technology. Volume IV* (Leiden, 1956), 122–4.

fruits of newly planted trees for three years, whereas the fruit of the fourth year is for the heave-offering. Only in the fifth year one may use the fruits of newly planted trees. Is it likely that the Essenes wore white clothes because they wanted to avoid the risk of the use of dyes that were made of rinds of *orlah* fruit? Both in the case of the avoidance of oil as well as of dyes the matter is not that "oil" or "dyes" in themselves are impure or unfit, but that the Essenes, in matters of doubt, wanted to avoid all risks.

In either case, the point about the white dress is that they were undyed or colourless. The complete avoidance of dyes or of coloured garments also implied that the Essenes had no coloured vertical strokes (*clavi*) on their tunics, or notched bands on their mantles, but plain clothes, just as Philo tells.[66] Josephus probably refers to the same point when he relates that the Essenes swore that they would not express their leadership by means of dress or adornments. One of the accepted manners to express one's social position in one's dress was the breadth of the *clavi*. The Essene non-use of the coloured *clavi* would automatically result in a dress without any marks or signs expressing leadership.[67]

Josephus' description of manners and dress of the Essenes is comparable to anecdotes in Greek literature about dress, appearance and behaviour of philosophers or members of a school, such as Cynics, Pythagoreans, or gymnosophists. This description does not serve to characterize the Essenes in their own terms, but to highlight certain features for a foreign audience. Josephus' interpretation of the Essene custom of avoiding oil is his "attempt to explain to his Greek readers (or to himself) the reason for the custom practiced by the Essenes without, however, being properly informed."[68] Perhaps Josephus knew the reasons for the Essenes' white dress, but he did not think it necessary to explain them to a non-Jewish audience.

How would the Essenes themselves have regarded the matter of dress? Josephus tells that each novice received an axe, a linen loincloth, and white dress. The first two items are related to a new kind

---

[66] See also the more exhaustive discussion in Magness, *Archaeology*, 195–6.

[67] On the absence of decorations on the tunics of slaves see Hamel, *Poverty and Charity*, 77–8.

[68] Meir Bar-Ilan, "The Reasons for Sectarianism According to the Tannaim and Josephus' Allegation of the Impurity of Oil for the Essenes," in Schiffman, Tov, and VanderKam (eds.), *The Dead Sea Scrolls*, 587–99 at 598.

of physical behaviour. The axe has to be used to dig a hole in the
ground, into which one should defecate, and which one should thereafter fill again with earth.[69] The loincloth should be used to cover
one's loins, instead of being naked whenever one bathed. Both items
are related to everyday (or almost everyday) behaviour, which was
different from that one was used to before applying for Essene
membership.

   At first sight, the white dress does not have a new instrumental
function like the other two, although Magness calls attention to
another aspect, related to the wearing of linen, namely that linen,
contrary to wool, would cause less sweat.[70] The important point here
is the function of the white dress as compared to clothes in general.
The issue was not only a halakhic one, related to dyes, but also a
social and political one. Wearing white clothes without distinctive
marks was an act of protest against a society of inequality, extravagance, and the blurring of distinctions between men and women.
Giving a white dress to a novice was a kind of first initiation rite,
by which the novice was asked to commit himself to the way of life
of the group.

   Social function should not be confused with halakhic reasoning.
The Enochic *Book of Watchers*, which is often labelled as "Essene,"
bluntly ascribes the art of dyeing to the wrong teachings of Asael.
The least we can say is that we have a second century B.C. text that
is critical of dyes. The possibility that dyes are unfit, for example
because of *orlah*, is not enough reason to avoid coloured clothes altogether. One could have ruled out certain kinds of dyes and toler-
ated other kinds. Yet, in a group which was very strict in all kinds
of respects, one may expect this kind of ruling, namely that it is best
to avoid dyes altogether. This relatively minor halakhic point may
have been one of the main markers of Essene identity.

COMPARING PYTHAGOREANS AND ESSENES

Correspondences between Essenes and Pythagoreans have been
observed from Antiquity up to modern times. With regard to the

---

[69] See recently A. Baumgarten, "The Temple Scroll, Toilet Practices and the
Essenes," *Jewish History* 10 (1996) 9–20.
[70] Magness, *Archaeology*, 201.

white dress of both groups one encounters the problem that the
sources are not explicit with regard to the reasons for being dressed
in white, and that the descriptions stem from different times. The
reasons seem to have evolved in Pythagoreanism. Based on the analysis given above, one may observe the following correspondences and
differences. Both Pythagoreans and Essenes promote a life of asceticism
and frugality and are opposed against extravagance and immodesty.
Hence both groups favour the wearing of plain simple white clothes
instead of expensive extravagant dyed clothes. In neo-Pythagorean
texts such white clothes are called "pure." This is not explicitly the
case in Josephus, but may be implied. In both cases the wearing of
white sets these groups apart from other groups and society at large.
Yet, the reasons for wearing white are not in all respects the same.
In neo-Pythagoreanism, "white" or "pure" dress is identical to clothing made of non-animal material, though some authors seem to per-
mit wool. In the descriptions of the Essenes we do not see such a
vegan approach. On the other hand, the Pythagoreans do not share
the halakhic reasons for avoiding dyed clothes.

Both in Pythagorean texts and in some Jewish texts like *1 Enoch*,
dyed or coloured garments are associated with hetaerae or lustful
women, whereas white is the colour of chastity. The preference for
the "virginal" colour white thereby also expresses the attitudes of
these groups towards immodest female sexual behaviour, and, in
extension, towards sex in general. As such, white dress also expresses
an ascetic puritan attitude towards the body. In this respect, the
Essene white dress belongs to the same category as the axe and the
loincloth, namely that each of these three items, which were given
to candidates, are related to rules that restrict bodily behaviour.

APPENDIX: QUMRAN AND WHITE CLOTHING

Did the members of the Community living near Qumran dress like
the Essenes? Among the textiles found at Qumran, none has positively been identified as belonging to garments. This is in distinction
to the finds in the Cave of Letters, and in Masada, where many
remnants of garments have been found.[71]

---

[71] For a succinct description of the textiles, see Magness, *Archaeology*, 196–7.

None of the Dead Sea Scrolls refers explicitly to axe, loincloth, or white dress, nor does any of the preserved fragments refer to the wearing of white clothes or avoidance of coloured clothes or dyes. For want of direct evidence, scholars refer to 1QM VII 10–11, which describes the clothes of seven priests participating in the battle against the enemy. These are qualified as "garments of white byssus" (בגדי שש לבן), and it has been suggested that

> the addition of "linen" to every item, including the girdle, plus the special emphasis on "white," may well be an indication of the Essene fondness for white garments.[72]

However, the enumeration of the list of clothes of the priests is largely dependent on Lev 16:4, the clothes which the high-priest is to wear on Yom Kippur, and there is no reason to relate this to the Essenes.

Indirect evidence concerning Qumran sectarian clothing and attitudes towards dress may be found in isolated remarks. The *Community Rule* discusses the person who takes out "his hand" from under his clothes while he is dressed in rags so that his nakedness becomes visible.[73] It is not certain that the text really refers to rags, or whether "his hand" should be interpreted literally, or as a euphemism for one's penis. Yet, the rule fits Josephus' statement that the Essenes wore their clothes until they were no more than rags.

A fragmentary text called *Ordinances* (4Q159) expands on the commandment against transvestism of Deut 22:5:

> No woman shall wear man's clothes (כלי נבר). [No man is to] [7]be covered with woman's mantles (שלמות אשה), and he is not to dress in a woman's tunic (כתונת אשה), for such is an abomination (4Q159 2–4 6–7).[74]

The formulation is close to that in Deut 22:5, but includes the reference to a woman's tunic. Above we saw that archaeological findings and textual evidence indicate that one of the main differences between men's and women's clothes were the colours. The typically sectarian formula which is found in fragment 5 of the work, "interpretation

---

[72] Beall, 79; see also Magness, *Archaeology*, 202.

[73] 1QS VII 13–14. The key words are והואה פוח, "while he is dressed in rags" and ידו "his hand." See the discussion by Magness, *Archaeology*, 194.

[74] DJD, V, 8. A similar rule against transvestism has been reconstructed by Joseph Baumgarten, in 4Q271 3 3–4 (DJD, XVIII, 175–6).

of,"[75] may suggest that this was a sectarian text, even though the
ordinances discuss matters such as marriage.[76] This "ordinance" consists of scattered quotations of the biblical text. The inclusion of the
rule on transvestism indicates that it was considered relevant, and it
may have served as a basis for wearing white clothes. In this connection one should note that the Hebrew Bible rarely relates Israelite
men to coloured clothes (except of course in the case of ritual dress
of priests). The main exception is Joseph, if the כתנת הפסים in Gen
37 is, as suggested by the LXX, a many-coloured tunic (χιτῶν ποικίλος).
Perhaps it is for this reason that *Jubilees* 34 does not refer to the
multi-colouredness of this dress at all.

Indirect evidence for a negative judgment of coloured clothes is
present in the so-called *Visions of Amram*, found in multiple copies in
Qumran cave 4. Amram sees two angels in a vision, apparently the
angel of light and the angel of darkness, fighting over his own soul.
The text proceeds with a very damaged description of the appearance and names of these two angels. The description of the colour
and dress of the angel of light has not been preserved in the *Visions
of Amram*, but one may assume that these were white or luminous.
The point of interest here is that the description of the angel of
darkness says that "all his clothing was coloured" (צבענין).[77] This is
the same word that is used in the Midrash of Shemichazah and
Asael, which tells the secrets revealed by the Watchers to mankind
(corresponding to *1 Enoch* 8:1).[78] In this respect, there may be a connection between these *Visions of Amram* and the sixth Similitude of
the *Shepherd of Hermas*, where the angel of luxury and deceit appears
as a shepherd dressed in saffron-coloured clothes (τῷ χρώματι κροκώδη).[79]

---

[75] 4Q159 5 1 פשר] and 5 4 פשר הדבר].

[76] F.D. Weinert, "4Q159: Legislation for an Essene Community outside of
Qumran?" *JSJ* 5 (1974) 179–207 at 203 argues that frag. 5 "is not originally derived
from the same text as 4Q159," but the hand seems to be identical. Also L.H.
Schiffman, in J.H. Charlesworth *et alii* (eds.), *The Dead Sea Scrolls. 1. Rule of the
Community and Related Documents* (Tübingen-Louisville, 1994), regards frag. 5 as a sep-
arate composition.

[77] 4Q543 5–9 5 and 4Q544 1 13. See now the official edition by É. Puech in
DJD XXXI.

[78] See the text and translation in J.T. Milik, *The Books of Enoch. Aramaic Fragments
of Qumrân Cave 4* (Oxford, 1976), 322–9: "And 'Aza'el was appointed chief over all
kinds of dyes (צבעונים) and over all kinds of women's ornaments by which they
entice men to unclean thoughts of sin" (in some of the versions this phrase occurs
twice in the Midrash).

[79] J.T. Milik, "4QVisions de 'Amram et une citation d'Origène," *RB* 79 (1972)

In the Greek world dyes made from saffron stigmas were particularly associated with hetaerae. And, of course, as the most expensive spice in the world it is associated with luxury.

To sum up: the community that lived at Qumran cannot directly be identified with the Essenes described by Philo and Josephus, and there is no direct evidence that the Qumranites dressed in white. Nonetheless, indications in the texts preserved at Qumran do suggest that they too would have shared the same criticisms towards and avoidance of coloured clothes.[80]

77–97 at 81–2. See *Hermas* 61.5–62.1 (Sim. VI 1,5–2,1). For an overview of interpretations of this yellow dress see Norbert Brox, *Der Hirt des Hermas* (KAV 7; Göttingen, 1991), 334. See also Leutzsch, *Hirt des Hermas*, 475 n. 137.

[80] I would like to thank Jan Bremmer for his critical reading of an earlier version of this paper, and his many helpful bibliographical references on the Pythagoreans.

ORIGEN ON THE *ASSUMPTION OF MOSES*

JOHANNES TROMP*

At some time in the early first century C.E., in Jewish Palestine, a writing was composed in which the history of the Israelite people was related, extending from the entry into the promised land up to and including the end of time. This survey was cast in the mould of a prophecy revealed by Moses to Joshua, his successor as the leader of the people. To this prophecy the author attached a dialogue between Moses and Joshua, in which the former expressed words of reassurance to the latter, who doubted his capability of fulfilling his task of bringing the people into the land successfully. The writing was probably concluded by the story of Moses' death, and his assumption into heaven; this concluding part of the writing is lost. The writing was entitled the *Assumption of Moses* (*As. Mos.*) or, in Greek (quite possibly the language in which it was originally written): the ἀνάληψις Μωϋσέως.

There must have been some interest in this small book in the early church. It was known to several authors, including the theologian Origen (185–253/4) and the church historian Gelasius of Cyzicus († 476), who both have explicitly referred to it. The earliest reference to the *As. Mos.* is most likely that found in the Epistle of Jude (vs. 9). The *As. Mos.* was translated into Latin, and copied at least once, presumably in the sixth century C.E.

The production of this copy is the last trace of interest in the *As. Mos.* until its rediscovery in the nineteenth century. Some thousand years before that rediscovery, the text of this copy was sacrificed for the *Excerpts from Augustine* by Eugippius († after 533):[1] in a time when parchment was scarce, the pages of the codex containing the *As. Mos.* were erased and re-used for what was then considered a more useful purpose. With great difficulty, and not without damaging the material, the lower scripture could be deciphered for the edition of the text in 1861.

---

* Leiden.
[1] A.-M. Ceriani, "Fragmenta Parvae Genesis et Assumptionis Mosis ex veteri versione latina," in: *id., Monumenta sacra et profana* I (Milan, 1861), 11b.

In the course of time, the codex containing Eugippius' *Excerpts* disintegrated, and the pages containing the final part of the *As. Mos.* were lost. The disappearance of this final part of the *As. Mos.* is a loss both for students of early Judaism, and for students of the early church. There is reason to believe that Christians were interested in that part in particular: all extant citations but one refer to a scene in which the corpse of Moses was the object of a dispute between the archangel Michael and the devil. In fact, the part of the *As. Mos.* that has been preserved, contains little that could be useful for early Christian theologians: in that part, the downfall of Israel, but especially its eventual salvation through the establishment of God's kingdom, stands central,[2] and nothing is offered which could be interpreted in a Christian sense. One of the questions addressed in this article is why Christians were at first interested in this writing, and why they lost interest afterwards.

I have discussed the possible contents of the lost ending of the *As. Mos.* previously.[3] In the following pages, I shall discuss the matter anew, but from a different angle (that of the Christian interest in the *As. Mos.*), and in light of recently developed insights in the literary history of the *Life of Adam and Eve*.

1. Quotations of the *As. Mos.* in Early Christian Literature

In an earlier discussion of the possible quotations from the *As. Mos.* in early Christian literature, I have argued that most of the candidates assembled by A.-M. Denis,[4] are unlikely to be quotations from the *As. Mos.*, but rather speculations about the context of Jude 9, which was known to be a reference to the *As. Mos.* Four phrases that can be ascribed to the *As. Mos.* with certainty remained; three of these must stem from the lost ending. They are the following.

---

[2] N.J. Hofmann, *Die Assumptio Mosis. Studien zur Rezeption massgültiger Überlieferung* (JSJSup, 67; Leiden, 2000), chapter 2.

[3] J. Tromp, *The Assumption of Moses. A Critical Edition with Commentary* (SVTP, 10; Leiden, 1993), 270–285.

[4] A.-M. Denis, *Fragmenta pseudepigraphorum quae supersunt una cum historicorum et auctorum Judaeorum hellenistarum fragmentis* (PVTG, 3; Leiden, 1970), 63–67; cf. the discussion in R. Bauckham, *Jude and the Relatives of Jesus in the Early Church* (Edinburgh, 1990), 245–270.

(1) καὶ προεθεάσατό με ὁ θεὸς πρὸ καταβολῆς κόσμου εἶναί με τῆς διαθήκης αὐτοῦ μεσίτην.

This is a quotation of *As. Mos.* 1:14: *itaque excogitavit et invenit me qui ab initio creaturae orbis terrarum praeparatus sum ut sim arbiter testamenti illius*,[5] found in *Ecclesiastical History* II 17:17 by Gelasius of Cyzicus.[6]

(2) ἐπιτιμήσαι σοι κύριος.

Quoted in Jude 9, these words are certain to derive from the *As. Mos.* (as opposed to Zech 3:2, where an identical phrase occurs), because of the description of the scene in which they are said to be spoken: ὁ δὲ Μιχαὴλ ὁ ἀρχάγγελος, ὅτε τῷ διαβόλῳ διακρινόμενος διελέγετο περὶ τοῦ Μωϋσέως σώματος κτλ. The same scene is depicted in the following cases, where its source is explicitly identified as the *As. Mos.*

(3) ἀπὸ γὰρ πνεύματος ἁγίου αὐτοῦ πάντες ἐκτίσθημεν.

According to Gelasius, this phrase was quoted by one of the theologians present at the Council of Nicaea. It is one of several quotations used to prove that the Holy Spirit as a "member" of the Trinity played a role in the creation of the world. From testimony (1) it appears that Gelasius knew the *As. Mos.*, and it is therefore only reasonable to accept that his assertion is correct in this instance as well. The phrase is introduced by a reference to the context from which it was taken: ἐν βίβλῳ δὲ ἀναλήψεως Μωσέως Μιχαὴλ ὁ ἀρχάγγελος διαλεγόμενος τῷ διαβόλῳ.

(4) After this quotation in Gelasius' *Ecclesiastical History*, the next one follows immediately, introduced by the formula: "And again, he says": ἀπὸ προσώπου τοῦ θεοῦ ἐξῆλθε τὸ πνεῦμα αὐτοῦ, καὶ ὁ κόσμος ἐγένετο.

---

[5] In my edition of *As. Mos.* 1:14, the word *creaturae* has fallen out (as noted by W. Horbury, review in *Vetus Testamentum* 45 [1995] 398–403, esp. p. 401).

[6] Ed. G. Loeschcke and M. Heinemann, *Gelasius. Kirchengeschichte* (GCS, 28; Berlin, 1918). It can be argued that Gelasius' introduction to this phrase, Μωσῆς προσκαλεσάμενος Ἰησοῦν υἱὸν Ναυῆ, is not part of the quotation, but Gelasius' own reference (Hofmann, *Die Assumptio Mosis*, 95), even if these words are the almost exact equivalent of *As. Mos.* 1:6, *qui vocavit ad se Jesum filium Nave* (Tromp, *The Assumtion of Moses*, 78). To be on the safe side, I will leave out these words from the present discussion.

Apart from these four instances which can with certainty be taken to be testimonies of the *As. Mos.*, a special case was presented by a phrase found in Origen's *Principles* (written in the third decade of the third century, and preserved in Rufinus' Latin translation from the fifth century). This reference to the *Assumption* (or, in his words, *Ascension*) *of Moses* runs as follows:

> *in Ascensione Moysi, cuius libelli meminit in epistola sua apostolus Iudas, Michahel archangelus cum diabolo disputans de corpore Moysi ait a diabolo inspiratum serpentem causam extitisse praeuaricationis Adae et Euae.*[7]

> in the Ascension of Moses, to which booklet the apostle Jude refers in his epistle, the archangel Michael, when he is arguing with the devil about the body of Moses, says that because of the devil's inspiration, the serpent had become the cause of Adam and Eve's transgression.

The *As. Mos.* must indeed have contained a scene in which the angel and the devil disputed about the body of Moses, as can be safely concluded from the preceding instances. However, in my earlier treatment of this passage, I found reason to doubt that Michael's words as cited by Origen, "that because of the devil's inspiration, the serpent had become the cause of Adam and Eve's transgression," derived from the same writing.[8] The reasons for these doubts were the following.

(1) A reference to the original sin of Adam and Eve is surprising in a writing such as the *As. Mos.*, which does not seem to be particularly concerned with primeval history and the origin of sin.

(2) Adam, Eve and the serpent are at the centre of attention in another writing, nowadays usually designated as the *Life of Adam*

---

[7] *De principiis* III 2:1, ed. H. Crouzel & M. Simonetti, *Origène. Traité des Principes* III (SC, 268; Paris, 1980).

[8] D. Maggiorotti, "Testamento di Mosè (*Assumptio Mosis*)," in: P. Sacchi (ed.), *Apocrifi dell' Antico Testamento* IV (Brescia, 2000), 181–235; esp. 191, doubts whether Origen knew the *As. Mos.* at all, and has suggested that he followed the opinion of those who asserted that the apostle Jude quoted from it. Also, the traditions concerning the death of Moses may by the end of the second century have been developed to such an extent, that a kind of general mix-up of sources containing them would be conceivable—in that case, Maggiorotti concludes, the references of Gelasius (or at least nrs. [3] and [4]) may not be trustworthy, either. However, it will be argued below that Origen had good reasons for quoting the *As. Mos.*, and the suggestion that he simply guessed what was in it, without really knowing it, does not seem to be in accordance with the general nature of Origen's theological and exegetical work. Concerning Gelasius, Maggiorotti too easily brushes over the fact that he quotes *As. Mos.* 1:14 correctly, which proves that he knew the writing.

and Eve, but also known as the *Apocalypse of Moses*; a confusion of the *Assumption* and the *Apocalypse of Moses* on account of their similar titles seems well possible, the more so because the *Apocalypse of Moses*, in contrast to the *As. Mos.*, contains no revelations in the ordinary sense.

(3) A factor contributing to the emergence of such a confusion might have been that in the *Apocalypse of Moses* another dispute with the devil seems to occur, namely that of Seth with an animal (see below). In this context Seth rebukes the animal with the same words Michael used against the devil according to the *As. Mos.*: ἐπιτιμήσαι σοι κύριος, for in the Latin version of the *Life of Adam and Eve*, Seth is reported to say: *increpet te Dominus Deus*, the exact Latin translation of the Greek words.

I concluded that Origin's information concerning the contents of Michael's dispute with the devil must derive, not from the *As. Mos.*, but from the *Apocalypse of Moses*, to which I added in parenthesis: "whatever form it may have had when Origen knew it." Since then, however, much more has become known about the form which the *Life of Adam and Eve* may have had in the time of Origen, and it is now virtually certain that Origen cannot have quoted the phrase under discussion from that writing. A dispute between Seth and an animal does occur in the *Life of Adam and Eve*, but in its most primitive text-form, the animal is neither a serpent, nor the devil, and it is not accused of having caused Adam and Eve to sin.

2. THE GREEK AND LATIN VERSIONS OF THE *LIFE OF ADAM AND EVE* 10–12

In sections 10–12 of the Greek *Life of Adam and Eve* (perhaps to be dated to the second or third century),[9] the following story is told.[10] When Adam is lying on his deathbed, his wife Eve and their son Seth travel to paradise to try to obtain a medicine against death. On their way, they come across "an animal" (θηρίον) which attacks

---

[9] Cf. M.E. Stone, *A History of the Literature of Adam and Eve* (SBLEJL, 3; Atlanta, 1992), 53–58.

[10] For this and the following paragraphs, see also G.A. Anderson, "The Penitence Narrative in the *Life of Adam and Eve*," *HUCA* 63 (1992) 1–38, here quoted from G.A. Anderson et al., *Literature on Adam and Eve. Collected Essays* (SVTP, 15; Leiden, 2000), 3–42, esp., 33–40.

Seth (10:1). Eve reproaches the animal, asking it how it dares to attack "the image of God" to which it was subordinated (10:3). The animal answers by explaining that Eve's sin has caused a profound change in the order of creation. Later on in the story, when Eve is looking back on her and Adam's transgression in paradise, she recounts that as a result of their mistake, humankind has lost its garments of righteousness and glory (20:1–2; 21:6). Here, the animal informs her that "our (that is, the animals') nature, too, has changed" (διὰ τοῦτο καὶ ἡμῶν αἱ φύσεις μετηλλάγησαν 11:2), and the dominion of the animals has arisen because of Eve (11:1). Thus, Eve and Seth are confronted with the enmity between humans and animals which issued from God's curse of the serpent (cf. 26:1).

The conclusion to this episode is curious. Seth tells the animal to be silent and disappear from the image of God (that is, himself), and the animal obediently departs to its lair (12:1–2). This strange turn of events may be no more than an awkward way to end the episode. After all, Eve and Seth are on their way to the gates of paradise, and the story must continue.[11] Therefore, from the narrator's point of view, the animal has to disappear from the scene.[12]

In this form of the story, the animal is nothing more than some wild animal, part of nature that had been subordinate to humanity in paradise (15:2–3), but now forms a hostile environment (cf. 26:4).[13] The animal is not identified, neither as a snake, nor as any other kind of dangerous animal.[14]

Only in a secondary form of the story, represented by the Greek manuscripts EFW (fifteenth–seventeenth centuries), a copyist has apparently taken the animal to be the devil. In these manuscripts, the relevant clause in 10:1 reads as follows:

---

[11] On the use of suspense in the *Life of Adam and Eve*, see M.E. Eldridge, *Dying Adam with his Multiethnic Family. Understanding the* Greek Life of Adam and Eve (SVTP, 16; Leiden, 2001), 191–192.

[12] Three manuscripts, ATL (thirteenth–sixteenth centuries), represent a text of which the editor has attenuated the imperfection by adding that the animal had wounded Seth. This addition is preserved in the Georgian and Latin translations (see below). The texts of the manuscripts of the Greek *Life of Adam and Eve* are available in a diplomatic edition, presented in parallel horizontal lines, by M. Nagel, *La vie grecque d'Adam et Ève* I–III (Lille, 1974).

[13] T. Knittel, *Das griechische 'Leben Adams und Evas'. Studien zu einer narrativen Anthropologie im frühen Judentum* (TSAJ, 88; Tübingen, 2002), 113–114.

[14] For the animosity of animals against humankind, compare Philo, *De praemiis et poenis* 85–90. As particular examples of animals posing a threat, Philo mentions wolves, bears, lions, panthers, elephants, tigers, scorpions, serpents, crocodiles and hippopotamuses.

εἰσερχομένων ἐν τῇ ὁδῷ, ὑπήντησεν αὐτοὺς θηρίον ἀγρίωδες καὶ ἀνήμερον, ἤγουν ὁ ἀντικείμενος διάβολος, πολεμῶν μετὰ τοῦ υἱοῦ αὐτῆς Σὴθ ὡς ἰδέας θηρίου.

while they were on their way, a wild and untamed animal, that is to say, the adversary, the devil, came towards them, fighting with her son Seth in the form of an animal.

Originally, the addition identifying the animal as the devil may have been just a marginal gloss (ἤγουν often occurs in glosses). In the text as it stands in these manuscripts, the point of the story is ruined, and this form of the sentence is certainly secondary. Nonetheless, it shows that a reader of the *Life of Adam and Eve* could easily misunderstand this passage in light of the common interpretation of the story of Eve's transgression as having been caused by the devil speaking through the serpent.

An identification of the animal in the *Life of Adam and Eve* 10–12 is also implied in the Latin version. In the oldest text-form of this version,[15] the story as such is left intact: the animal (*bestia*) is not yet said to be a serpent, and the point that Eve's transgression has caused the rule of the animals[16] is well made (38[11]).[17] Only in Seth's words to the animal does it appear that the author of the Latin version must have associated it with the devil—the designation "enemy of truth" is clear proof of that: *Claude os tuum et obmutesce maledicte et inimice ueritatis* (39[12]). The reference to the animal's "lair" (σκηνή in the Greek version) is left out as no longer appropriate (*statimque effugit bestia, eumque dentibus suis uulneratum dimisit* 39[12]).

In later developments of the Latin text, Seth's speech is expanded, and the animal is explicitly identified with the serpent as a representative of the devil.[18] In the version of the manuscripts from England,

---

[15] In this part of the text represented mainly by manuscript *Pr*, ed. J.-P. Pettorelli, "Vie latine d'Adam et d'Ève. La recension de Paris, BNF, lat. 3832," *Archivum Latinitatis Medii Aevi* 57 (1999) 5–52.

[16] The translator of the Latin version, however, less felicitously rendered the Greek ἡ ἀρχὴ τῶν θηρίων with *initium bestiarum*, which may have been unclear to later copyists.

[17] It is likely that the mention of Satan in the Armenian version is a separate development within that branch of the tradition. The Georgian translation, generally agreed to be closely related to the Armenian, does not mention the devil, either. Cf. Knittel, *Das griechische 'Leben Adams und Evas'*, 116–117.

[18] On the secondary character of these text-forms as compared to that of ms. *Pr*, see J. Tromp, "The Textual History of the *Life of Adam and Eve* in the Light of a Newly Discovered Latin Text-Form," *JSJ* 33 (2002) 28–41.

the animal, as soon as it is introduced, is said to be the accursed snake: *subito uenit serpens bestia impietatis* (37[10]). In Seth's reproach of the animal, its diabolical character is emphasized: *Increpet te Dominus Deus! Recede a conspectu hominum et claude os tuum et obmutesce, inimice, maledicte, confusio ueritatis.*[19] Only at this stage of the development of the Latin text, therefore, do the words *increpet te Dominus Deus* occur.[20] It is likely that the editor of this text-form was dependent on Zech. 3:2 and Jude 9.[21] It is from these passages that the editors of the late Latin recensions must have learned that these are suitable words to rebuke the devil.

It is not clear to which century the original Latin version of the *Life of Adam and Eve* should be dated, but it can be maintained with certainty that it must have existed before the tenth century.[22] However, it seems highly unlikely that the text form containing the biblical words *increpet te Dominus Deus* was already available to Origen, around 200 c.e., or even Rufinus, in the second half of the fourth century. Therefore, my earlier suggestion that Origen mistakenly ascribed to the *As. Mos.* what actually was in the *Apocalypse of Moses*, must be withdrawn. Instead, Michael's words in his altercation with the devil over Moses' body should be included in the corpus of quotations from the lost ending of the *As. Mos.*

3. The Lost Ending of the *As. Mos.*

It must now be investigated if our understanding of the lost ending of the *As. Mos.* is changed or improved by the addition of this testimony. Before that, however, some remarks about the desirability of making sense of the quotations from the lost ending are in order.

---

[19] Ed. J.H. Mozley, "The 'Vita Adae,'" *JTS* 30 (1929) 121–149.

[20] They are maintained in one of the latest versions of the Latin *Life of Adam and Eve*, the text-form represented by the manuscripts from southern Germany: *increpet te dominus deus! Stupe, obmutesce, claude os tuum, maledicte, inimice ueritatis, confusio perditionis* (ed. J.-P. Pettorelli, "La Vie latine d'Adam et Ève," *Archivum Latinitatis Medii Aevi* 56 [1998] 5–104; spec., 18–67).

[21] In the Old Latin translations, the rendering of ἐπιτιμήσαι in Jude 9 seems to be rather consistently *imperet* or *imperat*; see W. Thiele (ed.), *Epistulae catholicae* (Vetus Latina 26; Freiburg, 1956–1969), 421–422; so also the Vulgate. The Vulgate of Zech. 3:2 reads *increpet*.

[22] J.-P. Pettorelli, "Deux témoins latins singuliers de la *Vie d'Adam et Ève*: Paris, BNF, Lat. 3832 & Milan, B. Ambrosiana, O 35 Sup.," *JSJ* 33 (2002) 1–27, esp., 26–27.

It has been suggested that no attempts at the impossible should be made, because the ensuing speculations run the risk of obscuring the meaning of the writing as a whole, burdening it with content matter which it may never have had.[23]

It is true that interpreters of the *As. Mos.* should not let themselves be disturbed by passages of the writing which are no longer there. A relatively large fragment of the work does exist, and it is possible to reach plausible interpretations of that fragment, so that a pragmatic attitude towards the fact that the document is incomplete, is to be recommended: for the purpose of understanding the *As. Mos.* insofar as it has been preserved, it is enough to assume that the writing probably ended with the end of the earthly life of Moses.[24] However, this does not relieve us from the task of trying to make sense of the few phrases preserved in the testimonies, even if that exercise is of an entirely different nature than interpreting the *As. Mos.* as it lies before us. The quotations suggest that Christian theologians were interested in this writing, but mainly in the part that is lost. This means that these quotations are the only clues to an answer to the question of why the church for a while chose to transmit this writing.

As remarked above, a reference to the original sin of Adam and Eve comes as a surprise in a writing such as the *As. Mos.*, because in the extant fragment no attention is paid to primeval history and the original sin. Naturally, this argument is worthless if it appears to be true that this reference comes from the lost ending of that writing, after all, so that we have to overcome our surprise, and imagine how it might have fitted in the context of the concluding part of the *As. Mos.*

It can be safely assumed that the main events described in the lost ending of the *As. Mos.*, included the prophet's death, his burial, and his assumption into heaven.[25] Presumably, the archangel Michael was presented as descending from heaven to bury Moses' body and take his soul with him. At some moment during this scene, the devil must have appeared and made objections of some kind to what was happening. However, it can be taken for granted that the archangel's

---

[23] Maggiorotti, "Testamento di Mosè," 192.
[24] Cf. Hofmann, *Die Assumptio Mosis*, 70.
[25] Differently: Bauckham, *Jude and the Relatives of Jesus*, 235–245.

words, of which a number survive in quotations, were supposed to effectively put the accuser to shame.

Speculating about the Epistle of Jude, vs. 9, exegetes from the fifth century onwards have adduced various grounds on which the devil may have protested against the ascension of Moses' soul into heaven.[26] Thus, it has been suggested that Moses' sins were an obstacle, or that the devil demanded that Moses be handed over to him as the master of matter (ὕλη).

However, it is unlikely that the author of the *As. Mos.* would have brought Moses' errors into the discussion. The stature of the prophet in the eyes of the author is so high (see especially 11:16–18),[27] that it can be ruled out that the biblical reports about Moses' sins were a point of even the slightest interest to him. Furthermore, the concept of the devil as the master of matter seems to be primarily at home in second-century anti-gnostic, Christian discussions, and may therefore be dismissed as later speculation about the scene described in Jude 9.[28]

The addition of Origen's reference to the corpus of quotations from the *As. Mos.* may be helpful in reconstructing an outline of the argument between Michael and the devil. In this reference, the archangel is pictured as recalling that it was the devil who had caused Adam and Eve to transgress. If this is supposed to be the answer to an argument of the devil's, one could guess that the devil had objected against at Moses' immortalization as such.

The devil's role as the accuser of somebody who is highly valued by God is well known from Old Testament and Jewish tradition. In the book of Job, Satan is described as making objections to God's praise of Job, because God has made it too easy for Job to be pious (Job 1:9–11). In Zech 3:1–2, Satan is envisioned as the accuser of Joshua, trying to prevent him from being consecrated as high priest. More particularly, the devil is regarded as one who is intent on people's death (e.g., *Jub* 1:20) and struggling to prevent them from reaching eternal life (1QM XIII 10–12; cf. Hebr 2:14).[29] According to *As. Mos.* 10, Israel will be exalted into heaven at the arrival of God's

---

[26] For this and the following paragraph, see Tromp, *The Assumption of Moses*, 275–280.

[27] Cf. Hofmann, *Die Assumptio Mosis*, 174–177, 191–193.

[28] Bauckham, *Jude and the Relatives of Jesus*, 244–245.

[29] Cf. A. Piñero, "Angels and Demons in the *Life of Adam and Eve*," *JSJ* 24 (1993) 191–214; esp., 203.

kingdom (10:8–9). God's first deed on that occasion, however, is to kill the devil (10:1; cf. Rev 12:10), whose presence is apparently thought to prevent Israel's obtaining such happiness until that day (cf. *1 Enoch* 10–11).

It is conceivable that in his dispute with Michael, who had come to bring Moses to heaven, the devil insisted that he should die. In that case, he may have pointed to the fact that God had imposed death on humankind as a reaction to Adam's sin, and that there were no grounds to except Moses from this general verdict on humankind. The archangel may have retorted that God, contrary to the devil, does not wish people to die. To make this point, the author may have made use of a common ethical pattern in Jewish literature from the first centuries B.C.E. and C.E.: God has given humanity the choice between righteousness and impiety, and thereby between life and death.

Whereas it may be that death is imposed on all human bodies, the souls of the righteous will live forever (as opposed to the souls of the unrighteous, for whom no such happy fate is in store). This is one of the teachings recurring in the *Psalms of Solomon*, e.g., 3:11–12; 13:11; 14:9–10; 15:12–13. It is also a major theme in the *Fourth Book of Ezra*. In this writing, death is presented as a punishment for the evildoings of man, but eternal life is said to be in store for the righteous in the next world (e.g., 7:45–48). In answer to Ezra's complaints about the universality of sin, it is said that evil is sown into the human heart (4:30), but so is the law (9:31). It may be that there are not many who are faithful to the law, but they are precious in God's eyes (7:60) and for them the bliss of the age to come is prepared (8:51–52). In short, the possibility exists to choose against evil and for God's commandments, and therefore, the possibility to escape eternal death exists, and one is invited to choose life (7:127–129).[30]

The views on death and afterlife in *4 Ezra* are complicated by the fact that its author seems to be deliberately trying to harmonise two conflicting notions of life after death: that of a survival of the soul after death, and that of the resurrection of the dead in the last days (see especially 7:75–80).[31]

---

[30] Cf. C. Münchow, *Ethik und Eschatologie. Ein Beitrag zum Verständnis der frühjüdischen Apokalyptik* (Göttingen, 1981), 89–91.
[31] Cf. M.E. Stone, *Fourth Ezra. A Commentary on the Book of Fourth Ezra* (Minneapolis, 1990), 65b–67a.

Closer to the subject matter of Michael's words may therefore be *Wisdom of Solomon* 2:23–3:4. In that passage it is stated that God has created (ἔκτισεν) man to be incorruptible (ἐπ᾽ ἀφθαρσίᾳ), as an image of God's own eternity, but that death arrived in the world because of the devil's envy. The souls of the righteous ones, however, are in God's hands: to fools it may seem they have died, but they are in peace, full of hope for immortality (ἀθανασία; cf. 8:17).[32] An important role in the creation of the world and of humankind is attributed to wisdom (e.g., 7:21; 9:1–2), and wisdom is little less than God's holy spirit (7:22–8:1), descending into holy souls and making them friends of God (7:27; 9:17).[33]

In Jewish literature from the period in which the *As. Mos.* was written, there appear to be clear and consistent relationships between the concepts of righteousness and piety, wisdom and the spirit of God, and immortality. Against this background, the surviving phrases quoted in Jude, and by Origen and Gelasius are conceivable as parts of Michael's answer to the devil's objections to Moses' immortalization.

After having the devil demand that Moses should die, referring to the story of Adam's sin, the author may have described how Michael rebuked the accuser (ἐπιτιμήσαι σοι κύριος) for being the cause of death in the first place (*a diabolo inspiratum serpentem causam extitisse praevaricationis Adae et Evae*). The devil's inspiration may then have been contrasted with God's inspiration: it is possible to let oneself be inspired by God, for we are all created by his holy spirit (ἀπὸ γὰρ πνεύματος ἁγίου αὐτοῦ πάντες ἐκτίσθημεν), that same holy spirit which permeates the entire creation (ἀπὸ προσώπου τοῦ θεοῦ ἐξῆλθε τὸ πνεῦμα αὐτοῦ, καὶ ὁ κόσμος ἐγένετο). For the author of the *As. Mos.*, the only way to cling to the Lord is through perfect obedience to his commandments (*As. Mos.* 1:10; 9:4–5; 12:10), mediated by Moses (1:14), that is, "the holy and sacred spirit" himself (11:16).[34]

---

[32] Cf. K. Martin Hogan, "The Exegetical Background of the 'Ambiguity of Death' in the Wisdom of Solomon," *JSJ* 30 (1999) 1–24.

[33] Cf. Philo (admittedly using a different concept of immortality), who in *De opificio mundi* 135 comments on Gen 2:7 that God insufflated man with the divine spirit (πνεῦμα θεῖον), so that man, although mortal according to the body, might partake in immortality through his mind (θνητὸν μὲν κατὰ τὸ σῶμα, κατὰ δὲ τὴν διάνοιαν ἀθάνατον).

[34] Cf. S. Schreiber, "Hoffnung und Handlungsperspektive in der *Assumptio Mosis*," *JSJ* 32 (2001) 252–271.

Obviously, this reconstruction is speculation, but it does show, in my opinion, that the phrases under discussion are conceivable in the context of the *As. Mos.* as a first-century Jewish writing. The contents of the quotations give no cause to regard them as part of a secondary addition or revision of the writing.[35]

4. Origen's Reasons to Quote the *As. Mos.*

Finally, it should be asked why Origen chose to refer to a somewhat obscure apocryphon to make his point that the original sin was caused by the devil's inspiration. In Genesis 3, the serpent is not associated with the devil. However, the association of both was considered obvious in Origen's age and before.[36]

On many occasions, Origen's contemporary Tertullian (*ca.* 160–*ca.* 220) simply identifies the snake of Genesis 3 with the devil, e.g., in *Adversus Iudaeos* 10:10 (= *Adversus Marcionem* III 18:7); *De carne Christi* 17:5.

Justin Martyr († 165) also regards the serpent in paradise as the devil himself. In his *Dialogus cum Tryphone* 39:6,[37] Justin says that one of the reasons why the Jews refuse to acknowledge Jesus as the Christ, is that they want to avoid being persecuted by the rulers, who are continually driven by that bad spirit, the serpent, to persecute the Christians (οἳ οὐ παύσονται ἀπὸ τῆς τοῦ πονηροῦ καὶ πλάνου πνεύματος, τοῦ ὄφεως, ἐνεργείας θανατοῦντας καὶ διώκοντες τοὺς τὰ ὄνομα τοῦ Χριστοῦ ὁμολογοῦντας; cf. 70:5; 125:4). In ch. 79, the Jew Trypho comes forward with the accusation that it is blasphemous to say that there are angels who have acted wickedly. Justin then proves that the bible itself says that this is so by pointing at several biblical passages, including Isa 30:4; Zech 3:1–2 and Gen 3:3–14: καὶ ὑπὸ Μωσέως ἐν ἀρχῇ τῆς Γενέσεως ὄφιν πλανήσαντα τὴν Εὔαν γεγραμμένον ἔχομεν καὶ κεκατηραμένον. That the serpent was none other than the devil is apparently obvious for Justin, for he does not explicitly equate the two (cf. 124:3). He does so in 103:5, where he explains

---

[35] Bauckham, *Jude and the Relatives of Jesus*, 269.

[36] Evidence for this association in Jewish tradition is extant, but scarce; cf. Piñero, "Angels and Demons," 210.

[37] Ed. M. Marcovich, *Iustini Martyris dialogus cum Tryphone* (PTS, 47; Berlin/New York, 1997).

the element νᾶς in Σατανᾶς as deriving from the Hebrew for "serpent," *naḥaš*.

The assumed association of the serpent with the devil probably also underlies Rev. 12:9, where the defeat of the devil is described: καὶ ἐβλήθη ὁ δράκων ὁ μέγας, ὁ ὄφις ὁ ἀρχαῖος, ὁ καλούμενος Διάβολος καὶ ὁ Σατανᾶς.[38]

However, the distinction between the serpent and the devil was not always completely lost. Theophilus of Antioch (*fl.* 180) clearly distinguishes the devil and the serpent, when he states that the devil spoke through the serpent's mouth: ὁ κακοποιὸς δαίμων, ὁ καὶ Σατὰν καλούμενος, ὁ τότε διὰ τοῦ ὄφεως λαλήσας αὐτῇ (*Ad Autolycum* II 28:6).[39] This is also the view explicitly expressed in the Greek *Life of Adam and Eve* (16:1–4).

Both the complete identification of the serpent and the snake, and the awareness that they can be regarded as separate personalities, come together in the curious phrase of Epiphanius (*ca.* 315–403): οὐκ ἦν δε αἴτιος μόνος ὁ φαινόμενος τότε ὄφις, ἀλλὰ ὁ ἐν τῷ ὄφει ὄφις λαλήσας (*Panarion* XXXVII 1:6).[40]

Origen himself sometimes refers in a casual way to the serpent as the devil's mouthpiece, e.g., in *Homilia in Jeremiam* XX 7.[41] In other instances, however, he is well aware that the book of Genesis contains no reference to the diabolical adversary.

In *Contra Celsum* IV 36,[42] Origen reports that Celsus had ridiculed the story told by the Jews, that a serpent had opposed God's commandments and prevailed over them. Celsus regarded this old wives tale as most impious, "making God a weakling from the very beginning, unable to make even a single man, whom he had created himself, be obedient." After pointing out that Celsus should have taken the story allegorically (as the Greeks themselves do with their own preposterous stories; IV 39), Origen explains that in this story "Adam" stands for humanity in general. To say that God is presented as

---

[38] L.J. Lietaert Peerbolte, *The Antecedents of Antichrist. A Traditio-Historical Study of the Earliest Christian Views on Eschatological Opponents* (JSJSup, 49; Leiden, 1996), 133–135.

[39] Ed. M. Marcovich, *Theophili Antiocheni ad Autolycum* (PTS, 44; Berlin/New York, 1995).

[40] Ed. K. Holl and J. Dummer, *Epiphanius II* (Berlin, ²1980).

[41] Ed. P. Nautin, *Origenes Werke* III (GCS, *sine numero*; Berlin, ²1983).

[42] Ed. M. Marcovich, *Origenes. Contra Celsum libri VIII* (VCSup, 54; Leiden, 2001).

weak, because he could not prevent one man from sinning, is then equivalent to objecting to the idea that evil exists at all (IV 40).

In this instance, Origen makes no connection between the serpent and the devil. However, in book VI he returns to the matter, where he discusses Celsus' objections to the Christian teaching concerning the devil. In Celsus' understanding, Christianity represented the devil as one who successfully opposes God in his efforts to do something good for humankind, thus impiously representing the great God as impotent (ὁ μέγιστος θεός, βουλόμενός τι ἀνθρώπους ὠφελῆσαι, τὸν ἀντιπράσσοντα ἔχει καὶ ἀδύνατει; VI 42). To show that the doctrine of an opposing power is not a Christian invention, but a revered teaching of great antiquity, much older than the Greek authorities produced by Celsus, Origen quotes from the books of Moses. He insists that the serpent, the cause of the expulsion from paradise, cannot have been anything other than something like the devil; his other examples include the destroying angel, and the goat sent into the desert. In the book of Job, even older than the Mosaic scriptures, the devil is explicitly named and depicted (VI 43). Origen also discusses why the devil should exist: God, far from being a weakling, introduced an adversary (ἀντικείμενος) into creation, in order to put men to the test and enable them to show themselves worthy of the ascent to things divine (ἄξιοι φανέντες τῆς εἰς τὰ θεῖα ἀναβάσεως VI 44).

From this passage in book VI, it is clear why Origen had waited with his identification of the serpent with the devil in the passage in book IV: Celsus did not just object to the story of the serpent, but to the idea of the devil as God's victorious opponent. Only after Origen had defended the Christian view on "the adversary," could he point to the serpent as a reference to this evil power. To mention the devil in his discussion of the serpent in book IV would have gravely damaged his argument at that stage.

It also emerges that, although the association of the serpent and the devil was self-evident within a Christian context, someone like Origen was aware that in other contexts it had to be made plausible that the devil played a role in the story of Genesis 3. In other words, Origen knew very well that the devil is not explicitly mentioned in the biblical version, and that the assumption that the serpent was associated with him is the outcome of exegesis, and therefore at best a likelihood.

Finally, it appears that in philosophical circles, such as those of Origen and Celsus, the notion of the existence of a power opposing God was a matter of contention. Therefore, it is not surprising that in *De principiis*, in which Origen for the first time in history systematically expounded a Christian theology, he pays quite some attention to the reality of the devil, that is, the powers which try to incite us to sin from the very beginning of creation (III 2:1). It is in this connection that Origen quotes the *As. Mos.*, of which he emphatically states that it was used by the *apostle* Jude.

Origen knew of course that the *As. Mos.* had no canonical authority (cf. his remark to that effect in *Homilia in Jesu Nave* II 1),[43] but he also knew that it was quoted in the Epistle of Jude. By mentioning that fact, he could transfer some of Jude's authority to the *As. Mos.*, and thereby strengthen the important point that the devil had been active in creation from the very beginning.[44]

CONCLUSIONS

Origen's statement that in the final part of the *As. Mos.*, the archangel Michael was portrayed as reproaching the devil because he had inspired the serpent to induce Adam and Eve to sin, is probably correct. The earlier suggestion that Origen might have mixed up the *Assumption* and the *Apocalypse* of Moses must be discarded.

The inclusion of this reference to the *As. Mos.* into the corpus of quotations from the lost ending of this writing contributes to our understanding of that part as a discussion of the human fate after death. It is conceivable that the story described how the devil denied the archangel Michael's right to bring Moses to heaven and how, in response, the archangel discoursed on various sorts of inspiration, that by the devil, or that by God's holy spirit. Moses had to die according to the flesh, but he was a righteous person and the embodiment of the holy spirit, and so his soul should rightfully be immortalized.

Although the interpretation of the transgression in paradise as diabolically inspired was common in the Christian exegesis of Origen's

---

[43] Ed. A. Jaubert, *Origène. Homélies sur Josué* (SC, 71; Paris, 1970).

[44] Cf. E. Bammel, "Die Zitate aus den Apokryphen bei Origenes," in: R.J. Daly (ed.), *Origeniana quinta. Papers of the 5th International Origen Congress* (BETL, 105; Louvain, 1992), 131–136; esp., 134–135; repr. in *id.*, *Judaica et Paulina. Kleine Schriften II* (WUNT, 91; Tübingen, 1997), 161–167; esp., 166–167.

time and before, Origen was aware that the association of the serpent with the devil was not explicit in Genesis 3. He regarded the usual interpretation of that story as correct, but was nonetheless happy to quote the *As. Mos.*, because in that writing the identification of the devil as the real evildoer was made explicit. As appears from Origen's discussion with the non-Christian philosopher Celsus, the concept of an evil force opposing God was not undisputed. Origen acknowledged the apocryphal character of the *As. Mos.* (for which reason he could not use the writing in his discussion with Celsus), but suggested that it still had some authority because it was used and quoted by the apostle Jude.

Finally, some remarks concerning the Christian transmission of the *As. Mos.*, as compared to that of the *Life of Adam and Eve*, may be made, in order to shed light on the phenomenon of the Old Testament pseudepigrapha as part of the Christian heritage in general.

The *As. Mos.* has travelled from Judea to Italy via Alexandria and Caesarea (where Origen worked), and Asia Minor (where the Nicene fathers quoted it). Early Christian writers found it worthwhile to quote its views on good and evil spirits. However, when it was no longer needed for that purpose (possibly because the Christian teachings on the spiritual world were no longer opposed), the writing came into disuse: insofar as the scribes of Northern Italy were concerned, the parchment on which it was written was more valuable than the text itself. Only by chance part of it survived.

The *Life of Adam and Eve*, too, travelled throughout the Roman empire and beyond. It is preserved in scores of manuscripts in many languages of Christendom. Its main usefulness seems to have been that a story about the first human beings is capable of incorporating changing and new views on the details of the human condition in general. Many readers of the story must have found it enjoyable and useful for the purpose of edification. In stark contrast to the five extant quotations from the *As. Mos.*, however, the *Life of Adam and Eve* is never quoted in theological discourses.

The question of why the Christian church adopted and transmitted the pseudepigrapha of the Old Testament, will have to be answered differently in each individual case. The interest vested by the church in non-canonical writings cannot be defined in a general manner, but should be determined by reading each and every document (and, in the event, each and every recension of a document) by itself. If this is true, it once more underlines the fact that the "apocrypha and pseudepigrapha" should not be treated as a separate corpus of texts.[45] In other words: from the perspective of its reception in the church, the *As. Mos.* has as much in common with, e.g., *1 Enoch* or the *Testament of Job*, as with the works of Flavius Josephus, Thucydides and Julius Caesar.

---

[45] Cf. J.-C. Picard, "L'apocryphe à l'étroit," *Apocrypha* 1 (1990) 69–117; repr. in: *id.*, *Le continent apocryphe: Essai sur les littératures apocryphes juive et chrétienne* (Instrumenta patristica 36; Turnhout, 1999), 13–51.

LA SAVEUR BIBLIQUE DU LATIN MÉROVINGIEN:
L'EXEMPLE DE LA *VIE DE SAINTE RUSTICULE,*
ABBESSE À ARLES (VIIᴱ SIÈCLE)

Marc Van Uytfanghe*

1. Le dédicataire du présent article est un éminent représentant des études paleochrétiennes telles qu'elles ont longtemps fleuri aux Pays-Bas, dans le sillage de la fameuse *École de Nimègue*. Certes, on n'envisage plus le "latin des chrétiens" comme Joseph Schrijnen († 1938) et Christine Mohrmann († 1988) l'ont défini à l'époque, c'est-à-dire comme une vraie *Sondersprache*, puisqu'on étudie plutôt, aujourd'hui, le latin tardif dans son ensemble, quitte à y intégrer des spécificités chrétiennes (lexicales principalement).[1] Force est cependant de préciser que le terme de *Sondersprache* pourrait toujours se justifier lorsqu'il s'agit de qualifier le latin biblique. Celui-ci, en effet, est une langue de traduction qui, en dépit de sa grande variété stylistique,[2] se démarque très sensiblement du latin classique en alliant une certaine *rusticitas* à une certaine couleur "exotique" (produite par les nombreux hébraïsmes et grécismes, y compris syntaxiques).[3] Ce mélange aboutit à une tonalité propre (*gravitas, suavitas, dulcedo . . .*) qui en son temps enchantait Goethe,[4] mais dont se ressentaient aussi, dans une certaine mesure, les traductions en langues vernaculaires.[5]

La Bible latine a façonné, on le sait, une bonne partie de la latinité médiévale, nourrissant de la sorte l'intertextualité la plus élaborée de

---

* Gent.

[1] Cf. J. Fredouille, "'Latin chrétien' ou 'latin tardif'?" in *Recherches augustiniennes* 29 (1996) 5–23; B. Colot, "'Latin chrétien' ou 'latin des chrétiens'? Essai de synthèse sur une terminologie discutée," in B. Bureau, C. Nicolas (réd.), *Moussylanea. Mélanges C. Moussy* (Louvain-Paris, 1998), 411–420.

[2] Déjà remarquée par saint Augustin: cf. J. Fontaine, *Aspects et problèmes de la prose d'art latine au IIIᵉ siècle. La genèse des styles latins chrétiens* (Torino, 1968), 38–39.

[3] Cf. J. Martin, "Volkslatein, Schriftlatein, Kirchenlatein," in *Historisches Jahrbuch* 41 (1921) 201–214; W. Suess, "Das Problem der lateinischen Bibelsprache," in *Historische Vierteljahrschrift* 27 (1970) 1–39.

[4] Cf. F. Stumemer, "Vom Satzrhythmus in der Bibel und in der Liturgie der lateinischen Christenheit," in *Archiv für Liturgiewissenschaft* 3 (1954) 233–283, ici p. 234.

[5] Les traductions médiévales étaient évidemment faites sur la Vulgate mais le constat vaut toujours pour les traductions ultérieures, faites sur les originaux: voir par ex. J. Lammertse, "De historische beteekenis der Statenvertaling," in *Schild* 19 (1938) 491–498.

cette période.[6] Cela vaut déjà pour les siècles du haut Moyen Âge, où, dans la Romania, la parole vive n'était pas encore sortie du "diasystème" latin.[7] J'ai examiné moi-même, sous cet angle, les textes hagiographiques mérovingiens du VIIe et de la première moitié du VIIIe siècle.[8] Je me propose d'analyser ici, à titre d'exemple, quelques passages de la *Vita sanctae Rusticulae abbatissae Arelatensis*.[9]

Cette *Vie* a sans doute été écrite peu après la mort de Rusticule († 632/633?) par un certain Florentius, prêtre de la région de Vaison, où la sainte était née (vers 555/556?) dans une famille de clarissimes d'origine romaine. Appelée d'abord Marcia, Rusticule fut enlevée, à l'âge de cinq ans, par un gentilhomme qui convoitait son héritage paternel. Après une intervention de l'évêque Syagrius d'Autun († vers 600) auprès du roi Gontran († 592) de Bourgogne, elle fut libérée et conduite au monastère Saint-Jean d'Arles (fondé par saint Césaire [† 542], dont elle fut élue abbesse à dix-huit ans. Plus tard, accusée auprès du roi Clotaire II († 628) d'avoir accordé l'asile à l'un de ses rivaux (Childebert), elle fut arrêtée. L'évêque Domnulus de Vienne († vers 614) se chargea alors de la défendre et Clotaire accepta finalement de la faire relâcher et renvoyer avec honneur à son abbaye, où elle reprit ses fonctions. Selon l'hagiographe, elle y mourut à l'âge de soixante-dix-sept ans.

Le texte a été édité en 1902 par Bruno Krusch, qui a malheureusement "sauté" quelques récits de visions, qu'on retrouvera dans l'ancienne édition de Jean Mabillon.[10] L'hypercritique éditeur des *Monumenta Germaniae Historica* voyait d'ailleurs dans la *Vita Rusticulae* l'oeuvre d'un faussaire vivant sous le règne de Louis le Pieux (814–840),

---

[6] À côté de la tradition biblique et chrétienne, il y a évidemment aussi la veine classique: cf. C. Mohrmann, "Le dualisme de la latinité médiévale," in *Revue des études latines* 29 (1951) 330–348.

[7] Comme le dit Michel Banniard, *Du latin aux langues romanes* (Paris, 1997), 21–29.

[8] M. Van Uytfanghe, *Bijbel en hagiografie in het Merovingische Frankenrijk (600–750). Een onderzoek naar denkvormen en taalexpressie in de zogeheten 'Dark Ages'*, I–II, diss. Gent, 1979 (je renvoie ici spécialement à la quatrième partie intitulée *Bijbel en taalexpressie*, I, 455–724). Voir le compte rendu en français de Jacques Fontaine dans *Analecta Bollandiana* 97 (1979) 387–396.

[9] Parmi les 19 textes que j'avais retenus pour mon corpus, cette *Vita* est parmi celles qui accusent une intertextualité biblique relativement dense.

[10] B. Krusch, in *Monumenta Germaniae Historica, Scriptores Rerum Merovingicarum*, IV, 1902, 339–351; à compléter par J. Mabillon, in *Acta Sanctorum Ordinis S. Benedicti*, II (Paris, 1669), 142–143 (chap. 11–16, selon une numérotation qui n'est évidemment pas celle de Krusch).

mais Pierre Riché l'a restituée, par des arguments probants, à l'époque mérovingienne.[11]

2.1. L'intertextualité biblique est assez prononcée dans cette *Vita*. Le premier niveau de stratification[12] regroupe les citations ou renvois. Il s'agit d'emprunts incontestables, insérés sciemment par l'auteur avec une fonction énonciative très claire (au niveau du contenu),[13] pourvus ou non d'une référence (directe ou indirecte)[14] à l'Écriture. Ils peuvent être explicites (l'usage moderne aurait alors recours à des guillemets)[15] ou implicites (c'est-à-dire enchâssés dans le tissu syntaxique de la phrase de l'hagiographe), textuels, quasi textuels ou partiels, limités à un seul passage biblique ou "contaminés" avec d'autres (éventuellement aussi avec des réminiscences ou syntagmes: voir *infra* sous 2.2 ou 2.3).

Ainsi,[16] décrivant le rapt de la jeune enfant *a quodam nobili*, l'hagiographe s'empresse de souligner que le Seigneur veillait sur elle: *Sed ille, qui* non dormit neque dormitat *in aevo*, qui custodit Israel, revelavit Spiritu suo sancto beatissimae Liliolae abbatissae[17] *monasterii, quod*

---

[11] P. Riché, "Note d'hagiographie mérovingienne. La Vita S. Rusticulae," in *Analecta Bollandiana* 72 (1954) 369–377.

[12] Sur la stratification choisie, qui est forcément sujette à discussion, voir Van Uytfanghe, *op. cit.* (n. 8), 475–485. Il n'est pas facile d'en proposer une qui soit adéquate partout et exempte de recoupements: cf. aussi M.A. Guillemin, "En marge du "martyre de Polycarpe". Le discernement des allusions scripturaires," in *Forma futuri. Studi in onore del Card. M. Pellegrino* (Torino, 1975), 462–469, ici p. 463.

[13] Sur ces différentes catégories fonctionnelles (1. Les typologies nominatives; 2. L'Écriture garante de sa propre [ré]actualisation; 3. L'"accomplissement" de paroles scripturaires; 4. L'Écriture en tant que référence normative et exemplaire; 5. L'emploi justificatif de l'Écriture; 6. L'énonciation d'idées, de concepts ou de sentiments au moyen de citations scripturaires), voir M. Van Uytfanghe, *Stylisation biblique et condition humaine dans l'hagiographie mérovingienne* (Bruxelles, 1987), 17–42.

[14] Par ex. *V. Rusticulae*, 6/342, 30–32: *Quae mox ut expergefacta fuisset, tamquam si eum legisset, ita memoriter recensebat, implens illud scripturae dictum*: Ego dormio, et cor meum vigilat (citation de Cant 5:2, avec référence directe, fût-elle vague); 8/344, 31–32: *Vere enim secundum apostoli dictum*, ut sapiens architectus fundamentum posuit (citation de 1 Cor 3:10, avec référence directe, plus précise); 22/348, 20–21: . . . *ad praemia laeta evocatur ad caelos, ut recipiat*, quod oculus non vidit nec auris audivit nec in cor hominis ascendit, quae sunt parata diligentibus Deum (citation de 1 Cor 2:9, dans une variante vieille latine, sans référence). Références indirectes: voir les exemples dans les paragraphes suivants.

[15] Voir par ex., dans la note précédente, la citation de Cant 5:2.

[16] En ce qui concerne les emprunts bibliques, on utilise ici les caractères non italiques pour les mots identiques (abstraction faite de leur désinence morphologique) et les caractères italiques soulignés pour les mots apparentés.

[17] Liliole succéda sans doute à Césarie, deuxième abbesse de Saint-Jean: cf. Riché, *op. cit.* (n. 11), p. 372.

sanctae recordationis urbis Arelatensis papa Caesarius fundavit, ut peteret... (3/341, 15–18). Le *sed ille, qui* annonce la citation implicite de Ps 120:3–4: *Non det im commotionem pedem tuum, neque dormitet qui custodit te... Ecce non dormitabit neque dormiet.* Plutôt que cette version de la Vulgate, l'auteur suit ici une leçon préhiéronymienne qu'on repère (paraphrasée) chez Cassiodore:[18] *... non dormit neque dormitat qui custodit Israel.*

Un peu plus loin, dans le récit d'une pêche miraculeuse (rassasiant ceux qui conduisaient à Arles l'enfant libérée), l'auteur évoque en ces termes l'assistance divine telle qu'il la trouvait garantie dans l'Ancien Testament: *Sed Dominus, qui non privat bonis eos qui ambulant in innocentia, ut eripiat animas eorum a morte et alat eos in privat fame, ipse per famulam suam tribuit egentibus donum misericordiae suae* (4/341/30–32). Ici, deux versets de psaumes différents ont été associés, en l'occurrence Ps 83:13: *Non privabit bonis eos qui ambulant[19] in innocentia. Domine virtutum, beatus homo qui sperat in te* (Vulgate), et Ps 32:18–19: *Ecce oculi Domini super metuentes eum, et in eis qui sperant super misericordia eius, ut eruat* (variante vieille latine: *eripiat)[20]* a *morte animas eorum et alat eos in fame.* L'antécédent *Dominus* et le pronom relatif *qui* font, ici encore, fonction de référence indirecte à l'Écriture. Au total, la *Vita* compte une vingtaine de passages appartenant à ce premier niveau (15 emprunts simples et 5 mixtes).[21]

2.2. Le deuxième niveau de stratification est celui des réminiscences. J'entends par là des emprunts qui dépassent l'usage stylistique d'expressions et de syntagmes d'origine scripturaire, mais qui ne sont

---

[18] *Expositio Psalmorum*, Ps 43:23 (éd. M. Adrieaen, *Corpus Christianorum, Series Latina*, 97, 400).

[19] Rusticule est "en route" vers Arles: l'hagiographe joue donc sur les deux sens (matériel et métaphorique) de *ambulare*.

[20] *Bibliorum Sacrorum Latinae Versiones Antiquae*, éd. P. Sabatier, II (Reims, 1743, réimpr., Turnhout, 1976), 64.

[21] Passages qui n'ont pas encore été cités (ni dans le texte ni dans les notes): a) emprunts simples: 2/341, 6–11: Mt 5:14–15; 6,343, 3–5: Cant 6:9; 7/343, 11–13: 2 Cor 6:4–5; 9/344, 10–14: Dan 13:44–45; 9/344, 16–18: Ps 36:15; 17/347, 9–12: Lc 2:14; 17/347, 15–17: Ps 33:4–5; 18/347, 23–25: Mt 6:14; 22/348, 36–40: Mt 25:20–21; 23/349, 9–11: 2 Tim 4:7–8; 30/351, 20–21: Joh 5:22–23; Mab 11/142, 7–9: 1 Cor 9:22; b) emprunts mixtes: 9/343, 35–37 + 344, 1: Act 7:59–60; Lc 23:24; 12/345, 20–23: Judith 13:7; Ps 33:23; Lc 1:52; Act 12:11; Gen 30:23; 1 Reg 17:26, 1 Cor 2:10; 22/348, 20–23: Mt 3:11–12; 13:30; Lc 12:42; 24/349, 34–35 + 350,1: Lc 4:41; Ps 29:8; 43–24. Il importe de signaler que l'auteur utilise très souvent une version *Vetus Latina*.

plus des "citations" ou renvois indéniables. Leur degré de "probabilité" ou de "reconnaissabilité" (qu'on me pardonne ce néologisme)
est donc moins élevé, même si le lecteur attentif y retrouve un ou
plusieurs fragments bien localisables dans la Bible latine; par ailleurs,
une certaine fonction énonciative (quoique plus subtile que sous 2.1)
dans le contexte de la *Vita* est toujours possible. Ces réminiscences
s'apparentent parfois, il est vrai, à des citations implicites partielles
(sans référence); il faut donc compter avec des cas limites, sujets à
discussion.

Clémentia, la mère de Rusticule, avait eu, si l'on en croit l'hagiographe, un songe prémonitoire: *vidit in extasi quasi* duos pullos columbarum *suo affectu enutrire* (2/340, 29–30). Ces deux jeunes colombes
rappellent évidemment le récit de la présentation de Jésus au Temple
chez Luc:... *et ut darent hostiam secundum quod dictum est in lege Domini,
par turturum, aut* duos pullos columbarum (Lc 2:24).

Dans le même songe, elle vit saint Césaire d'Arles rendre visite à
sa maison pour demander qu'une de ces deux colombes lui fût
offerte.[22] Voici le passage où Clémentia court à la rencontre de
l'évêque: *Quod illa* audiens, *sanctissimi viri gavisa adventu, in occursum eius
laeta properat, atque officiosissime eum* salutans, *ut* ingressu *suo,* benedictionem
suae domui largiretur, humili prece poscebat, ingressus*que domum, benedixit
eam"* (2/340, 33–36). La draperie biblique vient pareillement d'un
passage de l'Évangile de l'Enfance, du récit de l'Annonciation plus
précisément: *Et* ingressus *angelus ad eam, dixit: "Ave gratia plena, Dominus
tecum;* benedicta *tu in mulieribus". Quae cum* audisset, *turbata est in sermone
eius, et cogitabat qualis esset ista* salutatio (Lc 1:28–29).[23]

La suite du chapitre baigne dans la même atmosphère, tout en
combinant Luc 1 avec d'autres versets. L'hagiographe, en effet,
exprime l'étonnement de la mère de Rusticule devant le souhait émis
par saint Césaire: *At illa* haesitans intra semet ipsam, cogitabat, unde
hoc sciret, *quod haec illa apud se haberet,* dicens *se* huiusmodi *rem* non
habere (2/341, 1–2).[24] L'"hypotexte"[25] se compose respectivement d'Act

---

[22] Clémentia avait eu deux enfants, mais peu après le décès de son mari (sur-
venu le jour même de la naissance de Rusticule), son fils mourut à son tour.

[23] Ce passage inspire souvent, dans l'hagiographie, le songe prémonitoire de la
mère enceinte du saint, mais ici il s'agit d'une vision *post partum*.

[24] Clémentia avait proposé à l'évêque de prendre le repas chez elle, mais ne
souhaitait pas lui offrir des colombes. Elle ignorait, du reste, que Césaire parlait en
réalité de l'élection divine (comme *sponsa Christi*) de sa fille.

[25] Sur ces notions relatives à l'intertextualité (hypotexte, hypertexte, paratexte,
etc.), voir G. Genette, *Palimpsestes. La littérature au second degré* (Paris, 1982).

10:17 (*Et dum* intra <u>*se*</u> *haesitaret* Petrus, *quidnam esset visio quam vidis-set, ecce viri qui missi erant a Cornelio, inquirentes domum Simonis, astiterunt ad ianuam*), de Dan 4:16 (*Tunc Daniel . . . coepit* intra semet ipsum *tac-itus* cogitare *quasi una hora . . .*), de Lc 1:29,34 (*Quae cum audisset, tur-bata est in sermone eius, et <u>cogitabat</u> qualis esset ista salutatio . . .* Dixit *antem Maria ad angelum: "Quomodo fiet <u>istud</u>, quoniam virum* non *cognosco?"*), et de Lc 1:18 (*Et dixit Zacharias ad angelum:* "Unde hoc sciam? *Ego enim sum senex, et uxor mea processit in diebus suis"*). Ces quatre réminiscences sont vraiment contextuelles, du fait que les passages scripturaires con-cernés sont tous tirés d'un récit de vision.[26]

Il y a moyen de déceler, dans la *Vita Rusticulae*, d'autres spécimens de telles réminiscences "enchevêtrées," par exemple là où l'auteur décrit la réaction de la jeune fille lorsque sa mère lui fait apporter de riches cadeaux pour la faire sortir du monastère. *Sed illa, cuius* fidei fundamenta iam erant supra petram *firmissimam*, omnia tamquam stercus *respuens, una eademque perseverabat* immobilis (5/342, 23–25).Le verbe *stabilire* apparaît 14 fois dans la Vulgate, au perfectum passif par ex. dans Eccli 31:11: *Ideo* stabilita sunt *bona illius in Domino*. Mais le sujet du verbe passif et le syntagme prépositionnel viennent de l'image évangélique de la maison bâtie sur un roc: *Similis est homini aedificanti domum qui fodit in altum et posuit fundamentum super petram* (variante vieille latine: fundamenta supra petram)[27] (Lc 6:48). Le "rejet de tout comme si c'étaient des déchets" est emprunté à saint Paul: . . . *propter quem* omnia *detrimentum feci, et arbitror ut* (variante vieille latine: tamquam)[28] stercora (Philipp 3:8). Enfin, l'enchaînement de l'ensemble est encore recoupé par un autre verset paulinien où revi-ennent quelques mots clé (ou au moins leur radical): . . . *si tamen . . . per-manetis in* fide <u>*fundati*</u>, *et* <u>*stabiles*</u>, *et* immobiles *a spe evangelii, quod audistis . . .* (Col 1:23).

Lors du transfert de l'abbesse au palais de Clotaire (qui la blanchira finalement des accusations portées contre elle), les esprits immondes annonçaient son arrivée prochaine dans les cités qui se trouvaient sur son chemin: *In civitatibus vero, in quibus famula Dei ventura erat, vexati ab* spiribus immundis *ante plurimis diebus* adventum *eius* praenuntia-

---

[26] Act 10: la vision de Pierre concernant le centurion Corneille; Dan 4: le rêve de Nabuchodonosor; Lc 1: *les apparitions angéliques à Zacharie et à Marie*.

[27] Cf. *Itala*, éd. A. Juelicher, III, *Lucas-Evangelium* (Berlin, 1954), 69.

[28] Cf. *Vetus Latina*, éd. Beuron 24,2 (*Epistulae ad Philippenses et ad Colossenses*) (Freiburg, 1966), 191.

bant, dicentes "Ecce! *famula Dei iam* venit, *ut* nos torqueat *et de habitatione nostra eiciat, et quasi stadiis tribus aut quatuor venientes obviam ei, humiliter prosternebantur, confitentes atque* dicentes: *Cur* nos, *famula Christi,* torquere venisti *et de* domiciliis *nostris expellere*?" (13/345, 31–36).

Dans ce fragment transparaissent deux épisodes de l'Évangile où des démoniaques se manifestent, à savoir Mt 8:24: *Et ecce* [*daemonia*] *clamaverunt* dicentes: "*Quid nobis et tibi, Iesu, fili Dei? Venisti huc ante tempus* torquere nos?", et Mc 5:2–3: *et exeunti ei de navi, statim occurrit de monumentis homo in* spiritu immundo, *qui* domicilium *habebat in monumentis.* Ils se combinent avec une parole du protomartyr Étienne sur les tueurs de ceux qui prédisaient la venue du Juste: *Et occiderunt eos qui* praenuntiabant *de* adventu *Iusti* (Act 7:52). Signalons qu'on peut détecter, dans la *Vita*, une quinzaine de ces passages à réminiscences (7 simples et 8 mixtes).[29]

2.3. Au troisième niveau, on a affaire à de simples syntagmes ou *iuncturae verborum*, que frôlaient déjà certaines réminiscences "faibles" (tel élément de telle réminiscence "contaminée"). Le degré de probabilité de ces emprunts descend, en effet, encore d'un cran. Il s'agit de syntagmes ou de juxtapositions non syntagmatiques de mots (*iucturae*), qui figurent *aussi* dans la Bible latine. Reprises conscientes ou plutôt fortuites, orchestration scripturaire voulue ou plutôt spontanée, associative, du langage hagiographique? Cette question demeure très souvent sans réponse univoque, bien qu'une fonction énonciative (faible) ne puisse être exclue.

Voici quelques exemples potentiellement intertextuels avec un seul passage biblique. Dans son prologue, adressé à l'abbesse Celsa[30] et aux *virgines Christi* du monastère d'Arles, l'hagiographe leur assure qu'il s'est tenu scrupuleusement à leur propre relation écrite des faits et à la *testificatio perspicua* d'autres témoins oculaires: *ne tamen quicquam* *superflue* *aut non veraciter dictum esse* videatur (*praef.*/340, 7–8). Dans cette proposition optative, on décèle éventuellent un écho d'un texte du second livre des Macchabées sur la prière pour les morts: *nisi*

---

[29] Passages non encore cités: a) réminiscences simples: 3/341, 24–25: Act 9:15; 5/342, 13–15: Lc 7:12; 14/346, 9–11: Joh 20:19; 24/350, 3–4: Sap 16:21; Mab 14/142, 38–39: Ps 12:4–5; b) réminiscences mixtes: 2/340,38: Act 10:22; 1 Reg 17:37; Lc 1:28; Tob 7:20; 4/341, 38–40: Mt 4:19; 1 Tim 4:4–5; 25/350, 23–27: Ps 109:1. Mt 25:33; Apoc 5:1, 8–9; 14:3–4; 3 Reg 10:10; Mab 13/142, 27–28: Gen 27:45; 43:14; Ruth 1:5; Mab 16/142, 52–54: Mt 14:27; 1:20; Dan 12:1; Lc 1:19.

[30] Sans doute celle qui succéda à Rusticule.

enim eos qui ceciderunt, resurrecturos speraret, superfluum videretur et vanum orare pro mortuis (2 Mac 12:44).

Au premier chapitre, l'hagiographe recourt au stéréotype de la beauté corporelle de son personnage. *Erat itaque* pulchra facie *et eleganti corpore* (1/340, 26–27). Directement ou indirectement,[31] quelques mots reprennent la description du patriarche Joseph dans la Genèse: *Erat autem Ioseph* pulchra facie, *et decorus aspectu* (Gen 39:6). Un peu plus loin, quand Césaire d'Arles apparaît en songe à Clémentia, celle-ci entend dire le pontife: . . . *non hinc egrediar, priusquam* petitioni meae *satisfacias* (2/341, 3–4; cette *petitio* désigne le désir de l'évêque de se voir offrir l'une des deux colombes). Dans la Vulgate, Tobie dit à Ragouël: *Hic ego hodie* non *manducabo, neque bibam, nisi* prius petitionem meam *confirmes* . . . (Tob 7:10). Dans cet épisode de l'Ancien Testament, la *petitio* concerne également une fille.[32]

Amenée au monastère d'Arles, la jeune Rusticule se voit confier à l'abbesse Liliole,[33] qui entame tout de suite son instruction spirituelle: . . . *et edocens illam* omnem *fidei sanctitatem, adgregavit virginibus Christi* (5/342, 4–5). Il n'est pas exclu que cette phrase véhicule un souvenir vague de la promesse (faite par le Christ) de l'Esprit saint dans le quatrième évangile: *Paraclitus autem Spiritus Sanctus . . . ille vos docebit* omnia . . . *quaecumque dixero vobis* (Joh 15:26). Clémentia, quant à elle, demeura inconsolable après le refus de l'évêque arlésien Sapaudus († 586)[34] de faire sortir sa fille du monastère: *Haec audiens genitrix, nullam* consolationem accepit *sed maiorem ainimi* dolorem *sustinens, dirigit quosdam* . . . (5/342, 20–21). On y entend peut-être quelque chose du chagrin de Jacob qui, lui, avait perdu son fils Joseph: *Congregatis autem cunctis liberis eius ut lenirent* dolorem *patris, noluit* consolationem accipere . . . (Gen 37:35).

La première réaction du roi Clotaire II, qui venait d'apprendre que Rusticule aurait permis à Childebert (fils de Thierry II [† 613], le filleul et héritier du roi Gontran) de se cacher dans son monastère,

---

[31] Il s'agit, en effet, d'un topique hagiographique: cf. F. Grauss, *Volk, Herrscher und Heiliger im Reich der Merowinger* (Praha, 1965), 463–468 ("Die Schönheit des Heiligen").

[32] Tobie veut épouser Sara, la fille de son parent Ragouël, et y réussit avec l'aide de l'archange Raphaël. Dans le livre de Tobie il est question d'un marriage réel, dans la Vita Rusticulae Césaire "arrange" pour ainsi dire le marriage spirituel de la sainte dans le monastère arlésien fondé par lui.

[33] Cf. *supra*, la note 17.

[34] On le connaît aussi par d'autres sources, notamment Grégoire de Tours, *Hist. Francorum*, VIII, 39.

consista à ordonner une enquête minutieuse. Il la confia au patrice Riccimer lui-même, qui fut précisément (avec l'évêque Maxime [d'Avignon?]) l'un des dénonciateurs de l'abbesse:[35] . . . *iussit suprascripto principi, ut* diligenter *haec* inquiri *iuberet et sibi* denuntiaret (9/344, 7–8). L'injonction du souverain franc fait penser à celle d'Hérode (adressée aux Mages) se sentant menacé par la naissance du Messie. Ce cas pourrait même passer pour une quasi réminiscence de l'Évangile de l'Enfance chez Matthieu: "*Ite, et interrogate* (variante vieille latine: inquirite)[36] diligenter *de puero: et cum inveneritis*, renuntiate *mihi, ut et ego veniens adorem eum*" (Mt 2:8).

Lorsque l'enquête eut prétendument confirmé le faux témoignage de Riccimer et de Maxime contre Rusticule, le roi se mit en colère et envoya le duc Faraulfus[37] arrêter l'abbesse d'Arles: *Et amplius* furore accensus rex *misit quendam de obtimatibus suis nomine Faraulfum, qui suis eam praesentaret optutibus* (10/344,25–26). Ce vocabulaire, devenu plus ou moins stéréotypé il est vrai,[38] n'est pourtant pas sans rappeler par ex. le passage du livre d'Esther évoquant l'ire du roi perse Assuérus (après la désobéissance de la reine Vasthi): *Unde iratus rex, et nimio* furore *succensus interrogavit* . . . (Esth 1:12). Une fois innocentée, Rusticule effectua un retour triomphal à Arles: . . . *illud referam, cum quali* gaudio *vel* exultatione *a suis civibus est recepta* (17/347, 1–2). Cette juxtaposition plus ou moins redondante coule également de source dans la *narrativa* chrétienne; on peut en tout cas la localiser notamment dans la parole de l'ange à Zacharie (lui annonçant la naissance de Jean-Baptiste): . . . *et erit* gaudium *tibi, et* exsultatio, *et multi in nativitate eius gaudebunt* (Lc 1:14).[39]

De même, le topique hagiographique du troupeau laissé orphelin par la mort du saint (dans la présente *Vita*, il s'agit évidemment des consoeurs de l'abbesse: . . . *commendabat Domino filias, quas* orfanas *relinquebat, flentesque forti animo consolabatur* [23/349, 8–9]), comprend un syntagme du discours johannique de Jésus avant sa Passion: . . . *non* relinquam *vos* orfanos (Joh 14:18).[40] Le même chapitre sur la maladie et le trépas de Rusticule fait d'ailleurs un rapprochement moins

---

[35] Sur le contexte, voir Riché, *op. cit.* (note 11), 374.
[36] *Itala*, éd. A. Juelicher, I, *Matthäus-Evangelium* (Berlin, 1938), 8.
[37] Connu aussi par la *Vita Lupi episcopi Trecensis*, 10 (*MGH, SRM*, IV, 182).
[38] Cf. Van Uytfanghe, *Stylisation, op. cit.* (note 13), 212.
[39] Cf. aussi Ps 125:2: *Tunc repletum est gaudio os nostrum, et lingua nostra exsultatione.*
[40] Le thème de l'*orfanus* spirituel revient souvent dans le traditionnel *planctus* après la mort du saint: cf. Van Uytfanghe, *Stylisation, op. cit.* (note 13), 85 (+ note 123).

typique avec la Passion, selon saint Luc cette fois-ci: Die *itaque* sabbati illucescente *coepit modico frigore teneri* . . . (23/349, 4–5). Le sabbat, en effet, pointait aussi au moment de l'ensevelissement de Jésus: *Et* dies *erat parasceves, et* sabbatum illucescebat (Lc 23:54).

Ce troisième niveau d'emprunt donne lieu, à son tour, à une intertextualité biblique composite, où plusieurs passages s'emmêlent.[41] Revenons donc un instant à l'apparition de saint Césaire d'Arles à Clémentia. Une foiss réveillée, la mère de Rusticule ne cessait de se casser la tête à ce sujet: *At illa* expergefacta cogitabat intra semet ipsam, quid hoc esset, *et revolvebat in* animo suo, *quare ille qui defunctus fuerat sibi* apparuisset (2/341, 6–8). Dans cette phrase, le "patchwork" potentiel pourrait se ramener aux versets suivants: Gen 41:4: Expergefactus *Pharao, rursum dormivit* . . . (Pharaon s'éveille après un premier songe, où il vit les sept vaches grasses et les sept vaches maigres);[42] Dan 4:16: *Tunc Daniel* . . . *coepit* intra semet ipsum *tacitus* cogitare *quasi una hora* (voir déjà *supra*, sous 2.2: le songe prémonitoire de Nabuchodonosor); Lc 18:36: *Et cum audiret turbam praetereuntem, interrogabat* quid hoc esset;[43] Gen 24:45: *Dumque haec tacitus mecum* <u>*volverem*</u>, apparuit *Rebecca veniens cum hydria* . . .; Eccli 37:9: *A consiliario serva animam tuam; prius scito quae sit illius necessitas; et ipse enim* animo suo cogitabit.

Plus tard, quand Rusticule sera devenue effectivement *sponsa Christi* au monastère d'Arles, l'évêque Sapaudus tentera, on s'en souvient, de consoler Clémentia (qui l'avait supplié en vain de lui rendre sa fille): Consolare *ergo, quaeso, iam, dulcissima filia, et* noli flere *amissam* . . . (5/342, 18–19). Ces deux impératifs accusent une résonance bien biblique, ce dont témoignent notamment Is 40:1: Consolamini, consolamini, *populo meus, dicit Deus vester,*[44] et Lc 7:13 (parole de Jésus adressée à la veuve de Naïm): *Quam cum vidisset Dominus, misericordia motus super eam, dixit illi*: Noli flere.[45]

Comme abbesse, Rusticule se chargea de construire une nouvelle église conventuelle, dédiée à la Sainte-Croix.[46] Une vision céleste l'y

---

[41] Parfois, le quatrième niveau (celui des "vocables") y entre déjà.
[42] Cf. aussi Act 16:27: Expergefactus *autem custos carceris* . . . *volebat se interficere*.
[43] Cf. aussi Exod 4:2; 18:14; Num 23:11; 3 Reg 21:5.
[44] Cf. aussi Eccli 38:17 (. . . *fer luctum illius uso die, et* consolare *propter iustitiam*) et 38:24.
[45] Cf. aussi 2 Esdr 8:9; Tob 5:26; Jer 22:10; Lc 8:52; 23:28.
[46] Sur le contexte, voir Riché, *op. cit.* (note 11), 372 (relation entre les monastères d'Arles et de Poitiers, voyage de sainte Radegonde à Arles).

encouragea: *Dehinc demonstratum est eidem per revelationem aedificium mirae magnitudinis* in caelo aedificatum, *quem (= quod)* intuens, *iubetur a Domino, ut similitudinem illius fabricaret in* terris (8/343, 22–24). L'expression biblique pourrait provenir ici à la fois d'une doxologie du Livre d'Amos (Amos 9:6: *Qui* aedificat in caelo *ascensionem suam, et fasciculum suum super* terram *fundavit . . .*) et du récit de la première multiplication des pains chez Marc (Mc 6:41: *. . .* intuens *in* caelum, *benedixit, et fregit panes . . .*).

À la suite de la fausse accusation dont elle fut la victime, l'abbesse fut contrainte de quitter son monastère, où règne désormais un désarroi absolu: Conversus est *illis* dies in nocte, *dulcedo* in amaritudine, cantica in luctu, lux *in* tenebris, vita *in* morte;[47] *omnes omnino mori magis quam piissima matre absente vivere cupiebant* (11/345, 12–14). Dans cette accumulation d'antithèses[48] résonne encore la parole d'Amos (Amos 5:8: *Facientem Arcturum et Orionem, et* convertentem *in mane tenebras, et* diem in noctem *mutantem;* 6:13: *Numquid currere queunt in petris equi, aut arari potest in bubalis, quoniam* convertistis in amaritudinem *iudicium, et fructum iustitiae in absinthium?* 8:10 *. . . et* convertam *festivitates vestras* in luctum, *et omnia* cantica *vestra in planctum*), et aussi celle d'Isaïe (Is 5:20: *Vae qui dicitis malum bonum, et bonum malum; ponentes tenebras lucem et* lucem tenebras; *ponentes amarum in dulce, et dulce in amarum*) et de saint Paul (Rom 7:10: *. . . ego autem mortuus sum; et inventum est mihi mandatum, quod erat ad* vitam, *hoc esse ad* mortem).[49]

Un dernier exemple évoque avec admiration le recrutement d'un nombre élevé de moniales sous l'abbatiat de Rusticule: O *quanta, Domine, dispensato procurationis tuae, quae per famulam tuam Rusticulam tantum* gregem de luporum *faucibus* ereptum *tuo* ovili *collocasti!* (Mab 11/142, 5–6). La métaphore "pastorale" utilisée ici est commune à bien des hagiographes,[50] mais sa formulation se ressent toujours tant de l'Ancien Testament (cf. *Mich* 2:12: *pariter ponam illum quasi* gregem *in* ovili; 1 Reg 17:37: Dominus *qui* eripuit *me de* manu leonis, *et de* manu ursi *. . .*) que du Nouveau (Mt 10:16; *mitto vos sicut oves in medio* luporum; Joh 10:16: *fiet unus* ovile *et unus pastor*).[51] Au total, ces

---

[47] La distinction entre *in* + abl. et *in* + acc. se fait plus vague en latin tardif.

[48] Cf. M. Van Uytfanghe, "La formation du langage hagiographique en Occident latin," in *Cassiodorus* 5 (1999) 143–169, ici 158–162.

[49] Les antithèses du type *dies – nox, lux – tenebrae, vita – mors* sont évidemment très courantes dans la Bible et la littérature chrétienne en général.

[50] Cf. Van Uytfanghe, *Stylisation, op. cit.* (n. 13), 82 (+ note 113).

[51] Cf. aussi Joh 10:1. Dans les *Vies* monastiques, on a affaire à un rétrécissement

syntagmes et *iuncturae* se chiffrent, dans la *Vita*, à une certaine de cas potentiels (67 de type simple et 32 de type mixte).[52]

2.4. Tout en bas de l'échelle, on pourrait encore distinguer un quatrième niveau, celui des "vocables" individuels (certains entraient déjà dans des composés du niveau 3). L'exhaustivité théorique m'incite à en faire mention, mais sa portée est plutôt secondaire. Il est, en effet, d'autant plus difficile de déterminer si un simple mot a été emprunté à la Bible que les éléments lexicaux spécifiquement scripturaires s'étaient depuis longtemps intégrés dans le vocabulaire du latin tardif. Tout au plus peut-on attribuer une "couleur" biblique à certains vocables ou bien très fréquents dans la Vulgate ou les *Veteres Latinae*, ou bien employés dans une acception typiquement biblique, ou bien susceptibles d'évoquer un contexte scripturaire précis.

L'emploi du verbe *adstare* par exemple dans le récit de l'apparition de Césaire d'Arles à Clémentia (2/340, 32–33: . . . *videtur sibi, quasi domus familia nuntiaret, quod sanctus Caesarius urbis Arelatensis episcopus prae floribus* adstaret) n'est peut-être pas tout à fait fortuit, eu égard à la parole angélique adressée à Zacharie: *ego sum Gabriel, qui* asto *ante Deum* (Lc 1:19). De même, l'admiration de ceux qui avaient pu se régaler du grand poisson que la petite Rusticule, en route vers Arles, avait capturé dans le Rhône (4/341, 38–40: *Et* ammirantes super *hoc factum, dicebant*: "Vere *in hoc apparet quia multas animas ista per verbum Dei capiet et Christo domino cansecrabit*), n'est éventuellement pas sans harmoniques lexicaux avec des versets qui expriment la stupéfaction que Jésus lui-même suscitait (par ex Mt 7:28: *Cum consummasset Iesus verba haec,* admirabantur *turbae* super *doctrina eius*;[53] Mc 15:39. *Videns autem centurio ait . . .*: "Vere *hic homo filius Dei erat*).[54]

Dans un des "thrènes" que Clémentia adresse à l'évêque Sapaude (5/342, 11–12: *Quis nunc aetatem meam fovebit,* unica *quam habebam amissa?*), *unica* introduit une certaine ressemblance avec la prière du père du démoniaque épileptique dans Lc 9:38: *Magister, obsecro te,*

---

sémantique de la métaphore de la "bergerie", laquelle s'y identifie au monastère lui-même.

[52] Je m'abstiens d'énumérer ici toutes ces références, qu'on trouve in extenso dans Van Uytfanghe, *Bijbel, op. cit.* (note 8), 593–609.

[53] Cf. aussi Mc 11:18: *quoniam universa turba* admirabatur super *doctrina eius*.

[54] Le *multas animas . . . capiet* s'explique à partir de Mt 4:19 ("je ferai de vous des pêcheurs d'hommes").

respice in filium meum, quia unicus *est mihi*.[55] Le texte des Nombres sur la prétendue "oblation de jalousie" (Num 5:13: . . . *et testibus argui non potest, quia non* est inventa in *stupro*) pourrait avoir suggéré à l'auteur le verbe *invenire* (au passif + *in*) dans le récit des faux témoins envoyés auprès du roi par le patrice Riccimer: . . . *qui adserere deberent, quod culpabilis* inventa fuisset *beatissima virgo Christi* in *hoc falso crimine* (10/344, 24–25). Tout cela tient évidemment à un fil très ténu, comme c'est le cas d'autres mots tels que *baiulare*,[56] *contristari*,[57] *tribulare*,[58] *dispensatio*.[59]

Il arrive aussi qu'une *iunctura*, qui n'apparaît pas comme telle dans un texte scripturaire, suggère tout de même, par le contexte, une très légère teinte biblique des mots individuels. Ainsi, après avoir énuméré les archanges et les saints auxquels les sept autels de la nouvelle basilique étaient consacrés, l'hagiographe évoque les habitacles célestes que, par leur intercession, ils ont déjà préparés pour celle qui les vénérait: *Ipsi namque eidem sidereas* mansiones *paradisi suis interpellationibus* paraverunt, *quos tanto amore venerabiliter excoluit in terris* (8/343, 33–34). On peut penser ici à la fois aux "nombreuses demeures de la maison du Père" (cf. Joh 14:2): *In domo Patris mei* mansiones *multae sunt*) et au Royaume préparé depuis la fondation du monde pour ceux qui seront placés à la droite du Fils de l'homme (cf. Mt 25:34: . . . *possidete . . .* paratum *vobis regnum a constitutione mundi*).[60]

2.5. Qu'il me soit permis d'attirer également l'attention, hors classement si j'ose dire, sur la présence, dans la *Vita*, de certaines caractéristiques grammaticales et stylistiques du latin biblique (de celui des livres narratifs en particulier, les évangiles en premier lieu).

---

[55] Cf. aussi 2 Reg 1:26; Tob 6:15; Lc 7:12; 8:42.

[56] *V. Rusticulae*, 24/350, 3–4: *Quis umquam poterit . . . promere, quo ingenio* baiulabas *exiguitatem nostram*; cf. par ex. Lc 14:27. *Et qui non* baiulat *crucem suam . . . non potest meus esse discipulus.*

[57] *Ib.*, 23/349, 17–18: *Haec videntes virgines Christi* contristatae *omnes*; cf. par ex. Mt 17:22: *Et* contristati *sunt vehementer* (*contristare* est fréquent dans le Vulgate).

[58] *Ib.* 14, 346, 11–12: *"Beatissime amice Dei, adesto mihi nunc* tribulanti"; cf. par ex. Ps 30:10: *Miserere mei, Domine, quoniam* tribulor (*tribulare* est également fréquent dans la Vulgate).

[59] *Ib.*, Mab 11/142, 5–6: *O quanta, Domine,* dispensatio *procurationis tuae, quae per famulam tuam . . .*; cf. par ex. Eph 3:2: *si tamen auditis* dispensationem *gratiae Dei, quae data est mihi in vobis.*

[60] Il va sans dire qu'il faut prendre en compte ici toute une concrétisation postbiblique de l'eschatologie *post mortem*, telle qu'on la trouve par exemple dans le IVᵉ livre des Dialogues de Grégoire le Grand. Pour d'autres exemples de ces vocables à tonalité biblique potentielle, voir Van Uytfanghe, *Bijbel, op. cit.* (note 78), 609–612.

Pour illustrer mon propos, j'épingle quelques phrases: 1/340, 18–19: . . . *factum est, ut nasceretur eis filius*; 2/341, 2–3, 35, 38–39: *At ille dixit ad eam . . .; At ille reluctari coepit et ad se eam trahere; Domini vero gratia praestitit virtutem famulae suae . . . Et ammirantes super hoc factum, dicebant. "Vere in hoc apparet, quia multas animas consecrabit"*; 9/343, 35–36: *Quadam die cum in basilica sancti Petri hora meridie quievisset, vox ad eam facta est et vocavit eam nomine suo, dicens . . .*; Mab 15/142, 41–46: *Quadam nocte . . . cum sopori dedita fuisset, apparuit ei quaedam virgo . . . inquirens ab ea utrum vigilaret, dixit: "Marcia, cognosce quia quando de hoc corpore migraveris, mecum . . . portionem habebis". Illa autem pavefacta sciscitabatur ub ea quisnam esset qui hoc illi diceret.* Mab 16/142, 54–57: *Haec eo loquante, ecce apparuit ante oculos eius persona quaedam horrenda . . . Cumque eum vidisset tremens, archangelum intuebatur auxilium ab eo petens. Qui conversus dixit: "Ne timeas . . ."*; 9/344, 6–7: . . . *et abeuntes ad regem Chlotharium accusaverunt eam. Ille autem haec audiens, commotus est . . .*; 11/345, 10–12: . . . *nec est qui . . . ferre valeat consolationum solatia . . . Ovile Christi . . . pro matris absentia ululatibus et gemitibus resonabat*; 12/345, 21–22: . . . *ipse misit angelum suum et abstulit obprobrium a filiis Israel*[61] *revelavitque per Spiritum suum sanctum . . .*; 13/345, 34–35: . . . *venientes obviam ei, humiliter prosternebantur, confitentes atque dicentes . . .*, 14/346, 13–14: *Haec ea dicente, disruptae sunt catenae et reserata sunt claustra . . .*; 18/347, 20–21: . . . *confusi atque conpuncti veniunt ad eam humiliter veniam postulantes atque pro sui culpa indulgentiam flagitantes*; 23/349, 1: *Factum est autem quadam die . . .*

Bien que la notion de "style biblique" ait quelque chose d'impressionniste et que certains traits *en soi* n'accusent rien de spécial par rapport à la latinité tout court, on reconnaîtra aisément, dans ces extraits, quelques phénomènes de la *consuetudo Scripturarum*:[62] la fréquence des pronoms démonstratifs devenus pronoms personnels et des adjectifs possessifs; l'usage élargi de certaines prépositions (*de, in, super . . .*); les tournures impersonnelles introduisant une phrase;[63] la parataxe (avec *et*), mais en même temps l'accumulation des participes présents (avec valeurs de circonstancielle) et, dans une moindre mesure, les temporelles en *cum* (qui, dans la Bible latine, rendent très sou-

---

[61] Cf. Gen 30:23: *Quae* (= Rachel) *concepit et peperit filium, dicens. Abstulit Deus opprobrium meum.* Autres références précises dans ce passage: voir *supra*, la note 21.

[62] Comme l'appelle saint Jérôme: cf. G.Q.A. Meershoeck, *Le latin biblique d'après saint Jérôme. Aspects linguistiques de la rencontre entre la bible et le monde classique* (Nijmegen-Utrecht, 1966), 64.

[63] Ainsi, *factum est autem* traduit le grec ἐγένετο δὲ.

vent le participe aoriste du grec);[64] les complétives introduites par
quia (oti); la multiplication des conjonctions (ou adverbes) du type
autem, vero...; le style dialogué (*dixit, dicens*...) et le style synonymique
ou redondant; l'antéposition du verbe dans certains cas (influence de
l'hébreu?).[65]

3. Il serait cependant faux de conclure que la *Vita Rusticulae* ait été
rédigée dans un style biblique continu. Par ailleurs, peu de *Vies*
mérovingiennes sont dans ce cas:[66] leur langue est également nour-
rie par le latin classique et surtout tardif (les écrits patristiques, la
liturgie, les règles et l'office monastiques, etc.). La Bible n'épuise donc
pas toute l'intertextualité: à ce propos, on ne négligera surtout pas
les hagiographes antérieurs, par exemple Sulpice Sévère et certains
textes du Ve et du VIe siècle, utilisés notamment par l'auteur de
notre *Vita*.[67] Et si les hagiographes du VIIe siècle (tous clercs ou
moines) connaissent sans doute l'Écriture (ou du moins une partie
de celle-ci) par la lecture directe, ils se la sont sûrement appropriée
aussi (et peut-être davantage) par la voie indirecte (la liturgie par
exemple, qui pourrait précisément expliquer les souvenirs de versions
préhiéronymiennes).[68] Leur "mémoire musculaire" et leur "mâchonne-
ment des mots", si bien décrits par dom Jean Leclercq,[69] ont dû pro-
duire souvent une expression spontanée, sans que les auteurs eux-mêmes

---

[64] Cf. W.E. Plater – H.J. White, *A Grammar of the Vulgate* (Oxford, 1926), 30–31,
111; P.W. Hoogterp, *Étude sur le latin du Codex Bobiensis (k) des Évangiles* (Wageningen,
1930), 193–216.

[65] Cf. C. Lavergne, *L'expression biblique* (Paris, 1947), 84–85; E. Loefstedt, *Late
Latin* (Oslo, 1959), 89. Signalons encore le biblisme probable que constitue l'emploi
élargi du génitif de qualité (le *genitivus inhaerentiae*, par ex. praef/339, 33–34: *ortum
nativitatis sanctae recordationis domnae Rusticulae*; 1/340,23: *per hanc prolem fecunditatis suae*;
1/340,25: *in regenerationis fonte*; 17/347, 8–9: *hymnum exultationis*; 21/348, 9: *prolixitatis
meae sermo*, Mab 11/142,5: *dispensatio procurationis tuae*; le génitif augmentatif: 11/345,
10–11: *consolationum solatia*.

[66] Dans mon corpus de 19 textes, il n'y a que la *Passio Iusti Bellovacensis* (VIIe
siècle) et la *Vita Memorii Trecensis* (VIIIe siècle), deux récits assez courts, apparentés
aux Passions dites "épiques." Le mimétisme scripturaire continu y sert peut-être à
prévenir le soupçon d'inauthenticité.

[67] Cf. les références, dans l'édition de Krusch, à Sulpice Sévère et à trois *Vies*
de saints arlésiens (Honorat, Hilaire, Césaire).

[68] Par ailleurs, il faudra attendre l'époque carolingienne pour voir le triomphe
de la Vulgate en tant que tel.

[69] Cf. J. Leclercq, *Initiation aux auteurs monastiques du Moyen Âge. L'amour des lettres
et le désir de Dieu* (Paris, 1963[2]), 70–86.

aient toujours nécessairement su localiser les versets utilisés (même en cas de citations proprement dites).[70]

Cela n'a pour autant pas empêché l'intertextualité scripturaire d'avoir eu une fonction communicative. À part l'objectif précis de telle ou telle citation,[71] il s'agissait de "rehausser" le genre lui-même[72] par une tonalité biblique générale, mais aussi de suggérer par moments, et parfois d'une manière subtile (*sprachliches Jonglieren*, disait Karl Pivec),[73] une association avec telle personne, telle idée ou tel récit de l'Écriture (pensons au songe de la mère de Rusticule).

Est-ce que ces emprunts et allusions étaient discernés par les lecteurs ou les auditeurs? Cela dépendait évidemment du niveau de leur propre culture biblique.[74] Dans bien des cas, l'essentiel de la communication est dans les paroles l'hagiographe lui-même et le message peut "passer" même si l'on ne perçoit pas l'hypotexte biblique. Ailleurs, c'est plus difficile (cf. par exemple sous 2.1: la citation de Ps 120:3–4 dans *V. Rusticulae*, 4), voire impossible.[75] Dans notre *Vita* par exemple, l'hagiographe dit pourquoi son héroïne a mérité tout de suite après son trépas les *praemia laeta* du ciel: . . . *eo quod* triticum horrei *dominici familiae sibi commissae prudenter atque fideliter dispensaverit* (22/348, 22–23). Ici, le sens du texte se perd tout simplement pour quiconque n'y reconnaît pas l'image, mise dans la bouche de Jean-Baptiste par Matthieu (Mt 3:12) et reprise ensuite dans la parabole eschatologique de l'ivraie (Mt 13:20), du blé (triticum) que le Messie recueillera dans son grenier (horreum). La métaphore se prolonge dans celle de l'intendant fidèle et avisé (*fidelis dispensator prudens*) que le Maître établira sur ses gens pour leur donner en temps voulu leur ration de blé (Lc 12:42).[76]

---

[70] De là aussi les références parfois vagues (*ut scriptum est, ut ait scriptura*, etc.).

[71] Voir *supra*, la note 13.

[72] Sur les rapports entre l'Écriture sainte et l'hagiographie, voir M. Van Uytfanghe, "Le culte des saints et l'hagiographie face à l'Écriture: les avatars d'une relation ambiguë," in *Santi e demoni nell'alto medioevo occidentale (Settimane del CISAM)* 36 [1988] (Spoleto, 1989), t. I, 155–202.

[73] K. Pivec, "Die Bibel und das mittellateinische Schrifttum," in *Festschrift R. Heuberger*, (Innsbruck, 1960), 99–110, ici 106.

[74] Qui était sans doute très bas chez les auditeurs laïcs (mais la *Vita Rusticulae* était destinée en premier lieu aux moniales d'Arles, puisque le prologue s'adresse à l'abbesse Celsa: *in unius libelli opusculo conscriptum sancto coetui vestro obtuli lectitandum* [*praef*/340, 2–3]).

[75] Sur cette distinction, voir aussi P. Tombeur, "Réminiscences bibliques dans la 'Chronique' de Raoul de Saint-Trond," in *Archivum Latinitatis Medii Aevi* 30 (1960) 161–176.

[76] Dans la *Vita*, la métaphore se rétrécit évidemment en s'appliquant au seul milieu monastique (*familia*), dont l'abbesse fut responsable.

En somme, la *Vie de sainte Rusticule* nous fournit un assez bon exemple, me semble-t-il, de ce que pouvait être l'influence variée du langage biblique sur le latin littéraire (qui, alors, était principalement hagiographique) de l'époque de transition entre le latin tardif d'une part et la latinité médiévale et les langues romanes de l'autre.

A BIBLIOGRAPHY OF A. HILHORST

A. Books

1. *Sémitismes et latinismes dans le Pasteur d'Hermas* (Græcitas Christianorum Primæva 5; Nijmegen, 1976).
2. *Apocalypse of Paul. A New Critical Edition of Three Long Latin Versions. With fifty-four Plates* (Cahiers d'Orientalisme 21; Geneva, 1997). [with T. Silverstein].

B. Books Edited

1. *De heiligenverering in de eerste eeuwen van het christendom* (Nijmegen, 1988).
2. *Text and Testimony. Essays on New Testament and Apocryphal Literature in Honour of A.F.J. Klijn* (Kampen, 1988). [with T. Baarda, G.P. Luttikhuizen and A.S. van der Woude].
3. *Fructus centesimus. Mélanges offerts à Gerard J.M. Bartelink à l'occasion de son soixante-cinquième anniversaire* (Instrumenta Patristica 19; Steenbrugge, 1989) [with A.A.R. Bastiaensen and C.H. Kneepkens].
4. *Eulogia. Mélanges offerts à Antoon A.R. Bastiaensen à l'occasion de son soixante-cinquième anniversaire* (Instrumenta Patristica 24; Steenbrugge, 1991). [with G.J.M. Bartelink and C.H. Kneepkens].
5. *Mane Novum. Christelijke Latijnse teksten uit de tweede tot de negende eeuw. Aantekeningen bij de Latijnse teksten* (Emmeloord, 1992). [with M. van Assendelft, G. Dölle, W. Palmen, A.-M. Palmer-Foster and E. Smits].
6. *The Scriptures and the Scrolls. Studies in Honour of A.S. van der Woude on the Occasion of His 65th Birthday* (VTSup, 49; Leiden, 1992). [with F. García Martínez and C.J. Labuschagne].
7. *Early Christian Poetry. A Collection of Essays* (Supplements to Vigiliae Christianae, 22; Leiden, 1993) [with J. den Boeft].
8. *Studies in Deuteronomy in Honour of C.J. Labuschagne on the Occasion of His 65th Birthday* (VTSup, 53; Leiden, 1994). [with F. García Martínez, J.T.A.G.M. van Ruiten and A.S. van der Woude].
9. *Evangelie en beschaving. Studies bij het afscheid van Hans Roldanus* (Zoetermeer, 1995). [with H.S. Benjamins, G.D.J. Dingemans, J. van Slageren and R. Steensma].
10. *The Apostolic Age in Patristic Thought* (Supplements to *Vigiliae Christianae* 70), Leiden – Boston 2003 (forthcoming).

C. Other Editorial Activities

Periodicals

Journal for the Study of Judaism (Leiden) [since 1981; Secretary since 1998]
Filología Neotestamentaria (Cordoba) [since 1988]

Series

Supplements to the Journal for the Study of Judaism (Leiden) [since 1996]
Studies on Early Christian Apocrypha (Leuven) [since 1995]

D. Articles

1978

1. "De visserstaal van de apostelen," *Theocreet* 10/1 [October, 1978] 3–14.

1982

2. "L'Ancien Testament dans la polémique du martyr Pionius," *Augustinianum* 22 (1982) 91–96.
3. "Darius' Pillow (1 Esdras iii.8)," *JTS* 33 (1982) 161–163.

1983

4. "The Wounds of the Risen Jesus," *EstBib* 41 (1983) 165–167.

1984

5. "Refreinlied over het leven van Christus," in A.F.J. Klijn (ed.), *Apokriefen van het Nieuwe Testament I* (Kampen, 1984), 95–101. [with A.A.R. Bastiaensen].
6. "De Handelingen van Paulus," in *Apokriefen van het Nieuwe Testament I*, 154–196.

1985

7. "De Brief aan de Laodicenzen," in A.F.J. Klijn (ed.), *Apokriefen van het Nieuwe Testament II* (Kampen, 1985), 187–190.
8. "De Briefwisseling van Paulus en Seneca," in *Apokriefen van het Nieuwe Testament II*, 191–200.
9. "De Openbaring van Paulus," in *Apokriefen van het Nieuwe Testament II*, 210–249.
10. "Theologie en Latijn," *Theocreet* 17/1 [December, 1985] 32–36.

1986

11. "De houding van de christenen ten opzichte van de profane cultuur," *Hermeneus* 58 (1986) 82–89.

1987

12. "De benaming grote en kleine profeten," in F. García Martínez, C.H.J. de Geus and A.F.J. Klijn (eds.), *Profeten en profetische geschriften* (Kampen and Nijkerk, [1987]), 43–54.
13. "Ficta ac Facta: op zoek naar een klankwisseling in Grieks en Latijn," *Hermeneus* 59 (1987) 252–255.
14. "De Latijnse taal verbindt de katholiek aan zijn verleden," *NRC Handelsblad* 18.34 [9 November, 1987].
15. "Acta Iustini," in A.A.R. Bastiaensen (ed.), *Atti e Passioni dei Martiri* (Scrittori greci e latini; [Milan], 1987), 47–57, 391–396, 606–607.
16. "Martyrium Pionii," in *Atti e Passioni dei Martiri*, 149–191, 453–477, 610–612.
17. "Malachias Angelus," *Wiener Studien* 100 (1987) 175–184.
18. "Ex 4,10: ¿una variante textual ignorada en Orígenes?," *EstBib* 45 (1987) 493–496.

1988

19. "Biblical Metaphors Taken Literally," in T. Baarda, A. Hilhorst, G.P. Luttikhuizen and A.S. van der Woude (eds.), *Text and Testimony. Essays on New Testament and Apocryphal Literature in Honour of A.F.J. Klijn* (Kampen, 1988), 123–131.
20. "A Bibliography of A.F.J. Klijn," in *Text and Testimony*, 276–285.

21. "Hermas," *RAC* 14 (Stuttgart, 1988), 682–701.
22. "Termes chrétiens issus du vocabulaire de la démocratie athénienne," *Filología Neotestamentaria* 1 (1988) 27–34.
23. "De Latijnse taal verbindt de katholiek aan zijn verleden," *Vereniging voor Latijnse Liturgie, Bulletin* 41 (March, 1988) 20–22. [Reprint of 14].

1989

24. "'Servir Dieu' dans la terminologie du judaïsme hellénistique et des premières générations chrétiennes de langue grecque," in A.A.R. Bastiaensen, A. Hilhorst and C.H. Kneepkens (eds.), *Fructus centesimus. Mélanges offerts à Gerard J.M. Bartelink à l'occasion de son soixante-cinquième anniversaire* (Instrumenta Patristica 19; Steenbrugge, 1989), 177–192.
25. "Latijn op de Petrus- en Pauluskerk," *Van Zoys tot Soest* 9/4 [Spring, 1989] 3.

1991

26. "The Epistola Anne ad Senecam: Jewish or Christian? With a New Edition of the Text," in G.J.M. Bartelink, A. Hilhorst and C.H. Kneepkens (eds.), *Eulogia. Mélanges offerts à Antoon A.R. Bastiaensen à l'occasion de son soixante-cinquième anniversaire* (Instrumenta Patristica 24; Steenbrugge, 1991), 147–161.

1992

27. "Inleiding" [to chapter 1, "De christenen en de Romeinse staat"], in M. van Assendelft, G. Dölle, A. Hilhorst, W. Palmen, A.-M. Palmer-Foster and E. Smits, *Mane Novum. Christelijke Latijnse teksten uit de tweede tot de negende eeuw* (Emmeloord, 1992), 11–14.
28. "Inleiding" [to chapter 2, "De christenen en de klassieke cultuur"], in *Mane Novum*, 85–88.
29. "De nieuwe Bauer," *NTT* 46 (1992) 104–108, 152.
30. "Christine Andrina Elisabeth Maria Mohrmann. Groningen 1 augustus 1903—Nijmegen 13 juli 1988," *Jaarboek van de Maatschappij der Nederlandse Letterkunde te Leiden* 1990–1991 (Leiden, 1992), 121–129.
31. "The Speech on Truth in 1 Esdras 4,34–41," in F. García Martínez, A. Hilhorst and C.J. Labuschagne (eds.), *The Scriptures and the Scrolls. Studies in Honour of A.S. van der Woude on the Occasion of His 65th Birthday* (VTSup, 49; Leiden, 1992), 135–151.
32. "Was Philo Read by Pagans? The Statement on Heliodorus in Socrates Hist.Eccl.5.22," *The Studia Philonica Annual* 4 (1992) 75–77.

1993

33. "The Cleansing of the Temple (John 2,13–25) in Juvencus and Nonnus," in J. den Boeft and A. Hilhorst (eds.), *Early Christian Poetry. A Collection of Essays* (Supplements to Vigiliae Christianae, 22; Leiden, 1993), 61–76.
34. "Paganism and Christianity in the Philopatris," in H. Hokwerda, E.R. Smits (†) and M.W. Woesthuis (eds.), *Polyphonia Byzantina. Studies in Honour of Willem J. Aerts* (Mediaevalia Groningana 13; Groningen, 1993), 39–43.

1994

35. "Deuteronomy's Monotheism and the Christians. The Case of Deut 6:13 and 10:20," in F. García Martínez, A. Hilhorst, J.T.A.G.M. van Ruiten and A.S. van der Woude (eds.), *Studies in Deuteronomy in Honour of C.J. Labuschagne on the Occasion of His 65th Birthday* (VTSup, 53; Leiden, 1994), 83–91.

36. "A Bibliography of C.J. Labuschagne," in *Studies in Deuteronomy in Honour of C.J. Labuschagne*, 289–294.
37. "Heidenen, joden en christenen in Smyrna. De verdedigingsrede van de martelaar Pionius in de vervolging van Decius," *Hermeneus* 66 (1994) 160–166.
38. "Le texte sur la résurrection de Jésus dans le ms. *k* de la *Vetus Latina* (Mc. 16,3). Note philologique," *Revue Bénédictine* 104 (1994) 257–259.

1995

39. "Waar woont God? Handelingen 7,48–50 en het kerkgebouw," in H.S. Benjamins, G.D.J. Dingemans, A. Hilhorst, J. van Slageren and R. Steensma (eds.), *Evangelie en beschaving. Studies bij het afscheid van Hans Roldanus* (Zoetermeer, 1995), 33–48.
40. Translation from the French of W. Rordorf, "Socrates in de christelijke literatuur van de eerste eeuwen," in H.S. Benjamins, G.D.J. Dingemans, A. Hilhorst, J. van Slageren and R. Steensma (eds.), *Evangelie en beschaving. Studies bij het afscheid van Hans Roldanus* (Zoetermeer, 1995), 69–93.
41. "The Apocryphal Acts as Martyrdom Texts: The Case of the Acts of Andrew," in J.N. Bremmer (ed.), *The Apocryphal Acts of John* (Studies on the Apocryphal Acts of the Apostles, 1; Kampen, 1995), 1–14.

1996

42. "The Escorial Fragment on the Heavenly Jerusalem," in R.I.A. Nip, H. van Dijk, E.M.C. van Houts, C.H. Kneepkens and G.A.A. Kortekaas (eds.), *Media Latinitas. A Collection of Essays to Mark the Occasion of the Retirement of L.J. Engels* (Instrumenta Patristica, 28; Steenbrugge and Turnhout, 1996), 223–228.
43. "Tertullian on the Acts of Paul," in J.N. Bremmer (ed.), *The Apocryphal Acts of Paul and Thecla* (Studies on the Apocryphal Acts of the Apostles, 2; Kampen, 1996), 150–163.

1997

44. "Sint-Jan apostel en evangelist. Jacobus de Voragine Legenda Aurea hoofdstuk 9," in A. Gaalman and T. Graas (eds.), *Sint-Jan apostel en evangelist. Vijf eeuwen Sint-Jan, verbeeld in het Bossche Bisdom. Catalogus bij de tentoonstelling in het Sint-Janscentrum te 's-Hertogenbosch, 5 september t/m 5 oktober 1997* ('s-Hertogenbosch, [1997]), 21–30. [with C. Hilhorst-Böink].
45. "Az apokrif akták mint mártírium-szövegek: az András-akta vizsgálata," in I. Czachesz (ed.), *Tanítványok, csodatevők, mártírok. Tanulmányok az apokrif apostol-aktáról* (Újszövetségi-patrisztikai kutatások, 4; Budapest, 1997), 184–196. [Translation of 41].
46. "Das Lebensende des Ezechiel," *Analecta Bollandiana* 115 (1997) 249–51.

1998

47. "The Text of the *Actus Vercellenses*," in J.N. Bremmer (ed.), *The Apocryphal Acts of Peter. Magic, Miracles and Gnosticism* (Studies on the Apocryphal Acts of the Apostles, 3; Leuven, 1998), 148–160.
48. "Jacobus de Voragine, de Gulden Legende: de heilige Cosmas en Damianus. Vertaling: Carolien Hilhorst-Böink en Ton Hilhorst naar handschrift München clm 13029," in K.W. Zimmerman (ed.), *One Leg in the Grave: The Miracle of the Transplantation of the Black Leg by the Saints Cosmas and Damian* (Maarssen, 1998), 12–17.
49. "Appendix: Jacobus de Voragine, Legenda Aurea: Cosmas et Damianus," in *One Leg in the Grave*, 61–62. [with C. Hilhorst-Böink].

50. "Erotic Elements in the *Shepherd* of Hermas," *Groningen Colloquia on the Novel* 9 (Groningen, 1998), 193–204.
51. "Kruimels van de *Cena Cypriani*," *Hermeneus* 70 (1998) 220–222.

1999

52. "Biblical Scholarship in the Early Church," in J. den Boeft and M.L. van Poll-van de Lisdonk (eds.), *The Impact of Scripture in Early Christianity* (Supplements to Vigiliae Christianae, 44; Leiden, 1999), 1–19.
53. "The Noah Story: Was it Known to the Greeks?," in F. García Martínez and G.P. Luttikhuizen (eds.), *Interpretations of the Flood* (Themes in Biblical Narrative: Jewish and Christian Traditions, 1; Leiden, 1999), 56–65.
54. "Het proto-evangelie naar Jakobus," *Schrift* 181 (February, 1999) 19–23.
55. "Het evangelie volgens Petrus," *Schrift* 181 (February, 1999) 25–30.
56. "A Visit to Paradise: *Apocalypse of Paul* 45 and Its Background," in G.P. Luttikhuizen (ed.), *Paradise Interpreted: Representations of Biblical Paradise in Judaism and Christianity* (Themes in Biblical Narrative: Jewish and Christian Traditions, 2; Leiden, 1999), 128–139.
57. "Bijbelwetenschap bij de kerkvaders: haar prestaties en haar beperkingen," *Kleio* 28 (1999) 174–188.
58. "Sind die Hebräer träge geworden? Zu den Aussagen über die Adressaten in Hebr 5 und 6," *Filología Neotestamentaria* 12 (1999) 161–166.

2000

59. "De Gulden Legende," *Tijdschrift voor Geschiedenis* 112 (2000) 49–54. [with C. Hilhorst-Böink].
60. "Erwähnt P.Oxy. LXIII 4365 das Jubiläenbuch?," *Zeitschrift für Papyrologie und Epigraphik* 130 (2000) 192.
61. "The Acts of Andrew and Matthias: Is It Part of the Original Acts of Andrew?," in J.N. Bremmer (ed.), *The Apocryphal Acts of Andrew* (Studies on the Apocryphal Acts of the Apostles, 5; Leuven, 2000), 1–14. [with P.J. Lalleman].
62. "Fourth Maccabees in Christian Martyrdom Texts," C. Kroon and D. den Hengst (eds.), *Ultima Aetas. Time, Tense and Transience in the Ancient World. Studies in Honour of Jan den Boeft* (Amsterdam, 2000), 107–21.

2001

63. "The Heavenly Palace in the *Acts of Thomas*," in J.N. Bremmer (ed.), *The Apocryphal Acts of Thomas* (Studies on Early Christian Apocrypha, 6; Leuven, 2001), 53–64.
64. "The Prooimion of the Eisagoge: Translation and Commentary. Edited by B.H. Stolte and R. Meijering," *Subseciva Groningana: Studies in Roman and Byzantine Law* 7 (2001), 91–155. [with W.J. Aerts, Th.E. van Bochove, M.A. Harder, J.H.A. Lokin, R. Meijering, S.L. Radt, J. Roldanus, B.H. Stolte and N. van der Wal].

2002

65. "The Bodmer Poem on the Sacrifice of Abraham," in E. Noort and E. Tigchelaar (eds.), *The Sacrifice of Isaac: The Aqedah (Genesis 22) and its Interpretations* (Themes in Biblical Narrative, 4; Leiden, 2002), 96–108.

2003

66. "Poésie hébraïque et métrique grecque. Les témoignages des Anciens, de Philon d'Alexandrie à Boniface de Mayence," Accorinti, D. – Chuvin, P. (eds.), *Des Géants à Dionysos. Mélanges de mythologie et de poésie grecques offerts à Francis Vian* (Alessandria, 2003), 305–29.

67. "Abel's Speaking in Hebrews 11.4 and 12.24," in G.P. Luttikhuizen (ed.), *Eve's Children. The Biblical Stories Retold and Interpreted in Jewish and Christian Traditions* (Themes in Biblical Narrative, 5; Leiden, 2003), 119–127.
68. "De Latijnse uitgaven van de *Legenda Aurea* en het werk van de bijbelvertaler. Enkele opmerkingen bij de legende van Sint Vedastus," in A. Berteloot – H. van Dijk – J. Hlatky (eds.), *"Een boec dat men te Latine heet Aurea Legenda"*. *Beiträge zur niederländischen Übersetzung der* Legenda aure (Niederlande-Studien 31), Münster – New York – München – Berlin 2003, 53–64 [with C. Hilhorst-Böink].

Forthcoming

"The Apocalypse of Paul: Earlier History and Later Influence," in M. McNamara (ed.), *Apocalyptic and Eschatological Heritage: The Middle East and Celtic Realms* (Dublin, 2003).
"Romantic Fantasies: Early Christians Looking Back on the Apostolic Period," in A. Hilhorst (ed.), *The Apostolic Age in Patristic Thought* (Supplements to *Vigiliae Christianae* 70), Leiden – Boston 2003.

E. Book Reviews

1980

1. J.-M. Poinsotte, *Juvencus et Israël. La représentation des Juifs dans le premier poème latin chrétien* (Publications de l'Université de Rouen, 57; Paris, 1979), *JSJ* 11 (1980) 110–111.

1982

2. E. Tov, *The Text-Critical Use of the Septuagint in Biblical Research* (Jerusalem Biblical Studies, 3; Jerusalem, 1981), *JSJ* 13 (1982) 214–216.
3. B. Dehandschutter, *Martyrium Polycarpi. Een literair-kritische studie* (BETL, 52; Leuven, 1979), *NTT* 36 (1982) 72–74.

1983

4. J. Allenbach, A. Benoît, D.A. Bertrand, A. Hanriot-Coustet, E. Junod, P. Maraval, A. Pautler and P. Prigent, *Biblia Patristica, Supplément: Philon d'Alexandrie* (Paris, 1982), *JSJ* 14 (1983) 52.
5. D. Ambaglio and L. Troiani, *Ricerche di storiografia antica II* (Biblioteca di studi antichi, 24; Pisa, 1980), *JSJ* 14 (1983) 88.
6. H. Schreckenberg, *Bibliographie zu Flavius Josephus. Supplementband mit Gesamtregister* (ALGHJ, 14; Leiden, 1979), *JSJ* 14 (1983) 89.
7. W. Horbury and B. McNeil (eds.), *Suffering and Martyrdom in the New Testament. Studies Presented to G.M. Styler by the Cambridge New Testament Seminar* (Cambridge, 1981), *JSJ* 14 (1983) 93–94.
8. F.J. Bautz (ed.), *Geschichte der Juden. Von der biblischen Zeit bis zur Gegenwart* (Beck'sche Schwarze Reihe, 268; Munich, 1983), *JSJ* 14 (1983) 186.
9. R.A. Bitter, *Vreemdelingschap bij Philo van Alexandrië. Een onderzoek naar de betekenis van πάροικος* (Diss. Utrecht, 1982), *JSJ* 14 (1983) 186–187.
10. H. Jacobson, *The Exagoge of Ezekiel* (Cambridge, 1983), *JSJ* 14 (1983) 202–204.

1984

11. P. Sacchi (ed.), *Apocrifi dell'Antico Testamento* (Classici delle religioni, 38; Turin, 1981), *JSJ* 15 (1984) 150–152.
12. G.C. Bottini, *La preghiera di Elia in Giacomo 5:17–18. Studio della tradizione biblica e giudaica* (SBF Analecta, 16; Jerusalem, 1981), *JSJ* 15 (1984) 165–166.

13. U. Offerhaus, *Komposition und Intention der Sapientia Salomonis* (Diss. Bonn, 1981), *JSJ* 15 (1984) 195–196.
14. H. Schreckenberg, *Die christlichen Adversus-Judaeos-Texte und ihr literarisches und historisches Umfeld (1.–11. Jh.)* (Europäische Hochschulschriften 23.172; Frankfurt am Main, 1982), *JSJ* 15 (1984) 206–209.

1985

15. J. González Luis, *La versión de Símaco a los profetas mayores* (Madrid, 1981), *JSJ* 16 (1985) 132–133.
16. H. Heubner and W. Fauth, *P. Cornelius Tacitus, Die Historien. Band V: Fünftes Buch* (Wissenschaftliche Kommentare zu griechischen und lateinischen Schriftstellern; Heidelberg, 1982), *JSJ* 16 (1985) 134–135.
17. M. Himmelfarb, *Tours of Hell: An Apocalyptic Form in Jewish and Christian Literature* (Philadelphia, 1985), *JSJ* 16 (1985) 135–137.
18. D. Piattelli, *Concezioni giuridiche e metodi costruttivi dei giuristi orientali* (Università di Roma, Pubblicazioni dell'Istituto di diritto romano e dei diritti dell'Oriente Mediterraneo, 58; Milan, 1981), *JSJ* 16 (1985) 149–151.
19. M. Pucci, *La rivolta ebraica al tempo di Traiano* (Biblioteca di studi antichi 33; Pisa, 1981), *JSJ* 16 (1985) 151–152.
20. A. Schenker, *Psalmen in den Hexapla. Erste kritische und vollständige Ausgabe der hexaplarischen Fragmente auf dem Rande der Handschrift Ottobonianus graecus 398 zu den Ps 24–32* (Studi e Testi, 295; Vatican City, 1982), *JSJ* 16 (1985) 156–157.
21. J.R. Busto Saiz, *La traducción de Símaco en el libro de los Salmos* (Textos y Estudios "Cardenal Cisneros," 22; Madrid, 1985), *JSJ* 16 (1985) 263.
22. R. Kuntzmann and J. Schlosser (eds.), *Études sur le judaïsme hellénistique. Congrès de Strasbourg (1983)* (Lectio divina, 119; Paris, 1984), *JSJ* 16 (1985) 264–266.
23. C.R. Holladay, *Fragments from Hellenistic Jewish Authors. Volume I: Historians* (SBLTT 20, Pseudepigrapha Series 10; Chico, California, 1983) *JSJ* 16 (1985), 269–271.
24. A. Mendelson, *Secular Education in Philo of Alexandria* (Monographs of the Hebrew Union College 7; Cincinnati, 1982), *JSJ* 16 (1985) 277–279.
25. A. Pietersma, *The Acts of Phileas, Bishop of Thmuis (Including Fragments of the Greek Psalter). P. Chester Beatty XV (With a New Edition of P. Bodmer XX, and Halkin's Latin Acta), Edited with Introduction, Translation and Commentary. With Full Facsimile of the C.B. Text* (Cahiers d'Orientalisme 7; Geneva, 1984), *JSJ* 16 (1985) 287–288.

1986

26. F.E. Greenspahn, E. Hilgert and B.L. Mack (eds.), *Nourished with Peace. Studies in Hellenistic Judaism in Memory of Samuel Sandmel* (Homage Series; Chico, California, 1984), *JSJ* 17 (1986) 104–106.
27. J. Paramelle, with the collaboration of E. Lucchesi, *Philon d'Alexandrie, Questions sur la Genèse II 1–7. Texte grec, version arménienne, parallèles latins. Interprétation arithmologique par J. Sesiano* (Cahiers d'Orientalisme 3; Geneva, 1984), *JSJ* 17 (1986) 113–115.
28. A. Pietersma and C. Cox (eds.), *De Septuaginta. Studies in Honour of John William Wevers on His Sixty-Fifth Birthday* (Mississauga, Ontario, 1984), *JSJ* 17 (1986) 115–117.
29. M. Cimosa, *Il vocabolario di preghiera nel Pentateuco greco dei LXX* (Quaderni di "Salesianum," 10; Rome, 1985), *JSJ* 17 (1986) 244–245.
30. C. Estin, *Les Psautiers de Jérôme à la lumière des traductions juives antérieures* (Collectanea Biblica Latina, 15; Rome, 1984), *JSJ* 17 (1986) 245–248.
31. H.W. Hollander and M. de Jonge, *The Testaments of the Twelve Patriarchs. A Commentary* (SVTP, 6; Leiden, 1985), *JSJ* 17 (1986) 252–255.
32. A.A. Mosshammer (ed.), *Georgii Syncelli Ecloga Chronographica* (Bibliotheca Scriptorum Graecorum et Romanorum Teubneriana; Leipzig, 1984), *JSJ* 17 (1986) 262–263.

1987

33. C. Truzzi, *Zeno, Gaudenzio e Cromazio. Test e contenuti della predicazione cristiana per le chiese di Verona, Brescia e Aquileia (360–410 ca.)* (Testi e ricerche di Scienze religiose, 22; Brescia, 1985), *Nederlands Archief voor Kerkgeschiedenis* 67 (1987) 80–81.
34. B. Gerhardsson, *The Gospel Tradition* (CB NT Series, 15; Malmö, 1986), *JSJ* 18 (1987) 90.
35. A.H. Jones, *Essenes: The Elect of Israel and the Priests of Artemis* (Lanham, 1985), *JSJ* 18 (1987) 91.
36. C. Orrieux, *Zénon de Caunos, parépidèmos, et le destin grec* (Centre de recherches d'histoire ancienne, 64; Paris, 1985), *JSJ* 18 (1987) 98–99.
37. M. Harl, *La Genèse. Traduction du texte grec de la Septante, introduction et notes* (La Bible d'Alexandrie, 1; Paris, 1986), *JSJ* 18 (1987) 235–237.

1988

38. V. Saxer, *Bible et hagiographie. Textes et thèmes bibliques des Actes des martyrs authentiques des premiers siècles* (Bern, 1986), *NTT* 42 (1988) 345–346.
39. A. Konikoff, *Sarcophagi from the Jewish Catacombs of Ancient Rome: a catalogue raisonné* (Stuttgart, 1986), *JSJ* 19 (1988) 106–108.
40. D.T. Runia, *Philo of Alexandria and the Timaeus of Plato* (Philosophia Antiqua, 44; Leiden, 1986), *JSJ* 19 (1988) 258–259.
41. F. Schmidt, *Le Testament grec d'Abraham. Introduction, édition critique des deux recensions grecques, traduction* (TSAJ, 11; Tübingen, 1986), *JSJ* 19 (1988) 263–264.

1989

42. E. Bammel, *Jesu Nachfolger. Nachfolgeüberlieferungen in der Zeit des frühen Christentums* (Studia Delitzschiana III/1; Heidelberg, 1988), *JSJ* 20 (1989) 84.
43. P. Harlé and D. Pralon, *Le Lévitique. Traduction du texte grec de la Septante, introduction et notes* (La Bible d'Alexandrie, 3; Paris, 1988), *JSJ* 20 (1989) 90–91.
44. J.P. Martín, *Filón de Alejandría y la génesis de la cultura occidental* (Colección "Oriente-Occidente," 4; Buenos Aires,1986), *JSJ* 20 (1989) 100.
45. W. Schneemelcher (ed.), *Neutestamentliche Apokryphen in deutscher Übersetzung. 5. Auflage der von Edgar Hennecke begründeten Sammlung. I. Evangelien* (Tübingen, 1987), *JSJ* 20 (1989) 109–110.
46. A.-M. Denis and Y. Janssens, *Concordance grecque des pseudépigraphes d'Ancien Testament. Concordance, corpus des textes, indices* (Louvain-la-Neuve, 1987), *JSJ* 20 (1989) 219–221.
47. A. Enermalm-Ogawa, *Un langage de prière juif en grec. Le témoignage des deux premiers livres des Maccabées* (CBNT Series, 17; Stockholm, 1987), *JSJ* 20 (1989) 221–222.
48. A. Piñero, L. Vegas Montaner, G. Aranda Pérez and F.-J. Martínez Fernández, *Testamentos o discursos de adiós* (Apócrifos del Antiguo Testamento, 5; Madrid, 1987), *JSJ* 20 (1989) 253–254.
49. R. Radice and D.T. Runia, *Philo of Alexandria. An Annotated Bibliography 1937–1986* (Supplements to Vigiliae Christianae, 8; Leiden, 1988), *JSJ* 20 (1989) 254–256.
50. F. Rehkopf, *Septuaginta-Vokabular* (Göttingen, 1988), *JSJ* 20 (1989) 256–257.
51. B. Virgilio (ed.), *Studi Ellenistici, II* (Biblioteca di studi antichi, 54; Pisa, 1987), *JSJ* 20 (1989) 260–261.
52. Helmut Engel, *Die Susanna-Erzählung. Einleitung, Übersetzung und Kommentar zum Septuaginta-Text und zur Theodotion-Bearbeitung* (OBO, 61; Freiburg, 1985), *Bibliotheca Orientalis* 46 (1989) 442–445.

1990

53. C. Haas, *De geest bewaren. Achtergrond en functie van de pneumatologie in de paraenese van de Pastor van Hermas* (Diss. Leiden; The Hague, 1985), *NTT* 44 (1990) 267–268.
54. R. Bodenmann, *Naissance d'une exégèse. Daniel dans l'Eglise ancienne des trois premiers siècles* (Beiträge zur Geschichte der biblischen Exegese, 28; Tübingen, 1986), *JSJ* 21 (1990) 95–96.
55. A. Le Boulluec and P. Sandevoir, *L'Exode. Traduction du texte grec de la Septante, introduction et notes* (La Bible d'Alexandrie, 2; Paris, 1989), *JSJ* 21 (1990) 123–126.
56. G. Rinaldi, *Biblia Gentium: Primo contributo per un indice delle citazioni, dei riferimenti e delle allusioni alla Bibbia negli autori pagani, greci e latini, di età imperiale. A First Contribution towards an Index of Biblical Quotations, References and Allusions Made by Greek and Latin Heathen Writers of the Roman Imperial Times* (Rome, 1989), *JSJ* 21 (1990) 272–275.
57. G. Stemberger (ed.), *Die Juden. Ein historisches Lesebuch* (Beck'sche Reihe 410; München, 1990), *JSJ* 21 (1990) 291–292.

1991

58. N. Fernández Marcos and J.R. Busto Saiz, *El texto antioqueno de la Biblia Griega. I. 1–2 Samuel* (Textos y Estudios «Cardenal Cisneros,» 50; Madrid, 1989), *JSJ* 22 (1991) 134–136.
59. W. Schneemelcher (ed.), *Neutestamentliche Apokryphen in deutscher Übersetzung. 5. Auflage der von Edgar Hennecke begründeten Sammlung. II. Band. Apostolisches. Apokalypsen und Verwandtes* (Tübingen, 1989), *JSJ* 22 (1991) 152–153.
60. J.W. Wevers, *Notes on the Greek Text of Exodus* (SBLSCS, 30; Atlanta, Georgia, 1990), *JSJ* 22 (1991) 153–155.

1992

61. J. van Amersfoort and J. van Oort (eds.), *Juden und Christen in der Antike* (Kampen, 1990), *JSJ* 23 (1992) 99–100.
62. G.H.R. Horsley, *New Documents Illustrating Early Christianity, Volume 5. Linguistic Essays* (Macquarie University, N.S.W., Australia, 1989), *JSJ* 23 (1992) 114–117.
63. P.W. Pestman, *The New Papyrological Primer, Being the Fifth Edition of David and Van Groningen's Papyrological Primer* (Leiden, 1990), *JSJ* 23 (1992) 128–129.
64. E. Tov, *The Greek Minor Prophets Scroll from Nahal Hever (8HevXIIgr) (The Seiyâl Collection I). With the Collaboration of R.A. Kraft and a Contribution by P.J. Parsons* (DJD, 8; Oxford, 1990), *JSJ* 23 (1992) 140–142.
65. N. Fernández Marcos and J.R. Busto Saiz, *El texto antioqueno de la Biblia Griega. II. 1–2 Reyes* (Textos y Estudios "Cardenal Cisneros," 53; Madrid, 1992), *JSJ* 23 (1992) 254–255.
66. J.W. van Henten (ed.), with the collaboration of B.A.G.M. Dehandschutter and H.J.W. van der Klaauw, *Die Entstehung der jüdischen Martyrologie* (Studia Post-Biblica, 38; Leiden, 1989), *JSJ* 23 (1992) 267–269.

1993

67. C. Dogniez and M. Harl, *Le Deutéronome. Traduction du texte grec de la Septante, introduction et notes* (La Bible d'Alexandrie, 5; Paris, 1992), *JSJ* 24 (1993) 89–91.
68. M.A. Knibb and P.W. van der Horst (eds.), *Studies on the Testament of Job* (SNTS MS, 66; Cambridge, 1989), *JSJ* 24 (1993) 118–119.

1994

69. A. Aejmelaeus, *On the Trail of the Septuagint Translators. Collected Essays* (Kampen, 1993), *JSJ* 25 (1994) 312–314.
70. D.T. Runia, *Philo in Early Christian Literature. A Survey* (CRINT III.3; Assen, 1993), *JSJ* 25 (1994) 330–333.

1995

71. P. Geoltrain, J.-C. Picard and A. Desreumaux (eds.), *Apocrypha. Le champ des apocryphes 2, 1991: La fable apocryphe II* (Turnhout, 1991), *REAug* 41 (1995) 145–147.
72. A.-M. Denis, *Concordance latine des pseudépigraphes d'Ancien Testament. Concordance, corpus des textes, indices* (CC, Thesaurus Patrum Latinorum, Supplementum; Turnhout, 1993), *JSJ* 26 (1995) 350–351.
73. C. Dogniez, *Bibliography of the Septuagint. Bibliographie de la Septante (1970–1993)* (VTSup, 60; Leiden, 1995), *JSJ* 26 (1995) 354–358.
74. S.R. Llewelyn with the collaboration of R.A. Kearsley, *New Documents Illustrating Early Christianity (Volume 7). A Review of the Greek Inscriptions and Papyri Published in 1982–83* (Macquarie University, N.S.W., Australia, 1994), *JSJ* 26 (1995) 368–369.
75. H. Schreckenberg, *Die christlichen Adversus-Judaeos-Texte und ihr literarisches und historisches Umfeld (11.–13. Jh.)* (Europäische Hochschulschriften, 23.172; Frankfurt am Main, 1995³), *JSJ* 26 (1995) 378–379.

1996

76. C. Carozzi, *Eschatologie et Au-delà. Recherches sur l'*Apocalypse de Paul (Aix-en-Provence, 1994), *VC* 50 (1996) 94–99.
77. A. Carlini, with the collaboration of L. Giaccone, *Papyrus Bodmer XXXVIII. Erma: Il Pastore (Ia–IIIa visione). Edito con introduzione e commentario critico. Appendice: Nouvelle description du Codex des Visions par R. Kasser, avec la collaboration de G. Cavallo et J. van Haelst* (Cologny-Geneva, 1991), *VC* 50 (1996) 417–419.

1997

78. N. Brox, *Der Hirt des Hermas. Übersetzt und erklärt* (Kommentar zu den Apostolischen Vätern, 7; Göttingen, 1991), *Jahrbuch für Antike und Christentum* 40 (1997) 220–224.

1999

79. L.V. Rutgers, *The Hidden Heritage of Diaspora Judaism* (Contributions to Biblical Exegesis and Theology 20; Leuven, 1998²), *NTT* 53 (1999) 149–150.
80. J.A. Fitzmyer, *To Advance the Gospel: New Testament Studies. Second Edition* (The Biblical Resource Series; Grand Rapids, 1998), *JSJ* 30 (1999) 99–100.
81. R. Katzoff, Y. Petroff and D. Schaps (eds.), *Classical Studies in Honor of David Sohlberg* (Ramat Gan, 1996), *JSJ* 30 (1999) 103–104.
82. R.J. Zwi Werblowsky and G. Wigoder (eds.), *The Oxford Dictionary of the Jewish Religion* (New York, 1997), *JSJ* 30 (1999) 116–117.
83. N. Fernández Marcos, *Introducción a las versiones griegas de la Biblia*, 2ª edición revisada y aumentada (Textos y Estudios "Cardenal Cisneros," 64; Madrid, 1998), *JSJ* 30 (1999) 341–342.
84. N. Fernández Marcos and J.R. Busto Saiz, with the collaboration of M.V. Spottorno Díaz-Caro and S.P. Cowe, *El texto antioqueno de la Biblia Griega. III. 1–2 Crónicas* (Textos y Estudios "Cardenal Cisneros," 60; Madrid, 1996), *JSJ* 30 (1999) 343–344.
85. M. Lamberigts and P. Van Deun 1995 (eds.), *Martyrium in Multidisciplinary Perspective. Memorial Louis Reekmans* (BETL, 117; Leuven, 1995), *JSJ* 30 (1999) 352–353.

86. S.R. Llewelyn, *A Review of the Greek Inscriptions and Papyri Published 1984–85* (New Documents Illustrating Early Christianity 8; Grand Rapids, 1997), *JSJ* 30 (1999) 353–354.

87. S. Schechter, *Aspects of Rabbinic Theology: Major Concepts of the Talmud* (Peabody, Massachusetts, 1998 [= 1909]), *JSJ* 30 (1999) 365.

88. A.M. Schwemer, *Studien zu den frühjüdischen Prophetenlegenden* Vitae Prophetarum. *Band I. Die Viten der großen Propheten Jesaja, Jeremia, Ezechiel und Daniel. Einleitung, Übersetzung und Kommentar. Band II. Die Viten der kleinen Propheten und der Propheten aus den Geschichtsbüchern. Übersetzung und Kommentar* (TSAJ, 49–50; Tübingen, 1995–1996). *Beiheft. Synopse zu den* Vitae Prophetarum (Tübingen, [1996]), *JSJ* 30 (1999) 365–367.

89. J.W. Wevers, *Notes on the Greek Text of Genesis* (SBLSCS, 35; Atlanta, Georgia, 1993), *JSJ* 30 (1999) 367–368.

90. M.H. Williams, *The Jews among the Greeks and Romans: A Diasporan Sourcebook* (London, 1998), *JSJ* 30 (1999) 368–369.

2000

91. P. Bettiolo, A. Giambelluca Kossova, C. Leonardi, E. Norelli, L. Perrone (eds.), *Ascensio Isaiae. Textus* (C Series Apocryphorum, 7; Turnhout, 1995). E. Norelli, *Ascensio Isaiae. Commentarius* (CC, Series Apocryphorum, 8; Turnhout, 1995), *VC* 54 (2000) 111–114.

92. R. Hanhart, *Studien zur Septuaginta und zum hellenistischen Judentum, herausgegeben von Reinhard Gregor Kratz* (Forschungen zum Alten Testament 24; Tübingen, 1999), *JSJ* 31 (2000) 91–92.

93. A. Lehnardt, *Bibliographie zu den Jüdischen Schriften aus hellenistisch-römischer Zeit* (JSHRZ, 6.2; Gütersloh, 1999), *JSJ* 31 (2000) 96–97.

94. S.E. Porter (ed.), *Handbook of Classical Rhetoric in the Hellenistic Period 330 B.C.–A.D. 400* (Leiden, 1997), *JSJ* 31 (2000) 108–109.

95. K. Demoen, *Gregorios van Nazianze. Ernstig spel. Een keuze uit zijn poëzie. Inleiding, keuze, vertaling en commentaar Kristoffel Demoen* (Obolos, 12; Groningen, 2000), *Tetradio* 9 (2000) 231–233.

2001

96. P.W. van der Horst, *Mozes, Plato, Jezus. Studies over de wereld van het vroege christendom* (Amsterdam, 2000), *Tijdschrift voor Geschiedenis* 114 (2001) 263–265.

97. P. Boned Colera and J. Rodríguez Somolinos, *Repertorio bibliográfico de la lexicografía griega (RBLG)* (Diccionario griego-español. Anejo III; Madrid, 1998), *JSJ* 32 (2001) 296–298.

98. P. Borgen, K. Fuglseth and R. Skarsten, *The Philo Index: A Complete Greek Word Index to the Writings of Philo of Alexandria* (Grand Rapids, 2000), *JSJ* 32 (2001) 298–299.

99. D.J. Harrington, *Invitation to the Apocrypha* (Grand Rapids, 1999), *JSJ* 32 (2001) 307.

100. J. Sievers, *Synopsis of the Greek Sources for the Hasmonean Period: 1–2 Maccabees and Josephus,* War *1* and Antiquities *12–14* (Subsidia Biblica, 20; Rome, 2001), *JSJ* 32 (2001) 354–355.

2002

101. A.-M. Denis and collaborators, with the collaboration of J.-C. Haelewyck, *Introduction à la littérature religieuse judéo-hellénistique (Pseudépigraphes de l'Ancien Testament)* (2 vols.; Turnhout, 2000), *JSJ* 33 (2002) 101–102.

102. N. Fernández Marcos, *The Septuagint in Context: Introduction to the Greek Version of the Bible. Translated by Wilfred G.E. Watson* (Leiden, 2000), *JSJ* 33 (2002) 103–104.

103. K.H. Jobes and M. Silva, *Invitation to the Septuagint* (Carlisle, Cumbria, and Grand Rapids, 2000), *JSJ* 33 (2002) 105–107.

2003

104. R.S. Bloch, *Antike Vorstellungen vom Judentum. Der Judenexkurs des Tacitus im Rahmen der griechisch-romischen Ethnographie* (Historia Einzelschriften, 160; Stuttgart, 2002), *JSJ* 34 (2003) 60–63.
105. E. Bons, J. Joosten, S. Kessler, P. Le Moigne and T. Muraoka, *Les Douze Prophètes, Osée: Traduction du texte grec de la Septante, introduction et notes par E. Bons, J. Joosten et S. Kessler. Avec la collaboration de P. Le Moigne. Introduction générale aux Douze Prophètes par T. Muraoka* (La Bible d'Alexandrie, 23.1; Paris, 2002), *JSJ* 34 (2003) 63–64.
106. C. Dogniez and M. Harl (eds.), *Le Pentateuque d'Alexandrie, Texte grec et traduction. Avec une introduction par M. Alexandre, J.-M. Auwers, M. Casevitz, G. Dorival, J. Moatti-Fine, M. Hadas-Lebel, A. Le Boulluec, O. Munnich, D.T. Runia* (Paris, 2001), *JSJ* 34 (2003) 71–72.

REFERENCES TO ANCIENT TEXTS

I. GREEK AND LATIN PAGAN TEXTS

Aelian
Var. hist. 12.32   302

Apuleius
Apol. 56   303
Metam.
5.1   63
7.7, 8.16, 10.6   70

Aristophanes
Eccl. 390–391   39
Ran. 448   62

Aristotle
Gen. an.
II 3.736 27–29, 39   190
Metaph.
986a 23   261
1004b 27,35   261
1058a 13; 1066a 15   261
1072a 31; 1093b 12   261

Caesar
Bell. gall.
1.9.3, 18.3   148
5.6.1   148

Censorinus
De die natali 24.1–3   39

Cicero
Att. 2.3.2   60
Nat. d. 2.51f.   156
Resp. 5.1   148

Claud.
Epithal. 55   61
Phoenix 101–105.108–110   157

Diodorus Siculus
10.9.6   303
12.21.1   305

Diogenes Laertius
2.78   306
5.67   303

8.19   303
8.33   303

Dionysius of Halicarnassus
Ant. rom. 3.61   94

Ennius
Frg. 156   148

Epictetus
Ench. 42   47

Euripides
Bacch. 794k   47

Hadrian
Eisagoge 132   117

Hesychius > 394   60

Homer
Il.
VII   96
VII.49   91
VII.58–61   90, 97
VII.59,61   92
VII.327–335   96
XIII.62   92
XIV.286–291   90–91
XVII.66–67   302
XXIV.290–321   96
XXIV.347   92
Od.
1.320   92, 97
5.337   92
7.114   61
10.504–540   169
13.222   92

Horace *C.* 1.38.4   60

Iamblichus
Pythagorean Life
56   304
63   302
100, 149, 153   303

Virgil		*Georg.*	
Aen.		1.293	31
4.26; 6.462	31	2.149–50	61

II. JEWISH TEXTS

1. *Hebrew Bible*

Genesis		41:4	350
1–11	264	43:14	347
1–3	263	49	179
1:1	27	49:11	278
1:2	187, 196	50	48
1:11	28	50:10	232
1:14–17	172	50:15–17.19–20	49
1:27	81–82, 192	50:20	49–51
2–3	272		
2	270	*Exodus*	
2:4–25	264	3:8	278, 282
2:7	81–83, 192, 334	3:17	282
2:8	59, 281	3:21f.	160
2:9	272	4:2	350
2:10	265, 266	11:2	160
2:10–14	229, 263, 264,	12:2	27
	266–267,	12:35f.	160
	269–270, 272,	13:5	282
	279	15:8.10	222
2:11–14	266	17:6	265
2:13	265	18:14	350
2:18	163, 193	19:4	95
2:21	194	19:8	295
2:23	194	20:4	108
3	196, 335, 337,	20:5	197
	339	24:10	175
3:3–14	335	24:16	294
3:19	81	28:17–20	174
3:23	69	31:12	298
3:21	193	32:13–14	278
3:24	167, 169	33:3	282
6:1–4	194	33:24	278
6:5ff.	194		
6–8	187	*Leviticus*	
6–9	241	8:36	289
22:3	167	16:5	319
24:45	350	16:23	311
26:19	170	19:23–25	315
27:45	347	20:24	282
28:12	170	26:46	287, 289
30:23	344, 354	27:34	289
37	320		
37:23.32	112	*Numbers*	
37:35	348	5:13	535
37:39–50	47, 49	13:27	282
39:6	348	20:11	265

3. Qumran Texts

4. Philo

5. Josephus

6. *Targums*

7. *Rabbinic Texts*

III. CHRISTIAN TEXTS

1. *New Testament*

2. *New Testament Apocrypha*

NHC II.26.12f.	190	BG 58.1–7	196
NHC II.29.6	187	BG 58.4–7, 10–14	194
NHC II.29.28–30	195	BG 58.14–20	196
NHC II.30.3–4	195	BG 58.17; 59.17	187
NHC III.15.24; 18.14.18; 23.20	190	BG 60.19–61.7	88
NHC III.24.6.10	190	BG 61.7–62.3	194
NHC III.24.7f.	192	BG 62.3–63.14	194
NHC III.25.2	190	BG 63.8–9	193
NHC III.29.5, 22	187	BG 64.13–71.2	196
NHC III.30.17–21	88	BG 67.14–18	193
NHC III.34.7; 34.14	190	BG 69.1–5	193
NHC III.37.23	187	BG 71.2–5	196
NHC IV.1	88	BG 73.4	187
NHC IV.22.24; 23.2	192	BG 73.16–18	194
NHC IV.45.30–46.2	195	BG 73.18–74.5	195
NHC IV.46.11–13	195	BG 74.6–10	193
BG 20.19–22.16	99	BG 74.13–16	195
BG 22:17–26:21	192		
BG 31.11f.	192	*Visio Pauli*	
BG 36.16ff.	188	3–10.45	263
BG 38.1–10, 15–17	192	19–30	267
BG 39.1–51.20	192	19,20	268
BG 45.5–11	196	21	267
BG 45.9	187	22	267–269
BG 46.2–6	188	23	263, 267,
BG 48.14–49.2; 49.9–51.1	190		269–270, 278,
BG 52.17–54.4	193		281, 283
BG 55.2–6.9–13	193	24	61, 268
BG 55.18–56.3	194	25–28	268–269
BG 56.14–17	193	31	267–268
BG 57.8–19	194	45	269, 281

3. *Ancient Christian Writers*

Ambrose		1.7–8	30
Abr. 2.11.80–81	26	1.7–11	32
Noe 19.70	26	1.10, 12–13, 16	33
Patr. 11.47	25	1.17–32	38
Exc. 2.59	162	1.18	31
Exp. Luc.		1.18–20	34
2.81; 7.12	25	1.32	33
4.17	248	2.5	29
4.33	249	4.9–10	29
7.29; 6.35	26	*In Psalm.*	
10.75	28	45.14	36
Hex.		45.15	35
1.13–14	28		
5.24	30	Aristides	
5.85, 88	30–32	*Orationes*	
5.88–89	38	16.4	153
Hymn.		144D:425f.	156
1.1–5	29		
1.1–16	37	Arnobius	
1.5–8	31	*Adversus Gentes* 2.71.1f.	154

Maximus of Turin
Serm. 99   25

Minucius Felix
Oct. 16.5   3

Nilus of Ancyra
Epistularum Liber IV 61   10

Opus imperfectum in Matthaeum
PG 56 col. 667   249–53

Origen
Catenae in Iohannem
520.12; 521.1   25
Cels.
1.15   148
4.36, 39   336
4.40   337
4.51   148
6.2   4
6.42, 43, 44   337
8.47   4
Comm. Rom. 178.1   25
Dial. 1.20   67
Ep.Afr. 11.85.49   67
Ep. Greg. 2.19–44   160
Hom. Jer. 20.7   336
Hom. Jes. Nav. 2.1   338
Or. 28.9–10   246
Princ. 3.2.1   326, 338

Polycarp
Pol. Phil. 4.3; 9; 13   105

Passio Mariani
6.9–10   60
6.11–12   63

Passio Montani et Lucii
1   63
6.15   66
7.5   60
12.1   56

Passio Perpetuae et Felicitatis
2.1   57
3.4   68
4.3   60
4.5   56
4.6   57, 59
4.8   60
4.29   71

6.3   57
8.4   65
11   58
11–12   72
11.1   56, 70
11.8, 9 57
12   58
12.1   57
12.5   57, 65
13   57, 59, 72
13.4   57
14   63
14.1, 3   56
15.2, 3 70
17.1–2   57
18.7   57
18.9   71
21.1.4   57

Passio Philippi 11–13   62

Passio sancti Felicis episcopi 1   64

Paulinus of Nola
Carmen
18.146ff.   68
27, 511, 516, 542–555   10

Prudentius
Cathemerinon
1   37
5.2   29

Shepherd of Hermas
Mand. 12.1.1–2   247
Sim. 6.1.5–2.1   321
Vis. 4.3   312

Tatian
Address to the Greeks 10   93
Oratio 31, 35   154

Theodoret of Cyprus
Curatio affectionum Graecarum
2.114   148
7.6   10
QO
3.18–19   116
127.7–13   109
181.11–14   115
241.24–242.2   114
248.19–20   109

4. *Medieval Texts*

5. *Erasmus*

SUPPLEMENTS

TO THE

JOURNAL FOR THE STUDY OF JUDAISM

49. LIETAERT PEERBOLTE, L.J. *The Antecedents of Antichrist.* A Traditio-Historical Study of the Earliest Christian Views on Eschatological Opponents. 1996. ISBN 90 04 10455 0

50. YARBRO COLLINS, A. *Cosmology and Eschatology in Jewish and Christian Apocalypticism.* 1996. ISBN 90 04 10587 5

51. MENN, E. *Judah and Tamar (Genesis 38) in Ancient Jewish Exegesis.* Studies in Literary Form and Hermeneutics. 1997.
ISBN 90 04 10630 8

52. NEUSNER, J. *Jerusalem and Athens.* The Congruity of Talmudic and Classical Philosophy. 1996. ISBN 90 04 10698 7

54. COLLINS, J.J. *Seers, Sibyls & Sages in Hellenistic-Roman Judaism.* 1997. ISBN 90 04 10752 5

55. BAUMGARTEN, A.I. *The Flourishing of Jewish Sects in the Maccabean Era: An Interpretation.* 1997. ISBN 90 04 10751 7

56. SCOTT, J.M. (ed.). *Exile: Old Testament, Jewish, and Christian Conceptions.* 1997. ISBN 90 04 10676 6

57. HENTEN, J-.W. VAN. *The Maccabean Martyrs as Saviours of the Jewish People.* A Study of 2 and 4 Maccabees. 1997. ISBN 90 04 10976 5

58. FELDMAN, L.H. *Studies in Josephus' Rewritten Bible.* 1998.
ISBN 90 04 10839 4

59. MORRAY-JONES, C.R.A. *A Transparent Illusion.* The Dangerous Vision of Water in Hekhalot Mysticism: A Source-Critical and Tradition-Historical Inquiry. 2002. ISBN 90 04 11337 1

60. HALPERN-AMARU, B. *The Empowerment of Women in the* Book of Jubilees. 1999. ISBN 90 04 11414 9

61. HENZE, M. *The Madness of King Nebuchadnezzar.* The Ancient Near Eastern Origins and Early History of Interpretation of Daniel 4. 1999. ISBN 90 04 11421 1

62. VANDERKAM, J.C. *From Revelation to Canon.* Studies in the Hebrew Bible and Second Tempel Literature. 2000. ISBN 90 04 11557 9

63. NEWMAN, C.C., J.R. DAVILA & G.S. LEWIS (eds.). *The Jewish Roots of Christological Monotheism.* Papers from the St. Andrews Conference on the Historical Origins of the Worship of Jesus. 1999.
ISBN 90 04 11361 4

64. LIESEN, J.W.M. *Full of Praise*. An Exegetical Study of Sir 39,12-35. 1999. ISBN 90 04 11359 2

65. BEDFORD, P.R. *Temple Restoration in Early Achaemenid Judah*. 2000. ISBN 90 04 11509 9

66. RUITEN, J.T.A.G.M. VAN. *Primaeval History Interpreted*. The Rewriting of Genesis 1-11 in the book of Jubilees. 2000. ISBN 90 04 11658 3

67. HOFMANN, N.J. *Die Assumptio Mosis*. Studien zur Rezeption massgültiger Überlieferung. 2000. ISBN 90 04 11938 8

68. HACHLILI, R. *The Menorah, the Ancient Seven-armed Candelabrum*. Origin, Form and Significance. 2001. ISBN 90 04 12017 3

69. VELTRI, G. *Gegenwart der Tradition*. Studien zur jüdischen Literatur und Kulturgeschichte. 2002. ISBN 90 04 11686 9

70. DAVILA, J.R. *Descenders to the Chariot*. The People behind the Hekhalot Literature. 2001. ISBN 90 04 11541 2

71. PORTER, S.E. & J.C.R. DE ROO (eds.). *The Concept of the Covenant in the Second Temple Period*. 2003. ISBN 90 04 11609 5

72. SCOTT, J.M. (ed.). *Restoration*. Old Testament, Jewish, and Christian Perspectives. 2001. ISBN 90 04 11580 3

73. TORIJANO, P.A. *Solomon the Esoteric King*. From King to Magus, Development of a Tradition. 2002. ISBN 90 04 11941 8

74. KUGEL, J.L. *Shem in the Tents of Japhet*. Essays on the Encounter of Judaism and Hellenism. 2002. ISBN 90 04 12514 0

75. COLAUTTI, F.M. *Passover in the Works of Josephus*. 2002. ISBN 90 04 12372 5

76. BERTHELOT, K. *Philanthrôpia judaica*. Le débat autour de la "misanthropie" des lois juives dans l'Antiquité. 2003. ISBN 90 04 12886 7

77. NAJMAN, H. *Seconding Sinai*. The Development of Mosaic Discourse in Second Temple Judaism. 2003. ISBN 90 04 11542 0

78. MULDER, O. *Simon the High Priest in Sirach 50*. An Exegetical Study of the Significance of Simon the High Priest as Climax to the Praise of the Fathers in Ben Sira's Concept of the History of Israel. 2003. ISBN 90 04 12316 4

79. BURKES, S.L. *God, Self, and Death*. The Shape of Religious Transformation in the Second Temple Period. 2003. ISBN 90 04 12954 5

80. NEUSNER, J. & A.J. AVERY-PECK (eds.). *George W.E. Nickelsburg in Perspective*. An Ongoing Dialogue of Learning (2 vols.). 2003. ISBN 90 04 12987 1 (set)

81. COBLENTZ BAUTCH, K. *A Study of the Geography of 1 Enoch 17-19*. "No One Has Seen What I Have Seen". 2003. ISBN 90 04 13103 5

82. GARCÍA MARTÍNEZ, F., & G.P. LUTTIKHUIZEN. *Jerusalem, Alexandria, Rome*. Studies in Ancient Cultural Interaction in Honour of A. Hilhorst. 2003 ISBN 90 04 13584 7

83. NAJMAN, H. & J.H. NEWMAN (eds.). *The Idea of Biblical Interpretation*. Essays in Honor of James L. Kugel. 2003. ISBN 90 04 13630 4

ISSN 1384-2161